Multilingual America

Multilingual America

*Transnationalism, Ethnicity,
and the Languages
of American Literature*

EDITED BY

Werner Sollors

A LONGFELLOW INSTITUTE BOOK

New York University Press

NEW YORK AND LONDON

NEW YORK UNIVERSITY PRESS
New York and London

Grateful acknowledgment is made to Dr. Jeannette Langer for permission to quote from her work and to Harvard University Press
for permission to quote from *Special Sorrows: The Diasporic Imagination of Irish, Polish, and Jewish Immigrants in the United States.*
Copyright © 1995 by the President and Fellows of Harvard College

Library of Congress Cataloging-in-Publication Data
Multilingual America : transnationalism, ethnicity, and the languages
of American literature / edited by Werner Sollors.
    p.   cm.
"A Longfellow Institute book."
Includes bibliographical references (p.   ) and index.
ISBN 0-8147-8092-X (clothbound : acid-free paper). — ISBN
0-8147-8093-8 (paperback : acid-free paper)
    1. Multilingualism—United States.   2. American literature—
History and criticism.   3. United States—Literatures—History and
criticism.   4. Ethnicity—United States.   I. Sollors, Werner.
P115.5.U5M85   1998
404'.2'0973—dc21   98-6851
                         CIP

New York University Press books are printed on acid-free paper,
and their binding materials are chosen for strength and durability.

Manufactured in the United States of America

10 9 8 7 6 5 4 3 2 1

Contents

Acknowledgments

The publication of *Multilingual America* was supported by a grant from the European Association for American Studies (EAAS), and I am grateful to Rob Kroes and to Heinz Ickstadt for their enthusiastic endorsement of this project. I am deeply indebted to Niko Pfund at New York University Press for his unflagging support, past and present. I wish to thank David Gutiérrez and Peggy Pascoe of the 1996 American Studies Association (ASA) Program Committee for their initial encouragement, the ASA Executive Director John F. Stephens for publishing my plea "For a Multilingual Turn in American Studies" (out of which the introduction to the present volume grew), Jeff Finlay for posting it on INTERROADS, the electronic list for "International / Comparative Perspectives on the Study of American Culture," all the discussants for their responses on the list, and Robert Allison, Jules Chametzky, Thomas J. Ferraro, and Jessica Hook for some very helpful comments and suggestions. I also found the responses to related presentations in Warsaw, St. Louis, Kansas City, Cadenabbia, Trondheim, Rome, Berlin, and, of course, Cambridge useful in writing the final version of the present introduction. Many commentators and participants in the audience at EAAS and ASA panels as well as students and readers have helped to advance the project embodied by these essays. Steven G. Kellman examined the entire manuscript at an earlier stage and made many valuable comments and suggestions in his reader's report; and I hope that those that could not be incorporated in the present volume will be heeded in future publications on this topic. Valerie Jaffee edited a first version of the volume, Maria Chung, Rebecca Kiley, and Brandon Walston proofread various essays; and Despina Gimbel and Jessica Hook were the expert editors who saw this book through all stages of production, including all multilingual corrections in the copyedited manuscript and the page proofs.

My deepest thanks go to all contributors to *Multilingual America*. With the exception of the 1996 statement by the Linguistic Society of America, the volume consists entirely of fresh, previously unpublished work. Several of the essays and parts of the introduction were first presented at Longfellow panels of the European Association for American Studies and of the American Studies Association or were developed in the context of the new Discussion Group on "Non-English Literature of the United States" in the Modern Language Association, the leading members of which are also among the contributors to *Multilingual America*. The Longfellow Institute work has also prompted activities in other associations such as the American Comparative Literature Association, the American Literary Translators Association, the Nordic Association for American Studies, the Norwegian-

American Historical Association, the Société Imaginaire, the Amerikahaus Berlin, the TransCoop Foundation, and the Centro di Studi Americani, and in journals ranging from the *Antioch Review* to ÀCOMA and from *Lingua Franca* to *Amerikastudien*. To these and all the others who have given me indications of a positive feedback on the topic of American multilingualism I wish to acknowledge my indebtedness.

Introduction
After the Culture Wars;
or, From "English Only" to "English Plus"

Werner Sollors

> We Americans have yet to really learn our own antece-
> dents, and sort them, to unify them. They will be found
> ampler than has been supposed, and in widely different
> sources. Thus far, impress'd by New England writers
> and schoolmasters, we tacitly abandon ourselves to the
> notion that our United States have been fashion'd from
> the British Islands only—which is a very great mistake.
> —Walt Whitman

In many countries of the world the learning of languages other than the respective country's official tongue is considered part of an educational agenda that political conservatives and radicals alike unhesitatingly endorse. The European Union, for example, which has more official languages than the United Nations, actively supports language acquisition in educational institutions from grade schools to universities.[1] According to a 1996 survey, nearly 60 percent of Europeans have learned a second language, the most popular among which are English (33 percent), French (15 percent), and German (9 percent). This is not just a matter of teaching the leading languages of the European Union itself. In Sweden, for example, all public school children have the right to receive at least two weekly hours of language instruction in one of an amazing list of 124 accepted tongues—with the result that 80 languages were taught in Swedish schools in 1993, the less-well-known ones by traveling or part-time teachers; and British schools, too, offer an expanded officially approved list of "modern foreign languages" that may be taught privately by immigrant groups.[2] There are also established forms of official bilingualism; for example, in Italian South Tyrol/Alto Adige, state employees in the public sector must be able to answer their customers' questions in both German and Italian, and all laws (though not the instructions enclosed with pharmaceutical products) must be published bilingually.[3] This legal protection of minority languages brings obvious benefits to all citizens who learn the other language—not just in a vague cultural sense but also as an employment condition for public service jobs.

There are, of course, important differences between protecting and preserving the languages of historical or new minorities (or majorities) within the same political entities and the learning of second languages, ranging from world languages to local *linguae francae* to any language at all. Many countries have enjoyed the presence of at least one of these forms of bilingualism. The Linguistic Society of America was right in reminding the public in 1996 that "the vast majority of the world's nations are at least bilingual, and most are multilingual, even if one ignores the impact of modern migrations."[4] Yet some multilingual countries do not have much of a consciousness of either form of bilingualism: by adhering to a monolingual ideal, they tend to deny the historical significance and continuing presence of other languages, be it as mother tongues or as the result of school instruction. It is this ideal of monolingualism that seems to have captivated the contemporary United States—despite the fact this country has an impressive multilingual past and present all the same.

No matter how many American citizens may look back to different linguistic pasts and family documents, or be fluent in other languages now, U.S. politicians and educators have supported the steady scaling down of required language education—from the elementary grades all the way through graduate school.[5] World citizenship as an educational ideal is believed to be attainable in English alone, the concept of "language rights" is little known, and the word "bilingualism" carries the association of a social burden (and a problem for the bilinguals themselves), as if it were a bad but fortunately only transitory alternative to "proficiency in English."[6] Multilingualism is a goal neither for the Right nor for the Left in the United States today.

Conservatives who otherwise profess to demand more rigorous educational programs have not been eager to include languages in their popular listings of what "every American needs to know." The fear of linguistic "Balkanization" or Canadian-style disunity looms large. As E. D. Hirsch put it, "Linguistic pluralism enormously increases cultural fragmentation, civil antagonism, illiteracy, and economic-technological ineffectualness."[7] Hence an "English only" movement has captured the conservative imagination.

To suggest that the U.S. educational system should rest on an unquestioned ideal of monolingualism that is uninformed by the existence of American multilingualism, past and present, would mean to propose adopting an educational ideal that is at variance with virtually all comparable countries in the world (including the United Kingdom, the homeland of the English language). "English only" is likely to make the United States exceptional and to put the country at an international disadvantage in several respects. Ironically, the "English only" slogan gained wider currency at the same time that NAFTA would make the intensified teaching and learning of at least Spanish and French more desirable. John Edward Philips has commented on how the "frightening" pervasiveness of U.S. monolingualism today has "serious national security implications"—which he illustrates with the situation in the Gulf War, when "the U.S. military was forced to depend to a large extent on Arab

Americans, since so few other Americans have had any Arabic instruction."[8] And James W. Crawford wonders whether the U.S. failure to develop its language resources might give the economies of other countries "competitive advantages." He asks: "In a global economy, how long can the United States thrive without a more rational policy for conserving, developing, and managing language resources?"[9] The alternative of "bilingualism" and "proficiency in English" may also be a faulty one, for minority-language speakers, whose number has greatly increased again during the 1980s, are to a very high degree proficient in English, too. It is a myth that bilingualism lowers language performance in first languages; and no educational program or well-thought-out political platform should be based on it.[10]

Would not a focus on "English plus other languages" mean a further strengthening of English as the public language and a clearer understanding of language rights of minorities (and thus be likely to reduce social conflicts), bringing about a higher degree of literacy in English as well as more bilingual and multilingual fluency for everybody in the age of transnationalism?[11] Promoting "English plus other languages" is likely to prepare students better for world citizenship and reduce cultural friction at home by providing more vehicles of understanding between the English-language majority and historical and newly immigrated linguistic minorities. It enhances language rights by strengthening a fuller understanding of American history and by highlighting the need for translation in courts, in front of juries, and in other important public arenas.[12] A multilingual turn toward "English plus" might constitute the much-needed corrective for an absurd-seeming conservative agenda.

In fact, an "English plus" approach offers significant personal and social benefits. It seems doubtful whether "English only" education, based on the false myths of a monolingual past, of monolingual civil harmony, and of the supposedly better language skills of monolingual people, makes for more civic cohesion than would a fuller understanding of the pervasive multilingualism in U.S. history and society and a greater emphasis on language-learning today. The negative aspects of monolingualism in an age of transnationalism make it hard to understand how an "English only" slogan could ever pass as a "conservative" policy.

Liberals and radicals have also remained uninterested in the larger issues of a polyglot country in a globalized economy and an increasingly transnational world. Some multiculturalists believe that multilingualism might be tied to a nostalgia for a premulticultural America in which only a few classical or European languages were considered a sign of cultivation. These multiculturalists seem to fear that multilingualism would reinstate a colonial suppression of subgroups and minority cultures. Kevin McNamara, for example, writes that "language instruction equates the language as a whole with the linguistic habits of a particular, dominant subgroup," and he adds that the French he "learned had nothing to do with Creole, Cajun, Caribbean, or even Belgian French."[13] The question is, however, whether an English-only multicultural focus will prepare him better to read Cajun or Creole than will an even poorly particularized course in French. Furthermore, a multilingual turn is by no means compelled to exclude French Creole or Arabic or Chinese or any other relevant language or dialect from its purview; yet multiculturalism has largely been an "English-only" movement (though it professes to abhor that slogan). As Gerald Early put it in commenting on the provincialism of what he calls the multiculturalism craze, "multiculturalists generally do not see learning foreign languages as a major part of their educational reform."[14] Early's point is well taken, yet his use of the term "foreign" also suggests how natural the notion of an Anglophone United States has become even to its critics. Recently voices have been raised that propose, in Mary Louise Pratt's words, "expunging the term foreign to refer to languages other than English" for it applies neither to Spanish nor to "French, Cantonese, Italian, or Japanese—to say nothing of Lakota, Navajo, or Cree."[15] Would it be more appropriate, perhaps, to speak of American tongues, or the languages of America?

With the exception of some discussions of Spanish, multiculturalism has paid very little attention to linguistic diversity, past or present. This is all the more surprising since multilingualism would seem to be so easily linked with the multiculturalism debate. The absence of "language" as a variable in the debate may have contributed to the dominance of racially based identifications and the pervasiveness of identity politics. Recently, critical opinion has deplored this state of affairs, and Walter Benn Michaels, for example, has attempted to analyze "cultural pluralism" and "multiculturalism" as inevitably based on "race," for the "modern concept of culture is not . . . a critique of racism; it is a form of racism."[16] And David Hollinger has described the obsolete harshness of the "ethnoracial pentagon," by which citizens of the United States are currently defined as African-Americans, Latinos, Native Americans, Asian-Americans, and Euro-Americans, and made the invitation to move "beyond multiculturalism" by creating new cosmopolitan forms of voluntary affiliations that would widen the cirle of the "we."[17] Both of these approaches could be made more compelling if the issue of language were included in their reflections, for language provides a model for an understanding of culture that need not be based on race, and language acquisition may be one way of making voluntary affiliations, widening the circle of the "we," and at least in part "becoming what one is not."

Giving multiculturalism an "English plus" character is likely to extend the beneficial sides of multiculturalism by helping to correct one of its major blind spots, for how can one talk convincingly about "cultural diversity" without talking about language? How can one advocate a better understanding of others without learning the others' language? Should not true multiculturalists support both forms of bilingualism—the protection of mother tongues and the acquisition of important world languages, and, in fact, of any language? School instruction at all levels of education could motivate anybody to undertake the intensive study of a second language as early in life as possible. This goal is a desirable one for all students independent from their particular backgrounds—but it may also be realistic to take into consideration the fact that a language connected with a student's family background or partial ancestry may enhance motivation.

Perhaps it is some anxiety about ending the (predominantly Anglophone) "culture wars" that has kept the opposing sides engaged in continuing these skirmishes—and leaving language out of the game. Yet why do the conservatives not advocate an education in which they could both prepare children for the twenty-first century and preserve the American tradition? Why do conservatives not propose the teaching of more Arabic and Japanese and Chinese and European languages in order to prepare the next generation for a conversation with the world? Why do they not advocate the teaching of Cotton Mather's Latin (and Spanish) writings, of Dutch, Spanish, French, and Russian colonial texts, of the Founding Fathers' Latin and French, and of the widespread multilingualism of many nineteenth-century intellectuals, in order to stress the sense of an American tradition?

Instead of complaining about the colonizing effect of languages (hardly a convincing argument when advanced in English only), why do the radicals not demand the teaching of all languages spoken by the growing number of today's immigrants? Why do they not propose the study of the many languages used by American women, by members of ethnic minorities, by slaves, or by workers—and make available for multicultural education texts such as all extant works in Native American languages, Arabic slave narratives, letters by Swedish maids, antislavery writings by German Americans, Spanish-language writing insofar as it is not colonial or religious, multilingual radical newspapers, gay and lesbian literature in different languages, and the non-English part of the Asian-American tradition? Whatever their different goals might be otherwise, could not conservatives and radicals alike fight for the reintroduction of language requirements and serious professional instruction on all levels from kindergarten to graduate school? Is it absurd, naive, unrealistic, or eccentric to make such proposals?

The blind spot of language is shared by the "conservative" and the "radical" sides in the multiculturalism debate. This is not just a matter of cultural politics; it also takes its toll in scholarship and in historical consciousness. The field of American literary studies is a good case in point. Originally, an "Americanist" was a person who studied American Indian languages. Later, writing about "American literature" meant describing, analyzing, and criticizing works that were written or published in many different languages in the various colonies and in the United States. Yet while the "culture wars" have been raging between Left and Right, in the various fields of literary and historical study and in literary histories of the United States, the multitudes of texts written in languages other than English have quietly slipped from view. Though such areas as black studies have benefited from the massive work of textual recovery undertaken by such leading scholars as Henry Louis Gates, Jr., there are some other areas in which we know less now than scholars did at the beginning of the century—and multilingualism is certainly one such area.

After World War I, with all its efforts at Americanization, there was still a sense left in the world of scholarship that "language and literature of the United States" was a field not limited to English. Thus, the old *Cambridge History of American Literature* of 1917–1921 stressed that the "language of the people of the United States has been English even more prevailingly than their institutions and their culture"—yet it included more than sixty pages on "Non-English Writings."[18] Written by Albert B. Faust, Edward J. Fortier, Nathaniel Buchwald, and Mary Austin, these specialized sections focused on German, French, Yiddish, and "Aboriginal" texts, but other parts of the *History* also paid attention to non-English authors so that the old reference work touched upon writers from Lorenzo Da Ponte to Victor Séjour and on texts from Franz Daniel Pastorius's *Bee-hive* to the Leni Lenape epic, the *Walam Olum*, that will now need to be reintroduced to the general reader and the specialist by a new direction in scholarly work.[19] The authors of the *Cambridge History* generally still assumed that their readers were likely to be fluent in French, German, and Latin. And it was also in the same period that H. L. Mencken paid notable attention, in *The American Language* (1919), to the non-English elements of his topic.[20]

As late as 1946, Robert Spiller's *Literary History of the United States* included a chapter by Mencken, "The American Language"; a section by Stith Thompson, "The Indian Heritage"; and an entry by Henry A. Pochmann and others, "The Mingling of Tongues," that closely followed and abridged the old *Cambridge History* in delineating German, French, and Yiddish writing, while adding new and shorter sections on Spanish, Italian, and Scandinavian texts.[21] In contemporary literary histories, however, readers may be invited to pause for a moment and reflect on the many voices that were silenced, yet they will find little space dedicated to descriptions of non-English writings of the past. In contemporary critical studies, even some that focus on "the American language" and modernist American literature around World War I, the existence of non-English speech communities in the United States and the production of American literary texts in languages other than English are barely mentioned.[22] In contemporary anthologies, from Norton's and Heath's to the Library of America edition of American poetry, only a few non-English texts are included, typically only in an unproblematized English translation.[23] Literary histories, critical studies, anthologies, and even bibliographies of literature of the United States nowadays inevitably present English-only materials and often imply a monolingual Anglophone reader. A representative example of the "natural" way in which this exclusion takes place can be found in *Asian-American Literature: An Annotated Bibliography*, a comprehensive work of nearly three hundred pages published under the auspices of the Modern Language Association, which includes the following, telling declaration of limits: "[W]e exclude works written in Asian languages, unless they have been translated into English."[24] As many other examples could illustrate, non-English languages of the United States have been marginalized in the field of American studies, even when it has intersected with ethnic studies or has been undertaken with a multicultural focus, as well as in comparative literature, and in literary histories of the United States as well as in histories of French, German, Spanish, Scandinavian, and other relevant literatures. This is a great, great loss.

There are, of course, noteworthy exceptions to the rule, such as many contributions to Wolodymyr T. Zyla and Wendell M. Aycock's two-volume collection, *Ethnic Literatures since 1776: The Many Voices of America* (1978); Brom Weber's essay "Our Multi-Ethnic Origins and American Literary Studies" (1975), a programmatic call for an exploration of multilingual American literature; and some recent entries, especially on Spanish-language writing, in histories of American literature.[25] And Marc Shell's essay "Babel in America; or, The Politics of Language

Diversity in the United States" (1993) was a manifesto for a return to the factor of languages in American culture.[26] Nonetheless, the task that is still ahead is formidable. There are many, many American texts that were written in languages ranging from indigenous Amerindian tongues and from Spanish, French, Dutch, German, and Russian colonial writings to immigrant literature in all European, many Asian, and some African languages. At Harvard's Widener Library alone, for example, a database search has shown that there are more than 120,000 imprints published in the United States in scores of languages other than English, and the list of only those multilingual American newpapers that were under the surveillance of the U.S. postmaster in 1917 is sixty single-spaced pages long and includes more than two thousand titles of periodicals in languages ranging from Ruthenian to Syrian, Bohemian to "Spanish-Jewish" (Ladino), Tagalog-Visayan to Rumanian, as well as bi- and trilingual formats such as Polish-Latin, Danish-Norwegian-Swedish, or German-Hungarian.[27] These little-studied texts raise important issues of language policies, national identity, and education, and they are especially suited to international scholarly collaboration.

The files of the National Archives, the Library of Congress, the American Antiquarian Society, and the American Immigration Archives, and the shelves of numerous other libraries and research institutions are well stocked with unexamined multilingual materials; and exploring the histories of American polyglot publishing centers could keep whole teams of readers busy.[28] Many libraries and academic institutions offer scholarships to students, teachers, or translators—for example, the Recovering the U.S. Hispanic Literary Heritage project at the University of Houston, the New Netherland Project at the New York State Library in Albany, the American-Scandinavian Foundation in New York City, or, for international Americanists, such Rockefeller Residency fellowships as those at the University of Iowa. Among the many texts to be uncovered and studied are not only works of interest to sociologists of immigration, linguists, and cultural historians but also forgotten novels, plays, short stories, and poems—the aesthetic merit of which can be assessed only after a careful examination of the many sources and comparisons with the Anglophone canon. Students and professionals who know, or are willing to learn, languages other than English are likely to find it intellectually rewarding to enter the study of multilingual America at this time. I believe that we are just at the beginning of what may become a major reexamination of American literature and history in the light of multilingualism. As the result of a large collaborative effort, a comprehensive history of multilingual literature of the United States may soon be in the making.

Multilingual America is a first step in that direction, but it cannot possibly provide full coverage of the vast field that is its topic, and about which so relatively little is known to today's scholars. The selection has been guided, rather, by the principle of putting together exemplary analyses that explore issues that have broader implications for the study of other texts, of different language groups, or of related problems, and for an understanding of American multilingualism in general. The essays are presented here in the hope that they might help to stimulate a new historical consciousness, serve as models for new research, and open up a much-needed discussion of American multilingualism.

Many contributions call attention to the significance of language for various fields of study, others place language in the context of ethnicity or religion. Some essays concentrate on transnational language negotiations between English and another mother tongue, others deal with acquired and invented languages. A few contributions focus on languages that have been used in the United States, and most examine literary articulations of the languages they study—including prose fiction, poetry, drama, essay, sermon, and journalism. Many essays investigate languages other than English, some offer bilingual and multilingual comparisons, and a few read exemplary English-language writings in the context of multilingualism. Often the issues of linguistic and cultural interactions move to the foreground, for many American languages have coexisted in great proximity, and some have shared the same city, the same newspaper, the same street, the same building, the same family, and the same individual. Several essays offer substantive and affirmative answers to the question whether multilingual literature can be part both of the American tradition and of other literatures, thus forcing reconsiderations of the nation-state framing of much literary historiography. Some language areas are covered by overviews, others by representative case studies, and many languages regrettably do not receive any treatment at all in this collection. I can only hope that this volume will help to inspire new work on American literature in such languages as Greek, Vietnamese, Arabic, Russian, Hindi, Lithuanian, Dutch, Basque, Japanese, or Gullah; more investigations of writings in Hawaiian languages; and fresh studies of American texts that were written in acquired languages such as Latin or Esperanto.

All scholarly work included in *Multilingual America* is original and published here for the first time. Ranging from graduate student to practicing professional to professor emeritus (though the profile is, on the whole, rather on the young side), the contributors also represent different disciplines (history, English, comparative literature, American studies, modern languages, history of science, Judaic studies, and library science); they come from different countries (Norway, Germany, France, Italy, Turkey, Israel, China, Canada, and the United States); and they have studied a great variety of languages, ranging from Pueblo to Ladino, and including Spanish, Hebrew, German, Norwegian, Yiddish, French, Italian, Portuguese, Turkish, and English, as well as mixed languages, sign language, and ISOTYPE. Their efforts bring into new focus the "Languages of What Is Now the United States" (rendered at times by the acronym "LOWINUS," for short); and their work has, in many cases, developed in some association with the Longfellow Institute.[29]

Multilingual America is divided into seven parts and a brief research guide. The collection opens with "Literary History, Old and New," a part dominated by overviews that highlight, in a representative fashion, the many challenges that multilingualism presents to American literary history. The second part, "The Many Languages of American Literature," investigates a few exemplary cases at close range: an old Spanish-language play from the Southwest, a Welsh novel published in Utica, New York; responses to nationalism, transnationalism, cosmopolitanism, and "the Jewish question" in American Yiddish writing; Chinese American writers in their relationship to China and America; and a contemporary New Jersey poet who writes in Turkish. Such examples explore some of the ways in which multilingual literature has negotiated the demands of two or more literary traditions in constituting texts. The third part, "Yekl and Hyde: Different-Language Versions of the 'Same' Texts," is devoted to three case studies of a particularly fruitful issue in American literary studies. What are the literary and cultural questions that the doubling of the "same" texts as Yiddish/English, French/English, or Chinese/English raises? What does this "Jekyll and Hyde" game tell us about multilingual double-consciousness? Part 4, "Multilingualism as a Way of Life," explores, again in exemplary cases, the American elements in Hebrew sermons, assimilation in the German-language universe of newspaper and stage, comedy in the Italian-American theater, and Polish-language stories of immigration, assimilation, and American Polonization. The fifth part, "Melting Glots," confronts the pervasive issue of codeswitching, of mixed and "impure" languages, that has sometimes been used to justify the exclusion of literary texts that employ such languages from national literary histories into which such "impurities" would not seem to fit. What kinds of literary languages are Franglais, Portinglês, Yinglish, Italglish, Spanglish, or Germerican? Is their comic effect a result only of the desire for "pure" languages and traditions? Or do such languages embody double-consciousness as a cultural ideal (as Doris Sommer suggests)? Part 6, "Multilingualism and English-Language Writing," offers exemplary and suggestive readings of James Fenimore Cooper and Cynthia Ozick, as well as reflections on rereading American literature in a multilingual context. How does American literature in English look from a multilingual perspective? The seventh part, "Languages and Language Rights," turns to the serious political and historical problems of languages and language rights, focusing on an "almost lost" Indian language, the suppression of sign language for deaf people in the United States, and the creation and Americanization of ISOTYPE, and ends with the 1996 "Statement on Language Rights" by the Linguistic Society of America.

If a collection of this nature were accompanied by an appropriately exhaustive bibliography, it would have to be a massive multivolume set (which would be both costly and soon in need of updating). In the age of electronically available library catalogues and databases, there are alternatives, however, and in the last section some of these methods of researching multilingual literature are briefly and suggestively demonstrated.

The scholarly work assembled in *Multilingual America* includes case studies and groundbreaking bibliographic work, historically focused contributions on language creation and suppression, and close readings of representative texts. The collection presents new views of multilingualism as a historical phenomenon and as an ongoing way of life. It does so by taking seriously the task of examining the history of discrete language groups and their literary productions, as well as by crossing language boundaries (in comparative work centering on shared themes or genres) and paying attention to the many superimpositions of existing languages onto one another (in codeswitching, bilingual puns, and in "hybrid tongues"); by investigating newly invented languages; and by reflecting on the effects of multilingualism on English writing in the United States.

Multilingual America suggests much-needed reexaminations of the notions of assimilation and pluralism; it revives and gives new substance to Randolph Bourne's famous brief for a "Trans-National America";[30] it gives the approaches to ethnicity as an "invention" a new turn and new materials and shows how American languages could participate simultaneously in Americanization and in ethnicization; it presents many difficult negotiations with two or more languages with a rare sense of inwardness; it invites the reader to think of many little-known and fascinating authors and texts as part of American literature and to make the move from an "English only" to an "English plus" approach; and it thereby suggests that, as more work will be done in the future, new generalizations about the United States may be needed to reflect the history and culture of multilingual America more fully. Walt Whitman's prophetic warning may yet come to bear fruit.

NOTES

A word is probably needed concerning the use of "America" in the title, and throughout the text, of this collection to stand for "United States." Though the citizens of other countries in the Americas rightly stress that this usage tends to marginalize their existence, I find it difficult to avoid the noun "America" and impossible to do without the noun and adjective "American" ("United Stateser"? "USian"?). Furthermore, such terms as "Asian Americans," "Native Americans," or "African Americans" are employed even by critics of the *pars pro toto* use of the term "America" and can be avoided only by lengthy and clumsy circumlocutions. Since hyphenated languages and ethnic groups in the United States (of some importance to this collection) have also often been discussed with the suffix "-American" and since neither Canada nor Latin America but the United States is the focus of this volume, I have chosen to use the popular terms under which the United States is best known internationally and most widely discussed nationally.

1. See, for example, the impressive "LINGUA program for the promotion of language-learning" that is part of the European Union's SOCRATES program, Rue Montoyerstraat 70, B-1040 Brussels, Belgium; e-mail <infodep@erasmus.be>, world wide web page at http://cwis.usc.edu/dept/annenberg/voll/issue1/hutchison/about_erasmus.html.

2. Ingrid Gogolin, "Sprache und Migration," in *Ethnische Minderheiten in Bundesrepublik Deutschland: Ein Lexikon*, ed. Cornelia Schmalz-Jacobsen and Georg Hansen (München: C. H. Beck, 1995), 488–490.

3. See *The Autonomy Statute of Trentino-South Tyrol: A Possible Paradigm for Ethnic Pacification in the Central Danubian Area* (Trento: Associazione Italo-Tedesca di Sociologia with support of the United States Institute of Peace at Washington, February 1994), 27, 29–30. See also the multilingual website http://www.provinz.bz.it/LPA/authonomie/3statut.html.

4. "Statement on Language Rights, 1996," reprinted in full in part 7 of this volume.

5. A recent survey by the Modern Language Association showing that enrollment in foreign-language instruction has continued to decline in the 1990s has not generated much public discussion. See "Results of the Modern Language Association's Fall 1995 Survey of Foreign Language Enrollments," *MLA Newsletter* 28.4 (Winter 1996): 1–2. According to the executive director of the American Studies Association, the majority of academic Amer-

icanists in the United States is now monolingual, with the exception of "native speakers who happen to be US residents/scholars, or with folks in (mainly comparative) literature or ethnic studies where language is required" (personal communication from John Stephens, December 3, 1996).

6. See, for example, Phyllis Schlafly, "Bilingualism Is the Wrong Way To Go" (December 20, 1995), posted on http://www.heritage.org/townhall/columnists/schlafly/schl122095.html, a piece that juxtaposes bilingual education and fluency in English. Her use of the phrase "e uno plures" (in order to deplore cultural fragmentation) shows that this columnist is so convinced of her cause as to find it unnecessary to work on her Latin.

7. E. D. Hirsch, *Cultural Literacy: What Every American Needs to Know* (New York: Vintage Books, 1988), 91. By contrast, the Linguistic Society of America emphasized in its 1996 "Statement on Language Rights" that "where diverse linguistic communities exist in one country, they have generally managed to coexist peacefully. Finland, Singapore, and Switzerland are only three examples. . . . Multilingualism by itself is rarely an important cause of civil discord." The difference between Hirsch's and the Linguists' position merits careful study and discussion.

8. John Edwards Philips, comment posted at http://www.georgetown.edu/crossroads/interroads/philips6.html in July 1997 as part of a larger INTERROADS discussion of American multilingualism.

9. James W. Crawford, INTERROADS thread at http://www.georgetown.edu/crossroads/interroads/crawford.html. Citing Heinz Kloss, *The American Bilingual Tradition* (Rowley, Mass.: Newbury House, 1977), Crawford points out that a larger percentage of American elementary school students received foreign-language instruction in 1900 than today.

10. See "Myths about Bilingualism," posted on the web at http://www.nethelp.no/cindy/myth.html. See also James Crawford, ed., *Language Loyalties: A Source Book on the Official English Controversy* (Chicago: University of Chicago Press, 1992), 313–394, and INTER-ROADS discussion at http://www.georgetown.edu/crossroads/interroads/crawford.html.

11. For the "English Plus" slogan, see the National Education Association's advocacy and its web page at http://www.nea.org/info/engonly.html, and the impressive and extremely helpful website of *Issues in US Language Policies*, http://ourworld.compuserve.com/homepages/JWCRAWFORD/engplus.htm, reported also by Luisanna Fodde on INTERROADS at http://www.georgetown.edu/crossroads/interroads/fodde.html.

12. For the problem of court interpreters, see *Civil Rights Issues Facing Asian Americans in the 1990s: A Report of the United States Commission on Civil Rights* (February 1992), 168–169; see also Crawford, *Language Loyalties*, 225–312, and Martha Minow's work on the Supreme Court's decision to permit the exclusion of bilingual jurors in the *Hernandez v. New York* decision of 1991, "Equalities," *Journal of Philosophy* 88 (1991): 633–644.

13. INTERROADS discussion in July 1997, posted at http://www.georgetown.edu/crossroads/interroads/mcnamara.html.

14. Gerald Early, "American Education and the Postmodernist Impulse," *American Quarterly* 45.2 (June 1993): 220.

15. Mary Louise Pratt, "Comparative Literature and Global Citizenship," in *Comparative Literature in the Age of Multiculturalism*, ed. Charles Bernheimer (Baltimore: Johns Hopkins University Press, 1995), 64. The programmatic definitions from 1975 and 1993 of the field of comparative literature in the United States make clear that, if anything, it has become *more* acceptable in the past two decades to work with only English translations of non-English originals, in effect making all languages except English more "foreign" than ever; see the Greene report and the Bernheimer report in the same volume, 35 and 44.

16. Walter Benn Michaels, *Our America: Nativism, Modernism, and Pluralism* (Durham: Duke University Press, 1995), 129.

17. David A. Hollinger, *Postethnic America: Beyond Multiculturalism* (New York: Basic Books, 1995).

18. William Peterfield Trent et al., *The Cambridge History of American Literature*, vol. 3 (repr., New York: Macmillan, and Cambridge, England: University Press, 1943), 572–634.

19. These authors and texts are part of the large sampling of non-English literature of the United States, ranging from Native American and colonial languages to many immigrant tongues and French and Arabic works by African Americans, in *The Longfellow Anthology of American Literature*, ed. Marc Shell and Werner Sollors (Baltimore: Johns Hopkins University Press, forthcoming).

20. H. L. Mencken, *The American Language* (1919; 4th ed. 1936; repr., New York: Knopf, 1951).

21. Robert Spiller et al., *Literary History of the United States* (1946; fourth ed. repr., New York: Macmillan, 1975), 663–702.

22. Michael North's excellently researched study *Dialect of Modernism: Race, Language, and Twentieth-Century Literature* (New York: Oxford University Press, 1994), for example, provocatively casts "race" as "the American language" and examines numerous instances of minstrelsy and masking. While North offers a close reading of T. S. Eliot's French poem "Mélange Adultère de Tout" in the light of Deleuze and Guattari (84–86), mentions in passing post–World War I legislation prohibiting the use of languages other than English in American private and public schools (24), and discusses the "linguistic and racial" culture wars of the 1920s at chapter length (127–146), he surprisingly limits his discussion to the tension between standard English and English dialect in debates about "the American language" and modern literature—at the expense of all other American languages.

23. It is still a promising sign that the *Norton Anthology of African American Literature* includes at least one non-English text, Victor Séjour's fascinating short story "Le Mulâtre." The *Heath Anthology* also opened its pages to a few American texts that needed to be translated into English; yet see Te-hsing Shan's fine and exemplary critique, forthcoming in the *Longfellow Anthology*, of the *Heath Anthology*'s English-only rendition of two Chinese-American Angel Island poems, in inverted order, as if they were one—with an effect that strengthens the political protest.

24. King-Kok Cheung and Stan Yogi, eds., *Asian-American Literature: An Annotated Bibliography* (New York: Modern Language Association, 1988), vi. The reason given is that this will help "keep the bibliography to a manageable size"—which implies that the Asian-language publications by Asian Americans must be sizeable. Other excluded items are individual poems, archival and private materials, and student publications. A new turn in Asian-American studies can be witnessed in the scholarship of Te-hsing Shan, Xiao-huang Yin, Qian Jun, and Shen Shuang.

25. Zyla and Aycock, *Ethnic Literature since 1776* (Lubbock: Texas Tech University Press, 1978), the Proceedings of the 1976 Comparative Literature Symposium. Brom Weber, *Chapbook* 2 (Davis: University of California Library, 1975). See also Eric Sundquist's informative discussion of Spanish-language writing in Sacvan Bercovitch, ed., *Cambridge History of American Literature, vol. 2, Prose Writing, 1820–1865* (Cambridge: Cambridge University Press, 1995), 169. "Immigrants and Other Americans," my own contribution to Emory Elliott's *Columbia Literary History of the United States* (New York: Columbia University Press, 1988), 568–588, also constituted an attempt to take multilingualism seriously in a chapter of American literary history.

26. *Critical Inquiry* 20.1 (Autumn 1993).

27. Widener information courtesy of Marc Shell and Kenneth Carpenter; the listing of the U.S. postmaster general was provided by Peter Conolly-Smith, who is currently researching the multilingual press during World War I.

28. Among many particularly rich sources are "The Chicago Foreign Language Press Survey," a translation project issued by the Works Projects Administration in Chicago in 1942, available on microfilm, and "The Immigrant in America: A Microfilm Collection" (264 microfilm reels with guides).

29. The Longfellow Institute was created at Harvard University in 1994 in order to pull together past efforts of studying the multilingual writings of the United States; it was named after the polyglot poet whose translations and whose pioneering work in comparative literature helped to develop literary study across linguistic boundaries. See Daniel Zalewski's article "Tongues Untied: Translating American Literature into English," *Lingua Franca* (December/January 1996/97): 61–65, and the web page located at http://www.fas.harvard.edu/~lowinus/.

30. See Randolph S. Bourne, "Trans-National America," *Atlantic Monthly* 118 (July 1916): 86–97; reprinted in *Theories of Ethnicity: A Classical Reader* (Basingstoke: Macmillan, and New York: New York University Press, 1996), 93–108.

Part I

Literary History, Old and New

"Where is the rest of me?"—Ronald Reagan once asked at a poignant moment. It might very well be the question that American literature should be asking of many of its contemporary critics and interpreters. For although a first groundwork of scholarship on American multilingualism was laid early on, readers now generally assume that American literature means as much as literature of the United States written in English.

The overviews of this section stand for many other parts of "the rest" of American literature. Alide Cagidemetrio's survey constitutes an invitation to extend its engagement with multilingualism backward into the colonial period, forward into the twentieth century, and to flesh it out with close comparative readings; and Orm Øverland's, Michel Fabre's, and Aviva Ben-Ur's exemplary surveys of historical, ethnic, and regional segments of single-language groups not only present informative descriptions and interpretations but also may inspire students and scholars interested in other groups and languages.

"The Rest of the Story" is the history of American multilingual literary production, a history that fell into near-oblivion in the period from World War I through the Cold War. Proceeding comparatively and historically, and focusing on genre rather than isolating by language, Cagidemetrio's essay also offers a model answer to the question how writing in different languages could be related to the Anglophone tradition. The colonial languages may be too often identified with a colonialist project by contemporary multicultural critics (as if a quietly embraced "English-only" multiculturalism were an adequate response to that problem!). Yet there was much writing of specific interest to multicultural concerns, not only in English, the best-known colonial language of the United States, but also in Spanish, Dutch, French, and Russian. (Discussions of Spanish-language texts and issues follow in two later sections of *Multilingual America*.)

American literature in French is hardly well known today; and in "The New Orleans Press and French-Language Literature by Creoles of Color," Michel Fabre provides an overview of one important segment of Francophone writing in the United States. He examines the antebellum and post–Civil War literature, its cultural contexts in Louisiana and France, and its relationship to "white" Francophone writing, and reflects on the writers' silence on the slavery issue while they deal with such themes as plaçage very critically. Fabre's discussion provides the larger intellectual and political context for such outstanding and currently reclaimed literary figures as Michel Séligny, Victor Séjour, or Joanni Questy and such important essayist-journalists as Armand Lanusse, Rodolphe Desdunes, and the Belgian Jean-

Charles Houzeau—who passed for black in New Orleans.[1] Orm Øverland's essay, "From Melting Pot to Copper Kettles: Assimilation and Norwegian-American Literature," focuses on Norwegian-language writings by Waldemar Ager, Ole A. Buslett, and Dorthea Dahl and could serve as a model for future projects of discussing non-English literature of the United States in the context of American social and intellectual history. In his careful analysis of the Norwegian-Americans' reaction to Americanization as a double bind, and of their writings on the melting pot and their constructions of homemaking myths, Øverland complicates past accounts of linguistic and ethnic assimilation. In "The Ladino (Judeo-Spanish) Press in the United States, 1910–1948," Aviva Ben-Ur presents her fully researched findings on a little-known American language, Ladino—the language based on old Castilian and developed in the Ottoman Empire by Sephardic Jews expelled from Spain. Ben-Ur reviews Ladino journalism, including Moise Soulam's social columns, the documentation of Ladino theater, and the debates about Ladino language against the background of its speakers' ethnic transformation.

NOTES

1. A new edition of Michel Séligny's short stories has been prepared for publication in Montreal by Frans C. Amelinckx. A bilingual edition of Victor Séjour's selected drama and prose is being edited by Mary Lynn Weiss for the Du Bois Institute and the Longfellow Institute at Harvard University; Séjour is also the subject of a new book by Charles O'Neill, and his short story "Le Mulâtre" appears bilingually (the translation by Andrea Lee) in the *Longfellow Anthology*, and in another English translation in the *Norton Anthology of African American Literature*. Rodolphe Desdunes is at the center of recent work by Diana Irene Williams. And Jean-Charles Houzeau, a collection of whose writing has been translated into English by Gerard Denault, is a central topic of Shirley Thompson's dissertation-in-progress.

Chapter One

"The Rest of the Story"; or, Multilingual American Literature

Alide Cagidemetrio

On the Monolingual Origins of Literary Histories

"One nation . . . one language," Theodore Roosevelt said in 1917 and meant "the language of the Declaration of Independence," summoned in defense of a nation he felt was threatened by the Babel of immigration. A similar position shaped the authoritative *Literary History of America* (1900), written by Barrett Wendell, the professor of English at Harvard University who pioneered in teaching American literature. His *History* constituted the foundation of a discipline, characterized by Wendell as the study of the contribution that was made by "America," in the course of three centuries, to the "literature of the English language." For Wendell, language, and not race, descent, or blood, was the unique imprint of nationality. Reminding his readers of that "old legend of Babel," he cautioned them to consider how in that remote past the "confusion of tongues broke every bond of common kinship," and how, as an outcome, "the races which should hold together through the centuries sprang afresh from men who newly spoke and newly thought and newly felt in terms of common language." This insistently "new" common language appears to connect the past of Babel seamlessly to the future of America. The typical "new" language, Wendell added, is of course "this English of ours," and "we Americans are English-speaking still; and English speaking we must always remain." Thus the country's literary genealogy was located in Chaucer, Spenser, Shakespeare, and the King James version of the Bible, and its history was best told by always relating English-language writing in America to the body of English literature.[1]

Of course, by claiming an English descent, Wendell was following his predecessors, notably Charles F. Richardson, whose *American Literature* (1886), inspired as it was by a faith in Anglo-Saxonism, strongly adheres to an assimilationist rhetoric. For Richardson, it is not language but "race" that constitutes the body of American literary expression into which other "races" simply merge: "the American Irishman, or German, or Frenchman, notwithstanding his love for fatherland, soon loses somewhat of his former nature, under the potent influence of the new conditions and of the dominant Saxon temper." Consequently, "all the non-English folk have little affected the literature of the country," and moreover, "the numbers and power of the Dutch in New York, the Swedes in Delaware, and even the English Friends in Pennsylvania, acted at first as a hindrance to a literature necessarily English, and in intellectual sympathy with prevalent English ideas."[2] Whereas Richardson explained his notion of American literature—defined as *"isolated inheritance, working freshly"*—according to the principle of the "survival of the fittest," Wendell shaped a monolingual "canon" in a "colonial" perspective. The implied readers of Wendell's history were European literati, or the Europeanized Americans, men of taste who could appreciate the extent of the achievement of literature written in English. By the middle of the nineteenth century, American literature could, in Wendell's view, deservedly be compared with that of the motherland, the ground for comparison resting on the positive assumption of a commonality of origin.

This commonality of origin, the family history of American literature, appears to be nonetheless a point to be made rather than a foregone conclusion by 1900. Thomas Wentworth Higginson, for example, in *A Reader's History of American Literature* (1903, coauthored with Henry Walcott Boynton) humorously challenged those stubbornly nativist "chroniclers" of American literature who refuse to recognize that even the most recent works "confess" an "English ancestry." Higginson relates the anecdote of an Irishman who, suddenly come into a large fortune and a vast manor, asks Gilbert Stuart to provide him with a family portrait gallery. When Stuart wonders how he is to paint it in the absence of ancestors, the Irishman replies: "You have only to paint me the ancestors that I ought to have had." Accordingly, Stuart produced "a series of knights in armor, judges in bushy wigs, and fine ladies with nosegays and lambs, to the perfect satisfaction of his patron."[3] While Higginson is challenging nationalistic pride and blind refusal of any link with the late motherland, now the British Empire, he also suggests that any genealogical origin is an invention. Higginson's Anglophilia prevents him from seeing that he himself adopts the Irishman's answer when it comes to his own literary portrait gallery.

By the turn of the last century, the "imagined ancestry" for American literature was actively, and even too insistently, pursued within an English-only arena that politically celebrated the renewed "special relationship" with Britain. In the same year as Higginson's history, William P. Trent, Wendell's counterpart at Columbia University, told his story not as an argumentative account of the historical relation between Britain and the United States but through symbolic paradigms, iconized in the pair of opposite portraits, the English Cavalier and the Puritan. Nor does Trent deem it necessary to keep historical accuracy while engaged in the construction of mythical linguistic and literary purity and recording in passing that the original English immigrants were "later reinforced by small bodies of Dutch, Swedes, Huguenots, and Germans and in the next century by some Highlanders." If the vast numbers of non-English immigrants who arrived before and after the first English migrants could be condensed into such a statement, then it is not surprising that in the pursuit of collective ancestors, the Indians fared no better and disappeared from these literary men's accounts, since, in Richardson's words, "they had no poet, and they died."[4]

Given such competitors, it is Wendell's history that offers the most sophisticated
and authoritative account of the classic American literary tradition, not substantially different from what we still know and practice today, even if we remember
the additions, or the omissions, that were the consequence of this general procedure
and that have been addressed by the "reconstruction" of American literature
through the traditions of literature by women, by people of color, by ethnics, and
so forth. Wendell's *History* was the first to suggest, and to use as an operating
device, the notion of the "lag" of American literary expression behind the development of that of the mother country England, and to locate in the period of transcen-
dentalism the emergence of a cultural independence measured by the unmistakable
presence of aesthetic value in American literary works. Richardson had spoken of a
"Saxon-Greek Renaissance in the New World" and Wendell applied the notion of
a "Renaissance" to the New England writers before F. O. Matthiessen was to make
it famous. The New England Renaissance was nourished by the heritage of immigrants who "were native Elizabethans,—stern and peculiar, but still temperamen-
tally contemporary with Shakspere and the rest," whereas the other immigration
and the expansion of cultural production beyond the boundaries of this ideal region
constituted "the rest of the story," the fitting title of the last section of the *Literary
History of America*.[5]

In the account of this "rest," sociological and moral-ideological criteria of evaluation prevail over aesthetic ones that guide the assessment of "canonic" literary
production. This can be seen, for example, in the striking exclusion of Walt Whitman from the pantheon of American poetry. Whitman is presented in the course of
a description of New York, a metropolis grown out of bounds, where "material
development" overwhelmed any intellectual potential, a place shaped by "foreigners," more like Paris, Vienna, Berlin, ancient Rome, or Babylon than "ancestral
America." Topsy-turvy and unnatural, New York provides Wendell with the appropriate context for his disdain for Whitman's poetry: he finds its style of an "excres-
cent, abortive kind" and its eccentricity "foreign"; hence he views its author as "less
American" than others, and suggests that this prophet of egalitarian democracy
could have found more congenial materials for his expression "in those European
regions which have been most disturbed by French Revolutionary excess."[6] Wendell
knew that Whitman was representative of a "newer" America, a metropolis of
immigration and variety, threatening to demolish a linguistic-literary model the
excellence of which he recognized, but the decadence of which he feared and saw
under the pressures, including aesthetic pressures, of emergent modernity. Therefore
Wendell also remained silent on the numerous literary texts written in other languages and connected with cultural systems different from his English model,
though they may have been present in the American scene of his days, not only in
the audacity of Whitman's poetry but also in the writings of immigrants who came
precisely from those European countries that had been variously affected by the
French Revolution and its aftermath.

"Each generation should produce at least one literary history of the United States,
for each generation must define the past in its own terms."[7] Thus opens Robert
Spiller's *Literary History of the United States* (1946), declaring his post-Eliotic sense

of both familiarity with and distance from that other history, published during World War I, the *Cambridge History of American Literature* (1917–1921). For Spiller and his collaborators, the parallel between their country and ancient Rome and the Roman Empire—that Wendell had abhorred—reappears and provides a sense of unity and exemplarity to literature of the United States (no longer "American literature") in which they trace the change from a colonial literature to "a world literature," as the last chapter is entitled, which places the end of the story in 1945, at the end of World War II. "The slow emergence of an articulate racial mixture—a race of races, as Whitman called it," is located at the ideological center of the literary history of the United States, while the notion that it originated in a "transported" and "transformed" European culture remains in place. Crucial to this transformation is the parallel between the "creative translation" of the English language into the American language, which, in turn, is also understood as the language that emerged from the "translation" of other, different tongues. The "American" language—no longer Wendell's "English"—is thus the first of "*melting pots*," the necessary national glue in a society in which unity cannot be based on "blood or hereditary traits." An authoritative contributor, H. L. Mencken writes the chapter "The American Language" for Spiller's *History*; it defends the nineteenth-century idea that American English is descended directly from that creative transformation of the language in Elizabethan England and that therefore the Americans, more than the English, have retained linguistic "audacity." For Mencken, this American linguistic dynamism is shown in the ability to incorporate the vitalizing effect of the mixed idioms of the frontier—including elements of Indian languages—and of the immigrants, especially the Dutch, German, French, and Spanish.[8]

One might think that the notion of an American language and its "Elizabethan" capacities, might lead, when applied to literary history, to an extension of victorious "amalgamation" onto the literature written on the national territories in languages other than English. Yet this happens only in part. One finds in the 1946 *History* a chapter dedicated to the Indian heritage, and non-English works are grouped together in a chapter compiled by Henry A. Pochmann, tellingly entitled "The Mingling of Tongues." This procedure is hardly an expression of Spiller's "generation," for it goes back to, and closely follows, the *Cambridge History of American Literature,* which presented a much more detailed account of aboriginal, German, French, and Yiddish texts (by Mary Austin, Albert B. Faust, Edward J. Fortier, and Nathaniel Buchwald), to which Pochmann merely adds brief treatments of the Spanish, Italian, and Scandinavian contributions. More important than this indebtedness is the fact that Spiller's *History* hardly tells the story of the emergence of American literature in analogy to the American language, for it is the logic of the "cultural island," to use David Bowers's term of 1944,[9] which Spiller's contributors have followed in structuring their accounts: the unity of the chapter is subdivided according to the language of each work; each language has its own sharply compressed history, and connections with English-language literature or with literary works in the language of origins are missing. The notion of the "cultural island" of each language group is furthermore established precisely by the omission of any relationship between literary expression and American historical context. An obvious example is that of Francophone literature of Louisiana, which has made such important contributions to American national literature, and specifically to that of the South. Yet while Spiller's *History* gives ample space to the southern regional tradition and its historical context, there is no reference there to the history or to the cultural production of French Louisiana.

Such forms of linguistic separatism, or worse, complete exclusion, on the basis of language alone, have continued to shape not only literary histories of more recent years but also anthologies and handbooks. The *Encyclopedia of Southern Culture* (1989) is a good example here; its editors assume that "the South" is primarily a "cultural" entity, in the sense given this term by Clifford Geertz: "an historically transmitted pattern of meanings embodied in symbols, a system of inherited conceptions expressed in symbolic forms."[10] Paradoxically, in the treatment of the "symbolic form" of literature the contributions of French Louisiana are completely ignored, with the single exception of Charles Gayarré, who is listed between George Washington Cable and Kate Chopin as a "regionalist," without further linguistic or cultural specifications. While the *Encyclopedia* includes French, Spanish, and Creole among the languages spoken in the South, and dedicates entries to literary dialect and creolization, the discussion of *literary* expression is limited to Anglophone works of such authors as William Gilmore Simms or Joel Chandler Harris, without reference to French or Spanish works. The legal suppression of French in Louisiana in 1868—when French could no longer be taught in secondary schools—and the ultimate publication of all legislation in English only also do not receive sufficient attention in the *Encyclopedia*, and very little is offered in it about the reaction of the intellectuals who, in 1876, founded the Athénée Louisianais, whose bulletin, *Comptes Rendus,* became the organ of resistance of French literary expression up to the twentieth century.

French literature in Louisiana is not even incorporated in national literary accounts as a "conversion" story from one language to another, or as a part of the development of southern literature in English, including that of George Washington Cable and Kate Chopin with their distinctive patois dialogues. Lost to memory in the United States, such literature is not recorded as part of French literature either but as the subfield of colonial literature in French.

This loss is exemplary for many other such losses, and what follows is the outline of a survey of prose and poetry from the first half of the nineteenth century, mainly in French, German, and Spanish, that did not find their way into American literary histories (or were mentioned only in isolation as unrepresentative of American literature) and have largely been forgotten in the intervening years.

A Modest Proposal for Rewriting Literary History

The dominance of English as the language of amalgamation and of literary use, its tradition in the United States so rich but also so fiercely defended, undoubtedly helped to render invisible all possible relations with different linguistic-literary systems. However, in an era in which the multicultural version of national history, of the study of literature, and of the transformation of the "canon" has been so much discussed and so widely adopted, one could also take again into consideration the multiplicity of languages and of American literary texts that employed them. One could examine, for example, whether *The Columbiad* (1807) by Joel Barlow, or even earlier, *The Conquest of Canaan* (1785) by Timothy Dwight, foundational texts of the American epic tradition, might not be aesthetically inferior to the *Walam Olum,* the poem of the Leni-Lenape transcribed in pictographic form, translated, and, in 1833, published alongside the original by Constantine Rafinesque, a cosmopolitan naturalist born in Constantinople of a French father and a Greek mother. Or one might wonder about the function of the hymns in German— such as the seven hundred contained in *Das Paradisische Wunderspiel* (1776) by Conrad Beissel (and others)—in the development of a poetic-religious language from Edward Taylor to Emily Dickinson; or about the significance of American theater in French, German, or Spanish for the national tradition of drama; or why a history of the American novel does not discuss side by side Kate Chopin, or William Faulkner, and Charles Etiénne Gayarré, Alfred Mercier, or Sidonie de La Houssaye. Or one may ask if writings on American manners, society, and politics, like Alexis de Tocqueville's *La Democratie en Amerique* (1837), cannot be helpfully reread together with works like *Viaje a los Estados Unidos del Norte de America* (1834) by Lorenzo de Zavala, a Mexican with democratic and anti-Spanish leanings, or the *Bericht über eine Reise nach den Westlichen Staaten Nord-Amerikas und einen mehrjährigen Aufenthalt am Missouri (1824–27)* by Gottfried Duden, the author, among other works, of an annotated edition and translation of Tocqueville, whom Francis Grund answered promptly, and with amused sarcasm, in *Die Aristrokatie in Amerika* (1837).

How many examples of autobiographic writing or of travel writing are there in other languages? It may suffice here to remember Lorenzo Da Ponte, whose *Memorie* were written and published in different versions in New York (1807–1830), or the slave narrative written in Arabic by the Muslim slave Omar ibn Said (*The Autobiography of Omar ibn Said, Slave in North Carolina,* 1831), or *Aus Zwei Weltteilen* by Marie Hansen Taylor, a woman's inside view of mid-nineteenth-century cultural life written by the highly educated wife of Bayard Taylor, a Germanophile who authored, among many other works, a translation of Goethe's *Faust,* in a stylized English that had a German ring to it.

With such a comparative and translingual focus one could reexamine the major literary genres that were employed in the first half of the nineteenth century, and it might be helpful to present a brief overview of the relations that existed between the English tradition, the only one known today, and those in other languages. This would mean continuing the work started a century ago by critics like Alcée Fortier (*Louisiana Studies,* 1894) or Albert B. Faust (*The German Element in the United States,* 1909) and connecting it with Anglo-American literary history.

A first multilingual examination of the early-nineteenth-century novel, for example, would pair James Fenimore Cooper with Charles Sealsfield, his contemporary rival for public attention and commercial success in the United States and in Europe. Sealsfield (1793–1864), or Carl Postl, was a polyglot former monk from

Moravia who spent a part of his life in the United States, as planter, trader, journalist, ardent supporter of Jackson, traveler, and, perhaps, Bonapartist spy, but who had his tombstone in a Swiss country cemetery inscribed with the words "Bürger von Nord-amerika." His works were published in Germany, Switzerland, and America, at times simultaneously. He wrote a historical novel on the white-Indian conflict in English, *Tokeah, or the White Rose* (1828), and rewrote it in German as *Der Legitime und die Republikaner*; he also wrote, in German, *Virey* (1834) and *Nord und Süd* (1843), large novels set in Mexico. He was known in Europe and America as "the great unknown" because, like Walter Scott before him, he published his works anonymously—both German and American editions—and was reviewed and admired in such journals as *Knickerbocker* and *Edinburgh Magazine*. His erratic biography, and the mystery he added to it, present interesting questions about the relationship between language, nation, and literature: in Europe he was known as an American author, and German reviews like *Das Ausland* presented some of his works as German translations from English originals, though they were often pirated from Sealsfield's own German originals. This happened also with *Lebensbilder aus der westlichen Hemisphäre — Life in the New World; or Sketches of American Society* (1843), a collection of short narratives portraying several types from the "people": aristocratic and passionate southern planters, elegant eastern ladies, squatters, and western desperadoes.

Sealsfield had already published a similar collection, *Das Kajütenbuch oder Nationale Charakteristiken — The Cabin Book or National Character Sketches* (1840), his most widely read book, whose sketches deal with Texas on the eve of the war, providing a remarkable treatment of the reasons and conflicts among the various colonists, French, Spanish, and Anglo-Saxon. Lost on the prairie, they symbolically wander in different directions, only to find themselves together in the same place again and again. Sealsfield was uncommonly keen on political argumentation and succeeded in communicating his passionate enthusiasm for American scenery through a detailed attention to its peculiarities, its geography and naturalistic aspects. His descriptions were so effective that a later writer, the Irish American Mayne Reid (1818–1883) excerpted them—in English translation—in his *Wild Life* (1856). William Gilmore Simms, in turn, rewrote in *Guy Rivers* an episode from Sealsfield's story "Ralph Doughbys Brautfahrt." And Henry Wadsworth Longfellow, one of his admirers, was reading Sealsfield's Louisiana sketches in *Lebensbilder* while working on his own *Evangeline* (1847).

In the first decades of the nineteenth century there was a strong interest in history-related works, poems, essays, or novels, and a number of them were equally written in languages other than English. With Cooper and Simms, besides Sealsfield, one should mention Félix Varela, a New York priest, who published anonymously in Spanish *Jicoténcal* (1826), a novel only recently rediscovered, telling of Cortez's conquest; or the "Indian" novels from Louisiana, such as *Le Soulier Rouge* (1849) by Charles de la Bretonne (?–1876)—alias D'Artlys, alias Jacques de Roquigny—and *Whip-Poor-Will* (1847) by Amedée Bouis, a Creole of Italian origin, who migrated to Paris, where he became a prolific writer. The most famous historian in the Creole tradition was Charles Gayarré (1805–1895), and his authority was also recognized by the post–Civil War supplement of the *Encyclopedia Americana* (1865). Gayarré's *Essai historique sur la Louisiane* was published in New Orleans in 1830, four years earlier than the first volume of the *History of the United States* by George Bancroft, with whom Gayarré shares not the language but the mythic method of romantic historiography. In 1846, three years after the publication of the epic account of the Spanish Conquest by William Prescott (*History of the Conquest of Mexico*, 1843), the revised and enlarged edition of the *Essai* appears in print, richer than before in "patriotic" episodes and materials for fictional treatment (*Histoire de la Louisiane*, 1846–1847; *History of Louisiana*, 1866). Indeed, the story of Gayarré's *Histoire* is the source of *Louisiana* (1845) by Louis Armand Garreau, the first historical novel set in colonial times, and of Charles Testut's *Saint Denis* (1845) and *Calisto* (1849). Testut was one of the most prolific Creole novelists and editor of magazines such as *La Revue Louisianaise*, *Les Viellées Louisianaises*, and *La Violette*. *Feuilletons*, or novels by installments, were profusely published on their pages, testifying to the interest of the reading public and to the literary fervor from the 1840s to the Civil War. Testut himself recorded a lively literary community in his *Portraits Litteraires de la Nouvelle Orleans* (1850). The publication of "feuilletons" in New Orleans was not confined to French only; novels in German were published by the *Louisiana Staats-Zeitung*; one of them, *Die Geheimnisse von New Orleans* (1854–1855) by Baron Ludwig von Reizenstein (1826–1885), was in the multilingual tradition started by the *Mystères de Paris* by Eugène Sue (1842) in France and continued in the United States from the anonymous fragment *Die Geheimnisse von Philadelphia* (1850) to *Les Mystères de la Nouvelle Orleans* (1853–1854) by Charles Testut, *Die Geheimnisse von St. Louis* (1854) by Heinrich Börnstein, and *Cincinnati; oder, Geheimnisse des Westens* (1854–1855) by Emil Klauprecht; and later *I misteri di Mulberry Street* (1893) and *I misteri di Bleecker Street* (1899) by Bernardino Ciambelli. The "mysteries" of Baron von Reizenstein, however, deviate from the common line taken by Sue and by his descendants, since race and sex prove to be at the core of them. A black Messiah—who reminds us of Jean Toomer's *Cane*—comes to punish the whites for their racial crimes; and sexual squalor is redeemed by a lesbian love affair that appears to challenge sexual domination and patriarchy. Von Reizenstein was also—long before Vladimir Nabokov—a butterfly specialist, and as such inspired his friend George Washington Cable to write the novella *The Entomologist* (1899).

Race and slavery are the subject matter both of historical and of contemporary narratives. Among the works by the numerous French-speaking, African-American authors, *Monsieur Paul* (1863) by Joanni Questy (?–1869) should be mentioned; it is the story of an illegal and clandestine marriage between a romantic Frenchman and a young woman of color. The Santo Domingo revolution is the historical setting of "Le mulâtre" (1837), the first short story known to be written by an African American, Victor Séjour (1817–1874), who was born and grew up in New Orleans, and then became a well-known playwright in Paris. Between 1855 and 1861 appeared also the short stories by Michel Séligny (1808?–1868), a free man of color, who tells melancholy stories from the past of the region. A response in French to *Uncle Tom's Cabin* is found in *Le Vieux Salomon*, written by Charles Testut in

1858, and a German one in *Sclaverei in Amerika, oder: Schwartzes Blut* (1862) by Friederich Armand Strubberg (1806–1889). Strubberg, who went back to Germany in 1854 after thirty years of an adventurous life in Maryland and in Texas, became famous for his American stories; exoticism and "western" adventures are the happy formula for novels such as *Carl Scharnhorst, Abenteuer eines deutschen Knaben in Amerika* (1863) and *Der Sprung vom Niagarafall* (1864), published under the pseudonym of "Armand." Strubberg's *Sclaverei in Amerika* is an interesting attempt at analyzing the evils of slavery in a trilogy, *Die Quadrone*, *Die Mulattin*, and *Die Negerin*. In each novel appears the same type of heroine but with a different shade of color. She is repeatedly exposed to the conflict between love and slavery, confronted with men who are either racists or liberals, and always ends up triumphing over adverse circumstances or escaping to Europe with her beloved who has been converted to abolitionism. In *Carl Scharnhorst*—which had fifteen editions before 1900 and several translations into English—the issue of slavery is at the core of the relationship between Carl, an immigrant boy from Germany, and Dan, a black boy who becomes his friend and guide in the wilderness. Before Huck Finn, Carl has to face the moral dilemma between obedience to the law and personal loyalty, and he is ready to sacrifice himself in order to prevent Dan's return to slavery. Pretending to be Dan and offering himself to his masters turns out to be a successful trick, however, and both boys can enjoy an equal and unlimited freedom at the end.

Strubberg followed in the footsteps of Friedrich Gerstäcker (1816–1872), the author of *Die Flusspiraten des Mississippi* (1847), a vigorous traveler of the West, from Arkansas to California, and beyond to the Argentine pampas, and a vigorous writer of the mythical modern pioneer, the protagonist of *Die Regulatoren von Arkansas* (1845), *Gold, Ein Californisches Lebensbild* (1856), and especially *Nach Amerika! Ein Volksbuch* (1855), in which he tells the adventurous story of a group of German immigrants, from their landing in New Orleans to their voyage up the Mississippi and their settlement experiences. Its sequel, *In Amerika* (1876), begins in the last year of the Civil War and centers on the lives of those same immigrants who have become citizens, served as soldiers in the war, and are now active participants in the chaos of Reconstruction, in the violent climate after the fall of the South when the Ku Klux Klan was founded. Though excessively long and unnecessarily complicated, *In Amerika* is worth reading as a fascinating and historically rather persuasive "panorama" of the American scene from 1864 to 1872. The Civil War also provides setting and conflict for two later novels, *L'habitation de St. Ybars* (1881) by Alfred Mercier, and *Die Familie Nelville* (1889) by Balduin Möllhausen.

The immigraton experience is central to the work of Otto Ruppius (1819–1864), *Der Pedlar* (1857) and its sequel, *Das Vermächtis des Pedlars* (1859), novels that contrast life in the metropolis New York and that on the Alabama plantations. Surprisingly, the *pedlar* here is not a Yankee but a Jew who becomes the "magic helper" of the protagonist, a young German whom he teaches English and on whose life he keeps a vigilant eye. Ruppius had come to America after 1848, in a wave of political immigration that is also reflected in *Anton in Amerika* by Reinhold Solger (1817–1864), perhaps the best novel in German of the time. Published in installments between 1858 and 1861, *Anton in Amerika* appeared posthumously as a volume only in 1872. Anton is a literary descendant: he is the immigrant son of Anton Wohlfahrt, the protagonist of one of the most famous German "social novels," *Soll und Haben* (1855) by Gustav Freytag. The American story is in part a New World rewriting of plot and intention of social analysis of its antecedent; it shows the living conditions in New York and in New England, highlighting class conflicts but also ethnic differences within an array of characters that includes Irishmen, Germans, Frenchmen, and Franco-Africans.

In 1838, in New York, the octogenarian Lorenzo Da Ponte died. The author of the librettoes of *Cosi' fan tutte* and *Don Giovanni*, he had also written and published verses (*Poesie varie*, 1830; *Versi composti da Lorenzo Da Ponte per la morte d'Anna Celestina, sua virtuosissima e adorata consorte*, 1832; *Storia americana*, 1835). In 1840, William Cullen Bryant (1794–1878) edited an anthology of poetry, *Selection from the American Poets,* that may well be considered exemplary of the verse production in English, and only slightly different from *The Poets and Poetry of America*, published two years later by Rufus Griswold, whose critical authority shapes the "canon" with the inclusion of Emerson, Poe, Longfellow, and of numerous other poets, known to the literary historian as the "Fireside Poets," the forgotten authors of regional, nature verses in a musty language. These poems could be advantageously compared with the poems collected in *Les Cenelles* (1845), an anthology edited by Armand Lanusse (1812–1867) that collects the works of African-American poets, and is representative of the degree of maturity reached by Louisiana poetry in French. Camille Thierry (1814–1875) appears the most interesting poet in this collection, even if his most ambitious work, *Les Vagabondes* (1874), was published later in France. *Les Vagabondes* contains the poetical portraits of three New Orleans characters: Mariquita, a Spanish woman of aristocratic descent who has become a prostitute; Haricot, a French nobleman abandoned by his family; and Magloire d'Hoquincourt, a black prince who yearns to go back to Africa on a quest for his father's crown, lost in a battlefield.

Contemporary German-language poetry can be read in the collection *Deutsch in Amerika* (1892), which G. A. Zimmerman edited, selecting poems among those published in newspapers and magazines. Some authors were political exiles from 1848 and their verses—like those by Konrad Krez (*An Mein Vaterland*) and Gustav Brühl (*Poesien des Urwalds)*—are political and imbued with nostalgia for a lost cause and a lost country. The "creolization" of German—the Pennsylvania German or Dutch—characterizes an oral poetic tradition that becomes written with Henry Harbaugh (1817–1867), and his posthumously published *Harbaugh's Harfe* (1870). In the Southwest another oral tradition, that of the *corridos* was being transferred to print in newspapers like the *New Mexican*, founded in 1849. These were ballads telling of conflicts between Latin and Anglo cultures, episodes of frontier life, and legends of Indian wars. Cultural conflicts and historical poetry appear also in French verses, such as those of the poem on the battle of New Orleans, *Milhuit-centquatorze et Milhuitcentquinze* (1838) by Tullius St. Céran, and *Les Anglais à la Louisiane* (1845) by Urbain David; Auguste Lussan had instead dedicated to Napoleon *Les Impériales* (1841).

Among the contemporaries of Bryant and Emerson—whose *Poems* appeared in

1847--two brothers writing in French, François Dominique and Adrien Rouquette distinguished themselves for their verses. Both interpreters of the love of nature and of the Louisiana landscape, they were appreciated in France by such figures as Hugo and Beranger. François Dominique Rouquette (1810–1890) wrote *Le Mechacébéennes* (1839) and *Les Fleurs d'Amérique* (1856), in which he shows his romantic passion for primitive life and for its representatives, black and red "bon sauvages"; Adrien Rouquette (1813–1887) was a mystic inspired by the beauty of nature to be enjoyed in perfect solitude, as it is shown in *Antoniade ou la solitude avec Dieu* (1860) or *Les Savanes* (1840). Adrien Rouquette lived among the Indians, to whom he dedicated a novella, *La nouvelle Atala; ou, la fille de l'esprit* (1879), a kind of rewriting of Chateaubriand's work. He was a picturesque figure, well known in New Orleans literary circles, and a friend of George Washington Cable and of Lafcadio Hearn, for whom he wrote "Chant d'un jeune Creole: a mo zami grek-angle', L. H."

Let me conclude this brief sketch of American literary tendencies in some of the different languages that were used in the first half of the nineteenth century by saying that its purpose was merely to suggest the extent to which the national "ear" heard languages other than English, or, as the historian of the language Harry Morgan Ayres perceived it, in *The Cambridge History of American Literature*—at nearly the same time as Theodore Roosevelt's pronouncement that I cited at the beginning—"Italian-American, Yiddish-American, Scandinavian-American, German-American yammering in our ears."[11] Ayres felt the need to "rationalize" the American linguistic Babel, while Henry A. Pochmann was fully appreciative of its contribution. Thus Pochmann concluded his essay "The Mingling of Tongues" in Spiller's *Literary History of the United States* with: "The early desire to cast the Old World into a mythical melting pot has given place to a conviction that the immigrant serves his adopted country best when he is steeped in the traditions of his fatherland; that various and lively regional cultures increase the vitality of the culture of the United States."[12] Being aware of linguistic diversity, and of the need to "rationalize" and appreciate it, is only a short step away from being aware of the linguistically diverse literature of the country. Yet the work begun by *The Cambridge History of American Literature* and by the *Literary History of the United States* is still to be done, and we still need to integrate this, the "rest of the story," in what the literary historians of the early twentieth century came to call the "main stream."

NOTES

1. Barrett Wendell, *A Literary History of America* (New York: Charles Scribner's, 1900, repr. 1905), 3.

2. Charles F. Richardson, *American Literature, 1607–1885*, 1886 and 1888; repr., New York: G. P. Putnam's, 1904), 1, 22–23.

3. Thomas Wentworth Higginson and Henry Walcott Boynton, *A Reader's History of American Literature* (Boston: Houghton Mifflin, 1903), 2.

4. William P. Trent, *A History of American Literature, 1607–1865* (New York: D. Appleton, 1903), 5.

5. Wendell, 445; 449–518.

6. Ibid., 471.

7. Robert Spiller et al., *Literary History of the United States* (1946; 4th ed. repr., New York: Macmillan, 1975), vii.

8. Ibid., 663–693.

9. David F. Bowers, ed., *Foreign Influences in American Life* (Princeton: Princeton University Press, 1944).

10. Quoted in Charles Reagan Wilson and William Ferris, eds. *Encyclopedia of Southern Culture* (Chapel Hill: University of North Carolina Press, 1989), xvi.

11. Harry Morgan Ayres, "The English Language in America," in *The Cambridge History of American Literature*, vol. 3, *Later National Literature*, ed. William Peterfield Trent et al. (1921; repr., New York: Macmillan, and Cambridge, England: University Press, 1943), 568.

12. Spiller, 693.

Chapter Two

The New Orleans Press and French-Language Literature by Creoles of Color

Michel Fabre

The *gens de couleur* in antebellum Louisiana distinguished themselves from other African Americans by jealously preserving their Latin culture. Generally better educated than "American" free blacks (80 percent of them were literate in 1850), they had more than one thousand children attending schools often staffed by French-born teachers, and some of their children pursued studies in France. These "aristocrats of manners," who were, at the same time, pariahs in the neither-white-nor-black category, stood as far as possible from the slaves, whom quite a few of them owned, and consistently attempted to win a degree of acceptance from whites. This seldom occurred openly, even among the literary and artistic elite, in spite of the various links that existed between the two races. These men generally met among themselves in mutual help societies favoring cultural expression, such as the Société d'Economie, the Francs Amis, the Jeunes Amis, or the Association des Artisans.

During the antebellum period, the literary production of the *gens de couleur libres* of New Orleans represents a substantial output. The reasons for this blossoming, the identity, motivation, and outlook of the various writers, deserve close attention. They were generally New Orleans–born teachers, craftsmen, and shopkeepers who took to writing. Their travels, education, and readings made them very much part of the French metropolitan tradition, whose literary lions—Victor Hugo, Musset, Alexandre Dumas, Lamartine, Béranger—and progressive intellectuals, from Lamenais to Fourier, influenced them. Their works, occasionally published or performed in Paris, were mostly printed in regular white Louisiana newspapers, with the major exceptions of *L'Album littéraire* and *Les Cenelles*.[1]

The post–Civil War literature appeared in the colored press. Dealing principally with political issues and general news, the colored press made room for poetry and short stories at a time when fiction often initially came out by installments in newspapers. The period of Reconstruction until 1877 corresponds to the careers of *L'Union* (1863–1864) and *La Tribune de la Nouvelle Orléans* (1864–1869); the final period covers the life span of *The Louisianan* and *The Crusader* (1890–1897), at a time when the *Comptes-rendus de l'Athénée Louisianais*, edited by French-speaking whites now bent on retaining for themselves the name "Creole," vainly attempted to stem the tide of the English language in Louisiana.

From colonial times, the free colored population had grown regularly in Louisiana, fostering a generally-well-off elite, which included a handful of famous names in applied sciences (inventor Norbert Rillieux) and the medical profession (Louis and Armand Roudanez), many musicians, such as composer Edmond Dédé, and a few artists, like sculptor Eugène Warbourg and painter Jules Lion. The literary and artistic production of this group was closely linked with that of white Creoles and immigrant Frenchmen, with whom many of them studied, worked, and/or were linked by blood ties. That no colored press existed during the antebellum period was not due to lack of support but to antiabolitionist regulations and the suspicion in which free blacks were generally held. That they should have contributed to the local white newspapers, even though they were not permitted to sign their names in full, is all the more remarkable.

In *The Negro in Louisiana, Aspects of His History and His Literature* (1937), Creole of color Charles B. Roussève deals extensively with five early writers only: a poet who signed himself as Hippolyte Castra; Joseph-Colastin Rousseau, whose poem "Pauvre enfant" (Poor child) appeared in *La Réforme* on April 12, 1846, and who wrote a pamphlet, *Les Contemporains*; Michel Séligny, a teacher and the founder of the Académie Sainte-Barbe, whose numerous pieces were published only in the local press; Joseph Beaumont, "the Creole Béranger" who told the true story of Toucoutou, who wanted to pass for white, in Creole dialect but was never published; finally, Lucien Mansion, who not only employed his fortune to help colored people migrate to Haïti and Mexico in the mid-1850s, when their legal condition became worse, but championed their cause in grandiloquent verse after the war.[2] But this handful represented only a fraction of a literary set. In 1845, Armand Lanusse had no difficulty gathering a collection of eighty-five poems by seventeen authors, all belonging to his milieu, when he prepared *Les Cenelles*.

The first review of this colored elite, *L'Album Littéraire, Journal des Jeunes gens, Amateurs de literature* (1843), brandished the Latin maxim "Homo doctus in se semper divitias habet." This was a claim for the superiority of education over moneymaking and racial origin. A short-lived publication officially edited by a white (probably French-born) schoolteacher, J. L. Marciacq, this was the first journal of this kind in Louisiana.[3]

Most of the works in *L'Album* are unsigned, or signed by initials. Such precautions probably went along with the habit of depriving free men of color of the same complete identity as whites; indeed evading the laws prohibiting writings likely to arouse the slave population was not rendered necessary by the benign character of this publication. For example, the issue of July 1, 1843, prints an unsigned essay, "Philosophie de l'Histoire," in which the author condemns war, alludes to the "material" struggle (no echo of Marx!), yet never mentions slavery. There is an innocuous ode to friendship by Emile Torrégh; an elegy by Bo[we]rs on the death of a young woman; an "Essai poétique" on another dead lover by [Joanni] Q[ues]ty; a tribute from A. B. to a French lady; a story of female bravery by C. D. about "Une Louisianaise en 1814"; and finally, the second installment of "Un Scélérat."

In the July 15, 1843, issue, one finds a critique of social injustice under the title "Horreurs du jour" (The horrors of the day), but it remains general. The verse is bland, such as an ode to sleep; likewise, the poet's spleen is mostly due to the death of a mother in "Le Désenchantement" by T[éren]ce Rouquette. Of greater interest, M. F. L[iotau]'s "Une nouvelle impression" condemns a mother who urges her daughter to accept "plaçage":

> L'amour n'a plus d'attraits, une mère éhontée
> Aujourd'hui vend le coeur de sa fille attristée
> Et la vertu n'est plus qu'un vain mot qui se perd. (p. 81)

> [Love has lost its appeal; today a shameless mother is selling the heart of her bereaved daughter and virtue is only a vain word that gets lost.]

This practice, current at the time, is described as shameful. The girl hopes that God will forgive her future living in sin, and the poet admonishes the mother:

> Et vous que Dieu fit mère! . . . oh! ne craignez-vous pas
> Pour votre pauvre enfant un si cruel trépas! (p. 81)

> [You whom God made a mother, oh, don't you fear for your unhappy child such a cruel death?]

A short story, "Marie," by "Un abonné" (a subscriber), echoes the same theme. Here, the young woman commits suicide after her mother whips her into yielding to a rich protector. She is evidently a "quadroon," like the girl in "Un mariage de conscience" in the August 15, 1843, issue. This story, signed by Armand Lanusse, is not lacking in literary qualities. The narrator was already in the cathedral when a young pious woman flung herself to the foot of the altar and confided her woes to the Virgin loud enough for him to catch every word of it. Her tragedy is that of *plaçage*:

> Un jour, ma mère m'apprit que celui que j'aimais, ayant son consentement, l'avait chargée de me proposer de m'unir à lui. Je ne dissimulai point ma joie à ma mère et je répondis que je serais heureuse de devenir l'épouse de Gustave. Mais quand celle qui me donna le jour voulut me faire comprendre que ce jeune homme, occupant dans la société un rang plus élevé que le nôtre, ne pouvait s'unir légitimement à moi, je cachai ma tête dans mes mains et me retirai, le coeur indigné, car ce n'était donc que comme une maîtresse et non comme une épouse que Gustave me recherchait.
> Je ne voulus plus le revoir.
> Quelque temps s'était écoulé depuis que j'avais pris cette résolution, lorsqu'un jour ma mère me dit: "Mais ma fille, puisqu'une condition que tant de jeunes personnes recherchent dans ce pays te répugne, que ne contractes-tu un *mariage de conscience*?" . . . C'est un pacte où la loi n'a aucune part mais auquel un prêtre donne tout le caractère d'un engagement légitime. "Alors, ma mère, il ne me reste plus d'objection," lui dis-je. (p. 134)

> [One day my mother told me that the man I loved, had obtained her consent and asked her to propose that I be united to him. I did not hide my joy and replied that I would be happy to become Gustave's wife. But when the one who gave birth to me

tried to make me understand that this young man, whose station in society was higher than ours, could not become my legitimate spouse, I hid my head in my hands and retired with an indignant heart, since Gustave only wanted me for his mistress, not his wife.
I refused to see him any more.
Some time had elapsed since I had taken this resolution when my mother said to me: "But, daughter, since a condition which so many young women in this country are seeking is repugnant to you, why don't you contract a *marriage of conscience*?" . . . Law has no part in this contract but a priest brings to it all the characteristics of a legitimate union. "Then, mother, I have no longer any objection," said I.]

Marie was a faithful companion and bore her lover a child, who died. She became mad with sorrow and jealousy when he took a white wife. She ran out of the cathedral and threw herself under the carriage of the newlyweds.

"Mais elle était donc folle?" demanda d'une voix pleine de compassion la dame de la calèche. "Oui, madame," m'écriai-je, "elle était devenue folle parce qu'un lâche, abusant de sa simplicité, l'avait indignement trompée, et ce lâche, madame, c'est. . . ." "Fouette les chevaux!" cria soudain au cocher le pâle personnage qui sortit tout à coup de sa stupeur. Le cocher obéit à cette injonction, les chevaux partirent . . . et la dame se pencha vainement vers moi pour saisir les dernières paroles que ma bouche venait de prononcer. (p. 137)

["But she was mad, wasn't she?" the lady in the carriage asked in a compassionate voice. "Yes, madam," I exclaimed, "she lost her mind because a coward abused her simplicity and basely betrayed her, and this coward, Madam, is. . . ." "Move on," the pale-faced individual who suddenly came out of his stupor shouted to the coachman. The coachman plied his whip, the horses darted off . . . and the lady vainly leaned towards me to catch the last words which my mouth had just uttered.]

Lanusse also denounces the connivance between the Catholic church and the wealthy whites (colored fathers are markedly absent from this literature) who perpetuate a practice that insults female virtue and weakens the institution of marriage. In the same issue of *L'Album Littéraire*, the fable "Le coq et le renard" (The rooster and the fox) (probably by colored teacher Ludger Boguille), regrets the propensity of the fledgling hens (the quadroons) to leave their rooster (the male Creole of color) in order to follow the fox (the white man) who can offer them more.

The issue of August 1, 1843, also contains three unsigned essays that deplore in an allusive way the state of social affairs in Louisiana. The first piece laments the meager attention shown the poet and berates the city-bred vices. The second one, "Tout est crime" (Everything is a crime), is content with proclaiming universal brotherhood. The essay in the next issue, "Aux Louisianais," firmly requests that instruction be granted to all, although the author specifies that he would like a reform, not a revolution. A novelette, "Le chêne du chemin du bayou" (The oak tree on Bayou Road) by Questy, has personal revenge as a motif, as does the other story in this issue, "Une Vengeance," which is set in Spain. The poems show no commitment: the persona of Questy's "Prière" only asks God to grant him a peaceful sleep; and in "La nuit en pensant à toi" (At night, while thinking of you), he claims to be jealous of his lover's dreams. "Idées," by Camille Thierry, likewise evokes a sentimental, not an intellectual, crisis. "Deux ans après" (Two years later), an anonymous homage in verse, gives thanks to a friend who provided support for the author. (Later publication in *Les Cenelles* reveals that the friend was Auguste Populus and the author Michel St. Pierre, who contemplated suicide.) Though we may suppose that slavery concerned a few of those writers, they never take it for a theme, even indirectly. In *Nos Hommes et notre histoire*, Rodolphe Desdunes later insisted upon the fact that Manuel Sylva, in his "Essai Littéraire," speaks of his ancestral land as a free and pleasant country. Yet the lines quoted by Desdunes are no proof that Sylva combated the slave system in which he was living.[4]

A member of the Société des Artisans, founded in 1834, young Victor Séjour reportedly read his first poetic attempt to this assembled brotherhood on the anniversary of the association. It was a satire of the Société d'Economie, a rival association reputed to be overly exclusive. There is no doubt that such meetings of cultural or mutual aid associations allowed their members to try their talents in front of choice audiences. But how can one measure the ideological commitment of these writers? Desdunes asserts that Victor Séjour considered the racial problem in his writings, yet his pale negritude surfaces in only one of his twenty-odd plays performed in Paris, where he went at age nineteen and died in 1874.[5] The only story in which he deals with race issues, "Le mulâtre," set in Cap Haïtien, appeared in 1837 in the Paris-based *Revue des Colonies*, edited by Cyrille Bissette, a colored abolitionist from the Antilles.

One wonders why so few of these works offer a critique of the social and racial system. Is it due to the severe sanctions that, after 1840, attempted to discourage any criticism of slavery? We know that such laws often failed to be applied and dissuaded mostly agitators from outside the state. In my opinion, the lack of racial protest in the pages of *L'Album Littéraire* can be easily explained if we remember that its contributors wrote for a group of free people of color, with a good education and some wealth, whose efforts, in cultivating *belles-lettres à la française*, were destined to help them forget the disdain of most whites, not to change society.

There was no great difference between white and colored Creole poetry in the antebellum press. *La Louisiane* had decided never to publish unrequested verse. *L'Abeille*, however, printed much unsigned poetry like "L'églantine et la rose" (The dogwood and the rose) (August 22, 1829) or "Chanson d'un faiseur de bardeaux" (The shingle cutter's song) (March 4, 1837) next to signed poetry by well-known whites, such as a song by Tullius St. Céran honoring the company of the Tirailleurs d'Orléans, in response to Béranger's "Les tombeaux de Juillet" (November 12, 1853); or Constant Lépouzé's homage to St. Céran (August 22, 1835) and his "Ode sur les trois journées" on the 1830 upheaval in Paris (September 3, 1836). So did the English-language edition, *The Bee*. In 1840, *Le Courier* ran "Réflexions à propos des cendres de Napoléon" (about the return of the emperor's remains to the Invalides Church) by Henry T., possibly the young colored lawyer Henry Train, who later published in *La Tribune*. *La Gazette des Opelousas* had a page called "Variétés," which is a tantalizing miscellany of near-anonymous literary works. It printed the poem "A Mademoiselle ***" by (colored?) "M." and his four-page "Roman à propos d'un bal" in early 1842. It ran "Episode du 8 Janvier 1815" by

"Sé[lign]y," as well as (white) Delegorgue Cordier's "La pauvre nourrice" (The destitute wet nurse) and an unsigned song, "Ne me parlez pas d'amour," both on March 19, 1842. Identifying authors is often guesswork. A "Romance"—unsigned, but with a female persona called Malvina—, which appeared in the July 30, 1842, *Gazette des Opelousas*, recalls "A Malvina," a piece by Valcour B. in *Les Cenelles*, but is it really by him? One finds "Si tu m'aimais" by "W." (August 13, 1842) and "Rêverie," a prose poem ending with acrostics on *Athenais*, as well as an "Amélie" poem (unsigned) in September 1842. On October 15, 1843, "Romance: Est-ce pour moi, est-ce pour lui?" precedes the (unsigned) story, "Juanita la folle." All of those may well be by colored poets. On December 2, 1843, the fragment of a novel "Doute et amour" is also unsigned. But all "feuilletons" are by whites in *L'Abeille*, for example, "Madame de Montron" by Frédéric Soulié, followed by "Le Club des assassins" by Théophile Gautier, except "Le Comte de Monte-Cristo" by Alexandre Dumas in 1848.

Much better known by literary historians than *L'Album Littéraire*, *Les Cenelles* has been hailed as the first anthology of Negro poetry ever published in the Americas. Armand Lanusse thus broke new ground in 1845, with the collaboration of sixteen free male Creoles of color of New Orleans. The first poem to bear a date—a tribute from Valcour B. to his French teacher of classics, Constant Lépouzé—was composed as early as 1838. These poems mostly treat of love, generally conceived as desperate passion. Death is very present, often as a Romantic pose, though recurrent epidemics of yellow fever or cholera decimated relatives, friends, and lovers. Male friendship is often celebrated. And joy occasionally bursts out when love is requited, as in Michel St. Pierre's "Tu m'as dit je t'aime" (You told me, "I love you"). At times, it blends with love for the homeland, as in "Un an d'absence" (After a year away from home):

> La fortune cruelle
> M'exila de ces lieux,
> Mais je revins fidèle,
> Brûlant des mêmes feux.
> Au beau pays de France,
> Je pleurais mes amours . . .
> Sur la rive étrangère,
> Ah, pouvais-je être heureux? . . .
> O ma blonde créole,
> Pour moi plus de revers! (pp. 42–43)

> [Cruel fate exiled me from this place but I return faithfully, burning with the same fire. In the fair land of France I pined for my love. . . . How could I be happy on that foreign shore? . . . O, my fair haired Creole my setbacks are ended!]

Pierre Dalcour, who thus sang his return to "green savannas" and his blue-eyed belle, alludes to evils encountered in France. In fact, he had been sent there to study and, unable to bear the injuries of segregation after his return home, he died an exile in Paris. The only words in the poem that might hint at his actual situation in

Louisiana, "la fortune cruelle / m'exila de ces lieux," are a figure of style. In this perspective, it seems that the feeling of disillusionment that pervades the volume is as much part and parcel of the attitudes of the French Romantic school as an echo of the existential situation of Creoles of color in the 1840s. Only "Epigramme" by Lanusse explicitly criticizes the institution that degrades the female *femme de couleur*:

> "Vous ne voulez donc pas renoncer à Satan?"
> Disait un bon pasteur à certaine bigote
> Qui d'assez gros péchés, à chaque nouvel an
> Venait lui présenter l'interminable note.
> "Je veux y renoncer," dit-elle, "pour jamais;
> Mais avant que la grâce en mon âme scintille,
> Pour m'ôter tout motif de pêcher désormais,
> Que ne puis-je, pasteur,—Quoi donc?—Placer ma fille?" (p. 48)

> ["Don't you wish to renounce Satan?" a good priest was asking one devout woman who, on every New Year's day, came with an endless list of rather big sins. "I wish to renounce him," she said, "for ever, but before grace enlightens my soul, in order to have no reason to sin from now on, I wish I could, Reverend—What?—*Place* my daughter?"]

Once more, Lanusse presents a scathing critique of (unofficially) institutionalized white (sexual) supremacy. Yet Lanusse was also published in the white Creole press, if we are to believe an 1852 mention of him by Charles Testut. The same goes for several other poets. Bowers contributed to several newspapers, according to Roussève. His "L'orphelin des tombeaux" (The orphan among the tombs), included in *Les Cenelles,* was reprinted from *La Lorgnette* (December 11, 1842).

The dedication of *Les Cenelles* (Mayhaw berries) made it an offering "to the fair sex of Louisiana," because these poems, often written on the spur of the moment or upon request, essentially dealt with love. They were entertainment; for instance, Michel St. Pierre composed "A une demoiselle . . ." for a girl who requested lines for her album, and his "Couplet" was aimed at "a damsel at whom a pistol had been fired." Pierre Dalcour called "La Foi, l'Espérance et la Charité" (Faith, hope and charity) a proposal to a religious-minded dame written as a penalty in a society game. Numa Lanusse's lively "Couplets" were destined to be sung at a friend's wedding. Several poems are variations on a given word, not to mention the many acrostics that Joanni Questy sent to dailies.

A large number of these poems are "romances" on tunes generally indicated by the poets, like that of "Heureux habitans . . ." or "un air de yelva." These songs often recall the style of the French bard François Béranger, though they lack his edge. Nicol Riquet composed in this fashion scores of songs that were never published but reportedly remained popular among colored Louisianans (Desdunes, 57). His offering to *Les Cenelles* is a merry "Rondeau redoublé" (Doubled roundelay), dedicated to the Francs Amis brotherhood. One also finds humor in "A mon petit lit" (To my little bed) by Lanusse, and in "Mon vieux chapeau" (My old hat) by M. F. Liotau:

> Oh! si dans sa bonté
> Dieu me faisait la grâce
> De prolonger ma race,
> Que je serais flatté
> De voir, avant que j'aille
> Dans un monde nouveau,
> Un garçon de ma taille
> Mettre mon vieux chapeau. (p. 115)

[Ah, if in His kindness God were gracious enough to give me descendents, I would be most flattered, before going to a new world,
to see a lad my size with my old hat on his head.]

From all the evidence, those writers preferred not to mention their humiliating
situation due to racial prejudice to their colored audience. If their writings were
also addressed to white readers, it was to those few Creoles or Frenchmen they were
familiar with, their educated friends and peers. In his introduction, Lanusse is
explicit:

> Nous publions donc ce volume dans le but de faire connaître les productions de
> quelques jeunes amants de la poésie qui ne jalousent pas sans doute les beaux
> succès obtenus sur la scène ou dans le monde littéraire par des poètes louisianais qui
> ont eu le bonheur de puiser le savoir aux meilleures sources de l'Europe, car ces
> derniers seront *toujours pour les premiers un sujet d'émulation mais jamais un objet
> d'envie*. (Emphasis mine)

> [We therefore publish this volume with the aim of presenting the productions of young
> lovers of poetry who assuredly are not envious of the fine success achieved on the
> stage or in literary circles by Louisiana poets who were fortunate enough to draw their
> knowledge from the best European sources, for *the latter will always be a subject of
> emulation, but not an object of jealousy for the former*.]

The last sentence is conciliatory, even deferential, rather than subtly ironical, for it
was frequent, at the time, for the sons of "placées" and white protectors to pursue
their studies in France in the same schools as their white half-brothers.

In his 1892 essay, "La Littérature française de la Louisiane," Alcée Fortier, a
white Creole, did not specify that *Les Cenelles* was a collection of works by men of
color. By then, admittedly, the output of the despised *sang mêlés* was needed to
bolster up the dwindling volume of literature in French discussed in l'Athénée
Louisanais. But it is a fact that, during the antebellum period, there was more
complicity and fraternal emulation than rivalry between the colored and white
Creole writers, when the status of the former and the privileges of the latter were
not seriously challenged. One can often speak of outright collaboration: for example, *Le Courrier de la Louisiane* willingly announced the publication of *L'Album
Littéraire* in June 1843. Conversely, Michel Séligny, Joanni Questy, and several
others regularly sent "Communications" to the white press and the acceptance of
such works was nearly routine before the Civil War. One is only mildly surprised
to discover that a protracted literary exchange in *La Réforme* in 1846 took place
between colored, not white, poets.

In response to a satire written by L[éon]. S[indos]., an "Acrostiche Satirique" appeared on April 18, 1846:

> Laisse en repos la plume et reprends la truelle
> Elève-bachelier du bon Myrtil Courcelle,
> On dit: "*De profundis!*" sur tes grands vers ad-hoc
> Nourris dans l'ignorance, ensevelis en bloc.
> Sous la rime d'un fat, abimé du hasard!
> Insultant au physique un émule de l'art,
> Ne crois pas infiltrer ta fierté *léontine*
> Dans les coeurs pratiquant sous l'égide divine!
> On écrase du pied tes insectes rampants,
> Symboles du mépris de tes traits sans piquant.
> > TOUJOURS.

> [Let your quill rest and take the trowel again, student-graduate of good old Myrtil Courcelle. One says "De Profundis" over your grand *ad hoc* verse, nurtured in ignorance and buried wholesale under a fatuous rime, impaired by chance! Abusing physically a rival in this art, don't think you will instill your leonine pride into hearts which practice under God's shield. We trample your crawling insects, reflections of your despicable witless barbs. EVER.]

This may have come from the pen of Mirtil-Ferdinand Liotau, who published in *Les Cenelles* "A un ami, qui m'accusait de plagiat," in which he wrote:

> Il est passé, St. Léon, ce bel âge
> Où tu faisais notre admiration.
> Avec le temps a fui ton doux langage:
> Tu n'as gardé que ta présomption.
> De ranimer ton ardeur poétique,
> St. Léon cesse, elle est morte chez toi. (p. 177)

> [It is gone, St. Leon, the fair age when you provoked our admiration. With time your sweet talk has fled: you have retained only your presumption. Don't try to rekindle your poetic fire; desist, St. Leon, it is dead within you.]

The Léon Sindos who was listed in the 1843–1844 city directory as a grocer residing on Bayou Road had indeed been apprenticed to master builder Courcelle.

The acrostics were followed by an "Avis" requesting Sindos not to pursue with satire, and several communications. One of them derided the lack of wit of M. S[indos].; another, signed "Les amateurs de bonne satire," mocked his long efforts and his inanity; still another was supposedly a "Requête de M. S., poète satirique, pour entrer à l'Académie." *La Réforme* of April 19, 1846, printed a rebuttal in verse from "a friend of Mr. S.," against the asinine satirists ("sur les amateurs de bonne satire qui montrent un bout d'oreille d'âne"). The next day, it ran the following "Communiqué" from Ever:

> Afin de maîtriser, s'il est possible, la malicieuse interprétation que des amis,
> quand même!, de M. S*** ont donnée à un hémistiche de l'acrostiche qui a

été publié dans la *Réforme* du 16 courant, nous déclarons hautement n'avoir mentionné le nom de Mr. C. (que nous ne connaissons que de nom) qu'à l'effet de faire connaître au lecteur que Mr. S*** a été son apprenti, rien de plus. Nous déclarons aussi nous être servi de l'adjectif "bon" sans équivoque ni arrière-pensée.

[In order to limit, if possible, the malicious reading that friends of M. S***—he has a few—have made of half a line in the Acrostics in the issue of the 16th instant, we affirm that we mentioned the name of Mr. C., whom we do not know personally, only to let the reader know that M. S. once was his apprentice, nothing more. We declare that we used the epithet "good" unequivocally and without any implication whatsoever.]

On May 28, 1846, V. B. (probably Valcour B.), in a letter to the editor, protested that the exchange had turned into offensive personal attacks and ridiculed the group at great length. The same issue ran another acrostics in response:

A M. S*** et à son ami "pot".
Si l'apôtre V. B. consultait son confrère,
Il n'eut pas mis en pot: des oreilles sans sel
Ni piment, c'est trop fade. . . . allons, missionaire,
Dimanche vous viendrez au comptoir solennel
Offrir en sacrifice à "Soufflet le critique"*
Six pots de cornichons de la même fabrique.
(* Par amusement)

[To M. S*** and his friend the Pot.
If apostle V. B. had consulted his fellow-worker, he wouldn't have made preserves: ears without salt or pimiento are too bland. . . . Well, missionary, on Sunday you'll go to the solemn counter to present "Bellows turned critic"* with six jars of pickled cucumbers of the same ilk.

(*For the fun of it)]

This was signed "Soufflet" (meaning "kitchen bellows"). On June 7, the exchange continued with "Un Grand Ignorant, Consorts et Compères" (A great ignorant, his fellows and associates) deriding "M. Nigaudinos V. B., polichinelle scientifique et latin" as a stupid puppet, stuffed with pedantry and Latin. This spirited exchange, all between colored Creoles, sounded more like a shopkeepers' quarrel or the prank of high school alumni than like *belles lettres*, but as a result of it the editor of *La Réforme* promised to make his paper a real "journal politique et littéraire." On June 17, 1846, he announced that an association was being formed under the name "Les Jeunes littérateurs." He appealed to all young people interested in literature, mainly those who had been involved in the exchange, to come and read the rules of this association. And he announced the forthcoming publication of a sixteen-page pamphlet containing the writings of M. S., Grand Ignorant, Petit Impur, and other "Amateurs de la bonne littérature." No copy of this publication has been found.

It is remarkable that *La Réforme* should have helped Creoles of color organize a literary society at a time when Louisiana laws were restricting free blacks' moves to charter associations. It indicates close collaboration. Indeed several local newspapers were quite open to the writings of colored Creoles. Michel Séligny's contributions began with *Le Franc Parleur* in 1836. In *L'Abeille de la Nouvelle Orléans*, one finds obituaries and essays by him commending religious practice, such as "Le Père Antoine" (March 16, 1840) or "Article sur les prédicateurs du carême" (April 7, 1849); and a dozen short stories like the picturesque "Le pêcheur de la Guadeloupe" (April 17, 1849). To *Le Courrier de la Louisiane,* from 1841 to 1857, he contributed nine sad and sentimental stories, set in America, like "Un drame au lac Pontchartrain," or in France, like "La petite fille d'Aurillac"; as well as a report from Paris on the success of *Fils de la nuit,* the drama by his friend Séjour in 1856. *La Renaissance Louisianaise* ran three stories by Séligny: "La dentelle révélatrice," "La petite mendiante de Chambéry," and "Mademoiselle de Bectause," set in Vichy and Lyons, from May to November 1861.[6] Auguste Populus reportedly had rhymed acrostics in several issues of *La Renaissance.*

Camille Thierry, the son of a Bordeaux merchant and a Louisiana quadroon, ended his life in France, where his *Les Vagabondes, poésies américaines* was published jointly by Lemerre in Paris and De Laporte in Bordeaux in 1874. Most poems had appeared in antebellum periodicals: "Abd-el-Kader" in *La Chronique de la Nouvelle Orléans* of April 16, 1848; "Mariquita la Calentura," "Diane de Poitiers," "Lubie" (Whim), "La femme déchue" (The fallen woman), "Le clair de la lune" (In the moonlight), "Le général Magloire d'Hocquincourt" (In honor of an African prince who dreamed of reconquering his father's crown), "A une Américaine," and "Girardot" in various issues of *L'Orléanais.* And *Le Courrier de la Louisiane* significantly published his tribute in verse to the well-known white Creole poet Tullius de Saint-Céran, on January 7, 1850. After Thierry's death, one could still read his "A ma muse" in *Le Dimanche* (March 5, 1876), and two more poems were reprinted in the *Comptes-rendus de l'Athénée Louisianais* (January 1878). All those periodicals were run by French-born or Creole whites. Interestingly, Edouard J. Fortier did not mention Thierry's race when he praised *Les Vagabondes* in *Les Lettres françaises en Louisiane.*[7] He simply emphasized the deep rootedness of the "Indigenous poems" of *Les Cenelles* in the soil of Louisiana. By 1915, the output of the *sang mêlés* had been conscripted into the volume of literature in French.

From all evidence, the colored Creoles *literateurs* did not lack commitment, as their wartime and postwar careers revealed. If their antebellum production remained silent on the slavery question, which was in no way a pressing existential concern for them, they consistently attacked the "plaçage" system through which the white males deprived them of lighter-skinned companions, thus asserting their supremacy. And their production was often characterized by proud dignity as well as learned allusion.

The second period of the literary production of the colored Creoles depended principally upon the colored press and had a new, highly visible ideological tenor. By 1860, the group represented about one-tenth of the total New Orleans population of 150,000. Many were well-off, a few lived in luxury—like the Francis Dumas family who invited General Butler to a seven-course dinner served on solid silver. The presence of the Federal troops after the capture of New Orleans in April 1862 gave them free expression, although it occasionally plagued their everyday lives and greatly impaired their special status because the troops refused to distinguish between free men and freedmen. In November 1863, the *gens de couleur libres* availed themselves of the services rendered to the state, their loyalty to the Union, and their paying taxes to claim the right to register and vote. Again, they sent a delegation of their Union Radical Association in January 1864 but were kept away from the polls by General Nathaniel P. Banks. A few Creoles despaired and passed for whites. Others followed a more committed political line.

The brothers Roudanez and a few friends judged the time was ripe to campaign for civil rights. They launched *L'Union* in September 1862. While studying medicine in Paris, Dr. Louis Charles Roudanez had come under the influence of socialist thinkers like Louis Blanc and Ledru-Rollin. His newspaper was a "Mémorial Politique, Littéraire et Progressiste." The editorials reflected the opinions of Paul Trévigne, the son of a light-skinned aristocratic veteran of the battle of New Orleans. They addressed the French-speaking Creoles of color in the state, not the bulk of the black population, which consisted mostly of English-speaking freedmen. Well-written, its lively rhetoric frequently interspersed with erudite quotations, the paper is interesting from a literary point of view. Its contributors and correspondents were thoroughly familiar with Latin and French classics up to the Enlightenment and also with Abbé Grégoire, Balzac, and Comettant. From a literary as well as a political/social viewpoint such writings should not be overlooked. Rousseve quotes "The enslaver and the enslaved," an unsigned article in the *Union* of September 23, 1863. On August 9, 1865, one finds several essays on administering justice and one on "Le parti conservateur."[8] English-speaking writers, too, provided a few pieces. The paper's press also printed *L'Opinion de l'Avocat-Général Bates sur le droit de citoyenneté* in 1865.

Politically, *L'Union* remained a caste newspaper: it took the distinction between free man and freedman for granted, while provoking the resentment of conservative Southern whites, who threatened to kill Trévigne and to set fire to the newspaper's office. According to Edward Laroque Tinker, some intimidated associates of Roudanez stopped publication in June 1864. But Roudanez bought back the press in order to launch, the following month, *La Tribune de la Nouvelle Orléans*, enriched with an English edition, which claimed to be "the organ of the oppressed classes." At first published three times a week, it became a daily in October.

For two years it was the most impressive press organ of the city, with regular correspondents from Paris, Boston, and Mexico City, and more abundant news from France than that provided by other papers. It published letters to the editor from such illustrious persons as Garibaldi and Victor Hugo. Like the *Union*, the *Tribune* prided itself upon the literary culture and refinement of its contributors. It ran exciting serials; one of them dealt with "John Brown, le Christ des Noirs." This was followed by a life of Haitian mulatto rebel Vincent Ogé, by French West Indian Melvil Bloncourt. Several stories as well as much poetry by local citizens of color graced its pages, but *La Tribune* is also precious for its detailed recording of their cultural activities.

At first the organ of the Creoles of color, the *Tribune* took quite openly the side of the freedmen, even before Belgian Jean-Charles Houzeau became its editor in chief in late 1864 and wrote spirited editorials under the pseudonym "C. J. Dalloz." An astronomer at the Royal Observatory in Brussels who had left Europe because of his Republican beliefs, Houzeau soon passed for black and did not lack courage as a reporter when a mob of former Confederates and the city police stormed the liberal meeting at Mechanics Hall in July 1866. Under his direction, *La Tribune* was at the service of the Republican Party and benefited from the news of its American Press Association. It became more exclusively political. Its French-language edition continued to appear but the interesting local news faded from its pages. In the same radical line, the *Tribune* press printed pamphlets, among them *Les Droits de l'Homme* (1865), in which Dr. Joseph Chaumette asked for the abolition of slavery in all its forms:

> Vive la Liberté, la Déesse immortelle:
> A la vie, à la mort, nous combattrons pour elle!
> Le triomphe est à nous, assistés du Seigneur,
> Qui protège le faible et punit l'oppresseur. (Roussève, 117)

> [Long live Freedom, that immortal goddess: for life and until death
> we shall fight for her! Triumph is ours, with the help of the Lord,
> who protects the weak and punishes the oppressor.]

The first black vote in Louisiana, in November 1865, sent Henry Clay Warmoth to Congress. Now the official organ of the Republicans, the *Tribune* enjoyed a national audience. Free copies were sent to major American newspapers and to representatives in Congress. During its existence it denounced the initial project for a state constitution and was the champion of universal suffrage and complete political equality between the races. It criticized the Louisiana state system, the measures taken by General Banks that threatened to turn the freedmen into "serfs for the Union." It fought segregation in public transportation and the decrees limiting educational facilities for colored. It made proposals for a cooperative running of the plantations, reflecting Charles Fourier's socialist principles. With the support of Aristide Mary and Thomy Lafon, two wealthy Creoles of color, the *Tribune* initially received the support of Oscar Dunn, the promoter of the Association d'aide aux affranchis. But shortly after Louisiana was readmitted into the Union in 1867, the paper attacked those leaders of the Republican Party who attempted to turn black voters into docile instruments of their own interests. During the campaign for the 1868 elections, it fought the conservative Republicans. Yet Dunn was elected lieutenant-governor of the state, defeating Francis Dumas, who ran on the *Tribune*-supported radical ticket. Dr. Roudanez sank $35,000 in the venture to keep the paper's integrity. In November 1868, Houzeau quit and the *Tribune* stopped publication. From March 1869 to 1870, it survived, on a weekly basis, but no longer published much literature.

L'Union and *La Tribune* thus carried the works of many colored Creoles, works that deserve a systematic study from a literary point of view. Although Trévigne and Roudanez rarely signed their editorials and articles, one finds prose and poetry in French from the pens of Questy, Lanusse, Mansion, and others and a few pieces in English, sometimes by the same authors.

Before *L'Union, La Renaissance Louisianaise* had started a trend toward more commitment. On July 14, 1861, "La Muse de l'Hélicon" by Armand Lanusse was still nonpartisan, but it was followed by the patriotic pro-Confederate appeal, "Enfants du Sud," written on November 16, 1861, by white F. Colin. Of course, *L'Union* supported the Federals. In late June 1863, it ran a fine panegyric of the black hero of Port Hudson, "Le Capitaine André Cailloux et ses compagnons d'armes" by E. H.—possibly Emile Honoré, who became the first colored secretary of state of Louisiana in 1877. In the contemporary *Black Republican*, too, one could find many equally embattled poems in English, like "On the Shores of Tennessee" by Louise de Mortié, a colored philanthropist from Boston (April 22, 1865); "The Lost Chief" by Colonel Charles Alpine, alias Miles O'Reilly (May 13, 1865); "Charge of the Black Regiment at Port Hudson" by George M. Boker; and much verse glorifying Lincoln, including the ode on Lincoln's burial by William Cullen Bryant.

In *La Tribune*, earnest social writing predominated even in verse: "Le triomphe des opprimés" (Triumph of the oppressed) (November 8, 1864, unsigned) heralded the glory of the black volunteers fighting the forces of slavery. "L'ignorance" (March 21, 1865) by "Henry" extolled learning. He signed his poem "Washington et Lincoln" (May 17, 1865) Henry Train, which allows us to identify him as the colored New Orleans attorney who worked in partnership with Josiah Fisk. Train's "Hommage au poète," dedicated to Dr. Chaumette (June 11, 1865), "Epitre familière à ma muse" (July 2, 1865), "Résignation" (June 18, 1865), and "La rébellion du Sud en permanence"(September 24, 1865) are all concerned with the political situation. So were seemingly lighter pieces, like the unsigned "Communication d'outre-tombe, Cantate à mes amis," supposedly from the late Béranger, claiming that the day of universal suffrage had come (December 17, 1865). A poetic exchange about God allowed comparison of "Il est" [He is] by Antony and "Il n'est pas" [He is not—on the tyrant's side] by Armand Lanusse in September 1866. Indeed, through his letters to the editor, Lanusse was an eloquent political contributor to *La Tribune*. On May 12, 1867, Joanni Questy himself challenged the conservatives in his poem "Aux conservateurs." "Au père Chocarne" (April 12, 1867), about the misuse of religion, and "Sonnet" (June 16, 1867), both by "Pierre L'Hermite," were equally polemical.

Radicals of both races now worked side by side, and much research is still needed to identify several authors. Did "La liberté et l'esclavage" by Ad. Pecatier (August 13, 1865), "Le triangle sacré," a celebration of Freemasonry by Sneitz (April 28, 1867), and Camille Naudin's "Le souvenir des morts"(July 28, 1867) all come from the pens of whites? Antony—whether this was his first name or a pseudonym inspired by Alexandre Dumas's famous drama—was probably colored and contributed "Les trois perles," written at Grand Lac (May 26, 1867), "Combat de l'aigle républicain et du copperhead" (September 23, 1866), and "A Theodule Delassize," dedicated to the city surveyor of conveyances (December 20, 1866). But how can one identify "Yacoub," who dedicated his first poem to Duhart, who responded with "Poésie! Vox Dei!" (October 25, 1866)? And "Aster," whose denunciation of a traitor to the freedmen's cause, only designated this villain as "l'oeil droit de Philippe" [the right eye of Phillipe] on February 26, 1869? And "Stenio," who contributed, "S. . . . . a L.," in praise of a beloved woman?

Pierre Adolphe Duhart, a teacher who had studied in France and succeeded Questy at the head of the Institution Couvent, used the pen name "Lélia." His first published piece, "Poésie à Mademoiselle ***" came out in *La Renaissance Louisianaise* on October 18, 1862. One or two plays by Duhart were staged successfully at the Théâtre d'Orléans, now the showcase of colored Creole culture: *Lydia* in 1865 (according to Desdunes), and a four-act drama, *Lélia ou la victime du préjugé*, which was applauded in June of the following year. *La Tribune* published his romantic story "Trois Amours" in August and September 1865, after his "Simple histoire"(on March 9–10), as well as two dozen poems, mostly sentimental pieces, like "Tristesse" (June 2, 1867). Is the poem on love, "L'amour," signed "Berthe D.. . . ." also by Duhart? At any rate, he signed his full name to "L'astre s'est levé," a confident hymn to progress on December 2, 1866.

Eugène Victor Macarty, who sometimes acted with Duhart, was mostly known as an accomplished musician, actor, and baritone, but he also published poems in the *Tribune*, among them "La fleur indiscrète" on July 22, 1866. By Michel Séligny, one could read a political essay, "Marcellus à Junius" (October 22–24, 1867). By cigar-maker Lucien Mansion, *L'Union* printed an "Hommage au sexe" in three installments (September 22–October 3, 1863). And after his "La Sensitive" (October 20, 1867), his "Elégie à Armand Lanusse" (late 1868), and "L'Avenir" (The future), dedicated to Duhart on January 1, 1869, the ailing *Tribune* ran his "La couronne d'amour" (The crown of love) as late as January 21, 1869. Joanni Questy contributed articles and poems in October and November 1867; on January 1, 1869, he sent a poetic "Lettre à Nath[alie Populus, a fellow teacher]," followed by "Dépèche télégraphique" (January 26, 1869) and "Dors!" about the accidental death of a hunter (February 8, 1869).

Southern resentment was intense after the Civil War, but not all whites were opposed to African-American leaders, although their allies now were immigrants rather than Creoles. French-born Dr. Charles Testut, whose first volume of poetry, *Echos* (1849), was followed by his *Portraits Littéraires* (1850), included several Creoles of color among his sketches of fifty-two contemporary writers.[9] He proudly printed his friend Camille Thierry's "Remerciement," in his *Fleurs d'Eté* (1851). His novel *Le Vieux Salomon* (completed as early as 1858 but published only in 1872) was as thoroughly opposed to slavery as *Uncle Tom's Cabin*, to which it has been compared. In 1871, Testut, who had already founded eight short-lived newspapers, launched *L'Equité*, "journal de progrès universel," in order to promote racial reconciliation and harmony. He was soon detested by his Catholic associates, however, because of his attacks against the pope and his support of Freemasonry, so much so that the press of *Le Propagateur Catholique* refused to continue to print *l'Equité* after the third issue.[10] During the postwar period, another small, white-run publication also came to reinforce the colored press: *Le Sud*, edited by Charles de la Bretonne under the pseudonym "Jacques de R." appeared for the first time on the symbolical date of July 4, 1873. It was just as pro-black as *L'Equité* and replied vigorously to the caricatures that *Le Carillon,* edited by the racist Dr. Durell, made of the black leaders. *Le Sud* even alluded to the taboo topic of racial intermixture in Louisiana and to the "tar brush" that had touched even the supposedly most-lily-white families. If one recalls that the white Creoles were now busy asserting their racial superiority by all possible means, among them the denial of the appellation "Creole" to the *gens de couleur libres*, one might consider Charles de la Bretonne as a forerunner of George Washington Cable, whom the white Creoles disliked so much for the same reasons. But the Creoles of color did not contribute to those papers. Besides, in spite of his French-sounding name, J. Willis Menard, who sent his "Anniversary poem, July 4, 1867" to the English-language edition of the *Tribune*, was not a Creole. A teacher who also edited the *Radical Standard* from 1865 on, he was probably the major colored English-speaking poet living in New Orleans at the time.

It is impossible not to see the third period as a phase of decline. During the years 1860–1880, English became the standard language in Louisiana, even though Creole patois survived in rural areas and French was still in use in the novels of Sidonie de la Houssaye and Alfred Mercier. To maintain their traditions and their language, a few white Creoles founded a cultural association, l'Athénée Louisianais, under the impulsion of Dr. Mercier, on November 24, 1875. Its journal, *Les Comptes-rendus de l'Athénée Louisianais,* printed poetry, fiction, and essays that included interesting studies of the Creole language, songs and texts in Creole, even translations of a few French fables in Creole. In spite of the widening gap between white and colored Creoles, a few colored writers were published, such as Nathalie Populus in the 1890s. On April 23, 1886, Lucien Mansion's "La Folle," a fine poem about a girl abandoned by her lover, its meter closely imitative of "Les Djinns" by Victor Hugo, appeared in the *Comptes Rendus*.

But poetry by Creoles of color was far less abundant than before the war. The most famous names of the preceding generation were fast disappearing: Séligny and Lanusse died in 1868, Questy the following year, Séjour in Paris in 1874, and Thierry in Bordeaux in 1875. During the next half century Creole literature in French declined as inexorably as did the French language in Louisiana. Admittedly, speeches in French were still allowed in the two chambers of the state legislature until 1880, and sermons in French were still current in Catholic churches, but, in 1916, purportedly to cut costs, the state ceased publishing legal announcements in French. Such publication had ensured the survival of the nearly centenary *Abeille de la Nouvelle Orléans,* which came to an end. French was now spoken only at home in a few aristocratic and ancient Creole families, or at the meetings of learned societies like the Athénée Louisianais. This may explain why we find only a couple of colored writers in the French language during this period: Victor-Ernest Rillieux and Rodolphe Desdunes. There was only one black newspaper with a regular French edition, the *Crusader*.

Victor, the brother of the inventor Norbert Rillieux, divided his time between caring for his small business and writing much poetry. Only a few of his poems saw print. In 1895, three years before his death at age fifty-six, the press of the *Crusader* printed *Les Feuilles mortes,* his free adaptation of *Leyendas Espagnolas* by Gustave A. Becker. The composer Edmond Dédé set to music Rillieux's poem "Si j'étais lui," Lawrence Dubuclet did so with his "Le Timide." Rillieux's "Le Docteur noir," probably inspired by Alfred de Vigny, was still unpublished when Desdunes came across it in the early twentieth century. Was this due to its resolutely vengeful tone? It is the story of a black slave who refuses to cure his master in retaliation:

> Te souviens-tu que dans ta rage,
> Frappant ma femme et mon enfant,
> Sous les coups de ton fouet sauvage
> Tu les fis mourir lentement?
> Quand je souffrais de ta vengeance,
> Tu te riais de ma douleur,
> Mais aujourd'hui, vil oppresseur,
> Je me ris de ton impuissance.
> Tremble, et redoute mon pouvoir,
> Je suis, je suis le docteur noir.[11]

> [Do you recall that, in your fury, hitting my wife and my child, you killed them slowly under the blows of your cruel whip? When I suffered from your vengeance, you scoffed at my sorrow. But today, vile oppressor, I laugh at your impotence. Tremble, and fear my power; I am, I am the black doctor.]

In November 1894, when the last prewar Creole of color militant for civil rights died, Rillieux composed "Une pensée sur la tombe de Lucien Mansion," which the *Croisé* printed as a tribute. In the same spirit, the paper ran, on June 16, 1894, two tributes to a distinguished educator: "Mme Louisa Lamotte" by Nathalie Populus and "Retour au berceau maudit" by Victor Rillieux. Both commemorated the return to New Orleans, after her father's death, of a Creole of color who had taught in Paris and directed the girls college at Abbeville, in the North of France.

Rillieux's narrator expresses his hatred of segregation in the United States and his love for France when he exclaims:

> Pars! fuis l'ingrat berceau pour la plage chérie,
> Où la science est tout et la race pour rien! . . .
> Au faîte de ta gloire au beau pays de France
> Laisse parfois vers nous s'envoler tes baisers. . . .

> Car quelle autre à ta place ayant tout en partage,
> Eût, parmi nous, daigné reconnaître son sang?
> Puis d'une foule amie acceptant l'humble hommage,

Eût osé se montrer, brillant au premier rang
  Sous leur ciel noir d'orage?[12]

[Go, flee your ungrateful cradle for the cherished shore where
knowledge is all and race is nothing. . . . At the top of your fame in
fair France, let your kisses fly towards us at times. . . . For who else,
in your all-embracing condition, would have acknowledged her
blood ties with us? Then, accepting the humble homage of a friendly
crowd, would have dared to appear, radiant in the first rank, under
their black stormy sky?]

Written during the "nadir of African-American history," when "their" discrimination and violence broke records, this piece celebrates those who did not give up the
cause of the Negro. Later, Rillieux would compare civil rights champion Ida B.
Wells to Judith and Joan of Arc in "Amour et dévouement":

Oh, jamais! car ta race abhorrant tous les crimes,
Des deux rôles choisit le rôle des victimes
  A celui des bandits
Dont les rifles, le lynch, le bûcher, la potence
Et les sombres forfaits sont par l'intolérance
  Dans tout le Sud bénits.[13]

[Oh, never, because your race, detesting all crimes, chooses between
two parts, that of the victim instead of the bandit's whose rifles,
lynching, stake, gallows and dark deeds are blessed by intolerance
throughout the South.]

Several Creoles of color thought of celebrating their own group. In the weekly
Louisianan, run by former acting governor P. B. S. Pinchback from Christmas 1870
to 1881, there appeared in 1875–1876 several installments of "A Centennial History of the Louisiana Negro." Commemorating American independence, Paul Trévigne evoked the contributions of French-speaking Creoles like Questy, Séligny,
Lanusse, and inventor Honoré Roth. This was notable because the moderate Republican newspaper rarely published articles by Creoles until it changed editors and
became reconciled with the Roudanez group. To the French-language edition, *Le
Louisianais*, which started in 1880, Adolphe Duhart contributed a monologue, "La
pluie" (It will rain) and "Une légende," concerning the Sainte Chapelle in Paris in
September 1881. The paper also printed a poetic tribute to André Cailloux by
"William" (November 8, 1879); "Pour les pauvres," a poem by D. L. (October 29,
1881); and Charles Testut's "Le Quatorze Juillet 1789," celebrating the coming
proletarian revolution as a prelude to universal reconciliation (August 6, 1881).
With those writers, one may mention (colored) Louis Nelson Fouché, who compiled
a *Nouveau recueil de pensées, opinions, sentences et maximes . . .* (1882), more
remarkable for its eclecticism than its originality.

Government clerk Rodolphe L. Desdunes was a key member of the Comité des
Citoyens, an association for the defense of the civil rights of black people, and he
contributed regularly (in English) to the *Daily Crusader* and the *Louisianan,* also to

the short-lived *Louisanais*. Possibly inspired by the vignettes written by Trévigne, he later completed the first history of the Creoles of color. This volume, *Nos hommes et notre histoire*, appeared in 1911 in Montreal. In spite of lacunae, errors, and a tendency to turn history into hagiography, it has been a standard reference for all those who have written on the group.

Of the poets in *Les Cenelles*, Desdunes writes:

> Nous voulons sauver de l'oubli les noms de ces dix-sept créoles qui, au prix des plus grands sacrifices, se sont donné la peine d'écrire un livre pour notre gloire, alors qu'ils étaient soumis à toutes sortes de privations civiles, politiques, et sociales, sans même avoir la liberté de se plaindre. (p. 14)

> [We wish to save from oblivion the names of the seventeen Creoles who, at the cost of great sacrifices, took the pains to write a book to our glory, while they were forbidden even to complain about all the civic, political and social deprivations they were subjected to.]

Desdunes again praised famous Creoles in his "Ode à Thomy Lafon" and in his sonnet "Au Comité des Citoyens," dated September 30, 1893, and printed in the *Crusader*. This bilingual newspaper served as a mouthpiece of the Citizens' Committee in its fight against racial discrimination, which became rampant after radical Reconstruction. A weekly in 1891, then a daily, the *Crusader* was owned by Dr. Louis A. Martinet, who was elected to the legislature during Reconstruction and taught at the new, all-black Southern University. The paper attacked discriminatory measures and denounced the hypocrisy of the Catholic clergy who allowed segregation in local churches. It invited all African Americans to fight in order to preserve their dignity. For instance, a piece by Lucien Mansion's son, Numa, "Le Paria américain," detailed the injustices and vexations that all blacks had to endure (June 23, 1894). One also finds in the *Crusader* a few letters and statements signed by white champions of the Negro cause, such as Bishop Ireland and lawyer-cum-novelist Albion W. Tourgée. It attempted to be the successor of *La Tribune*. yet its influence was limited, mostly because civil equality for African Americans was a "lost cause" at the time.

Besides occasional poems by Victor Rillieux and regular articles by Rodolphe Desdunes, one finds in the *Crusader* contributions by Paul Trévigne, who edited the French section, *Le Croisé,* from 1892 to 1896, and rendered a tribute to Dr. Charles Roudanez on March 22, 1890; a laudatory vignette on Mme. Lamotte by Nathalie Populus: a tribute to the late Joanni Questy by Lucien Mansion (both on June 16, 1894), and Mansion's poem "La Folle" (May 26, 1894). In addition, the press of the *Crusader* printed such works as *Les Feuilles mortes,* by Rillieux, and Desdunes's *Hommage rendu à la mémoire d'Alexandre Aristide Mary*, the philanthropist who had generously placed his large fortune at the disposal of committed men of color. In August 1893, it printed a pamphlet, *The Violation of a Constitutional Right,* which denounced the difficulties encountered by an honorable colored citizen when his white neighbors tried to drive him from the summer house he had bought in Mandeville. Paul Armand Desdunes, Rodolphe's brother, was a fine poet. Eight of his poems were included by E. Maceo Coleman in *Creole Voices*.[14] They apparently had had no chance of seeing print before: Creole literature in French had practically become extinct in Louisiana before the start of the First World War.

NOTES

1. *L'Album Littéraire, Journal des Jeunes gens, amateurs de littérature*. La Nouvelle-Orléans: J. L. Marciacq, 1843. Armand Lanusse, ed. *Les Cenelles*. La Nouvelle-Orléans: H. Lauve, 1845.

2. Charles Roussève. *The Negro in Louisiana, Aspects of His History and Literature*. New Orleans: Xavier University Press, 1939.

3. Only four issues of *L'Album littéraire* have survived. The first available one carries the words "Volume l, 1er Juillet 1843" (pages numbered 75–96); it refers to a previous issue and announces a semimonthly publication of twenty-four pages only. The issue dated August 1, 1843, is labeled "5eme livraison" (pp. 97–120). The issue dated August 15, 1843, is labeled "6eme livraison" (pp. 121–144). Tinker mentions an issue dated October 15, 1843, which has not been found. All translations are mine, except indicated otherwise.

4. Rodolphe L. Desdunes. *Our People and Our History*. Translation and notes by Sister Dorothea Olda McCants. Baton Rouge: Louisiana State University Press, 1973. (Translation of *Nos hommes et notre histoire*. Montreal, 1911.) The English-language version in Desdunes reads:

> To the songs of a thousand birds, to those of the nightingale,
> I dared to mingle my voice in a Spanish melody.
> Oh, I sang about Adèle and to my mother dear,
> I sang about all the delights of a beautiful country.

(1973 ed., p. 58)

5. Desdunes. *Our People and Our History*. In *Le Martyre du Coeur* (1858), a Jamaican black, Placide, plays an important part in moving the drama along to a happy ending. He is the esteemed steward of the Nepteuil family fortune by will of Clarisse's father. He proudly tells Lerdac, the villain who aspires to marry Clarisse for her money: "I am not your nigger." At his death, Séjour left an unpublished five-act drama, *L'Esclave*, which has not been found. See Charles E. O'Neill. *Victor Séjour: Parisian Playwright from French Louisiana*. Lafayette: University of Southern Louisiana, 1996. 130–133.

6. Professor Frans C. Amelinckx will publish a collection of Séligny's short stories in Montreal. I am indebted to him for a complete bibliography of Séligny, and to Professor J. John Perret for his help in identifying several authors. I also wish to thank the American Antiquarian Society for a grant that allowed me to work on the Edward Laroque Tinker collection in July 1993.

7. Edouard J. Fortier. *Les Lettres françaises en Louisiane*. Québec: Imprimerie l'Action sociale, 1915.

8. Roussève. *The Negro in Louisiana*. 122–123.

9. Charles Testut. *Portraits littéraires de la Nouvelle Orleans*. New Orleans: Imprimerie des Veillées, 1850.

10. Edward Laroque Tinker. *Les Ecrits de langue française en Louisiane au 19eme siècle. Essai biographique et bibliographique*. Paris: Honoré Champion, 1932. Repr. Kraus, 1970.

11. Roussève. *The Negro in Louisiana*. 118.

12. Mathé Allain and Barry Ancelet, eds. *Littérature française de la Louisiane; anthologie*. Bedford, N.H.: National Materials Development Center for French, 1981. 197–198.

13. Allain and Ancelet. *Littérature française.* 199.

14. Edward Maceo Coleman, ed. *Creole Voices, Poems in French by Free Men of Color First Published in 1845.* Washington, D.C.: Associated Publishers, 1945.

Chapter Three

From Melting Pot to Copper Kettles
Assimilation and Norwegian-American Literature

Orm Øverland

In the past, much lip service has been paid to the American melting pot. Today, when some hail the ideal of a multicultural America and others nostalgically evoke an image of a once-unified American culture, it may be useful to remind ourselves that American definitions of "American" have tended to exclude rather than include.[1] Throughout the nineteenth century and up to the beginning of the First World War in Europe, the dominant Anglo-American response to the immigrant wishing to enter American society may be summed up as "Although you may call yourself an American and try to behave and think like an American, you are and will remain a foreigner." We may call this response Anglo-exclusivity, even though Anglo-Americans until recently did not have any ethnic identification. They were American.

The official attitude toward immigrants changed abruptly in 1914, when the threat of war made many Americans question the loyalty of their large European-born population.[2] The Americanization campaign of the four war years had a strong impact on public opinion and led to a new but equally exclusionary response to the immigrant in America: "If you want to stay here you must forget who you have been and become like us." While the first of these responses challenged the immigrant's dream of entering the land of promise, the other, which may be characterized as Anglo-conformity, threatened the immigrant's identity. Since the Americanization movement was spearheaded by the president, Woodrow Wilson, and a former president, Theodore Roosevelt, and led to extreme public and private reactions against immigrant languages and cultural expressions, the threat was perceived as real and immediate by many immigrant leaders and spokespersons.[3]

While Americanization as an officially sponsored national movement was limited to the four-year period 1914–1918, Americanization as a factual process has been at work from the time the first immigrant entered the United States. Immigrants did not come with the conscious intention of preserving their national or ethnic identity. Indeed, an awareness or construction of such an identity may depend on confrontation with perceived others and the consequent need to create distinguishing "boundaries."[4] As large numbers of immigrants from one country or region congregated in concentrated rural or urban areas, secular and religious institutions that served to foster a sense of a shared distinguishing identity were created. Many immigrants, however, seemed more eager to enter America and have their children become indistinguishable from other Americans than to celebrate their ethnicity.[5] Indeed, the antihyphen propaganda of Americanization was internalized by many immigrants, as may be seen in the many instances where immigrant parents would never speak their own language in the presence of their children. Consequently, immigrant spokesmen, whose identities were based on so ephemeral a foundation as a transitional immigrant culture, made the preservation of such cultures their main goal. In this work they made battle on two fronts: on the one side striving to create an ethnic loyalty involving the maintenance of language and culture, on the other arguing against the Americanization pressures from without.

Few immigrant spokesmen were able to regard the complex and difficult process of acculturation with such equanimity as the journalist and writer Johannes B. Wist (1864–1923), editor of the most-long-lived American newspaper in the Norwegian language, *Decorah-Posten* (1874–1972). Our culture is and must be transitional, he would caution his colleagues who more optimistically spoke of a long-lived ethnic culture distinct from both its Old World origin and New World context.[6] In the last volume (1922) of his satirical trilogy about the Americanization of a Norwegian immigrant in Minneapolis and the Red River Valley, Wist's narrator reflects on the effect of the two contradictory attitudes of Anglo-conformity and Anglo-exclusivity:

> If you asked these young people of Norwegian descent what nationality they were, they would immediately answer (not without some indignation at being asked such a question) that they naturally were Americans. What else could they be? But if you asked a Yankee what kind of people these immigrant children were, they would always answer without hesitation that they were foreigners or Norwegians. It was not unusual to hear more or less cultivated Americans use expressions such as "half-civilized foreigners" or "dirty Norwegians" about the native-born American descendants of Norwegian immigrants of the second or third generation.

Consequently, he wryly observes, "while it was your duty to be an American, you did not really have permission to be one."[7]

For many other immigrants or descendants of immigrants, the experience of exclusion was too painful to allow for the satirical distance so typical of Wist's view of the immigrant's situation. One effect of this is the panegyrical mode of so many of the popular accounts of the contribution of specific ethnic groups to the United States. A representative book in this genre is Michael Musmanno's *The Story of the Italians in America* (1965), where the opening chapter is the standard litany of early arrivals and achievements in filiopietistic histories of American immigrant groups. Musmanno tells of Italians in America before the Puritan Pilgrims and Italians who have fought American wars. Then, however, he interrupts his litany with a bitter childhood memory that implicitly explains his need to begin his book by arguing that Italian Americans have a right to call America their home. "At twelve years of age," he writes, "I fell in love with a very pretty girl who had recently arrived from England and sat at a desk across the aisle from mine in the country schoolhouse of Stowe Township, Pennsylvania." He decided that he would marry her when he grew up and got a friend to present his proposal. The next day his friend could report that he had "talked to Penelope and she said she loves you. . . . But she says she can never marry you because you are a foreigner." And Musmanno observes: "I was born in America; she had been here seven months. She was an American, I was a foreigner. . . . I did not even attempt to argue the question with her because I accepted what everybody said and believed. Italians were foreigners."[8]

The stamp of being a foreigner in your own country called for a counterargument, and Musmanno's strategy of claiming both a long Italian-American history and Italian-American heroes and martyrs is typical of what I have called homemaking mythologizing, the creation of a filiopietistic history that demonstrates that your group has as much right to the name "American" as do the Anglo-Americans. Such homemaking myths were told in more or less developed narratives and systematized forms in most immigrant groups of European origin and may be classified as myths of foundation (stories demonstrating that "we were here first . . . or at least very early"), myths of blood sacrifice (stories of how "we fought America's wars"), and myths of ideological contributions (stories of how "our traditional values are America's values").[9] In the present article, however, my main concern is with some immigrant literary responses to the apparently opposite insistence on Anglo-conformity, the demand that the immigrant forget the past in order to become an American. The Americanization movement of the First World War made the very hyphen itself into a symbol of potential disloyalty, and both Wilson and Roosevelt insisted that the hyphen and the use of languages other than English were incompatible with true or 100 percent Americanism.

In his essay "Theories of American Ethnicity," Werner Sollors reminds us not only of the distinction between the two kinds of assimilation labeled "melting pot" and "Anglo-conformity" but also of how the former, a metaphor of the creation of a new nationality on the basis of all the contributing nationalities to the American nation, has often been used to actually mean the latter, that is the demand for a kind of cultural suicide as the price of acceptance.[10] Indeed, few who have had full membership in the "new nationality" have demonstrated any eagerness to take part in the change of identity implied in the metaphor of the melting pot as a creative force. We should keep in mind that the two most powerful and influential visions of an open, all-inclusive concept of what it means to be "American" have both been expressed by outsiders, literally by foreigners. Moreover, both were published in London. Crèvecoeur, a Frenchman who had lived for some years in the colony of New York before the Revolution and whose relationship with the United States was that of a diplomat, defined the American both in material ("*Ubi panis ibi patria*") and ideal (the "new man, who acts upon new principles") terms and Zangwill, a British Jewish dramatist, glorified the American as a new kind of human being, the product of the great American melting pot.[11] Compared to these inclusive views of the meaning of "American" expressed by outsiders, Americans, or rather Anglo-Americans, have more often given exclusive answers to Crèvecoeur's question "What is an American?" Zangwill's melting-pot metaphor quickly gained popularity in the years after his play was first produced in the United States in October 1908, but its primary implication, especially during the period of the Americanization movement, was Anglo-conformity. The melting process as a negative removal of distinctive features rather than a creative blending of such features was the message of the many melting-pot, pageant-like pantomimes staged in the heyday of Americanization. One such pantomime at Henry Ford's plant is described by John Higham; the report of another, "America, the Melting Pot of the Nations," organized by a local branch of the Minnesota Women's Committee for Americanization, appears in the *Americanization Bulletin* dated February 1, 1918:

> Eleven children representing the different nations that chiefly come to our shores were dressed in the native costumes. As far as possible each child represented the land of his own nationality or that of his ancestors and was correspondingly placarded. The children marched in, were welcomed by Uncle Sam, who gave each a flag and helped him up the ladder into the melting pot. . . . Then Uncle Sam stirred the pot and the audience sang "America" with great enthusiasm. As they came out of the pot, Uncle Sam welcomed into citizenship the newly made Americans, dressed to represent the visiting nurse, the Salvation Army worker, the Y.M.C.A. worker, the Y.W.C.A. worker, the Knight of Columbus, Boy Scout, Camp-Fire Girl, Red Cross Nurse, and a soldier and a sailor. At the end each graciously accepted a flag.[12]

There is no account of such a pantomime where the clothes worn on leaving the pot are inspired by the variety of styles worn into it.

The Norwegian-American novelist and journalist Waldemar Ager (1869–1941) insisted there could be only one interpretation of the melting pot: it was merely Anglo-conformity in disguise. He polemicized against Americanization and the melting pot and developed his own view of a multicultural America in a series of essays published in his journal *Kvartalskrift* (Quarterly) from 1916 to 1920, two on "The Melting Pot" and four others in a series with the common title "The Great Leveling."[13] Here the melting pot is given a sinister meaning far from Zangwill's triumphant metaphor of the creation of a new kind of human being. The melting pot, Ager insisted, was primarily a metaphor of destruction, more about the killing of the old man than the creation of the new. As he put it in his essay "The Melting Pot" in 1916, "The taking on of the character of the 'new man' is of secondary importance. Discarding the 'old man' is by far the more significant issue" (78).

Ager has three main reasons for warning against the sacrifice involved in the melting-pot process. The Anglo-American or, as Ager calls him, "the self-designated American" has no intention of taking part in this process, no wish "to absorb in himself the Russian, Pole, or Jew, but he wants these people to intermingle their traits with each other" (77–78). Indeed, he explains, "From an 'American' point of view, the melting pot is . . . not for 'Americans.' It is its function to denationalize those who are not of English descent" (85). Second, the aim of the process is in his view not a worthy one, justifying the sacrifice it demands: "We Norwegians would . . . gladly melt ourselves in American culture, but we resist when we find out that it is not American but really English." To Ager, an American culture would be one in which all ethnic groups were given equal respect and to which they all contributed. In effect, one immigrant group is given such a dominant position that "we encounter a culture which is regarded as being American, but on closer examination we find that it is 'English' and that it has no more valid claim to be native here than the Norwegians' *norskdom* (Norwegianness) or the Germans' Germanness" (79). And third, the process is entirely a negative one, one characterized by Jane Addams in 1905 as "the American process of elimination."[14] The result of such elimination may be observed, says Ager, in "the majority of Norwegian Americans in the cities [who] have cast off their old dress without having been able to don the new one. Culturally speaking, they are naked" (79). In effect, he sees the elimination process of the melting pot as a way of controlling the immigrant masses and making them into a permanent class of robots: "If this process succeeds, then one can imagine a servile, weak, and imitative lower class, which has lost the strongest and most forceful traits of its character and which subordinates itself to the only pure race. This latter race will become a kind of automatic upper class." Then "the people of non-British descent who are made over in this manner may come to form a dead weight in the nation instead of constituting its major source of energy as they now do" (85).

As did most of his contemporaries, Ager wavers ambiguously between speaking of the melting of races and the melting of traditions. At times it seems that it is the popular biological concept of mongrelization that is implied, as when he warns that one may not be able to "melt together the different races without losing their strongest, most characteristic, or attractive qualities" (78). In keeping with quite common usuage, however, Ager as well as his friend and colleague Ole Edvart Rølvaag speak of a "race" where one today would speak of a "culture," and in other passages it is quite clearly a cultural rather than a genetic melting down that is his prime concern, as when he deplores the Norwegian Americans who can no longer read "Norwegian classics . . . and an English or American book does not interest them. . . . [I]t is extremely seldom that such an 'assimilated' family knows the name of a single modern American writer" (79). Ager explores the consequences for one immigrant of an assimilation that means the elimination of his culture without the acquisition of a new one in his novel *On the Way to the Melting Pot*, published in Norwegian in 1917, when the Americanization hysteria was at its peak.[15]

The trajectory of the male antagonist, Lars Olson, is similar to that of David Levinsky in Abraham Cahan's novel *The Rise of David Levinsky*, of the same year: he acquires the necessary ruthlessness and skills to succeed in business but loses his soul. Assimilation, the road to the melting pot, is a process in which the immigrant discards all distinguishing traits, all vestiges of the culture of the old country, and becomes an empty shell, good for little else than extinction in the melting pot. At the end of the novel Olson, as seen by the female protagonist, Karoline Huseby, has been "melted down to money and prestige." She recognizes, however, that his fate is a common one and, moreover, a necessary preparation for entry into "the great melting pot":

> First they stripped away their love for their parents, then they sacrificed their love for the one they held most dear, then the language they had learned from mother, then their love for their childhood upbringing, for God and man, then the songs they learned as children, then their memories, then the ideals of their youth—tore their heritage asunder little by little—and when one had hurled from his heart and mind

everything which he had been fond of earlier, then there was a great empty void to be filled with love of self, selfishness, greed, and the like. . . . Thus they readied themselves for the melting pot's last great test. (197–198)

Ager's central thesis, that the melting pot is for the spiritually and culturally stunted and defective, is made rather explicit in an extended metaphor of an industrial process involving a melting of useless scraps and wrecked parts to make new patented machines. The manager of the factory where this work is done explains that "he could not recall having seen a single typewriter, an electric motor, a usable sewing machine or piece of farm machinery wander into the melting pot." Even though the particular machine produced by the factory is said to be an improvement on existing ones, other machines are never purchased to be melted down. Only useless scrap metal is employed in the process because it is the cheapest available raw material. The message is clear: it does not make economic sense to melt down products, even inferior products, that have a function and still can serve a purpose. As if this were not sufficiently clear, we are also told that the manager, who did not hold the masses of new immigrants in high regard, was particularly suspicious of those who appeared to have Americanized themselves. Moreover, it is not only his factory that depends on immigrant labor: "A French cook prepared his food, a Belgian kept his garden in order, his clothes were sewn by a Swedish tailor, and a Norwegian girl cared for his children. In his club, however, he only socialized with members of his own race" (173). Regardless of our lowly social status and nonacceptance by the Anglo-Americans, the author admonishes his fellow immigrants, it is we, the immigrants of America, who are crucial to the machinery of the nation, as well as to the creation of that variety that is the essence of being American.

Through a social satire that involves a large gallery of minor characters, as well as through the contrasting stories of his two main characters, Ager exposes the destructive effects of Americanization on the individual, on the family, and on society as a whole. In the first chapter a dinner party sets the satirical tone. Before the guests arrive, Mrs. Omley is nervous and flustered. The experienced housewife, who knows little English but peppers her Norwegian dialect with the few English words and phrases she has picked up, has to consult every now and then with her daughter Sophy, who is able to read the cookbook and who pretends to know very little Norwegian: "She was preparing an American-style dinner, and that was no simple task" (1). After the meal the men gather on the porch to discuss politics and compare the United States with backward Norway while the women sit in the living room and talk with pride about the Americanization of their children. Much of the satire and some of the subplots are concerned with how the rush to the melting pot creates an unbridgeable gap between the generations, as for instance in the case of the mother whose inability to communicate with her English-speaking children drives her into mental illness. Lars Olson, a newcomer, is present at the dinner and is impressed by all he sees and hears. After most have left, he chats with another guest and observes, "It's strange that more Norwegians don't make the journey to America." "It's just as strange that more Norwegians don't make the journey back to Norway," the older immigrant responds. "You have to pay for what you get here too, and some things get plenty expensive, and what you pay with you don't get back again." Lars, however, ironically believes he is speaking of the higher prices in America and is confident that this will be compensated by a higher income (21).

In his readiness to assimilate, Lars illustrates the author's thesis that Americanization is a process of "discarding the 'old man.' " When Karoline, the girl he has left behind, eventually comes to join him, they soon drift apart as she shies away from the changed Lars and he reacts to her lowly status as a maid and her stubborn refusal to admire and aspire to the superficial world of the Americanized second generation. To demonstrate that Karoline's way is an *American* alternative to the road to the melting pot, Ager resorts to a frequently used cliché in Norwegian-American fiction, a cliché introduced by Hans A. Foss and employed by writers as different as Simon Johnson, Dorthea Dahl, and Jon Norstog: she is met with approval by the family of her employer, "a New Englander of the old school" (110). On the Seventeenth of May, Norway's Constitution Day, she wears ribbons of red, white, and blue while serving at a party and is chastised by one of the guests, who turns out to be "some kind of Scandinavian" (114), for not appreciating her new country. Her employers respond with requests for pieces of her ribbons and hoist the American flag in recognition of her holiday. As so often in Norwegian-American fiction, it is those who are loyal to their own ethnicity who receive Anglo-American recognition.

Lars continues to climb, marries the daughter of his employer, and takes over the business. Karoline returns to Norway, where she discovers that she has become an American. She often dreams "about the big country on the other side of the ocean"; like Jacob Riis, she could not hold back "a great outburst of joy one day when she saw a steamship sail past bearing the American flag" (179). But Ager's novel does not conclude, as did Riis's celebrating autobiography, *The Making of an American*.[16] Not only is Americanization a deadening process, but there seems little hope for the preservation of a vital ethnic culture. Ager underlines the pessimistic message of his novel by dispatching the two young characters who have shown the most resistance to the melting pot in the conclusion. Karoline, who meanwhile has made a second try in America, returns to the old country, and Henry Nelson, a character who in *Ragged Dick* fashion acquires wealth by perseverance and the good luck of marrying the Yankee boss's daughter, goes west with his wife to homestead and regain their lost happiness with a new beginning.

Ager is but one of several American authors of the early nineteenth century who took a bleak view of assimilation and created immigrant protagonists who did not fare much better than did Lars Olson on their way to the melting pot. One such character is Abraham Cahan's David Levinsky; another is Upton Sinclair's Jurgis Rudkus. The theme of the opening chapter of *The Jungle* (1908), describing the wedding celebration of Jurgis and Ona, is what Ager called "the great leveling," the wearing away of the traditions and culture of the homeland and the acquisition of worthless scraps of a new one to which they are strangers. After a while the fiddler no longer plays the music they have brought with them from Lithuania but an American tune, "one which they have picked up on the streets; all seem to know the words of it—or, at any rate, the first line of it, which they hum to themselves, over and over again without rest: 'In the good old summer time—in the good old summer time! In the good old summer time—in the good old summer time!' There seems to be something hypnotic about this, with its endlessly-recurring dominant. It has put a stupor upon every one who hears it, as well as upon the men who are playing it." Before his eventual awakening to a new life in socialism, Jurgis loses his humanity along with his culture.

Rølvaag polemicized against Americanization and the melting pot in essays collected in *Omkring fædrearven* (Concerning our heritage) in 1922. Some of Rølvaag's characters who demonstrate the consequences of the same negative process of assimilation as those of Ager, Cahan, and Sinclair are the miserly couple Louis and Lizzie in *To Tullinger* (Two idiots) (1920) and his eponymous hero of *Peder Victorious* (1929) and its sequel, *Their Father's God* (1931). Rølvaag was concerned with the internalized "American process of elimination"; two other American authors who wrote in Norwegian, Simon Johnson (1925) and Hans Rønnevik (1926), created paragon representatives of their ethnic group who hold high their cultural values in the face of the powerful but evil forces of Americanization both outside and within their group.[17] The fact that ethnic cultures have survived even though they have undergone radical changes and that few descendants of immigrants would accept either the negative or the positive fictional characters as versions of themselves or their parents does not detract from the "truth" of the visions of these writers who were so deeply concerned both with the future of a society that seemed unable to embrace its immigrants and with the future of these immigrants who seemed so ready to leave behind their cultural baggage.

Their older contemporary, Ole A. Buslett (1855–1925), responded to the Americanization frenzy by inadvertently making use of a traditional alternative vision of the United States as a multicultural federation of peoples. His story written in the dramatic mode, *Veien til Golden Gate* (The road to the Golden Gate), was published as a pamphlet in 1915.[18] Buslett was by no means the first to see a multicultural future for the United States. In 1876, a young immigrant and aspiring poet and novelist, Bernt Askevold, not only thought "that the Norwegian language could be sustained for centuries, particularly if the Norwegian book trade . . . Norwegian newspapers, associations, societies, schools, libraries, etc., will continue to thrive" but that the English language in the future would be limited to certain regions of the United States, and that the country would be divided into linguistic regions much like Europe, with German (which to him was "the world's foremost civilized language") as the dominant American language.[19] Askevold's vision has a ninety-years-older antecedent, published anonymously in 1785 without any indication of publisher or place of publication: *The Golden Age: or, Future Glory of North-America Discovered by an Angel to Celadon, in Several Entertaining Visions*.[20] The Angel shows Celadon a future America with large regions reserved for the many different ethnic groups. There is a Savagenia for the Native Americans, a Nigrania for the African Americans, and "in all those vast spaces westward to the great ocean, there may be seats hereafter for sundry foreign nations.—There may be a French, a Spanish, a Dutch, an Irish, an English, &c. yea, a Jewish State here in process of time.—And all of them united in brotherly affection, will at last form the most potent empire on the face of the earth" (11–12). Buslett's "Veien til Golden Gate" is in this tradition, if we may speak of a tradition when none of the parties to it seem to be aware of one another.

Buslett's vision of a multicultural American future is presented in a dialogue between his two protagonists, Haakon and Rosalita, at the end of his allegory. The Yankee Slough, a swampy area on the way west that swallows those who try to make shortcuts on the different roads that run from Castle Garden to the Golden Gate, has an allegorical function similar to that of the melting pot in Ager's destructive version of that metaphor. Central to the plot is the direction of the roads that go from one side of the continent to the other and represent the different modes of Americanization. The Golden Gate, however, does not of course simply define the western edge of the continent but is also the gate to the Promised Land, just as Castle Garden, on the Atlantic, was where immigrants were processed in New York before beginning their journey of Americanization.

At the end of the story Haakon and Rosalita are looking toward the West and the Yankee Slough through a powerful telescope, and Haakon explains that "it'll take ages before the slough is filled in and becomes firm ground." Looking out on the Norwegian-American area that borders on the Yankee Slough, Rosalita sees a land of great beauty, but she also sees that the road that runs through it is a road of memories: "The endless stretch of land sloping down to the Slough is like a heavenly dream.—There's one farm after the other.—Towns here and there.—Churches, many churches, along the long road that skirts the Slough. And I can see monuments—great men and great women—cut in stone in the gardens that border the road." Haakon urges her to "look over at the other side, the German side." She "lets out a long whistle" of admiration and observes that "their settlement, too, stretches down to the very edge of the Slough." They also observe the French settlement that borders on the Slough, "as French as in the countryside around Quebec."[21] "Their road is much the same as ours," says Haakon. "It, too, was to have been redirected from their settlement and into the Slough, but their Road Master has seen to it that the Slough only gets their waste." Indeed, from all sides they can see waste material blowing into the Slough, and Rosalita asks, "Once, when the Slough has been filled, won't we have good land—the very best land—where we now have the Yankee Slough?" Haakon agrees: "The Slough will become land wonderful beyond conceiving. But it won't remain a Yankee Slough. Many have property rights that extend into the Slough and the settlements will expand on their waste deposits. . . . There'll be more and more common waste that accumulates, and (since we are always traveling on each others' roads) also a common jargon, a language we are constantly sending back and forth across the ocean and to the Old World, where it'll be adapted and 'mixed.' We'll have to be patient and make use of a long yard stick in this country of ours."

So the present Yankee Slough of Anglo conformity will be transformed in the distant future to a true American melting pot, such as that envisaged by Celadon, Crèvecoeur, and Zangwill. And the vision of Haakon and Rosalita includes not only a new American nation, where all the present nations have merged, but a new American language, to which the many languages of the immigrants have also made their contributions. Indeed, it is suggested that the new language may become a universal one with influences going "back and forth across the ocean and to the Old World. . . ." The great American experiment of bringing together the peoples of the world and their many languages, Buslett suggests, may in turn give the world a language that can be shared by all. But this cannot come about through a deliberate Americanization effort but by a natural development over a long period of time.

But in 1915 Americanization was an urgent project. Suddenly, the war had made the question of the loyalty of those who spoke incomprehensible languages a crucial issue. Could a Babel be a nation? Would those who did not speak English be loyal to the United States? In 1920 one of the promoters of Anglo-conformity, Wentworth Stewart, wrote of "eliminating" such "handicaps of Americanism" as radicalism and foreign languages in *The Making of a Nation*.[22] To the zealots of Americanization, the long-term view of Buslett and other spokespersons for multiculturalism probably seemed as unacceptable as the long-term view of civil rights reform in Mississippi expressed by Faulkner in *Go Down Moses* (1942) and *Intruder in the Dust* (1949) must have seemed to impatient black citizens of that state.

Not the direction but the straightness of the immigrants' road to the Golden Gate is the disputed question in Buslett's allegory. His hero and heroine represent the American second generation who are ethnic Americans rather than immigrants. Their parents represent the two extremes of the immigrant responses to America, described in such different novels as Rølvaag's *Giants in the Earth* (1927) and Roth's *Call It Sleep* (1934). The two fathers are restless and rootless and always on the move to new land and new beginnings in the West, and Haakon's mother is sustained by her nostalgic memories of the old country. In both cases they lack the second generation's sense of home and rootedness in America. To Buslett and others, it seemed obvious that a condition for permanent ethnic settlements in the United States was a strong sense of belonging to specific permanent neighborhoods.[23]

The so-called road commissioners try to convince Haakon and his mother that they should let them build a new and straight road to the Golden Gate right through their clover field behind their home. These road commissioners represent the ethnic spokesmen for Americanization, and the allegorical implication of their plan is that it is the most valuable part of the ethnic heritage that must be sacrificed to Anglo-conformity. They explain that they will not take away the old road that passes by their modest home, but Haakon sees that it will have little meaning to hold on to a private piece of an old and crooked road when all others soon will be traveling on the new and straight public road into the Yankee Slough. Moreover, their ethnic memory is on the old road, and with the new one this memory will be lost. The road commissioners lose this round and they are seen to sink into the Yankee Slough and disappear as they survey their new road. "The entire Slough is a graveyard," explains Haakon. "All road surveyors who left their own nation in an attempt to find a faster route to the Golden Gate have been lost out there in the Slough."

Writing in 1915, Buslett could have reason to believe in the vitality of the culture represented by his two ethnically conscious and forward-looking second-generation protagonists for whom neither Norway nor Anglo-America but a Norwegian America was home, for the Americanization craze of the First World War years had just begun and his and other ethnic cultures seemed strong and healthy. Newspapers flourished and Buslett's and Ager's dream of an independent Norwegian-American literature seemed closer to realization than ever before. More than ten years later, however, when Rølvaag at the end of his life wrote the pessimistic concluding volumes of his trilogy, the external pressure of the official Americanization movement may no longer have been so strongly felt, but the ethnic Norwegian language-based culture, which had seemed so healthy in the previous decade, was nevertheless rapidly withering. To the natural attrition of the second and third generations was added the drastic drop in the immigration rate. Census figures show a gradual decline in the number of Norwegian-born Americans from 403,877 in 1910 to 363,863 in 1920 and 347,852 in 1930. The decline in language maintenance, however, was far more drastic than these numbers may suggest. One way of measuring language maintenance is to consider the statistics provided by the Norwegian Lutheran Church in America of language use in the services of its congregations. As Einar Haugen has demonstrated, there was a significant decline in the use of Norwegian in the 1920s. In 1917, 73.1 percent of all services were in Norwegian; by 1925 most services were in English; and in 1930 only 37.1 percent were in Norwegian. The use of Norwegian for the instruction of the young declined even more rapidly and had "practically ceased" by 1928.[24]

One writer who considered the nature of ethnic survival through and after the journey to the melting pot was Dorthea Dahl (1881–1951). Buslett and Johnson, writing in Norwegian and publishing in the Midwest, may be said to have had a marginal relation to American literature, but they were central figures in the literature of their ethnic group compared to Dahl, who was one of the few women writers to gain recognition, and who, moreover, lived in distant Moscow, Idaho, on the outskirts of the Norwegian-American culture that had its centers in the midwestern states of Illinois, Wisconsin, Minnesota, Iowa, and North Dakota. She wrote one of her best stories, "The Copper Kettle," in 1930, after it was obvious that the multicultural vision of Buslett, Ager, and Rølvaag had come to naught. She wrote it for a literary magazine in Chicago published and edited by a group of young, educated, and urban people, compared to whom she may have felt much like the old and battered kettle of her story.[25] This was, moreover, the first time she ventured outside the world of church publishers, something that may have added to her sense of having become a relic. But in her story it is the discarded and dirty old copper kettle that is discovered to have value and that is brightened up and handled lovingly by the couple who have decided to give it to the young Anglo-American woman who has taught them to cherish it.

In Dahl's story, as in so many immigrant fictions, the old ways have been found not good enough for the new country by the immigrants themselves and have been discarded. Here the immigrant farmer Trond's immigrant heritage is both metaphorically and literally a copper kettle that he has inherited from his father, who had inherited it from his father. But the kettle that he had packed into his emigrant chest with such expectations of bliss is declared junk and placed in a shed by his wife, Gjertrude, who had already been two years in America when Trond arrived and who had learned American ways as a maid "in a nice American family." In Dahl's story, as in the Ager novel, it is an Anglo-American who recognizes the value of the immigrants' discarded heritage, much like a Jane Addams in a settlement house trying to teach immigrant women to appreciate their songs and their embroidery. This theme of immigrants who disparage their own folkways in their haste to become real Americans is pervasive in Norwegian-American fiction.

However, as I have suggested in my introduction to the translation of this story in Shell and Sollors's anthology, Dahl's attitude toward the immigrant culture is different from that of both Buslett and Ager. They militantly tried to protect the immigrant culture against outside pressures and from internal disintegration; Dahl wrote from a different perspective. By 1930, it was quite clear to her that the melting pot had done its work and that the Norwegian language in which she mostly wrote would not survive as an American literary language. But even though a vital immigrant culture was already a thing of the past, she looks forward to its survival of sorts as an American ethnic culture where English is the only natural language. With little regret she celebrates the copper kettles, the museum-like pieces that may remain as memorials of what the immigrants once brought with them but that can have no place at the center of the American lives of their descendants.

NOTES

1. The view that in the past American culture was unified compared to the present situation is implied in the metaphors of "disuniting" and "fraying" in recent books critical of a multicultural concept of America: Arthur M. Schlesinger, Jr., *The Disuniting of America: Reflections on a Multicultural Society* (New York: Norton, 1992), and Robert Hughes, *The Culture of Complaint: The Fraying of America* (New York: Oxford University Press, 1993).

2. The 1920 census has a total population of 105 million and of these more than a third were either foreign-born (14 million) or had a foreign-born parent (22 million). Roger Daniels, *Coming to America: A History of Immigration and Ethnicity in American Life* (New York: HarperCollins, 1990), 274–275.

3. The standard work on the Americanization movement is still Edward George Hartmann, *The Movement to Americanize the Immigrant* (New York: Columbia University Press, 1948). Key statements made by Roosevelt and Wilson may be found in Philip Davis, ed., *Immigration and Americanization: Selected Readings* (Boston: Ginn, 1920).

4. See Fredrik Barth, introduction to *Ethnic Groups and Boundaries: The Social Organization of Culture Difference* (Boston: Little, Brown, 1969); repr. in Werner Sollors, ed., *Theories of Ethnicity: A Classical Reader* (Basingstoke: Macmillan, and New York: New York University Press, 1996), 294–324.

5. For a discussion of the transitional nature of an immigrant culture, see the first chapter of my *The Western Home: A Literary History of Norwegian America* (Northfield, Minn.: Norwegian-American Historical Association, and Champaign, Ill.: University of Illinois Press, 1996).

6. See his essay "Our Cultural Stage," originally given as a speech in Minneapolis in

1904, and the response by Waldemar Ager, "Our Cultural Possibilities," both translated in Odd S. Lovoll, ed., *Cultural Pluralism versus Assimilation: The Views of Waldemar Ager*, introduction by Carl H. Chrislock (Northfield, Minn.: Norwegian-American Historical Association, 1977).

7. Johannes B. Wist, *Jonasville: Et kulturbillede* (Decorah: *Decorah-Posten*, 1922), 113–114. For a more complete account of Wist and the other writers discussed here, see my history of Norwegian-American literature, note 5, above.

8. Michael A. Musmanno, *The Story of the Italians in America* (Garden City, N.Y.: Doubleday, 1965), 7.

9. See my *Home-Making Myths: Immigrants' Claims to a Special Status in Their New Land*, Odense American Studies International Series. Working Paper No. 20 (1996); "Home-making Myths: The Creation of Ethnic Memory," in Waldemar Zacharasiewicz, ed., *Remembering the Individual/Regional/National Past* (Vienna: Stauffenburg, 1997); and "Old and New Homelands—Old and New Mythologies: The Creation of Ethnic Memory in the United States," in Dag Blanck and Harald Runblom, eds., *Migrants and the Homeland* (Uppsala, Sweden: Studia Multiethnica Upsaliensia/Acta Universitatis Upsaliensis, 1997).

10. Werner Sollors, "Foreword: Theories of American Ethnicity," *Theories of Ethnicity*, x–xliv. See in particular his section "Assimilation and Pluralism," xxv–xxix.

11. J. Hector St. Jean de Crèvecoeur, *Letters from an American Farmer* (London, 1782). (See any of various reprints, e.g. Harmondsworth: Penguin Books, 1981.) Israel Zangwill, *The Melting Pot: Drama in Four Acts* (New York, 1909).

12. John Higham, *Strangers in the Land: Patterns of American Nativism, 1860–1925*, corrected and with a new preface (New York: Atheneum, 1963; first edition, 1955), 247–248; *Americanization Bulletin* (U.S. Department of the Interior, Bureau of Education), 1 (February 1, 1919): 14–15. It may be noted that the Minnesota pantomime did not express an all-Protestant ideal of America.

13. "Smeltedigelen," *Kvartalskrift* 12 (April 1916): 33–42; "Til hr. A. H. Lindelie" (a polemic), ibid. 12 (October 1916): 108–113; and "Den store udjævning," 13 (July 1917): 73–89; 13 (October 1917): 100–115; 15 (April, July, October 1919): 37–50; and 16 (1920): 9–16. With the exception of the second and fourth essay in the "Leveling" series, these are translated in Lovoll, *Cultural Pluralism versus Assimilation*. References are to this translation.

14. Jane Addams, "Immigration: A Field Neglected by the Scholar," Convocation Address at the University of Chicago, published in *The Commons* 10 (January 1905) and reprinted in Davis, *Immigration and Americanization*, 3–22.

15. Waldemar Ager, *Paa veien til smeltepotten* (Eau Claire, Wis.: Fremad, 1917); translated by Harry T. Cleven and published as *On the Way to the Melting Pot* (Madison, Wisconsin: Prairie Oak Press, 1995). References are to this translation.

16. Jacob A. Riis, *The Making of an American* (New York: Macmillan, 1901). Riis tells of his joyful experience of seeing "a ship flying at the top the flag of freedom, blown out on the breeze till every star in it shone bright and clear," while he was lying sick in the home of a friend in Denmark, on the last page of his autobiography: "I knew then that it was my flag; that my children's home was mine, indeed; that I also had become an American in truth. And I thanked God, and, like unto the man sick of the palsy, arose from my bed and went home, healed."

17. Abraham Cahan, *The Rise of David Levinsky* (New York: Harper & Brothers, 1917); Upton Sinclair, *The Jungle* (New York, 1908), the quotation is from the 1960 Signet edition, 24; Ole Edvart Rølvaag, *To Tullinger* (Minneapolis: Augsburg, 1920), revised and translated

as *Pure Gold* (New York: Harper & Row, 1930); *Peder Seier* (Oslo: Aschehoug, 1928), translated as *Peder Victorious* (New York: Harper & Row, 1929); *Den signede dag* (Oslo: Aschehoug, 1931), translated as *Their Fathers' God* (New York: Harper & Row, 1931); Simon Johnson, *Frihetens hjem* (The home of freedom) (Minneapolis: Augsburg, 1925); and Hans Rønnevik, *100 procent* (Carlisle, Minn.: author, 1926).

18. Ole A. Buslett, *Veien til Golden Gate* ([Minneapolis]: author, [1915]). Quotations are from my translation in a forthcoming anthology edited by Marc Shell and Werner Sollors with the tentative title *The Longfellow Anthology of American Literature* (Baltimore: Johns Hopkins University Press). See the introduction to this translation for a discussion of the writing and publishing of the story.

19. Bernt Askevold, "Norsk-amerikansk literatur," *Budstikken* (Minneapolis newspaper), 14 and 21 November 1976. The editor found Askevold's speculations on the possibility of future linguistic regions in the United States somewhat fanciful and commented in a footnote that "this will probably remain a *pium desideratum.*"

20. Sollors discusses Celadon's vision in his foreword to *Theories of Ethnicity*, xxvi–xxvii.

21. Buslett's choice of nationalities here is not fortuitous. Not only were the German Americans the largest non-British ethnic group, they also had a tradition of what we may call separatism. In the early nineteenth century, that is, before there was a Germany, there were several movements to establish a German state within the United States "in which the German language is as much the popular and official language as the English is now, and in which the German spirit rules." Franz Löher (Cincinnati, 1847) as quoted in Kate A. Everest, *How Wisconsin Came By Its Large German Element* (Madison: State Historical Society of Wisconsin, 1892), 10. The acculturation of the French-Canadian Americans in the Northeast "has, in some respects, been slower than that of other groups," notes the historian Roger Daniels (1990, 261).

22. Wentworth Stewart, *The Making of a Nation: A Discussion of Americanism and Americanization* (Boston: Stratford, 1920). His third chapter has the title "Eliminating the Handicaps of Americanism."

23. This is the message of his story "—Og de solgte ut" (—And they sold out), published in Augsburg's Christmas annual, *Jul i Vesterheimen*, in 1913. The common development, however, especially in urban areas, has rather been that one ethnic group has succeeded another, creating what Werner Sollors has called an "Ethnic Palimpsest" (1995). See his essay with this title in Vidar Pedersen and Zeljka Svrljuga, eds., *Performances in American Literature and Culture. Essays in Honor of Professor Orm Øverland on His 60th Birthday* (Bergen: University of Bergen, 1995).

24. Einar Haugen, *The Norwegian Language in America: A Study in Bilingual Behavior*, 2 vols. (Philadelphia: University of Pennsylvania Press, 1953), 262–263.

25. Dorthea Dahl, "Kopper-kjelen," *Norden* 2 (December 1930): 18–19, 27–28, 31. References are to my translation in the forthcoming anthology edited by Marc Shell and Werner Sollors.

Chapter Four

The Ladino (Judeo-Spanish) Press in the United States, 1910–1948

Aviva Ben-Ur

Between 1890 and 1924, thirty thousand Jews from the Ottoman Empire (Turkey and the Balkans) poured into the United States. Most of these immigrants (approximately twenty thousand by the early 1920s) settled in New York City.[1] Although among them were Greek- and Arabic-speaking Jews, the majority spoke Ladino, or Judeo-Spanish, the language their ancestors had transmitted after their exile from the Iberian peninsula four hundred years earlier. Ladino, a language whose creation is identified primarily with the Spanish Expulsion, developed in the Ottoman Empire and is based on medieval Castilian, with admixtures of French, Hebrew, Arabic, Greek, Turkish, and other regional languages. Until the early twentieth century, Judeo-Spanish was almost always written in Hebrew, as opposed to Latin, characters.[2]

One of the most important literary achievements of the Judeo-Spanish people is the Ladino press. Judeo-Spanish scholar Haïm Vidal Sephiha does not exaggerate in declaring that worldwide, the Ladino press, during its first 136 years of existence, was as important to the Jewish community as *responsa* literature had been in previous centuries.[3] Sephiha notes that "had it had time to develop, [the Judeo-Spanish press] would probably have produced masterpieces comparable to those of Yiddish literature."[4] In a similar vein, Professor Edouard Roditi postulates that the Ladino press "might . . . have fathered a whole movement of modern Judeo-Spanish writing similar, though perhaps on a smaller scale, to the Yiddish Renaissance in Eastern Europe and the Americas."[5] Professor Tracy K. Harris notes that the Judeo-Spanish press was a means through which Sephardim maintained and vitalized their language and literature, and was often the only channel through which they kept abreast of events occurring in the outside world.[6]

The American Judeo-Spanish press, printed in Hebrew letters and founded primarily by immigrants from Salonika,[7] was originally created to assist new immigrants in their cultural and economic adjustment to the United States. The difficulties common to Jewish immigrants in this country were more numerous in the case of Sephardic newcomers from the Middle East and Balkans because, due to their unfamiliar physiognomy and language, and their ignorance of Yiddish, many of the existing Ashkenazic communal organizations did not recognize them as Jews.[8]

Moreover, many of these Ashkenazic organizations did not suit the cultural, linguistic, and religious needs of the Sephardim. For these reasons, Sephardic Jews found employment particularly difficult to secure, and they struggled to form their own religious, cultural, and political organizations.[9] One of the most vibrant of these independent endeavors was the Judeo-Spanish press. The Sephardic press, as a record of the multifaceted immigrant experience of Oriental Jewry, is the richest and most encompassing primary source on the struggles this community faced and is an eloquent testimony to the cultural, religious, and political transformation Ladino speakers underwent in their adopted land.[10]

The American Ladino press roughly coincides with the era between the Young Turk revolution in 1908 and World War II, a period that Spanish scholar Paloma Díaz-Mas identifies as the second and most prolific of three in the history of the Judeo-Spanish press.[11] The first enduring American Ladino newspaper, *La Amérika* (1910–1925), was joined by at least eighteen others of varying lifespans until the complete demise of the American Ladino press in 1948. All known Judeo-Spanish tabloids in the United States, with the exception of *El Mesajero* (The Messenger), which appeared in Los Angeles from 1933 to 1934, and *El Emigrante* (The Emigré), which appeared in New Brunswick, New Jersey, in 1917, were published in New York.[12] To date, there exists no definitive bibliographical account of all Ladino newspapers published in the United States, and there may indeed have been additional short-lived periodicals or bulletins from other major centers of American Sephardic settlement, including Atlanta, Chicago, Indianapolis, and Montgomery, that have remained undocumented.

Ladino newspapers in the United States varied politically and religiously, and reflected the ideological diversity of their editors and readership. New York witnessed the birth of a number of publications of a socialist bent, notably *El Progreso* (Progress, 1915–1920, later renamed *La Boz del Pueblo,* and still later, *La Époka de Nu York*) and the aforementioned, *El Emigrante. La Amérika* tended to be religiously traditional and critical of atheist political movements. *La Vara* (The Staff, 1922–1948), describing itself on its masthead as a "serious-humorous newspaper," devoted itself to social satire. The bulletins of the Sephardic Brotherhood of America—a New York burial, mutual aid, and communal society founded in 1915 by Salonician immigrants—focused on the history and activities of the organization and included some articles on improving the social and educational status of Sephardic immigrant women.[13] The monthly magazine *El Luzero Sefaradí* (The sephardic beacon, 1926–1927), described by its editors as a national and apolitical review of science, art, and literature, focused primarily on non-Sephardic themes, with the exception of a number of controversial articles on Sephardic-Ashkenazic tensions in America and the value and beauty of the Judeo-Spanish language. Whatever their orientation, American Ladino newspapers were, almost without exception, dedicated to the social and intellectual betterment of Sephardic immigrants.

The American Ladino press enjoyed an extremely wide circulation. Judeo-Spanish newspapers that published their subscription lists reveal a readership as near as Alabama and Seattle and as distant as South America, Cuba, Constantino-

1. The masthead of *La Vara* (The staff), the last Judeo-Spanish newspaper published in the United States. This issue, dated Friday, February 20, 1948 (corresponding with the Hebrew date, the 10th of Adar, 5708), was the last ever printed. Due to the illness of the tabloid's last editor, Albert (Alberto) J. Torres (1892–1970), this issue received very limited circulation and today exists only in hard copy, in the possession of a handful of individuals. The headline reads "Embargo de armas para Sion trokará" (Arms embargo for Zion will be changed). Note that the word "Sion" is misprinted on the masthead. The Hebrew word above the two hands shaking reads "ehad" (one), and the Ladino words on the two globes read "el mundo" (the world).

ple, Western Europe, and the cities of the Balkans. *La Amérika,* which published a list of its agents in 1915, reveals a readership as widespread as Havana, Río de Janeiro, Buenos Aires and Río de Santa Fé (Argentina), Mexico City, Salisbury (Rhodesia, Africa), Vienna, London, Belgrade (Serbia), and Jerusalem.[14] In 1928, *La Vara* boasted 16,500 subscribers, a significant increase from the 9,000 tallied in 1926.[15] Though this figure pales in relative comparison to the Yiddish-language *Forward,* which at its peak in the 1920s had more than a quarter of a million subscribers,[16] it is significant when one considers the social fragmentation, illiteracy, and economic disadvantages that were the lot of many Sephardim both in the Ottoman Empire and the United States. These subscription figures are also placed in perspective when one considers that the Judeo-Spanish speaking population of the world was estimated at 350,000 for the years 1900 and 1925.[17] In comparison, the Yiddish-speaking population of the world in 1900 and 1925 was 7 million and 8,200,000 respectively.[18]

In reality, it is somewhat misleading to compare the American Ladino press in its heyday to the American Yiddish press at its peak. The former is better compared to the earlier stages of the Yiddish American press (1870 to about 1905), which Arthur Goren refers to as "a long period of gestation." This period began with the launching of the first Yiddish American newspaper, the *Yidishe Tseitung* (Jewish Journal), which appeared irregularly until its demise in 1877. All together, nine Judeo-German journals appeared in the 1870s, but only one survived. Goren attributes the failure of the early Yiddish press to the relatively tiny size of the Yiddish-speaking population. In 1870, there were approximately 15,000 Yiddish speakers in New York, a number that ballooned to 35,000 a decade later. Goren also notes that most immigrants were not accustomed to tabloids, having come from provinces where orthodoxy dominated and where secular influences were slight.[19] We have noted earlier that approximately 20,000 Oriental Jews, the majority of whom were Ladino speakers, settled in New York City from 1890 to 1924. Considering that between 1910 and 1924, fourteen known Ladino periodicals appeared, the survival and vitality of the Ladino press in the United States compares favorably, if not remarkably, to its Yiddish counterpart.

Given the social and linguistic isolation of Ladino-speaking immigrants, it is safe to declare that the Judeo-Spanish press was largely an internal conversation. There are examples of Ashkenazim who, seeking a rapprochement with Sephardim, or building upon their knowledge of and interest in modern Spanish, did correspond with the editors of the Ladino press and even subscribed. For example, in 1915 an Ashkenazic Jew named Max Schurman, a researcher for the Bureau of Jewish Education, sent a letter to *El Progreso* indicating that with his modest knowledge of Spanish he was able to read that Ladino newspaper with some effort, and appreciated the editors' "toilsome mission."[20] From personal experience, the present writer may add that she is aware of one non-Jewish professor of linguistics, currently teaching at the City University of New York, who subscribed to *La Vara* in the 1940s. These instances, however, are extremely isolated, and generally, the contributors to Ladino newspapers were able to express themselves much more candidly than had these publications appeared in a more widely accessible language. This candid aspect of the Ladino press is generally characteristic of other foreign-language American Jewish tabloids, which were, as Jonathan D. Sarna notes, "often bolder and more critical of America and American Jewish life than English-language ones."[21]

Some officials of the greater Jewish community, however, were indeed aware of the Judeo-Spanish press. *The Jewish Communal Register of New York City* for the years 1917–1918 lists *La Amérika* and *La Boz del Pueblo* in its accounting of Jewish periodicals published in New York City. The list was prepared by Joseph Margoshes of the Yiddish *Der Tog* (The Day) and is based on tabloids that were available at the New York Public Library and the Library of the Jewish Theological Seminary of America.[22] An article in the same issue, written by Samuel Margoshes of the Bureau of Education, also mentions "La Renasansia" (*sic*) and "El Kierbatch Amerikano" (*sic*). The author apparently had some knowledge of Judeo-Spanish, given his declaration that "[f]rom the editorials of 'La America' it is rather difficult to decide what policy it pursues, but 'La Bos del Pueblo' is pronouncedly socialist." Commenting on the state of the Ladino press, Margoshes wrote pessimistically,

> For one reason or another, the Judeo-Spanish press has failed get a grip on the oriental community. All the four papers combined have a circulation not exceeding 1,500, which is pretty low considering the size of the oriental community in New York City [20,000, according to Margoshes]. The limited circulation of the Ladino press may perhaps be explained by the fact that the oriental community does not form a unit even linguistically, some oriental Jews speaking Arabic, some Greek, and the rest other languages, while not all of them understand Ladino.[23]

Margoshes was correct in citing the ethnic heterogeneity of the Oriental Jewish population, but he failed to take into account the fact that the vast majority of these immigrants did indeed speak Judeo-Spanish. In any case, Margoshes's analysis would have been drastically different had he reported after 1922, the year the extremely popular tabloid *La Vara* was launched. As noted above, 9,000 Sephardic Jews subscribed to this newspaper in 1926, and this number ballooned to 16,500 by 1928.

From the point of view of the editors, the Ladino press was anything but a lucrative endeavor. Moise Gadol, for example, editor of *La Amérika,* operated his Lower East Side press at great financial personal loss, particularly given that existing Jewish organizations, Sephardic and Ashkenazic alike, failed to provide financial support for his publication.[24] The entire fifteen-year history of *La Amérika* was one of financial struggle. *La Amérika* cost $3,000 a year to operate, and Gadol received only $1,500 in contributions yearly. He supplemented his income with the sale of various books at the editorial offices, the profits from his printing services, and the proceeds from his export business. In his words, "[I do] all of this only for the sake of serving my Jewish nation, since, given the numerous languages I know, I could earn my living much better [elsewhere] and earn a profit in America."[25] His hyperbolic contention, on the tenth anniversary of the publication of *La Amérika,* that his newspaper had been responsible for drawing Sephardic immigrants to the United States and for effecting a rapprochement between Sephardim and Ashkenazim certainly contains much truth (and much irony, given some of the acerbic comments he directed against his Yiddish-speaking brethren).[26]

Some aspiring Ladino journalists solicited the Sisterhood of New York's historic Spanish and Portuguese Synagogue (whose congregation was founded in 1654) for funds to launch Ladino tabloids. In September of 1915, Salonician-born Maurice S. Nessim, struggling to secure funds for his proposed Judeo-Spanish weekly, wrote Sisterhood president Alice Menken of his desire, assuring her that his paper would be "independent of any doctrine" and would "only reflect the social condition of the Sepharadim *[sic]* Jews in America." Perhaps attempting to appeal to Menken's sense of female leadership, Nessim declared, "My mother came last week from abroad, and as we consider her the head of our family, I spoke to her on that score [launching a Ladino newspaper]. When I assured her that the Sepharadim Jews are craving for a real paper, she agreed with me and offered only $200 for that purpose. . . ." Nessim requested at least $300 from Menken but was rebuffed by her apparent denial of the need for such a tabloid (only Nessim's correspondence is available). "I do not agree with you," he responded, "when you say that the Spanish-speaking Jews are not numerous enough in America to have a newspaper of their own."[27] One suspects that Menken's decision to withhold funds went beyond issues of population size. Contrary to his earlier promise, the editorials Nessim published in his newspaper, launched in 1915 as *El Progreso,* were highly political and were interpreted by American wartime censors as "communist propaganda." Nessim was eventually forced into French exile in November of 1919.[28]

The editors of the Ladino press belonged to the cultural and intellectual elite of the Sephardic East. Many had benefited from the education provided by the Alliance Israélite Universelle and other European schools and had enjoyed successful careers in their native lands. Before immigration, Albert J. Levi ([?]–1962), one of the editors of *La Vara,* had graduated from L'École Normale of Salonika and had served as editor of the Ladino daily *El Liberal* (The liberal) of that city. His longtime partner, Salonician-born Moise B. Soulam (1890–1967), had attended both the Alliance and the Turkish college Idadie. Before emigrating, Soulam had launched his own newspaper in Salonika and had also served on the staff of Moise Levy's *El Kirbach* (The whip), a Salonician satirical journal. *La Vara,* the weekly Albert J. Levy founded with Moise B. Soulam as assistant editor, was the longest-running, and perhaps most creative, Ladino newspaper of the United States.

In the early years of Sephardic immigration, when Oriental Jews encountered linguistic barriers and ethnic prejudice at Ellis Island, the American Ladino press served as a channel through which Sephardim could appeal to their brethren for assistance. Sephardic leaders understood that on account of language barriers and idiosyncratic last names, Sephardic immigrants were not recognized as Jews by the Ashkenazic officers of the Hebrew Immigrant Aid Society, the very officers who were authorized to intervene on their behalf. In the Ladino lingo of the Lower East Side, the immigration experience at Ellis Island was known as *la izla de las sufriensas* (the island of suffering) or *el kastigar* (the scourge).[29] Especially memorable is the letter of the twenty-four-year-old Salonician upholstery merchant Itshak Azriel, who found himself detained at Ellis Island, suspected of an unspecified ailment. ". . . I have made so many sacrifices, both financially and temporally, and furthermore, I have spent a good fortune on the voyage," he despaired. Azriel, whose Salonician companions had already been released, begged the editor of *La Amérika* to procure someone to vouch for him: "Now, I implore you with all of my heart to make efforts on my behalf and come to my aid and reclaim me quickly, before it's too late, and I am returned to my country, as they have threatened, and afterwards, who knows what could happen?"[30] After two unsuccessful attempts to obtain sponsors to reclaim Azriel, Moise Gadol made an appeal to Washington and secured Azriel's release.[31] Two weeks later, a letter of Azriel's appeared in *La Amérika* entitled "How I Was Liberated From Ellis Island." It expressed his appreciation for a newspaper that labors "in favor of all of our Sephardic immigrants."[32]

One of the most vibrant features of the Ladino press was the quasi-fictional advice columns by Moise B. Soulam under the noms de plume, "Tía Satula" (Aunt

Satula), "Bula Satula," "Ham Avraham," and "Ham Moshón."[33] Soulam began to contribute his column within a week of his arrival in New York, and it proved to be one of the longest-running features of the American Ladino press, spanning from 1913 until 1934. The columns, which ultimately evolved into "Postemas de Mujer" (Pet peeves of a woman) and "Postemas de Ham Moshón" (Pet peeves of Rabbi Moshón), opened with a recounting of an outrageous anecdote of inappropriate social behavior and ended with a satirical commentary directed at Sephardic female and male immigrants of New York. They are revealing of the extreme self-consciousness Sephardim felt as immigrants with a distinct language and "Oriental" mores, and represent an attempt to Americanize Sephardic readers through social satire. Though the stated purpose of the columns was "to proffer good morals to the people, and to counsel women [and men] to take the right path in this blessed city," Soulam's contributions were also meant to offer consolation in times of trouble. The installments dealing with the Great Depression, for example, are among the most poignant and are filled with uplifting Ladino adages such as "Ay días klaros i días eskuros, i todo ay ke tomarlo kon pasensia" (There are clear days and cloudy days, and everything must be endured with patience).

The American Ladino press is also a rich source for Sephardic community activism. The bulletins of the Sephardic Brotherhood of America, for example, offer information on female participation in organizations such as the Brotherhood's Committee of Education, which in 1922, under the direction of Fanny Angel, Rebecca Nahoum Amateau, and other Sisterhood volunteers, organized a series of lectures of "general interest." From an article in *La Vara* in 1924, we learn that one of these lectures, given by Angel, was on "love and sex," and that Angel was to be commended as "the first of our Sephardic women to speak with courage in public."[34]

Judeo-Spanish newspapers are also an excellent source for documenting the history of the Ladino theater of the Lower East Side and other Sephardic-American communities. Theater groups served an important function by providing social activities for both performers and audience members, and were a means through which Sephardim expressed political and social activism, since many shows donated their proceeds to local Sephardic clubs, to both local and overseas charities, and to the victims of the two world wars. From the first few years of its inception, the Ladino press faithfully printed announcements of upcoming performances and offered critical reviews, describing drama plots, naming individual actors, and commenting on the quality of performances.[35]

The Judeo-Spanish press records many fascinating interactions between Ashkenazic and Sephardic immigrants, many of them betraying intraethnic tensions. In 1915, a Russian-born Jewish girl wrote to the editor of *La Boz del Pueblo* of an amorous encounter with a Sephardic youth. Clara met Jack at a ball organized by the Judeo-Spanish newspaper, but she was not certain of his religious affiliation. "At first glance," she wrote, "I thought him Italian. The way he spoke, his countenance and his gestures were like those of the Italians. But later, when we began seeing each other, he swore to me that he is a Spanish-speaking Jew." Though the two were in love, Clara's parents objected to the union because they did not believe that Jack was indeed Jewish. Addressing the editor, Clara wrote, "Now, I beg you to tell me through your esteemed newspaper if it is possible, that a Jew who doesn't speak Jewish, and doesn't look Jewish, can nevertheless have a Jewish soul." The editor was annoyed that this Ashkenazic girl "is still not up to par with her knowledge on Judeo-Spaniards in America." ". . . Yes, 'Clara,' " the editor replied, "the boy speaking Spanish, having Italian gestures, who can read our newspaper, is Jewish. . . . No, we don't see any inconvenience in the intermarriage of Sephardim with Ashkenazim. There are many examples of Sephardim living with Ashkenazim in the greatest harmony."[36]

The transformation of the ethnic identity of Ladino-speaking Jews manifests itself distinctively throughout the Ladino press. Having constituted more than 90 percent of all Jews in the former Ottoman Empire, Sephardic Jews encountered a new reality on American soil, where they were now a tiny minority in a sea of Ashkenazic Jews. Their struggle to redefine themselves in relation to their Eastern and Central European coreligionists proved to be a major preoccupation. To distinguish Middle Eastern and Balkan Sephardim from old Sephardim, descendants of Iberian Jews who had immigrated to America via Western Europe, South America, and the Caribbean, Ladino-speaking Jews became known as "Oriental Jews." The communal organization founded for them in 1912, in fact, was known as the Federation of Oriental Jews of America, and *La América,* on its masthead, described itself as an "Oriental Spanish-Jewish" tabloid until as late as 1915. Once Sephardi immigrants realized the connotations of the word "Oriental," a semantic battle ensued. The term was deemed objectionable not only because it also referred to peoples known today as "Asians" but also because of its negative connotations of backwardness and economic and cultural disadvantage. Contributors to the Ladino press protested that the only acceptable nomenclature was "Sephardim" and pointed out that Ladino was a Western language, not an Oriental tongue. Furthermore, they argued, the word "Sephardic" conjured up images of the most glorious epoch in Spanish Jewish history, when medieval Spanish Jews flourished culturally and literarily under Islamic rule.[37]

According to a tradition dating to medieval times, Iberian Jews traced their origins to the royal house of David and were descended from a long line of "kings and princes." Even after the Spanish expulsion, Sephardic Jews continued to perceive themselves as the chosen of the Jewish people. Their widespread poverty and the failure of many Ashkenazim to recognize them as Jews shook the self-confidence of immigrant Sephardim. The disdain among many Sephardim for the Judeo-Spanish language as "jargon" and "uncultured," inculcated by the Alliance Israélite Universelle of Ottoman lands, was accentuated in the United States. As Sephardic intellectual leaders became exposed to studies in modern Spanish, moreover, the idea of Ladino as a corrupted tongue began to gain currency. In a 1916 article on modern Spanish proverbs, Dardanelles-born Maír José Benardete, who was to become a renowned scholar and professor of Hispanic and Sephardic studies, asked rhetorically, "Is it [Ladino] really a language?"[38] Both Moise Gadol and Ben-Tsion Behar, a contributor to *La América,* lamented the use of Ladino because it bore with it memories of the anti-Jewish persecutions in Spain.[39]

These language battles can be compared to parallel conflicts among Ashkenazi Jews, whose journalists also fought over the propriety of the use of Yiddish as the means of communication among American Jews. Many of these intellectual leaders deemed Judeo-German "the jargon of the uneducated masses," and some even sought to substitute "a heavily Germanized Yiddish style and vocabulary."[40] Others, mostly radicals, adopted a more pragmatic approach, viewing Yiddish as "a transitory phenomenon" to be exploited for purposes of political unification until the Americanizing of the Jewish labor force was accomplished.[41] Particularly intense debates between Zionists, who advocated Hebrew as the key to national redemption, and Yiddishists, who regarded Hebraicists and the culture they sought to cultivate as elitist, heat up the pages of the Yiddish press in the 1890s and early 1900s.[42] While these internal debates bear some striking parallels to the linguistic controversy bubbling in Sephardic circles, the conflicts of Ladino speakers bear a distinctive flavor and conjure up elements of a unique experience, one that encompassed Inquisitorial oppression, legendary ethnic nobility, and the secularizing forces of the Alliance Israélite Universelle.

The editors of the American Ladino press were remarkable personages; extraordinarily energetic and creative, and filled with a zeal for effecting the betterment of their community. Yet for all their idealism, these editors were not without imperfections. As Joseph M. Papo notes, one major factor in the demise of the Sephardic press was intragroup fighting between various competing periodicals, melees that sometimes even resulted in lawsuits.[43] Still, it was another factor that played a central role in the eclipse of the press. Professor Jane Gerber observes that the Ladino press was ultimately the "victim of its own success," acculturation being the primary reason for the demise of the last Judeo-Spanish newspaper in 1948.[44]

JUDEO-SPANISH NEWSPAPERS PUBLISHED IN THE UNITED STATES

The following list represents all known Judeo-Spanish periodicals published in the United States and provides, where available, the names of their editors, cities of publication and publication lifespans. My information is based on the research of previous scholars and, where this research is inaccurate or incomplete, my own research and first-hand knowledge. I have omitted from this essay detailed bibliographical information on the American Ladino press, including archival holdings and biographical details of editors, as such information extends beyond the framework of this volume. I should stress that this bibliography, while it represents the most inclusive list of American Ladino periodicals to date, is by no means definitive, and at the time of this writing, I am still waiting for a number of institutes and libraries to confirm their holdings and to send me issues and publications I have not yet examined.

The existence and lifespans of many American Ladino newspapers remain nebulous. Much work must be accomplished in order to establish dates, archival holdings, and previously overlooked titles definitively. Only then can scholars begin a comprehensive assessment of the multidimensional contribution of the Ladino press. As this brief survey has intended to demonstrate, the Judeo-Spanish press is a rich, and largely unexplored, source for the history of Ladino-speaking Jews in the United States.

1. *La Ágila* (The eagle). 1910. New York. Editor: Moise S. Gadol.
2. *La Amérika* (America). 1910–1925. New York. Editor: Moise S. Gadol.
3. *La Ágila* (The eagle). 1912. New York. Editor: Alfred Mizrahi. Coeditor: Behor Hana.
4. *La Renasensia* (Renaissance). 1912. New York. Editor unknown.
5. *El Progreso / La Boz del Pueblo / La Époka de New York* (Progress / The voice of the people / The epoch of New York). 1915–1920. New York. Editors: Maurice S. Nessim; Alfred Mizrahi
6. *El Emigrante* (The emigré). 1917. New Brunswick, N.J. Editor: Albert J. Covo.
7. *El Kirbach Amerikano* (The American whip). 1917. New York. Editor: Albert J. Levi.
8. *La Renasensia* (Renaissance). 1917–1922. New York. Editors: Shimon (Simon) S. Nessim; Robert Fresco. Organ of the Agudat Zionist Maccabee.
9. *El Amigo* (The friend). 1918[?]. New York. Editor: Albert J. Covo.
10. *El Proletario* (The proletarian). 1918. New York. Editor unknown. Organ of the Sephardi Branch of the Arbeiter Ring (Workmen's Circle; an affiliate of the American Socialist Party).
11. *El Ermanado* (The brotherhood). 1920[?]–1938[?]. New York. Numerous editors. Organ of the Sephardic Brotherhood of America.
12. *La Luz* (The light). 1921–1922. New York. Editor: Shimon (Simon) S. Nessim. Asst. Editor: Maurice Benrubi.
13. *La Vara* (The staff). 1922–1948. New York. Editors: Albert J. Levi; Albert J. Torres. Asst. Editor: Moise B. Soulam.
14. *El Amigo* (The friend). 1923[?]–1932[?]. New York. Editor unknown. Publisher: New York committee for the Insane Asylum of Salonika.
15. *El Luzero Sefaradí* (The Sephardic beacon). 1926–1927. New York. Editors: Albert J. Levi; Moise B. Soulam.
16. *The Sephardic Bulletin.* 1928–1930. New York. Editors: Robert Franco; Victor Tarry.
17. *El Sol.* 1930[?]. New York.
18. *El Mesajero* (The messenger). 1934–1935. Los Angeles. Editor: Dr. Robert Benveniste. Publisher: Sosiedad Paz i Progreso (Peace and Progress Society).
19. *The Sephardi.* 1940[?]/1943–1959[?]. New York, N.Y. Editor: Joseph M. Papo.

NOTES

I would like to thank the following individuals for their scholarly guidance: Dr. Jonathan Sarna of Brandeis University; Dr. Denah Lida, professor emeritus of Brandeis University; and R. Dr. Marc D. Angel of Congregation Shearith Israel; the following individuals for their bibliographical assistance: Dr. Charles Cutter, James Rosenbloom, and Nancy Zibman of Brandeis University's Judaica and Special Collections; Mary Moynihan of Brandeis University Library's Inter-Library Loan; and Susan Tobin, archivist of Congregation Shearith Israel; and the following individuals for their interviews: Linda Ezratty Rosenberg, editor of *The Sephardic Brother*; Dr. Joel Halio, grandson of the late Albert J. Torres; and Benjamin Soulam, son of the late Moise B. Soulam. I would also like to thank Temple University's Center for American Jewish History and the Jewish Historical Society of New York for awarding me fellowships to further my research on Moise S. Soulam and his advice columns. Finally, I wish to express my gratitude to Dr. Joe Halio and Robert Bedford of the Foundation for the Advancement of Sephardic Studies and Culture for providing me with the masthead of *La Vara*. All translations and transliterations from the Ladino and translations from the French are mine.

1. This is a conservative figure, based on Marc D. Angel, *La America: The Sephardic Experience in the United States*, Philadelphia: The Jewish Publication Society of America, 1982, p. 6. In 1923, *La Vara* estimated the Ladino-speaking population of New York and the United States at 35,000 and 50,000, respectively. See Albert J. Levi, "El Menester de Un Jurnal Kotidiano Se Aze Fuertemente Sentir," *La Vara*, 12/14/23, p. 2, and "Por La Prima Vez en la Istoria de los Sefaradím de América: Grandioza Kompanía de Publisidad Sefaradít" (editorial announcement), ibid., p.4. In 1934, the American Sephardic population was estimated at 75,000. See "A Los Lektores de 'La Vara': Nuestra Seksión en Ingléz," *La Vara*, 8/10/34, p. 8.

2. See Tracy K. Harris, *Death of a Language: The History of Judeo-Spanish*, Newark: University of Delaware Press, 1994, p. 56. According to Harris, the use of Latin letters increased only in the twentieth century, particularly in the field of journalism. Harris notes that the first Ladino newspaper printed in Latin letters was the Rumanian tabloid *Luzero de la Pasensia*, which appeared from 1886 to 1889. Throughout this essay, for reasons of simplicity, I refer to the language of the Sephardim as Ladino or Judeo-Spanish. For a discussion of the controversy regarding nomenclature, see Harris, pp. 20–29.

3. Haïm Vidal Sephiha, *L'Agonie des Judéo-Espagnols*, Paris: Editions Entente, 1977, p. 106. Sephiha's arithmetic eludes me; he refers to "ces cent trent-six dernière années," indicating that his survey of the Ladino press ends in 1978. According to him, the first Ladino newspaper, *La Buena Esperansa*, originated in Smyrna in 1842, and by 1973, only two Ladino newspapers remained worldwide, one published in Tel Aviv and one in Constantinople. The Tel Aviv Ladino newspaper Sephiha was probably referring to is *La Luz de Israel* (published in Latin letters), which folded in 1990. Sephiha has documented 344 titles, exceeding Moshe David Gaon's accounting of 296. See Gaon, *HaItonut BeLadino: Bibliografia* (A bibliography of the Judeo-Spanish [Ladino] press), Tel Aviv: Monoline Press, 1965. The Judeo-Spanish press appeared on five continents—Europe, North America, South America, Africa, and Asia—and in the following countries: England, Austria, Bulgaria, Egypt, the United States, France, Greece, Hungary, Israel, Mexico, Rumania, Czechoslovakia, Turkey, and Yugoslavia. It also appeared in the British crown colony of Gibraltar and on the island of Curaçao. See Sephiha, *L'Agonie des Judéo-Espagnols*, pp. 100–101.

4. Sephiha, *L'Agonie des Judéo-Espagnols*, p. 106. "Elle [la presse] constitue en outre une littérature en gestation, qui si elle avait eu le temps de se développer aurait probablement donné des chefs-d'oeuvre comparables à ceux de la littérature yiddisch. . . ."

5. Edouard Roditi, "The Slow Agony of Judeo-Spanish Literature," *World Literature Today* 60 (Spring 1986): 244–246, at p. 245.

6. Harris, *Death of a Language*, p. 130.

7. The founders of the two longest-lived Ladino periodicals in America, Moise S. Gadol (*La Amérika*) and Albert J. Levi (*La Vara*), were of Bulgarian and Salonician origin, respectively. Gadol is also thought to have launched *La Ágila* in 1910; Levi also launched *El Kirbach Amerikano* and *El Luzero Sefaradí*. Behor Hana, former editor of *La Boz de Izmir*, who was coeditor with Alfred Mizrahi of the short-lived *La Ágila* (1912), was probably from Izmir. I have not yet identified the patrimony of Alfred Mizrahi, who was also editor of *La Époka de Nu York*. Albert J. Torres (publisher of *La Époka de Nu York*, cofounder and business manager of *La Luz*, editor of *La Vara*, and business manager of *El Luzero*

Sefaradî), Maurice S. Nessim (*El Progreso*), Albert J. Kovo (*El Emigrante*; the 1918[?] *El Amigo*), Shimon S. Nessim (*La Renasensia; La Luz*), and Moise B. Soulam (*La Vara; El Luzero Sefaradî*) were all from Salonika. I have not yet identified the patrimony of Maurice Benrubi (cofounder and assistant editor of *La Luz*) and Robert Fresko (*La Renasensia*), though I suspect that they too were born in Salonika. Many of the editors of and contributors to the annual reviews of the Sephardic Brotherhood of America, including Ralph Hasson, were of Salonician origin. I have no information on the editors of the *Sephardic Bulletin*. The committee for the Insane Asylum of Salonika in New York, which published the later *El Amigo*, was most likely made up of Salonician Jews. The existence of New York's *El Sol* and its editor is unconfirmed. Avram Galante is the only scholar who mentions this tabloid, and he dates it to 1930. See his *Histoire des Juifs de Turquie*, vol. 9, Istanbul: Editions Isis, 1985 (first published 1926), p. 225, and "La Presse Judéo-Espagnole Mondiale," *Hemenora* 8–10 (July/August/September 1935): 186–199. Dr. Robert Benveniste, editor of *El Mesajero*, was probably from Rhodes, given that the bulletin's sponsoring organization, Sosiedad Paz i Progreso of Los Angeles, was founded by Jews of that island. *The Sephardi* counted among its editors Palestinian-born Joseph M. Papo, a Ladino-speaking Sephardi, and John J. Karpeles, whose ethnic origins are unknown to me at this time.

8. Ashkenazim are Yiddish-speaking Jews, in this case, of Eastern European origin. During the Middle Ages, the biblical place-name, "Ashkenaz" came to be identified with Germany, and "Sefarad" with Spain; hence, "Ashkenazic" and "Sephardic."

9. For histories of the immigrant experience of Ladino speakers in the United States, see Angel, *La America*, and Joseph M. Papo, *Sephardim in Twentieth Century America: In Search of Unity*, San Jose and Berkeley, Calif.: Pelé Yoetz Books and Judah L. Magnes Museum, 1987 (henceforth, *SITCA*). See also Diane Matza, "Sephardic Jews Transmitting Culture Across Three Generations," *American Jewish History* 79 (Spring 1990): 336–354, and Jack Glazier, "Stigma, Identity and Sephardic-Ashkenazic Relations in Indianapolis," in *Persistence and Flexibility: Anthropological Perspectives on the American Jewish Experience*, ed. Walter P. Zenner, Albany: State University of New York Press, 1988, pp. 43–62.

10. See my "Nuestra Kolonia: A Report on the Sephardic Community of the Lower East Side as Conveyed Through the Judeo-Spanish Press, 1910–1925" (unpublished manuscript researched and prepared under the direction of Dr. Jane S. Gerber for the Komunidad Project of the Lower East Side Tenement Museum), May 1995.

11. Paloma Díaz-Mas, *Los Sefardíes: Historia, Lengua y Cultura*, Barcelona: Riopiedras Ediciones, 1986, pp. 167–68. The first and last periods are 1845–1908 and 1945 to the present.

12. For information on the Ladino-speaking Jews of Los Angeles, see Daniel J. Elazar, "Sephardim in North America," *The Other Jews: The Sephardim Today*, New York: Basic Books, 1989, pp. 162–183, at p. 175; Papo, *SITCA*, pp. 294–299; and Stephen Stern, *The Sephardic Jewish Community of Los Angeles*, New York: Arno Press, 1980. In 1910, the Sephardic population of New Brunswick swelled to such a degree that Oriental Sephardim made up nearly one-third of that city's Jewish population of 2,500. For several years, New Brunswick represented the largest Sephardic community outside New York City. See Papo, *SITCA*, p. 270.

13. See my "Ladino (Judeo-Spanish) Press," in *Jewish Women in America: An Historical Encyclopedia*, ed. Paula Hyman and Deborah Dash Moore, N.Y.: Routledge, 1998, pp. 781–785.

14. "Lista de Nuestros Ajentes," *La América*, 11/12/15, p. 5. Even with this geographic

diversity, Gadol claimed only just under one thousand subscribers. See "La Kestión de los Dokumentos Turkos," *ibid.*, p.2.

15. Harry Linfield, *The Communal Organization of the Jews in the United States, 1927,* New York: American Jewish Committee, 1930, p. 175. The figures are tabulated from "Claimed Circulation." In 1927, the claimed circulation of *La Vara* was sixteen thousand, indicating that, if these figures are accurate, this tabloid increased its readership by seven thousand in the span of one year. Linfield does not list subscription figures for *El Luzero Sefaradí;* see p. 174.

16. Paul Mendes-Flohr and Judah Reinharz, "The American Experience," in *The Jew in the Modern World,* ed. Mendes-Flohr and Reinharz, Oxford: Oxford University Press, 1980, pp. 354–417, at p. 383. In 1916, the year during which Judeo-German journalism in the United States reached its acme, the American Yiddish daily press enjoyed a readership of two million. This figure is not surprising, considering that between 1880 and 1914, more than two million Eastern European Jews immigrated to the United States. See Arthur A. Goren, "The Jewish Press," in *The Ethnic Press in the United States: A Historical Analysis and Handbook,* ed. Sally Miller, New York: Greenwood Press, 1987, pp. 203–228, at p. 212.

17. Arthur Ruppin, *Soziologie der Juden,* vol. 2, Berlin: Jüdischer Verlag, 1931, p. 131. As Sephiha has noted, Ruppin's figures are misleading, given that the quality of Judeo-Spanish knowledge has steadily declined; see Sephiha, *L'Agonie des Judéo-Espagnols,* p. 95.

18. Ruppin notes that these figures represent 60.6 percent and 54.7 percent of world Jewry, as opposed to Ladino-speaking Sephardim, representing 3 percent and 2.3 percent in 1900 and 1925. In 1991, Joshua A. Fishman estimated the world Yiddish-speaking population at more than three million, and the Yiddish-speaking population of the United States at a million and a quarter. See Fishman, *Reversing Language Shift: Theoretical and Empirical Foundations of Assistance to Threatened Languages,* Clevedon: Multilingual Matters, 1991, p. 194. In 1994, Harris estimated the world Ladino-speaking population at sixty thousand but did not provide an estimate for the United States. See Harris, *Death of a Language* pp. 19, 255.

19. Goren, "The Jewish Press," p.211.

20. "Tribuna Libera," *La Boz del Pueblo,* 11/26/15, p. 3. Given the flawlessness of the Ladino, this letter was probably translated from the English.

21. Jonathan D. Sarna, "The History of the Jewish Press in North America," in *The North American Jewish Press,* The 1994 Alexander Brin Forum, Waltham, Mass.: Brandeis University, 1995, pp. 2–7, at p. 5.

22. *The Jewish Communal Register of New York City, 1917–1918,* New York: Lipshitz Press, 1918, p. 619.

23. Samuel Margoshes, "The Jewish Press in New York City," in ibid., pp. 596–616, at pp. 610–611.

24. Papo, *SITCA,* pp. 68–70.

25. "La Kestión de los Dokumentos Turkos," *La Amérika,* 11/12/15, p. 2.

26. Ibid., and Papo, *SITCA,* p. 79. See also Albert J. Amateau, "The Sephardic Immigrant from Bulgaria: A Personal Profile of Moise Gadol," *American Jewish Archives* 42, 1 (1990): 57–70.

27. Letter from Maurice S. Nessim to Alice Menken. Archives of Congregation Shearith Israel's Sisterhood.

28. Papo, *SITCA,* p. 82. Interestingly, a few months after the tabloid was launched, Menken, writing on behalf of the Sisterhood, sent a letter of congratulations to *La Boz del*

Pueblo, wishing those involved success in their "admirable work." Regrettably, with the exception of "admirable work," Nessim only paraphrases the letter in the January 7, 1916, issue of his paper. See "La Sisterhood Apresia La Boz del Pueblo," p. 1. (Nessim's summary of the letter is, of course, in Ladino.)

29. "Rosh A-Shaná 5676" (no author given), *La Amérika,* 9/8/15, p. 2.

30. "Letra de Ellis Island," *La Amérika,* 6/11/15, p. 8.

31. "Itshak Azriel Delivrado de Ellis Island," *La Amérika,* 6/18/15, p. 1.

32. "Komo Fui Delivrado de Ellis Island," *La Amérika,* 6/25/15, p. 6.

33. Ham, the Ladino pronunciation of the Hebrew word "haham," or wise man, denotes "rabbi."

34. "Aktividades de la Kolonia: Enteresante Konferensia," *La Vara,* 11/21/24, p. 7.

35. See my "Ladino (Judeo-Spanish) Theater," in *Jewish Women in America: An Historical Encyclopedia,* ed. Paula Hyman and Deborah Dash Moore, N.Y.: Routledge, 1998, pp. 781–785. An account of the American Judeo-Spanish theater, parallel to the work of Elena Romero, remains a desideratum. See Elena Romero, *Repertorio de Noticias Sobre el Mundo Teatral de los Sefardíes Orientales,* Madrid: Instituto Arias Montano, 1983. For a brief overview of the Sephardic theater in Seattle, see Marc D. Angel, "The Sephardic Theater of Seattle," *American Jewish Archives* 25, 2 (November 1973): 156–161.

36. "Tribuna Libera: Lo Ke Nuestros Lektores Pensan: Porke No?" *La Boz del Pueblo,* 5/26/16, p. 6.

37. See, for example, Ben-Sion Behar, "Sefaradím, Ma No Orientales," *La Amérika,* 10/29/15, p. 2.

38. "Tribuna Libera: Lo Ke Nuestros Lektores Pensan" (letter from Meyer [Maír José] Benardete), *La Boz del Pueblo,* 4/28/16, p. 6.

39. "Por La Lingua" (no author given), *La Amérika,* 12/9/10, p. 1, and Ben-Sion Behar, "Sefardím, Ma No Orientales."

40. Goren, "The Jewish Press," p. 212. On language wars, see also David Wolf Silverman, "The Jewish Press: A Quadrilingual Phenomenon," in *The Religious Press in America,* ed. Martin E. Marty et al., New York: Holt, Rinehart, and Winston, 1963, pp. 125–172. pp. 125–126, 135–136 and 144–145.

41. Goren, "The Jewish Press," p. 214.

42. Ibid.

43. Papo, *SITCA,* pp. 89–90 and "Pasado, Prezente i Futuro de la Prensa Sefaradít en Amérika" (signed "Reporter"), *El Progreso,* 5/26/16, p. 5. See also " 'El Progreso' No Pudo Progresar" (no author given), *La Amérika,* 12/17/15, p. 3.

44. Jane Gerber, *The Jews of Spain: A History of the Sephardic Experience,* New York: Free Press, 1992, p. 270.

Part II

The Many Languages of American Literature

Spanish is America's oldest colonial language and, after English, now also the foremost postcolonial language in the United States. It is the language with the highest growth rate—having replaced German as the second most frequently spoken language (after English) in the United States.

In " 'Los Comanches' at Alcalde: Two Centuries of Tradition," Sandra Dahlberg examines the history and recorded versions of the traditional Spanish-language play "Los Comanches," a representative work based on an oral tradition about an event in the 1770s that is still being presented in New Mexico today. Dahlberg compares the version used in the performances that continue the oral tradition and the printed text (which goes back to 1907), and finds that the "errors" that the editor of the print version corrected may very well have been "deliberate constructions" employed to render nuanced dialect differences of Comanche and New Mexico Spanish. This raises the larger question of how easy it may be, especially in working with "mixed" languages, to confuse language incompetence, resulting in errors that editors have to correct, and sophistication in the conscious and nuanced employment of "impure" language elements for aesthetic or other purposes. Such aspects of the language may be an indication of a "mixed" location, which is also what characterizes whole bodies of literature. For example, Welsh-language literature, the existence of which is a well-kept secret in the United States, may have a location that permits connections both with Welsh national projects and with Anglo-American literary trends. Melinda Gray's "Language and Belonging: A Welsh Language Novel in Late Nineteenth-Century America" offers an assessment of R. R. Williams's Welsh-language American novel *Dafydd Morgan* (1897) and shows how Williams fits into the American realist moment (embodied, for example, by the English-language writer William Dean Howells, who, incidentally, was of Welsh descent) while also paying attention to the ways in which his novel was a response to calls for a Welsh national literature.

In " 'The Quintessence of the Jew': Polemics of Nationalism and Peoplehood in Turn-of-the-Century Yiddish Fiction," an essay that resonates with Øverland's findings on melting pot and pluralism in Norwegian-American writing, and with Gray's focus on William Dean Howells and Welsh-American literature, Matthew Jacobson takes selected writings by Jacob Gordin and by Abraham Cahan (whose first novel *Yekl: A Tale of the New York Ghetto* was presented in English by Howells in 1896) as an occasion to place their apparently domestic concerns with American assimilation and pluralism in the transnational contexts of nationalist and cosmopolitanist responses to "the Jewish Question." In "Redefining Chinese American Literature from a 'LOWINUS' Perspective: Two Recent Examples," Te-hsing Shan focuses on Chinese-American writings from Yan Geling to Chin Yang Lee and asks why one might stress the Chinese or the American connection (as Frank Chin did at different stages of his career). Shan proceeds to show how even the attempts at "reconstruct-ing" American literature that were undertaken by the group responsible for the *Heath Anthology* remained tied to an English-language focus, and goes on to call attention to some general problems that future investigators of multilingual America will need to heed in order to reflect the transnational and transcultural border-crossings that characterize their materials.

Gönül Pultar's "Ethnic Fatigue: Başçıllar's Poetry as a Metaphor for the Other 'Other Literature,' " offers a full reading of Turkish-language poetry in the United States and returns to the questions of ethnic identity and assimilation that concern several other contributors as well. Her close and subtle readings of the modern free verse by Seyfettin Başçıllar (who is also the chief meat inspector in New Jersey) focus on his "American" themes and on the broadly applicable issue of what she calls "ethnic fatigue." All essays in this section examine works at the transnational cross-sections of American literature in English and of such national literatures as Spanish, Welsh, Chinese, and Turkish. The varied approaches presented here do not only set out to compare English-language writings with American literature in other tongues and to complement the English-only version of American literary history, but also attempt to correct past blindness to the transnational dimensions of American ethnic literature.

Chapter Five

"Los Comanches" at Alcalde
Two Centuries of Tradition

Sandra L. Dahlberg

The folkloric traditions of New Mexico provide provocative insights into the tur-moil of early Spanish settlement and into the bicultural influences that were formed as a result of centuries of Hispano and Indian interaction. When the Spanish arrived in New Mexico with an ensemble of Franciscan friars, the Franciscans used morality plays and folk dramas to introduce Christianity to the Indians.[1] Near present-day Alcalde, New Mexico, the Oñate party celebrated its arrival in the region by staging a performance in 1596 of "Los Moros y Cristianos," a folk drama that recounted the expulsion of the Moors from Spain as a result of divine intervention. This folk drama was presented to facilitate the religious conversion of the Indian populations, as well as to portray a Spanish military "show of force" in order to secure the political compliance of the Indians.[2] As the region became predominantly Catholic and came securely under Spanish control, secular plays emerged within the oral traditions based on uniquely New Mexican historical incidents, one of the most noteworthy of which is "Los Comanches," which is based on a series of events that occurred in the 1770s.[3] Today, in the shadow of the Oñate monument, Alcalde's "Los Comanches" tradition is thriving.

"Los Comanches" represents a syncretization of the secular ritualization of mili-tary conquests and depictions of frontier settlement with the sacred traditions of Catholicism during the Christmas season. The *Nuevomexicano* Christmas season heralds a series of festivals honoring the sacred and the secular. During Advent, singing townspeople reenact the search by Mary and Joseph for shelter before the birth of Jesus. This dramatic procession is called "Las Posadas."[4] Each night, the procession knocks on a different door, moving successively closer to the church courtyard where the community nativity is located. On Christmas Eve, "Los Pas-tores," another Christmas folk drama, portrays a group of shepherds traveling toward the star of Bethlehem. Enrique Lamadrid notes that the "shepherd's play has been popular in New Mexico since colonial times when Franciscan friars dram-atized the story of Christ to convert the Indians."[5] These folk dramas provide, as they did in medieval Europe, a means by which communities can participate in the miracles of Christmas. Yet, *Nuevomexicano* traditions are also unique in their deliberate combination of the sacred and the secular dramatic productions within the Christmas season. In Alcalde, as in other communities in northern New Mexico, "Los Comanches" is presented after the religious festivals of "Los Pastores" and "Las Posadas," and in conjunction with another integral component of *Nuevomexicano* culture, "Los Matachines."[6]

"Los Matachines" and "Los Comanches" are two of the most enduring of the secular dramatic traditions in New Mexico. According to Aurora Lucero-White, "Las Matachines" has much appeal because "this drama is the only folk manifestation common to both the *Hispanos* . . . and to the Indians."[7] "Los Matachines" is a dance drama that was introduced to New Mexico by don Diego de Vargas in 1692 to commemorate the Spanish reconquest of New Mexico after the Pueblo Revolt of 1680. The essence of the drama is defined as "a struggle of good and evil, of the old and the new, of the conquerors and the conquered, a new spirit is born, a new harmony is celebrated."[8] To portray this newly born harmony, "Los Matachines" uses characters as old as the first Spanish-Indian encounters in the New World—it is the story of Malinche and Cortés.[9] In Alcalde, "Los Matachines" is performed the day after Christmas. Juxtaposing "Los Matachines" with "Los Comanches" is somewhat understandable in that both dramas depict important events in *Nuevomexicano* history and dramatize, when performed together, a progression of Spanish conquests in the New World and in the region.

Even though the "Los Comanches" tradition is thriving today in Alcalde, performers and organizers vividly recall the difficulties of the near past and voice concerns about the play's viability in the future. The World War II years, and the decade following, nearly ended the "Los Comanches" tradition at Alcalde. Not only were numbers of young men lost to the war effort, those who remained or returned from the war found no future or stability in Alcalde's post–World War II economy. As a result, whole families moved west to California in search of factory and defense industry jobs. The mass migration left few people to perpetuate the old customs. According to Alfredo Montoya, who currently organizes the "Los Comanches" performances in Alcalde, the folk drama was not performed in the community for nearly an entire generation, even though it was an integral aspect of community life. Arthur Campa, who published a study of "Los Comanches" in 1942, wrote: "This drama will continue until the camp grounds, gasoline stations, and night clubs displace it, a time when primitive America will lose all the color and genuineness that today makes it interesting and invigorating."[10] Campa published his study when oral traditions such as "Los Comanches" were most threatened, and he recognized that it would be difficult for the "color and genuineness" of these communal plays to withstand the onslaught of an automotive, individualistic, and media-centered era.

By the late 1950s, however, the young people of Alcalde began expressing interest in the folk traditions of their elders, including "Los Comanches." In response to this interest, Alcalde resident Alberto Vialpando, a professor of Spanish at the College of Santa Fé who had participated in "Los Comanches" performances before the war, led a community effort to reconstruct the text of the drama "a lo mejor de nuestra memoria" (to the best of our memory).[11] Vialpando not only determined to revive the drama, he created a written text for Alcalde's previously oral art form. Vialpando and his collaborators were able to reconstruct, or revoice, this oral literature because of their proximity to the tradition, even though a span of more than twenty years separated them from the last performance. As Eric A. Havelock noted, "[F]or an oral culture learning or knowing means achieving close, empathetic, communal identifications" with the oral literatures.[12] In this case closeness and communal identification facilitated the recovery of "Los Comanches."

Vialpando was apparently unaware of two published versions of the folk drama by Aurelio Espinosa (1907) and Arthur Campa (1942). Working entirely from memory, he offers an apology in the script's prologue for the "many errors" committed in the collaborative effort because no extant "manuscript" existed from which to work. However, it must be noted that Vialpando's reconstruction of a dormant oral tradition compares very favorably to both of the previously published scripts, with entire speeches matching verbatim.[13] Of course, there are differences between these texts as well, some of which are quite striking, including additional characters, omitted characters, and some redistribution of speeches. The Alcalde script is also much shorter than both the scripts published by Espinosa or Campa, and it varies significantly from the performance described by Lorin W. Brown in 1938.[14] The timing of Campa's (1942) and Brown's (1938) recordings of "Los Comanches" performances is incredibly fortuitous. Records of "Los Comanches" performances are rare, and the accounts that do exist are from different northern New Mexico communities (El Pino and San Ildefonso Grant).[15] Even with community variations in the presentation of "Los Comanches," as well as the gap of time between, the details given by these witnesses furnish important information regarding "Los Comanches" in general and its tradition at Alcalde in particular.

The most visible difference between Vialpando's script and those published by Espinosa and Campa is the absence of the Barriga Dulce character. Analysis of these previously published scripts and earlier eyewitness accounts of the play makes evident that Barriga Dulce was a central role in these pre-war versions of the drama, providing a mirror in which the actions and/or motivations of the other characters, and society, could be interpreted. By the 1930s, when both Campa and Brown witnessed performances of "Los Comanches," the clownish aspects of Barriga Dulce were pivotal to plot and structure. Campa described Barriga Dulce as "some sort of a tag-along intended for a clown, no doubt. He usually rides a burro and watches the battle from a safe distance shouting whatever comes into his head."[16] Brown, a writer for the Federal Writers' Project (in the Works Progress Administration) between 1938 and 1941, also recorded oral histories and traditions of New Mexicans, including "Los Comanches" and the portrayal of the Barriga Dulce character. According to Brown, after the opening challenges and boasts by Cuerno Verde and Fernández, the attention shifted to Barriga Dulce:

> Here, Barriga Dulce, the comedian of the play, a boastful character who hides under the wagon [representing the Spanish camp] when the Indians attack, comes forward and cuts a ludicrous figure, as in his oversized helmet and with his enormous horse pistol he starts out to trail the Indians. He very bravely follows the trail, shouting

threats of vengeance to the empty air, but as soon as the Indians are sighted dancing around their two captives, he turns and flees for camp, stumbling and falling in his haste and terror.[17]

In both instances, Barriga Dulce's antics created a comic tone, which provided a more complex presentation of the serious issues of war with the Comanches and the subsequent conquest of them than is presented today in Alcalde. Just as the festive traditions of "Los Pastores" and "Las Posadas" enable the Christian community to participate in sacred history, folk dramas such as "Los Comanches" allow *Nuevomexicano*s to reenact the events associated with the Spanish colonial era.

Although the character of Barriga Dulce is no longer presented in the Alcalde version of "Los Comanches," two female captives remain part of the drama. Campa recorded that the performance he saw at El Pino began with Barriga Dulce mishandling a trade with the Comanches: "The Indians have advanced before the battle and tried to trade with the clownish Barriga Dulce, taking possession of the two hostages of war referred to as 'Las Pecas.' "[18] The performance Brown witnessed at San Ildefonso had two boys taken captive after the Indians' first charge on the Spanish camp, the battle during which Barriga Dulce cowered under the wagon.[19] At Alcalde today, these captives appear only briefly at the end of the play, and they are Indian women.

The play begins in Alcalde with both parties, Spanish and Comanche, gathered to discuss the possibility of establishing a treaty. Juan Antonio Romero, an Indian ambassador, claims to have had in his possession a written order for a treaty, but on the way to the meeting he lost it. Later in the play, Tabaco recalls a treaty that he had previously established with the Spanish (at Taos) on behalf of the Comanches. Tabaco bitterly rejects peace when he suspects duplicity on the part of the Spanish captain. In this entire process, the captives are silent and inactive; they are just there. After all the speeches are given and the battle begun, Oso Pardo and Tabaco steal the two captives and ride out of the churchyard. It is the retreat of Oso Pardo and Tabaco that signals the end of the folk drama.[20]

The presence of the captives in the drama at Alcalde was, without either Barriga Dulce or the pretext of ransom, understandably puzzling to Alfredo Montoya, Alcalde's *mayordomo* currently organizing the "Los Comanches" performances.[21] Because Montoya and the other contemporary Alcaldeans were unable to contextualize the roles of the captives fully, these roles and the emphasis placed on the captivity scene has been progressively diminished. Vialpando, who is at present quite elderly and ill, was unable to provide Montoya more information about these characters. Certainly, without the character of Barriga Dulce botching a trade or cowering for cover while the Spanish camp is under attack, the captives could simply become disjointed props. In the performances recorded by Campa and Brown prior to World War II, the scene in which the captives were taken triggered anticipation of an impending retaliation by the Spanish, and the safe return of the captives after the final battle provided closure and reinforced the Spanish victory. Today, however, the captives are taken at the end of the drama, when the resolution has already been offered in the form of a Comanche defeat; therefore, the theft of the captives could be interpreted as undermining the Spanish victory. Not surprisingly, Montoya and other participants question the inclusion and placement of these characters in the current "Los Comanches" performances.

When we compare other elements of Alcalde's presentation of "Los Comanches" to the earlier accounts and scripts, the main parts, those of Cuerno Verde and Fernández, remain consistent with the earlier scripts but are significantly shortened. Of the supporting characters, the portrayal of Tabaco remains the most constant. Tabaco's speech, as first published by Espinosa in 1907, varies only slightly from Alcalde's present text despite the reduction in the length of the script as a whole. In his speech, Tabaco recounts some of the Spanish-Comanche history, particularly stressing the Taos treaty negotiations, at which he represented the Comanches. Tabaco tells Cuerno Verde that his personal sense of integrity will not allow him to participate in the upcoming battle if he believes the attack against the Spanish to be an unwarranted act of aggression on the part of the Comanches, or if the Comanches are deliberately violating the Taos treaty.

> No quiero ser enemigo
> No quiero ser mas traidor;
> Gozar quiero del empleo
> Que tengo de embajador.
>
> [I do not want to be your enemy
> I do not want to be a traitor anymore;
> I want to enjoy the role
> That I have as ambassador.][22]

When Tabaco is stating his hesitancy to attack, we are to understand that he is assessing the impetus that led to the present state of war. Tabaco is trying to decide whether Cuerno Verde is justified in his intended move to violence. At Alcalde today, with Barriga Dulce absent, the complexity of the historical issues at stake are voiced through Tabaco, the former ambassador; Tabaco's assessment is somber without the antics of Barriga Dulce.

It is not known why the character of Barriga Dulce is no longer represented in the Alcalde play. Perhaps Barriga Dulce's liveliness, along with his self-deprecating clowning, contradicted the sobriety with which Alcalde celebrates its heritage. Today, in keeping with Vialpando's introductory remarks, the play solemnly commemorates the Spaniards' actions and celebrates Spanish heritage. It may be that in the diasporic aftermath of the 1960s when Alcalde was recovering this "lost" tradition, buffoonery may not have seemed appropriate. And, it is not known exactly when Barriga Dulce was removed from Alcalde's performances. It is entirely possible that Alcalde had crafted a more somber play even before the war. One thing is certain, it is by design that "Los Comanches" is a serious production in Alcalde, one in which clear distinctions are made between the Spanish and the Comanche characters. In Vialpando's "Los Comanches" script, a stage direction states that Romero's speech should be given "en un lenguaje español muy cortado" (in very broken Spanish).[23] Actually, most of the Indian characters at Alcalde speak in fairly broken and heavily accented Spanish. Other speech irregularities, some very subtle, are provided for Spanish characters as well, and there are indications that this irregular speech is not unique to Alcalde.

Espinosa's 1907 text is the first published version of "Los Comanches," and in preparing his manuscript for publication, Espinosa readily admitted to minor syntactical rearrangement to ensure clarity of thought and to ease the poetic meter. Espinosa indicated that his editing work was necessary to "correct" some language errors as well. In analyzing the language issues Espinosa concluded:

> The author of Los Comanches was not . . . a learned man, as can be judged from his work. While the language is in good Spanish, it is very simple, almost the language of the uneducated. At the same time, there are passages, which compare favorably with the verses of the Araucana and the language of the Golden Age.[24]

Espinosa seemed intrigued by this incongruous contradiction in usage and skill, uneducated simplicity and poetic quality. He imputed to the copyists these "dialectic peculiarities":

> The fact that the original ms. was not printed, however, may account for many poor passages in our play as we now have it. I do not believe, for instance, that the author of Los Comanches would confuse the pronouns vosotros and ustedes in the same sentence, as we find repeatedly in our ms. These are undoubtedly the copyists' errors, if not our copyist the one before him or others for in New Mexican Spanish vosotros is not used, hence ustedes crept in here and there until the ms. came to be in the present state of confusion in this respect.[25]

Certainly, errors did occur in the copying process, especially if we consider the variable quality and clarity of hand-produced "originals." But the extant published texts, including Espinosa's, also provide evidence that many of the discrepancies in both diction and usage may be deliberate constructions to capture dialectical nuances that defined both the Comanche and New Mexican Spanish.

Most of the "dialectical peculiarities" follow consistent patterns in language misuse and are concentrated in specific characters. For instance, these substandard usage errors are most heavily concentrated in the Comanche parts. Espinosa, whose expertise was in diachronic linguistics, was expert in recognizing the minute distinctions between eighteenth-century New Mexican dialects and those of Peninsular or Mexican Spanish of the same era, as well as the adaptations in the language up to the first decades of this century. Based on his expertise, Espinosa assigned many of these errors to "obviously New Mexican" origins. In other words, Espinosa recognized the vernacular nature of particular language constructions and concluded that an inattentive copyist slipped into his own language patterns while copying the text, which resulted in a confusion between standard Spanish and regional usage. Yet, what if the author of "Los Comanches" used these "errors" to capture and portray the flavor of a variety of New Mexican dialects, perhaps even idiolects based on local speech patterns? In an art form so thoroughly grounded in the oral tradition, in which pronunciation itself provides meaning, as shown in Vialpando's stage direction to use broken Spanish, then perhaps Alcalde's preservation of the "dialectical peculiarities," reinforces the possibility that they were not entirely erroneous.

First and foremost in this determination is the centrality of "Los Comanches" to New Mexican oral traditions. These "Los Comanches" oral traditions, not any of the published versions, are the actual basis of Alcalde's present text. According to Montoya, neither he, Vialpando, nor any of the other people involved in the script's reconstruction were aware of published texts of the play. Alcalde's current format evolved entirely from the oral traditions, passed on from player to player, from generation to generation. As is to be expected, the "Los Comanches" of Alcalde today differs from earlier productions and the presentations of the drama in other communities. Yet, the similarities that exist between these various portrayals indicate the parts of the drama that have the most cultural value. In oral traditions, details endure when they retain value for the storyteller and the listener, or the player and the audience in the case of "Los Comanches." When long segments of speeches match exactly those that were previously performed (and published), even when riddled with syntactical errors, we have to assume that value exists, at least in part, because of the incorrect pronunciation or usage.

Espinosa stated in his introduction to "Los Comanches" that his edition "is practically an exact reproduction" of the Chaves manuscript, although "in a few instances slight changes were made, all of which are mentioned in the notes."[26] While the following comparisons may seem meticulous, especially in light of Alcalde's much shortened script, the consistency of the remaining script with the Chaves manuscript (before Espinosa's changes) are remarkable and speak to the consistency of the traditions. In Tabaco's speech, for instance, Espinosa showed the character saying, "*Y así, vete á preparar*" (And so, go prepare yourself). Espinosa states simply that "the ms. reads componer" (to compose) for which he made the change to the standard use of *preparar*.[27] In the Alcalde performance nearly ninety years later, Tabaco says, "*Y así vete á componer*."[28] The "misuse" of the language, according to Montoya, is done deliberately to accentuate the language barriers between Comanche and Spanish. The misspoken words, he explained, were necessary to reinforce the fact that the Comanches were speaking Spanish as a second language.[29] In comparing Vialpando's text with the Espinosa text, it is important to keep in mind that Vialpando was a professor of Spanish and also expert in the Spanish language. Yet, his text makes the same "errors" that Espinosa attributed to "poor copyists." Therefore, Vialpando's use of *componer* was deliberate and certainly not a result of ignorance or sloppiness.

Vialpando still attends the "Los Comanches" celebrations in Alcalde, but his protégé, Montoya, now organizes the annual production. Montoya has been actively involved in Alcalde's "Los Comanches" performances for more than twenty years and is working to ensure the future of "Los Comanches" at Alcalde. One critical factor that Montoya encounters when organizing the folk drama and selecting a cast is finding competent horsemen. The entire performance of "Los Comanches" is conducted on horseback and the riders must be skilled enough to make intricate moves within a fairly restricted space, at the edge of which are rows of unprotected onlookers, many of whom are small children. The players must be able to conduct their horses through the mock battles, complete with pistol shots and lance thrusts that occasionally make contact with the animals. Although this is not injurious to the horses, an unsure rider and/or a nervous horse could have danger-ous results for the rider and for the audience. Montoya stresses that it takes a great deal of expertise to control horses under these chaotic circumstances. During the final battle scene, for example, twelve or more horses may be engaged in jostling, charging, pressing, or rearing up to simulate warfare. Montoya laments the fact that most of Alcalde's younger generation cannot ride well enough to participate in the drama. On the other hand, of those community members now participating in the drama, Montoya reports renewed interest in horsemanship and increased vigor for the presentation and choreography of the horses, elements he feels are vital to the survival of the drama at Alcalde.

The battle depicted in "Los Comanches" occurred in 1779. The century and a half following was turbulent for all of New Mexico: Mexico gained its independ-ence from Spain only to lose New Mexico and the rest of the Southwest region to the Americans after the Mexican-American war in 1849. Statehood was not conferred upon New Mexico for another seventy-two years, but the English lan-guage and the Anglo-American culture imposed upon the people of New Mexico were meant to diminish the use of Spanish, a move that would necessarily impede the folk traditions that the language supported. Then, World War II and its economically inspired diaspora almost ended centuries of Hispano traditions. In spite of these vast changes, "Los Comanches" survived. Its current version may incorporate some new names, but the essence of the drama and the actual speeches are consistent with the earlier renditions. These variations in Alcalde are understandable, given the circumstances under which Alcalde's script was recon-structed. According to Walter J. Ong:

> The way verbal memory works in oral art forms is quite different from what literates in the past commonly imagined. In a literate culture verbatim memorization is com-monly done from a text, to which the memorizer returns as often as necessary to perfect and test verbatim mastery. In the past, literates have commonly assumed that oral memorization in an oral culture achieved the same goal of absolutely verbatim repetition . . . [not recognizing that] instances of simultaneous recitation in oral cul-tures were hardly sought for.[30]

Vialpando and the other Alcaldeans who rerecorded "Los Comanches" did not intend to perpetuate a written text but to vocalize the speeches according to their understood essence. What is amazing is the level of consistency between the contem-porary oral tradition, which is not based on a verbatim rendition, and a textual copy of earlier versions of the play. Some redistribution of speeches is to be expected in the re-memory process and the subsequent translation to textual form.

When Alberto Vialpando resurrected "Los Comanches" for Alcalde, he may not have realized that he was also testifying to the vitality of an oral tradition and to the integrity of an oral memory spanning two centuries. As a result of his desire to recapture a tradition that he found valuable to his community and to his sense of identity, and as a result of Montoya's careful guidance of "Los Co-manches" these past decades, Alcalde is looking forward to a third century of "Los Comanches."

NOTES

1. Arthur L. Campa, "Spanish Religious Folktheatre in the Spanish Southwest (First Cycle)," *University of New Mexico Bulletin, Language Series* 5.1(1934): 5–43.

2. Gaspar Pérez de Villagrá, Juan de Oñate's chronicler, described the first enactment of the play "Los Moros y Cristianos" near present-day Alcalde in his epic poem. See Gaspar Pérez de Villagrá, *Historia de la Nueva Mexico*, eds. Michael Encinias et al. (Albuquerque: University of New Mexico Press, 1992), xxxi, and XVI, lines 102–116. Villagrá said that the Spanish used the drama as a militaristic show of force presented to the Acoma Indians.

3. The folk drama "Los Comanches" depicts a series of historical battles that occurred in northern New Mexico in the 1770s. Sandra Dahlberg, "Having the Last Word: Recording the Cost of Conquest in 'Los Comanches,' " in *Recovering the U.S. Hispanic Literary Heritage*, vol. 2, ed. Erlinda Gonzales-Berry and Chuck Tatum (Houston: Arte Público Press, 1996), 133–147.

4. Enrique R. Lamadrid, *Tesoros del Espíritu: A Portrait in Sound of Hispanic New Mexico* (Embudo: El Norte/Academia, 1994), 98.

5. Ibid., 93.

6. Performances of "Los Comanches" have, in the past, been attributed to a number of communities in northern New Mexico. However, as far as I can determine, Alcalde is the only community in which "Los Comanches" has consistently been performed since its reintroduction in 1960. The elders of Alcalde contend, however, that before World War II, Alcalde hosted performances every December 27 as well. The people of Alcalde also assert that although other communities perform "Los Comanches," Alcalde has the oldest performance history with a consistent yearly production. No physical records exist to substantiate or dismiss Alcalde's claim.

7. Aurora Lucero-White, "*Los Hispanos*: Five Essays on the Folkways of the *Hispanos* as Seen Through the Eyes of One of Them," in *Hispano Culture of New Mexico*, ed. Carlos E. Cortés (New York: Arno, 1976), 32.

8. Lamadrid, *Tesoros,* 17.

9. Sylvia Rodríguez, "Defended Boundaries, Precarious Elites: The Arroyo Seco Matachines Dance," *Journal of American Folklore* 107 (1994): 248–267.

10. Arthur L. Campa, "Los Comanches: A New Mexican Folk Drama," *University of New Mexico Bulletin, Language Series* 7.1 (1942): 22.

11. Alberto Vialpando, "Los Comanches" (manuscript), Alcalde, New Mexico.

12. Walter J. Ong, *Orality and Literacy: The Technologizing of the Word* (New York: Routledge, 1990), 45–46.

13. The use of the term "manuscript" in conjunction with the play "Los Comanches" is problematic because it is unknown whether the play was first a literary text that was absorbed into the oral traditions of New Mexico and evolved differently from community to community. On the other hand, copies of scripts, or at least one—the Chaves manuscript—did exist and prompted the publications of both Espinosa and Campa. Yet, it is not known whether the Chaves manuscript was constructed similarly to Vialpando's Alcalde script, that is, transcribed into a literary format from the oral tradition.

14. The Alcalde text is, in essence, the same text as was published by Espinosa and Campa. However, those plays numbered 515 and 715 lines, respectively. The Vialpando script has 273 lines.

15. San Ildefonso is only about seven miles south of Alcalde and is a Pueblo community. I was unable to locate El Pino.

16. Campa, "Los Comanches," 16.

17. Lorin W. Brown, *Hispano Folklife of New Mexico: The Lorin W. Brown Federal Writers' Project Manuscripts* (Albuquerque: University of New Mexico Press, 1978), 42.

18. Campa, "Los Comanches," 18.

19. Brown, *Hispano Folklife,* 42.

20. Vialpando, "Los Comanches."

21. Alfredo Montoya, personal interview, 23 January 1996, Española, New Mexico. Lucero-White, "Los Hispanos," 25: "Each year the parish or visiting priest appoints *mayordomos* (a fiesta council) to take charge of the preparations for the year's fiesta. The council appoints collectors and these go from house to house soliciting contributions to defray the necessary expenses of the fiesta. If the amount does not come up to the expectations of the *mayordomos,* they have to make up the deficit from their own pockets. This insures the success and continuance of the fiesta." At Alcalde, Alfredo Montoya is the *mayordomo* who oversees the presentation of "Los Comanches."

22. Vialpando, "Los Comanches."

23. Ibid.

24. Aurelio M. Espinosa, "Los Comanches: A Spanish Heroic Play of the Year Seventeen Hundred and Eighty," *University of New Mexico Bulletin, Language Series* 1.1 (1907): 19.

25. Ibid.

26. Ibid., 18.

27. Ibid., 45, fn 87.

28. Vialpando, "Los Comanches."

29. Montoya, personal interview, 23 January 1996.

30. Ong, *Orality,* 57–58.

Chapter Six

Language and Belonging

A Welsh Language Novel in Late-Nineteenth-Century America

Melinda G. Gray

Through the 1980s and 1990s, as the multiculturalism debates have played out, there has been persistent scrutiny of the American literary canon and the notion of canonicity itself. This attention has provided a range of challenges to an official literary canon, and in part because each challenge struggles against its own version of the official canon, there have also been descriptions of the ways in which literary canons evolve and function and the purposes they have served.[1] Current scholarship has been particularly interested in investigating the interplay of the processes through which national or cultural identities and literary canons are formulated. Studies of ethnicity and literature, for example, have afforded points of entry for discussion of the constructedness of notions of national identity and canonicity.[2] Such projects aim for revision of the "long established practice of compartmentalizing American literature into mainstream and ethnic" canons that William Boelhower described in 1984. They also encourage experimentation with more dialogical paradigms for the study of literature of the United States, and foster inquiry into the processes by which such categories are set up and the functions that they serve (or that they have served in the past).[3]

The nineteenth-century literature of the United States has proven fertile ground for such projects. In the late nineteenth century, immigration into the United States and the rapid diversification of the population have been tied by Eric Hobsbawm to the rise of American nationalism: "The basic political problem of the U.S.A., once secession had been eliminated, was how to assimilate a heterogeneous mass—towards the end of our period, an almost unmanageable influx—of people who were Americans not by birth but by immigration. Americans had to be made."[4] A substantial body of writing grew from the immigration experience, and it was partly in this writing and in response to it that a national identity was fashioned. The editors of one recent volume of revisionist essays, *American Realism and the Canon* (1994), write that this period, in which realism was a dominant literary mode, was "one of unprecedented literary diversity. The realist mode was flexible enough and of sufficient range, the realist era itself hospitable enough, that a multitude of women writers and minority writers produced and published texts that, albeit at times covertly, gave voice to the most urgent concerns of race and ethnicity, gender, class, section, and region."[5] As Wendell V. Harris and others have pointed out, the anthologies and reviews published in this period testify that the critical establishment was aware of and relatively open to this diversity.[6]

The urgency with which the call for a national literature was heard in this period of increasing literary production is another reason attention to late-nineteenth-century American literature offers particular promise for such projects. The writings of William Dean Howells, whose *Criticism and Fiction* (1891) was the foundational text of American realism, closely examined the question of a national literature. In the editorials that he published from "The Editor's Study" in *Harper's Monthly Magazine* between 1886 and 1892, Howells described "fidelity to experience and probability of motive" as the "essential conditions of a great imaginative literature"; his own work aimed to cultivate these conditions in the United States.[7] In his day, Howells's publications in widely read journals and his prominence in literary circles (the Cambridge group) gave his ideas far-reaching currency. His book reviews and his friendships with younger writers helped to establish the idea of a national literature and to give it shape.[8]

What Howells takes for granted in his formulation of a national literature is the correspondence between language and nation: the idea that American identity could be represented through the medium of only one national language. Although Howells does not directly address the connection between national language and national identity, this connection strongly informs his criteria for an author's credence and tenure. An author gains authority, Howells insists, through writing that aims for "true" or realistic representation. He supports his realist aesthetic, itself heavily invested in the idea of progress (toward truth), with a critical rereading of the Russian and European "classics," such as Balzac, Zola, and Tolstoy. Thus he makes reference to "a time, just passing away, when certain authors were considered authorities in certain kinds, when they must be accepted entire and not questioned in any particular. Now we are beginning to see and to say that no author is an authority except in those moments when he held his ear close to Nature's lips and caught her very accent" (*CF*, 14). In the United States, then, "Nature's very accent" necessarily varied according to the region or the state in which a writer lived in order to mark the particularity of that writer's experience. The author gained his authority when he convinced his audience that he was able to communicate with nature, that his relationship with the natural world (and with the truth borne there) was an intimate one, that they spoke the same language. It was the translative or interpretive function that gave Howells's writer authority and allowed his writing a belonging to American literature.

The apparent paradox inherent in Howells's notion of a national literature stands out even more clearly in a later essay, "The Great American Novel" (1912). Here he argued that "our novelists are each bound by the accident of his birth to this locality or that; and we do not believe we shall ever have a truly United States novel till some genius is born all over the Union" (*CF*, 349). For Howells, American literature was wholly bound up with the regional, with local experience shared and made intelligible to audiences located outside a writer's region and beyond a writer's particular experience.

The accessibility of the local and the particular is also an essential ingredient in Howells's understanding of a national language. When he praises the use of "local parlances" in regional fiction, Howells explains that he means "dialects" of English. For Howells, dialect writing performed the crucial function of nativizing and authenticating the English language as American. It did so by demonstrating the potential for a single language to contain the diverse speech of "the common people." "For our novelists to try to write Americanly, from any motive," Howells writes, "would be a dismal error, but being born Americans, I would have them use 'Americanisms' whenever these serve their turn; and when their characters speak, I should like to hear them speak true American, with all the varying Tennesseean, Philadelphian, Bostonian, and New York accents" (*CF*, 65–66). The accent represents difference in a way that leaves it intelligible and accessible. The idea is that language itself has a nationalizing function, that it creates a "common people," a people who have their language in common. In Howells's work, the language of the United States is the seat of a compelling tension between the drive to depict the truth as it might be heard, in all its particularity, and the desire to create a utopian universalizing language that he calls "American."

Howells's work clearly supports the traditional link between linguistic and national unities that Benedict Anderson has more recently identified: "[F]rom the start, the nation was conceived in language, not in blood, and . . . one could be 'invited into' the imagined community."[9] That which holds Howells's Americans apart from one another (regional differences) can be overcome through dialect writing, which communicates difference without sacrificing accessibility. That which binds them is inheritance, but an inheritance that must also be constructed through language. Thus Howells's Americans, "being born in America," speak an "inherited English," and Howells writes "in the hope that our inherited English may be constantly freshened and revived from the native sources which our literary decentralization will help to keep open" (*CF*, 64). In the same passage, Howells urges linguistic modification, in order for the English language used in America to become "American." Like literary tradition, the English language must evolve and progress so as to differentiate itself from British English and to help naturalize the idea of America. Matthew Frye Jacobson has also described the relationship between linguistic and national unities: "Literary figures become the guardians of the language itself (often considered the most important basis of national unity); their artistic merit reflects no less than the 'national genius'; and their creations tap and represent the 'national memory.' "[10] The role of national language in Howells's work on American literature invites us to turn Jacobson's statement on its head and to ask how much language (and specifically that need for accessibility that Howells's own comments on language communicate) has determined—and guarded—our collection of national literary figures.

In spite of his willingness to review and to promote the works of lesser-known American writers, his interest in languages (he learned French, German, Italian, and

Spanish), and his belief that American writers could learn from European and Russian masters, Howells showed little interest in the work of those who were writing in the United States in languages other than English. That Howells had some awareness of this body of writing is apparent from his memoir *Years of My Youth* (1916), where he writes that in 1857, while living in Columbus, Ohio, "there were so many Germans in Ohio that an edition of the laws had to be printed in their language, and there was a common feeling that we ought to know their language, if not their literature." Howells is clear that the Germans he knew in Columbus were not American: "I never afterward met them at American houses; the cleavage between the two races in everything but politics was absolute" (118). The German language, like the German "race," is an "alien" tongue, not at home in America, and the German poetry Howells learns to read is Schiller, Germany's national poet. However, when later he became news editor at the *Ohio State Journal*, part of his work entailed "[looking] through the exchange newspapers which flocked to us in every mail" and selecting and translating useful passages for publication in the *Journal*: "We had French and Spanish and German exchanges, and I sometimes indulged in a boyish vanity by prefacing a paragraph from these with such a sentence as, 'We translate from the *Courrier des Etats Unis*,' or 'We find in *La Cronaca* of New York,' or 'We learn from the *Wachter am Erie*,' as the case might be."[11] These writings appealed to him as a source of information and as a way to heighten his own editorial authority (i.e., by displaying his own linguistic dexterity, by allowing him publicly to catch and to interpret "nature's very accent").

Recent scholarship has begun to consider a body of writing (newspapers, novels, poetry, and essays) from nineteenth-century America in languages other than Howells's American English.[12] This literature has been generally overlooked (as in *American Realism and the Canon*, which does include work on immigrant writers), or it has been read as ethnic literature.[13] Insistence that the topography of the English language describes the boundaries of American literature is symptomatic of continued investment in a paradigm that holds "ethnic" and "mainstream" literatures separate from each other and is continuous with that nineteenth-century nativist perception of immigrant cultures as "alien." To describe this literature as ethnic, however, or otherwise to contain it as a body of literature separable from mainstream American literature and peripheral to American literary history, threatens its perception as "minor, ephemeral, local, aesthetically inferior, and thus easily dismissable" and buries the traces of its contributions to and dialogue with other literature published at the same time.[14]

That such writings have yet to be widely considered in scholarship on American literature suggests two related sets of questions. First, there seems to be some confusion about how to read these works: Can we call them "American" (though for Howells they were something other than American)? Do they make sense—is it meaningful to read them now—in the context of that always shifting and possibly expanding group of texts that constitutes a canon of American literature? What do they have to tell us in the context of those schools of thought and literary practice that have identified themselves as American? To what extent have these writings been shaped and influenced by, or in dialogue with, the ideas (and ideals) of Howells and his contemporaries?

This first inquiry generates a second, broader set of questions about the way American literature and literary scholarship has conceived of language. To what extent have we expected language, and all the cultural baggage that attaches itself to language, to create naturalized barriers comparable to those described by "nation"? Is it possible for a language to assume a nationalizing function even when it is not the official language of a particular nation or community?

Insofar as it has been asked, the question of whether we can call these works "American" has most often been answered by the preemptive assumption that they are meaningful only for a readership that isn't generally described as American and therefore that they have no national significance. Howells's American writers are "born Americans" and presumably writing for an American audience. Despite the American writer's interpretive function, he shows little ambivalence in his identification (no signs, for instance, of bilingualism). The reluctance to consider these works in relation to literature in English echoes Portes and Schauffler's recent assertion that at the turn of the century "bilingualism on the part of immigrants was frowned upon . . . due to the association of non-English languages with the existence of large ethnic communities which lay beyond the pale of the English-speaking population, out of sight but never out of mind."[15]

Current descriptions of canonicity return to questions of audience and readership. For example, Matthew Jacobson's recent work on immigrant nationalisms in the United States at the turn of the century suggests one possibility for why these works might have appeared unavailable to scholars of American literature. His study of Irish, Polish, and Jewish literatures of the United States reveals the strength of many immigrant communities' attachments to their native lands. Immigrants often thought of themselves as exiles and emigrants: "the beleaguered peoples left behind—imagined as nations—retained a central position in the migrants' ideological geographies."[16] Perhaps it is a tacit recognition of these immigrant nationalisms, in conjunction with an idea of language as an intrinsically nationalizing force, that has kept literary critics from considering so-called foreign-language literatures in the United States at the turn of the century. The assumptions are that the languages in which these writings were composed tie them more closely to the cultural traditions of their homelands than to Howells's America, that representational writings in other languages than English were not composed for, and not trying to be intelligible to, American audiences, and consequently, that these works have more to teach in the context of other national literatures.

The critics' hesitation to read this writing as American is often mirrored in the individual works themselves, where questions of national allegiance and belonging are of central concern. In an essay on representation in immigrant fiction, Susan Harris declares that "in writing about immigrants within an American context, [writers newly arrived] had at first only available to them the forms already developed in that culture, and these were inherently biased against sympathetic representations of the Other."[17] As Jacobson has shown, however, many of the "newly arrived" had available to them both the literary forms and preoccupations developing in the United States and those developed in the literatures of their native countries. The incorporation of both Old and New World themes and concerns in much of this writing produced an intricate play of identification.

Writing in native tongues other than English in the United States also meant writing to audiences for whom the representation of self and other was not tightly formulated. Some writers, like R. R. Williams of L'Anse, Michigan, who wrote in the Welsh language, experimented with the literary forms and concerns developing in the United States in order to articulate the process of identifying as American. Williams, a frequent contributor to the Welsh journals in the United States, reflected in 1896 on his own career and "the changes forty years have accomplished: an old man with a white head now; another language and an audience of Americans to address!"[18] Williams wrote in a moment of uncertainty, when the audience for the Welsh-language journals in which he published was dwindling. As he wrote, the journals' audience was shifting from *Cymry*, Welsh, to *Americiaid*, Americans. Williams was in fact writing that shift; his essays and his single novel imagined American identity (the nature of *Americiaid*) through the medium of the Welsh language.

To read R. R. Williams's novel now is to recognize that spirit of experimentation described by the editors of *American Realism and the Canon*. *Dafydd Morgan* (1897) is preoccupied with questions about its own readership and belonging, with its own literary allegiances: the patchwork of its form, thematics, and cultural referents asks that it be read as both Welsh and American. Roughly the first half of the novel describes Dafydd Morgan's childhood in North Wales, the debate and discussion surrounding the decision of a neighboring farmer to move his family to the United States, and Dafydd's own decision to make the journey. The novel takes its structure in part from the letters that cross back and forth between Wales and America. There, in the territory of Wisconsin, Dafydd buys land, marries his childhood sweetheart, and builds a home for his new family. Unlike the novel's author, Dafydd is bilingual when he arrives in the States.[19] He is a model citizen, first in North Wales and then in the community of Welsh and German immigrants with whom he settles. He easily negotiates the transition between his country of origin and the country in which he settles without seeming to break with his native community or betray its traditions and values. The novel worries about the consequences of moving to America, about the survival of family ties. Crossing to America is imagined as oedipal conflict; by making this journey, the novel asks, will a son betray his father and his fatherland and break up the home? Despite the novel's concern with the possible trauma of crossing, however, every equilibrium is maintained: fiction disseminates virtue, loyalties and tradition remain unbroken, and paternal authorities remain intact and powerful. One can be American, the novel insists, without having to stop being Welsh.

This essay will conclude with a discussion of some of the ways in which *Dafydd Morgan* wants to situate itself in relation to Welsh literature and culture and how, too, the novel lays claim to an American belonging; these two gestures (toward "being American" and "being Welsh") are interwoven in the novel, often inextricable from each other. Williams's novel came into being in the context of at least two important cultural institutions imported from Wales to the United States: the eisteddfod, a festival of literary and musical competition, and the Welsh-language press, which allowed for wide geographical participation in the competitions by giving them publicity and by printing winning poems and essays along with the adjudicators' commentaries. Together, the eisteddfod and the press helped to create a larger sense of Welsh community in the United States, where immigrant settlements tended to be scattered and small. Thus, *Dafydd Morgan* was awarded the prize of $20 for best entry on the theme "*Dylanwad Addysg yr Aelwyd*" (The importance of learning at the hearth) at the 1896 Eisteddfod of Middle Granville, New York.[20] In 1897, the novel was published by the proprietor of *Y Drych* (The mirror), an internationally circulated Welsh-language newspaper whose offices were in Utica, New York.[21]

Dafydd Morgan can be read as a response to a call for an invigorated Welsh national literature at the end of a century in which Welsh language and culture had come under attack in Britain. In the late nineteenth century, Wales produced its first widely acclaimed "Welsh novelist," Daniel Owen of Mold. Following Daniel Owen's death in 1895, the American journals published articles calling for additional Welsh novels and novelists. At least one other nineteenth-century American eisteddfod sponsored a competition for novels, although *Dafydd Morgan* may well be the only novel written in Welsh in the United States that was published as a book.[22] In a brief prefatory notice to *Dafydd Morgan*, the adjudicator of the Granville competition makes a bid for readership on the grounds of national solidarity: "I applaud the venture of publishing R. R. Williams's winning story. . . . I hope the author will receive the support he deserves from his compatriots."[23]

The fact that the novel was neither reissued nor translated speaks to the risk involved in publishing a Welsh novel in the United States; the journals would have had to market a novel to a relatively small and geographically dispersed population of Welsh readers, who, in spite of their desire to support a national Welsh literature, might also have been concerned about the morality of reading fiction. Hywel Teifi Edwards writes that many nineteenth-century Welsh readers had been educated in Methodist Sunday schools to believe that novels made inappropriate reading material: "As late as 1900 . . . the Reverend Evan Rees, a highly successful *awdlwr* [poet], saw fit to explain the dearth of Welsh novels as proof of the nation's pursuit of higher things. With hand on heart he declared that 'The religion of Wales cannot abide any kind of pretence. That is why it frowns on even the best of novels.' "[24] In the preface to *Dafydd Morgan*, Williams confesses some of his own anxiety over writing a novel: "That the competition called for 'fiction' was a bit of a stumbling block to my mind. . . . I feared that by undertaking to write, I would be dishonoring the memories of my mother and father, as well as my old teachers in the Sunday schools of Capel Coch"(*DM*, 3). However, Williams is not always looking back over his shoulder. *Dafydd Morgan* makes explicit reference to both Welsh and American literary influences: not only to Daniel Owen but also to Washington

Irving, Lew Wallace, and Stephen Crane. These references suggest that the novel's ideal readers would have shared with other American readers an exposure to and interest in those novels popular in the United States at the time.

Williams defends his literary endeavor by arguing for the "new" genre's potential usefulness, by calling on the American tradition into which he enters, and by invoking in the story a spirit of progress and innovation. However, the novel shows repeated signs of that struggle, which haunts the preface, to come to terms with its own medium: "These things are facts," Williams's narrator insists in a passage on the best way to raise a child, "without a ghost of fiction in them, having been discerned through the experience of centuries"(*DM*, 31). To contend with this "ghost of fiction," the novel incorporates a historical voice (the voice of truth). By the time he decided to enter the eisteddfod, Williams wrote, novels had "changed for the better" and could be used to teach the disciplines of progress: science and history. The connection Williams makes between writing novels and writing history also shows him at work to establish the set of conventions within which his novel could be read. The novel associates progress with the United States by making a contrast between a concrete "historical" present (the United States) and a hazy, romantic past (Wales). The first part of the story, set in Wales, takes its cue from the historical romance. The opening passage situates Dafydd's childhood home in a fairy-tale past, vague and arbitrary:

> At the bottom of one of the most beautiful valleys in Caernarvonshire, North Wales, one hundred years ago, was one of the loveliest and best farms of the shire. It encompassed only eighty acres of ground; thus, not for its expanse did it exceed the farms adjacent to it, but in its pleasing design and in its highly cultured and honest inhabitants. The farm was called Trefnusfaes (Tidy Field); truly the name was suited to this farm, every foot of it. (*DM*, 17)

America, on the other hand, gets specific dates and historical facts. Williams uses an abundance of detail in chronicling the history of the United States and particularly the history of the state of Wisconsin, in which Dafydd finally buys land. By anchoring the story in fact, Williams literally makes a place for the Welsh novel in the United States.

Williams's concern with the moral usefulness of fiction and with the novel as an instrument of instruction recalls Howells's similar investment in realistic writing. It is interesting, then, to ask why the realist aesthetic doesn't enter more strongly into Williams's novel. The story of immigration might be full of conflicts and travail, and the novel does suggest that conflict, particularly in early conversations between Dafydd and his father. By the end of the story, however, Dafydd's parents genuinely support their son's move, and the distance between Wales and Wisconsin, which, at the outset, had seemed vast, is made to seem almost inconsequential by a series of visits between the two families. There are moments in the story when the narrator specifically turns away from a painful reality, as when Dafydd takes leave of his family to go to America:

> And as all the ruptured love beginning and ending with the meanest word of the language, "farewell," bruises human sentiment, I will draw the curtain across the

scene, and I will leave it to the reader to gaze on it and to expound on it through his imagination, if he so wishes. I find it better to turn from the scene, and so that's what I will do, by calling the reader's attention to something more comforting. Let us look instead at the father and mother of the handsome lad; these comfort themselves with the heartfelt knowledge that they have fulfilled their duty on the hearth as parents to their firstborn, who now turns away to make his own home. Through their bank in Bangor, he and his father arrange for him to receive for his use a thousand pounds in a New York bank. (*DM*, 131–132)

By writing the history of Welsh family in such a way, the novel expresses the necessity of bridging this immense distance, of negotiating that which might be felt as an overwhelming loss or betrayal. The novel creates continuities between the past and all that is left behind, and that which is new in the present because it wants to construct a place for the novel in Welsh literature.

By trying to make a place for the Welsh novel in the United States, *Dafydd Morgan* recalls the idea frequently expressed in the nineteenth century, that America might be a better home than Wales for the Welsh language. In the second half of the nineteenth century, social and educational policies initiated a decline in the number of Welsh speakers in Wales. The Anglican Church sponsored one study in 1847 that described what it saw in Wales as moral degeneration and cultural backwardness, which it ascribed mainly to the influences of Welsh women and the Welsh language.[25] Hywel Teifi Edwards has shown that poets and writers used America to represent the possibility of a better place for the Welsh language. They imagined that if the language were to fail in Wales, a renaissance was awaiting it in America. Sensitive to the irony, Edwards notes the imperial impulse in some of the writings: "Perhaps the Welsh language was destined to lose a country and to win a continent."[26] Yet the romanticism of one passage he includes is also charged with the hope that by crossing the Atlantic, the Welsh language might attain some force of presence and shake off the shame that it had accrued for its speakers in Wales:

> The nations flow westward. And perhaps our own nation will bloom again there, strong and successful; and perhaps the sweet sounds of the Welsh language will be heard on the shores of the great Ohio, or mingling with Niagara's thunder, when there are only the occasional poet and sad antiquarian wandering at the base of Snowdon, and on the banks of the Dee, whispering longingly, "Wales that Was!"[27]

Williams's novel participates in the generalized worry over the fate of the language by wanting to reassociate Welsh with truth and morality. By moving its hero from Wales to the United States and by including didactic passages on good mothering and wifely virtue, the novel writes the Welsh family into a history of community, morality, and material success. At the end of the story, Dafydd has bought land and built a new home with the same name as his parents' home in Wales: Trefnusfaes. Apparently, then, nothing has changed between the beginning and end of the story, which has traveled from one clean hearth to the next; yet Williams's readers would have understood that Dafydd's American hearth, removed as it was from condemnation of the Welsh home, was more authentically "tidy" than his parents'.

By setting "The Importance of Learning at the Hearth" as the topic for competition, the Granville eisteddfod provides Williams's novel with the means of responding to a set of concerns proper to nineteenth-century Welsh literature. The thematics and rhetoric of the hearth were very popular in nineteenth-century American poetry and so offer the best example of a cultural code that functions in the novel for both Welsh and American readerships. James H. Justus writes of the reverence inspired by the so-called Fireside Poets (Longfellow, Lowell, Bryant, Holmes, and Whittier), which by the end of the nineteenth century had garnered for them the status of "national poets" in the United States. In the work of the Fireside Poets, as in Williams's novel,

> the fireside . . . is both symbolic and generative. It represents the centrality of the domestic affections in the general ethical idealism of the day, an impulse that historically incorporated the home, the church, and the school so effectively that the civic and religious virtues absorbed from the pew and the schoolboy's bench were merely extensions of the homely virtues taught and learned beside the hearth, the mother's knee and the father's chair.[28]

Justus also argues that attention to the hearth in this poetry balances a "rhetoric of care" and that the lessons of the hearth were designed to compensate for the poet's awareness of hardship in the world around him. Insofar as it incorporates a struggle to maintain the integrity of the home, *Dafydd Morgan* upholds Justus's observation. In Williams's novel, it is the hearth and the spiritual "path" that begins at the mother's knee that must compensate for rupture and loss:

> The child begins at the hearth. There is no better description of the consequences of this than in the Holy Book: "Show a child to the head of his path, and as he grows old he shall not depart from it." This path originates on the hearthstone; the parents start their children out on it, and there they will be seen when they have matured into old men and women, when the hands which supported them as they took their first steps have decayed in the soil of the valley! (*DM*, 34–35)

At the novel's close, Dafydd's parents respond in a letter to the news that he intends to stay in the United States:

> In spite of your suggestion that you might stay [in America] for a while, your letter has made us very happy. Your asking for our permission and blessing on all your movements and adventures there affords us much comfort, for we see that you are keeping to the path on which we started you out, here at home. This is an inexpressible comfort to your mother and myself as gray hair and old age overtake us. (*DM*, 153–154)

Here, too, the path that begins on the hearth creates continuity out of the discontinuities of departure and old age. Williams's novel operates on the basis of this desire to build over what might seem discontinuous, to span at least two possible readerships. In this sense, the novel is open and intelligible even to the contemporary reader, and it accords with Howells's wish that fiction should "speak the dialect, the language, that most Americans know—the language of unaffected people everywhere" (*CF*, 51).

NOTES

1. See, for example, Wendell V. Harris's well-known "Canonicity," in *PMLA* 106 (January 1991): 110–121.

2. See Werner Sollors, ed., *The Invention of Ethnicity* (New York: Oxford University Press, 1989).

3. William Boelhower, *Through a Glass Darkly: Ethnic Semiosis in American Literature* (Venice: Edizioni Helvetia, 1984), p. 34.

4. Eric Hobsbawm, "Mass-Producing Traditions: Europe, 1870–1914" in *The Invention of Tradition*, ed. E. Hobsbawm and T. Ranger (Cambridge: Cambridge University Press, 1983), p. 279.

5. Tom Quirk and Gary Scharnhorst, eds., *American Realism and the Canon* (Newark: University of Delaware Press, 1994), p. 19.

6. See Harris's description of E. C. Stedman's *Victorian Anthology* (1895) in "Canonicity," p. 114; see also Quirk and Scharnhorst, *American Realism and the Canon,* on William Dean Howells's support of lesser-known writers (women, ethnic minorities, et al.).

7. William Dean Howells, *Criticism and Fiction and Other Essays* (New York: New York University Press, 1959; 1891), p. 15; hereafter cited in the text as *CF.*

8. Stephen Crane, Frank Norris, Sarah Orne Jewett, and Paul Laurence Dunbar were several whom Howells assisted.

9. Benedict Anderson, *Imagined Communities: Reflections on the Origin and the Spread of Nationalism* (London: Verso, 1983), p. 145.

10. Matthew Frye Jacobson, *Special Sorrows: The Diasporic Imagination of Irish, Polish, and Jewish Immigrants in the United States* (Cambridge: Harvard University Press, 1995), p. 94.

11. Howells, *Years of My Youth and Three Essays*, ed. David J. Nordloh (Bloomington: Indiana University Press, 1975), pp. 117, 127.

12. See, for example, Werner Sollors, "Immigrants and Other Americans," in *Columbia Literary History of the United States*, ed. Emory Elliott (New York: Columbia University Press, 1988), pp. 568–588.

13. The works that do get critical attention are usually those that were translated into English not long after their original dates of publication, for example, the Norwegian-language works of Ole Rølvaag.

14. Boelhower, pp. 34–35.

15. Alejandro Portes and Richard Schauffler, "Language Acquisition and Loss Among Children of Immigrants," in *Origins and Destinies: Immigration, Race, and Ethnicity in America*, ed. Silvio Pedraza and Ruben G. Rumbaut (Belmont, Calif.: Wadsworth, 1996), p. 433.

16. Jacobson, p. 2.

17. Susan Harris, "Problems of Representation in Turn-of-the-Century Immigrant Fiction," in Quirk and Scharnhorst, *American Realism and the Canon*, pp. 127–142.

18. Williams wrote for *Y Drych* (The mirror) for at least twenty-five years, between 1880 and 1905. He also wrote for *Cyfaill o'r Hen Wlad* (Friend from the old country), which ran from 1838 to 1933. This passage comes from *Y Drych* (Utica, N.Y.), January 30, 1896, p. 1: "Y cyfnewidiad a wnaeth deugain mlynedd—hen wr penwyn yn awr—iaith arall a chynulleidfa o Americaniaid i'w hanerch!"

19. Dafydd is bilingual from childhood, unlike the novel's author. In *Y Drych*, May 21, 1895, Williams wrote that in 1853 when, at the age of seventeen, he sailed from Liverpool to New York, only one of the thirty people aboard the *Col. Cuttis* spoke English.

20. On American eisteddfods, see E. G. Hartmann, *Americans from Wales* (Boston: Christopher, 1967). For a history of the eisteddfod, see Hywel Teifi Edwards, *The Eisteddfod* (Cardiff: University of Wales Press, 1990).

21. On its front page, *Y Drych* (est. 1851) advertised overseas subscription rates, explained that it had "a large circulation, with subscribers in every State and Territory of the Union, in Great Britain, and the British Dependencies," and declared itself "The American Organ of the Welsh People."

22. This information is accurate to my best knowledge. The Welsh journals did serialize historical romances, but they were generally more interested in poetry and essays.

23. "Yr wyf yn cymeradwyo yr anturiaeth o gyhoeddi Ffugchwedl fuddugol R. R. Williams. . . . Gobeithiwyf y derbynia yr awdwr gefnogaeth deilwng gan ei gydgenedl," R. R. Williams, *Dafydd Morgan, neu Ddylanwad Addysg yr Aelwyd* (Utica: T. J. Griffiths, Argraffydd, Swyddfa y Drych, 1897), p. 10; hereafter cited in the text as *DM*.

24. Edwards, *The Eisteddfod*, p. 28.

25. For more about this, see Prys Morgan, "From Long Knives to Blue Books," in *Welsh Society and Nationhood*, ed. R. R. Davies et al. (Cardiff: University of Wales Press, 1984).

26. Hywel Teifi Edwards, *Codi'r Hen Wlad yn ei Hol 1850–1914* (Raising up the old country) (Llandysul: Gwasg Gomer, 1989), pp. 147–148: "Fe allai fod y Gymraeg wedi'i thynghedu i golli gwlad ac ennill cyfandir."

27. Ibid., p. 148. (My translation.) Edwards takes the passage from an article entitled "Y Gymraeg, a'r Dyfodol" (The Welsh language and the future), which appeared in the Welsh newspaper *Y Faner* on August 1, 1866.

28. James H. Justus, "The Fireside Poets: Hearthside Values and the Language of Care," in *Nineteenth Century American Poetry*, ed. A. Robert Lee (London: Vision Press, 1985), pp. 146–165. See also Thomas Wortham, "William Cullen Bryant and the Fireside Poets" in *Columbia Literary History of the United States*, ed. Emory Elliott (New York: Columbia University Press, 1988), pp. 278–288.

Chapter Seven

"The Quintessence of the Jew"
Polemics of Nationalism and Peoplehood in Turn-of-the-Century Yiddish Fiction

Matthew Frye Jacobson

Among the first and most famous pieces of Yiddish literature in the United States is *Yekl*, Abraham Cahan's account of a tragicomic Russian Jew who wants nothing more than to become, in his words, "a real Yankee feller." Because it found its way into English early on (it appeared in Yiddish in 1893 and in English in 1895), the novella has attracted more critical attention and has reached a wider audience than any other piece of Yiddish-American fiction. Indeed, *Yekl* was introduced to an English-speaking audience, amid much fanfare, by none other than the "Dean of American letters," a laudatory and enthusiastic William Dean Howells.

Howells's involvement seems to have forever stamped *Yekl* as a certain kind of novel accomplishing certain kinds of cultural work: Cahan has become a cultural ambassador, by most accounts, who served up the Jewish ghetto and made it accessible for an audience far broader than the Yiddish-speaking readership of the Lower East Side. From the outset the piece was received on the American literary scene as a work about America itself—about the trials and tribulations of immigrants *to* America, about the prospects of absorption *by* America, about the ghetto, a new and fascinating (if troubling) social zone *in* America. While Cahan's keen depiction of "ghetto types" has been noted over the years, more often it is the ghetto itself that commands critical attention in the United States. The novella, at bottom, becomes a work about its own setting.[1]

But it may prove a fruitful exercise to translate *Yekl*, as it were, back into Yiddish. What if the novella had never been rendered in English? What if it existed only in its original Yiddish version, and there had been no dean of American letters to popularize it among the genteel readers of the *Atlantic Monthly*? What would we be saying about it then? The novella is doubly paradigmatic: on the one hand, the Yiddish text is paradigmatic of a polemic current regarding the meaning and basis of Jewishness that ran through much Yiddish writing on both sides of the Atlantic in this period; the American, English-language reception of the novella, on the other hand, is paradigmatic of a certain blindness in American literary history to the transnational dimensions of "ethnic" literatures. The work of resituating *Yekl* within the Yiddish culture of the immigrant ghetto and its transnational intelligentsia is instructive not simply because there is still a great deal to say about the piece but because what there is to say no longer has much to do with "America" at all—with America as an idea, America as an ideal, or America as a piece of failed magic. *Yekl*, in Yiddish, that is, engaged transnational debates regarding the essence of Jewish character—its basis, its nature, and its possibilities; debates occasioned by the complex of crises known at the time as "The Jewish Question." The historic convergence in the 1890s of horrific pogroms in the East (to which Jews were so vulnerable because they had not assimilated at all) and the anti-Semitic upsurging around the Dreyfus Affair in the West (to which Jews were so vulnerable because they had assimilated so thoroughly) raised urgent and perplexing questions about the Jews' collective destiny. In this context the literary/political theme of "Americanization"—as in *Yekl*—represented not simply a melting-pot *American* tale but another of the possible fates to be met by the Jews, alongside their terrorization in Russia and their demonization in France. The porous texture of an American political culture deemed so desirable and inviting by some "Yekls" newly arrived from the Old World raised questions about the social possibilities inhering in Jewish identity—not just collective destiny but the very basis of Jewish collectivity.[2]

A rereading of *Yekl* in this context, moreover, opens a window on a range of Yiddish literary productions of the period, including the stories, sketches, and dramatic works of Leon Kobrin, Jacob Gordin, and Bernard Goren; and the poetry of Morris Winchevsky, Abraham Liessen, and Morris Rosenfeld. Like *Yekl*, these works were generated within a social and political context in which Yiddish thinkers on both sides of the Atlantic were absorbed with the question of Jewish identity itself, and its ideal relation to the other racial, ethnic, religious, or national identities on the world scene. *Dos pintele yid*, the quintessence of the Jew, was a sharply contested notion precisely because its properties—whatever they turned out to be— seemed to hold the key to collective action and hence to collective well-being.

At the heart of much Jewish political discussion in the late nineteenth century was the pressing question, on the Yiddish left, of whether Jews should enter the international workers' movement as Jews or as (assimilated) members of the various host countries within which they lived. The question was not a simple one: on the one hand, what did Jewish identity even *mean* in the context of a secularized socialist movement?—what did Jewishness consist of in the case of the nonreligious "Jew"? And on the other hand, as long as even secularized, assimilated Jews continued so often to be persecuted *as* Jews, how could the international workers' movement expect them so readily to drop their identity as specifically *Jewish* workers?

Polar philosophies crystallized around this question throughout the 1880s and 1890s—cosmopolitanists at one end of the spectrum, nationalists of various stripes (including labor Zionists) at the other. Even for some Jews the anti-Semitic violence of the Russian peasantry in the 1880s looked like a lamentable phase in an otherwise promising political awakening on the part of "the Russian people"; Jews should stop thinking of themselves as Jews at all, and should applaud (as Russians) the seeming rise of a Russian proletarian movement. For others, the Russian pogroms were the most powerful proof of the primacy of Jewish identity, offering a stark, dramatic plea for a Jewish movement of self-defense or even a Jewish homeland.[3] In both cases the conception of Jewish identity held the key to broader interpretations of Russian politics and socialist organization.

It was none other than Abraham Cahan who most clearly laid out the argument in favor of a distinctly Yiddishist commitment to socialism—a formula by which neither the "Jewish" nor the "worker" in Jewish working-class identity could be dismissed. At an international convention of socialists in Brussels in 1891, Cahan introduced a resolution calling on the socialist movement to denounce (and implicitly, *re*nounce) anti-Semitism of all stripes. "The Jews are persecuted," he argued:

> Pogroms are made upon them. They are insulted, they are oppressed. Exceptional laws are made for them. They have been made into a separate class of people with no rights. These people with no rights want to struggle right alongside all other proletarians and they request a place in the ranks of the social democracy. The anti-Semitic Russian press attacks the Jews, and tries to create the impression that everyone hates us, including the workers. I therefore demand that you declare before the world that this is a lie—that you are the enemy of all exploiters, Christian as well as Jewish ones; that you love Jewish workers as well as Christian ones.[4]

This complex, often strained commitment to both socialism and Jewishness was at the very center of Yiddish discussion in the 1890s and after. It colored the editorial policy of papers like the *Jewish Daily Forward*; it crystallized in the General Jewish Workers' League (the Bund) in 1897; and it provided both the context and the thematic grist for much Yiddish poetry, drama, and fiction from the 1890s onward—including Cahan's *Yekl*.[5]

The wrongheadedness—even futility—of transcending one's *Yiddishkayt* was the very crux of *Yekl*. The plot centers on a blustery and misguided immigrant bent on shedding his Russian Yiddish self and becoming a true Yankee. So intent is he on this transformation that when his wife and son join him in America after a prolonged separation, he recoils, ashamed of their "foreign" demeanor. Under the spell of his Yankee aspirations, Yekl then falls in love with Mamie Fein, a partly Americanized, royally pretentious woman whom he has met in an East Side dancing school. Yekl ends as a "defeated victor," achieving his freedom from the greenhorn Gitl through divorce, yet sensing vaguely that he has been duped by his own elusive measures of success and happiness.

In this character sketch of a familiar ghetto type, Cahan challenges the tenets of cosmopolitanism on two counts. First, *Yekl* counters the frequent cosmopolitanist argument that nationalism is necessarily divisive and that assimilation is necessarily a unifying principle, the key to workers' solidarity across ethnic or national lines. On the contrary, in the American context, assimilation itself was among the supreme expressions of bourgeois aspiration. Yekl's quest to become an American "feller" led to Mamie Fein, her money, and the petit bourgeois dream of opening a dancing school of his own. Assimilationism led to Yekl's self-absorption and his sense of superiority to his coworkers. Finally, it led to his fully inhuman attitude toward his wife and compatriot, Gitl: "I am an American feller, a Yankee—that's what I am! What punishment is due me, then, if I cannot stand a shnooza like her?" " 'Ah, may she be killed, the horrid greenhorn!' he would gasp to himself in a paroxism of despair."[6]

Cahan underscored the theme of assimilationism as a regressive impulse by the recurrent equation of Americanization with nobility, an unambiguous intimation for his largely socialist readership. Upon her first glimpse of the Americanized Yekl, Gitl remarks that he looks "like a *poritz* [nobleman]"; and later, confronted with her own mirror image wearing a department store hat, she sees herself as "quite a *panenka* [noblewoman]." Likewise, when Mamie Fein sweeps through Gitl's apartment for the first time, "apparently dressed for some occasion of state," Gitl comments sarcastically, "She looks like a veritable *panenka*. . . . Was she born here?"[7] In the world of Yekl, assimilation provided no "broad" alternative to "narrow" nationalism. On the contrary, kindness and decency themselves depended upon a humble acceptance of *Yiddishkayt*: one of Yekl's rare moments of clarity, a momentary resolution to reform and fulfill his obligation to Gitl, was attended by Old World memories of "the Hebrew words of the Sanctification of the Sabbath" and a homely vision of "a plate of reeking *tzimes*."[8]

Cahan's argument that assimilation was undesirable, moreover, was underpinned by an iron contention that it was in fact impossible. This second layer, Cahan's version of *dos pintele yid*, comprised a constellation of images of which this "plate of reeking *tzimes*" was but one element. The complex as a whole linked naturalized notions of lineage and kinship ("race" in the broadest instance, "parentage" in the narrower instance) to naturalized conceptions of patriarchal order. Cahan locates *dos pintele yid* within the rhythms of nature, firmly lashed to notions of race and sex also presumed to be natural.

Yekl's bid to become a real Yankee feller is futile. On the grounds of "race," the thin veneer of Americanization is ever betrayed by "his Semitic smile" and his "strongly Semitic" eyes. As one of his sweatshop rivals chides, "He thinks that shaving one's mustache makes a Yankee!"[9] Indeed, it is his attempt to transcend his "natural" self that renders Yekl the buffoon that he is. On the question of whether Judaism is a system of religious belief or a more fundamental element of one's being, *Yekl* is unequivocal: a Jew, even if fallen away, will always be a Jew. Hence when William Dean Howells identified Cahan as a "Hebrew" and described his ghetto sketches as "so foreign to our race and civilization," he was not merely expressing an Anglo-Saxon parochialism. This racialist view of the essential "difference" between Hebrew and Anglo-Saxon was embraced on both sides of the presumed barrier.[10]

Further, this racialized (which is to say, biologized) view of an immutable *Yiddishkayt* has a second dimension: for Cahan, as for many of his male colleagues, notions of *Yiddishkayt* invariably intersected notions of masculinity, femininity, maternal duty, and patriarchal authority. In the case of *Yekl*, sexuality, like "race," naturalized the Jewish quintessence. The buffoon-hero's hope of transcending his Old World self is limited by overlapping and enveloping complexes of parentage-as-race and parentage-as-patriarchy. Yekl's doomed quest to escape his own *Yiddishkayt* is played out almost entirely on the terrain of gender and sexuality. The question of identity that so plagues him is cast as a choice between two women: the cultural conservatism of Gitl, or the rather thin assimilationism of Mamie Fein. Yekl's momentary surrender to "the grip of his past," his fleeting acceptance of *Yiddishkayt* and his memory of "reeking *tzimes*," is attended by a very particular image of Judaism and the Jewish home: "seated by the side of the head of the little family and within easy reach of the huge brick oven is his old mother, flushed with fatigue, and with an effort keeping her drowsy eyes open to attend, with a devout mien, her husband's prayer." And again in the final scene, Yekl dimly acknowledges his mistakes and imagines undoing them in these terms: "What if he should now dash into Gitl's apartments and, declaring his authority as husband, father, and lord of the house, fiercely eject the strangers, take [his son] into his arms, and sternly command Gitl to mind her household duties?"[11]

The gender relations evoked throughout the novel replicate precisely and literally the sexual division of labor that constitutes an essential prop of traditional Judaism. Women were to supply men's physical needs, freeing men for the more important matters of the spirit—including the spiritual needs of women themselves. It was because of their biological function as mothers that women were discounted as legal members of the quorum in prayer; and it was this maternal capacity and its "natural" limitations that Jewish men were to acknowledge in their daily benediction, thanking God "for not having made me a woman." Cahan thus taps a powerful current of social authority—at once Talmudic and biologic—answering assimilationist aspirations not only with racial certainties of immutable Jewish selfhood but with an eternal Judaism rooted in patriarchy and the eternal feminine. Yekl's futile assimilation-as-denial is ultimately contrasted with Gitl's more organic transformation: with her neighbor Mrs. Kavarsky's help ("Be a mother to me"), Gitl loses her "rustic, 'greenhorn like' expression" without betraying her Judaism.[12]

Cahan was not alone among male writers in linking a stable, persistent *Yiddishkayt* with notions of immutable, conserving femininity. Hence these are the scenes that most captured the unconquerable spirit of *Yiddishkayt*: a once-pious woman, having fallen under America's ungodly spell, reawakens on Yom Kippur and once again feels at one with "the children of Israel . . . massed together in every corner of the globe." An Americanized, "fallen" woman of the ghetto reclaims her Old World self when the chant of the Kol Nidre, drifting up from a shul across the street, awakens in her a nearly pious "sadness in the soul." "I am not Jenny!" she cries. "I am Zlate." A daughter of the ghetto, a freethinker overcome by melancholy on Passover, can only ask herself, "Why is this night different from every other night?"—and yet feel certain that it is. A mother of the Old World, upon hearing that her emigrant daughter has married a Christian, rends her garments and recites a prayer for the dead. And as the grip of her parental authority loosens in the New World, another matriarch angrily denounces her daughter as a *shikse*—a non-Jewish woman.[13] All of these sketches and the many others like them—by Bernard Goren, Leon Kobrin, and Abraham Reisen—served the same polemic purpose as Cahan's *Yekl*: they countered cosmopolitanist certainties that *Yiddishkayt* should—or *could*—be shed like an unwanted garment.

There is some overlap, to be sure, between the complementary themes of the culture-bearing power of the feminine and the recuperative power of Jewish ritual (the power of the Hebrew words during Yekl's fleeting reawakening, for instance). But in his controversial sketch "What Is He?" Leon Kobrin developed the gendered aspect of this Yiddishist argument even as he captured the nationalist spirit of so much Yiddish literature in America. He had originally written the story in the first person of a man, but he later recast it and added the subtitle, "From the Diary of a Socialist Mother."[14]

"What Is He?" is a monologue in the voice of a freethinking socialist who begins to suspect that in casting off Judaism she has robbed her little boy of his childhood's rightful magic. "What does my little five-year-old . . . know of *Yiddishkayt*? What kind of Jew is he?" she asks. As she reflects on the beauty, the mirth, and the depth of feeling in the Jewish tradition, her question becomes, "Where is the poetry of my Nikolai's childhood?" What is there in socialism and the freethinker's concern for broad humanity that could take the place of Hannukah, Pesach, and Purim in the lives of activists' children? The *sotzialistke* finally works herself up from this simple reflection to a plaintive accusation leveled at the cultural tenets of Jewish socialism: "How come the socialists among other peoples do not take their national holidays away from their children?"

In response to the wave of critical letters that flooded the editorial offices of the *Abend blatt* in response to the sketch, Kobrin wrote a second, even stronger statement, titled "Yes, What Is He?" "What is my Nikolai?" asked the *sotzialistke* again. "What will he grow into in this indefinite grey reality?—in this mish mash of ours, without life, without light, and without the sunny warmth of a festive childhood?" Reviewing the Jewish calendar of festivals and recounting its joys at length, Kobrin's *sotzialistke* exclaims, "What poetic nectar for the spirit of a child!" *Yiddishkayt*, these sketches argued, was being unnecessarily sacrificed on the altar of cosmopolitanism. Like young Nikolai, the Jewish socialist in the age of Dreyfus was "cut off from his own people, but had no bonds with the stranger."[15] And again, it was the Jewish mother, never to be estranged from tradition, who stepped forward to make the case.

Such Yiddishist arguments did not go unanswered. The most vocal and active polemicist among the cosmopolitanists was Jacob Gordin, whose realist dramas were singlehandedly redirecting the Yiddish theater in New York. "He who will make of a man a nationalist will drag that man back," Gordin insisted in his much-heralded debate with Yiddishist Chaim Zhitlowsky.[16] Indeed, his popular plays in the realist mode were antinationalist in intent. But there was more than mere irony entailed in the effort to minimize the significance of Jewish identity through literary and dramtic works cast in a language spoken only by Jews. Both the cosmopolitanist intent and its pitfalls are ever discernible in Gordin's writings.

In "What Sings the Jew," for instance, a festive, motley gathering of emigrants entertain one another on shipboard en route from Hamburg to New York by performing their national anthems. When the cry went up that it was the Jews' turn, "Only a mournful, ironic smile played on their lips." There was, of course, no song to sing. But to everyone's surprise (and to the Gentiles' derision), "Israelik the pauper" agreed to sing. He sang the Kol Nidre, and Gordin's jeering onlookers were transformed by the Jewish song: "Unwillingly each of the goyim began to feel and to understand that he was hearing an old, holy, historical song which told of many human troubles and sufferings, which bitterly lamented the lost past and asked with pain what would be found in the future. . . . A melancholy feeling stole into the heart of everyone."[17]

The promise held up by the story's content—that humanity may indeed be united above the narrow divisions of national anthems like "Deutschland über alles" or "Jeszcze Polska nie zginela"—is broken by its Yiddishist narrative frame. Like the classic Yiddish tales by Sholem Aleichem, I. L. Peretz, and Mendele Macher Sforim, Gordin's story is founded on types and prototypes. Israelik can only be understood to represent "a Jew," and hence the transcendent power of his song can only suggest the superior ethics and culture of Judaism. With its emphasis on group identity even as it describes a universalizing sentiment, the tale is chauvinistic in spite of itself: in sharp contrast to the goyim, whose behavior is mean-spirited and whose songs are divisive, "the Jew" emerges as the moral superior in the social relations in this microcosm of humanity, just as only the *Jewish* tradition has the power to unite peoples across ethnic or national boundaries. The tale simultaneously holds out and revokes the cosmopolitanist promise of true internationalism.

Or again, "In Prayer Garments—A Fact" was Jacob Gordin's answer to those, like Cahan and Kobrin, for whom Jewish socialism was rooted irretrievably in Jewish identity. For Gordin, a persistent ethnic attachment leads only to despair: "Jacob knew that he was a Jew, and, as a Jew, he was born only to have worries, had children only to have worries, and with his troubles he *schlepped* himself over from Russia to America—to have worries." One morning, as he stood by the window with his prayer garments on, watching the "worried and depressed" passersby and listening to his children begging for food in the next room, and as he asked himself whether there was no other joy in life than "the love of one's God," he opened the window and leapt out. Fully comprehending this man's life and his death, those who gathered around his body on the street below "dared not tell a lie"—they dared not utter the prayer for the dead, "Blessed be the true judge."[18] Through the refusal of the passersby to "tell a lie," to recite the prayer, Gordin rejects the Jewish tradition as politically paralyzing. Nonetheless, his tale conveys a totalizing experience of uniquely Jewish "worries" that undermines the argument that Jewishness can be shed like an unwanted garment. "This little song about the Jewish quintessence and about the Jewish soul is very beautiful and sweet," he would argue in his famous debate with Yiddishist Chaim Zhitlowsky, "but it is no more than a lyrical feeling." And yet his own stories portrayed a Jewishness that ran much deeper than sweet little songs.[19]

Despite the stubborn limitations of cosmopolitanist polemic in Yiddish, Gordin's works do attest to the currency of the debate over the "quintessence of the Jew" for this generation of immigrant writers; and his works do help to identify the proper ideological context within which so much Yiddish cultural production in America emerged. Here, as in Cahan's writing, it is not so much "America" that is at issue but "the Jew" himself.

Many of these works seem to address purely "American" themes of immigration, settlement, readjustment, and "assimilation," but they ultimately demonstrate a deeper, more abiding commitment to questions and passions actually transnational in scope. While the novels, stories, and plays of Abraham Cahan, Leon Kobrin, and Jacob Gordin indeed depict life in the New World in its various dimensions, so are they framed by questions of Jewishness whose derivation and urgency have less to do with American life than with the crisis for Jews posed by vicious pogroms in the East and the Dreyfus Affair in the West. At the heart of Yiddish-American fiction, beneath an announced concern for questions of "Americanization" or "assimilation," lingered a vigorous Old World debate over nationalist and cosmopolitanist responses to "the Jewish Question." The most famous such work, indeed, was Israel Zangwill's *Melting Pot* itself—the play that has given us our most familiar metaphor for a distinctly American brand of diversity, notwithstanding Zangwill's engagement in the Jewish Question and in the debate over territorialism. The literature of immigration may represent a crucial chapter in American literary history, to be sure, but it is important to keep in mind that many immigrant writers counted themselves primarily *emigrant* writers, and it was not always the *Americanness* of the chapter that was foremost on their minds as they were writing.

NOTES

1. Jules Chametzky, *From the Ghetto: The Fiction of Abraham Cahan* (Amherst: University of Massachusetts Press, 1977).

2. This argument is condensed from Matthew Frye Jacobson, *Special Sorrows: The Diasporic Imagination of Irish, Polish, and Jewish Immigrants in the United States* (Cambridge: Harvard University Press, 1995), chapter 1. See Calvin Goldscheider and Alan Zuckerman, *The Transformation of the Jews* (Chicago: University of Chicago Press, 1984); David Vital, *The Origins of Zionism* (Oxford: Oxford University Press, 1975); Salo W. Baron, *The Russian Jews Under Tsars and Soviets* (New York: Schocken, 1964); Moses Rischin, *The Promised City: New York's Jews, 1870–1914* (Cambridge: Harvard University Press, 1962); Walter Lacqueur, *A History of Zionism* (New York: Schocken, 1978).

3. Baron, *Russian Jews*; Vital, *Origins*; Lacqueur, *History of Zionism*.

4. Abraham Cahan, *Bleter fun mayn leben* (New York: Forverts Association, 1926), vol. 3, pp. 158, 158–165.

5. Jacobson, *Special Sorrows*, chapter 3.

6. Abraham Cahan, *Yekl, the Imported Bridegroom, and Other Stories* (New York: Dover, 1970), pp. 70, 44.

7. Ibid., pp. 35, 36, 40, 52.

8. Ibid., pp. 30–31.

9. Ibid., pp. 3, 5, 6.

10. Howells, quoted in Bernard G. Richards, "Abraham Cahan Cast in a New Role," in Cahan, *Yekl*, p. vii. On turn-of-the-century versions of racialized Jewishness, see John M. Efron, *Defenders of the Race: Jewish Doctors and Race Science in Fin-de-Siecle Europe* (New Haven: Yale University Press, 1994); Sander Gilman, *The Jew's Body* (New York: Routledge, 1991); Sander Gilman, *The Case of Sigmund Freud: Medicine and Identity at the Fin de Siecle* (Baltimore: Johns Hopkins University Press, 1993); Sander Gilman, *Freud, Race, and*

Gender (Princeton: Princeton University Press, 1993); and Matthew Frye Jacobson, "Looking Jewish / Seeing Jews: 'Race' and Perception," in *Becoming Caucasian: Vicissitudes of Whiteness in American Political Culture* (Cambridge: Harvard University Press, forthcoming).

11. Cahan, *Yekl*, pp. 30, 89. Susan Kress, "Women and Marriage in Abraham Cahan's Fiction," *Studies in American Jewish Literature* 3 (1983): 26–39.

12. Paula Hyman "The Other Half: Women in the Jewish Tradition," in Elizabeth Koltun, ed., *The Jewish Woman: New Perspectives* (New York: Schocken, 1976), pp. 105–113, at 109; Saul Berman, "The Status of Women in Halakhic Judaism," in Koltun, *Jewish Woman*, pp. 114–128; Anne Goldfeld, "Women as Sources of Torah in the Rabbinic Tradition," in Koltun, *Jewish Woman*, p. 258; A. Cohen, *Everyman's Talmud* (New York: Schocken, 1975), pp. 159–161; Adin Steinsaltz, *The Essential Talmud* (New York: Bantam, 1976), pp. 137–144; Cahan, *Yekl,* pp. 65, 83.

13. Bernard Gorin, "Yom Kippur," *Abend Blatt*, September 12, 1899, p. 2; Leon Kobrin, "Jenny's Kol Nidre," in *Gezamlte shriften* (New York: Hebrew Publishing, 1910), pp. 197–209; Leon Kobrin, "Anna's Ma-nishtane," in *Abend Blatt*, March 25, 1899, p. 2, and *Gezamlte shriften* pp. 675–679; Leon Kobrin, "Borekh dyan emes," in *Gezamlte shriften*, pp. 197–209, and "Ver iz shuldig?" in *Gezamlte Shriften*, pp. 87–101.

14. Leon Kobrin, "Vos iz er?" The version collected in *Gezamlte shriften*, pp. 614–620, dated 1897, has a male narrator. The version that Kobrin quoted and discussed years later in his autobiography, *Mayn fuftzik yohr in America* (New York: YKUF, 1966), pp.191–200 (also dated 1897), and a somewhat shorter variation that ran in *Abend Blatt*, May 18, 1899, p. 2, both have a female narrator and bear the subtitle "oys a togbukh fun a muter a sotsialistke."

15. Leon Kobrin, "Yo, vos iz er?" in *Mayn fuftzik yohr*, pp. 191–200.

16. Jacob Gordin, "Natzionalismus un asimilatzion," in *Ale shriften* (New York: Hebrew Publishing, 1910), vol. 4, pp. 281, 267–284.

17. Jacob Gordin, "Vos zingt der yid?" (c. 1897) in *Ertzaylungen* (New York: Der internatzionale bibliotek, 1908), pp. 116–121.

18. Jacob Gordin, "In tales un tfilin: a fakt" in *Ertzaylungen*, pp. 93–95.

19. Gordin, "Natzionalismus un assimilatzion," p. 272.

Chapter Eight

Redefining Chinese American Literature from a LOWINUS Perspective

Two Recent Examples

Te-hsing Shan

August and September 1996 witnessed the publication in Taiwan of two significant Chinese American writings: Yan Geling's novel *Fu Sang* and Chin Yang Lee's collection of short stories *Ch'i-p'ao ku-niang* (*Changsan Girl* is the title of the English-language edition).[1] The Chinese reading public viewed them primarily as Chinese literary works proper,[2] or as works by the Overseas Chinese in their mother tongue about Chinese immigrants in the United States. However, *Fu Sang* and *Ch'i-p'ao ku-niang* are of special interest when viewed from the perspectives of Chinese/Asian American literature, the LOWINUS (Languages of What Is Now the United States) Project of the Longfellow Institute, and transnational and cross-cultural literary production.

Yan started her Chinese writing career in 1981 and published three novels in China before she came to the United States in 1989. In 1990, while majoring in fiction writing at the University of Chicago, Yan began to publish works in Taiwan. She since has published seven books there and has received several important literary awards.[3] In the recent, prize-winning *Fu Sang*, Yan tells the story of the title character, a nineteenth-century San Francisco prostitute, constructed out of 160 historical documents she unearthed in San Francisco libraries. In a metafictional mode, the female narrator, who identifies herself as a fifth-generation Chinese American married to a white husband, at times directly addresses this legendary Chinatown prostitute who lived more than 120 years ago.[4]

Lee, born in 1916 in Hunan, China, and best known in the English-speaking world as the author of *Flower Drum Song* (1957), published his first collection of short stories in Chinese, *Ch'i-p'ao ku-niang*, at the age of eighty.[5] His tales of Chinese Americans living in Los Angeles, especially at Monterey Park (the famous "Little Taipei"), are interesting in themselves. The story behind the writing and production of *Ch'i-p'ao ku-niang*, however, may be even more fascinating to scholars interested in literary and cultural production as well as transcultural and transnational border crossings.

Several things emerge when these two books are considered side by side and in the LOWINUS context. These issues include the use of the Chinese language, the significance of immigrant literature, the relationship of immigrant literature to the home country and the adopted country, the numerous agents in transnational literary production (i.e., the role of literary mechanisms such as Chinese literary supplements and literary awards), and various methods of contextualization (in Chinese literature, American literature, Chinese American literature, and Overseas Chinese literature).

The question of "how to connect"—that is, of how to make these works relevant to the Chinese-speaking world, especially to literary consumers in Taiwan—has almost become an obsession of Yan, Lee, and Ya Hsuan (who introduces Lee's collection).

Yan's introduction to *Fu Sang* and her remarks on receiving the *United Daily News* critics' award in 1995 forcefully express her longtime concern with "immigrant" literature and with challenging the center/margin dichotomy suggested by this term (it should be noted that the audience she addresses is Chinese speaking rather than English speaking). The introduction and her remarks, together with some of the metafictional comments in the novel, indicate the author's concern about Chinese immigrants in the United States over the past few years.[6] Short as they are, Yan's comments are rich and inextricably intertwined with her theme and technique, as she brings the narrator into a metafictional dialogue with a fellow Chinese American woman who lived in San Francisco more than a century ago.[7]

Yan's argument is that it is the task of the storyteller to present a tale that is not only interesting, but also significant, exposing hidden qualities of human personality. The charm of the story lies in its illumination of the fickle and unpredictable nature of human beings. To explore the possibilities of human nature, the storyteller must create situations through which the inner qualities of the characters may be evoked. The situation of the immigrants—those who have left their home country and find themselves strangers in a strange land—is undoubtedly a uniquely compelling one. To Yan, "the specific situation of the immigrants induces this particular kind of sensitivity" (*Fu Sang*, iii).[8] Citing four renowned immigrant writers—Joseph Conrad, Vladimir Nabokov, Milan Kundera, and Isabel Auendene (Allende)—Yan asserts that the experience of immigration "has decisively broadened and deepened their perspective and thinking" (iii–iv).

To Yan, the center/margin dichotomy and the statement that "immigrant literature is marginal literature" are rather questionable, if not unacceptable, for "literature is about human beings. Everything that enables writers' understanding of human environment, events, life forms should be treated the same—it makes no sense in distinguishing the center and the margin" (iii). Following this reasoning, the concept of literary orthodoxy makes little sense as well, because "where there are Chinese, there should occur orthodox, mainstream Chinese literature" (iii). In other words, geographical centrality does not guarantee the centrality of a literary work. The fact that *Fu Sang* won the *United Daily News* critics' award in a contest open to works in Chinese written anywhere in the world substantiates Yan's argument.

While in *Fu Sang* the author's treatment of the American protagonist's fascination with the mysterious Oriental prostitute is quite Saidian, Yan's concept of archeology and history is undeniably Foucaultian. In her remarks on receiving the *United Daily News* prize, Yan talks about her "excavation" of long-forgotten documents in the various libraries of San Francisco and marvels at "the inexhaustible richness of the history of the early Chinese immigrants" (v). Most significantly, she discovers "a peculiar phenomenon":

> Different people with different perspectives will construct totally different stories/histories. Heroes in the eyes of the Chinese might prove to be scoundrels in the eyes of the Americans. As a consequence, history is never real, objective. . . . Being an immigrant—this most fragile, sensitive life form—can generate the most verisimilitudinous reaction toward the cruel environment and is thus doomed to be dramatic, tragic. (v)[9]

Finally, Yan appreciates the critics' attention to *Fu Sang*, as "this concern will lead all Chinese communities' concern toward the immigrant literature" (v). This remark paradoxically confirms Taiwan's somewhat self-important claim to be the center of Chinese culture, and thus undercuts Yan's questioning of the concepts of norm, center, orthodox, and mainstream.[10] Despite this apparent incongruity, Yan is able in five short pages to express cogently her ideas about the task of the storyteller, the interaction between character and situation, the peculiarity of the immigrant situation, the significance of the excavation and construction of the immigrant literature, the problem of the center/margin dichotomy and literary orthodoxy, and the status of the Chinese diaspora.

To most Chinese readers, Lee is a legendary yet seldom read writer. Among his eleven English publications of the past four decades, only three have been translated into Chinese.[11] One question raised by the publication of Lee's first collection of short stories in Chinese, then, is how to market this esteemed but largely unfamiliar writer to the Chinese-speaking world. The task is to make him relevant to the Taiwanese, who at the close of the twentieth century are exposed to so many attractions outside of literature. The strategies adopted by the publisher indicate some interesting phenomena.

Because news coverage may not be extensive, pertinent to marketing, and lasting in the reader's memory, direct mail in the form of the publisher's book-club newsletter is used to target the book's audience. All told, however, the most powerful advertisement is still the book itself. Lee's sixteen stories are bracketed by an introduction, significantly entitled "The Ice-Breaking Journey—The Bilingual World of Chin Yang Lee's Writings,"[12] and Lee's two autobiographical accounts—"My Memory" (focusing on his family and his earlier career) and "My Search for Roots" (having to do with the writing of *Ch'i-p'ao ku-niang*).

Needless to say, the introduction plays a pivotal role in orienting the reader's response. Ya Hsuan, the writer of the introduction—hailed by Lee as "the promoter of my Chinese writing" (*Ch'i-p'ao*, 8)—negotiates between Lee's status as a novice at writing in Chinese and the desire to make him relevant to the target audience.

The apparent Sinocentrism of the introduction may have more to do with Ya Hsuan's effort to connect Lee to the Chinese reading public than with an endeavor to position Lee in a bilingual context.

The occasion on which Ya Hsuan and Lee became acquainted is of particular significance. At the invitation of the Association of Chinese Writers around the World,[13] Lee visited Taiwan in April 1995 with a group of other Chinese American writers, including Maxine Hong Kingston and Aimee E. Liu. During his visit, he met with many writers, cultural workers, and scholars—among them Ya Hsuan, a modern poet and the general editor of the Literary Supplement of the *United Daily News*.[14] In correspondence later, Ya Hsuan encouraged Lee to write in Chinese. With the help of a bilingual dictionary, Lee embarked on his Chinese writing career.

Several points may be drawn from Ya Hsuan's introduction and Lee's appendices, which are aimed at establishing Lee's Chinese connections. The first, quite understandably, concerns the Lee family. Both the introduction and the appendices emphasize Lee's family background: his grandfather and father passed the civil examination of the Ch'ing Dynasty; his eldest brother was the Dean of the College of Liberal Arts of Peking Normal University and Mao Tse-tung's teacher in Chinese literature; four of his eight brothers engaged in writing or music; and he himself came to the United States for advanced studies, first at Columbia University and then at Yale University. This autobiographical account creates the impression that because Lee is from such a highly educated family, his becoming a writer was simply a matter of course.

Second, the list of Lee's English publications indicates that all eleven of his English works concern Chinese people at home and abroad; at least four of them are about Chinese Americans. The autobiographical sketch describes the start of his writing career, his attitude toward writing, and so on. Lee also writes about his debut novel, *Flower Drum Song*, although it remains for Ya Hsuan to situate Lee in the Chinese American literary scene.

As a literary editor in Taiwan whose object is to win as large a Chinese audience for *Ch'i-p'ao ku-niang* as possible, Ya Hsuan values the sojourner mentality of Overseas Chinese writers, who either write in Chinese and publish their works in their motherland (such as Pai Hsien-yung, Nieh Hua-ling, Cheng Ch'ou-yu, Yang Mu, and Yu Li-hua)[15] or write in English directly about things Chinese (Lin Yutang and Chiang Yi).

In comparison with authors like Lin and Chiang, the younger generation of Chinese American writers—among whom Kingston, Liu, Amy Tan, and Shawn Wong are mentioned—are praised for "opening up new horizons for the Chinese literature [*hua-jen wen-hsueh*][16] all over the world and foreshadowing various possibilities" (*Ch'i-p'ao*, 3). Moveover, the publication of Lin's *My Country and My People* and *The Art of Living* in the 1930s and the successful Broadway performance of Lee's *Flower Drum Song* in the 1950s are singled out as "two great events which marked the historical turning point in the development of Chinese American literature" (3). Lin and Lee are thus dubbed "the two heralds in the pioneering team of Chinese American literature" (3).

In his introduction, Ya Hsuan dutifully describes the characteristics of *Ch'i-p'ao ku-niang*, including Lee's masterful command of the Chinese language (4), the common theme of Chinese Americans' social identity and efforts to merge into the American mainstream society (4–5), the merit of the short-story form to represent the Chinese American community by means of collage (5), the use of a humorous and light-hearted tone to dispel former ethnic stereotypes (5), and the life-like characterizations derived from Lee's longtime observation of Chinatown (6–7).

Several observations can be made here. The first and foremost involves Yan's and Lee's Chinese connections and their attitudes toward these connections. Both authors came from Mainland China (though their journeys were separated by more than four decades) and both now live in the United States. Both are currently writing in their mother tongue for their Chinese reading public—mainly in Taiwan—and cherish this opportunity to connect with their readers. This accounts for their mixed feelings of familiarity, strangeness, respect, nostalgia, and even anxiety. For despite cultural and linguistic ties, there is a physical and a psychological distance between these authors and their readers in Taiwan.

Taiwan's various mechanisms of cultural production play an indispensable role in establishing literary ties. In addition to the Association of Chinese Writers around the World (in Lee's case), the literary supplements of Taiwan's newspapers provide writers with literary awards or at least space for them to gain both fame and fortune. This time-honored literary forum publishes and promotes their works both before and after they appear as books under the sponsorship of the local publishers. Thus the relationship between Taiwan's literary milieu and Chinese American writers (especially those writing and publishing in Chinese) is much closer than most Americans would expect.

Another factor strengthening the authors' Chinese connections is the subject of their writings: Chinese Americans. We can hardly imagine that their works—no matter what their origins—would gain so much critical attention if they had nothing to do with Chinese Americans. In other words, different as their works may appear to be, they all address one common theme: the Chinese diaspora. Yan's emphasis on the immigrant situation and Ya Hsuan's stress on Lee's Chinatown experience are two examples of this focus.

The question remains, however, to what extent should one emphasize this connection? While it is very difficult to offer a satisfactory answer, one thing is certain: an undue emphasis on the "sojourner mentality" of Chinese Americans will do more harm than good.[17] Even Ya Hsuan, who stresses this mentality at the beginning of his essay, points out that "one common theme of *Ch'i-p'ao ku-niang* is the attempt to show the various situations of the Chinese Americans' gradual merging into the mainstream society under the impact of external environment" (4).

This emphasis on the Chinese connection readily reminds us of Frank Chin's long introduction to *The Big Aiiieeeee!* (1991), which highlights the significance of the Asian connection to Asian American literature and advocates the establishment of a heroic tradition based on classical Chinese literature. This is in sharp contrast to the introduction to the earlier *Aiiieeeee!* (1974), published nearly two decades ago. In the first manifesto, Chin and his coeditors held firmly to what they named "the Asian American literary sensibility" and which they regarded as neither Asian nor American. King-Kok Cheung designates these two introductions as efforts first to "disconnect" and then to "connect" with the Asian/Chinese tradition under different social and historical contexts.[18]

Several things can be said about Chin's attitude toward writers with Chinese ties. Chin's recent emphasis on the Asian connection has a strategic purpose—to use rich Asian resources for the sake of identity politics.[19] This motive demonstrates that "identity" is fluid, unfixed, changeable, and ongoing, and that Chin has tried to establish the most useful contexts for his own ideas and ideals under different circumstances.

Nevertheless, it is clear that Chin's emphasis on the Asian connection is by no means a wholesale acceptance of everything Asian or Chinese. Here enter the politics and problematics of authenticity. Chin's longtime concern with the distinction between the real and the fake has almost become an obsession. He severely criticizes Jade Snow Wong, Maxine Hong Kingston, Amy Tan, David Henry Hwang, to name some "representative" Chinese American authors, for being "fake" writers who misrepresent the Chinese/Asian Americans and their cultural traditions in order to cater to the tastes of white American society. Lee and Lin, whom Ya Hsuan praises, are also among the writers criticized by Chin.[20] Despite their Chinese connections, Lee and Yan, neither of whom are American natives or—at present—write in English, are even further outside the boundaries drawn by Chin.

We may further compare Lee and Yan with the various categories of Chinese American writers mentioned by Ya Hsuan, and examine more closely their Chinese connections. The first group is made up of writers who write and publish in Chinese and whose reputations are established in the world of Chinese literature. As mentioned earlier, they received their education up to the college level in Taiwan and then went to the United States. The second group consists of those who write in English about things Chinese, such as Lin Yutang and Chiang Yi.[21] Ya Hsuan seems to blur the distinction between this second group and the third, those commonly accepted as Chinese American writers proper, such as Kingston, Tan, Shawn Wong, and Aimee E. Liu. These are American natives and write in English about things (Chinese) American.[22] As we can see, what separates the three groups of writers are language and target audience (Chinese or English speaking), content (things properly Chinese or otherwise), origin (China, Taiwan, or elsewhere), and whether they are "ABCs" (American-born Chinese) or "FOBs" (fresh off the boat)—to be more specific, whether they are American natives, naturalized Americans, or simply sojourners.

Much can be said about the problematics of language, the main concern of the LOWINUS Project. The multiethnic and multilingual situation in the United States is undeniable, but there are different and competing ways of addressing it. The American literary canon has been characterized primarily as WASP, male, heterosexual, middle-class, and East Coast. Although *MELUS* focuses on multiethnic literature in the United States,[23] it takes English for granted as the language of this literature. Paul Lauter calls for a comparative approach to the literatures of America, yet his "canon-broadening" *Reconstructing American Literature* and *The Heath*

Anthology of American Literature show that his "literatures of America" are limited to English works in the United States.[24] With respect to Asian American literature, Cheung's definition includes literature in Canada and writers such as Lin Yutang and is thus more inclusive than Chin's concepts of Asian American literary sensibility or Asian American heroic tradition. Her annotated bibliography of Asian American literature paved the way for interested scholars, though Cheung mentions somewhat apologetically the reasons that she did not include printed materials not in English (14–15).[25]

The uniqueness of the LOWINUS perspective is thus highlighted by its contrast with previous attempts to reconstruct or redefine American literature. Its major merits include exploring the possibility of multilingual American literature, putting the concept of multi-ethnicity and especially multilingualism into practice, and unearthing literatures not in English that have long existed yet been unduly neglected. Significant and unprecedented as it is, this ambitious project is not without difficulties.

First, there is the problem of the ambiguous position and function of the English language. LOWINUS, on the one hand, challenges the concept of the English language as *the* lingua franca or even *the* national language; yet in practice, the United States, with such diverse linguistic communities, must have some kind of common linguistic tool if communication is to occur at all. And this linguistic tool, at least now, must be English.[26] The publication of *The Longfellow Anthology* in a bilingual or trilingual edition (one language always being English) demonstrates that this is the case.

Second, the discussion of various groups of Chinese American writers indicates that there are various degrees of Chinese connections. Several kinds of "Chinese literature" can thus be distinguished. The first is *chung-kuo wen-hsueh* (Chinese literature proper).[27] To this only the first group of writers, such as Pai Hsien-yung, Nieh Hua-ling, Cheng Ch'ou-yu, Yang Mu, and Yu Li-hua, belong. The other two categories are *hua-wen wen-hsueh* (literature written in the Chinese language) and *hua-jen wen-hsueh* (literature written by people of Chinese descent). Authors are thus categorized respectively as *hua-wen tso-chia* (those writing in the Chinese language) and *hua-jen tso-chia* (writers of Chinese descent). However, the lines between these three groups are sometimes difficult to draw.

Moreover, from the LOWINUS perspective, these other-than-English languages are relatively strong and powerful in comparison with languages not included in the LOWINUS Project, for they must have already produced distinct literary and cultural traditions. And the subject preferably deals with the immigrants of that linguistic community in the United States. Otherwise, they are read as "foreign" rather than American literature, because both the content and the language are not commonly understood and accepted as "American."

These writers live in the United States and write in Languages of What Is Now the United States. Few would question the practice of designating works in English by these authors as American. However, the treatment of works written in Chinese about things Chinese as American literature, while perhaps irrelevant to the American audience in general, may seem totalizing and even hegemonizing to people of other countries and cultural traditions. Works that have been regarded by Chinese readers as Chinese or Overseas Chinese literature are now classified as American. The problem of how to avoid appearing too expansionist must be constantly considered. In other words, the trap of geographical determinism is something to be dealt with carefully.

The last but not the least difficulty is the question of what L. Ling-chi Wang calls "the structure of dual domination."[28] The relationship between Chinese American literature and, on the one hand, Chinese literature, and, on the other hand, other American literatures, is quite complicated. Chin's navigation of these two powerful relationships over the decades exemplifies the complications involved. The previous paragraph discusses possible domination from the American perspective. The other side of "dual domination" can be inferred from Ya Hsuan's introduction to Lee's work, which sometimes verges on Sinocentrism (although this may simply be a strategy to appeal to a larger portion of the Chinese reading public). If U.S.-centrism or Eurocentrism is to be avoided, Sinocentrism should be as well. This problem is exactly what Yan is addressing when she challenges the dichotomy of center and margin.

The above discussion of the LOWINUS Project does not detract from its significance. As mentioned earlier, the LOWINUS perspective has already opened up a new terrain of possibilities and produced many concrete achievements. In fact, without this multilingual perspective, this article would have been impossible. It discusses recent works written in Chinese—one of the "languages of what is now the United States"—in order to demonstrate the possibilities created by this perspective and the intricacies it involves. In short, the LOWINUS Project at once unsettles and redefines long-held ideas about American literature (and even Chinese literature, as in the present case) and yet has many theoretical and practical challenges to be confronted.

NOTES

I would like to thank Werner Sollors, Maria Chung, Valerie Jaffee, Lee Yu-cheng, David Der-wei Wang, and Rebecca Kiley for their comments on an earlier version of this paper.

1. A note on the transliteration of Chinese names in this paper and its implication should be given here. The two predominant transliteration systems from Mandarin into English are the Wade-Giles system (which scholars from Taiwan usually adopt) and the *Pinyin* system (which people from Mainland China adopt), and each individual may have his/her own way of transliterating his/her name. Moreover, some people prefer to keep the Chinese way of placing the surname before the given name; others follow the Western way by putting the surname after. In this paper, the name of Chin Yang Lee, already an established writer in the English-speaking world, follows his own way of transliteration (with the given name before the surname); the name of Yan Geling, who came from Shanghai, China, follows the *Pinyin* system; and all other names abide by the Wade-Giles system, with the surname before the given name. Hence, Chin Yang Lee, *Changsan Girl* (Taipei: Chiu-ke, 1996), but Yang Geling, *Fu Sang* (Taipei: Lien-ching, 1996).

This instance demonstrates the complexity within the seemingly homogeneous group known as the Chinese Americans. A case in point is Peter Feng's observation on Asian American cinema: "[T]here are maybe three or four Chinese American cultures. . . . [I]f we draw a distinction between Japanese American and Chinese American Cinema, don't we also have to make distinctions between New York and San Francisco Chinese Americans, between pre- and post-Communist China immigrants, between Mandarin and Cantonese speakers?" (p. 33 in Peter Feng, "In Search of Asian American Cinema," *Cineaste* 21, no. 1–2 (1995): 32–36). The following discussion will show how varied Chinese American literature can be.

2. The term "Chinese literary works proper" refers to literary works written by the Chinese in the Chinese language and published by Chinese publishers for the Chinese reading public.

3. Yan twice won the *Central Daily News* literary award for fiction (1991 and 1993), the *United Daily News* first prize award for short-story writing (1994), and the *China Times* critics' award for short-story writing (1994). The novel *Fu Sang* won the *United Daily News* critics' award (1995). It was serialized in the literary supplement of the *United Daily News* before appearing in book form. Her "Shao-nu Hsiao-yu" (A girl named Hsiao-yu), a short story about two lovers from Mainland China who try to become naturalized Americans, was adapted and made into a movie in Taiwan by a female director. According to *China Times* (November 7, 1997, p. 23), the American scholar Cathy Silber is now translating *Fu Sang* into English and a Hong Kong producer plans to make this novel into a film. Yan came from Mainland China, wrote her works in the United States about Chinese Americans, and published her works in Taiwan and won many awards. Her achievement in the literary scene of Taiwan is better than most of the writers living in Taiwan.

4. While much can be said about this metafictional technique, as well as the distinction/interaction between fact and fiction, history and storytelling, this is not the focus of my paper and will be mentioned only in passing.

5. The *Columbia Literary History of the United States* mistook Lee's year of birth for 1917. His first and most famous English work, *Flower Drum Song,* was made into a Broadway show and a Hollywood film and thus acquired an unexpectedly large audience for any piece of Chinese American writing in the 1950s, probably even greater than that of Jade Snow Wong's *Fifth Chinese Daughter*. In addition to the sixteen short stories, *Ch'i-p'ao ku-niang* contains an introduction by Ya Hsuan, two appendices by Lee, and a list of Lee's works (all written in English).

6. Yan mentioned *Fu Sang*, "On the Other Shore," "A Girl Named Hsiao-yu," and "Landlady" specifically (*Fu Sang*, iv), though many more of her works are on this subject. In his critical essay on Yan, K'ang Cheng-kuo calls her collection of short stories *Shao-nu Hsiao-yu* (A girl named Hsiao-yu) "hsin yi-min hsiao-shuo" ("the new immigrant story"). "On the Other Shore" was published in *Hai-na-pien* (On the other shore) (Taipei: Chiu-ke, 1995), pp. 43–69. "A Girl Named Hsiao-yu" and "Landlady" were published in *Shao-nu Hsiao-yu* (A girl named Hsiao-yu) (Taipei: Erh-ya, 1993), pp. 25–53 and 55–78. The "Yi-ken te K'uang-wei—Lun Yan Geling te Hsin Yi-min Hsiao-shuo" (The taste of uprootedness—on Yan Geling's new immigrant story) was published in the *Central Daily News* (October 15–16, 1996), p. 18.

7. As a matter of fact, the situation of Chinese immigrants, especially the new immigrants from China of whom Yan is one, is the recurring theme in her recent collections of short stories. The scope of this paper does not allow me to discuss Yan's other immigrant stories and comments on the immigrant literature. However, Yan's idea about the immigrant literature finds its fullest expression in her introduction to *Fu Sang*, which is significantly entitled "Mainstream and Margin." Moreover, her acceptance remarks on receiving the

award are also given a meaningful title, "Excavating the Sorrow and Anger of History." (These titles are translated.)

8. In her afterword to *Shao-nu Hsiao-yu*, Yan also remarks that being far away from her home country is like "the transplantation of life," which makes her "amazingly sensitive" (248).

9. The metafictional comments in *Fu Sang* explicitly express the questioning of the authenticity of history (205) and the recognition that there can be various versions of a historical event (276). And the whole narrative can be seen as Yan's effort to confront the immigrant situation of both Fu Sang and the female narrator verbally.

10. Although Yan is spatially distanced from both Mainland China and Taiwan, her anxiety over the center/margin dichotomy may prove to be superfluous, for as the winner of several important literary awards in the world of Chinese creative writing, Yan has already been a focus of critical attention.

11. *Flower Drum Song* had a Hong Kong translation that is no longer available. *Lover's Point* and *The Sawbwa and His Secretary* had Taiwan translations—the former was without the author's permission and the latter's publisher no longer exists.

12. It is interesting to note in passing that the title "P'o-ping chih-lu" (Ice-breaking journey), ostensibly a literal translation of an English idiom, was used to describe the Republic of China (on Taiwan) premier's secret visit in August 1996 to Eastern Europe under pressure of the People's Republic of China. Here, this trite English metaphor, a fashionable expression in Taiwan, in effect suggests Ya Hsuan's endeavor to break the ice between Lee and his Chinese reading public.

13. The exact English translation of *Shih-chieh Hua-wen Tso-chia Hsieh-hui* should be "the Association of the Writers in Chinese around the World." In other words, "Chinese Writers" here refers to "writers writing in Chinese," rather than "writers of Chinese descent." However, judging from the visitors invited, it is clear that the latter was the case. So far as Lee is concerned, the publication of *Ch'i-p'ao ku-niang* extends his identity from just the second to both the first and the second. According to my contact with two of the invited writers (Maxine Hong Kingston and Amy Ling), literally and metaphorically they did not speak the language of the local writers with whom they were asked to meet. It was only during the Second Conference on Chinese American Literature sponsored by the Institute of European and American Studies, Academia Sinica, that they found people who spoke English and had read their works.

14. This is one of the leading Chinese newspapers in Taiwan. Among the Chinese newspapers this media enterprise publishes internationally is the *World Journal* in North America.

15. All five writers received their education in Taiwan up to the college level and then went to the United States. They have all stayed in the United States except for Yang Mu, who returned to Taiwan in 1996 to serve as the dean of the College of Liberal Arts and Social Sciences, National Tung-hua University. Yu's novel *Yi-ke T'ien-shih te Ch'en-lun* (One fallen angel) appeared in November 1996 under the imprint of the publisher of *Ch'i-p'ao ku-niang*. As a writer of eighteen novels and short-story collections, Yu has long been considered one of the representatives of *liu-hsueh-sheng wen-hsueh* (overseas [Chinese] student literature). In this most recent novel, she relates the tragic life of a Chinese American girl who had been sexually abused by her uncle and ended up in an American jail after having killed her abuser. This is a very unusual story in Chinese American literature.

16. The nuance and complexity of this term will be explained later.

17. Historically, white Americans took this "sojourner mentality" as an excuse to expel the Chinese immigrants. One of the most notorious events in American legal history was the

enactment of the Chinese Exclusion Law in 1882, which barred a specific ethnic group. For an in-depth inquiry into the racialized foundations of the U.S. national culture from the Asian American perspective, see Lisa Lowe's "Immigration, Citizenship, Racialization: Asian American Critique," in her *Immigrant Acts: On Asian American Cultural Politics* (Durham, N.C.: Duke University Press, 1996). Recently, many people have written about the change from *luoye guigen* (returning to one's home country) to *luodi shenggen* (taking root where you are), from *hua-chiao* (overseas Chinese sojourner) to *hua-jen* (people of the Chinese descent), from *qiao* (sojourner) to *qiao* (bridge [between two cultures]). See L. Ling-chi Wang, "Roots and the Changing Identity of the Chinese in the United States," in *The Living Tree: The Changing Meaning of Being Chinese Today*, ed. Tu Wei-ming (Stanford: Stanford University Press, 1994), 185–212. Also Him Mark Lai, *Ts'ung Hua-ch'iao tao Hua-jen: Erh-shih Shih-chi Mei-kuo Hua-jen She-hui Fa-chan Shih (From Overseas Chinese to People of Chinese Descent: A History of the Development of the Chinese Americans in the Twentieth Century)* (Hong Kong: San-lien shu-tien, 1992). Also Victor Hao Li, "From Qiao to Qiao," in *The Living Tree*.

18. Frank Chin, "Come All Ye Asian American Writers of the Real and the Fake" in *The Big Aiiieeeee! An Anthology of Chinese and Japanese American Literature*, ed. Jeffery Paul Chan et al. (New York: Meridian Books, 1991), 1–92. King-Kok Cheung, "Asian and Asian American: To Connect or Disconnect?" Lecture at National Taiwan University, February 25, 1993.

19. With regard to this observation, Lee Yu-cheng rightly remarks, "The emphasis on the Asian connection in fact also provides Chin with a critical space to foreground his literary masculinism in Asian/Chinese tradition, with which he tries to deconstruct the stereotype about Asian/Chinese Americans in mainstream or white people's cultural imaginaries." Email to the author, November 27, 1996.

20. The introduction to *Aiiieeeee!* states: "C. Y. Lee and Lin Yutang, born and raised in China, are secure in their Chinese culture, and unlike Chinese Americans, are Chinese who have merely adapted to American ways and write about Chinese America as foreigners. . . . [T]heir being Chinese precludes their ability to communicate the Chinese American sensibility." Frank Chin, Jeffery Paul Chan, Lawson Fusao Inada, and Shawn Wong, eds. *Aiiieeeee! An Anthology of Asian-American Writers* (Washington, D.C.: Howard University Press, 1974), 23–24.

21. It should be pointed out that although Lin was best known in the English-speaking world as an advocate of Chinese culture, he also wrote a novel on Chinese Americans under the title *Chinatown Family*, which, to some extent, was another way of advocating for Chinese culture and representing (or misrepresenting) Chinese Americans. Lin Yutang, *Chinatown Family* (New York: J. Day, 1948).

22. By this definition, Chin and Kingston belong to the same category, in spite of Chin's desperate effort to tell the real from the fake.

23. As described in each issue of *MELUS*, "Founded in 1973, *MELUS* endeavors to expand the definition of American literature through the study and teaching of African American, Hispanic, Native American, Asian and Pacific American, and ethnically specific Euro-American literary works, their authors and their cultural contexts."

24. Paul Lauter, *Canons and Contexts* (New York: Oxford University Press, 1991), 48–96, 21. Paul Lauter, general editor, *The Heath Anthology of American Literature* (Lexington, Mass.: D. C. Heath, 1990). Paul Lauter, ed., *Reconstructing American Literature: Courses, Syllabi, Issues* (Old Westbury, NY: Feminist Press, 1983).

25. Te-hsing Shan, "An Interview with King-Kok Cheung," *Tamkang Review* 24, no. 1 (1993): 1–20.

26. Furthermore, the fact that English is an international language is undeniable, whether people around the world like it or not. Recently, the Education Reform Committee in Taiwan even suggested that elementary school students should receive formal English-language training, though junior and senior high school students have already had this kind of compulsory training for decades. Also, many high school and college students in China nowadays are eager to learn English. The dominating power of the English language is in contrast to Samuel P. Huntington's recent observation that "the proportion of the world's population speaking English is small and declining. . . . A language foreign to 92 percent of the world's population is not the world's language" (40). Samuel P. Huntington, "The West: Unique, Not Universal," *Foreign Affairs* 75, no. 6 (1996): 28–46. Also, the fact that most people around the world use the English language to communicate on the Internet demonstrates its predominance—both as a linguistic tool and as a cultural force. Small as the population of Internet users may be, its substantial influence is far greater than its size would seem to indicate.

27. In fact, this is also extremely complicated, given the fact that the Chinese literary canon is mostly characterized by the works of the male intelligentsia of the Han people at the expense of other ethnic and linguistic groups and classes, and of female writers. In comparison with American literature, much more has to be done with respect to the multilingual and multi-ethnic situation of Chinese literature.

28. L. Ling-chi Wang, "The Structure of Dual Domination: Toward a Paradigm for the Study of the Chinese Diaspora in the U.S.," *Amerasia* 21, no. 1–2 (1995): 149–69.

Chapter Nine

Ethnic Fatigue
*Başçıllar's Poetry as a Metaphor
for the Other "Other Literature"*

Gönül Pultar

> I have spoken of a voice telling me things. . . . It did not
> use the words that Moran had used when he was little.
> —Samuel Beckett, *Molloy*

Turkish Immigration to the United States and Literature Produced by Turks in the United States

Turkish immigration to the United States has a long history that is still largely untapped. Certain characteristics are nevertheless evident. During Ottoman times, it was sporadic and relatively negligible, with the percentage of "ethnic" Turks themselves among the "Turkish" immigrants being rather low. The usual pattern, moreover, was to eventually reintegrate into the homeland.[1] A society with a predominantly different culture, as well as another language and another set of mores, appeared too positioned in the ontological space of the Other for Turks to imagine forging an identity in it. On a more mundane level, lacking a *communitas* of their own, most felt déclassé in an "age of innocence" they could not penetrate. Although communication was not what it is nowadays, they still managed to maintain ties with the *heimat*, and some went back after 1923 to help build the newly formed Turkish Republic.[2] This event itself was a tremendous sociopolitical upheaval that sent members of the ancien régime abroad, and thus to the United States as well.

The immigrants who came later were not any more the polyethnic subjects of the *Sublime Porte* but the citizens of a "developing" country that later was to experience Marshall Plan aid. They came in admiration of Uncle Sam and in anticipation of striking gold and finding freedom. It is a bitter irony that Muzaffer Sherif, now known as one of the founders of American social psychology, had to leave Ankara University and Turkey during the 1940s because he was hounded there as a communist. Sherif may be categorized also as one of the precursors of the "brain drain" that has characterized recent Turkish immigration. Then, of course, Turkish-

Americans are part of those ethnic groups that benefited largely from the 1965 immigration law that stopped privileging the Europeans. Turkey, moreover, is on the "green-card lottery" that allots the so-called diversity-visa.

One dominant trait among Turkish-Americans seems to be the loss of diglossia starting with the second generation. Although the dramatic and unethical suppression of language is of course that performed by authorities, more widespread is always the one performed by mothers, those well-meaning women who wish their offspring to "succeed," and who speak English with their children, regardless of whether they themselves are in good command of it or not. That is what seems to be the trend among Turkish-American families.

Turkish has been used formally among Turkish-Americans in periodicals they publish, most of which have had short life spans.[3] Certain Turkic Americans also use Turkish for their publications, such as the Crimean Tatar Americans' *Kırım Türkleri Amerikan Birliği Yayın Organı*.[4] Whether Turkish or Turkic, such publications are mainly for communicative purposes within the community.

The discussion of Turkish-language writing, for ends other than journalism, presents at once many difficulties, largely because it is totally unknown and unrecognized. Much literary archeology still needs to be done to get a true picture of this particular genre. In earlier times, certain Turks who wrote in Turkish during their temporary stays in the United States, such as Halide Edib Adıvar (1882–1964), who lived in the United States during the 1930s, published their writings that had Turkish themes and preoccupations in Turkish in Turkey, while at the same time penning texts in English. Today poets such as Talat Sait Halman, Seyfettin Başçıllar, and Mustafa Ziyalan and authors such as İlhan Arsel and İlhan Başgöz write in Turkish on United States soil and get published in Turkey. At the same time, Halman and Ziyalan write poetry in English, and Başgöz and again Halman, as academicians affiliated with United States universities (Indiana University at Bloomington and New York University, respectively), also write and publish in English.

When they write in Turkish, these poets and authors do not interpellate the American mainstream, or multicultural America; nor do they interpellate the Turkish reader from their position as Americans. That is their most salient feature, and one that makes Turkish-language writing on United States soil problematic.

In fact, believing that in Rome one must do as Romans do, and taking for granted the superiority of English, the medium of communication of the global superpower, Turks who have migrated to the United States have usually decided that Turkish had no place in their public lives and expressed themselves in English, and their preoccupations became more American than Turkish. Such is the case of Güneli Gün, who wrote her novel *On the Road to Bagdad* (1991) in English.[5] Although it takes place in Ottoman lands during Ottoman times, within a stereotypical Orientalist framework, the novel is very much a critique of the American way of life with such features as take-out food, the pursuit of happiness through individualism, and the freedom the pursuit connotes, chased so relentlessly at the expense of all else.

Educated Turkish-Americans, who have been broken into American academic discourse, have written in English also partly because they have lost their Turkish, having been schooled out of it. Such is the case with Shirin Devrim, who wrote her autobiography, *A Turkish Tapestry: The Shakirs of Istanbul* (1994), in English.[6] It presents a notable case of double audience because she subsequently rewrote it, taking out chunks that described Turkey to Americans that would be redundant to a Turkish readership, and had it published in Turkey, rendered into Turkish by a translator, Semra Karamürsel, as *Şakir Paşa Ailesi: Harika Çılgınlar* (The Shakir Pasha family: Those marvellous madcaps, 1996).[7] Much as Devrim herself did the rearranging of the text, the mediation of the translator prevents us from considering it a work in Turkish composed on United States soil. However, it is very much a Turkish work in essence, capturing the spirit of an İstanbul that is timeless and (the Ottoman-Levantine one) gone forever at the same time; it also depicts a pre-Saddam Iraq. It falls into the tradition of American autobiographical writing: this first-generation Moslem woman immigrant, descended from the Ottoman *haute noblesse* and the step first cousin of King Faysal, Iraq's last monarch, finds her Israel in the New World, cultivating corn on her Harvard-graduate, WASP husband's Long Island farm.

Thus, writing in Turkish, the Turkish-American appears to remain Turkish; writing in English, she or he adopts the attitude of the consensual American. The putative juncture at which the two dialectical selves of Turkish-Americans meet posits the parameters of the problem. The Turkish-Americans' position within American society is itself sufficiently ambiguous. On the one hand, because they are white Caucasians, Turkish-Americans are regarded as being "too good" to be eligible for affirmative action and the like, and easily pass in many instances for the Eurocentric establishment white. On the other hand, as migrants to the culture, to the land, and to the ideology, they see themselves not perhaps at the bottom of the pit, as Günter Wallraff declares Turks are in Germany, but nevertheless as barred, in societal and existential terms, from participating or integrating: they are not versed in, nor cognizant of, a certain Western Weltanschauung, and find themselves apprehensive of a Judeo-Christian tradition they have been conditioned to perceive as inimical.

To this ambiguity is juxtaposed the further complicating issue of the Turkish sense of exceptionalism, "imagined"—whatever the historical facts may be—from 1923 onward by the founding fathers of the Republic, and drummed since, in Jacobean fashion, into every schoolchild of Kemalist Turkey. This has created a sense of belonging that far transcends blood as well as geographical location. To illustrate, what is an occasion for celebration in many ethnic groups in America, the acquisition of United States citizenship, is usually a source not of pride but of shame among Turkish-Americans, who feel the need to explain it away apologetically as due to professional obligations.[8]

This is then further complicated by the sense of "megaethnicity"[9] that pan-Turkists entertain and that is in the process of being reinvented, since the fall of the Soviet Union, through discussions centering around the concept of *turcité*. The Euro-Turks, as they have fashioned themselves in Germany and other EU states, who wish to integrate but not assimilate are accepted into the *turcité*. Whether the American Turks should also or could also be included has not been debated yet.

The ongoing fragmentation in the United States that may give way to a greater ethnic consciousness among Turkish Americans may raise such an issue in the future. *Turcité* is of import within the American context as it rejoins the Americans of various Turkic descent (Tatars, Uzbeks, Kazakhs, etc.). In effect, Alexandre Bennigsen remarks that Polish Tatars in the United States, although they may maintain a Polish identity insofar as, for instance, they will retain Polish cuisine, do not mix socially with Polish Americans but with other Tatars (Crimean, Volga).[10]

Of course, these are broadly outlined general trends, and individual cases do show variations. To illustrate the interplay of the issues I have presented above, I will discuss the Turkish-language poetry of the Turkish-American poet Seyfettin Başçıllar, a United States citizen who has been living in the United States since 1966. I will then contextualize Başçıllar's poetry within the wider spectrum of American studies. I will argue that the sense of "weariness" that is a salient feature of his poetics is a widespread syndrome, which I term "ethnic fatigue," that finds expression today in the surfacing of literatures in languages other than English.

Seyfettin Başçıllar's Turkish-Language Poetry

Seyfettin Başçıllar (1930–) was born in Kilis, in southeast Anatolia, and went to Ankara to study, graduating as a veterinarian. In fact, it is as a veterinarian that he works in the United States. He has been in meat inspection for the past thirty years, and now holds the position of Meat Poultry Circuit Supervisor for Northern New Jersey.

Başçıllar is what one may call a born poet. He wrote his first poem in elementary school, at the instigation of a teacher, for the school paper. While in high school, he won a poetry award in 1949 with his poem "Umut" (Hope). During his university years in Ankara he met other aspiring poets and authors (some of whom have since become prominent poets and authors), attended poetry "evenings," and made the acquaintance of well-known poets of the day then living in Ankara. In 1952, while still a university student, he had a poem, "Saat On Buçuk Treni" (The ten-thirty train), published for the first time. His first collection of poems, *Önce Bulut Vardı* (First there was the cloud), which he now considers to be juvenilia, came out in 1959. This was followed by *Altın Çağı Ölümün* (The golden age of death) in 1961.[11]

His subsequent collections of poems, after his move to America, comprise poems he composed while living in the United States: *Çiçek ve Silah* (Arms and the flower), published in 1969; *Sokak Şarkıları* (Songs of the street), published in 1973; *Unutulmasın* (Lest we forget) published in 1989; and *Kıyısızlık* (Landlocked), published in 1993.[12] Another collection, "Gül Sesleri" (The sounds of the rose), is awaiting publication. These books were all published in Turkey.

The back cover of *Unutulmasın* indicates that Başçıllar has been living in the United States since the 1960s, but the fact has not been explicitly publicized. Unlike the 1993 Turkish translation of Gün's *On the Road to Bagdad*, advertised with much fanfare, with Gün hailed as the Turkish woman author who wrote in English and got published in America (and then butted against a reactionary wall of silence by the critics, who did not share her concern with American issues), Başçıllar's books are not acknowledged as coming from abroad, as being written on foreign soil. So he is accepted as another Turkish poet, enjoying the succès d'estime with which most poets have to contend.

It must be said that much Turkish literature was composed outside what are now the boundaries of the present Republic of Turkey (for instance, *Manas*, said to be the longest epic in world literature, originating from what is now the post-Soviet republic of Kirghizistan). The very recent example of Turkish literature coming from Germany (not to be confused with German literature by Turkish authors such as Akif Pirinçci) itself makes Başçıllar's "American" poetry unproblematically Turkish.

Said to be influenced by the poetry of Max Jacob,[13] and written in free verse as well as in rhyme, Başçıllar's poetry exhibits a continuity in both form and content that makes it possible at first to overlook his immigration to America. The content appears almost conventional: nature, love, death, the beauty of İstanbul, the celebration of his native (Anatolian) Southeast, and the rendering of legends, such as that of "İnce Memed" (Memed my hawk),[14] the Robin Hood–like outlaw, which the novelist Yaşar Kemal also transposed in the novel of the same name. Transpiring through the verses and inextricably intertwined are such compelling themes as loneliness, exile (*sürgün*), migration (*göç*), and *hüzün*, that untranslatable word connoting sadness and melancholy, a sort of *tristessa*, which, looked at from one angle, are all traditional motifs in Turkish poetics.

Göç has always been a major theme in Turkish literature. It is more than the modus vivendi of a nomadic people, as tradition has it that the Turks have been. There is probably no Turk whose family has not been touched by *göç* in one way or another, and Turkish literature reflects it, not only in ancient epics that are "still very much alive in the oral tradition in Turkey and in the Turkic republics"[15] but also in the body of literature called *gurbetçi* (a neologism literally meaning the "migrationist") that grew out of the Gastarbeiter experience in Europe. Perhaps Nazım Hikmet best epitomized the feelings of the exile-emigré with his "Gurbetlik zor zanaat kardeşim" (Being away from one's land is no easy art, my friend).

Turks are a nation of immigrants. Turks migrated to Anatolia from Central Asia, and then to the Balkans, to the Arabian peninsula or to Africa as these were conquered, whether as settlers, as "colonial" administrators, or as exiles, deported as political "malefactors." Before long, the migration had been reversed, from Bosnia and the Peloponnese, from the islands in the Aegean, as the empire was no more and the *patria* shriveled. *Göç* also denotes internal migration, from the rural areas to urban centers, as Başçıllar himself experienced it. Thus, looked at from a purely Turkish angle, the *göç* in his poems can be shrunk in significance to the age-old migration of the Turks, and to his own migration from his native Kilis to metropolitan Ankara, and then abroad.

However, his poetry does not record his personal history. There is especially no explicit mention of Başçıllar's move to America, which must have made an even greater impact on him than his progress to Ankara, all the more since it was triggered by his realization that his leftist leanings would impede his career in

Turkey. Thus, Başçıllar's poetry is different from that of Aras Ören, writing in Germany, in his *Berlin Üçlemesi* (Berlin trilogy), immediately propelling the protagonist of the book-length poem to Naunynstrasse, Cafe Bauer, Hotel Adlon, and Bayerische Zelt, deliberately hurling the average Turkish reader into an alien universe.[16] It is also different from that of Atilla İlhan, who announces in the third person that he is departing for France with "the last passenger to board was called Atilla İlhan / . . . / he got on board carrying his typewriter," and then goes on to describe almost every single itinerary of his days in Paris, enumerating every street he crossed, every café he sat in.[17] Başçıllar, on the other hand, appears almost ashamed of his move to America, with a shame that connotes more shyness than guilt.

Instead, "all the world's a stage" Başçıllar seems to be saying, with his allusions to many countries and metropolises around the world. This is especially evident with the first "American" book, *Çiçek ve Silah*. Mentioning Casablanca along with San Francisco and İstanbul in the same poem as in "Bir Adam" (A man),[18] he blurs the tracks to obliterate the fact that the "man" writes from the United States. "Akdeniz" (The Mediterranean) transports the reader across ages, far away from the Turkish scene as well as from the American one, with the mention of the Acropolis, Athens, Naples, Rome, Carthage, Italy, France, Spain, Egypt, and Africa.[19] "Uzak Doğu" (Far East) mentions Japan and China, and contains the verse "Kırık Moğol bir gece" (A broken Mongolian night).[20] That is to say, the moment the setting is not purely Turkish, it apparently becomes cosmopolitan, and he gives the impression of wanting to arrive at a universal truth transcending time and territory. Mentioning Moses, Jesus, and Mohammed in the same poem, "Akdeniz,"[21] a trend he repeats in poems in other books, as in "Gazeller" (*Gazel*s) in *Unutulmasın*,[22] he seems to want to arrive at a synthesis of all three faiths. From that point of view, he gives the impression of a much-traveled man who has seen it all, of a sage, recalling the *aşık*, the Anatolian troubadour, or the wandering scop, so to speak.

The comparison with the scop is not idle. It must be said that, coming from "the provinces," Başçıllar is a country man, possessing a poetic language that is at once limpid, and denuded very much in the vein of Old English poetry, unencumbered by the Ottomanisms (words of Arabic or Persian origin) that more urbane contemporary Turkish poets such as İlhan or Halman cannot help utilizing. "It is a mother tongue which has at its source the poetic language of Karacaoğlan and Dadaloğlu [Anatolian folk poets of the seventeenth and nineteenth centuries, respectively]," he wrote to me, in answer to my naive question as to how he had been able to retain Turkish so (the way Yale-educated Devrim was unable to do).[23]

The poet Cemal Süreya, a friend from his Ankara days, relates that already in his early twenties, Başçıllar had been exposed to a deep poetic culture and was very much versed in Turkish poetry.[24] It is the strength of that culture, as well as the security it has provided, that has sustained Başçıllar, the mainstream inspector, as a Turkish poet, enabling him to write poetry in Turkish, within the framework of a poetics based on Turkish folk poetry. Yet he is also the mainstream man, the immigrant who was able to achieve his American Dream. "I have been successful in

my profession [as a veterinarian] and have received many awards," he also wrote
in the same letter, apparently seeing no contradiction between the two facets of his
life.

And sure enough, overlooking the medium of expression and viewing Başçıllar's
poetry as that of an American immigrant at once yields a different picture, one that
remained somewhat concealed as part of the cosmopolitan setting, amid the so
much more familiar Turkish elements.

A poem in the first book of his American period, *Çiçek ve Silah*, is entitled "Köle
Kadının Türküsü" (The ballad of the slave woman):

> Oğlum içerde kırbaçlanırken
> Çok yaşa kıralım marşı çalınır.
> Ben de aynı şeyi söylerim içten
> Çünkü başka şarkımız kalmamıştır.
>
> Kocam meydanlarda kurşunlanırken
> Armağanlar gider kraliçeye.
> Ben de yüreğimi yollarım o en
> Tatlı kinlerimle sana ey ece![25]

> While they're whipping my son in there
> The band is playing long live the king.
> I chant the same tune by myself
> As they usurped the songs that we sing.
>
> While they're shooting my husband in the square
> Gifts are being carried to the queen.
> I have a present as well for her:
> My heart, full of rancor and of spleen.

The king and queen in the poem, ostensibly leading the reader away from the
American scene, should not detract us; the slave woman's woes reflect a very
American drama. A passage in the same vein is also found in a poem in *Unutulma-
sın*, entitled "El Tropicana":

> Beyaz adam uyur
> Serin gölgelerde
> Uyur elbette,
> Bu gemiler kimin
> Beyaz adamın,
> Bu silahlar kimin
> Beyaz adamın,
> Bu asker, bu polis
> Beyaz adamın,
> Bu zincir, bu kırbaç
> Beyaz adamın.
> Beyaz adam avcı,
> Beyaz adam papaz,
> Beyaz adam tüccar,
> Beyaz adam gelmiş,
> Gitmek bilmiyor.[26]

The white man sleeps
In cool shades
He can indeed sleep,
Whose ships are these
The white man's,
Whose weapons are these
The white man's,
This soldier and this cop
The white man's,
This chain, this whip
The white man's.
The white man is a hunter,
The white man is a priest,
The white man is a tradesman,
The white man has come,
He just doesn't know how to leave.

The search for American elements thus yields many allusions in *Çiçek ve Silah* to life in America, with even the word "flower" in English,[27] to Vietnam and to the whole atmosphere of violence that is often considered typically American. *Sokak fiarkıları* contains poems with specifically American titles, such as "Niagara."[28] That book, the second American collection of poems, has three sections. The second starts with:

Hüzün köprüleri kurdum
Tuna nehri üstüne[29]

I erected bridges of sadness
Across the river Danube

The third section announces his coming to terms with his new life:

Umut köprüleri kurdum
Mississippi üstüne[30]

I erected bridges of hope
Across the Mississippi

And in the third book, *Unutulmasın*, he finds himself a new man, in "Öğret Bana" (Teach me):

Yeni dillenmiş bir çocuk gibiyim
Adımı öğret bana[31]

I am like a child who just learned to speak
Teach me my name.

He makes out the balance sheet of his life in "Elli Yaş" (Fifty years old), registering that he has a wife and kids now, and asking:

Umduklarım neydi?
Nedir bulduklarım?[32]

What did I expect?
What did I find?

It is finally in that book, in "Mektup" (Letter), that he is able to acknowledge having left Turkey.[33]

The *hüzün*, the sadness/melancholy of the transplant, is also openly acknowledged in "Zormuş" (Difficult to bear):

> Otuz yıl oldu, unuttum çoktan
> Duruşunu, saçlarını, yüzünü
> . . . .
> Anımsamak ve yeniden unutmak
> Zormuş zor ayrılmanın hüznü.[34]

> It has been thirty years, and I have long since forgotten
> Her bearing, her face, her hair
> . . . .
> To remember and then having to forget again.
> I didn't know separation would be this difficult to bear.

What "wife of youth," outgrown or left behind, has come to haunt him?

Even the title of a poem such as "Yalnızlığı Çalan Saat" (The clock that strikes loneliness) is telling.[35] In another poem, "Şehirler Anası" (City mother), he says:

> . . . içim dışım çorak
> . . . .
> Daha hızlı yaşamak . . . daha
> Unutkan . . . herkesin isteği bu
> Dolduramıyor zaman içimizdeki boşluğu.[36]

> . . . I am barren inside out
> . . . .
> Live faster . . . more
> Forgetful . . . that's all people want
> Yet time cannot fill the void in us.

In "Artık Gel" (Well now, come) in *Kıyısızlık*, the fourth and most recent book, he tells an imaginary woman that

> . . . unutuyor
> Kilis Kilisliğini
> . . . .
> İmkansız bir hüzün gibi
> . . . .
> Yalnızlığın kumaşı yırtılıyor birden[37]

> Kilis forgets its Kilisness
> . . . .
> As a sadness become impossible
> . . . .
> Loneliness is being suddenly torn apart

and then he entreats her to make him wait no longer:

Artık gel
Büyük aşkı, erişilmez olanı getir![38]

Well now, come
Bring along a love, the unattainable!

"Kilis forgets its Kilisness." The smalltown boy has learned that "you can't go home again." In fact, the poet himself realizes that deracination in the United States is complete when he finds that "the ten-thirty train," which presumably took him to his native Kilis in Anatolia, doesn't leave at ten-thirty any more ("*Artık on buçukta tren kalkmıyor*") in the poem that he entitles "Saat On Buçuk Şiiri 2" (The ten-thirty poem 2).[39] Finally, in "Saat On Buçuk Şiiri 3" (The ten-thirty poem 3), he explains that he ran after it, but could not catch it. "That train I missed never passed again":

Koştum koştum yetişemedim
Saat on buçuk trenine.
Ve hiç geçmedi o kaçan tren[40]

Başçıllar uses the conventional framework of the *göç* theme in Turkish poetics, which has become depersonalized through timeless use, and the just as traditional and worn-out theme of *hüzün*, poignant yet impersonal, to describe a personal drama. Their imbrication functions as a smokescreen obscuring the process of deracination of the first-generation immigrant that is accompanied inevitably by a regret for what he has been in the company of loved ones, defaced but not erased from memory. The transplant with awards in town and wife and kids at home, whose public success in mainstream America is a personal failure, has reached the other end of the rainbow, and found, as Ernest Hemingway would put it, "*nada y nada y nada.*" In this age, still very much one of middle-class romance, his soul is yearning for the impossible, searching for a love that is unattainable, for more than just an Annabel Lee. This is also a dream, perhaps another American Dream, that of transcending the boundaries of the American predicament. The Turkish language and the seemingly prevailing Turkish character of the poetry help to mask the very American tension.

This is not a poetry of anger, or of frustration, even if the plight of the blacks or the Indians is mentioned in some poems. Perhaps it is not in vain that Başçıllar, the mainstream inspector, was unable to write in English of what had no place in his life in English. Neither is his poetry the condemnation of the American Dream, as *The Rise of David Levinsky* may be said to be. This is the hidden side of the American Dream, the cost in spiritual terms of achieving it. It is as if the poetry were reflecting a sort of postcoital sadness.

Başçıllar's poetry is the expression of the loneliness that assails one, the nostalgia that surfaces in unguarded moments. Forced to "live fast," the transplant is too busy to prove to himself and to others that it has been worth the while. The sadness is a mere "moment," triggered in the following poem by the occasion of the New Year's Eve, entitled "Bir Yılbaşı Gecesi" (A New Year's Eve) in *Unutulmasın*:

Şarkım yanık dudakları arıyor
dinle!

Biraz Antep,
   biraz İzmir,
      biraz Erzurum,

Çal çalgıcı, bu yılbaşı gecesinde
Yurdumdan uzak ve yorgunum.

Dışarda kar mı yağıyor ne,
Nedir bu içki, bu kahır?
Ben bu kenti sevmiyorum bu gece
Benim gönlüm şimdi uzaklardadır.

Bir ev, çocukların altın saçları
Savrulur zaman salıncağında,
Ve anneler ince, ürkek, uçarı
Gençliğinin en güzel çağında.

Nereye gitti onlar şimdi nerde,
Nerde güneşi bol bahçeler?
Biz değil miydik yaşayan o günlerde?
Hepsi geçti, gelecekler de geçer.

Zaman savruluyor, içelim onu,
İçelim bir daha akmıyacak bu çeşmeden,
Bir yaprak gibi mevsim sonu
Yorgun başımız yastığa düşmeden

fiarkım eski dudakları buluyor
      dinle!
Biraz Kilis,
   biraz Ankara,
      biraz Erzurum.

Çal çalgıcı,
Çal ki bu yılbaşı gecesinde
Yurdumdan uzak ve yorgunum.[41]

My song is searching burning lips,
      listen!
A bit of Antep,
   a bit of İzmir,
      a bit of Erzurum,

Play musician, on this new year's eve
I am far away from my country and feeling weary.

Looks like it is snowing outside,
What is this drink, this ordeal?
I do not love this city tonight
My heart is now faraway.

A house, children with golden hair,
Blown away in the cradle of time

And mothers delicate, frightened, wanton
In the prime of their youth.

Where did they go now, where,
Where are the gardens abounding in the sun?
Were we not the ones living those very days?
They're all gone now, the future ones will also pass.

Time dissipates, let us drink it,
Drink from this fountain that will not flow again,
Before our weary heads fall on the pillow
As a leaf at the end of the season.

My song is finding old lips
     listen!
A bit of Kilis,
  a bit of Ankara,
    a bit of Erzurum.

Play on musician,
Play on this new year's eve
When I am faraway from my homeland and feeling weary.

What is this sense of "weariness" that emerges from the sadness, the *tristessa* of the transplant, articulated with such melancholy during a moment of *défaillance* by a persona of poetry that seems to encompass the whole of the poetry, as one big cry in the desert? What does it symbolize/signify? I suggest that this "ethnic fatigue," as I would like to term it, is a syndrome, perhaps long in the making, now surfacing more compellingly than ever, that is an apt metaphor for the other "other American literature," the non-Anglophone one. In the remainder of the essay, I attempt to contextualize the significance of "ethnic fatigue" within the field of American studies.

Ethnic Fatigue

The correlation(s) among language, literary expression, and ethnicity, even in the absence of nationhood and/or nation-statehood, or especially in the absence of nationhood and/or nation-statehood, have been much written about. What is to be noted is that this other "other literature" is being foregrounded at a historical moment that, for the time being, can best be called the post–Cold War period. The historical juncture at which it is surfacing is as important as the fact that it is.

The worldwide consensus has it that the Cold War was won by the United States and lost by the Soviet Union. The spoils were an ever-growing search inward in the United States itself. Americanists, "observers," and decision makers at all levels started to scrutinize, examine, feel the pulse of the victor, the other partner in that grandiose chess game, on the lookout for the likelihood of the existence of phenomena similar to that which had afflicted *homo sovieticus*. Indeed, the United States had not come out unscathed, making people wonder whether it was not the secret loser. The unspeakable, hidden, taboo fear and question, whether the fate of the United States would resemble that of the Soviet Union, took shape apprehensively in most minds, and could not be dismissed, although neatly "bracketed," as a perfect example of the Husserlian epoché.

And indeed, American exceptionalism has begun to be questioned; it dawned suddenly that the myth and symbol school had long been over; and that *homo americanus* was not what he or she had seemed to be. At best, he or she was Janus-faced, and it is the other physiognomy, which had been revealed already for a long period of time for anyone who wished or was forced to see it, that could not be ignored any more. On the contrary, it had been crystallized over the years, with the impressive body of scholarship and criticism that had been amassed. To give but one example, Jean Fagan Yellin dispelled any remnants of "received opinion" of *Incidents in the Life of a Slave Girl* by Harriet A. Jacobs "as a false slave narrative" or "an antislavery novel that [its original white editor L. Maria] Child had written."[42] This new aspect almost gained the upper hand, requiring a new symbology and a new mythography, relegating Plymouth Rock as well as Ellis Island to a vacuous past, and tending to privilege the experience of Richard Rodriguez over that of Cotton Mather.

It is now held to be self-evident truths that the land on which the United States was established was no *virgo intacta*; that Jefferson was himself a slaveowner; that the Declaration of Independence does not mention "nation" but "people," and that the democracy, equality, and social justice it foresaw was for the white male only; and that Crèvecoeur did not remain an "American farmer" all his life, and moreover ended his days in his native France. It has just been revealed that the French sent Lafayette to America merely as a way of weakening the British.[43] Paradoxes and ironies like these steer the definition of Americanness to a renegotiation.

It has become equally evident, because not emphatically refuted, that America is an "imperium";[44] but that it lost its "imperial" character the day it became indebted to Japan;[45] and that, thus, it may not be totally incongruous to project the fate of other empires onto that of the United States.

Mainstream intellectuals were quick to seize the occasion to both be on the vanguard and supply their mea culpa. To give an example out of many, Shelley Fisher Fishkin wrote in *Was Huck Black?*:

> This book suggests that we need to revise our understanding of the nature of the mainstream American literary tradition. The voice we have come to accept as the vernacular voice in American literature—the voice with which Twain captured our national imagination in *Huckleberry Finn*, and that empowered Hemingway, Faulkner, and countless other writers in the twentieth century—is in large measure a voice that is black.[46]

Of course, Bakhtin had already explained to us the dialogic character of voice, and students of American literature had known for long that Huck's idiom was Negro talk. What is interesting, within the context of American studies, is not what Fishkin is saying but how she is expressing it. She is not discussing "canon" or "restructuring" but the nature of mainstream literature itself, which, she simply says, was influenced by black folk. This is not exactly what W. E. B. Du Bois had in mind. It is nevertheless representative of a holistic view of American literature, very much prevalent, which takes for granted a literature of English expression, governed by a unified code derived from English literature, whatever "black" elements may transpire from its content. In this academic conundrum, "English" and "white" are synonymous, and Başçıllar's cry in the desert, reflecting an American drama, is expulsed, problematizing his "ethnic fatigue."

Fishkin reduces the societal makeup of the United States into a hue-blind, simplistic binary opposition between blackness and whiteness, which she conceptualizes unproblematically as a homogenous, monolithic construct—while at the same time denying entry to Spider Woman, Ultima, and the rest.

Even Arthur Schlesinger does better, when he uses the epithet "Anglo" in his mea culpa that "the smelting-pot . . . had, unmistakably and inescapably, an Anglocentric flavor. . . . This tradition provided the standard to which other immigrant nationalities were expected to conform, the matrix into which they would be assimilated."[47]

Against a totalizing matrix of Anglo-whiteness, non-Anglo white immigrants, such as Başçıllar, proved loyal conformists. For them to protest that they were different would have been self-immolation, a fall from the pedestal construed so zealously by the founding fathers. It would have led to self-banishment from a community they stood so much to gain by joining and had already lost so much to in the process of integration and assimilation. Yet as "whiteness" itself was being questioned, and bilingualism demanded clamorously by a Latino community that regards the English language as a Foucauldian prison, they have realized that they are "weary," atavistically weary of expressing themselves in English. Like Samuel Beckett's Moran, they are very much aware that the language of power does not "use the words that Moran had used when he was little."[48]

In a society said to be multicultural, ethnic fatigue is the manifestation of the outcome of the enforced biculturalism that so many Americans, whether white or nonwhite, whether willingly or unwillingly, experienced while adhering to Anglocentricism as the *mode d'emploi* of Americanization. For, although societies can be multicultural, individuals cannot. At best they can be cosmopolitan and polyglot. The *lebenswelt* of the Americans, when it is not monocultural, is inherently bicultural, not multicultural. It is now the "other" cultures, the *egos* that are literally *alter*, hidden for so long, refusing to remain mere palimpsests any more, that are surfacing through their literatures.

It cannot be a coincidence that, during the same period, the English (of Great Britain) have decided to appropriate American literature of English expression as part of their own culture and heritage. Penguin Books published *American Literature* (1988) as the ninth volume of its New Pelican Guide to English Literature series.[49] This occurred just when the efforts covering almost a century of so many scholars (to whom Americanists should pay the greatest tribute) had seemed at last to have given fruit irreversibly, and American literature was seen as a national literature distinct from the English one. Pelican Books, by considering and reclaiming American Literature as part of "English Literature," has clarified matters, put things in perspective. American literature of English expression is only a British postcolonial literature, albeit the most illustrious one. Literature in English in the United States is part of English literature. It cannot claim any status of unicity in America.

The atavistic "ethnic fatigue" that cannot be suppressed any longer seems poised to lead to no less than a paradigm shift, the parameters of which will have to be "imagined," "invented," for a long time to come. It may be that this will force open the still-taboo question concerning the future of the United States. Alternatively, the resultant variegation may paradoxically reinforce the commonality of American-ness, its basic core, rather than the other way around. It may, either way, lead to, and be paralleled by, a renewed interest in national identity, as opposed to culture and ethnicity, which have replaced it, gradually but firmly, since the end of World War II. Then, American literature may certainly acquire a new face, calling for reconceptualization, and relegating perhaps literature of English expression by non-Anglos to the status of sub-postcolonial literature.

And of course it will mean much uphill work. Just as Eric Sundquist found that overcoming a "fundamental conception of 'American' literature" remained diffi-cult,[50] "consent" for non-Anglophone "American" literature, that will inevitably entail the cognizance of a plethora of other literary traditions, may prove to be a bigger hurdle. While the new paradigm may not be far from signaling the end, in the long run, of the English department as traditionally conceived in the United States, its main task will have to be to address with renewed urgency the question Werner Sollors posed in *The Invention of Ethnicity*: "What is the active contribu-tion literature makes . . . ?"[51]

In this era said to be postnationalistic, Turkish-American poet Seyfettin Başçıllar's Turkish poetry, published in Turkey yet concerned with an American drama, be-trays an ethnic "fatigue" that finds no readily visible echo within the range of mainstream American literature. As such, this cry in the desert emerges as a meta-phor for non-Anglophone American writing, the intentional monoglossia that is surfacing at present. It is evident that now that the genie is out of the bottle, work to unearth more and more texts will continue. Years ago Elias Lönnrot painstak-ingly assembled the fragments that would combine into *Kalevala*, and thus virtually created Finland. It remains to be seen if the pieces of the puzzle to be gathered in the United States will fuse to create a polyphonic, polyglossic American epic, that will be both very old and very new at the same time.

NOTES

1. Talat Sait Halman, "Turks," *Harvard Encyclopedia of American Ethnic Groups,* ed. Stephan Thernstrom (Cambridge: London: Harvard University Press, The Belknap Press, 1980), p. 993.
2. Ibid.
3. Ibid., p. 995.
4. Alexandre Bennigsen, "Tatars," *Harvard Encyclopedia of American Ethnic Groups,* p. 989.

5. Güneli Gün, *On the Road to Bagdad: A Picaresque Novel of Magical Adventures, Begged, Borrowed, and Stolen from the Thousand and One Nights* (Claremont, Calif.: Hunter House, 1991).

6. Şhirin Devrim, *A Turkish Tapestry: The Shakirs of Istanbul* (London: Quartet Books, 1994).

7. Şirin Devrim, *Şakir Paşa Ailesi: Harika Çılgınlar* (İstanbul: A.D. Yayıncılık Anonim Şirketi, 1996).

8. See Halman, p. 995.

9. See Renat Taziev, Ronald Hatto, and François Zdanowicz, "La Turcophonie: naissance d'un nouveau monde?" *Dire* (Volume 5, Numéro 2, Hiver 1996), pp. 26–27.

10. Bennigsen, p. 990.

11. Seyfettin Başçıllar, *Önce Bulut Vardı* (İstanbul: Yeditepe, 1959); *Altın Çağı Ölümün* (İstanbul: Yeditepe, 1961).

12. Seyfettin Başçıllar, *Çiçek ve Silah* (İstanbul: Yeditepe, 1969); *Sokak Şarkıları* (İstanbul, Yeditepe, 1973); *Unutulmasın* (İstanbul: Cem Yayınevi, 1989); *Kıyısızlık* (İstanbul: Broy, 1993).

13. Cemal Süreya, introduction to *Unutulmasın*, p. 5.

14. *Unutulmasın*, p. 47.

15. Warren Walker, "Triple-Tiered Migration in The Book of Dede Korkut," in *The Literature of Emigration and Exile*, ed. James Whitlark and Wendell Aycock (Lubbock: Texas Tech University Press, 1992), p. 25.

16. Aras Ören, *Berlin Üçlemesi* (İstanbul: Remzi Kitabevi, 1980), pp. 15–19.

17. My translation of "son yolcunun adı attila ilhandı . . . yazı makinasıyla binmişti," from "tatyos'un kahrı" (tatyos's distress), *Sisler Bulvarı* (Boulevard of fogs) (Ankara: Dost Yayınları, 1960), p. 124.

18. *Çiçek ve Silah*, p. 12.

19. Ibid., pp. 72–74.

20. Ibid., pp. 19–20. All translations of Başçıllar's poems are mine.

21. Ibid., p. 74.

22. *Unutulmasın*, p. 147.

23. Private letter, 25 May 1996.

24. Introduction to *Unutulmasın*, p. 5.

25. *Çiçek ve Silah*, p. 7.

26. *Unutulmasın*, p. 13.

27. *Çiçek ve Silah*, pp. 68–69.

28. *Sokak Şarkıları*, p. 24.

29. Ibid., p. 25.

30. Ibid., p. 47.

31. *Unutulmasın*, p. 20.

32. Ibid., p. 38.

33. Ibid., p. 51.

34. Ibid., pp. 56–57.

35. Ibid., p. 77.

36. Ibid., p. 83, 86.

37. *Kıyısızlık*, p. 22.

38. Ibid.

39. Ibid., p. 81.

40. Ibid., p. 84.

41. *Unutulmasın*, pp. 103–104.

42. Harriet A. Jacobs, *Incidents in the Life of A Slave Girl: Written by Herself*, ed. Jean Fagan Yellin (Cambridge: Harvard University Press, 1987), pp. vii, xxv.

43. See Gilles Perrault, *La Revanche Américaine* (Paris: Fayard, 1996).

44. Edward Said, *Culture and Imperialism* (London: Vintage Books, 1993), p. 7; see also, *inter alia*, Sacvan Bercovich, "Introduction: The Music of America," *The Rites of Assent: Transformations in the Symbolic Construction of America* (New York: Routledge, 1993), pp. 1–28.

45. As maintained by Gore Vidal, quoted in *National Identities and Postamericanist Narratives*, ed. Donald E. Pease (Durham: Duke University Press, 1994), pp. 225.

46. Shelley Fisher Fishkin, *Was Huck Black?* (New York: Oxford University Press, 1993), p. 4.

47. Arthur Schlesinger, *The Disuniting of America: Reflections on a Multicultural Society* (New York: Norton, 1992), p. 28.

48. Samuel Beckett, *The Beckett Trilogy: "Molloy," "Malone Dies," "The Unnamable,"* trans. the author, with *Molloy* translated in collaboration with Patrick Bowles (London: Picador, 1976), p. 62.

49. *American Literature*, vol. 9 of *The New Pelican Guide to English Literature*, ed. Boris Ford, 9 vols. (Harmondsworth: Penguin Books, 1982–1988).

50. Eric Sundquist, *To Wake the Nations: Race in the Making of American Literature* (Cambridge: Harvard University Press, 1993), p. 7.

51. Werner Sollors, "Introduction: The Invention of Ethnicity," *The Invention of Ethnicity*, ed. Werner Sollors (New York: Oxford University Press, 1989), p. xiv.

Part III

Yekl And Hyde
Different-Language Versions of the "Same" Texts

A joke told twice in different settings may evoke remarkably different reactions. This is similar to the situation that some writers (or their editors and translators) seem to have accommodated when they offered the "same" tales in different versions. Many writers have written alternative versions of an existing story or play—for example, as comedy and as tragedy. Some authors have expressed their ambivalence about their own works by rewriting and transforming them and publishing them twice; others rewrote or permitted rewritings in order to accommodate different audience expectations—as do good tellers of jokes.[1] In the cases of some bilingual or multilingual American authors, the different versions were also written in different languages. Comparisons between the different-language versions thus open up to scrutiny the ways in which the literary coding of a work as "English" or as "Yiddish"—or as "Italian-American" or as "Chinese"—might work; the different texts also make plastic the ways in which authors (or their translators and editors) would respond to at least two communities of readers; and their doubling—in the manner of Robert Louis Stevenson's famous novella to which Abraham Cahan's choice of the (non-Yiddish) name "Yekl" (for Yiddish "Yankele") in the English version may be alluding—highlights the interactions of different cultural trajectories in single texts.

Jules Chametzky has shown pioneeringly how Cahan, in some of his stories, varied the plot lines in the English and Yiddish versions, excising the socialist editor's voice and adding a happy ending as well as more caution in matters of sexual frankness for the "American" audience.[2] In this section, Aviva Taubenfeld's " 'Only an 'L': Linguistic Borders and the Immigrant Author in Abraham Cahan's *Yekl* and *Yankel der Yankee*" extends Chametzky's approach to one of Cahan's most famous texts and compares the English and the virtually unknown Yiddish versions of Cahan's first novel. Her focus on the linguistic mediation that was needed in English but not in Yiddish, on the differing representations of dialect in his two linguistic mediums, and on the omission of profanities in the English version shows how fruitful it is to apply comparative literature models to American studies and to read different-language texts by the same authors against each other. In "The Strange Case of Luigi Donato Ventura's *Peppino*: Some Speculations on the Beginnings of Italian American Fiction," Mario Maffi confronts a similar situation in the case of Luigi Ventura's Peppino, an early "Italian-American" novella that was first published by the author in *French*, and only later in a remarkably altered, largely cleaned-up English version that was coauthored by Ventura and S. Shevitch, a Russian immigrant.

Along the same lines of inquiry, Xiao-huang Yin's "Worlds of Difference: Lin Yutang, Lao She, and the Significance of Chinese-Language Writing in America" examines tendencies of greater freedom and complexity and less concern about "American" responses that distinguish Chinese-American literature written in Chinese from works that were written in English. He contrasts Lin Yutang's cheery *My Country and My People* with his political protest writing that appeared only in Chinese, his "whitewashed" English-language opinions with his left-wing leanings in Chinese that are further suggested by his participation in China's social reform movement. Yin's essay culminates in the provocative suggestion that Lao She's *Rickshaw Boy*, which differs quite significantly between the Chinese original publication and the English translation by Evan King, may, despite popular critical assumptions, very well have been written once with a Chinese pessimistic conclusion and once with an American happy ending, with the author's consent.

It is tempting to believe that the "world of difference" that separates different-language versions of the same texts can be accounted for by finding an editor, a translator, or a powerfully seductive mentor figure who always comes from another ethnic group or a more dominant location—a Howells, a Shevitch, or a King. Yet what if it turned out, as Yin suspects in the case of Lao She, that the writer *wanted* the different versions, that the Dr. Jekyll who authored the original was also the Hyde who altered it for English-language consumption?

More comparisons of literary variants in linguistically differentiated media could offer a particularly fruitful approach to studying the differences between "English-language" and "non-English" literature of the United States, or at least to the ways in which specific authors have imagined these differences. Such studies could also continue Benedict Anderson's pioneering work by focusing on the pressures exerted upon authors by two, at times conflicting, "imagined communities."[3] The study of literary texts that were written in two languages by their authors—as were Charles Sealsfield's *Tokeah; or, The White Rose/Der Legitime und die Republikaner* (of 1833, briefly mentioned by Cagidemetrio), Abraham Cahan's *Yekl*, Luigi Ventura's *Peppino*, Lao She's *Rickshaw Boy*, and doubtlessly many other works—can throw some light on the question of the differing roles language has played in constituting "culture." The problem presented by different-language versions of the "same" text is thus fruitful in exploring the murky boundaries of language and culture, and it makes manifest and plastic the kinds of cultural interactions that may go into the production of literary texts.

NOTES

1. Compare the following example, taken from *Neither Black Nor White Yet Both: Thematic Explorations of Interracial Literature* (New York: Oxford University Press, 1997):
In 1792 J. F. Ducis adapted *Othello* for the Parisian stage and claimed in the "aver-

tissement" that, unlike the English, the French—even at the height of the Revolution, as Jan Kott has remarked—would not tolerate the violent Shakespearean ending. Ducis made the threshold for the limits of pity and fear explicitly dependent on "national character." He believed that whereas for the English it might be acceptable to see Othello push a pillow again and again on Desdemona's mouth until she suffocates, the French spectators would never tolerate this. "A tragic poet is therefore forced to conform to the character of the nation to which he presents his works." This is an "unquestionable truth" for Ducis; and in order to please his French audience, he offered the change—happily, it was quite "easily made," as he points out—of substituting a happy ending ("dénouement heureux") that seemed more appropriate to the nature and morality of the theme. However, Ducis printed both the original and his alternative conclusions, thus leaving theater directors the choice of presenting a violent or a happy ending.

2. Jules Chametzky, *From the Ghetto: The Fiction of Abraham Cahan* (Amherst: University of Massachusetts Press, 1977), 43–74.

3. Benedict Anderson, *Imagined Communities: Reflections on the Origin and Spread of Nationalism* (London: Verso, 1983; rev. ed. 1991).

Chapter Ten

"Only an 'L' "

Linguistic Borders and the Immigrant Author in Abraham Cahan's Yekl and Yankel der Yankee

Aviva Taubenfeld

"*Yankel*—Yankee: it's a difference of only an 'L,' nothing more!" quips one of the characters in the virtually unknown Yiddish version of Abraham Cahan's English novel *Yekl: A Tale of the New York Ghetto*.[1] This juxtaposition of languages and the communities they signify epitomizes the belief that the division between ethnic identities is primarily linguistic. A solitary letter separates the East European immigrant Yankel from the Yankee—the "L" of language or *loshon* in Yiddish. Yet until the immigrant successfully adopts the language of the dominant culture, direct communication between the two communities remains impossible. Any dialogue must take place through the mediation of an interpreter.

With his English novel, Cahan placed himself in this role of interpreter, crossing the linguistic border in order to depict an aspect of the immigrant community to the American population whose language and identity it was struggling to adopt. At the same time, Cahan, a Russian Jewish immigrant living on the Lower East Side, sought to establish himself as an American author by using a story from his ethnic community as his literary vehicle. To do so, he had to create multiple linguistic and narrative devices to bridge the gap between the immigrants he portrayed and the American audience he sought. Yet despite his attempts and the intercession of respected Americans on his behalf, none of the prominent literary journals of the time would accept his manuscript for publication; no one wanted to hear his immigrant character's story. In extreme frustration, Cahan crossed back into the familiar milieu of the Jewish immigrant community, publishing *Yekl* in Yiddish under the title *Yankel der Yankee* for an audience composed of insiders in the world of the protagonists and author.

Perhaps it is because the novel was eventually published in English that critics have all but forgotten the Yiddish text, assuming it to be simply a translation of *Yekl*.[2] But an examination of the two works reveals that the difference between them is more than just an "L"; *Yankel der Yankee* is not a literal rendering of Cahan's novel into his native tongue. No longer serving as an intermediary between disparate cultures when writing for Jewish immigrant readers, Cahan reconstructed his narrative and self-representation within the Yiddish text. He altered his narrative voice, refigured his relationship to his readers and characters, and freed himself from multiple constraints on language and subject matter. Within the insular space of the Yiddish paper, Cahan could respond to and liberate himself from the demands of an American audience. Reading this text alongside the better-known English novel provides poignant insight into what it meant for the Jewish immigrant to strive for acceptance as an American author.

To appreciate fully the crucial distinctions between the two texts, we must first examine the story of their genesis. This history, recorded in Cahan's memoirs and recounted in part by several critics,[3] reveals Cahan's intense desire to fashion himself into an American artist, as well as the attempts of others to mold him into a figure consistent with their expectations of an immigrant writer. Cahan undertook his first English-language novel only after receiving encouragement from novelist William Dean Howells, the self-proclaimed champion of young Realist writers. Howells first met Cahan in 1892 while researching the unionization of New York sweatshops for his utopian novel, *A Traveler from Altruria*. Three years later, after having come across Cahan's short story "A Providential Match," Howells invited the author to his home and said of his story: "It is not a serious thing. But it convinced me that you must write. It is your duty to write."[4]

Apparently uncertain about which subjects would appeal most to an American audience and what might be considered a "serious thing," Cahan presented a list of potential themes to his friend James K. Paulding, Jr., grandson of the early American Realist James Kirk Paulding and a man whom Cahan viewed as a "real American."[5] Paulding selected the story of the uneducated, working-class immigrant Jake Podkovnik, who throws off his Old World values with his given name (originally Yankel) and attempts to become a Yankee. Jake's image of himself as an American is threatened by the arrival of Gitl, the wife he had left behind in Lithuania three years before; her European clothing and Yiddish speech remind Jake of the past he has tried so hard to negate. After failing to Americanize his wife sufficiently or rapidly enough, Jake leaves her for another, more Americanized woman, Mamie Fein, only to find that he has lost both his family and his freedom.

This story ultimately became the plot of Cahan's first novel. The other potential protagonists and themes on the list he presented to Paulding remain unknown. We know only that Paulding—America's representative in Cahan's eyes—believed it was Jake's story that the immigrant author should tell his American readers, and Cahan heeded his advice.

Segments of the Jewish community, including the more Americanized German Jews along with several recently arrived Russian Jewish intellectuals, later condemned Cahan's thematic decision. As he reports in his memoirs:

> Their criticism, chiefly after the book's appearance in English, was based on the declaration that I should have chosen for my tale a more important and more likable type than Yekl—that I should have shown the Americans a prettier sample of our Quarter—an educated, interesting idealist, for example, one who sacrifices his own advantage for the common good.[6]

Like other minority intellectuals of the time,[7] these Jewish critics were tremendously concerned about the impression representations of their community would make on members of the dominant culture. As one reviewer expressed in the *American Hebrew*, the English-language weekly of the German-Jewish population:

> There are no doubt Yekls in the Ghetto; they were there a score of years ago, before anything was done to lift the denizens of New York's submerged tenth out of the slough of despond; there is however, vastly richer material there today for the novelist than our author has chosen, material that would give the Gentile reader a better opinion of the Russian Jew, and at the same time make a more readable novel.[8]

What the "Gentile reader" would think of the Jew was of utmost concern to the German Jewish community, which wished to be perceived as the enlightened Jews who lifted their poor, East European brethren "out of the slough of despond." They considered Cahan's exposition of the underside of the Ghetto as "an offense only slightly less heinous than treason."[9] Addressing the same issue of "racial betrayal" from a middle-class American perspective, novelist and critic Nancy Huston Banks asks in her review of *Yekl* for *The Bookman*:

> Does Mr. Cahan wish us to believe that the types and phases of the life of the Ghetto thus presented by him are truly representative of his race? That it is as sordid, as selfish, as mean, as cruel, as degraded as he has here shown it to be? . . . If, then, these likenesses and these views are reproduced from life, was it wise to develop the pictures?[10]

Banks confirms the fears of the Jewish critics by adding that Cahan's narrative provides "frank revelations of racial weaknesses."[11]

In the face of such criticism, Cahan defended his thematic choice to his community. "I did not write the novel with the goal of advertising our Jewish population," he states bluntly in his autobiography.

> The question in belle letters is not what kind of people the author presents, but how he presents them and whether they have a natural relation to the artistic plan of his work. I am sure that my theme touches on a situation that mirrors our immigrant life in a characteristic manner and that this has much more meaning than advertising the Jewish people.[12]

Cahan's primary concerns were the realism, artistry, and thematic probing of his novel. He sought to depict the average immigrant, not the educated elite, and he wished to be evaluated by the artistic merit and truth of his representation, not as an advocate of his "race."

But in order to be judged as a Realist artist, Cahan first had to win a hearing for his work. Once he had selected the subject of the novel and completed the manuscript, Cahan again solicited the aid of "real Americans." He immediately brought his work to Paulding and then Howells for their approval and suggestions. While he praised the novel profusely, Howells strongly opposed the story's working title, *Yankel the Yankee*, telling Cahan, "That's all right for vaudeville, but not for a story like yours."[13] Howells felt that the title sounded too artificial and undignified, and that it might keep publishers from taking the work seriously. His comment led to a change in the title as well as in the corresponding Yiddish name of the protagonist from Yankel to Yekl. "Yekl" is not an actual Yiddish name, and it has been suggested that Howells chose this appellation for the character who attempts to alter his identity because of its similarity in sound to that of the most famous literary dual personality, Dr. Jekyll.[14] Whatever the reason for his choice, what is most significant is that a non-Yiddish-speaking American was the one to provide the name for the immigrant protagonist and the title for the immigrant author's text. Howells imposed his standards upon the Old World identity of the character along with the American experience of the novelist. He also added the subtitle "A Tale of the New York Ghetto," in an attempt to lure readers with the promise of a local-color novel.[15] Possibly believing that a "true American" was needed to mediate further between the immigrant author and the American public, Howells insisted on bringing *Yekl* to potential publishers himself. He took complete control over the destiny of Cahan's manuscript.

Yet despite Howells's influence, none of the editors of the prestigious journals of the time would agree to publish the novel. Their responses explicitly reveal the prevailing attitudes toward Realist literature, Jewish immigrants, and the intersection of the two.[16] In his autobiography, Cahan reports that the editor of *Harper's Weekly* returned the manuscript with a note saying "the life of an East Side Jew wouldn't interest the American reader."[17] The editor of another journal wrote to Howells: "You know, dear Mr. Howells, that our readers want to have a novel about richly dressed cavaliers and ladies, about love which develops in the fields while they are playing golf. How can a novel about a Jewish immigrant, a blacksmith who became a tailor here and whose ignorant wife becomes repulsive to him possibly interest them?"[18]

When Cahan went to retrieve his manuscript from *McClure's*, Associate Editor John S. Phillips remarked: "You describe only Jews. Someone reading your novel is likely to think that there are no other people but Jews in America."[19] Phillips believed that American novels must depict "Americans," not Jews, excluding Jews from this national identity. While he acknowledged Cahan's talent, the editor encouraged him to use it for the creation of "Art." "Art should concern itself with beautiful things," he expounded. "A dancing school on the poor East Side, ignorant people, a man who isn't true to his wife. What do these have to do with Art?" A lengthy debate over aesthetics and Russian Realism ensued. Near its conclusion Cahan argued, "Do you believe then that a flower is more beautiful than the beautiful soul of a peasant?" to which Phillips replied: "Does your Yekl have a beautiful soul?"[20] It seemed impossible for the immigrant author writing realistically about the bleaker aspects of his community to present his work to the American public.

Although frustrated by these rejections and what he considered the "primitive" views of American critics,[21] Cahan refused to compromise his concept of literature and its role in depicting characteristic aspects of the ethnic community. Instead of rewriting his novel along the lines suggested by the American journal editors, Cahan decided to translate his work into Yiddish and to publish it in serialized form in the *Arbeiter Tseitung*, the socialist newspaper of the Jewish labor union, where it ran in sixteen weekly installments from October 18, 1895, through January 31, 1896. The Yiddish text is thus a product of Cahan's frustrations and despair at ever being able to tell his story to members of the dominant culture. As he recalls in his memoirs: "My main reason [for translating the text] was my impatience to see it published—if not in the original, at least in translation. . . . I also became interested in seeing what kind of impression the novel would make on our Jews—on the same human world that it depicts."[22] Cahan was clearly aware of the shift in his position when writing for an immigrant audience. No longer a mediator between two cultures, with his Yiddish publication Cahan brought Jake's story home, back to the world from which it had sprung.

When writing for a Yiddish-speaking audience, Cahan released himself and his work from Howells's influence. Most significantly, he retained the original title *Yankel der Yankee* and the Yiddish name "Yankel" for his protagonist. "I knew that Howells was right in contending that the title sounded like a device," Cahan acknowledged. But "for our readers it was a well chosen title, or so I thought, and my heart would not allow me to do away with it."[23] While seeming to imply that a title "too vaudeville" for Americans was appropriate for the less sophisticated Yiddish reader, Cahan's comment also reveals his greater comfort writing for the Yiddish-speaking community. Within the confines of its language and newspaper, he could follow his heart, write as he pleased, and trust his own insights into his audience's taste, rather than feeling compelled to conform to the advice of a Howells or Paulding.

And yet, Cahan did not publish the Yiddish text under his own name; instead he used the pseudonym "Socius," one of several he wrote under for the *Arbeiter Tseitung*. Although many of his Yiddish readers may not have known that the Latin word "socius" means comrade, they certainly would have recognized the similarity between this term and "socialist." Cahan's pen name thus provides a guide for readers of the *Arbeiter Tseitung* to interpret his work within a socialist framework. It also declares comradeship between the author and his working-class, immigrant audience.

At the same time, the use of the pseudonym also reflects Cahan's ambivalence about identifying himself as a Yiddish novelist. Until the middle of the nineteenth century, Yiddish had functioned primarily as the spoken vernacular of East European Jewry and the vehicle of popular religious education, particularly for women and other "simple folk."[24] It lacked cultural prestige, especially among newly Westernized Jewish intellectuals. Only with the increase in urbanization, industrialization, and secularization did Yiddish become for some the language in which to express Jewish nationalism and secular ideologies. It was then that secular Yiddish literature was born.[25] Even so, many, if not most, Jewish intellectuals in the late nineteenth century still did not take Yiddish seriously. They referred to it contemptuously as the "zhargon," or jargon, holding it beneath European literary languages.[26] Although historian John Higham identifies Cahan as the individual who did more than anyone to encourage the creation of secular Yiddish literature and culture in the United States,[27] Cahan himself wrote that at the turn of the century, the term "Yiddish Literature" was something of a joke.[28] While he published "serious articles" in the Yiddish press under his own name, he wrote his Yiddish feuilletons and fiction in the *Arbeiter Tseitung* under the pseudonym "Socius,"[29] refusing to identify himself openly as a "jargon" author.

Ultimately, however, Cahan did claim his Yiddish novel *Yankel*. He revealed himself as its author immediately after the English edition of the work was finally accepted for publication. In the eighth installment of *Yankel der Yankee* (December 6, 1895) under the byline Socius stand the English words: "Copyright, 1895, By Abraham Cahan," and the pseudonym never appears again in any of the subsequent installments of the Yiddish novel. In striking English letters, Cahan demonstrates his preferred identity as an American author on the Yiddish page. He gives status to his Yiddish novel and to himself as a writer through his English work, declaring himself Abraham Cahan, American author. This remarkable statement reveals the complexity of Cahan as a Jewish-American writer. The original rejection of his English novel impelled him to write a bolder, less constrained Yiddish version of the same. But it was the ultimate publication of the English text that gave him a sense of pride and legitimacy as an author.

Within the texts themselves, we find that authorship for Cahan is an American identity. He represents himself and the activity of writing very differently in his Yiddish and English novels. *Yekl* opens with a third-person omniscient narrator describing a sweatshop and its inhabitants: "The operatives of the cloak shop in which Jake was employed had been idle all morning. It was after twelve o'clock and the 'boss' had not yet returned from Broadway, whither he had betaken himself two or three hours before in quest of work."[30] Thus begins Cahan's English novel. In contrast to its formal narrative voice, *Yankel* opens with the following:

> I knew him. I met him a few times when his troubles were greatest. I know his story with all its details. But I will tell it only in short, simply tell it. Sketch it, paint it, perform it—that I will not even attempt. I will be very satisfied if I succeed in just telling it to you as if we were talking at a table.[31]

Never in the English version of the text does the narrator identify the protagonist as a personal acquaintance. He does not wish to associate himself so closely with his narrative world. But he also cannot project himself directly into the homes of his audience; the immigrant writer could never have presumed to share a table with his American readers. Two characters present in the Yiddish novel do not appear at all in the English work: the "I" of the first-person narrator and the "you" of "the reader." "I" and "the reader" can share the Yiddish text with the protagonists because all inhabit the same cultural and linguistic space. Despite differences in class and education, they can meet within the medium created by and for them— the Yiddish newspaper.

Yet at the same time that he expresses comfort and familiarity with his audience and characters in *Yankel*, Cahan effaces the artistic construction of this Yiddish narrative. Clearly, the Yiddish novel is just as artistically contrived as the English. Although the first-person narrator of *Yankel* claims simply to transcribe the story told to him by Jake, the narrator's actual omniscience belies this claim. Not only does he know Jake's version of his story, but he can relate conversations among characters that Jake never heard, and he has insight into the unspoken thoughts and emotions of all of the characters. Nevertheless, Cahan chooses to (mis)represent himself in the Yiddish text as merely a conduit between Jake and the readers.

The difference in Cahan's view of his authorship and art in the two texts is further illustrated by the virtual erasure of the author figure from the Yiddish novel. The English work includes an unnamed character who writes and reads Jake's letters. We are told in *Yekl* that "neither Jake nor his wife nor his parents could write even Yiddish, although both he and his father read fluently the punctuated Hebrew of the Old Testament or the Prayer Book. Their correspondence had therefore to be carried on by proxy."[32] The inability of the Podkovnik family to communicate directly is symptomatic of their illiteracy and also of the cultural and psychological chasm between the Old and New Worlds. Their proxies not only pen their letters; they decide what should be communicated. "What else shall I write?" the letter writer asks Jake. "How do *I* know?" Jake responds. "It is you who can write; so you ought to understand what else to write."[33] The proxy is not merely a scribe but an author whose duty it is to describe the lives of particular immigrants to their families back home who are both physically and culturally alienated from their Americanizing relations.

The letter writer's vocation mirrors that of Cahan in the English text. In *Yekl*, the author serves as Jake's proxy, writing his story for readers outside the protagonist's linguistic and cultural community with whom the immigrant cannot communicate on his own. But both Cahan and the letter writers have additional, personal agendas. They earn money from their work, but even more important, they see their writing as a means of achieving some degree of personal recognition. Cahan tells us that the proxy who wrote the letter from Jake's family informing him of his father's death was "ambitious to impress the New World" with his scholarship and language.[34] He, like Cahan, is anxious to prove his talents to an American (albeit, in his case, immigrant) audience.

No such ambitious proxy is required for Jake's story to be told within his own community. In *Yankel*, Cahan describes the letter writer in only two lines. The narrator of this text tells us merely:

> In a few weeks, he [Jake] received a letter saying that his father had died. After the letter was read to him, the past suddenly came to him in such bright colors as he had not recently experienced. . . . With a sad heart, he went from the cigarette and newspaper *stand* of the little Jew who read and wrote his letters.[35]

The reduction of the author figure to a mere mention and the complete omission of the description of his writing process from the Yiddish text can be read as a statement of the difference in Cahan's perception of himself in the two editions of the novel. In *Yankel*, Cahan chooses to represent himself as the "I" of the narrator but not as an author. He omits the character of the letter writer and repudiates the artistry of the novel, claiming for it instead the status of a simple storytelling—a retelling of the real-life tale related to him by his acquaintance Jake Podkovnik. In the English version of the text, Cahan never uses the intimate first person but represents himself instead through the figure of the letter writer and the presence of a third-person narrator with an authorial voice distinct from that of his characters. Cahan perceives himself as the teller of the Yiddish story, but as the author of the English novel.

The act of interpretation is integral to Cahan's conceptualization of authorship. He sees himself as artist and author in the English text partly because he must devise multiple strategies for communicating across the dividing line between the worlds of his characters and his audience. As proxy for the immigrant community, he had to create a language through which his characters could communicate with an American audience. As Jules Chametzky asserts, Cahan's experiments with language and voice in all of his English works reflect his attempt to convey the Jewish immigrant's experiences to an American audience.[36] In *Yekl*, Cahan represents his characters' speech by creating a fictionalized written dialect.

The language spoken on the Lower East Side was a distinctly American Yiddish. In the fourth edition of his *American Language*, H. L. Mencken reports Cahan as saying:

> The Americanisms absorbed by the Yiddish of this country have come to stay. To hear one say "Ich hob a billet für heitige vorstellung" [I have a ticket for today's show] would be as jarring to the average East Side woman, no matter how illiterate and ignorant she might be, as the intrusion of a bit of Chinese in her daily speech.[37]

Jews in English-speaking countries did not use such Germanicized, European Yiddish. Instead, they would be more likely to say: "*Ich vel scrobbin dem floor, klinen die vindes, un polishen dem stov,*" Cahan once described jokingly.[38] To represent this Americanized immigrant Yiddish speech to his American audience in *Yekl*, Cahan very deliberately devises a unique linguistic code in which to write his novel.

He first translates the Yiddish idiom into English. "I represented in English words the way that such a Yekl, for example, speaks, and I transmitted characteristic Yiddish phrases, such as 'the black year should know him' in a literal English translation," he relates in his memoirs.[39] Cahan also incorporates twenty transliterated Yiddish words into his narrative; he defines these words in footnotes below the text so as not to disrupt the story with excessive explanatory material. These Yiddish words are employed primarily when there are no English equivalents, such as for "*cheder*" (defined in a footnote as "a school where Jewish children are instructed in the Old Testament or the Talmud").[40] Transliterated Yiddish is also used to relate puns and wordplays popular on the Lower East Side. For instance, the reversal of fortunes experienced by many immigrants in the New World is represented with the linguistic exchange: America is the land in which "a shister [shoemaker] becomes a mister and a mister a shister."[41] Although clearly indicating the potential for both achievement and failure in America, this rhyme represents success linguistically as an American experience. English is the language of the "mister"; Yiddish delineates the impoverished Jew, the "*shister*." At the same time that it speaks of economic possibilities, this phrase also reflects upon the status of the languages it employs, with Yiddish represented as the poor ethnic jargon—the shoemaker's language. The speech of only the most un-Americanized characters contains transliterated Yiddish words, serving to highlight the foreignness of these individuals. Jake's newly arrived wife, Gitl, for example, describes her Americanized husband as a *"poritz"* ("Yiddish for nobleman," as the footnote tells us);[42] she can conceptualize his transformation only in Old World economic and linguistic terms.

In addition to his translation of the characters' Yiddish and transliteration of key Yiddish phrases, Cahan also represents his protagonists' significant insertion of English words into their Yiddish speech. Cahan renders these words typographically. "English words incorporated in the Yiddish of the characters of this narrative are given in italics," he tells his audience in a footnote following Jake's first speech.[43] These words are written as Cahan believes they are pronounced by the residents of the ghetto. "Of course" becomes " *'f caush,"* and "furniture" becomes *"foinitsha"* in the mouths of Cahan's characters. The author also seeks to distinguish the characters' regional accents and individual peculiarities of speech, thereby emphasizing the diverse and multinational nature of the Jewish ghetto. While the Lithuanian-born Jake says, "Vot'sh a madder," his Galician letter writer says, *"Vot's der madder."*[44] Similarly, Gitl responds, "I am *salesfiet,"* when her neighbor Mrs. Kavarsky instructs her to "say that you are *saresfied."*[45]

While enabling immigrant characters to communicate with their American audience, these three linguistic devices—the translation of Yiddish into English, the transliteration of Yiddish words, and the typographical representation of the English incorporated into the characters' speech—underscore the distance between the two language communities that the immigrant author must traverse in attempting to portray one to the other realistically. These devices also highlight the artistry of the language of the text. The English novel provides a graphic representation of spoken language. It is precisely the sketch, painting, and performance of language that Cahan tells his Yiddish readers he will avoid in *Yankel.*

Told to the same community from which it emerged, *Yankel's* story can be communicated more directly to its readers. Unlike the English work, it requires no invention of language, no "author"—only a narrator to relate the tale. Translation and italicization are not required to represent the way in which the characters converse in *Yankel.* The characters' speech is written in their native Yiddish, and the English words they insert into their language are given in English in the midst of the Yiddish text. Cahan renders these words in Hebrew characters. Thus Yiddish readers find "Dot'sh a' kin a man I am," "never mine," "ekshkuzsh me, Mrs.," "a hell of a lot," and many other English words written in the letters of their mother tongue just as they had been inserted into the immigrant characters' and readers' daily speech.

Through his insistent use of dialect in both his English and Yiddish texts, Cahan depicts the immigrants' attempt to assert their American identity through language. The discourse strategy of using more than one language in a single communicative episode, known to linguists as "code switching," has proven a common and significant element of immigrant speech.[46] The amount of English immigrants insert into their speech reflects the extent of their acculturation. Reflecting his first stop in the New World as well as his desire to prove himself something of a Yankee, Jake speaks "Boston Yiddish"—a Yiddish, which Cahan explains to American readers,

"more copiously spiced with mutilated English than is the language of the metropolitan Ghetto."[47] With the very first words he utters in the English novel, Jake
seeks to distinguish himself from his coworkers in the sweatshop on the basis of his
self-proclaimed Americanization:

> When I was in Boston, I knew a *feller*, so he was a *preticly* friend of John Shullivan's.
> He is a Christian, that feller is, and yet the two of us lived like brothers. . . . How,
> then would you have it? Like here, in New York, where the Jews are a *lot* of *green-
> hornsh* and can not speak a word of English? Over there every Jew speaks English
> like a stream.[48]

Seeking to separate himself from the "greenhornsh" of New York, Jake colors his
discussions in both editions of the novel with expressions such as "Oh, didn't he
knock him out off shight!" and responds to challenges to his new identity with
"Dat'sh a' kin' a man I am!" However, his need constantly to declare his Americanness through language reveals Jake's underlying anxiety that he has failed to rein-
vent his national identity.

The arrival of Gitl three years after his own emigration poses a tremendous
threat to Jake's American self. He is embarrassed and repulsed by Gitl's Old World
clothing and the wig she wears, which characterizes her as a pious married Jewess.
Being identified as the husband of such a woman transforms Jake back into the Old
World Jew he is trying to negate. To reassert his own American identity, Jake
believes that he must either remake or reject his wife. At first he buys Gitl new
clothing and demands that she replace her wig with a high-crowned hat. He insists
that she learn English words so that through language she can prove both herself,
and by extension her husband, American. On the trip home from Ellis Island, Jake
immediately begins instructing Gitl in the "five or six score English words and
phrases which the omnivorous Jewish jargon has absorbed in the Ghettos of English-speaking countries."[49] To her question "Where do you eat your *varimess*?" he
responds, "Don't say varimess. . . . [H]ere it is called dinner."[50] But Gitl resists using
language in the way that Jake demands. "*Dinner*? And what if one becomes fatter?"
she retorts, punning on the Yiddish word for thinner.[51] Gitl jokingly turns English
into Yiddish, resisting the American identity implied by English use and forced
upon her by her husband. Thus when Jake's Americanized dancing-school partner,
Mamie Fein, invades the Podkovnik home speaking only English, Jake feels compelled to take complete control of Gitl's speech. "Say 'I'm glyad to meech you.'"
"Shay 't'ank, you ma'am!'" "Say 'cull again!'" he commands, using Gitl and her
language as props in the performance of his own American identity.[52]

The characters' use of English in *Yekl* received much criticism. While some
praised the dialect, many critics found it highly offensive. A reviewer for the *Commercial Advertiser* complained:

> The worst blow has fallen. A Yiddish dialect story is out. Readers who have tried to
> keep up with the development of this sort of literature still remember what delight
> they felt in the rollicking humor of Irish and German dialect. The splendor of wild
> west colloquial exaggeration aroused admiration. The new negro dialect . . . puzzled

us a little, but was not without certain compensations for its intricacies. Then came the Swedish, the mountaineer and a few other dialects of romance. . . . We even tried to enjoy the Bowery slang dialect. . . . Now comes a story in the most hideous jargon and we are asked to give it a place in literature because it represents still another dialect alleged to be spoken on the east side. . . . It tells us that the Russian-Polish-Lithuanian-Bessarabian Jews that swarm and seethe in Suffolk and Hester streets have adopted a set of catch phrases from American talk, mostly slang, which they mispronounce most vilely and repeat like parrots in season and out of season.[53]

While expressing disgust with Jewish jargon in particular, the hostility of the reviewer's statement seems to betray larger anxieties about American culture. For this critic, the division of English into multiple dialects seems to portend a fracturing or radical and terrifying mutation of American language and society. Howells expresses similar concerns in his review of *Yekl* entitled "New York Low Life in Fiction." "What will be the final language spoken by the New Yorker?" he asks:

We shall always write and print a sort of literary English, I suppose, but with the mixture of races the spoken tongue may be a thing composite and strange beyond our present knowledge. Mr. Abraham Cahan, in his "Yekl, A Story [sic] of the New York Ghetto" (Appleton's), is full of indirect suggestions upon this point. Perhaps we shall have a New York jargon which shall be to English what the native Yiddish of his characters is to Hebrew, and it will be interlarded with Russian, Polish, and German words, as their present jargon is with English vocables and with American slang.[54]

Like the writer for the *Commercial Advertiser*, Howells seems threatened, though intrigued, by the language of Cahan's characters. While he takes comfort in the notion of a "pure" and idealized written language, he fears that the "mixture of races" in New York will make spoken English "strange" to native speakers and transform the American city into an unfamiliar, foreign metropolis.

Later critics have also been troubled by the use of dialect in *Yekl*. Irving Howe remarks that it is a "promising work that suffered from too close a rendering of immigrant dialect into English."[55] Others find it uncomfortably close to anti-Semitic portrayals of Jews in English fiction.[56]

But while they raise important and telling objections to Cahan's construction of his immigrant characters, many of these critics ignore the second voice in the English text—the language of the story's third-person narrator. Seeking to mediate further between his subject and his audience and to guide his readers through the world of the Lower East Side, Cahan creates a "superior narrator," one who provides inside information about Jewish immigrant culture.[57] This narrator describes the ghetto, the sweatshop, and the dancing school in great detail for his American audience.

The role of the narrator in *Yekl* is perhaps best demonstrated in Cahan's famous depiction of the Suffolk Street ghetto:

Suffolk Street is in the very thick of the battle for breath. For it lies in the heart of that part of the East Side which has within the last two or three decades become the Ghetto of the American metropolis, and, indeed, the metropolis of the Ghettos of the world. . . . You find there Jews born to plenty, whom the new conditions have deliv-

ered up to the clutches of penury; Jews reared in the straits of need, who have here
risen to prosperity . . . —in fine, people with all sorts of antecedents, tastes, habits,
inclinations, and speaking all sorts of subdialects of the same jargon, thrown pellmell
into one social caldron—a human hodgepodge with its component parts changed but
not yet fused into one homogenous whole.[58]

As the narrator explains to his readers, the Jewish immigrants are coalescing not in
what Israel Zangwill called the "melting pot" of American society but in the
separate cauldron of the ghetto. Just as their language is transforming into American Yiddish, not English, for now, at least, they are becoming American Jews, not
Americans.[59] As such, even with the translation and representation of the immigrants' speech in this novel, they are judged incapable of expressing the entirety of
their experience to Anglo-American readers because of the cultural and class differences implied by their origins and dialect. Cahan feels that a "superior narrator" is
needed to explain immigrant society and culture to an American audience in its
own language. And his narrator therefore speaks what may be described as osten-
tatiously correct standard English.

Yet while attempting to articulate further the experience of the immigrant, the
language of the narrator in *Yekl* exists in extreme tension with the speech of the
characters. In depicting Jake's posture of cool superiority upon entering the dance
academy that he frequents before the arrival of his wife, the narrator remarks with
perhaps intentionally humorous stilted diction: "Jake was the center of a growing
bevy of both sexes. He refused to unbend and to enter into their facetious mood,
and his morose air became the topic of their persiflage."[60] Within moments, Jake
joins the crowd and shouts, "Alla right! . . . Gentsh, getch you partnesh, hawrry
up!"[61] The sound of what Cahan calls Jake's "mutilated English" clashes with the
high tone of the narrator.[62] Similarly, when Mrs. Kavarsky cuts Gitl's hair in a final
attempt to make the young wife pleasing to her husband, the narrator reports,
"Gitl's unwonted appearance impressed Jake as something unseemly and meretri-
cious."[63] Framing this sentence on either side are Mrs. Kavarsky's *"Goot-evenik,*
Mr. Podkovnik" and Jake's declaration "It becomes her like a-a-a wet cat!" The
narrator's genteel gloss seems to mock the language of his characters. Their vastly
different capacities for expression in English are most clearly demonstrated in the
love scene between Mamie and Jake on the rooftop of her tenement building. Using
rather florid language, the narrator describes the setting:

> When they reached the top of the house, they found it overhung with rows of half-
> dried linen, held together with wooden clothespins and trembling to the fresh autumn
> breeze. Overhead, fleecy clouds were floating across a starry blue sky, now concealing
> and now exposing to view a pallid crescent of new moon. . . . A lurid, exceedingly
> uncanny sort of idyl it was.[64]

The disparity between the language of this description and the words spoken in this
scene is striking. "Mamie, come shomeversh! I got to shpeak to you a lot," Jake
demands. *"Vot's de madder*, Jake? Speak out!" she responds.[65] Chametzky writes
that this love scene poignantly illustrates the immigrants' struggle to express themselves in a "new, imperfectly assimilated language . . . [that] could not in the mouths

and hearts of these immigrants achieve mature felicity."⁶⁶ At the same time, however, this scene also reveals the immigrant author's desire to prove that, unlike his
characters, he has achieved complete and refined expression in his adopted language.

This conflict in voice throughout the novel seems to disclose Cahan's deliberate
attempt to distance himself linguistically from the characters he portrays and the
world with which his audience would have most certainly identified him. The
language of Cahan's narrator in *Yekl* removes him from the confines of the Lower
East Side even as it implies intimate knowledge of the life within. Although Cahan
was a crucial part of this community, his narrative voice places him outside the
"human hodgepodge," its jargon, and its destiny. The narrator speaks much more
like his imagined audience than like his immigrant characters. His voice allies with
the unmarked and linguistically unaccented world of his English readers. Against
the tale of Yekl's failed Americanization, Cahan strives to narrate his own transformation into an American, and in particular, an American author. He resists identification solely as a writer of dialect literature, claiming a more mainstream, dominant American voice and identity even as he represents the immigrants and their
speech in his work.

But this deliberate demonstration of American artistic identity appears fraught
with anxiety, much like Jake's attempts to prove himself a Yankee. In the English
version of the novel, Cahan explicitly describes Jake's speech and gestures in terms
of performance. He refers to Jake's exhibitions of his knowledge of boxing as "the
performances of his brawny arms and magnificent form," his initial aloofness in the
dance academy as "an affected expression of *ennui*," and says of Jake's exuberant
American waltz, "throughout the performance his face and his whole figure seemed
to be exclaiming 'Dot'sh a kin' a man *I* am!' "⁶⁷ Particularly in the opening of *Yekl*,
Cahan refers to Jake's spectators as an audience. The presser and three women in
the sweatshop "formed an attentive audience to an impromptu lecture upon the
comparative merits of Boston and New York by Jake," and the "feminine portion
of Jake's audience" finds him particularly attractive.⁶⁸ Yet Jake remains consistently
insecure about his ability to enact his American identity successfully before the
members of his audience whom he considers more Americanized or more educated
than himself. In one instance, when his respected coworker Mr. Bernstein mocks
Jake's emulation of uneducated American athletes, the narrator tells us that Jake
feels "anxious to vindicate his tastes in the judgment of his scholarly shopmate and
in his own."⁶⁹

A comparison of these moments in *Yekl* and *Yankel* allows us to draw an
analogy, which would otherwise be impossible to make, between the anxiety experienced by the protagonist and that of the immigrant author writing for an American audience. None of the passages cited above appears in the Yiddish text. While
Jake clearly seeks to demonstrate his Americanness in *Yankel der Yankee*, the words
"performance," "flaunting," "affectation," and "audience," which pervade the English novel, are virtually absent from the Yiddish. As an advocate of assimilation,
Cahan may not have wanted to upset his Yiddish readers by emphasizing the
affectation and crude performances involved in what Cahan believed was their

crucial use of English and adoption of American manners. But while this theory may account for the absence of references to affectation and audience in the Yiddish work, it does not explain the presence of these words throughout the English novel. Their frequent mention in the English text seems to reveal the author's, or at least the narrator's, greater self-consciousness regarding his own performance and audience when speaking to American readers.

Anxiety of this sort does not exist at all in the Yiddish text. The narrator in *Yankel* does not seek to distinguish himself from the world he describes as he does in *Yekl.* The languages of the narrator and characters are much more alike in the Yiddish version of the novel than in the English. Cahan does not elevate the Yiddish of the narrator above that of the characters; he does not limit the use of American Yiddish in this work to the speech of the characters. Even the narrator uses a tremendous number of English words in *Yankel der Yankee.* "Boarder," "tenement," "greenhorn," "bedroom," "floor," "pants," "shop," "strike," "saloon," "supper," "corset," "price," "rocking chair," "side bangs," "respect," parlor," "fellow," "single man," and at least forty others are all part of the narrative. Often when Cahan borrows these English words, he adapts them to the grammar of Yiddish. Thus we get verbs such as "stoppen," "gemoved," and "bluffst," and plural nouns including "warehauser" and "shepper" (shops).

Although the narrator's English lacks the errors present in the character's dialogue, it too frequently becomes accented by the very nature of Yiddish phonetics. For instance, because Yiddish lacks the /w/ sound, the word "sidewalk" must be transliterated in a way that would lead it to be pronounced "sidevalk." Likewise, /j/ is written as "dz" leading to pronunciations such as "Dzake" and "dzentleman." In this way, the author's English in the Yiddish text necessarily allies him with the minority rather than the dominant language community.

Many of Cahan's contemporaries were outraged by his use of English in his Yiddish writing. "He spit on our language," cried the Yiddish writer Joseph Opatashu. Others condemned Cahan for "cheapening the Jewish word."[70] One critic, Menakhem Boraisha, commented: "He prepared gradually for that which in his opinion is inevitable—assimilation."[71] But in all of his Yiddish work, Cahan refused to write in the Germanized, flowery Yiddish of many intellectuals of the time, a writing style that would have kept his work, like theirs, out of the reach of the masses. As a socialist seeking to appeal to a proletarian Jewish audience, Cahan insisted on writing in "plain Yiddish," the way it was spoken on the street, and in America, the language of the street was full of English expressions. Cahan believed that popular usage grants literary license.[72]

For this reason, Cahan includes common English profanities in the text of *Yankel der Yankee.* In this version of the novel, when Jake thinks about Gitl in a moment of kindness, he declares: "I will get used to her. She is a *damn shight* better than all the *dancing school goils.*"[73] The same line is rendered as follows in the English: "I shall get used to her. She is a ——— *shight* better than all the dancing-school girls."[74] All such profanities are similarly stricken from the English text. When Mamie taunts Jake in the Podkovnik's home, she says in the Yiddish, "A married man! You must have *a hell of a lot* of things to pay for,"[75] while in the English

Cahan writes: "Vy, a married man! . . . You got a ——— of a lot o' t'ings to pay for. . . . But what a ——— do *I* care!"[76] The same words that may be used in one text must be deleted from the other. Cahan cannot represent the real language of immigrants like Jake and Mamie to American readers. The constraints of the American publishing industry force him to tone down the realism of his English text. Cahan must censor himself and his characters or be censored.

The deletion of all "hells" and "damns" from *Yekl* may also reveal Cahan's perception of his American audience as more genteel than the proletarian readers of the Jewish labor press. It is likely that he tailored his English text for a predominantly female audience. Responding to criticisms of *Yekl* as "unpleasant," Cahan's friend Hutchins Hapgood, author of *The Spirit of the Ghetto,* wrote: "Strong compensating qualities are necessary to induce a publisher or editor to print anything which they think is in subject disagreeable to the big body of America readers, most of whom are women."[77] Howells too was keenly aware of the fact that women composed the primary audience for novels in the United States.[78] Most likely, Cahan also would have known that unlike the working-class men and women who read the Yiddish newspaper, the majority of his American readers would be middle-class females. He could not write for them in the same way as he did for his Yiddish audience. He could not represent American speech as openly. Yet despite his reluctance to offend this audience with blatant profanity, Cahan insists on representing his character's speech as closely as possible within the limits of propriety. He therefore leaves blanks in the dialogue, inviting his readers to insert the missing "hell" or "damn" on their own. If they do so, the readers, and not the author, are implicated for the use of such language.

Throughout the English novel, Cahan is particularly cautious with regard to his comments about American women. Mamie is said to mimic the condescending smile of a "rich American lady" in *Yankel,*[79] but of "some uptown ladies" in *Yekl.*[80] And when Mrs. Kavarsky rails at Jake for rejecting Gitl, she asks sarcastically in the Yiddish: "Do you think an American girl would make you a better wife?"[81] while in the English she declares: "Do you think a stylish girl would make you a better wife?"[82] Missing from the English text altogether is the narrator's remark that "on that very day, Mrs. Kavarsky had a mishap with a Negro woman, a customer who had moved while still owing a few dollars."[83] Cahan maligns the black American woman to readers within his own community but refrains from doing so before his American audience.[84] Perhaps he was unsure of how this comment would be received by his American audience, or perhaps he was concerned about his own vulnerable position as a minority member. Clearly, within the safe confines of the Yiddish newspaper, Cahan feels that he can openly acknowledge tensions between ethnic communities and give voice to the prejudices of his own community. The absence of such comments from *Yekl* seems to reveal concerns of audience, while their presence in the Yiddish portrays a tenser, more ambiguous relationship to America that could be more openly discussed in this text.

Immigrant anxiety and hostility toward the unknown America and American is generally more explicit in the Yiddish text. When Gitl first recognizes her husband's disdain for her, she wishes she could find a pious Jew to pray on her behalf or an old peasant woman to concoct a love potion. Suddenly recalling that she now resides in an unfamiliar world, she exclaims in *Yekl*: "But then, alas! who knows whether there are in this terrible America any good Jews or beggar women with love potions at all! Better she had never known this 'black year' of a country!"[85] In the Yiddish, Cahan pushes further: "Why did she come here? Better she had never known of the thieving America!"[86] The age-old recourses for dealing with crisis have vanished, and Gitl blames America for leaving her helpless. America has stolen Gitl's husband; America has destroyed her happiness. Although clearly voicing the sentiments of a distinct character, Cahan (or his editor) refuses to use the phrase "thieving America" in the English text.

Surprisingly, however, certain expressions of hostility toward the immigrants' adopted land are included in the English *Yekl* but not in *Yankel*. Upon learning that her husband has been seen courting Mamie Fein, Gitl runs to Mrs. Kavarsky and says in the English text:

> "*Oi*, as my ill luck would have it, it is all but too true. Have I no eyes, then? He mocks at everything I say or do; he can not bear the touch of my hand. America *has* made a mountain of ashes out of me. Really, a curse upon Columbus!" she ejaculated mournfully, quoting in all earnestness a current joke of the Ghetto.[87]

The Yiddish text breaks off after the mention of the touch, ending with intimations of sexual rejection that are glossed over more quickly in the English. But the English novel seems to speak more stongly against America in this passage; the curse upon Columbus is included in *Yekl* but not in *Yankel*. However, the curse is tempered by the explanation that it refers to a ghetto joke taken seriously by the literal-minded Gitl. This explanation assigns the curse to both the local-color aspect of the novel and a peculiarity of the character, rather than leaving it to seem like a potential attack on America by the author. Furthermore, all open criticisms of America are ultimately revoked at the end of the English novel, where the final explicit mention of the country is given in terms of highest praise. Mrs. Kavarsky declares to Gitl, who has been recently divorced from Jake and now intends to marry the educated Mr. Bernstein: "You ought to say Psalms for your coming to America. It is only here that it is possible for a blacksmith's wife to marry a learned man."[88] Significantly, no such tribute can be found in the Yiddish text. By articulating the characters' ambivalence toward the country and population into which they hope to assimilate, Cahan acknowledges and validates the experience of many of his immigrant readers.

While *Yekl* attempts to interpret immigrant culture to American readers, *Yankel*, like most of Cahan's Yiddish work, seeks to articulate and thus alleviate the painful struggles of the immigrant to adapt to American life. In the Yiddish novel, Cahan appeals to his immigrant audience's sense of loss and dislocation from the lives they left behind in Europe. In the English story, Jake's previous life is not described until page 10; the work opens in the New World, the common ground of its characters, author, and audience. The Yiddish version, however, begins in the Old World: "Without any embellishment and without any hurry, let me just tell you what kind of person he was. At home he was a blacksmith."[89] *Yankel* comes from the town of

Povodye, the author from elsewhere in Lithuania, the audience from all over Eastern Europe, but by calling the thousands of places they left behind "home" and invoking their shared experiences, the narrator helps to turn the "hodgepodge" of the Lower East Side into siblings of a new family and to establish a unified ethnic community in America. He creates his characters, audience, and himself into a people with a common history and home even before their arrival in the United States.

Cahan frequently invokes his Yiddish reader's sense of shared history and religious custom. He describes *Yankel* as having "a heavy voice with sharp finishes like yeshivanikers [Talmud students],"[90] and he depicts the character's quasi-assimilation into Russian culture in the Old Country with the comment: "He learned very quickly to speak Russian with mistakes like beans and sing military songs which he sang as he worked the bellows mixed with the 'Kol Ma'aminim' or the new melodies of the cantor's 'Hallel.' "[91] If this statement had been included in the English text, it would have required much background explanation. However, Cahan's Yiddish readers would have immediately recognized his reference to the sacred prayers of the Jewish festivals and High Holidays. They would also have laughed at the alias selected by Mamie's rival, "Jenny the Worrier" (called "Fanny the Preacher" in the English text), when she secretly reports to Gitl on Jake's relationship with Mamie. In *Yekl* she tells Gitl that her name is Rosy Blank, a play on her milky complexion, which is quick to color. In *Yankel* she calls herself Esther Blank, an amusing reference to Purim, the Jewish holiday of masking, whose heroine is Queen Esther. Thus even as she declares her name, Gitl's informant winks at the knowing audience, admitting her disguise. Knowledge of religious practice would have also enabled Yiddish readers to perceive the extent of Jake's secularization in the single sentence referring to his obligation to say the Kaddish prayer upon the death of his father. While *Yekl* lacks all mention of this filial duty, in *Yankel* Cahan explains: "He wanted to say the evening prayers and recite the Kaddish, but it was already too late for services."[92] The breach of his sacred responsibility to the dead reveals to a Jewish audience just how assimilated Jake has become. When writing in Yiddish, Cahan has at his disposal a language steeped in cultural references that he can deploy with confidence because of his own and his readers' intimate knowledge of this culture and its people. Cahan does not, and most likely cannot, use English in the same way.

Even Cahan's omissions in the Yiddish text speak clearly of the relationship between the author, readers, and subject matter. In describing Yekl's departure from his family, Cahan writes in the English:

> Three years had passed since Yekl had for the last time set his eyes on the whitewashed barracks and on his father's rickety smithy, which, for reasons indirectly connected with the Government's redoubled discrimination against the sons of Israel, had become inadequate to support two families; three years since that beautiful summer morning when he had mounted the spacious *kibitka* which was to carry him to the frontier-bound train; since, hurried by the driver, he had leaned out of the wagon to kiss his half-year-old son good-bye amid the heart-rending lamentations of his wife, the trem-

ulous "Go in good health!" of his father, and the startled screams of the neighbors
who rushed to the relief of his fainting mother.[93]

In the Yiddish, the narrator simply states: "Because of Jewish persecutions, the
smithy was unable to provide for two families, and that is why Yankel had to leave
for America."[94] Lack of details particular to Jake's leave-taking effectively allows
the immigrant audience to recall their own experiences and to engage with the text
on an extremely personal level unavailable to the American reader.

Dozens of Yiddish readers actually wrote back to the text, responding with
stories of their personal experiences. The novel facilitated individual expression. As
Cahan records in his memoirs:

> The story in Yiddish had immediate success. From various sources, our editor received
> letters in which some man or other believed that it depicted him; or this or that woman
> was convinced that she is the Gitl of whom the story is told. People thought that the
> entire tale presents a picture of their own lives or of a life with which they are per-
> sonally familiar.[95]

Readers accepted Cahan's representation of *Yankel der Yankee* as the simple transcription of a true story. They claimed it as their own, further erasing both its
artistry and author.

The English text did not achieve its goals to the same extent that *Yankel* did.
Despite Cahan's considerable attempts to represent and establish himself as an
American author through his English novel, even critics who praised the work
marginalized its author. In his rave review, which provided a brief entree for Cahan
into New York literary society, Howells wrote of the narrative voice with which
Cahan sought acceptance as an American and American artist: "I had almost
forgotten to speak of his English. In its simplicity and its purity, as the English of a
man born to write Russian, it is simply marvelous."[96] Despite his praise, Howells
highlights Cahan's foreignness, accidentally or deliberately identifying his mother
tongue as Russian rather than Yiddish (de-emphasizing his Jewishness and allying
Cahan more closely with the Russian Realists whom Howells admired). Furthermore, Howells writes that Cahan is "already thoroughly naturalized to our point
of view; he sees things with American eyes, and he brings in aid of his vision the far
and rich perceptions of his Hebraic race; while he is strictly of the great and true
Russian principle in literary art."[97] Although Cahan's triple consciousness is considered a great asset to his work,[98] it prevents him from being naturalized in anything
other than his vision. Only his eyes have the privileged perspective and status of a
native-born citizen. He may have "our point of view," but he is certainly not one
of us. The invocation of Hebrew as "race," implying biologically determined, immutable characteristics, fixes Cahan's identity in heredity, making complete assimilation impossible.

Howells's remarks in this review shed new light on his insistence on eliminating
the title *Yankel the Yankee*. Too vaudeville? Possibly, but perhaps more accurately,
too threatening. By changing the protagonist's name from Yankel to Yekl, Howells
eliminates the possibility for the pun on Yankel and Yankee. For Howells, the

difference between the two must exceed language. It is too easy for an immigrant to learn English. Language acquisition, for Howells, cannot be the primary criteria for becoming an American. As he comments in his review of Cahan's *The Imported Bridegroom and Other Stories*, published in 1898:

> It will be interesting to see whether Mr. Cahan will pass beyond his present environment out into the larger American world, or will master our life as he has mastered our language. But of a Jew, who is also a Russian, what artistic triumph may not we expect?[99]

Howells announces surprising alternatives for Cahan's future: either he will pass quietly into "our" world or he will master us. Howells does not suggest that Cahan will remain in his present environment among the immigrants, which indeed he does. And yet the prospect of his invading American society causes Howells to take refuge in the obscure negative question "what may not we expect" and to proclaim Cahan's ethnicity as Jewish and Russian. Although clearly a danger for the future, particularly if not limited to "artistic triumph," Cahan has thus far, according to Howells, mastered only American language, not life. His race and native tongue exclude him from the dominant society even as his mastery of its language distinguishes him from the immigrant masses he depicts.

Cahan's successful translinguification, demonstrated by his English novel, denies him identity of any sort. Above or at least distanced from his characters, yet not at home in the world in which he imagines his American audience, the immigrant author writing in English stands, as it were, on the "L" between Yankel and Yankee, looking into each community but entering neither.

NOTES

I am greatly indebted to Isaac Taubenfeld for his expert assistance with the translation of the Yiddish text. I would also like to thank Werner Sollors, Priscilla Wald, Robert Ferguson, Sylvia Taubenfeld, and Daniel Schloss for their input at various stages of this project.

1. Abraham Cahan, *Yankel der Yankee*, Arbeiter Tseitung 18 October 1895: 6. Cahan's serialized novel, *Yankel der Yankee*, was published in the Yiddish socialist newspaper *Arbeiter Tseitung*, in sixteen weekly installments between 18 October 1895 and 31 January 1896. His English novel, *Yekl*, was published by Appleton in 1896.

2. In the only published book-length study of Abraham Cahan's fiction to date, Jules Chametzky mentions the existence of the Yiddish text in passing. See Chametzky's *From the Ghetto: The Fiction of Abraham Cahan* (Amherst: University of Massachusetts Press, 1977), 68. While Chametzky does not compare *Yekl* and *Yankel der Yankee*, he does, however, provide a skillful comparison of Cahan's early Yiddish work "Mottke Arbel and His Romance" to the English version of that story (published under the title "A Providential Match"). His study establishes an important model for reading Cahan's English and Yiddish works against each other.

3. The fourth volume of Cahan's five-volume autobiography, *Bletter fun Mein Leben* (New York: Forward Association, 1928), contains the story of the events leading up to the creation of *Yekl* and *Yankel der Yankee* as well as of the reception of these texts. Chametzky

provides a useful summary of the publication history that draws heavily on Rudolph Kirk and Clara M. Kirk's excellent article "Abraham Cahan and William Dean Howells: The Story of a Friendship," *American Jewish Historical Quarterly*, 52 (September 1962–June 1963): 27–57.

4. Cahan 28.

5. Ibid., 34.

6. Ibid.

7. Harlem Renaissance artists and intellectuals engaged in similar debates about how to represent African Americans to readers outside their culture.

8. Rev. of *Yekl*, by Abraham Cahan, *American Hebrew*, 17 July 1896: 275.

9. "Chronicle and Comment," rev. of *Yekl*, by Abraham Cahan, *Bookman* January 1900: 428.

10. Nancy Huston Banks, "The New York Ghetto," rev. of *Yekl*, by Abraham Cahan, *Bookman* October 1896: 157–158.

11. Ibid., 158.

12. Cahan, 44.

13. Ibid., 36.

14. I am indebted to Professor Werner Sollors for this insight.

15. Ronald Sanders, *The Downtown Jews: Portraits of an Immigrant Generation* (New York: Dover, 1987), 201.

16. Chametzky, 67.

17. Cahan, 38. Unfortunately, the only known record of these correspondences exists in Cahan's autobiography.

18. Ibid., 39.

19. Ibid., 39.

20. Ibid., 39.

21. Ibid., 40.

22. Ibid., 42.

23. Ibid., 43.

24. Joshua A. Fishman, *Yiddish in America: Socio-Linguistic Description and Analysis* (Bloomington: Indiana University Press, 1985), 4.

25. Ibid., 7–9.

26. Sanders, 26.

27. John Higham, *Send These to Me: Jews and Other Immigrants in Urban America* (New York: Antheneum, 1975), 99.

28. As cited in Chametzky, 54.

29. Cahan, 42.

30. Abraham Cahan, *Yekl: A Tale of the New York Ghetto* (1896; New York: Dover Publications, 1970), 1. All cites to *Yekl* in this essay refer to the 1970 Dover edition of the text.

31. *Yankel,* 18 October 1895, 6.

32. *Yekl*, 26.

33. Ibid., 27.

34. Ibid., 28.

35. *Yankel*, 25 October 1895, 6. I have added italics to quotations from *Yankel der Yankee* to indicate words rendered by Cahan in transliterated English within the Yiddish text. Their significance will be discussed.

36. Chametzky, ix.

37. H. L. Mencken, *The American Language: An Inquiry into the Development of English in the United States*, 4th ed. (New York: Knopf, 1936), 636.

38. Abraham Cahan, *The Education of Abraham Cahan*, trans. Leon Stein, Abraham P. Conan, and Lynn Davison (Philadelphia: Jewish Publication Society of America, 1969), 356.

39. *Bletter*, 53.

40. *Yekl*, 10.

41. Ibid., 25.

42. Ibid., 25.

43. Ibid., 2. It is important to note that Cahan's technique of italicizing the English words incorporated into his character's Yiddish speech breaks down; italics is sometimes foregone and sometimes employed more conventionally for emphasis.

44. Ibid., 28.

45. Ibid., 85.

46. Monica Heller, introduction to *Codeswitching: Anthropological and Sociolinguistic Perspectives*, ed. Monica Heller (New York: Mouton de Gruyter, 1988), 1. In her study of recent Puerto Rican immigrants, "Constrastic Patterns of Codeswitching in Two Communities," in the same volume, linguist Shana Poplack concludes that in this community, "code switching per se is emblematic of their dual identity," 237. The deliberate interjection of English into the Yiddish speech of the community Cahan depicts similarly pronounces its identity as simultaneously East European Jewish and American.

47. *Yekl*, 2.

48. Ibid.

49. Ibid., 38; see also *Yankel*, 8 November 1895, 6.

50. *Yekl*, 38; *Yankel*, 8 November 1895, 6.

51. *Yekl*, 38; *Yankel*, 8 November 1895, 6.

52. *Yekl*, 49, 52, 52; *Yankel*, 29 November 1895, 5–6.

53. "In Yiddish Dialect," rev. of *Yekl*, by Abraham Cahan, *Commercial Advertiser* 1 August 1896, 14.

54. William Dean Howells, "New York Low Life in Fiction," rev. of *Yekl*, by Abraham Cahan, *New York World*, 26 July 1896, 18.

55. Irving Howe, *World of Our Fathers* (New York: Harcourt Brace Jovanovich, 1976), 525.

56. See, for example, Louis Harap, *The Image of the Jew in American Literature* (Philadelphia: Jewish Publication Society of America, 1974), 494–495.

57. Chametzky, 49.

58. *Yekl*, 13–14.

59. Werner Sollors, *Beyond Ethnicity: Consent and Descent in American Culture* (New York: Oxford University Press, 1986), 99. I am also indebted to Priscilla Wald for her insights on this subject.

60. *Yekl*, 17.

61. Ibid.

62. Ibid., 2.

63. Ibid., 68.

64. Ibid., 75.

65. Ibid., 74, 75.

66. Chametzky, 64.

67. *Yekl*, 3, 16, 20.

68. Ibid., 1, 3.

69. Ibid., 5.

70. See Harap, 489.

71. See Howe, 529.

72. Abraham Goldberg, *Pioneers and Builders: Biographical Studies and Essays* (New York: Abraham Goldberg Publication Committee, 1943), 287.

73. *Yankel*, 22 November 1895, 5. The line appears as follows:

זיא איז אַ דעם שײַט בעשער פֿאַר אַלע דענצינג שקול גאָיעלס....

74. *Yekl*, 45.

75. *Yankel*, 29 November 1895, 5. The line appears as follows:

די מוזט האָבען אַ העלל אָוו אַ לאָט זאַכען צו בעצאָלען.

76. *Yekl*, 50.

77. Hutchins Hapgood, *The Spirit of the Ghetto* (1902; Cambridge: Belknap Press, 1967), 248.

78. Howells frequently comments on the composition of the audience for fiction in the United States. See, for instance, his comments on women readers in his novels *A Hazard of New Fortunes* (1890; New York: Meridian Classic, 1983), 123, and *A Traveler from Altruria* (1894; New York: Sagamore Press, 1957), 25.

79. *Yankel,* 29 November 1895, 5.

80. *Yekl*, 50.

81. *Yankel*, 25 December 1895, 6.

82. *Yekl*, 69.

83. *Yankel*, 10 December 1895, 5.

84. It would be extremely useful to examine the original manuscript version of the English text written before the publication of *Yankel* as well as the manuscript of *Yankel* in order to determine whether the English text originally contained such language and was later edited and censored or if these incidents and words were added to the Yiddish text. I have been unable to locate any manuscript versions of the novels.

85. *Yekl*, 42.

86. *Yankel*, 15 November 1895, 6.

87. *Yekl*, 66.

88. Ibid., 88.

89. *Yankel*, 18 October 1895, 6.

90. Ibid.

91. Ibid.

92. Ibid.

93. *Yekl*, 11.

94. *Bletter*, 18 October 1995, 6.

95. Cahan, 43.

96. Howells, "New York Low Life," 18.

97. Ibid.

98. Higham, 96.

99. Reprinted in Kirk and Kirk, 41.

Chapter Eleven

The Strange Case of Luigi Donato Ventura's *Peppino*

Some Speculations on the Beginnings of Italian-American Fiction

Mario Maffi

By now recognized as "the foundational fiction for Italian-American literature,"[1] Luigi Donato Ventura's *Peppino* still remains, in many respects, a "strange case." Written in 1882, it was published three years later by William R. Jenkins, *Editeur et libraire français* in New York, in a series of *Contes Choisis*—"short stories and *nouvelles* by the best French writers, thus giving at every [sic] moderate price specimens of the very best French fiction"[2]—where it keeps company with Edmond About, Alphonse Daudet, George Sand, Georges Ohnet, and Guy de Maupassant.

And, indeed, the story of the Italian street arab Peppino, set in the immigrant Lower East Side of New York, is told by the Italian writer Ventura not in Italian but *in French*—or, at least, so it was published by Jenkins. No evidence is at present available that the novelette was ever published in Italian before, although the preface speaks of the book as of "cette édition française" (5). The fact that Italian words and sentences do crop up here and there, regularly followed, in brackets, by their translation into French, might show that *Peppino* was actually conceived and written in a language other than Italian.

In 1886, an *English* version also appeared. It was included in *Misfits and Remnants*, a collection of stories edited by Ventura himself and the Russian author S. Shevitch and published by Ticknor and Company in Boston. This version, however, as Cagidemetrio has shown, not only is far from faithful but carries no indication that might help solve the mystery.[3]

In the plurilinguistic panorama of fin-de-siècle American fiction, Ventura's novelette thus remains a "strange case"—something apart even from the genetic complexity and linguistic density of such a text as Abraham Cahan's *Yekl*, which was published in 1896. And this very "strangeness" stimulates not a few intriguing questions and hypotheses on the theme of the relationship of immigrant cultures to "America."

Peppino's plot is a very simple one. In a first-person narrative, which is also a kind of uninterrupted dialogue with the reader,[4] a down-and-out would-be writer in New York, Mr. Fortuna (which, in Italian, can be a synonym of Ventura), tells how, during one of his idle downtown strolls, he encountered Peppino, a twelve-year-old shoeshine. Struck by his honesty and maturity, Mr. Fortuna arranges for him to shine his shoes daily in his apartment, notwithstanding his landlady's dislike of that "sorte de brigand italien" (21). By and by, he comes to know Peppino's brothers (one is also a shoeshine, the other a violinist on the Coney Island pleasure boats) and one Sunday is invited to eat macaroni in their poor quarters—a chance to talk at length with these countrymen of his from a southern region, Basilicata.

Back in New York after a three-month voyage to the West, Mr. Fortuna falls ill and cannot pay the rent to his wolfish landlady, but, providentially, Peppino arrives and offers to pay with his savings. The shoeshine's gesture not only averts eviction but also brings luck: one of the articles Mr. Fortuna hopelessly keeps sending around to several American newspapers is finally accepted and a large sum awaits him. Peppino is asked to go and cash it. He never returns, however, and all attempts to find him are vain. For a week, many dark speculations crowd the writer's mind. But one day, just in front of Bellevue Hospital, Fortuna meets a pale and lame Peppino and discovers he had been run over by a lorry just after concealing the envelope with the money within an old book in Fortuna's apartment, in order to shelter it from the landlady's designs. Peppino did not know his friend's name, his two brothers were away from New York, and so he had to lie in his hospital bed, anguished at the thought of what Fortuna might have inferred from his disappearance.

The story ends with the little shoeshine being treated by "un honnête docteur américain, qui ne voulut pas accepter un sou pour les soins qu'il avait prodigués à Peppino" (64). So, "[q]uand vous passez, lecteur, par le coin de Prince Street, portez aussi vos dix sous à Peppino. Mais mon petit ami est modeste: ne lui dites jamais ce que je vous ai conté" (65).

In a way, Ventura's *Peppino* is thus a story in the poverty-and-honesty trend, that kind of extreme, stereotyped Dickensian subgenre that was so common in those very years both in Great Britain and the United States.[5] Still, the reading of this novelette allows a few considerations that help us place Ventura's work in the *corpus* of Italian-American literature.

First of all, it must be stressed that *Peppino* appeared at quite an early time as far as Italian immigration to the United States is concerned. In fact, although a steady trickle since the late 1840s, the inflow from Italy really took on impressive proportions in the 1880s, and it was only in the following years that a veritable Italian community took shape.[6] Although few literary personalities existed in the *colonia* even before (Lorenzo Da Ponte is perhaps the best example),[7] only later would its veritable mouthpieces emerge. In fact, Bernardino Ciambelli's Little Italy *feuilletons* and Edoardo Migliaccio's Farfariello sketches, just to name a few examples, started to appear in the press in the 1890s. Ventura's work can thus be considered an anticipation of Italian-American fiction, and as such it was instrumental in sedimenting attitudes and tropes. Diverse situations can indeed be traced in the text, in which a discourse on emigration and cross-cultural interaction clearly surfaces with specific traits.

From this point of view, the novelette clearly presents us with an Italian-American identity *in the making*, that is, going through a process of definition. In the book, this process has three main stages, which could be called the construction of America, the contrast with America, and the dialogue with America.[8] Let us briefly examine each of this stages.

The construction of America. Three Americas can be said to be at play in *Peppino*. As Fortuna recalls,

> "[J]'étais arrivé d'Italie . . . avec une idée . . . dans la tête. Je croyais que l'Amérique était un pays où l'argent courait les rues. . . . [L]'on m'avait fait croire qu'il n'y avait pas moyen de se loger modestement à New York à moins d'y mettre le prix de quinze dollars par semaine, et qu'en fait de nourriture il n'y avait que le menu de Delmonico ou de Martinelli de possible." (10–11)

The first America is thus the most obvious and common one: "America as the Promised Land," with its gold-paved streets and success within reach—an irresistible attraction for emigrants from all countries.

The second America is also a common one: the other side of the coin, made up of menial jobs and crude poverty, of money earned in toil and sweat, of tenements "d'une apparence triste et désolante . . . dans la partie de Crosby street où s'entassent pêle-mêle des êtres et des choses sans nom" (31–32).[9] In Fortuna's autobiographical (and even self-mocking) tale, this America of disillusionment is epitomized by a gradual descent through the body of the city—another classical trope in much urban and immigrant fiction, both American and European.[10]

> Comme je marchais en voyant les choses à travers un prisme, que je ne savais pas un traître mot d'anglais, et que je voulais coûte que coûte découvrir l'Amérique sans l'aide de personne, il m'arriva qu'en trois semaines je passai par toute la gamma chromatique de la musique à argent réduit, et que j'appris: Premièrement, à changer de logement et de *landlady* en descendant de quinze à dix, puis à cinq dollars par semaine, puis à ne plus pouvoir payer du tout. Duexièmment, à descendre de la hauteur de la vingt-septième rue à la profondeur d'un sous-sol où le dîner coûtait vingt-cinq sous, un verre de bière compris" (12).

Now, if these two Americas occupy a kind of inevitable and central position in almost all immigrant fiction, not so common is *Peppino*'s third America: the America back home. What Fortuna soon discovers is not only that these "birds of passage" conceive their stay in America as provisional, living and toiling in view of a rapid return, but that, back home, they are creating a kind of America-within-Italy. The talk Fortuna has with Peppino and his brothers, in front of their Sunday macaroni, is, from this point of view, illuminating:

> "Mais vous êtes logés comme des princes", dis-je au trio.
> "Nous sommes contents", me répondit le joueur de violon, "mais ce que vous voyez n'est rien, nous allons avoir notre maison là-bas".
> "Où là-bas?"
> "A Viggiano".
> "Etes-vous de Viggiano?"

"Certainement", ajouta Antonio, "nous aurons une belle maison dans Broadway".

Décidément je tombais des nues. Viggiano-Broadway: je n'y comprenais plus rien, et comme mes hôtes m'avaient offert un petit vin de Sicile bien noir et épais, je commençais à craindre que la liqueur ne leur eût monté à la tête. Par contenence je me mis à rire.

"Je vois bien que vous êtes Americain", reprit Philippe, "et que vous ne connaissez pas Viggiano. Eh, bien, voulez-vous que je vous dise ce que c'est Viggiano?"

"Qu'est-ce que cela lui fait Viggiano à ce Monsieur", interrompit Peppino, qui ne croyait pas que cela pût m'intéresser, et voulant de toute façon m'être agréable.

Cependant, comme je désirais beaucoup avoir le mot de cette énigme, je dis:

"Au contraire, racontez-moi cela, Philippe." (36–37)

What then follows is a graphic description of the first stage of the "chain migration" to America from the South of Italy, with "birds of passage" who come home rich and thus help create the myth. The reality that is thus unveiled to Fortuna is one that he (himself an emigrant from Italy, although from another region—possibly a northern one) does not know about and not even suspect exists. "Philippe" in fact so continues:

"C'est comme cela que nous arrivons en Amérique. Tous les mois nous allons chez *Signor Cantoni* et nous envoyons l'argent que nous avons ramassé, les uns en jouant, les autres en décrottant des bottes. Quand nous avons soixante dollars nous les envoyons au Syndic qui est un des nôtres, un de ceux qui maintenant est riche".

"Combien faut-il d'argent pour se dire riche là-bas?", demandai-je.

"Oh! avec quatre mille dollars on est très riche", ajouta Philippe.

"Et quelle garantie vous donne-t-on pour votre argent envoyé?"

"Nous ne domandons qu'un simple reçu, et nous dormons bien tranquilles, car avec cet argent l'on achète pour nous un terrain dans Broadway. Broadway, c'est le nom de notre grande rue qui est longue d'un demi mille, et qui a été baptisée par un syndic, qui avait été cireur en chef pendant dix ans dans le Broadway d'ici. . . . il y a trente ans, Viggiano n'était qu'un amas de masures, et maintenant tout le monde qui est de retour d'Amérique parle moitié anglais moitié italien—plus anglais qu'italien, et chacun possède une maison avec *swell front*. Ce ne sont pas de grandes maisons comme dans la Cinquième Avenue de New-York, mais c'est beau; rien n'y manque, c'est en briques blanchies à la chaux, avec des *swell front*."

Philippe appuyait sur le *swell front*.

Peppino battait des mains: Antonio prenait une mine béate, en fumant son cigare, et en observant de très près l'impression que cette singulière conversation faisait sur moi. En Italie je ne m'étais douté qu'il y eût un reflet de vie américaine dans les montagnes de la Basilicate. (38–40)

Peppino then reinforces this mythical image of an "America-in-Italy" by remarking that " 'le cousin Paolo a une chambre tapissée de cartes-annonces de New-York, que le monde lui envoie d'Amérique, et que nous ramassons partout dans les rues, et monsieur le curé a une malle recouverte de timbres-poste américains' " (40–41). And, to Fortuna's question, "Mais les affaires comment les traitez-vous?" Peppino quickly answers: "A l'américaine. Les autorités nous respectent parce que nous venons de l'Amérique, et nous appellent Américains. C'est comme une république chez nous et nous arrangeons nos petites affaires entre nous" (41). And Philippe concludes: "Ici nous sommes toujours pauvres, car l'argent c'est pour chez nous; ici, nous travaillons pour que nous puissions nous reposer quand nous serons vieux. Si vous saviez comme c'est beau Viggiano, nous avons des fleurs, et le soir tout le monde chante assis devant les *swell front*" (42).

The Contrast with America. Given these three Americas, it is clear that, in *Peppino*, the immigrant discourse defines itself first of all in terms of contrasts. Of these, the main one is between Old World and New World mores. Fortuna would rather have his shoes shone at home by Peppino, and this act (which surely relieves the boy from the public humiliation implicit in shoeshining in the streets but at the same time casts him in a sort of traditional, backward master-servant relationship) is severely criticized by Mrs. Stiffenton, Fortuna's landlady: "[I]ci en Amerique," she reminds him, "les messieurs les plus distingués, les plus riches, cirent leur bottes. . . . Je vous assure, Monsieur, que monsieur Gould et monsieur Vanderbilt cirent eux-même leurs bottes, oui, Monsieur, eux-même, parcequ'ils sont *gentlemen*" (23, 24).

The landlady's talk clearly belongs in the "American-democracy-vs.-European-aristocracy" tradition, with all its demagogical overtones and ambiguous implications (and an overt contradiction: the final use of the term "gentlemen," which seems to reverse the initial assertion). And, since Mrs. Stiffenton (quite an allegorical name!) is far from an agreeable character, it is obvious where the author/narrator's sympathies lie.[11] Fortuna concludes the episode with the (rather aristocratic, to be sure) comment: "je n'avais jamais rêvé de devenir propriétaire d'une boîte à cirer pour me livrer à la peinture en chambre de mes bottes" (24).[12]

But the contrast between Europe and America touches other aspects as well. Our first encounter with "la vieille, la sèche, l'austère" (21) Mrs. Stiffenton immediately takes the form of a religious polemic:

> Le soir de ce même jour, en revenant chez moi j'abordai mon hôtesse qui se tenait comme d'habitude dans une salle du rez-de-chaussée, salle noire, meublée de bancs et d'une table sur laquelle était placée en évidence une grande bible. Pour expliquer ma présence dans cette maison il faut que je dise que ma pauvreté m'avait réduit à prendre une chambre très modeste, chez une dame qui à ses fonctions de maîtresse de maison joignait celle de pasteur Méthodiste, je crois. Il venait chez elle tous les soirs quelques confrères, et des gens pauvres du quartier qui apportaient leur obole à d'autres pauvres imaginaires, lesquels se résumaient en une seule et unique pauvresse patentée—la vieille, la sèche, l'austère Mrs. Stiffenton. (20–21)

The Catholic Fortuna's comment, "[C]ette femme qui se disait chrétienne et traitait si mal le pauvre monde quand'elle ne pouvait en tirer aucun profit" (22), is clearly leveled not at religion at large but at the Protestant world in which he and Peppino (also an example of religiosity, but once more of the Catholic kind!) are now struggling to survive.

At the same time, the process through which the immigrant rebuilds his or her own identity in a new context also includes—at least initially—a defensive/aggressive attitude toward other ethnic groups. In Ventura's novelette, this attitude takes on rather blatant racist overtones on the only two occasions when this encounter with another group (namely, African American) occurs.

Peppino opens, in fact, with these words: "Si jamais vous allez à New-York, et que par une belle journée de mai vous entrepreniez un petit voyage, moitié affaires, moitié plaisir, dans la direction du bureau de poste, suivez mon conseil, ne prenez pas le tramway qui va par Union Square à la rue Barclay, vous étoufferiez entre duex matrones, ou vous seriez asphyxié entre deux nègres" (7). A few pages below, the little shoeshine is described as sweating over the shoes of an enormous (and apparently inebriated) black, who then walks away dissatisfied with Peppino's work, grunting, "[J]e ne sais plus quel *nègre mot*" (19). Olfactory and auditory revulsion thus serves to define the immigrant territory as opposed to that of other ethnic groups.

The Dialogue with America. But the immigrant discourse defines itself not only in terms of contrasts; it also develops in terms of (quasi-Bakhtinian) dialogism, that is, in terms of a continuous and often covert dialectic with American society and culture.[13] The novelette revolves in fact around a most common figure in those years—that of the street gamin. Just ten years before, in *The Dangerous Classes of New York, And Twenty Years' Work Among Them*, Charles Loring Brace had written a worried and scathing survey on the situation of "the outcast street-children grown up to be . . . the 'feeders' of criminals, and the sources of domestic outbreaks and violations of law."[14] A few years later, in 1890, with his photos and seminal book *How the Other Half Lives*, Jacob A. Riis would pick up the subject again, betraying all the uneasiness of the late-nineteenth-century Victorian American morality. And in the following years, a veritable flood of novels on the "street-arab figure" would flow from the pen of Horatio Alger, Jr., this time with didactic rather than sensational aims: boys on the street *could* become real Americans, epitomes of the "American success story."

Ventura holds some kind of "middle position" between these extremes. His marginal boy is engaged in surviving in the Big Metropolis, in the very midst of a Babelish downtown New York: he is streetwise, he can relate to different critical situations, he can speak (really and metaphorically) several languages, he has a "sound heart." But he is not interested in becoming a "real American": all he wants to do is go back to his small village in southern Italy, where the main street is called "Broadway."

Somehow, we have here another version of Huckleberry Finn, refusing to be "sivilized" (i.e., Americanized) and lighting out to the Territory (a territory that is not an unknown one ahead but a well-known one at home). Not by chance, the years of composition and publication of *Peppino* (1882 and 1885) are those of the final completion and publication of *Adventures of Huckleberry Finn*, another transgressive story of marginality and "sound heart."

All these elements (*Peppino*'s early apparition as compared to the development of an Italian-American community and literary world, its more or less covert meanings in terms of the relationship with America, its variation on a theme—that of the street boy—that holds the social and cultural foreground and impresses the contemporary collective imaginary) are by themselves, I believe, extremely important and will deserve a deeper analysis than the one possible here. But the text contains much deeper contradictions and questions.

Fred L. Gardaphé has argued that, like all "ethnic" literatures, Italian American literature too moves from the stage of oral (collective) tradition to that of the creation of a literary self.[15] From this point of view, *Peppino*, with its clear, often-surfacing storytelling ring and at the same time with its explicit, separate authorial I, could really work as a very early and "synthetic" example of that passage, and as such tell us much about these cultural, literary, and linguistic mechanisms. At the same time, however, John M. Reilly reminds us that

> ethnic literature can only be fully explained by an approach that studies writing as an expression of the cognitive orientations of the authors. Ethnicity is a constant among these orientations, but it is varied and modified by authorial disposition, assumptions about social and personal relationships, self-image, and assumptions about the way the natural and social world works.[16]

In dealing with *Peppino*, we should thus take into account Ventura's "disposition and self-image." And, of course, here—where language is directly and inevitably concerned—*enters French*: because here we have a recently immigrated Italian author who writes one of the earliest Italian-American texts in a language other than English (even incorporating the usual Italian words and idiolects) *but other than Italian as well.*

The obvious, inevitable questions are, Why French? What kind of a reading public was Ventura (or Mr. Jenkins) aiming at? Was there a comparable French American literary world in which *Peppino* could find a specific place (and this in the New York area, that is, out of the Louisiana region where one would expect to find such a literary world)? Or was Ventura (or Mr. Jenkins) thinking of the French-Canadian market? Or rather, Was Ventura using some kind of device, a mask, some sort of "signifyin' "—that is to say, dealing with a burning issue (that of immigration, at an early stage as far as Italian immigration was concerned, and thus of the contact/contrast with America) through linguistic indirection, that is, by writing in a language other than English?[17]

An interesting clue in this respect would be found precisely in *Peppino*'s English version, which, as we have seen, came out a year after. Here, in fact, besides other interesting differences,[18] the racist antiblack remarks and the religious polemic were struck out, and even Mrs. Stiffenton, though retaining the disagreable traits of the "landlady [rather Dickensian, at that] character," becomes mellower, even "worthy." But this English version was obviously meant for a much larger reading audience than the French one, and the difference is eloquent.

At the same time, if Ventura was really making use of some kind of "signifyin' " in the French *Peppino*, this strategy would also be in striking accordance with the early stages of Italian-American writing. Again, Gardaphé has drawn attention to the two cultural codes "carried to America through the oral traditions of southern

Italian culture," that is, "*omertà*, the code of silence that governs what is spoken or not spoken about in public, and *bella figura*, the code of proper presence or social behavior that governs an individual's public presence."[19]

Now, if we read the French *Peppino* through the magnifying lens of these two codes, not only is the perception reinforced of a text that is located at a crucial stage in the passage from an oral/collective tradition to a literary/individual one—*omertà* containing more collective, social implications; *bella figura* more individual, personal ones—but also a possible answer to the question "Why French?" can be inferred. French would in fact allow the writer to retain both the *omertà* code (not to speak in public—the *American* public—of things Italian) and the *bella figura* code (an Italian in the United States affording the luxury of writing in French). From this point of view, the English *Peppino*, with its erasure of so many contradictions at the level both of language and of content, would clearly imply a step backward.

However well founded these speculations might be, the fact is that Luigi Donato Ventura's *Peppino* continues to be a "strange case," and as such it requires further inquiry (or, perhaps more appropriately, *enquête*). The case is still open; or, as Sherlock Holmes would put it, "The game is afoot."

NOTES

1. Alide Cagidemetrio, Introduction to *Peppino*, in Marc Shell and Werner Sollors, eds., *The Longfellow Anthology of American Literature* (Baltimore: Johns Hopkins University Press, forthcoming).

2. From the back cover, Luigi Donato Ventura, *Peppino* (New York: William R. Jenkins, 1885). All future references are from this edition and will be indicated by page numbers in parenthesis in the text.

3. Cf. the introduction to *Peppino* by Cagidemetrio, who also offers several interesting interpretations in regard to the linguistic and cultural issues lying at the core of *Peppino*. It should be added that the novelette's mystery is paralleled by that surrounding its author, about whom very little is known. In her seminal work *The Italian-American Novel: A Document of the Interaction of Two Cultures* (Rutherford, N.J.: Fairleigh Dickinson University Press, 1974), Rose Basile Green limits herself to a brief résumé of the novelette, without any biographical data about Ventura other than the dates of birth (1845) and death (1912, but Cagidemetrio advances the latter to 1908). No mention of Ventura can be found in such recent books on Italian-American fiction as *From the Margin: Writings in Italian Americana*, ed. Anthony Julian Tamburri, Paolo A. Giordano, and Fred L. Gardaphé (West Lafayette: Purdue University Press, 1991), and Fred L. Gardaphé's *Italian Signs, American Streets: The Evolution of Italian American Narrative* (Durham: Duke University Press, 1996). Among the first scholars to become interested in Ventura was Frank Lentricchia, with his "Luigi Ventura and the Origins of Italian-American Fiction," *ItalianAmericana*, 1, no. 2 (Spring 1975):188–195 (I owe this bibliographical reference to Orm Øverland).

4. The opening sentence reads: "Si jamais vous allez à New York" (7); the closing one begins: "Quand vous passez, lecteur, par le coin de Prince Street . . ." (65). Between these two extremes, the narrator is constantly addressing the reader, in an *almost* Baudelairean

mode. This continuing dialogue with the reader might also betray the original destination of the story; in the preface, Ventura tells of having *read* the novel in Burlington, Vermont, where he held the chair of Italian at the local language college (4).

5. See, in particular, Arthur Morrison, *Tales of Mean Streets* (1894; Woodbridge, Suffolk: Boydell Press, 1983), and Jacob A. Riis, *Out of Mulberry Street* (New York: Century, 1898).

6. The Italian *colonia* in New York counted 700 persons in 1850; 1,500 in 1860; 2,700 in 1870; 20,000 in 1880; 115,000 in 1890; and 225,000 in 1900. See Ira Rosenwaike, *Population History of New York City* (Syracuse: Syracuse University Press, 1972). Also see Donna R. Gabaccia, *From Sicily to Elizabeth Street: Housing and Social Change Among Italian Immigrants, 1880–1930* (Albany: State University of New York Press, 1984), and Mario Maffi, *Gateway to the Promised Land. Ethnic Cultures in New York's Lower East Side* (Amsterdam: Rodopi, 1994; New York: New York University Press, 1995).

7. See, for instance, Francesco Moncada, "New York's 'Little Italy' in 1850," *Atlantica* (April 1937). For almost-contemporary depictions of the Italian *colonia* in New York, see Charlotte Adams, "Italian Life in New York," *Harper's New Monthly Magazine*, 62, no. 371 (April 1881), and Viola Roseboro, "The Italians of New York," *Cosmopolitan*, 4, no. 5 (January 1888).

8. Of course, instead of "United States," I purposely use here the term "America" for its "mythical" implications.

9. This passage bears a striking similarity to one by Brander Matthews, in *Vignettes of Manhattan* (1894): "that part of the city, . . . where architecture is as irregular, as crowded, and as little cared for as the population." Interestingly enough, when the English version came out, the reviewer of *The Literary World* suggested that Luigi Donato Ventura and S. Shevitch might be "aliases hiding the identity of some 'Brander Matthews and Leander Richardson'" (quoted in Cagidemetrio's introduction).

10. On this aspect, see Eric Homberger, *Scenes from the Life of a City: Corruption and Conscience in Old New York* (New Haven: Yale University Press, 1994).

11. In this regard, it must be remarked that the only female characters in the novel are landladies, and rather disagreeable ones. Here, gender motifs intertwine with sociocultural biases in a rather interesting and illuminating way.

12. As a matter of fact, a preoccupation with an aristocratic conduit often surfaces in the novelette. At the very beginning, for instance, just after the first introduction of Peppino to the reader, the narrator says: "Peppino est un aristocrate en son genre" (10). It is true that such a definition might easily be taken as a kind of peculiar recognition of the boy's "craftsmanship," but even so it reinforces the contrast between European (backward, still feudal) traits and American (democratic) ones. Ventura's use of the term "aristocrat" in this context reminds me of Jack London's use of it to define the top layers of the hobo world in *The Road* (1906) and Hutchins Hapgood's to characterize certain elements of the Bowery world in *Types from City Streets* (1910).

13. See Werner Sollors, *Beyond Ethnicity: Consent and Descent in American Culture* (New York: Oxford University Press, 1986).

14. Charles Loring Brace, *The Dangerous Classes of New York, and Twenty Years' Work Among Them* (New York: Wynkoop & Hallenbeck, 1872), p. ii.

15. See Fred L. Gardaphé, "From Oral Tradition to Written Word: Toward an Ethnographically Based Literary Criticism," in Tamburi, Giordano, and Gardaphé, *From the Margin*.

16. John Reilly, "Criticism of Ethnic Literature: Seeing the Whole", *MELUS*, 5, no. 1 (1978): 12

17. The reference here is, of course, to Henry Louis Gates, Jr.'s seminal *The Signifying Monkey: A Theory of African-American Literary Criticism* (New York: Oxford University Press, 1988).

18. The ending, for instance, is much more rhetorical and less facetious or even ironical (see Cagidemetrio's introduction).

19. Fred L. Gardaphé, *Italian Signs, American Streets*, p. 20. I believe Gardaphé's remarks apply not only to *southern* Italian culture but, more broadly, to Italian popular (peasant) culture, above all in its first impact/confrontation with America.

Chapter Twelve

Worlds of Difference

Lin Yutang, Lao She, and the Significance of Chinese-Language Writing in America

Xiao-huang Yin

The birth of Chinese-language literature in America can be traced to the mid-nineteenth century.[1] On April 22, 1854, the first Chinese newspaper in North America, *Kim Shan Jit San Luk* (Golden Hills News) was published in San Francisco.[2] The following decades saw Chinese newspapers and periodicals spring up in major Chinatowns throughout America. Although they varied in quality and scope, most of the newspapers contained some forms of literary works as a means of promoting circulation. A few of them, such as the *Chung Sai Yat Pao* (China-West Daily, 1900–1951), founded by Dr. Ng Poon Chew, an eminent Chinese journalist, and *Mon Hing Yat Bo* (Chinese World, 1891–1969), favored by Sui Sin Far (Edith Maude Eaton), the first Chinese-American woman writer, were especially known for dedication to publication of creative writings.[3]

Chinese-language literature in America began to enter a distinctively new phase in the post–World War II era, as an outcome of historical, social, and cultural forces that dramatically transformed the makeup and dynamics of the Chinese-American community. While the Chinese population in the United States grew from about 120,000 in 1950 to more than two million in 1995, the percentage of the native-born dropped from around 60 percent to 30 percent. Meanwhile, the arrival of large numbers of Chinese intellectuals in America has been a striking distinction of the new immigration from the old.[4] Although there were Chinese students and scholars in the United States as early as in the mid-nineteenth century, not until the postwar era did Chinese student immigration gain momentum. Statistics show that between the 1950s and the mid-1980s, nearly 150,000 students from Taiwan came to America for graduate education and advanced training; 97 percent of them settled in the United States after graduation. The last two decades also saw around 250,000 students and scholars from China studying in American institutions of higher learning. About 50 percent of them eventually settled in this country.[5]

The immense demographic change within the Chinese-American communities, especially the growing presence of highly educated immigrants, has helped Chinese-language literature develop at an unprecedented rate because the new immigrants have displayed strong interest and sustaining enthusiasm in works written in their mother tongue. Therefore, the past few decades saw a "renaissance" of Chinese publications in America. By the 1940s, many Chinese newspapers in America had been forced to close down because of the shrinking subscription rate—a result of the decline of immigration. With the influx of new immigrants, however, readership of Chinese newspapers witnessed quantitative and qualitative changes. In New York City, Chinese dailies increased from four in the 1940s to seven in 1975 and nine by 1987, most of them with international circulation. In Los Angeles County, there are now twice as many Chinese newspapers printed each day as there are Chinese households in the area.[6]

The thirst of new immigrants for publications in their mother tongue has led to the prosperity of Chinese-language literature. Riding the wave of readers' enthusiasm, from the 1950s on, most Chinese newspapers began to add *Fu Kan* (literary pages) to promote more creative writings in order to compete for the limited numbers of subscribers. Such a practice in turn attracted more readers. For example, Hu Shi, a leading Chinese writer and critic, showed great interest in poems published in various *Fu Kan* during his stay in New York in the 1950s.[7] Yu Lihua's best-seller *Fujia de Ernumen* (*Sons and daughters of the Fu family*) was a big hit when it appeared in serial in *Sing Tao Daily* (New York). *Meiguo Yuelian* (*The American moon*), a popular novel by Chao Youfang, stimulated such strong interest when it was serialized in *Zhong Bao* (*The Central Daily*) that the author received phone calls from readers who wanted to share their impressions of her portrayal of the protagonists in the novel.[8]

It is necessary to point out that the quantitative dimensions of newspaper reading of Chinese immigrants is a typical "American phenomenon." According to a Gallup study of urban life in China, even in the cities with the highest economic development, only about 42 percent of adults regularly read newspapers or magazines.[9] By contrast, nearly 90 percent of Chinatown residents in Philadelphia read Chinese newspapers.[10] On the other hand, the keen interest shown by Chinese immigrants in newspapers in their native language is a familiar scene in immigrant communities across America. "Out of 312 Russian immigrants in New York," a study finds, "only 16 regularly read newspapers in Russia. . . . [But] in America all of them are subscribers or readers of Russian newspapers."[11]

In general, three points stand out to offer useful glosses to understand characteristics of Chinese-language literature in America and its difference from writing in English by Chinese-American authors. First, Chinese-language writers enjoy a high degree of freedom that their counterparts writing in English do not have. Indeed, a hallmark of Chinese-language literature in America is the liberty it takes in themes and subject matter while remaining within the general corpus of Chinese-American writing. The fact that their audience is almost exclusively immigrants with strong traditional Chinese values frees the writers from feeling restrained by the social codes of mainstream society. As a result, Chinese-language writers do not worry about responses from outside critics and readers, they are more outspoken about problems in the Chinese community and larger society, and they have consciously spawned a unique cultural perspective to explore the Chinese-American experience. Their portrayal of controversial issues, such as Chinese attitudes toward other minorities, the rise of feminist consciousness among Chinese-American women and its implications, conflicts between immigrants and the native-born, and interracial love affairs, appears closer to the Chinese-American reality. For example, poverty and crime in Chinatowns draw considerably more attention from Chinese-language writers. We are made to see, through their penetrating observations, that a whole class of destitute Chinese immigrants exists below the poverty line. In their works, they clearly paint a picture that shows Chinese Americans are not all successful or a "model minority" group. In the story "Dou Tai" (Abortion), the author examines the lives of sweatshop women in San Francisco's Chinatown and their attitudes toward abortion. It demonstrates how sexual harassment and economic hardships force working-class Chinese women to choose abortion as a means of surviving in poverty-stricken inner-city ghettos.[12] One doubts if the author would write in such a shockingly honest way had she published the story in English.

Second, Chinese-language literature has always remained closely identified with the immigrant experience. While American-born Chinese writers tend to delve into the broad issues of ethnic identity, cultural conflicts, and sentiments of the native-born, Chinese-language writers are more dedicated to exploring compelling issues grounded in an immigrant sensibility, such as the agony of displacement, the dilemma of assimilation and alienation, and the struggle for survival in a strange land. Their works possess more complexities and richer colors regarding immigrant life, and they provide us with insight on how race relations, class identification, economic factors, cultural influence, and social environment affect the concerns and consciousness of Chinese immigrants.[13] For example, in the story "Ye Ben" (A visit at night), the author shows how recent immigrants with educational and urban backgrounds fit into a rapidly changing American society. With a strong desire to succeed in their adopted land, Chinese immigrants have become assertive and no longer shy away from racial confrontations. In the story, a Chinese immigrant urges his son to challenge anyone who bullies him:

> I tell you, in this country, whether you are right or wrong depends on if you have tough muscle and dare to fight. . . . Be quiet and patient? Forget it! If you're modest and self-giving, others would treat you like trash. The high-sounding Chinese doctrine of endurance, benevolence, and always putting others before you, don't work at all in this place.[14]

In other words, what distinguishes Chinese-language writers is their persistent focus on immigrants. The troubles of displacement and the mentality of being a marginalized person provide them with a unique angle to observe the losses and gains of life in a new country, as well as the differences and similarities between Chinese and other minority groups in multiracial American society. Their writing reflects the fact that the experience of Chinese immigrants does not fit the assimilation pattern or theories based on the experiences of other minority groups. It is such a depiction of the many facets of immigrant life that makes Chinese-language literature so relevant to the Chinese-American reality yet so different from works written in English.

Third, with a few exceptions, Chinese-language writers have rarely published in

English. This is not because writing in English is the province of the American-born. Many Chinese immigrant writers are well versed in English. Rather, they argue that until recently, for Chinese immigrant writers, creative writing in English often demands suppression and distortion of the Chinese sensibility that does not fit into the stereotyped portrayal of "Orientals" that is popular in mainstream American culture.[15] Such a critical opinion in part comes from their personal experiences. Many of them have encountered difficulty or subtle bias when they try to get their work that does not address popular Chinese stereotypes accepted by mainstream publishers. Yu Lihua's experience is an illustrative example. A prolific writer, she has published more than fifteen volumes of novels and collections of short stories in Chinese since her arrival in America in 1953. Regarded as precursor to the "literature of student immigrants," her works employ a wide range of narrative strategies and techniques to trace the lives of Chinese students and faculty on campuses across America. Her writing gains us an entry into the world of Chinese immigrant intellectuals that is little known to the public.

Ironically, Yu Lihua's career as an immigrant writer in America began with the publication of a prize-winning story in English. It is a romance about a young girl's journey to find her "lost" father along the Yangtze River. Shortly before her mother's death, the girl sets out to look for her father who left home many years before; but when she finally finds him, he does not recognize her. She then plays a heart-touching piano tune she learned from him in her childhood. The familiar and moving tune awakens her father's memory and conscience, and the father and daughter are finally reconciled.[16] This sentimental story helped Yu Lihua win the prestigious Samuel Goldwyn Creative Writing Award and raised her confidence about pursuing a career as a professional writer of English.

Unfortunately, Yu's subsequent writings in English—three novels about the lives of Chinese immigrants in America—were all rejected by publishers. "They [mainstream publishers] were only interested in stories that fit the pattern of 'Oriental exoticism'—the feet-binding of women and the addiction of opium-smoking men," Yu concluded. "I didn't want to write that stuff. I wanted to write about the struggle of Chinese immigrants in American society."[17] Convinced that only by conforming to these low expectations, would she fit the "ethnic niche" of the mainstream publishing market, Yu decided to engage primarily in Chinese writing. To her and her peers, writing in Chinese thus represents a vindication of their artistic integrity.

The allegation made by Yu that mainstream publishers tend to use their "gatekeeping" power to control and regulate the access of Chinese immigrant writers to readers is echoed by some American-born Chinese writers.[18] For example, Monfoon Leong recalled his works were repeatedly rejected by publishers because they thought his stories had "no readership" and that "they're not marketable." The collection of his short stories, *Number One Son*, written in the 1950s, was published posthumously in 1975 by an Asian-American publisher at the Leong family's own expense.[19] Furthermore, it is interesting that there exists a world of difference between works in Chinese and in English by the same authors. The phenomenon seems to indicate that because of a desire to win popularity in mainstream society,

Chinese immigrant writers are more likely to give up certain principles when they write in English. The controversy over Lin Yutang's writing is a case in point.

The author of more than thirty books in English, Lin Yutang (1895–1976) is perhaps the most widely read Chinese immigrant writer in America. His fame in the English-speaking world was first established with the publication of the best-seller *My Country and My People* (1935). Apparently, Lin's portrayal of the Chinese in the book as loyal, reserved, modest, obedient to elders, and respectful of authorities, and his interpretation of Taoism as a philosophy of patience and maintaining a low profile are in perfect keeping with the American view of "Orientals." For this reason, he was recognized as an exponent of China and Chinese civilization in the West,[20] and *My Country and My People* became a record-breaking success for a Chinese writer in America—eleven reprintings within two years. The fact that President George Bush quoted the book half a century later in his State of the Union Address to Congress attests to its immense popularity.[21]

Lin Yutang's subsequent writing further reinforced Western stereotypes of China and the Chinese. For example, elaborating on "the Chinese way of life" in his novel *Chinatown Family*, Lin asserts that the Chinese can succeed and get along with people everywhere largely because they know how to follow Taoist teaching to avoid confrontations: "He [Tom Fong, Sr.] had been pushed about in this country and he had made his way like water, that symbol of Taoist wisdom, seeking the low places and penetrating everywhere. . . . Laotse was right; those who occupy the lowly places can never be overthrown."[22]

However, while Lin Yutang's writing is lauded as a "cultural eye-opener" on China by mainstream readers, Asian American scholars have accused it of being "submissive" in tone and representing no more than an effort to exploit "Oriental exoticism" to boost his fame in the West. They argue that Lin's writing comes from "a white tradition of Chinese novelty literature," and it misrepresents the Chinese to court the popularity of mainstream readers in precisely the same way that Asian Americans find offensive. In fact, despite their conflicting views on many issues, Asian-American men and women scholars are all critical of Lin Yutang for his capitulation to "the white mentality," being "morally bankrupt," and buying his way into second-class white status.[23]

While Lin Yutang's English writing seems "whitewashed" to collaborate in rather than challenge the stereotyping images of the Chinese in the West, his works written in Chinese assume a surprisingly opposite role. In contrast to his polite and self-mocking tone, light-hearted jokes, and apolitical attitude that characterized his English writing, his writing in Chinese published during the same period was often highly political, angry, impassioned, and even rebellious. For example, in an essay that appeared shortly before *My Country and My People*, Lin expresses his concerns for the well-being of the Chinese people with sharp and sensitive feeling:

> I am not dreaming: I only wish there would be a good university managed by Chinese so that our children could have a place to study without having to attend schools run by *foreign devils*. . . . [Italics added.]
>
> I am not dreaming: I only wish there were a small piece of peaceful land in China where there are no wars, no exorbitant taxes. . . .

I am not dreaming: I only wish we Chinese could have the right to vote and dispose government officials. . . .

I am not dreaming: I only wish China could really ban opium and forbid anyone to use warships to carry opium. . . .

I am not dreaming: I only wish there would be no more corrupted and greedy officials and the government would not destroy people's property and lives so casually. . . .

I am not dreaming: I only wish the government could truly protect people, and would not tear down people's houses nor impose harsh taxes on peasants.[24]

In another essay, "Guoshi Weiyi" (China is in crisis), written after the publication of *My Country and My People*, Lin argued emotionally that the only way to save China was to stand up rather than to bow to foreign pressures and that the government must stop the practice of "spineless diplomacy."[25] Lin's bitter criticism of government policies and passionate defense of the rights of the people in these essays differed dramatically from his humble tone and the doctrine of "endurance and passivity" he preached in *My Country and My People*.

Lin Yutang became mainly a writer of English after he moved to the United States in 1936. But his occasional writing in Chinese still contains criticism and thorny remarks that were not seen in the English. In an essay for the Chinese press in 1943, Lin commented sarcastically on presidential elections in the United States "In not too long I will see a presidential election . . . I want to see who tell more lies to the people, the Republicans or the Democrats. If the Republicans are able to tell more lies, a Republican president will be elected; if the Democrats are able to tell more lies, a Democratic president will be elected."[26] These biting remarks certainly presented a sharp contrast to Lin's amiable words and songs of praise for America commonly found in his English writing.

Lin Yutang's progressive views reflected in his Chinese writing are no accident. He was a friend of left-wing Chinese writers such as Lu Xun and Yu Dafu, and a supporter of the student movement when he was teaching at Beijing Women's Normal University in the 1920s. Because of his radical ideas, he was wanted by the warlord regime and had to flee for his life. When the League of Defense for Chinese Democracy, a left-wing organization, was founded in Shanghai in December of 1932, Lin Yutang was elected as a member of its standing committee and participated in the organization's activities until he moved to America.[27]

There are different explanations for why Lin Yutang became so "whitewashed" in his English writing,[28] but two factors are worth mentioning. One is that he was thrilled by the fame and fortune brought by his role as "an interpreter of China to the West." Until the 1960s, Lin Yutang was the only Asian in America included in *The Picture Book of Famous Immigrants*, where his name was listed together with that of Eleutherie Irenee Dupont and Andrew Carnegie. Money also meant a great deal to Lin because he had been born and had grown up in an impoverished family. According to his daughter, Lin enjoyed enormous financial rewards for his publications in English: he made $36,000 in 1938; $42,000 in 1939; and $46,800 in 1940—extraordinary sums in those days.[29]

In addition, in his writing in English, Lin Yutang was influenced by his editors and agents, especially Pearl S. Buck, the foremost missionary writer on China, and her husband, Richard J. Walsh, publisher of the John Day Company, who brought out most of Lin's best-sellers. Lin's daughter recalls that Buck and Walsh played an extensive role in her father's choice of subject matter and themes.[30] Lin himself acknowledged this point in his preface to *My Country and My People*: "My thanks are due to Pearl S. Buck who, from the beginning to the end, gave me kind encouragement and who *personally read through the entire manuscript before it was sent to the press and edited it*, to Mr. Richard J. Walsh who offered valuable criticism while the book was in progress. . . ."[31] (Italics added.)

If Lin Yutang indeed followed the suggestions of his editors and agents in choosing themes and subject matter for his English writing, he is not alone among Chinese immigrant writers. Zhang Ailing (Eileen Chang), an eminent woman writer, was actually given plot and outlines by her agent for a novel (*The Rice-sprout Song*, 1956) she wrote in English.[32] An American agent of Anchee Min, author of the best-seller *Red Azalea* (1994), reportedly suggested to her that she add a story of lesbian affairs, as a means to appeal to the curiosity of readers, to her memoirs on her life in China during the Cultural Revolution.[33]

If the gap between Lin Yutang's writing in Chinese and English presents a fascinating example of how a Chinese writer may not always speak the same thing in each language, the fate of *Ruto Xiangzi* (*Rickshaw Boy*) in America reveals how a Chinese text can be altered to satisfy readers' sentiments when it is translated into English.

Ruto Xiangzi, the most successful work of Lao She (Shu Qingzhun, 1900–1966), was first published in serial form in 1936 in the periodical *Yuzhoufeng* founded by Lin Yutang in Shanghai.[34] A tragedy and social expose, the novel is based on a rather pessimistic and fatalistic view of life: the inevitable downfall and destruction of individuals, honest and hardworking though they may be, in an oppressed and "diseased society." At the end of the novel, Xiangzi (the hero) dies in poverty and his lover commits suicide after being trapped in a brothel.

The novel was translated into English by Evan King and published in 1945 under the title *Rickshaw Boy* by Reynal and Hitchcock (the same publisher that had brought out Lin Yutang's *My Country and My People*.)[35] Interestingly, in this translation, the last two chapters of the novel were completely rewritten; and the story ends with a happy reunion of the two young lovers. Well reviewed in mainstream magazines such as the *New Yorker* and *Saturday Review of Literature*, the novel won critical acclaim and was celebrated as the first "modern novel about China written for the Chinese, of the Chinese, and by a Chinese."[36] Reviewers also highly praised King's translation. One wrote, "There remains to say that the translation, sufficiently colloquial to give us the color of pungent Chinese phrases, is simple and pleasant to read."[37] Chosen by the Book-of-the-Month Club, the novel became a runaway best-seller. Ironically, the sweet and triumphant ending of the English version was particularly favored by the general reading public as well as critics. Unaware of its obvious clash with Lao She's original theme, reviewers all thought the hero's acting to rescue his lover from the brothel was "the climax of the story."[38]

The happy ending clearly undermined the novel's powerful message as a criticism of social injustice and contradicted in every way Lao She's intent in writing the book. Those who read the concluding chapters of King's translation and that of Lao She's original would wonder if the two are the same book. The Chinese text ends in this way:

> Handsome, ambitious, dreamer of fine dreams, selfish, individualistic, sturdy, great Hsiang Tzu (Xiangzi). No one knows how many funerals he marched in, and no one knows when or where he was able to get himself buried, that degenerate, selfish, unlucky offspring of society's diseased womb, a ghost caught in Individualism's blind alley.[39]

But King's translation ends in a dramatic and happy reunion of the hero and his lover:

> With quick movements he [Xiangzi] lifted the frail body up, folding the sheet about it, and, crouching to get through the door, he sped as fast as he could across the clearing into the woods. In the mild coolness of summer evening the burden in his arm stirred slightly, nestling closer to his body as he ran. She was alive. He was alive. They were free.[40]

The striking difference between the ending of the novel's English version and that of its Chinese text raises a question: How could this happen? Most critics suspect King rewrote the last two chapters without consulting Lao She. However, Lao She himself did not leave any written record nor make any public statement on this critical issue.[41] This is quite strange because Lao She lived in New York at that time, and during his stay in America (1946–1949), King's translation went through at least five editions in New York and London. Furthermore, it is doubtful whether King, a career foreign service officer, was able to make such a profound change entirely on his own. A former diplomat to China, King had never engaged in creative writing and did not seem to possess much literary talent. The only thing he had published by then was a research report on market and business activities in Hong Kong during World War II.[42] Carefully written and documented, the report must have been a valuable source of information to merchants and government bureaucrats. Nevertheless, it was dry and dull, and resembles not at all the rich literary flavor and local color of *Rickshaw Boy*. Therefore, it is difficult to believe that King himself was capable of rewriting the last two chapters of a modern Chinese classic and of making the change so artistically. The fact no reviewers discovered any flaws or inconsistency in those chapters of King's version attests to the quality of the work. Even Chinese critics agree that the rewriting was done "masterfully."[43]

More significantly, *Rickshaw Boy* is not Lao She's only work of which the English version differs substantially from its Chinese text. During his stay in New York, Lao She collaborated with Ida Pruitt to translate into English his novel *Sishi Tongtang* (Four generations under one roof). In rewriting the novel based on suggestions from the publisher, Lao She added thirteen episodes—nearly 20 percent of the manuscript—that he had dropped in the Chinese text. The English version, published under the title *The Yellow Storm*, was again chosen by the Book-of-the-

Month Club and became a best-seller.[44] Similar to the case of *Rickshaw Boy*, critics and readers at that time had no way of knowing *The Yellow Storm* differed significantly from its Chinese text.

Based on these facts, we *may* speculate that Lao She *might* have given some advice to King, or whoever worked with King, on how to rewrite the concluding part of *Rickshaw Boy* in English. The sweet ending, especially the rescue scene in which the hero carries his lover in his arms and rushes into the woods, would surely satisfy American readers whose literary taste was heavily influenced by Hollywood-style dramatics. Moreover, the happy ending, with two lovers being freed at last, may also have the aim of arousing pro-China sentiments among readers at the time. The novel came out on the eve of the victory in the Pacific war, a time when there were warm feelings among the American public toward China, a wartime ally. Lao She *might* have agreed that a triumphant ending of *Rickshaw Boy* could help improve the Chinese image and could imply that, like the hero of the novel, China faced bright prospects and was entering a new phase of hope and prosperity after the decade-long brutal Japanese invasion.[45]

To some extent, such a speculation is not far-fetched. Recent studies on Lao She have thrown some light on this issue. For example, Lao She's widow recalls that Lao She himself dropped the tragic ending of the Chinese text when he republished *Ruto Xiangzi* (*Rickshaw Boy*) in China in 1950. By then, Lao She had returned to Beijing and cast his lot with New China. He might have felt it was more appropriate to have "Rickshaw Boy" avoid a tragic end. Lao She even planned to write a happy sequel to the novel. "After liberation, Lao She wanted very much to write a sequel to *Ruto Xiangzi*," wrote Lao She's widow. "He wanted to write the new life of Xiangzi and his happiness."[46] It is also well-known that, during the 1950s, Lao She changed the sad endings of several of his major works because he thought they were too pessimistic to be consistent with the upbeat atmosphere in China after the Communist victory.[47] Although Lao She's life is an ultimate tragedy—he committed suicide during China's Cultural Revolution—he was optimistic about the fate of his native land when he was in America. A Chinese immigrant writer who met Lao She shortly before his repatriation was impressed by his confidence in China's future after the civil war.[48]

The fate of *Rickshaw Boy* in America and the discrepancy between writing in Chinese and English by Lin Yutang and other Chinese immigrant authors demonstrate how Chinese writers may speak differently in English. Overcome by an intention to present a world in the best possible light, they may make "conscious choices" to say what they believe mainstream audiences want to hear.[49] In this limited sense, a comment by Paul Celan, a noted German Jewish poet, can help us understand the significance of Chinese-language literature in America. Asked why he still wrote in German after he had left Germany, Celan replied: "Only in the mother tongue can one speak one's own truth. In a foreign tongue the poet lies."[50] Chinese immigrant writers may feel the same way.

NOTES

The author wishes to express his gratitude to Alex Kuo, Steven G. Kellman, Leo Ou-fan Lee, Amy Ling, and Adrienne Tien for their comments on this article.

1. I use the term "literature" here in a broad sense, including not only imaginative literature but also journalist essays and other forms of writings.

2. Li Chunhui et al., *Meizhou Huaqiao Huaren Shi* (A history of Chinese immigration to America) (Beijing: Dongfang, 1990), 250–256; Karl Lo and Him Mark Lai, comps., *Chinese Newspapers Published in North America, 1854–1975* (Washington, D.C.: Center for Chinese Research Materials, 1977), 2–3. The Massachusetts Historical Society has a copy of the newspaper in its collection.

3. Xiao-huang Yin, "Between the East and West: Sui Sin Far—the First Chinese American Woman Writer," *Arizona Quarterly*, 47:4 (Winter 1991), 49–84; Shih-shan Henry Tsai, *The Chinese Experience in America* (Bloomington: Indiana University Press, 1986), 128–132, 140; Victor G. and Brett De Bary Nee, *Longtime Californ: A Documentary Study of an American Chinatown* (reprint; Stanford: Stanford University Press, 1986), 201.

4. Roger Daniels, *Asian America: Chinese and Japanese in the United States since 1850* (Seattle: University of Washington Press, 1988), 303–306. I use the term "student immigrant" to refer to a person who enters the United States on student/scholar visa but later acquires immigrant status.

5. Peter Kwong, *The New Chinatown* (New York: Noonday Press, 1987), 60–62; Hsiang-shui Chen, *Chinatown No More* (Ithaca: Cornell University Press, 1992), 129; Qian Ning, *Liuxu Meiguo* (Studying in the USA), (Nanjing, China: Jiangsu Wenyi, 1996), 277–300. Also see *U.S. News & World Report*, September 20, 1993, 20–22.

6. Andy McCue, "Evolving Chinese Language Dailies Serve Immigrants in New York City," *Journalism Quarterly*, 52:3 (Summer 1975), 272–276; "War of Words—Chinese Style: Papers Fight for Readers Amid Rising Competition," *Los Angeles Times*, September 12, 1993, J1; Kwong, *The New Chinatown*, 37–39.

7. Tang Degan, "Xinshi Laozuzhong yu Disan Wenyizhongxin" (Founding father of new poetry and the Third Center of Literature), in *Haiwei Huaren Zhuijia Sanwenxuan* (A selection of essays by Chinese immigrant writers), ed. Mo Linshe (Hong Kong: Joint, 1983), 139–161.

8. Cao Youfang, *Meiguo Yuelian* (The American moon), (Hong Kong: Joint, 1986), 159–160.

9. *China: Nationwide Consumer Survey* (Princeton: Gallup Organization, 1994); *Zhongguo Daobao* (China guide; Los Angeles), August 26, 1994, 8.

10. Daisy Chang-ling Tseng, "Chinese Newspapers and Immigrant Assimilation in America: A Local Exploratory Study" (M.A. thesis, University of Pennsylvania, 1984), 67–70.

11. Werner Sollors, "Immigrants and Other Americans," in *Columbia Literary History of the United States*, ed. Emory Elliot (New York: Columbia University Press, 1988), 579.

12. Yi Li (Pan Xiujuan), "Dou Tai," in *Haiwei Huaren Zhuijia Xiaoshuxuan* (A selection of short stories by Chinese immigrant writers), ed. Li Li (Hong Kong: Joint, 1983), 84–116.

13. Hsian-yung Bei, "Wandering Chinese: Themes of Exile in Taiwan Fiction," *Iowa Review* (University of Iowa), 7:2/3 (Spring/Summer 1976), 205–212.

14. Zhuang Yin, "Ye Ben," in *Haiwei Huaren Zhuijia Xiaoshuxuan*, 310–311. Translation is mine.

15. My interview with Yu Lihua (Li-hua Yu) at her residence in Albany, New York, October 13, 1994. Also see Yu Lihua, *Youjian Zonlu, Youjian Zonlu* (Again the palm trees, again the palm trees), (reprint; Beijing: Youyi, 1984), 158, 270.

16. Yu Lihua, "Sorrow at the End of the Yangtze River," *UCLA Review*, March 1957, 1–13.

17. My interview with Yu Lihua. Also see Yu Lihua, "Xu" (Preface) in *Kaoyan* (An ordeal) (reprint; Hong Kong: Joint, 1983), 1.

18. Jeffery Paul Chan et al., eds. *The Big Aiiieeeee! An Anthology of Chinese American and Japanese American Literature* (New York: Meridian, 1991), xi–xvi, 1–51; Elaine Kim, *Asian American Literature: An Introduction to Its Social Context* (Philadelphia: Temple University Press, 1982), 3–22.

19. Monfoon Leong, *Number One Son* (San Francisco: East/West, 1975), vii–xiv.

20. Wing-tsit Chan, "Lin Yutang, Critics and Interpreter," *College English*, 8:4 (January 1949), 163–169.

21. *Meizhou Huaqiao Rebao* (Chinese American Daily; New York), February 11, 1989, 2.

22. Lin Yutang, *Chinatown Family* (New York: John Day, 1948), 148. Also see Mao-chu Lin, "Identity and Chinese-American Experiences: A Study of Chinatown American Literature since World War II" (Ph.D. diss., University of Minnesota, 1987), 73–84.

23. Frank Chin et al., eds., *Aiiieeeee! An Anthology of Asian-American Writers* (Washington, D.C.: Howard University Press, 1973), vii–xvi; Kim, *Asian American Literature*, 27–29. It is noteworthy that Chinese writers in Lin Yutang's time did not hold his English writing in high estimation either; they thought it, albeit elegant in style, rather superficial in substance. For example, in his novel *Weicheng* (Fortress besieged, 1946), Qian Zhongsu, a renowned writer and critic, mentioned Lin's English writing with a humorous yet biting touch. He placed *My Country and My People* alongside books such as *How to Gain a Husband and Keep Him* — listing them as favorite readings of a daughter of a Chinese comprador in Shanghai. Some Chinese critics also dubbed *My Country and My People* as *Selling Country and Selling People* because, phonetically, the word "my" in Chinese has the same sound as "selling" (mai). See Qian Zhongsu, *Weicheng* (reprint; Beijing: Renmin, 1990), 45; Lin Taiyi (Anor Lin), *Lin Yutang Zhuan* (Biography of Lin Yutang) (Beijing: Zhongguo Xiju, 1994), 136.

24. "Xinnian Zhimeng—Zhongguo Zhimeng" (New Year's dream: My wishes for China), *Dongfang Zazhi* (Shanghai), 1933. Reprinted in Lin Taiyi, *Lin Yutang Zhuan*, 104–106. Translation is mine.

25. Reprinted in Lin Taiyi, *Lin Yutang Zhuan*, 109–111.

26. Quoted from R. David Arkush and Leo O. Lee, trans. and eds., *Land Without Ghosts: Chinese Impressions of America from the Mid-Nineteenth Century to the Present* (Berkeley: University of California Press, 1989), 161–162.

27. Wan Jinping, *Lin Yutang Lun* (On Lin Yutang) (Xi'an: Shanxi Renming, 1987), 15–26.

28. For more information on this issue, see ibid., 29–32.

29. Lin Taiyi, *Lin Yutang Zhuan*, 158, 165.

30. Ibid., 131–49.

31. Lin Yutang, *My Country and My People* (New York: Reynal & Hitchcock, 1935), xviii. Reynal & Hitchcock was a division of the John Day Company.

32. Yu Qing, *Qicai Yinu — Zhang Ailing* (Zhang Ailing: A talented woman writer) (Jinan, China: Shandong Huabao, 1995), 122.

33. Anchee Min, *Red Azalea* (New York: Pantheon Books, 1994). I have received the information from several of my friends and colleagues.

34. Lao She and Lin Yutang were close friends. It was no accident that some of Lao She's most important works were first published in magazines founded or edited by Lin Yutang.

35. Lao She, *Rickshaw Boy*, trans. Evan King (New York: Reynal & Hitchcock, 1945). Evan King is the nom de plume of Robert Spencer Ward.

36. Hamilton Basso, "New Bottles, Old Wine," *New Yorker*, August 11, 1945, 61.

37. Harrison Smith, "Out of the Streets of China," *Saturday Review of Literature*, July 28, 1945, 12.

38. Quoted in *Two Writers and the Cultural Revolution*, ed. George Kao (Hong Kong: Chinese University Press, 1980), 38. Also see Smith, "Out of the Streets of China."

39. Lao She, *Rickshaw*, trans. Jean M. James (Honolulu: University of Hawaii Press, 1979), 249. Also see Perry Link, "End of *Rickshaw Boy*," in Kao, *Two Writers and the Cultural Revolution*, 50.

40. Lao She, *Rickshaw Boy*, 384.

41. Wang Renhua, *Lao She Xiaoshuo Xinlun* (New studies of Lao She's fiction) (Shanghai: Xulin, 1995), 216. Personal memories have not provided much help on this issue. George Kao said that Lao She told him King wrote the last two chapters himself, but Lao She's widow mentioned nothing on this critical issue in her memoir except to make a rather brief yet ambiguous comment: "So far we haven't got much information on Lao She's work during his stay in America." Lin Yutang's daughter, who saw Lao She frequently in New York at that time, recalled Lao She seemed to be pleased by the popularity of *Rickshaw Boy* in America. See George Kao, *Two Writers and the Cultural Revolution*, 30; Hu Jichin and Su Yi, *Sanji Lao She* (Random notes on Lao She) (Beijing: Beijing Renmin, 1986), 281; Lin Taiyi, *Lin Yutang Zhuan*, 188.

42. Robert S. Ward, *Hong Kong Under Japan's Occupation: A Case Study in the Enemy Techniques of Control* (Washington, D.C.: Department of Commerce, 1943).

43. Kao, *Two Writers and the Cultural Revolution*, 38.

44. Hu Jichin and Su Yi, *Sanji Lao She*, 278–289; Lao She, *The Yellow Storm*, trans. Ida Prutt (New York: Harcourt, Brace, 1951).

45. Incidentally, the discrepancy between *Rickshaw Boy* in Chinese and English resembles that in writings by Abraham Cahan. A renowned Jewish-American writer, Cahan made changes in his Yiddish novel when he turned it into English.

46. Hu Jichin and Su Yi, *Sanji Lao She*, 154.

47. Ibid., 282–283; Wang Renhua, *Lao She Xiaoshuo Xinlun*, 211–213, 216–218.

48. Weng Shaoqiu, *Wo Zai Jiujinshan Sishinian* (My forty years in San Francisco) (Shanghai: Shanghai Renmin, 1988), 36.

49. Discrepancies between Chinese and English versions of the same work can also be found in bilingual Chinese-American newspapers, largely because they aim at different readers. For example, the English version of *Sampan*, a Chinese-English weekly published in Boston, usually contains reports on Chinese and Asian cultural events and interviews of prominent Chinese and Asian Americans; its Chinese section covers more activities within the Chinese community.

50. John Felstiner, *Paul Celan: Poet, Survivor, Jew* (New Haven: Yale University Press, 1995), 46. Of course, Celan's comment comes from the context of a Jewish writer using the German language after the Holocaust. In addition, although there are writers who tend to tell the truth in their mother tongues, others may more likely do that in acquired languages.

Part IV

Multilingualism as a Way of Life

Multilingualism is not just a matter of a few established literary genres. The pressures of a multilingual society are palpable in monolingual texts of many genres in single languages, and can be measured by the presence of small thematic or linguistic elements. Neither journalism nor drama—and not even the orthodox sermon—can stay pure and untouched by the American multilingual environment.

Menahem Blondheim's "Divine Comedy: The Jewish Orthodox Sermon in America, 1881–1939" examines the little-known tradition of Hebrew Orthodox sermons printed in the United States, in which thematic references to American life, as well as such American elements as humor and chastisement, appear and give this tradition a distinctly New World flavor. In " '*Ersatz*-Drama' and Ethnic (Self-)Parody: Adolf Philipp and the Decline of New York's German-Language Stage, 1890–1920," Peter Conolly-Smith draws on his extensive research in the German-language press of New York City and here follows the career of the German-American playwright Adolf Philipp, whose career in delightful representation of English-German language interferences became enmeshed in the politically charged language debates of World War I. While linguistic assimilation may have been a stock element in broad comedy, it also marked the fate of a language community as a whole.

Anna Maria Martellone's "The Formation of an Italian-American Identity in the Italian-American Popular Theatre" continues her work on Italian-American cultural history with an examination of the immigrant theater; and her focus on code-switching, the funny linguistic mixture that has been called "Italo-Americanese" or "Italglish" invites comparison with Conolly-Smith's work on German-American comedy, Taubenfeld's examination of Yinglish and the whole section on "Melting Glots" that follows the present one. In "Crossings and Double-Crossings: Polish-Language Immigrant Narratives of the Great Migration," Karen Majewski reviews little-known Polish-language immigrant narratives and fictions from Julian Czupka to Helena Staś in which the experience of migration and the themes of the "grynhorn" and of ethnic tricksterism are subtly negotiated.

It is no coincidence that intersections of comedy and multilingualism emerge again and again in this section (and elsewhere in *Multilingual America*), for the comic interaction of different linguistic and cultural codes may well be one of the mainsprings of what has been called "American humor." What the essays in the-

189

following section also show is that the non-English parts of the American literary tradition constitute links between English-language literary and cultural trends and those present in many other languages. Thus American multilingual literature emerges as an ideal subject for American studies, comparative literature, and the various language fields.

Chapter Thirteen

Divine Comedy
The Jewish Orthodox Sermon in America, 1881–1939

Menahem Blondheim

The commotion in the vicinity of Norfolk Street, on 21 July 1888, was unusual even by the standard of New York's bustling Lower East Side. Thousands of Jews had flocked to the Beth Hamidrash Hagadol, New York's largest Orthodox synagogue. The sanctuary, with a seating capacity of two thousand, was packed by three thousand of New York's Yiddish-speaking Jews. Thousands more crowded on the streets surrounding the synagogue desperately trying to enter. The throngs were anxiously awaiting the inaugural sermon of Rabbi Jacob Joseph (1840–1902), New York's first and, as it would turn out, last chief rabbi.

Rabbi Joseph, formerly rabbi in Vilna, "Lithuania's Jerusalem," had been elected to the post by a group of Orthodox congregation leaders who had associated in an attempt to establish a framework that would manage the religious affairs and communal interests of the city's Orthodox immigrants. The New Yorkers had decided on Rabbi Joseph after two years of intrigue-ridden negotiations with the highest echelons of the East European rabbinate. On either side of the Atlantic it was understood that the chief rabbi's mission was to represent the European rabbinical elite in America. Building on his prestige and wielding his rabbinical authority, the chief rabbi was expected to provide leadership and bring peace to the strife-ridden community, order to its chaotic religious affairs, and pride to the immigrants struggling to accommodate to a bewildering new world.[1]

Rabbi Joseph was not the obvious choice. There were greater lights than he in what was considered the rabbi's supreme function, interpreting and applying Jewish law, and there were others with better credentials in communal authority and greater experience in public leadership. Yet Rabbi Joseph had qualifications that the New York Orthodox leaders could hardly overlook, in particular a fabulous reputation as an orator. Throughout the Jewish pale of settlement in Eastern Europe, Rabbi Joseph was recognized as one of the greatest, and most beloved, preachers of the times.[2]

The thousands surrounding Beth Hamidrash Hagadol in the hope of hearing the words of the famous preacher appeared to justify the most optimistic expectations of the members of the nominating committee. The local police found it necessary to call in reinforcements to try to control the excited crowds attempting to break into the synagogue. Only after threats, then use, of force, was the venerable rabbi, escorted by a throng of policemen, able to make his entrance into the building. The immense crowd fell silent as the rabbi walked up to the ark, kissed its curtain—the parochet—then approached the podium and began his homily, which focused on the midrash, "A precious stone hung from Abraham's neck."[3]

That precise moment was the peak of Jacob Joseph's American career. It was also the point from which it began to plummet. "He did not satisfy his audience here," noted dryly the wise and scholarly Judah David Eisenstein (1854–1956), vice president of Beth Hamidrash Hagadol. Although he preached the same sort of sermon to, demographically speaking, the same Eastern European sort of audience in both Vilna and New York, the latter would ultimately find Rabbi Joseph's sermons "loathsome."[4] Indeed, journalist Abraham Cahan reported, "[S]ome of the very people who drank in his words thirstily in Vilna left the synagogue in the middle of his sermon here." The inaugural sermon apparently fell flat, as did practically everything else the rabbi would attempt to do in America. Defeated and abandoned, both physically paralyzed and spiritually spent, a pauper Rabbi Joseph would pass away in New York, on 22 July 1902.[5]

A half century ago a practitioner of, and an authority on, Jewish homiletics, Shim'on Glicksberg, tried to explain the Rabbi Joseph fiasco by blaming "the air of America," which had "evaporated the taste" of Jacob Joseph's sermons. Glicksberg was arguing, in essence, that homiletics and exegetics did not travel well: "[Rabbi Joseph's] wise and sharp sermons failed in America, for they could not affect the hearts of New York's Jews, who had become distanced—through the effects of the new environment—from the style of the traditional sermon. . . . It was good for Vilna, not for New York." The sermon, it would appear, was highly sensitive to space, and there was something in the New York milieu that made a significant difference.[6]

In explaining the failure of great European preachers in America, Judah David Eisenstein pointed out two factors that, he thought, made a difference. "The simpletons—who constitute a majority of those attending the sermon in America—have become accustomed to quenching their [spiritual] thirst with the lukewarm, [and their hunger] with the bran which the preachers set before them in thundering voices, to the point of unsettling their nerves. Consequently they have lost their spiritual senses and their ability to discern between good and bad." Eisenstein distinguishes a new order of American preachers, hints that the composition of the audience had changed, and, moreover, suggests a process of transformation in its tastes. American audiences had become conditioned by popular, compelling, and unsettling sermons to a new style of preaching. Indeed, as early as 1887 a discerning New York rabbi, Moses Weinberger (b. 1854), cautioned prospective European immigrant-scholars that they would find it difficult to "satisfy the tastes of American sermon audiences."[7]

These early students and critics of the Orthodox American sermon seemed to concur that a near-instantaneous transformation had occurred in the traditional sermon upon its transplantation to America. Or perhaps a reversed perspective would be more appropriate: with the mass immigration of Orthodox Jews there emerged a new kind of Orthodox sermon, born in the U.S.A., which supplanted the traditional, East European rabbinical homily.

The history, literature, and theology of the Orthodox American sermon has remained a vast but unexplored continent.[8] Sermons were delivered weekly, sometimes even daily, by many hundreds of rabbis and reverends. Hundreds of thousands of American Jews heard these sermons, in hundreds of communities all over the United States, ever since Orthodoxy took root in America. Ironically, the history of this most public, commonplace activity has remained something of a hidden history.[9] Whatever the causes of the neglect of the Orthodox-American sermon, scarcity of research materials was not one of them. Immigrant preachers left to posterity an impressive corpus of sermonic literature, in Hebrew and in Yiddish, in books, pamphlets, periodicals, and in manuscript collections. In my best estimate, more than five hundred publications that include Orthodox sermons of the period under consideration are extant, besides many dozens of collections of sermons in manuscript. Moreover, this vast library contains numerous metasermons providing the preachers' analysis of American sermonics, and a host of reflexive comments presenting their own understanding of what they thought they were doing. These sermons-on-sermons and other explicit statements about the American pulpit serve as a useful key to opening this large library and making sense of it.

Given the state of the field, what appears necessary is a preliminary sketch of the most prominent contours of Orthodox immigrant sermonics, etched in very broad strokes.[10] Hence, the generous periodization proposed here, spanning 1881, when the immigration movement of East European Jews to the United States started accelerating in earnest, and the eve of the Second World War. By then the absorption process of the masses of immigrants—an influx that had peaked around the turn of century, significantly declined in the years of the First World War, dwindled thereafter, and practically subsided after passage of the immigration restriction laws of 1924—had generally been completed. While a strong case could be made for significant changes in the American sermon within this period, the proposed temporal framework still provides a degree of unity and coherence. This unity is, above all, generational: it encompassed the age of the first generation's "old Orthodoxy" as opposed to the modern- or neo-Orthodoxy of the subsequent generations of American-raised (and mostly -born) Orthodox Jews.[11] This was the era in which immigrant rabbis preached in Yiddish and in Hebrew to their fellow Yiddish-speaking immigrants.[12]

However abundant the materials, studying the sermon in the context of its time and place constitutes a methodological nightmare. The sermon, after all, is a one-time public, oral, experience; it is evanescent. The text of the sermon is at best only a reflection, a written echo of the verbal role of one participant in a public event, or as anthropologists would call it, a cultural performance. The full meaning of such performances emerges only in the process of playing them out, in the present case, through the social context of preaching and the cultural significance of the occasion.[13]

Not only does sermonic literature exclude the dimension of occasion, omit the roles of all participants other than the preacher and, to an extent, the effect of audience feedback on the sermon, it can hardly document the full range of the preacher's messages. While the text is capable of documenting verbal utterances, it leaves no record of the preacher's use of other "cultural media" that include intonation, accent and diction, gesticulation and emphasis, facial expressions and body language. As the Pinsk-born New York preacher Isaac Waltman explained apologetically in the introduction to his *Siach Yitzchak*:

> Seeing the book is very different from live hearing, it lacks the pleasantness of voice and the sweetness of melody, for there is time for tears and time for laughter. And while at times I had made my juniors laugh, when necessary I extracted tears even from flint stone.[14]

But the problems of documentation only begin with the complex ecology of the performed sermon. The reader of sermonic literature has no way of evaluating the reliability of what is presented as the text of a live sermon. He has first to ascertain whether the printed homily was ever delivered as a sermon, and if so, to evaluate the extent to which the text represents all that was said, nothing but what was said, in the same form in which it was said.[15] While these latter parameters inevitably vary from text to text, in the case of the immigrant sermon, one element in the gap between the oral and the written is consistent. A substantial majority of Orthodox American sermons were delivered in Yiddish but published in Hebrew. Built into the study of these texts, therefore, is a very significant distancing between the oral performance and the written record.

Fortunately for the study of American sermonics, there appears to have been a potent force working in the opposite direction, providing a degree of validity and authenticity to the texts as representative of the oral sermon, and a certain proximity to the life world of the sermonic event. This force was the great demand of American preachers for appropriate subject matter for their sermons. Indeed, much evidence suggests that an important share of American sermonic literature was produced to satisfy precisely this kind of demand, and it was therefore consciously attuned to the requirements of oral delivery. This dynamic cycle of sermon-to-text-to-sermon is manifest in many explicit statements in introductions to sermonic publications to the effect that the work contained "written utterances" that were actually delivered, and well received.[16] Thus Washington, D.C.'s Gedalia Silverstone (b. 1872), in his introduction to the second volume of *Beth Meir*, attributed the commercial success of his earlier volumes to the fact that the printed sermons were "arranged so that every preacher can preach directly out of the book with no need for omission or commission."[17] In his introduction to *Me'irat Einayim*, Silverstone felt secure enough to tease his potential clients; he asked that those who preached his sermons do so standing, rather than sitting down, since it would be "impolite" and inappropriate for the preacher to sit while the sermon he delivers stands in print.[18] Silverstone himself, it should be noted, drew from the texts of other American preachers, as is evidenced by his annotations to a volume he owned of sermons by a popular contemporary, Judah Leib Lazerow.[19]

Indirect evidence, too, indicates that much of the literature, rather than repre-senting an extension of the preacher's appeal to the public through a different medium, was intended for the use of other preachers. Numerous approbations to volumes of American sermons recommend the texts for repetition from the pulpit.[20] Even the Hebrew titles of volumes of sermons indicated their intended readership: *New Light for Preachers, Ideas and Materials for Preaching, Light [for the path] of the Preachers*, even *Sermons to Utter*.[21] In the long lists of subscribers to sermonic publications (*Prenomeranten*) that were commonly appended to the published work, one usually finds an outstanding representation of rabbis, preachers, and congregations.[22] The remarkable proliferation of anthologies of sermons in America and the publication of sermons in local rabbinical periodicals and handbooks un-derscores the great demand for sermonic subject matter. A major contemporary authority on Hebrew book culture in America, Ephraim Deinard (1846–1930), commenting on the overall output of homiletic literature in America, averred that "the publishers' income came not from the pockets of the people, for none would purchase books of sermons, only from the pockets of other preachers who are seeking building blocks and literary material for their sermons."[23] Considering the publication of sermons as an intermediate tool for diffusing the sermon from one pulpit to others would work to keep our sources honest to the real life world of the sermonic experience.[24]

The abundance and variety of Orthodox American sermonic literature can thus be attributed, at least in part, to strong forces on the demand side. Aspects of its structure would further indicate that the demand focused on local materials, prom-inent among them prepackaged modules and do-it-yourself sermons. A closer look at the institutional framework through which the Orthodox American sermon developed, as well as at characteristic attributes of its form and content, may well provide preliminary insights into the nature of the dynamics shaping this demand structure.

Immigrant Orthodox Jews seemed to have had an insatiable appetite for sermons. "Nowadays," complained Rabbi Shraga Rosenberg of New York (b. 1871) shortly after the turn of the century, "there are numerous leaders who deliver innumerable sermons. Our people have never heard as many sermons as they hear now." Ac-cording to Rosenberg, a dramatic organizational change occurred in the nature of the pulpit in America. "Formerly," he explained, "the rabbi preached only four times a year, on New Year, on the Day of Atonement, on the Sabbath of Repentance [between these two holidays], and on the Great Sabbath [preceding Passover]. But now, the rabbi preaches on each and every Sabbath. And in a number of syna-gogues, . . . the rabbi is required to preach three and four times on every Sabbath."[25] In still other synagogues the rabbi was expected to preach on weekdays as well. It also became expected of him to address the crowd on a variety of occasions, such as at the developing institution of the Bar Mitzvah celebration, at weddings and even anniversaries, at circumcisions and funerals, on the occasions of unveiling tombstones and the laying of cornerstones for synagogues and other communal buildings. The sarcastic New York commentator Rabbi Shmuel Hurwitz (1862–

1943) put it succinctly: America was "the land of the sermon." The prominent educator, author, and preacher Shmarya Leib Hurwitz (1878–1938) preferred the tag "the land of talk and preaching."

The rabbi, now required to "divide his waking hours" between a host of such "varied and strange affairs" was an excellent target for Shmuel Hurwitz sarcasm. "In this hour," he began illustrating the rabbi's crowded itinerary,

> he stands and eulogizes [not merely a simpleton, but] a simpleton's wife, and praises her profusely for not having strayed from the permissible interpretation of the depths of the Torah in her erudite study. . . . This of course all takes place on Sunday, for in America there is no time to die [on working days]. In this hour he travels to the world of the dead to sermonize at a tombstone unveiling ceremony and there he addresses the wood and stone. In this hour he performs the wedding ceremonies of pregnant and nursing brides, who find it difficult [to follow the custom and] fast on their wedding day.

The rabbi then returns to his synagogue and "as a dessert, [must] provide an American sermon to fit the gastronomic taste of the two legged creatures that appear at the synagogue at that time."[26] In the land of the sermon, preaching became an integral part of synagogue service, just as it was part of the liturgy in neighboring Christian churches.[27]

The great expansion of the sermon as a communal institution had obvious, far-reaching implications for the rabbi's craft and for the nature of sermonic literature. In Europe, observed Rabbi Isaac Bunin (b. 1871/72), where the rabbi's sermons were few and far between, his "words were dear" to the members of the community "who found them exceedingly attractive and benevolent." But America was different. Having to preach so often, the American rabbi faced a serious problem: "the audience is used to the rabbi's sermons and it has become much more difficult to satisfy them," and to provide "interesting novellae each and every time."[28] Consequently, the beleaguered American rabbi was driven, according to Shmuel Hurwitz,

> to purchase a homiletic library of all styles—in effect open an apothecary for mixing all sorts of essences to include jokes and jests. Combining these with his original style, brought from his alma matter, he mixes and readies a potion of incense in the fragrance of which the entire audience will bask with pleasure, even including the women.[29]

One of the most respected and most prolific American preachers, Abraham Aaron Yudelovitch (1850–1930), provided a glimpse of the dilemmas with which rabbis dealt in their literary workshop—that "apothecary" of Hurwitz's description. Yudelovitch, president of the Union of Rabbis and Preachers of North America, was invited to speak at a wedding. "Yes my brethren and fellow nationals, ladies and gentlemen [transliterated]," the egotistic rabbi addressed his crowd:

> What am I to do now? If I recite a pilpul in Jewish law as becomes a rabbi such as myself, you will laugh at me [and say] Rabbi Yudelovitch comes to a party, to a dance, and wants to impress us with his legal ingenuity. This is no place for that. And if I preach a sermon, you will laugh and say: we all know that rabbi Yudelovitch is the greatest preacher in the whole country. . . . [B]ut this is not the place to deliver his sermons. And If I speak empty words, a jocular speech, you will laugh at me and say:

from such a great rabbi as Yudelovitch we hoped to hear words of wisdom, not empty words and jokes.

Yudelovitch ultimately chose to repeat a popular proverb, "in place of the jester," but also added a midrashic exegesis. He, like many other rabbis who faced similar dilemmas and found what they considered an appropriate sermonic solution, went on to publish their creative responses. Yudelovitch himself published numerous volumes of sermons for the Sabbath and holidays. They were intended, as he wrote, for "many people" who "want to preach on the Torah, but have not a sufficient store of things to say." In publishing these works, wrote a smug Yudelovitch, he was merely fulfilling the biblical commandment "that thy brother [preacher] may live with thee" (Lev., xxxiii, 36).[30]

The vast body of American sermonic literature can thus be seen as a kind of rabbinical marketplace. The printing press became a forum in which preachers, overwhelmed by soaring demand for sermons, shopped for materials that would enable them to provide their audiences with "interesting novellae each and every time" they preached. In this marketplace they would find creative solutions that had worked for other preachers when put on the spot to deliver an appropriate sermon for an occasion their European mentors never imagined to require one. Here they would shop for "all sorts of ingredients, to include jokes and jests." Here, too, they would place their own wares on the bookshelf for the benefit of their colleagues.[31]

The beleaguered immigrant preachers became dependent on the market of sermons transcribed for them by their peers. They could not turn to the vast body of Jewish preaching accumulated throughout the ages, nor could they draw even on sermons they themselves had delivered or heard in the old country, for, as one of the only preachers successful both in Europe and in America, the outstanding Zionist spokesman Zvi Hirsh Masliansky (1856–1943) had explained,

> Here, in the land of freedom life has been completely changed, and with it the needs [of the audience]. And since my orations and spoken essays are the children of life, they too have changed. All that I had preached [since stepping onto the pulpit for the first time, a jubilee ago] overseas, I could not preach here. Because it is a central theme in preaching that not only the right thing for the right time is commendable, but also [the right thing] for the right place.[32]

Traditional homiletics and the sermons of the old country would not satisfy American audiences. The immigrant Orthodox publics, consisting of those "two legged creatures" to whom Hurwitz referred, demanded an "American sermon." What made a sermon American?

To begin with, an American sermon would have to be simple. In comparing sermons of popular American preachers such as Silverstone, Lazerow, and Abraham N. Galant to the publications of outstanding European authors of modern sermonics such as Yoseph Dov Soleveichik, Yosef Chaim Kara, Noach Rabinowitz, Chaim Rumshishker, or even Jacob Joseph, Ya'akov David Willowsky, and Zvi Hirsh Orliansky (who would ultimately preach in America), one is struck, overall, by the contrast in structure.[33] The European sermons tended to have a highly elaborate, complex edifice. Numerous scholarly digressions congested the already complex flow of central ideas.[34] American sermons, on the whole, appeared to present a much more compact, direct, and simple structure to frame a more restricted flow of ideas.

The characteristic intricacy of European sermons was due in part to the scale and to the nature of the sources it opened. Numerous complicated sources, often-times legal ones, were injected into the discussion, each requiring interpretation and elaboration, which, in turn, burdened the edifice. The texts used in anchoring American sermons tended to be much simpler. Occasionally, the central texts were simply biblical verses, or well-known midrashim such as those used by Rashi in his commentary on the Bible (the standard commentary in use), or those incorporated in the popular *Ein Ya'akov*. Moreover, the exegesis of classical sources, however simple, tended to be consistently sacrificed to a narrative created by the preacher himself.

If simplification of structure and of texts and prooftexts was condoned as a necessity, the shift in the sermon's focus from exegesis to free rhetoric, from dis-cussing traditional sources to the preachers' own narrative, was unacceptable to the more traditional practitioners. Lieber Kahan, preacher and legal scholar who began his American career in the South, offered a proverb that captured the contrast, or as he perceived it, the gap in values between these two distinct styles of preaching. In Kahan's proverb the traditional preacher was the bee, the new preacher was the spider. The former collected nectar from the flowers in the textual gardens of the sages and processed it into sermons as sweet and as wholesome as honey. Along came the spiders and began building webs of words extracted solely from their own bodies, "to the extent of not providing in their orations even a hint to the sayings of the sages." The architecture of the web, conceded Kahan, may indeed be won-derfully wise and aesthetically pleasing. But coming to the moral of the proverb, he pointed out that unlike the bee's extractions, the taste of the spider web was poisonous, and moreover, that the beautiful edifice was ephemeral, it could be destroyed by a single blow. A house, Kahan believed, if not grounded on the wisdom of the sages, could not stand.[35]

Criticism of sermons devoid of exegesis and scholarship, short on references to rabbinical texts and long on the analysis of news and politics and descriptions of everyday life, became a favorite target for criticism by the more traditional preach-ers. Not deep beneath the surface, the opposition to this new, seemingly unschol-arly, sermon reflected professional anxiety: after many years of study preparing for the rabbinate, rabbis feared the usurpation of the field by those who were not properly trained for the pulpit. One such scathing comment in reference to the "phony rabbis who desecrate God's name" was offered by Detroit's Yehudah Leib Levine (b. 1863) late in the nineteenth century: "Whoever has a slick enough tongue to offer jocular proverbs from the pulpit, they will take him as rabbi and teacher. Doing so they turn down an expert rabbi who had filled his stomach with Talmud and compilations of the law, should the latter not speak slickly."[36]

Even the learned, however, would ultimately have to make allowances to the demand for simpler, rhetorically pleasing, sermons. Chanoch Zundel Levine (b. 1882), in his 1938 *Drashot Shlemot* (Complete sermons), offered a general characterization that justified, in traditional terms, the exegetic style that came to dominate the American pulpit. Drawing on a talmudic distinction between two strategies of midrash, "drilling" and "stringing," he suggested that the former implied the opening and interpreting of a central text, deriving from it or attributing to it an idea on which the preacher wished to focus. In contrast, the stringer or "chain maker" strung his central idea from a series of texts and fragments and reached his point through collating—commonly torturing—them into a unified structure. In America, agreed Levine's contemporary, the essayist Shmuel Mirsky, "drilling" became the dominant style of preaching; "stringing" was generally abandoned.[37] Naturally, there was great demand for "drilling"-style materials in the sermonic marketplace. The vast body of "stringing" sermons was no longer useful.

Beyond the dramatic change in the institutional role of the sermon and the changes in its structure and strategy, the most marked change was in the topical focus of sermons. The overall tendency was a shift from intellectual and moral issues concerning law and ethics, which affected Jewish life in the abstract, to a powerful zoom-in on concrete everyday problems, immediately affecting the lives of audience and preacher. The topical venue of the sermon became the real world just outside the synagogue, its temporal focus became the day-to-day experiences and struggles of the immigrant public. This transformation would have far-reaching implications on both the role of the preacher and the function of the sermon.

Skimming through practically any volume of sermons published in the United States during this period may demonstrate how central groping with reality had become. Even the sermons that Chief Rabbi Jacob Joseph preached in the course of his American career point in the direction of the sweeping change in the sermon's orientation. Just prior to his immigration, the rabbi had published *Lebeit Ya'akov*, a collection of his Vilna sermons. Outstanding in their exegetical sophistication, the sermons in the volume were devoid of any hint of the ephemeral.[38] A subsequent 1896 edition of the book included a number of sermons Rabbi Joseph had preached in New York. In them, one finds explicit references to the circumstances of New York's Jewish community, most notably, discussions of the rabbi's ordeal in trying to bring order to the chaotic kosher meat market (an effort that played a major role in his downfall). Even the texts that the preacher opened in his American sermons hinted at his personal predicament. The sermon on the weekly portion of *Vayishlach* began with the biblical text describing the brothers' hatred of Joseph in contrast to Israel's love of him. Another sermon opened the midrash that begins: "Jacob wished to live in peace" but the peace was broken by the jealousy and enmity between his sons. After quoting the midrash, Rabbi Joseph wrote: "Why do they hate him [i.e., Joseph]?" In 1889, the communal organization that had nominated Rabbi Joseph published a pamphlet containing sermons he had delivered in New York. They too referred explicitly, and prominently, to the New York environment, spanning issues of kashrut, the secularization of the local Jews, and the lowly state of Jewish education in town.[39] Yet these adjustments only signaled the tide of sweeping change that had been taking place. For Rabbi Joseph, the adjustments appear to have been too little, and to have come too late.

Above and beyond its characteristic attributes with regard to structure and sources, exegetic strategy and style, topics and themes, an "American sermon" was one in which two ingredients came to be expected, in fact became paramount. The first was humor. The "bran," preached in a "thundering voice" by the immigrant preacher, could be expected to be eminently entertaining, at times downright hilarious. "Fable and flower and frolic," one rabbi would characterize the immigrant sermon, in what was a ringing Hebrew alliteration. "A system of excessive buffoonery," proposed another. "Jocular proverbs from the podium," according to a third.[40] Dov Ber Borochov (1872–1939) conceived the "major change which has taken place in the nature of American preachers in the past decades" in their becoming entertainers. "The entire sermon," lamented Borochov, "is no more than a medley of proverbs, and tales, and occasional jokes, and the preacher's supreme goal is to frolic the public mind. Indeed, the audience has come to view the preacher as a clown dancing on a rope." Shraga Rosenberg concurred, and took the theme one step further. "The severe deterioration in the calling of the religious leader in America" had made him not simply an entertainer but a comedian. His role was now "to jest in the face of the crowd, to dance and mock, and the more he succeeds in laughing in jests in his sermons the better."[41]

Ben Zion Eisenstadt (1873–1951) shuddered at the religious implications of this dominant thrust in the immigrant sermon: "The preachers . . . bring the masses to a state of laughter and light-mindedness, in the precise place of which the verse implores 'my sanctuary shall ye reverence!' " (Lev., xix, 30). Ze'ev Levy put it most explicitly, and in terms appropriate for the proverbially materialistic immigrant crowd. "The price of Orthodox Judaism is very low," he wrote in *Hadeah Vehadibur*: "For three dollars a year [in synagogue membership fees] you will get the opportunity to hear 'the artist of the ark . . . what is called in the Gentiles' language 'a comedian.' " A century later apocrypha would have a rabbi-turned-professional comedian, Jacky Mason, openly and humorously acknowledge that his second career was merely an extension of his first, albeit to larger audiences.[42]

The second dominant ingredient in the American sermon was reproof. However humorous, the immigrant sermon was at the same time scathingly critical of the congregation and pessimistic as to its future. And significantly, as so many quotations in the foregoing may illustrate, these two seemingly opposing elements—jokes and jeremiads—tended to appear in the same sermons. On the face of it, the emphasis on both humor and reproof could underscore the dominance of the latter. As court jesters knew for millennia, humor could help ease the tensions and antagonism bred of chastisement; it could serve as a sugar coating that would help the medicine of reproof go down.[43] This, however, does not appear to have been the case in the immigrant sermon. More than coexist, "laugh . . . and tears" appeared to merge in symbiosis.

Humor tended to be of the agonistic type; it underscored conflict, imbalance, paradox. Quite often it demonstrated a subversive streak, teasing the audience, poking fun at it and invoking laughter at its expense. It had a bittersweet texture and flavor. Concurrently, the American Orthodox jeremiad was anything but an elegiac lamentation. Chastisement and the depiction of an inevitable bleak future for Jews and Judaism in America was commonly dressed in thoroughly upbeat and amusing rhetorical forms. Irony was the trope of reproof. Chastisement was exercised through the satirical, sarcastic, and sardonic.[44]

Inexorably linked, comedy and reproof pointed in a single direction, both providing the audience with uses and gratifications. As the author of *Bigdey Srad* complained, the American rabbi

> descends to the level of the masses, his audience, and adjusts his tenor and perspective according to their whim. One time he laughs, another he cries. At times he cheers and sings, at times he wails and laments. At times he waxes poetic, at times he roars. At times he compliments and praises, at times he jests and criticizes. All—according to the wants and passions of the people whom he wants to please.[45]

Both comedy and lament were in demand. Both offered catharsis to the congregation.

But if audiences wanted both "jests and criticisms," rabbis and preachers felt very differently about either of the two. Chastisement was fine, indeed urgently called for, but comedy was an aberration, as Eisenstadt put it, an outright desecration of the sanctuary. In comment after reflexive comment concerning the American pulpit, authors of sermonics scolded their fellow preachers for their excessive use of comedy and for their paucity of reproof. They considered themselves working against the grain. They would not resort to frivolity and comedy, and would be daring enough to challenge and severely rebuke their congregations.

To an extent, these repeated criticisms were deserved, but a broader look at the confluence of immigrant sermons would suggest that they should not necessarily be taken at face value. Yes, a majority of preachers indeed incorporated humorous materials in their sermons, and yes, authors who congratulated themselves for criticizing their bread givers did indeed deliver jeremiads. But as it turns out, reproof was not the exception, it was the rule; and even those preachers who were most critical of their colleagues' jocularity did not necessarily refrain from "fable, and flower and frolic."

Thus the prominent Zionist spokesman Jacob Levinson (1875–1955), in his introduction to a volume of sermonic materials, bewailed "the jocular popular preachers who desecrate both preaching and synagogue with their jests." "Such an orator," Levinson affirmed, "won't find anything in this book of mine for his pathetic satchel." Five pages later Levinson quoted the midrash: "On what merit do the people abroad [i.e., in the Diaspora] live? On the merit of their observing [e.g., not working on] the Sabbath and holidays." The thrust of the midrash, proposed Levinson, can be directed at the sinful practices of Jewish factory and workshop owners in America, who take advantage of observant Jews who refuse to work on the Sabbath and therefore can't find a job, by paying a pittance for their labor on weekdays. These shop owners "abroad," namely in America, "live"—

make a handsome living—on the merit of their unfortunate employees "observing the Sabbath and holidays." Concluding this rendering of the midrash, Levinson added in parentheses: "I said this jocularly at a meeting."[46]

This is not to suggest hypocrisy, authors consciously distorting the record. Most rabbis and preachers must have genuinely thought that what they were preaching was, in essence, a jeremiad, even if it didn't look that way. Like the owner of the mask factory in Marcel Marceau's pantomime, they were stuck with a jolly-faced mask, behind which they felt genuine agony and exasperation at the state of the community. In contrast, their audiences may have worn a tearful mask listening to the preacher's critique of their spiritual, religious, and social shortcomings, his nostalgic lamentations of the passing of the pure and wholesome ways of the old home. Beneath it, they may well have felt gratifying relief that the severe bonds of strict established observance in its traditional European form had been broken. Or perhaps it was the other way around: the rabbi scolded and lamented, internally satisfied with fulfilling his calling and with the fact that traditional values were still relevant to the congregation. The audience may have laughed with the preacher describing their transgressions, or at the preacher and his hopeless and irrelevant reproof, his satire and sarcasm adding to the fun. But deep beneath the boisterous mask they may have lamented, with the rabbi, the passing of traditional values and old country ways, feeling, beneath the smirk, the sting of his satire and sarcasm and irony.

The American Orthodox sermon was a medium through which the immigrant Jews attempted to adjust to a changed world, a ritual drama, served to process the social drama that they were living out. Anthropologists explain that when the stable course of social life, proceeding peacefully on the basis of consensual norms, is disturbed by a significant change in either the internal consensus or in the environment that conditions social arrangements, a social drama is said to occur. The natural response to this kind of crisis is a process of collective soul-searching in which society reevaluates its performance in relation to its norms and values, as well as reexamines the fundamental norms themselves. This process of self-examination is commonly done, in a variety of cultures, through the use of drama, oftentimes ritual drama, acted out in the framework of cultural performances.[47]

Many characteristic features of the immigrant sermon fall into a pattern, given such a perspective. The dramatic expansion of the sermon's institutional framework—its greater frequency, its inclusion in the synagogue service, its spilling over into a variety of rites of passage and ceremonial occasions—reflected the depth and power of the social drama experienced by the uprooted, at the same time that it would demonstrate the sermon's effectiveness as a tool for processing the experience. The sermon's traditional educational functions represented in its intellectual sophistication and structural complexity gave way to the much more urgent needs of the community for a reflexive forum in which to process the social crisis. To serve its new functions effectively, the sermon would have to take the everyday dilemmas and problems of the immigrants seriously, to comment on them and relate them to the group's traditional value system. Chastisement and reproof would similarly represent the ongoing effort to set down ground rules and boundaries in an unexplored environment, to chart where change was permissible and where it was not.

Comedy, too, and its symbiotic attachment to reproof can be better understood within this framework. In a variety of cultures, ludic activity, including entertainment and comedy, characterizes the experience beyond the boundary of the secular, everyday life (an experience tagged liminal, or in industrial societies, liminoid). The mere humorous and jocular stance, which characterizes many forms of ritual drama, can be construed to express a position of doubt, of questioning the norms and values structuring the secular, economic world, therefore also contesting them; it suggests the possibility of its reform. The sermon, as transplanted to industrial, urban, modernized America, provided a liminoid experience. It critically surveyed, reviewed, and evaluated American life. Its criticism was expressed through explicit reproof as well as through its entertaining, ludic, jocular stance. Comedy and reproof went hand in hand.[48]

But pointing out a snug fit between the new sermon and its social and cultural setting does not amount to a historical explanation of its emergence. Indeed, it is unlikely that the nature of the new sermon was a conscious, a priori decision, a constructed strategy based on merging an analysis of the new social conditions on the one hand and the traditional sermon's potentialities on the other. Rather, the new sermon emerged through a process of trial and error, under pressures particular to the new environment. Immigrant preachers, in contemplating the nature of their sermons, provided a compelling analysis of this process and of the forces that engendered and shaped it.

According to this analysis, the decisive change in the institutional structures framing Jewish communal life unleashed the forces that would ultimately determine the nature of the American sermon. At the bottom of it all lay the basic difference between Europe and America in the church-state nexus. In the old country, where religion was established, the Jewish community had been a formally recognized civil entity, vested with quasi-political powers and with full authority over the religious affairs of its members and, to an extent, over civil functions too. Regulation of ritual slaughtering and kosher food, burials and cemeteries, registration of birth and death, marriage and divorce, all had been officially recognized communal functions. The community, therefore, held dominant sway, in fact a monopoly over the religious practices and the personal-status affairs of its members, and leveraged these extensive powers to exercise social control.[49]

Leadership of the communal structures was vested in the rabbinate and in a lay elite. The basis of the rabbinate's power had traditionally been its legal authority. Originally limited to religious issues, prominent among them jurisdiction over questions of personal status, the rabbinate's legal authority had expanded and was accepted by the community in a wide range of civil matters. This was due mainly to the lack of an effective alternative in the prejudicial, badly administered East European states. From this power base, the rabbinate went on to annex additional powers that were not necessarily a rabbinical prerogative. According to Jewish law, ordination is required only for deciding Jewish law. Performing marriages and divorces, teaching or preaching, just like circumcision and slaughtering, did not require ordination; they could be performed by any Jew. Nevertheless, the powerful position that the rabbinate had assumed within the communal framework made it the broker of all such religious functions. It was up to the rabbinate to decide who would preach, when and how. Communal rabbis usually reserved to themselves the delivery of a few sermons on outstanding occasions. In these sermons they attempted to dazzle their audiences by demonstrating the scale, scope, and depth of their scholarship, their virtuoso command of exegesis of both legal and midrashic sources, their originality and prowess in manipulating the sources to generate novelae, and their skill in weaving the complex, divergent elements into exquisite, unified structures. These sermons served to celebrate the eminence of the study of the Torah as the leading ethos of Jewish society and to reaffirm the rabbi's authority and social power, which was based on epitomizing it. The performance of sermons by communal preachers or wandering maggidim were subject to approval and authorization by the communal rabbi.

Freedom of religion, disestablishment of the church, and free incorporation in America annulled the power of the Jewish communal institution over the religious affairs of the immigrants. With the de facto abolition of the vestiges of its once quasi-political powers, the immigrants found that the institution in its entirety could be dispensed with; and with the dissolution of the communal framework, the rabbinate lost its traditional basis of power. Consequently, and as rabbis soon discovered, from the standpoint of leadership, America became "an upside-down world." "Tops were down, the lowly rose to the top" and people "walked on their heads": simpletons rose above the erstwhile leadership and trampled on it.[50] With their jurisdiction over issues of personal status no longer officially recognized, and with the general laxity in religious observance, the rabbis' legal authority lost its significance. The only query that comes before the rabbi nowadays, complained a contemporary in bitter humor, was "what do we need rabbis for?"[51]

For preaching, was a possible answer. "Indeed the times have changed," Rabbi Moses Weinberger evaluated the situation with his usual acuteness:

> The crown is lifted and the wreath removed from the heads of the rabbis in our times. Their edicts are no longer edicts and their decrees are no longer decrees. . . . And the nullification of rabbinical legal prerogative by the governmental authority leaves them with only the sermon. . . . However, in most places the sermon is also in danger, for orations which are not commodious . . . and properly arranged and adapted to the spirit of the times and to the spiritual tastes of the public will do no good. . . . For even the sermon, once under the sole and exclusive power of the rabbis is now under the power of the congregation.[52]

The rabbi's authority over the sermon was endangered from within and from without: from the congregation and from a competing order of unordained preachers.

In America, affiliation was voluntary. For those immigrants who chose to affiliate, the community was never a serious option. Instead, they formed numerous independent congregations. In the larger settlements these congregations competed fiercely with one another, even though they were usually defined by distinct European localities from which the nucleus of founding members originally came. With the proliferation of fiercely independent congregations and the lively competition among them, leaders attempted to re-create a communal-like framework led by prestigious rabbis and powerful laymen. The failure of the New York experiment and of its figurehead, Jacob Joseph, symbolized the futility of such attempts. The failure, moreover, had a chilling effect on further attempts to organize along the communal line. Rabbi Joseph's fate, in turn, symbolized the decline of the rabbinate that drew its power and authority from the communal framework.

The synagogue and its services became the focus of the new congregational infrastructure. With no leverage over the supply of religious and civil services other than liturgy, these synagogues competed in a free and open market for daily, Sabbath, and holiday services. Moreover, all congregations had to compete with alternative forms of leisure activity that became available to the immigrants. To survive, let alone to prosper, as independent social and economic entities, it was imperative upon the congregation to attract as many paying members as possible and to sell as many synagogue seats as possible to nonmembers.

Given the new synagogue economics in a competitive environment and under conditions of religious voluntarism, it became apparent that the demand side would dominate the design of American synagogue services. Adjustments would have to be made to increase the attractiveness of the services and to cater to popular tastes. Traditional Orthodox liturgy, it should be noted, was not originally all that pleasing. It was based on daily and weekly repetition of a fixed set of liturgical texts. Readings from the Bible and Prophets did change from week to week but all within the rigid confines of a yearly cycle of readings. Repetitive and routine, traditional liturgy would be an unlikely commodity to win favor even in a strong market for cultural performances.

But synagogue organizers and congregational leaders ultimately did find two features that could help them compete successfully in the gratification-market segment of communal togetherness and shared nostalgia. One was the recruitment of talented cantors who could provide an aesthetically pleasing musical performance. Gradually, they also came to recognize that a sermon preached weekly as part of the liturgical services could provide variety and novelty to the static, repetitive ritual. But not all sermons would fill the bill. Sophisticated explications of strings of recherché texts, ingeniously woven into a complex structure could gratify a limited circle of scholars. To attract the masses to the synagogue, week in and week out, a different sermon was called for. It would have to be long on entertaining features and short on scholarship; it would have to be easy to follow and to comprehend. It would have to be emotionally rather than intellectually stirring. Above all, it would have to be relevant, reflecting the perplexities of the immigrants' lives and addressing their dilemmas, rather than dwell on legal problems or on eternal religious and theological questions. At its best it would offer catharsis, whether through reproof or through comedy.

Should congregational rabbis fail to deliver the goods, the lay leaders had a ready alternative. The right to preach could be transferred to the host of self-styled "reverends" who appeared in the immigrant community. A uniquely American phenomenon, the reverends filled the vacuum in the supply of religious services caused by the disintegration of the official communal institution. Neither ordained nor necessarily well educated and learned, the reverends functioned as freelancers, performing marriage ceremonies, burials, Bar Mitzvahs, and religious divorces. If and when necessary, they preached to entertain and please the crowds. Rabbis could and did censure their new competitors in a barrage of colorful and poignant rebukes, but wars of words would lead them nowhere. If they wished to retain their hold on the pulpit—the only service they could perform that was in demand—they would have to assimilate the techniques of these competing "masters of the tongue" and adopt their tricks of the trade. They would have to "provide the public with proverbs and fables, with jokes and tales," and make the sanctuary "a house of plays and entertaining performances." As the record shows, many rabbis did precisely that.

Rabbi Zalman Friederman succinctly summarized the institutional and economic imperative for the emergence of the new American Orthodox sermon. Unmistakably alluding to the travails of the Children of Israel in Egypt, Friederman (b. 1863) averred that in America,

> The rabbis must satisfy the wants of the audience, for that is the foundation for their survival, since their prodders—the officers of the synagogues—order them: "expand the membership of the congregation increase the audience, attract the affluent to hear your sermons," so as to increase the income.

Many other immigrant rabbis, in commenting on the nature of the American sermon, concurred with Friederman's analysis.[53] Some added an artistic touch to their interpretation, their sarcastic and sardonic medium underscoring the thrust of their message. Thus, Rabbi Shmuel Maharshak pointed to the Jewish neighborhood's billboards as proof for his argument that congregations installed a rabbi solely because

> it forms a business proposition. For the officers of the congregations [can then] provide a portrait of the rabbi to go along with the portrait of the congregation's famous cantor on the broadsides which they distribute before the High Holidays, and add in large, bold letters: "so and so, the genius rabbi, our dear rabbi, the excellent preacher, a pearl-emitting mouth, who makes the ears of all his listeners ring, will preach and shake the hearts in his pleasant sermons in our synagogue . . ." and to the listeners it shall be pleasing.

It would only be natural, added Maharshak, "that after such a gross advertisement there would be great demand for the goods, namely many will purchase synagogue seats to enjoy the cantor's singing and the rabbi's sermon, and the managers' bounty will be plentiful."[54]

Immigrant Orthodox Jews demanded catharsis and entertainment, and a lot of it. They demanded a running commentary on the vicissitudes of their lives, an interpretation of significant public events and trends, and they demanded insights into the meaning of the bewildering dynamic world in which they were living. This would take place in a novel institutional setting, the congregation, created, advertised, and paid for by the members themselves. At the bottom of their tensions and perplexities lay the gulf between the two worlds they had known and experienced, the land of their fathers and the world they had entered. They expected that the former would provide a key to understanding the latter, as well as to the implications of the change. They also expected a new rendering of Old World values and traditions that would fit their present experiences. The strains on their formerly authoritative set of traditional values, norms, and world outlook, demanded an urgent repair job, and the immigrants would pay to have it done. It was now the immigrant masses who would select the most appealing ideas in the most attractive forms by the best spokesmen, in a free marketplace of ideas, of cultural performances, and of performers. Thus emerged the Orthodox American sermon.

The collapse of Old World structures of authority and power and the democratization of social and institutional life as experienced by Orthodox immigrants, made way for a congruent democratization of religious life and of its characteristic forms and practices. The Orthodox sermon in America emerged under the sway of forces on the demand side unleashed by this process of democratization. These forces were, in essence, the same as those that bred the Puritans' "plain style of preaching," then Jonathan Edwards's pastoral response to the swell of popular emotions leading into the Great Awakening, later yet Whitfield's and Finney's response to freedom's ferment in the Jacksonian period, and closer to the emergence of the Orthodox American sermon, Beecher's and Parker's response to public demands in a maturing democracy. The failure of Rabbi Jacob Joseph, in his attempt "to tell society what it should or should not do, without any regard to its immediate interests, whether emotional or economic," underscored the power of the democratizing forces in American religious life. Rabbi Joseph's successors in the American pulpit fully implement the thrust of what Perry Miller had described as the moral of the Great Awakening, "that the leader has the job of accommodating himself to the realities of human, and in any particular situation, of social experience,"[55] especially a revolutionary experience such as the adjustment to a new world.

But in a sense, this process of democratization had liberated the rabbis and preachers too. Coerced, to an extent, by their congregations, they came to face, head on, the challenges of the new environment to their traditions, and to challenge their environment with their group's heritage. Through these challenges American rabbis and preachers found a crucial social role and a unique and original voice. They could no longer resort to the luxuries of pietistic escapism justified through entrenched conventions and traditions of preaching and of religious leadership. Or conversely, rabbis and preachers could point to economic imperatives and to social compulsion to justify their abandonment of the restrictive conventions and standards of preaching and of leadership, thus legitimizing bold experimentation. This freedom to experiment would lead to more than a radical accommodation of the essence of their traditions to a changed world. Its real power was in the freedom to forge a new interpretation of America in light of their group's traditions.

The demands on the American pulpit for entertainment and catharsis gave rabbis and preachers their most powerful weapons. They used the license they were given to "jest and criticize" and bring about catharsis, to subversive ends. Their marginality in the new social world the immigrants made, gave them power in a community struggling on the margins of two worlds. Preachers would lament and chastise by the standards of a bygone world, knowing full well that by raising the standard of the past they were coming to terms with the present, shaping it in the process. Through comedy they would question the apparent meaning of America as forced on the immigrants' consciousness by the conventions of the host society; their marginality gave them the freedom to propose a counterculture.

Rabbi Joseph's more successful peers on the American pulpit would provide numerous sermons as a running commentary on secular daily life. They would compromise the discourse of eternal issues, traditional texts, their imported library of sermons, and their former styles of preaching. And like the sage of the Mishnah, Rabbi Akiva, who laughed and cried in response to the destruction of Jerusalem, they would stage a divine comedy when considering the past in its relation to the present, and the present in its relation to the past.

NOTES

Many thanks to Michael Kramer for much help and advice: "Like apples of gold among figures of silver is a word spoken in a proper manner" (Prov., xxv, 11).

1. The first authoritative accounts of the chief rabbi episode were presented by Judah David Eisenstein, a participant in the events and an early historian of the American Orthodox experience: *Ner Hama'aravy* (New York) 1, 12 (1895): 41–47; "The History of the First Russian-American Jewish Congregation," *Publications of the American Jewish Historical Society* (hereafter: PAJHS), 9 (1901); *Otzar Drashot* (New York: 1919), pp. 390–391; "New York," in *Otzar Zikhronotay* (New York: 1929), pp. 60–61, 106, 246–271; *Otzar Yisrael*, vol. 7. The seminal secondary account of Rabbi Joseph's American career is Abraham J. Karp, "New York Chooses a Chief Rabbi," PAJHS 44 (1955): 129–198.

2. On Rabbi Joseph's preaching in Europe, see Shimon Halevi Glicksberg, *Hadrashah Beyisrael* (Tel Aviv: 1940/41), pp. 439–440, 469–470; Shmaryah Leib Hurwitz, *Otzar Hatorah* (New York: 1926), pp. 81–83; Dov Katz, *Tnu'at Hamusar* (Tel Aviv: 1954/55), pp. 365–384; Zvi Hirsch Masliansky, *Kitvey Masliansky*, vol. 3 (New York: 1929), p. 169; Chaim R. Rabinowitz, *Dyokna'ot shel Darshanim* (Jerusalem: 1967/8), pp. 291–296. On the role of preaching in Rabbi Joseph's nomination, see Abraham Cahan, *The Education of Abraham Cahan* (Philadelphia: 1969), p. 394.

3. Rabbi Joseph had delivered his first sermon in America on the evening of the Saturday on which he arrived (7 July), to representatives of the communal committee. It focused on the verse "How beautiful are thy steps in sandals, O prince's daughter" (Song of Songs, vii, 3). See Eisenstein, *Zikhronotay*, pp. 60, 267; and cf. Jacob Joseph, *Lebeit Ya'akov* (Vilna: 1888/9), sermons 19–21, 63–71.

4. Eisenstein, *Zikhronotay*, p. 60; "New York." Karp does cite a series of positive responses to the inaugural sermon. These responses, however, appear to reflect the impressions of non-Orthodox observers who may well have been impressed more by the exercises of the inauguration than by the sermon itself. Other positive evaluations appear to have emanated from sources expressing the interests of the communal committee.

5. Abraham Cahan, "A Back Number," in *Grandma Never Lived in America: The New Journalism of Abraham Cahan*, ed. Moses Rischiu (Bloomington: 1985), pp. 72–73. Rabbi Joseph's death and his funeral turned out to be formative experiences in the development of

American Orthodoxy. Menahem Blondheim, "Harabanut Ha'ortodoksit Megala et America," in *Be'ikvot Columbus: America, 1492–1992,* ed. Miri Eliav-Feldon (Jerusalem: 1996); Arthur A. Goren, "Lezekher Giboreinu" (paper presented at the 1992 Annual Meeting of the Israeli Historical Society). See also Leonard Dinnerstein, "The Funeral of Rabbi Jacob Joseph," in *Antisemitism in American History,* ed. D. A. Gerber (Urbana: 1987); and *New York Times,* 29 and 31 July, 1 August 1902.

6. Glicksberg, *Hadrashah,* pp. 440, 469–470.

7. Eisenstein was referring to the American sermons of the Ridbaz [acronym for Rabbi Ya'akov David Willowski]: *Zikhronotay,* p. 108; and see Ridbaz's introduction to *Nimukey Ridbaz* (Chicago: 1904/5), especially pp. 2–3, and his more general evaluation of the decline of the contemporary sermon in the introduction to *Shut Beit Ridbaz* (Jerusalem: 1908/9). Moses Weinberger, *Hayehudim Vehayahadut Benew York* (New York: 1887), p. 27.

8. Glicksberg stated "that the American sermon is of great interest and awaits competent hands that would redeem it," *Hadrashah,* p. 471; Shmaryah Leib Hurwitz intended to publish a book on "the sermon and the preachers in America" but apparently never accomplished this goal: *Otzar Hatorah,* p. 80. Nathan M. Kaganoff, "The Traditional Jewish Sermon in the US" (Ph.D. diss., American University, 1960), focuses on sermons of the earlier period and of what may be considered Conservative preachers. Yet he also discussed immigrant Orthodox sermons of this period, especially pp. 140–150a. Aaron Mirsky published an important essay on Orthodox preaching in America: "Al Hadarshanim Vesifrut Hadrush Be'amerika," *Sefer Hashanah L'yhuday Artzot Habrit* (New York: 1938), 388–395; a revised version of which, entitled "Hed Hamagidim Be'amerika" appeared in a volume of his collected essays *Ertez Veyamim* (Jerusalem: 1953). More recent are the works of my student Kimmy Kaplan, "Bein Massoret Lemoderna: Harav Sivitz Vehadrush Haivry Be'amerika," *Mechkrey Yerushalayim Bemachshevet Yisrael* 11 (1993/4): 187–242; "Ha'eyn ze Olam Hafuch" (Ph.D diss., Hebrew University, 1996); and forthcoming, Menahem Blondheim and Michael Kramer, "The Orthodox Jewish Sermon in America: The Example of Judah Leib Lazerow's Mateh Yehuda," in *The First Longfellow Anthology* (of American literature in languages other than English). Sporadic references to Orthodox sermons in America, too numerous to list here, appear in biographies, and local and general histories of American Judaism. My own paper, read at the 1991 annual meeting of the Israeli Historical Society, and subsequently published (in Hebrew) as " 'And to the Listeners it shall be pleasing': The Orthodox Sermon in the US Between Rabbinic Supply and Public Demand," in *Popular Culture,* ed. B. Z. Kedar (Jerusalem: 1996), pp. 277–303, served as the basis of this present article.

9. English sermons, Reform and Conservative in particular, have fared much better. See, e.g.: Naomi Cohen, "Sermons and the Contemporary World," *Contemporary Judaism* (Jerusalem: 1984), pp. 23–44; Robert V. Friedenberg, *Hear O Israel: The History of American Jewish Preaching, 1654–1990* (Tuscaloosa: University of Alabama Press, 1989). The academic study of Jewish preaching was launched by Leopold Zunz's monumental *Die Gottesdienstlichen Vortraege Der Juden Historisch Entwickelt* (1832); its revised 1892 edition, translated into Hebrew and critically edited and introduced by Chanokh Albeck (*Hadrashot Beyisrael* [Jerusalem, 1974]) remains extremely useful. Good introductions in English to Jewish sermonics include Israel Bettan, *Studies in Jewish Preaching: Middle Ages* (Cincinnati: 1939); Marc Saperstein, *Jewish Preaching, 1200–1800: An Anthology* (New Haven: 1989), pp. 1–103; and the entry "Preaching" in *Encyclopedia Judaica.*

10. Given this "macro" orientation, a number of significant factors affecting the nature of the sermon were overlooked. Of these, one is the geographical: no attempt has been made

to differentiate between sermons of center and periphery, metropolis and town, large congregation and small, New York and San Francisco. Neither has an attempt been made to differentiate between sermons of distinct Orthodox factions such as Galician and Lithuanian Jews, Hasidic or Mitnagdic preachers and congregations, Zionist or non-Zionist orientations. Nor is any allowance made for the personal differences between preachers: greenhorns and veterans, old and young, popular or obscure, scholarly and learned or not quite so, prolific publishers or onetime publishers, are all treated alike. Further studies may well look into these interesting cleavages. However, the following outlines what appear to be major currents, those which in effect "swamped" all other variables.

11. A model application of the generational paradigm is Deborah Dash Moore, *At Home in America: Second Generation New York Jews* (New York: 1981), see especially pp. 3–17. Loyd P. Gartner, "Contemporary Historians of New York Jewry," in *Contemporary Judaism* (Jerusalem: 1984), provides an overview of the approach. For a contemporary analysis, see, e.g., A. Berman, *Hamidrash Vehahigayon* (New York: 1932), pp. 4–5.

12. In second- and third-generation neo- or modern-Orthodox congregations, rabbis, commonly American-trained, preached mainly in English. Based on an analysis of the listings in the *New York Communal Register* (New York: 1918) it appears that as early as 1918 the sermon was preached in English in approximately 10 percent of Orthodox congregations. See Jenne W. Joselit, *New York's Jewish Jews* (Bloomington: 1990), pp. 29–34. On the programmatic aspects of preaching in English, see Jeffrey S. Gurock, "Resisters and Accommodators: Varieties of Orthodox Rabbis in America, 1886–1983," in *The American Rabbinate* (Hoboken: 1985), pp. 46–48 passim. Good sources for neo-Orthodox sermons in English are the volumes of *Manual of Holiday and Sabbath Sermons* (or: RCA Manual), published since 1943, and Orthodox sermons in the annual *Best Jewish Sermons*, first published in 1954.

13. The literature on cultural performances from an anthropological perspective is vast. Representative of the approach are Milton Singer, *When a Great Tradition Modernizes: An Anthropological Approach to Indian Civilization* (New York: 1973), pp. 55–80; Victor Turner, *The Anthropology of Performance* (New York: 1986), pp. 21–32, 72–98. Clifford Geertz's seminal treatment of "cultural texts" in *The Interpretation of Cultures* (New York: 1973), e.g., pp. 448–453 is closely related to this approach.

14. Yitzchak Waltman, *Siach Yitzchak* (New York, 1926), p. 4.

15. The significance of the gap between the oral and the written has been brought out in a variety of disciplines. Walter J. Ong, *Orality and Literacy: The Technologizing of the Word* (New York, 1988), is a standard introduction, as are Jack Goody, *The Interface Between the Oral and the Written* (Cambridge, 1987); Viv Edwards and Thomas A. Sienkewicz, *Rappin' and Homer: Oral Cultures Past and Present* (Oxford, 1990). Saperstein, *Jewish Preaching*, pp. 5–15, is a good summary of the problem in the context of Jewish sermonics; Chava Turniansky, "Hadrshah Vehadrasha Bikhtav Kimtavachat bein Hatarbut Hakanonit Levein Hakahal Harachav," *Hatarbut Ha'amamit*, pp. 185–187 addresses the case of the popular Yiddish sermon in Eastern Europe.

16. E.g., Moshe Shim'on Sivitz, introductions to *Beit Paga* (Jerusalem: 1904/5), *Pri Yechezkel* (Jerusalem: 1908/9), *Zemach Hasadeh* (St. Louis: 1935/36), Shmuel E. Elkin, introduction to *Dvar Shmu'el* (St. Louis: n.d.), and Judah L. Lazerow, *Der Idisher Redner*, vol. 2 (New York: 1927), pp. 12–13; Yosef Yish'ayahu Margolin, *Drushey Maharshim* (New York: 1921/22), p. 9; Yosef Yish'ayahu Margolin, *Hama'aseh Vehamidrash* (Jerusalem: 1937/8), p. 5; Chanokh Zundel Levin, *Drashot Shlemot* (New York: 1938), 2; Shraga Rosenberg, *Bigdey Srad* (New York: n.d.), p. 3; Binyamin M. Livay, *Sefer Tehilim im Perush*

Nachalat Binyamin (St. Louis: 1933); Moshe Aharon Poleyeff, second introduction to *Be'er Avraham* (New York: 1939); Zvi Hirsh Dachowitz, introduction to *Hegyonai Vesar'apai* (New York: 1929); Menachem Hacohen Shoenbrun, introduction to *Minchat Cohen* (New York: 1909); and numerous other volumes.

17. Gedalyah Silverstone, *Beth Meir*, vol. 2 (Baltimore: 1912), p. 6; Silverstone claimed there to have sold the first volume of *Beth Meir* to more than two hundred rabbis, cantors, and preachers.

18. Gedaliah Silverstone, *Me'irat Einayim* (n.p.: 1924/25), p. 5; cf. introduction to *Kesef Nivchar*, vol. 2 (Washington, D.C.: 1920); introduction to vol. 3 (St. Louis: 1922/23). Other statements to the same effect in the introductions to other publications by Silverstone: *Darki Bakodesh* (St. Louis: 1924); *Matok Midvash* (Washington, D.C.: 1917), p. 7; *Shalhevet Esh* (St. Louis: 1927/28); *Otzar Nechmad* (St. Louis: 1926/27); and *Divrey Chen* (n.p.: 1924/25).

19. Yehudah Leib Lazerow, *Gan Yehudah* (Brooklyn: 1935). The annotated volume is in the National and University Library, Jerusalem (call number S46 A 990).

20. E.g., Shlomo Hacohen's approbation of Gershon Me'ir Boyarsky, *Regesh Amareinu* (Vilna: 1898/99); Jacob Joseph's approbation of Moshe Shim'on Sivitz, *Cheker Da'at*, vol. 1 (Jerusalem: 1898/99); Shalom Elchanan Jaffe to Ya'akov Ruderman's *Beit Ya'akov* (New York: 1908), and of Yehudah Joshua Falk Israelite, *Te'udat Yisrael* (Boston: 1915/6); Reuven Halevy Leibowitz of Ben Zion Eisenstadt, *Bilshony Milah* (New York: 1934); and numerous others.

21. Ben Zion Eisenstadt, *Or Lifney Hadorshim* (New York: 1916/17); Ben Zion Eisenstadt, *Or Chadash Lamatifim* (New York: 1918/19); Ya'akov Levinson, *Ra'ayonot Vechomer Lidrush* (New York: 1920); Gedaliah Silverstone, *Drushim Lehagid* (n.p.: 1931/32).

22. A good illustration of this process is the vast correspondence between Rabbi Tuvia Geffen of Atlanta and other American rabbis concerning the purchase and exchange of his publications. These papers are in the possession of the Geffen family in Jerusalem. Thanks to David Geffen for making this correspondence available to me.

23. Ephrayim Deinard, *Kohelet America* (St. Louis: 1926), p. 36.

24. Cf. Chayim Hillel Ben Sasson, *Hagut Vehanhaga* (Jerusalem: 1959), pp. 39–42, 54.

25. Rosenberg, *Bigdey Srad*, p. 95. See also Silverstone, *Beth Meir*, vol. 2, p. 5; Israelite, *Te'udat Yisrael*; Menachem Rizikoff, *Sha'arey Ratzon* (New York: 1931/32), p. 200; Judah Leiv Graubart, *Dvarim Kikhtavam* (St. Louis: 1932), p. 241; Shlomo Michael Neches, introduction to *Torato Shel Shem* (Jerusalem: 1930); Bernard Drachman, *The Unfailing Light* (New York: 1948), p. 281.

26. Shmu'el Hurwitz, *Hirhuray Lev Ragash* (New York: 1928), pp. 61–62.

27. The possible influence of Protestant practices on the Orthodox sermon deserves close attention. In evaluating this possibility, one should take into account the option of convergence, rather than direct influence, namely, that developments in the sermon of each denomination came in response to common background conditions, yet they occurred independently within each group. It should also be noted that notwithstanding the extensive criticism of aspects of the new style of Orthodox preaching (see below), contemporary critics did not suggest the possibility of a Protestant influence on the Orthodox sermon (Eisenstein, *Otzar Drashot*, p. 390, is a possible exception). The relation of the change in the Orthodox sermon to Jewish Reform influence (and the role of the Reform sermon as a possible intermediary to the Protestant preaching) is more complex and it deserves extensive discussion.

28. Yitzchak Bunin, *Hegyonot Yitzchak* (New York: 1953), p. 6; cf. Zvi Hirsh Hacohen, *Ginzey Drashot Vera'ayonot* (New York: 1933), pp. 137–139.

29. Hurwitz, *Hirhuray*, p. 61.

30. Avraham Aharon Yudelovitch, *Drash Av*, vol. 1 (New York, 1921), pp. 22–23 (most of the passage is quoted in Mirsky, "Hadarshanim"), and introduction to vol. 2 (New York, 1922).

31. Two outstanding attributes of sermonics in Orthodox-American book culture indicate their local focus. The ratio of American to European approbations is much higher in volumes of sermonics than that ratio in other genres (e.g., responsa); and the ratio of sermonic publications printed outside the United States (and thus more easily available to non-Americans) was much lower than in other genres. Blondheim, "Harabanut Ha'ortodoksit Megala et America."

32. Zvi Hirsch Masliansky, introduction to *Sefer Hahatafa*, vol. 1, part 1 (New York: 1929). Numerous other statements by American preachers emphasize the ephemerality of the sermon and the necessity of adapting it to changing times and places. See, e.g., Alexander Ziskind Levin, *Doresh Tov Le'amo* (New York: 1915/6), pp. 2–6, and the application of his principles, pp. 102–113, 149–166; Moshe Weinberger, *Darosh Darash Moshe* (New York: 1914), p. 56; Graubart, introduction to *Dvarim Kikhtavam*; Mordekhai Aharon Kaplan, *Ruach Ha'et* (New York: 1920), p. 4; Yosef Moshe Lehrman, *Imrey Moshe*, p. 51; Avraham Naftali Galant, introduction to *Mo'adim Lesimcha* (New York: 1928); Dov Aryeh Chayat, introduction to *Otzar Hara'ayon Vehamachshava* (New York: 1936).

33. The European preachers selected for comparison were those whom Glicksberg singled out as the most influential in the period just preceding the mass migration movement: see *Hadrashah*, pp. 427–456. The conclusions are based on a review of Yosef Dov Soleveichick, *Beit Halevy* (Warsaw: 1882); Yosef Chayim Kara, *Kol Omer Kra*, vol. 1 (Warsaw: 1866), vol. 2 (Pietrikov: 1879), vol. 3 (Warsaw: 1888), and vol. 4 (Warsaw: 1888); Noach Rabinowitz, *Toldot Noach*, vol. 2 (Warsaw: 1884); vol. 3 (Vilna: 1898); vol. 4 (Vilna: 1902); Yehoshua Helir, *Divrey Yehoshua Marpe Lnefesh* (Vilna: 1856); Yehoshua Helir, *Toldot Yehoshua* (Vilna: 1866); Yehoshua Helir, *Ohel Yehoshua* (Vilna: 1882); Chayim Elchanan Ben Yehudah, *Moreh Chayim* (Vilna: 1872); Willowski, *Nimukey Ridbaz*; Zvi Hirsh Orliansky, *Drashot Maharzha* (New York: 1922); Zvi Hirsh Orliansky, *Drashot* (New York: 1927). Jacob Joseph's European sermons are discussed below, note 38.

34. An outstanding example for the complexity a sermon can assume is the first sermon in Yehoshua Helir's *Ohel Yehoshua*, published posthumously and apparently not edited by the author. The sermon begins with nine postulates, then seven introductions. All these elements would ultimately be brought together by a single scheme.

35. Lieber Kahan, *Chidushey Chavivah* (New York: 1916), p. 49. This proverb is not original and may be found in the introduction to Yitzhak Ritbard, *Kohelet Yitzchak* (Vilna: 1899). See also Emanuel Rackman, Foreword, *RCA Manual, 1959*; Dov Ber Borochov, *Reshit Bikurim* (Jerusalem: 1932), pp. 48, 153; Yehudah Leib Levine, *Ha'aderet Veha'emunah* (St. Louis: n.d., but includes an approbation dated 1900/1), pp. 69, 80; Eli'ezer Adirim, *Ateret Zahav* (New York: 1919), p. 13; Yehudah Leib Lazerow, *Divrey Yehudah* (New York: 1910), p. 110; Judah David Eisenstein, introduction to *Otzar Drushim Nivcharim* (New York: 1918); but cf. Levy Yitzchak Kahanah, *Mas'at Beit Halevi* (New York: 1936), pp. 9–11, 133; Orliansky, *Drashot*, pp. 4, 6–7.

36. Levine, *Ha'aderet Veha'emunah*, p. 80. Levine's theme was common enough: Yudelovitch, *Drash Av*, vol. 4, p. 43; A. I. Rose, "Ha'emet Vehashalom," *Ha'ivry*, 1 Cheshvan 1896; Shmuel Halevi Blum, *Hatziklon* (New York: 1924), p. 15; among many others.

37. This distinction is, of course, fully congruent with the observations above as to the characteristic simplification of structure and flow of the sermon, the decline in use of intricate

classical texts, and the increased resort to free rhetoric. Chanoch Zundel Levine, *Drashot Shlemot al kol Haftarot Shmot* (New York: 1938), pp. 1–3; Mirsky, "Hadarshanim." For an alternative interpretation of "drilling" and "stringing" see Yitzchak Nissenboim, "Hadarshanut Vehadarshanim," *Hagut Lev* (Vilna: 1911), p. 7.

38. Jacob Joseph, *Lebeit Ya'akov* (Vilna: 1888); numerous other sermons delivered by Jacob Joseph in Vilna appear in Ritbord, *Kohelet Yitzchak*, and Yitzchak Ritbord, *Beit Yitzchak, Siach Yitzchak* (Jerusalem: 1910). Ritbard's versions of Rabbi Joseph's Vilna sermons include a number of those that were published in *Lebeit Ya'akov*. In several such cases Ritbord claims to present better and more complete versions of such sermons, e.g., *Kohelet Yitzchak*, pp. 74, 78.

39. *Lebeit Ya'akov* (Vilna: Baruch Y. Kahanah, 1896), pp. 105–120. Jacob Joseph, *Toldot Ya'akov Yosef Benew York* (New York: 1889), pp. 5–7, 14–15. The pamphlet was intended to be the first of a series of newsletters that were to report the rabbi's activities. Given the circumstances, the publication was discontinued after the first number. The first sermon in the pamphlet was apparently edited by Jacob Buchalter; the second was apparently written by the rabbi himself. Sermons attributed to Rabbi Joseph were occasionally published in the *New York Herald*, but they do not appear to have represented the rabbi's actual sermons.

40. Jacob Levinson, *Nitfey Ne'umim* (New York: 1943), p. 9; Hurwitz, *Hirhuray*, p. 63; Boyarski, *Regesh Amareinu*, p. 3.

41. Borochov, *Reshit*, p. 152; Rosenberg, *Bigdey Srad*, p. 97.

42. Ben Zion Eisenstadt, *Bilshoni Milah* (St. Louis: n.d.), p. 35; Avraham Ze'ev Levy, *Hade'ah Vehadibur* (Brooklyn: 1931), p. 26; and cf. Sivitz, *Beit Paga*, p. 48.

43. Moshe Shim'on, introduction to Sivitz, *Cheker Da'at*, vol. 2 (Jerusalem: 1898/99), and see the insightful discussion of this truism in Mendel Piekarz, *Bymay Tzmichat Hachasidut* (Jerusalem: 1978), pp. 122–129.

44. The subversive aspect of humor in the context of the ambiguities, conflicts, and tensions between assimilation and tradition in a marginal social position are discussed in Bernard Rosenberg and Gilbert Shapiro, "Marginality and Jewish Humor," *Midstream* 4, 2 (Spring 1958): 70–80. Useful also on this aspect are Stanley Brandes, "Jewish-American Dialect Jokes and Jewish-American Identity," *Jewish Social Studies* 45 (1983): 233–240; and Joseph Boskin and Joseph Dorinson, "Ethnic Humor: Subversion and Survival," *American Quarterly* 37, 1 (Spring 1985): 81–97. On irony as a traditional response to the conflict between the ideal and the practical and the resort to the (essentially Freudian) "hilarity of topsy-turvydom," see Israel Knox's somewhat problematic "The Traditional Roots of Jewish Humor," *Judaism* 12, 3 (1963): 327–337. On the social power of "community of laughter" in America (a concept shaped by Henry Bergson and Kenneth Burke), see Orrin E. Klapp, *Heroes, Villains, and Fools* (Englewood Cliffs, N.J.: 1962), ch. 3 (especially p. 69). An excellent introduction to standup comedy is Lawrence E. Mintz, "Standup Comedy as Social and Cultural Meditation," in *American Humor*, ed. Arthur E. Dudden (Oxford: 1987), pp. 85–96; to social aspects of comedy, Hugh Dalziel Duncan, *Communication and Social Order* (New York: 1970), ch. 27; and to Jewish humor, Elliott Oring, "The People of the Joke: On the Conceptualization of Jewish Humor," *Western Folklore* 42 (1983): 261–271; and Sarah Blacher Cohen, "The Varieties of Jewish Humor," in *Jewish Wry: Essays on Jewish Humor* (Bloomington: 1987), pp. 1–15.

45. Rosenberg, *Bigdey Srad*, p. 95.

46. Ya'akov Levinson, introduction to *Ra'ayonot Vechomer Lidrush* (New York: 1920), pp. 8–9.

47. E.g., Victor Turner, *From Ritual to Theater: The Human Seriousness of Play* (New York: 1982).

48. Victor Turner, *The Ritual Process* (Chicago: 1969); Turner, *Ritual to Theater*, pp. 30–44; Victor Turner, *The Anthropology of Performance* (New York: 1986), pp. 25–32; for a variety of applications of these ideas see the journal *Religion* (1985). Johan Huizinga, *Homo Ludens* (Hebrew edition, Jerusalem: 1984), pp. 131–143, 168–175, pioneered in relating ludic activity to cultural discourse; and Umberto Eco's *The Name of the Rose* (New York: 1983), remains a suggestive, popular read on such issues.

49. This analysis follows closely on Arthur A. Goren, *New York Jews and the Quest for Community* (New York: 1970), in particular, pp. 1–24. For a retrospective evaluation of Goren's approach, see the journal *American Jewish Archives* (1993). The application of the institutional imperative to the transformation of the sermon is modeled on Goren's interpretive scheme for the transformation of immigrant social traditions in America, as illustrated in his "Traditional Institutions Transplanted: The Hevra Kadisha in Europe and in America," in *The Jews of North America*, ed. Moses Rischin (Detroit: 1987), pp. 62–78.

50. A discussion of the conceptual and historical roots of these concepts and metaphors appears in Blondheim, "Harabamut Ha'ortodoksit."

51. Eisenstein, *Otzar Drashot*, p. 390, and cf. Shlomo Yitzchak Sheinfeld, *Tziunim Bederech Hachayim* (New York: 1928), pp. 199–200.

52. Weinberger, *Darosh Darash*, p. 56. Weinberger's analysis here is in full accord with his more general interpretation of the changed role of the American rabbinate as presented in his *Hayehudim Vehayahadut*.

53. The quotation is from Zalman Friederman, *Shoshanat Ya'akov* (New York: 1927), p. 8. Friederman presented the same essential interpretation in a more elaborate form in his *Nachalat Ya'akov* (New York: 1914), pp. 8–15. Numerous other authorities concur with this analysis: Weinberger, *Darosh Darash*, pp. 48–56; Shmu'el M. Fein, *Zikhron Shmuel*, vol. 2 (St. Louis: 1932), pp. 65–66; Mordekhai Doctor, *Drahshot Une'umim* (New York: 1922), p. 91; Sheinfeld, *Tziunim*, pp. 199–200; Hurwitz, *Hirhuray*, pp. 54, 62, 71; Eisenstadt, *Bilshoni Milah*, pp. 34–35; Yosef Fried, *Alumat Yosef* (Jerusalem: 1909), pp. 3–4; Avraham L. Gelman, introduction to Shmu'el Dov Maharshak, *Hegyoney Shmu'el* (St. Louis: 1934), p. 10; Sivitz, introduction to *Cheker Da'at*, vol. 2; Yesha'ayahu Hurwitz, "Perushim Udrushim al Haggadah Shel Pesach," commentary (1932) on the verse "yachol merosh chodesh" manuscript in the possession of the family.

54. Maharshak, *Hegyoney Shmu'el*, pp. 94–95, but see Marc Lee Raphael, *Profiles in American Judaism* (San Francisco: 1984), p. 135.

55. Perry Miller, "Jonathan Edwards and the Great Awakening," in *Errand into the Wilderness* (New York: 1956), pp. 153–66.

Chapter Fourteen

"*Ersatz*-Drama" and Ethnic (Self-) Parody
Adolf Philipp and the Decline of New York's German-Language Stage, 1893–1918

Peter Conolly-Smith

On March 2, 1913, the *New York World* published an interview with Adolf Philipp, managing director of the German-language Fifty-seventh Street Theater and, according to the newspaper, "the one German [theater] manager who has been able to make money in New York. . . . He is both author and composer of the plays in which he enacts the leading part." These plays were for the most part musical ethnic parodies that relied heavily on local color and the stereotypical Dutch-English dialect of the period.[1] Most were set in *Kleindeutschland* (the city's German immigrant enclave on the Lower East Side) and around New York, though some also featured acts set in the nearby countryside as well as other northeastern cities with large German immigrant populations. Judging by contemporary reviews, surviving programs, and what can be pieced together about Philipp's life and career, all poked affectionate fun at the community and its habits and, in so doing, encouraged (perhaps unwittingly, though it seems ever more consciously) German-Americans' adaptation to American life and the English language. Despite their irreverence (and maybe because of it) Philipp's plays enjoyed great popularity (the *World* noted that one had "reached 1,257 performances and is still running"), and it was Philipp himself who divulged the "secret of his success" to the newspaper: "I have given the German theatregoers in New York American musical comedy in German. I believe they prefer it to high-brow drama or even comedies by the leading German authors. The Germans in New York want something typically American, only they want to understand it. So I present my plays in German."[2]

Who was this German-American impresario, and what was the exact nature of his art? Modern encyclopedias of the American stage do not list his name, yet clearly he was a significant and highly prolific player in New York's turn-of-the-century theater scene. With more than twenty plays credited to his name (for none of which scripts have survived, despite the fact that most celebrated runs far in excess of one hundred consecutive nights), he stands apart from other German-American theater managers of the period, most of whom did not count on a play's remaining on the program any longer than a week or two. And with "American musical comedy in German," his chosen genre, too, diverged from the German-

American norm.[3] For conventional New York–based German stage managers (most notably Rudolf Christians of the prestigious but far less successful Irving Place Theater at fifteenth Street and Irving Place) still upheld the notion of an unassailable tradition of classical German drama (Goethe, Schiller, Lessing, et al.) as well as the more recent but equally distinguished moderns—Sudermann, Hauptmann, Schnitzler, and Wedekind, among others. To such "serious" German stage managers, the presentation of "American musical comedies" would have been unthinkable, whether in German or in any other language.[4]

Yet Philipp's success with just such fare is unquestionable. In the spring of 1918, the Irving Place Theater (after a season of Schnitzler, Sudermann, and Lessing) resorted to half-priced Monday night shows, but to no avail; a few months later, the theater was forced to close down for lack of patronage. Philipp, on the other hand (who had since moved to the larger Yorkville Theater on East Eighty-sixth Street, where he continued presenting his own plays) was able to raise his admission prices without repercussion during the same season and did not end his New York career until the next. Even then, he did so voluntarily, not for lack of patronage but because of his realization that the joint pressure of the war and the growing appeal of the American stage were making even as "popular" a German-language theater as his own an anachronism. Unlike Rudolf Christians at Irving Place, who retired a broken man, Philipp retired at the height of his popularity, although it quickly became apparent that his success had been inextricably linked to his fame within New York's immigrant community, and that his departure from that city ultimately resulted in the end of what for years had seemed a charmed career.

By sketching a brief outline of Philipp's colorful career, this chapter will attempt to show that his work was of vital importance in awakening within the immigrant audience a taste for the very traditions and genres of popular American theater that would ultimately prove his own undoing. Indeed, Philipp's plays represent a transitional link that helped bridge the gap from highbrow German drama to the popular American stage, a trajectory within which Philipp himself played a crucial role. Not only did his plots and characterizations anticipate those of popular American theater, his use of language familiarized the German immigrant ear with the vernacular of American life. Indeed, and despite Philipp's own claim that his plays were "American musical comedies in German," contemporary reviews in both the English and the German-language press make it abundantly clear that his plays contained, as one New York daily noted, "lots of English."[5] And it was by familiarizing the German audience with English, even if only the pidgin English spoken by his characters, that Philipp lessened its dependence on the German language—and the German-language stage—in its quest for theatrical entertainment.

Philipp's plays thus provided audiences with both a popular alternative to the highbrow tradition of German-language drama and an introduction to the English language that would ultimately prove crucial to the immigrant community's linguistic and cultural integration into the mainstream of American society. Not that Philipp hadn't once had typically "German," high-culture ambitions of his own. Brought over to New York in 1890 from the Hamburg stage in order to be the Irving Place Theater's lead tenor, Philipp left that prestigious playhouse three years later at the age of twenty-five. Striking out on his own, he leased the Germania Theater on Eighth Street between Broadway and Astor Place. There, he told the *World* some twenty years later, he initially "produced dramas by Schiller, Hauptman [*sic*] and Wildenbruch . . . but they never drew a corporal crowd." Another two years later he elaborated on the insight thus gained in an interview with the *Dramatic Mirror*: "[O]bserving that the other [Irving Place] theater [too] was not being well patronized, I discovered the reason in that plays from the pen of such poets and playwrights as Schiller and Goethe, who were as well known to the Germans in America as William Shakespeare, did not meet with the playgoers' approval. This gave me the good idea to write plays . . . showing German-American life," and thus began the first phase of his American career.

Philipp's American career can be divided into four distinct phases. The first, spanning the years 1893–1902, was marked by a previously-unheard-of series of fourteen consecutive box office hits of the ethnic-parody variety described above, all staged at the Germania Theater. Moving to Berlin, he produced one of his biggest successes, *Der New Yorker Brewer* (The New York brewer) under the title *Über'n Grossen Teich* (the play was presented for 1,300 consecutive nights in the German capital and was revived on New York's English-language stage as *From Across the Pond* in 1907). Philipp returned to New York in 1906, leasing the Wintergarten Zum Schwarzen Adler Theater on East Eighty-sixth Street from 1906 to 1911 and then the Philipp's Fifty-seventh Street Theater from 1912 to 1914. This, the second phase of his American career, may be considered Philipp's "French phase," during which he wrote a number of risqué musical comedies based on the successful farces of mistaken identities and wayward husbands then being imported from France with great financial success. Writing under the pseudonyms Paul Hervé and Jean Briquet, Philipp also translated a number of these plays into English, staging them to critical acclaim on Broadway and throughout the nation. Already a wealthy and well-known man, it was during this second phase that Philipp's fame and fortunes were to reach their height.

Leaving the city in 1914 to tour the English-language versions of his plays in California, Philipp returned in 1916 to assume comanagement of the Yorkville Theater on East Eighty-sixth Street with his fellow German impresario Georg Rachmann. In this, the third phase of his American career, Philipp revived a number of his ethnic parodies of years gone by to renewed success and also penned (and starred in) a number of new plays that followed the same formula, though now more consciously and explicitly "Americanizing" than ever. After wartime pressure placed too great a stigma on German-language theater for him to continue, Philipp retired from New York in September 1918, moving to California for the final phase of his career, during which he attempted, and failed, to break into the film industry and radio.

Although it is of most immediate interest in the context of this article, Philipp's first American phase is unfortunately also the one of which least is known. In spite of the fact that the ethnic parodies presented at his Germania Theater enjoyed great success and runs that were record-breaking in the history of German-American theater (his first and most famous, 1893's *Der Corner Grocer aus der Avenue A,* ran for a never-before-equaled 750 consecutive nights) there is not a single surviving script to tell us about the plays' contents or, more important, their use of German-English. Surviving theater programs, however, as well as interviews with Philipp himself and reviews of his plays provide useful clues that tell us much about the characters, situations, settings, and general flavor of his work, and that at least *suggest* the use to which language was put in Philipp's creative hands. Certainly, we may assume that what the *Brooklyn Eagle* wrote of *Ein New Yorker Brewer* was equally applicable to most other Phillip plays of this early period: "The play deals with the humors and woes of the German immigrants—is, indeed, a sort of *volks* play of the city."[6] In fact, the term *Volksstück* ("people's," or folk play, still used in Germany today to denote a farcical play concerning common people and set in everyday surroundings) is used to describe virtually all of the plays staged at Philipp's Germania Theater for which programs survive, and it is these programs, more than anything else, that provide the real clues to the nature of Philipp's craft.

The program for *Der Corner Grocer,* for example, billed as a *Volksstück mit Gesang in 5 Akten aus dem New Yorker Leben* (a folk play with song in five acts taken from New York life) describes the setting for three of those five acts (ostensibly in German, though partially in the very German-English pidgin Philipp's use of which I am trying to establish) as follows: "1. Akt.—Im Basement-Barbershop" (1. Act.—In the basement barbershop); "3. Akt.—Beim Corner Grocer" (3. Act—At the corner grocer's); and, most creatively of all, "4. Akt.—No use, dass man darüber talken thut" (4. Act—No use talking about it). Characters included, next to a number of humorously named German immigrant types (among them Herr Schlippenbach, Ulrike and Rosette Gerstenkorn, a brewer's widow and her daughter—"Gerstenkorn" means "barleycorn"—Herr Pannemann, and, not least, Hein Snut, the corner grocer himself), ethnic types such as McGynty (probably Irish), Mandelbaum (probably Jewish), and Jean (identified as *Diener*—"servant"— most probably French). The program also lists the following secondary characters, for whose descriptions (though again ostensibly provided in German) Philipp once more made creative use of the German-English pidgin: "Röschen Traubenfrost, *née* Federweisser, Landlady"; one nameless character simply described as "Sherif" (using the old-German spelling of the word with only one "f"); one described as "Detective" (which, though spelled nearly identically in both languages, would have exchanged the letter *c* for a *k* and would have omitted the final letter *e* in "proper" German), and one character—perhaps most interesting of all for the way the spelling of his vocation switched from English to German within one word—simply listed as "Policemann," in which the first part of the word, "police," corresponds to the correct English-language spelling, while the second, "-mann," corresponds to the German.

Observations such as these may seem overly subtle, but the process of linguistic change and shifting cultural allegiance is gradual, and it is only by noting subtleties of just this sort that we can hope to detect the nearly imperceptible inroads the English language was making into German (and the German-American theatergoing public) by means of Philipp's plays. Thus it is significant that a program for a later play, *New York Bei Nacht* (New York at night, dated 1896) no longer spells the word "Act" (as in "1. Act," "2. Act," and so on) in what would be the correct German manner ("Akt," with a *k*, as the word had been spelled in the program for the "Corner Grocer" three years earlier), but that it instead employs the correct, English-language spelling, A-c-t, as would all subsequent programs for Philipp's plays at the Germania from that date forth. A corresponding development is illustrated by the fact that there is again a secondary (and again nameless) law-enforcing character in this play, whose profession is no longer spelled as an amalgamation of the English and German terms, but in the correct, English-language manner: "Policeman." Though again subtle, these changes, too, must be considered an indication of the process of linguistic transformation at work in the larger context of Philipp's oeuvre.

And again (and perhaps more interestingly) the program's brief descriptions of the setting of each individual act provide us with at least an inkling of *New York bei Nacht*'s contents and structure. Apparently, this play did not begin in the city because its first act was entitled "Auf nach New York" (Off to New York) and featured as one of its characters Thomas Uhlfelder, "Mayor [the English-language term was used] und Postmeister [German for "Postmaster"] von Sheboygan," the latter a small and heavily German-populated town in Wisconsin. There can be little doubt that the action had shifted to New York by the second act, however, which presented "Ein Abend im Tingel-Tangel" (A night at the cabaret), where the characters were treated to such colorful acts of ethnic parody (within what was clearly itself an ethnic [self-] parody) as "Die 3 Geschwister [Sisters] Werris," "Die 3 Minstrels," "Die 3 Geschwister Barritani," and "Die Fünf [five] Estrudians." From here, the action moved to a site more commonly associated with *German*-American pursuits, "Vor dem Arion Ball," which could mean either "before" or "in front of" the ball of the Arion *Verein*, the latter one of the city's oldest and most respected upper-class singing societies.[7] Then on to another specifically American site, "Vor [which in this case definitely meant "in front of"] dem Madison Square Garden," then back again to the Arion ball before ending with "Eine Nacht auf der Bowery" (A night on the Bowery). For the last act of this mammoth play (more than thirty-five primary characters were listed, as well as dozens of "extras," including, in another amalgamation of German and English, a number of "Farmarbeiter" ("farm hands" or "workers"), who presumably made their appearance in the first, still rural act), Philipp once more put his penchant for Dutch-English to creative use, entitling his finale "Aber 'standen' muss man's können," which could mean either "But one must be able to stand it" or, perhaps, "But one must be able to stand." While the latter version is the less likely, it is not entirely unfeasible because one would indeed have to be *standhaft* ("resolute" or "steadfast") to endure an itinerary of such intense carousing through the city as that experienced by the play's characters in one single night. Just reading the two-page program leaves one with a sense of exhaustion, but in any case, it scored another hit; Philipp would later claim a run of 250 consecutive performances.[8]

Even more successful was 1894's *Der New Yorker Brewer und seine Familie*, which had a sensational run of 856 nights and was, as will be recalled, performed in Berlin 1,300 times before returning to New York as an English-language play,

From Across the Pond. The original program lists the play's five acts as having the following titles: "1. Grünhörner auf Ellis Island" (Greenhorns [the conventional term for newly arrived immigrants] on Ellis Island); "2. Ein unverhofftes Wiedersehen" (An unforeseen reunion); "3. Ein Tag auf Coney Island." (A day on Coney Island); "4. Danksagungstag in der 5. Avenue" (Thanksgiving Day on Fifth Avenue); "5. Danksagungstag in der Avenue B." (Thanksgiving Day on Avenue B). Thanks to its later English-language production, we even have a synopsis of the play's contents, if only those of the English-language version (which, as a comparison with the above-cited descriptions of the individual acts indicates, does not appear to have strayed too far from the original):

> Opening at Ellis Island with a shipload of immigrants, among whom a German, a Jew, an Irishman, and a Frenchman with six lovely daughters are chief, [Philipp] arranges for a meeting of all the new arrivals for a date five years later. By that time the German is running for alderman on the Bowery, the Irishman is on the police force, while the Frenchman has made money, engaged one of his daughters to an earl, and is too proud to speak to any of his poor shipmates. The German is defeated for alderman, and in the last act, which shows him as the keeper of a lemonade stand at Coney Island, all wrongs are righted and villains punished.[9]

The program for the original, German-language version of the play again lists characters as creatively named as Hulda Camillenthee (camomile tea), Jeremias Hitzköpfle (hothead), Hein Lehmkuhl, the titular brewer (played by Philipp himself), and the con artist Baron Egon von Donnersmark ("Nach Amerika gekommen um hier eine reiche Erbin zu finden—der Herr Baron reist nur durch Zufall im Zwischendeck" [Come to America in order to find a rich heiress—the *Herr Baron* is traveling in the steerage only by coincidence]). And again, the program provides some valuable clues as to the gradual process of cultural and linguistic transformation facilitated by Philipp's work. Situated in between his *Corner Grocer* and the later *New York bei Nacht,* we find that the program for *Der New Yorker Brewer* has not yet made the switch from the German spelling of the word "act" to the English because it is in this case still spelled a-k-t. Philipp's own role as (managing) "Director," however, is here already spelled in the correct, English-language fashion, with a *c* instead of a *k,* as it would have to be spelled in proper German (and is still spelled in the program for the earlier *Der Corner Grocer).* As befits a play as transitional in Philipp's larger body of work as *Der New Yorker Brewer,* we also find in its program another, transitional amalgamation of German and English: featuring secondary characters who are again law enforcement agents, the program for the play lists their occupation as "Policeleute" (Police people).

Judging by the large number of "police people" and other individuals maintaining law and order in Philipp's plays (other programs list, next to the requisite "Detectives" and the odd "Policeman[n]," judges, police commissioners, court clerks, and even coroners), his characters appear to have run into occasional difficulties with the law, which probably reflected quite accurately the reality of the lives of immigrants still struggling to gain a secure foothold in American society before the turn of the century. More interesting, perhaps, is the manner in which his plays changed settings from lower- to upper-class immigrant locales (from the Bowery to the Arion, for example, as in *New York Bei Nacht)* and then on to distinctly upper-class *American* locales (such as Madison Square Garden, or, as in the later *Der Butcher aus der Ersten Avenue,* from "der Butcherstore" to the Fifth Avenue home of Cesar Stackwitz, banker, "Einer von den 400" [One of the (upper) 400]), which indicates a prevailing interest in the process of social climbing. This concern for social advancement, presumably deemed desirable by the community at large and also of some importance to Philipp himself, as we shall see, is further evidenced by a number of Philipp's immigrant characters (recall, for example, *Der New Yorker Brewer*'s Baron Egon von Donnersmark, come to America "in order to find a rich heiress"). And again language is of central importance in the equation because social advancement for a foreign-language immigrant community almost inevitably requires a degree of linguistic integration into the host society.[10]

Given this connection between social climbing and linguistic assimilation, a review of the later, *English*-language production of *Der New Yorker Brewer* (staged as *From Across the Pond* at the Circle Theater in 1907, after Philipp's four-year hiatus in Berlin) is particularly insightful. "It is hardly necessary to say to any one who knows the German character that all the old habitués of the Germania Theater were on hand to welcome him," the *Telegram* observed in its review, then elaborated:

> It was curious to notice in this audience of old admirers men who to-day have become well known because of their wealth, &c. But, then, we must take into account that not only has New York moved upward, but that fortunes have doubled, tripled and tripled again in these last ten years. They laughed heartily at Adolf's foolish lines, they applauded mightily Adolf's high notes—but why should they not? It reminded them joyously of the old days when they lived in Spring Street or Rivington Street, days when they did not dream of having houses on Riverside Drive or apartments in Central Park West.

These comments provide as much insight into the connection between social climbing and the acquisition of English-language skills (recall that these now-wealthy "former habitués" of the Germania, who had quite possibly seen the play in its original, German-language version some ten years earlier, were here returning to see it in its *English*-language version at an American theater) as into the psychological (and also, as the review points out, the sheer *geographic*) distance these now-established immigrants felt from their erstwhile roots. Where once they might have delighted in the familiarity of seeing themselves satirized *as they were,* they now delighted in seeing themselves satirized as they *once* were but no longer considered themselves to be. In suggesting this, the *Telegram*'s review supports the notion that Philipp's plays allowed his patrons to laugh at, and in so doing increasingly distance themselves from, the way they were (and/or had been) stereotypically perceived by the host society, thereby facilitating their desire and ability to "become" American.[11]

That Philipp remained always aware of his own roots and that he was himself conscious of the connection between social climbing and linguistic assimilation are illustrated by the following "incident," recounted in the *Philipp Eno* of September

1, 1910. An in-house, promotional publication made available to his patrons after Philipp had himself left his former *Kleindeutschland* digs at the Germania Theater and moved to the more fashionable uptown quarters of the Wintergarten zum Schwarzen Adler Theater, only a few fragments of the *Philipp Eno* have survived to the present day, of which the following is one of the most interesting. Given his prolific nature as well as the control he liked to exert over everything associated with his name, it is likely that Philipp wrote the article himself. Even if not, its contents and use of language suggest that it was closely based on his own ethnic parodies, and in the absence of any surviving scripts, its story, entitled "Adolf Meets Fritz," is worth quoting in full:

> Adolf Philipp, while standing in front of his theater in East 86th Street the other day, spied an old gentleman coming down the street whose face seemed very familiar. His curiosity being aroused, he waited until the pedestrian approached nearer, and, on closer observation, found the subject of his thoughts to be an old fellow from his native city, whom he had not seen for more than twenty years. It was quite evident from the old man's appearance that his life had not been a bed of roses, as he was dressed very shabbily and wore a most dejected air. "Hello, Fritz," said Mr. Philipp, as the old fellow was passing by. The man spoken to stopped short, and looking inquiringly into the speaker's face, said: "You speak mit me, yes?" "Don't you remember me? My name is Adolf Philipp; I'm from your native town," said the German impresario. He scrutinized Mr. Philipp very carefully, and his face broadened into a grin, as he smilingly remarked: "Vell, vell, py chimminy, now I knowed it. But my, vot a leetle shafer you den vas. Since den—t'venty-five years—huh?" "Yes, it's all of that, but what are you doing for a living," answered the author. "Oh, I keep a small tailor shop, but no make money. But vot you do?" "I'm an actor and playwright." "So? Vot you means mit playwrights?" "Why I write plays for production, for theatres, for the actors, you know," responded Mr. Philipp. "Do you make monies mit such foolishness?" "Twenty-five or thirty thousand a year," he replied. "I vish I took to dat," said the old fellow as he departed on his way.[12]

The ingredients are all there: an old immigrant who speaks in the very German-English pidgin parodied in Philipp's earlier plays and who, as much by virtue of his use of language as by his "shabbiness" and stereotypical immigrant's profession, illustrates the impossibility of social climbing for those unable to adapt fully to the mores, values, and language of the host society; and an Americanized theater manager who feels a nostalgic distance from his roots and who was by this point in his career as fully established on the German-language stage as he was on the English-language stage (thanks to the "French" farces of his second phase, on which, see below). Philipp's success and own social advancement, meanwhile, are indicated as much by his very considerable income of "Twenty-Five or Thirty Thousand a Year" as (and in the context of this paper more significantly) by his perfect use of the English language.

For all the apparent ease with which he had transformed himself into a New World success story through his use of language, however, and notwithstanding his recognition of the social desirability of at least appearing to be perfectly fluent in English, still Philipp (ever the showman) would gladly revert to the old Dutch

English for comic effect if it served his unflagging efforts at self-promotion. In a letter sent to the *New York Herald* in 1912, for example (two years after his own publication, the *Philipp Eno*, had portrayed him as someone who spoke impeccable English) he offered his considered "Apinion" on himself. Providing a brief overview of his colorful early career in which he again emphasized, in hilariously bad and atrociously misspelled English, that his attempts to stage the classics had failed due to a lack of audience interest, he maintained that it was his recognition of the fact that German audiences wanted "to be entertained" that had inspired him to come up with *Der Corner Grocer,* the blueprint for most of his later successes. Of these, he concluded proudly, none had a run of less than "one hundred executive nights," the latter an example of Dutch English that might well have been considered "prizeless" by Mike and Meyer (the former vaudeville team of Dutch comedians Joe Weber and Lew Fields, perhaps Philipp's greatest competitors when it came to finding creative ways to merge the English and the German languages on-stage).[13]

The reference to Weber and Fields is not a gratuitous one here, for at this juncture it is necessary to take a closer look at what might have served as an inspiration for Philipp's plays other than the types, language, and milieu of *Klein-deutschland*. And undoubtedly, ethnic parodies such as the Dutch Act, as perfected by Weber and Fields around the very same time that Philipp was first putting pen to paper for *Der Corner Grocer,* will have figured prominently among his sources of inspiration. Themselves of immigrant stock (both were of Eastern European, Jewish descent, and both had grown up in the Lower East Side not far from the district's German enclave), Weber and Fields had been on the stage since the 1870s and made their first appearance when they were both just ten years of age. Though we may assume them to have been no less guilty of mythologizing their theatrical roots than were other personalities of the stage, it is interesting to note that Weber would later recall their first appearance to have taken place in the very heart of Little Germany, "at Turner's Hall . . . in the vicinity of the Bowery." Not that this location immediately suggested the Dutch Act to the young comedy team; as another source describes their first appearance, "they clog-danced their way onto the stage attired in snappy green knickers and singing, 'Two Irish Lads Are We,' " only to "be greeted with derisive cries from the German audience. They immediately took the hint, got fried egg hats, and changed their act overnight to German dialect. And so, as Mike and Meyer, they began to make theatrical history."[14]

Myth aside, it is not too much of an overstatement to declare that Mike and Meyer did make American theater history, and in the process turned Weber and Fields into wealthy men and household names, if not quite overnight. They developed a stock repertoire of costumes and established the standard conventions of makeup that were to be associated with the Dutch German for decades to come— bewhiskered Weber with his padded "brewer's" midriff and the lanky Fields adding a good five inches to his height with the aid of platform shoes. And while some theater historians have suggested that the appeal of the team's particular brand of comedy was first and foremost of a physical, slapstick nature (for the two were more often than not seen in violent on-stage altercation), I would suggest that it rested also in the hilarious vocabulary of German-English misnomers they established in their literally hundreds of Dutch Act exchanges over the years.[15] Consider, for example, the opening of their famous "Pool Hall" skit, to which—and here we again enter the realm of myth—they were allegedly inspired by observing two drunken Germans in a pool hall:

> *Mike:* I am delightfulness to meet you.
> *Myer:* Der disgust is all mine.
> *Mike:* I receivedidid a letter from mein goil, but I don't know how to writteninin her back.
> *Myer:* Writteninin her back? Such an edumuncation you got it? Writteninin her back! You mean rotteninin her back. How can you answer her ven you don't know how to write?
> *Mike:* Dot makes no nefer mind. She don't know how to read.[16]

As base as the humor of the skit may strike us today, there is about it something almost sophisticated in the way it addresses—albeit with tongue in cheek and perhaps unself-consciously—the importance, the pitfalls, and the sometimes inadvertent humor of language, literacy, and translation. Certainly, German-American audiences at the time appear to have taken this parody in the same playful spirit in which it was delivered. "Sensitive as they were about their cultural background," Richard O'Connor has noted, "the Germans apparently did not resent the caricature; perhaps it was too broad to be taken seriously, and in any case they could always laugh at the vaudeville conception of the Irish as equally stupid, intemperate and bellicose bog-trotters or the Jews as cunning and greedy knaves."[17] This they undoubtedly did, as much at vaudeville with its wide variety of ethnic parodies (of which Weber and Fields constituted only one example, if perhaps the one best remembered today) as at the productions of Adolf Philipp, which, as will be recalled, frequently featured a number of just these "other" ethnic types alongside the German immigrant caricatures in which he specialized (the Irish McGynty and the Jewish Mandelbaum in *Der Corner Grocer,* for example).

In fact, the ethnic parodies of Weber and Fields and other vaudeville comedians were undoubtedly very close to those presented by Philipp at the Germania Theater, with the significant difference, of course, that they were presented on the American (rather than German-American) stage, and that their humor depended more on a "Germanization" of the English language than an Americanization of the German. In such depending, I would suggest, American ethnic parodies and the sites in which they were presented further contributed to the trajectory of cultural and linguistic transformation and integration initiated for the German-American theatergoer at Philipp's Germania, for in the numerically overwhelming company of Americans, German immigrants among vaudeville audiences would even more self-consciously have laughed at—and thus consciously distanced themselves from—their own former selves. And why not, for the self-effacement implied by the acceptance of this form of humor was clearly tempered by the significant potential it held for the very social advancement toward which German immigrants strove. As Francis G. Couvares has noted, the "sympathetic, if somewhat ridiculous portrayals" offered by the Dutch Act "ratified the fact that those immigrants who had faced nativist hostility as recently as the 1850s, had become better integrated into the city—its skilled trades, commerce, and politics." Rather more bluntly, Richard O'Connor states, "If you can laugh at a man, you can't hate him too much." More recently, Miriam Hansen has noted that "the stereotypes [of ethnic burlesque] provided a foil for a new, ostensibly middle-class identity or, rather, for an identification with a specifically American myth of success that blurred all class and ethnic distinctions."[18]

Yet for all its arguably ameliorating and socially desirable potential, there remained significant and influential voices within the immigrant community that frowned severely on the stereotyping of the Dutch Act. The *New Yorker Staats-Zeitung,* for example, oldest and most respectable of New York's many German-language newspapers and ever the outspoken champion of *Kultur,* was not amused. "Such a ridiculous, impossible distortion, this small, pot-bellied fellow with his drooping mustache and dull eyes, replete with his wooden slippers, balloon-like hat, his long-stemmed pipe, beerglass, and pretzel," the newspaper lamented on American popular culture's conception of the German in 1913. "Where has one ever seen a German of this type. . . . We German-Americans do not laugh at him."[19] Catering to a solidly middle-class readership since its inception in 1834 and looking back on a long tradition of defending German from all inroads made by the English language (Carl Wittke has explicitly identified the *Staats-Zeitung* as one of several German-language dailies that were outspokenly opposed to the sort of "German-Americanisms" popularized by Philipp as well as Weber and Fields), the newspaper objected to the Dutch Act, we may assume, as much for its ungenerous physical portrayal of German immigrants as it did for the genre's threat to linguistic purity.[20]

Given the *Staats-Zeitung*'s distaste for linguistic amalgamations in general and the Dutch Act in particular, it is hardly surprising that the newspaper showed little enthusiasm for Philipp and his particular brand of comedy. Writing in 1910, *Staats-Zeitung* drama critic Albert Pulvermacher looked back on the history of New York's German theater during the 1890s, and commented,

> Around this time, Adolf Philipp established his Germania Theater on Eighth Street, a little episode that lasted for nine years. Originally come over as a singer of operetta, Philipp soon imagined himself to have discovered within the community a need for a site staging "folk" plays, whose manager, author, and star he was himself to be. . . . [H]e struck humorous chords with his "Corner Grocer"—embellishing farcical effects and Anglo melodrama with comical local color—and behold, the "folk" he had beckoned from around Avenue A and its environment came in droves, as it did also to his "Brewer" and "Landlady" as well as other plays, all of which bore a curious family resemblance to one another. As the plays became increasingly sentimental, however, and their humor too crude—on one occasion a limburger cheese was literally shot to pieces on-stage—they stopped being palatable even to the "folk" of Avenue A, and the "folk" diet stopped making good business. Philipp disappeared temporarily in 1897 . . . went to Berlin, where he served "Über'n Grossen Teich" [the German-language version of *From Across the Pond*] a mix of his best New York-grown local color farces, alongside dark barley ale. . . . The familiar diet of his "folk" plays was resurrected last year at the "Zum Schwarzen Adler" Theater [on East Eighty-sixth Street] and there proved itself to be nutritious still. . . . Now "Alma" lives there.[21]

The mention of "Alma" is a reference to Philipp's huge hit of 1909, *Alma, Wo Wohnst Du?* with which he moved into his second major American phase and achieved national fame as the "translator" (first "into" German; later, English) of purportedly French imports that he actually wrote himself under the pseudonyms Jean Briquet and Paul Hervé. No longer preoccupied with the lives of German immigrants, plays such as *Alma, Auction Pinochle, The Midnight Girl, Adele,* and *The Girl Who Smiles* told humorous stories of conniving chorus girls, wayward husbands, and shrewd wives; all scored huge hits for Philipp, first in German and later in English. The *New York Sun* would recall in its obituary of Philipp in 1936:

> "Alma, Where Do You Live?" a play written by Mr. Philipp, was the biggest hit in four years from 1909 to 1912 inclusive. It was played in both English and German, in Yorkville [the middle-class German-American section of Manhattan in which Philipp staged the play at his Wintergarden Zum Schwarzen Adler Theater] and on Broadway, and eventually in the Hinterlands, until the entire country was humming and whistling its merry tunes.

With characteristic aplomb, Philipp himself stated, "Some of my songs are being sung in public schools in the state of Wisconsin as folk songs."[22]

Though his noms de plume were no longer of interest for their playful use of language, the fact that Philipp insisted on hiding behind the pseudonyms "Briquet" and "Hervé" for a full six years as his plays took the nation by storm provides fascinating food for thought. Some contemporary sources later suggested that this was an expression of Philipp's "unusual modesty."[23] Given the delight he had earlier taken in ethnic masquerade and plays of cultural transition and transformation, however, I would suggest that Philipp's use of pseudonyms was perhaps less a function of "modesty" than a strategy that allowed him to continue deriving pleasure from his penchant for impersonation and ambiguous identities even after he had begun writing (or "translating") plays in(to) "straight" German (plays that were later translated into "straight" English equally devoid of linguistic implication). As early as 1907, on the occasion of the English-language performance of *From Across the Pond,* one source had noted that "Adolf Philipp, after writing the book and lyrics and composing the music, was likewise able, *perhaps by a dual personality,* to assist in its adaptation 'for the American stage.'" Similar reflections on the many roles assumed by Philipp can be found in reviews throughout his first and second American phases.[24] And what better way for Philipp to perpetuate his dual personality after he had abandoned ethnic parodies in favor of "French" farces than to hide behind the assumed names of two nonexistent writers. We can only imagine what a delight it must have been for this master of ethnic pastiche and impersonation to have confused American journalists searching the rosters of the French Academy for Hervé and Briquet (the latter actually the maiden name of his Franco-German mother) as he himself collected their royalties. In any case, when he decided that this true-life comedy of assumed identity had played itself out, Philipp "confessed" to his deceptions with characteristic flourish, effortlessly integrating the six-year episode into the myth of his career. Taking out a full page in the *New York Dramatic Mirror,* he presented an article entitled "A Remarkable Triple Identity":

> Yes, I am guilty of possessing a nom de plum, and as I have been caused a number of restless nights of late, due to the fact that some of the New York critics have been getting sort of suspicious as to who the two "French" authors, Paul Herve and Jean Briquet, are, I feel it is my duty to make a clear confession, and here it is: . . . in 1908, when everybody was producing French farces, I sailed for Europe on a vacation, and while in Paris I thought of writing a French farce but giving the public some music with it. . . . So I went to Chantilly, rented a nice little room and wrote a musical farce in three acts and called it "Alma, Where Do You Live?" When I had this manuscript finished I returned to America. Arriving in New York, at the dock I was met by several newspaper men who wanted news, and always being very friendly with the representatives of the New York press I told them that after a visit of several weeks in Paris I secured the American rights of several "French" musical farces which I proposed producing in New York in "German," at a little theater called "The Wintergarten" on the East Side. The first play of the "French" nature I presented was "Alma, Where Do You Live?" and when they insisted on knowing the authors of these imported works I thought of my French ancestors and told them that the book was by Paul Herve and music by Jean Briquet, with the American adaptation by myself. . . . After the Herve-Briquet trade mark was established I had to continue using those names and wrote "Adele" and "Auction Pinochle." . . . The latter was followed by "The Midnight Girl" and "The Girl Who Smiles," all by Paul Herve and Jean Briquet. I must say that all these plays have never been presented in France, but will be, after the war is over, and will then go abroad as an envious success from America.[25]

Not that Philipp had been entirely unsuspected of his multiple role-playing. Some reviewers, including one writing for the *Dramatic Mirror,* were voicing their doubts as to the existence of Hervé and Briquet (as well as, we should add, "F. Schuhmacher," the pseudonym under which Philipp wrote his controversial political play *Zabern,* on which, see immediately below) even before the playwright had made his confession. The *Mirror* had noted as early as 1914,

> If an American manager needs a hit, all he has to do is see Adolf. Adolf at once sees Paul Hervé, Paul Hervé sees Jean Briquet and—presto! you have a comic opera or a musical comedy guaranteed for four months with an option for a year or more. . . . Adolf deals in retail and wholesale hits, one-base hits and near hits, for the American market exclusively. All offers from Berlin, Vienna, and Paris ignored. Jean Briquet writes exclusively for this market. Paul Herve, ditto. F. Schumacher, ditto. All under the exclusive management of Adolf Briquet Paul Herve Schuhmacher Philipp.[26]

Less aware of Philipp's many identities but fully cognizant of the fact that the playwright had transcended at least the limitations of *national* identity, the *Los Angeles Examiner* wrote of Philipp around the same time,

> Most of his productions he has dashed off in German, produced and acted in them in German, at his German theater in New York, and then turned them into English. He is a German then, you ask. I do not know what nationality he claims. He was born in Paris, brought up in Germany, and made himself a rich man with his brains in New

York. Art knows no frontiers and laughs at geography; Mr. Philipps [sic] does not seem to be a citizen, nor a subject of any country; he is a Power himself.[27]

Just how effectively Philipp had in fact transcended the limitations of nationality, and just how little loyalty he felt to any one culture or country (in particular to Germany) is illustrated by his political play *Zabern* of 1914. Inspired by a military incident that almost led to war between Germany and France and that aroused the interest of the international press (and inspired also, perhaps, by his own French ancestry), Philipp wrote a play that took an aggressively pro-French and anti-German stance on the issue.[28] It was to prove the one near-fatal miscalculation in Philipp's otherwise perfectly orchestrated theatrical career, providing, as it did, the conservative and ever violently pro-German *New Yorker Staats-Zeitung* with the long-sought-for opportunity to blacken Philipp's reputation within the German-American community. Upon having seen the play, drama critic Pulvermacher was outraged. Not only was it filled with "stupid dialogue" of the "worst and most base humor" and contain, as he wrote in a follow-up several days later, "all sorts of lewd 'spice' . . . and tired elements of burlesque typical of Philipp's various New York 'folk' plays of the past"—*Zabern* was, worst of all, "a maliciously anti-German play" that "glorified the tricolor and figuratively mopped the floor with the German flag."[29]

The newspaper printed several aggressively anti-Philipp editorials and recommended that readers boycott the play altogether.[30] The controversy clearly hurt Philipp's reputation, and a month later, he withdrew all advertising from the *Staats-Zeitung* in retaliation and filed a suit for damages. As the *New York Review* reported several months later in an article entitled "Echo of 'Zabern' Play":

> Adolf Philipp filed a damage suit for $100,000, in which sum the German actor-manager claims he was injured by an article which appeared in Hermann Ridder's newspaper [the *Staats-Zeitung*] denouncing the production of "Zabern" . . . as malevolent and biased anti-German propaganda. Mr. Philipp claims that he is not only quite as loyal as "Herr von" Ridder, but a little more so and that before the bitter criticism of "Zabern" appeared in the *Staats-Zeitung* he was the histrionic idol of the German-American citizens of this city. After editor Ridder's paper jumped upon "Zabern" . . . Adolf Philipp's 57th Street Theater began to dwindle . . . the case is ordered to trial.[31]

Neither the German nor the American press covered the trial, and its verdict was never publicly disclosed (quite possibly, the matter was settled out of court). In any case, Philipp closed down his theater at the end of the season and left New York for California, where he spent several seasons touring his previously successful plays to great acclaim.[32]

Never one to be kept down, Philipp returned from his tour in the fall of 1916 to assume comanagement of the Yorkville Theater on East Eighty-sixth Street, just across the street from his own former Wintergarten zum Schwarzen Adler Theater. Despite his earlier criticism, even the *Staats-Zeitung*'s drama critic Pulvermacher had to give the playwright's first offering reluctant praise. A new musical comedy called *Sadie vom Riverside Drive* and starring Philipp as the male lead, the play told the story of a young American woman who lures wayward husbands—among them a duped German (Philipp)—into her Riverside Drive apartment to rob them. Although noting that "one may be slightly annoyed at so easily having walked into his trap," Pulvermacher conceded that "one will laugh, laugh, and laugh." The music, too, was vintage Philipp in Pulvermacher's estimation, full of "infectious tunes of whose origin one had best not inquire." But why dwell on the "unpleasant question" of plagiarism; in all, he readily and forgivingly admitted that "laughter of such genuine abandon and irresistibility has not been heard at a theater here in a long, long time."[33] And lest there be any doubt as to the language(s) in which this plot unfolded before the audience, another New York-based German-language daily, William Randolph Hearst's *New Yorker deutsches Journal,* offered the following observation: "One will amuse oneself royally, and even those with no command over the German language will be able to follow the action, as countless English phrases clarify the story."[34]

Philipp was back in full force, populating his most recent French vaudeville with ethnic types familiar from his earlier parodies and once more resorting to the same German-English pidgin. And the audience seems to have responded to his return with great enthusiasm: during a season in which none of the high-culture offerings at the competing Irving Place Theater remained on the playbill for more than a few days, Philipp held his Yorkville audience captive with *Sadie* for a full eight weeks, then followed it with a revival of his first play of the "French" phase, *Alma Wo Wohnst Du?* before returning unconditionally to his earliest roots by reviving his first New York success, *Der Corner Grocer von Avenue A.* After *Der Corner Grocer* had ended its successful five-week run, Philipp revived *Auction Pinochle* for the month of April, then presented *Ein New Yorker Brewer* until June 13.

By this time—the summer of 1917—the United States had joined the European war and the nation had been swept by a wave of anti-German hysteria that washed over all things German, including in particular the German language. In the months leading up to the war, German-Americans in New York and around the nation had filed for their naturalization papers en masse, and many German-language newspapers (including Hearst's *New Yorker deutsches Journal*) folded under the pressure. The few that survived (the previously belligerently pro-German *Staats-Zeitung* among them) now did a complete about-face in matters of politics, assuming a rabidly pro-American stance on the war in an attempt to prove their loyalty.[35] The Irving Place Theater, meanwhile, former temple of German *Kultur* (whose fortunes had been flagging since even before Philipp's return to New York and whose manager Rudolf Christians had attempted to attract audiences with pro-German propaganda plays during the period of American neutrality) was now singled out as an anti-American institution by the New York branches of the American Defense Society and the National Security League.[36] Crumbling under the pressure, Christians struggled to complete the season (which he ended early, on April 30) and announced that he was giving up his lease on the theater, which would henceforth be home to the Yiddish Repertory Theater under the leadership of Morris Schwartz.[37]

Even the career of Adolf Philipp, who had never aroused controversy for being "pro-German" (if anything, he had aroused controversy for being *anti*-German, as will be recalled of the *Zabern* incident), was in the end not able to resist the tribulations of war. True, the Yorkville Theater (by then commonly referred to as "*Philipp's* Yorkville Theater") weathered the stormy season of 1917–1918 without faltering; during the fall Philipp successfully revived his former ethnic parodies *Die Landlady* and *New York in Wort und Bild*, and in the spring he presented a new play, *O! Emilie*. Nothing is known of the last play except that it ran until June 3, well into the summer, and we can safely assume that like his others, it contained "lots" of English—if not quite enough to satisfy New York's various "loyalty leagues." By the season of 1918–1919, Philipp too had been singled out as a culprit in the eyes of those who held the German language responsible for all evil; on August 21, 1918, the *New York Telegraph* published an article stating that Adolf Philipp had "reformed." Abandoned by his former audience of "limburger eaters and sauerkraut devotees," the *Telegraph* claimed, Philipp, "like the Irving Place . . . has folded and will host American drama from now on." A similar article published in the *New York Star* bore the headline "Adolf Philipp sees the light" and noted that he "renounces German theater . . . and says the Yorkville will open as an American theater in September."[38] While it is untrue that Philipp had been abandoned by his audience—as we have seen, he continued his season until June 3, much longer than most other New York theaters—he had apparently, indeed, "seen the light."

Perhaps he was responding to an open letter that had been sent to him on June 4 by Mrs. William Jay, a fiercely anti-German patron of the arts whose pressure may have contributed to the Metropolitan Opera Company's withdrawal of all German-language opera a year earlier.[39] "In view of the prevailing loyalty of your patrons to the United States," she had written to Philipp, "I am making the suggestion that you consider the substitution of plays and operettas in the national language of this country and thereby win to your side the patriotic majority."[40] Philipp heeded the advice. In a statement published on August 19 on the front page of the *Staats-Zeitung* (which, along with its political about-face, now also displayed a far greater openness to the English language and Philipp's own "Americanizing" fare), the playwright announced to the public that "as both [the English-language] press and the far greater portion of the American population do not consider the further existence of a German theater to be justified or desirable under the present conditions, we willingly succumb to their verdict, all the more so because the owners of the Yorkville Theater will not permit us to produce German-language plays."[41]

Itself "converted," the *Staats-Zeitung* faithfully covered what little remained of the New York career of Adolf Philipp, whom the newspaper had on so many former occasions derided, criticized, and snubbed. On August 25, 1918, it announced approvingly that Philipp had written and planned to produce a "patriotic play" in the English language entitled *Tell That to the Marines*. It was, wrote the newspaper that had so long resisted the cultural and linguistic assimilation of its readership, a comical play that detailed the experience of a diehard German-American reluctantly converted to the American life style, his final submission illustrated by his purchase of Liberty Bonds and the fact that he willingly permitted his fully Americanized son to enlist in the marines. That a play of this nature was to be welcomed was illustrated by the many letters of approval Philipp had received from the German public, as stated by the *Staats-Zeitung* in an article published on September 1. The same article called the forthcoming production a "justification of all those who [unlike, ironically, the *Staats-Zeitung* itself] have unceasingly stood by the country of their choice." The *Staats-Zeitung* provided further advance publicity up until the very eve of the premiere and promoted the play heavily in a number of press releases far more detailed and positive than any ever before devoted to a Philipp production.[42]

The performance itself was lauded by the *Staats-Zeitung* as an "eminent deed." Philipp's trademark mixture of humor and pathos, formerly disdained, was now suddenly considered to be perfectly suited for the times. "All New York should see this play," drama critic Pulvermacher gushed. "Everyone should experience the great idea, the powerful, exciting plot, and the hearty humor of 'Tell That to the Marines.' It is a play that must interest all loyal citizens of this country equally, the native-born Yankee as much as the citizen of foreign birth." A week into its run, Pulvermacher wrote a long follow-up article in which he noted that Philipp had received many letters and telegrams of congratulations, and that the English-language press, too, was fully supportive of the play.[43] On the latter count, Pulvermacher was perhaps stretching the truth. Among the more gracious reviews in the New York press was that of the *Dramatic Mirror* — always a Philipp fan — headlined, "Adolf Philipp Begins Season at Yorkville with Patriotic Play":

> Adolf Philipp, a versatile author and manager, who has for many years been prominent in both German and English theatrical circles, figuratively hung a sign reading "Here English is spoken" outside his theater, the Yorkville, erstwhile home of the *ersatz* drama, and introduced a new regime there by presenting "Tell That to the Marines," which was announced on the program in large type as "an American play by American authors, with an American cast." This first production of a season in which Mr. Philipp proposes to present some ten more plays, both musical and dramatic, is a patriotic piece. . . . Each of the three acts . . . passed in the grocery store and home of Hein Schultz, a German-American [perhaps a distant cousin of the original *Corner Grocer von Avenue A*, Hein Snut?] who, although loyal, has a serious and interminably wordy row with his wholly American son immediately after he enlisted with the Marines [an indication that Philipp did perhaps after all manage to smuggle some "Dutch" English into the play]. But the squabbling was mainly due to a mistake about the boy's behavior with a manicure, who can, when occasion demands, double as a chorus girl. These complications [reminiscent as they are of a typical French vaudeville] were carried on for three solid hours.[44]

Reviewing *Tell That to the Marines* rather more viciously on September 27, *Variety* noted that it was "a bad play, a very bad one, crudely constructed and amateurish in treatment. The obvious plot is strung out by constant repetition of dialogue and situations." The review granted, however, that Philip had succeeded in "the assimilation of his former clientele . . . a portion of the dialogue is devoted to patriotic propaganda designed to impress the German-Americans, and judging by the applause accorded these outbursts they take it with avidity." A similarly unfavorable review appeared in the *Dramatic Mirror,* which panned even Philipp's performance as the converted German-American father, but also noted the effectiveness of the patriotic rhetoric designed to "assimilate the audience." Whatever the faults or merits of the play, it did not enjoy the longevity of former Philipp productions. A mere two weeks after *Tell That to the Marines* had opened, the *Staats-Zeitung* reported that Philipp had abruptly canceled the contracts of his ensemble players, paid off the staff, and closed down the theater. With that, one of the most colorful and successful characters in the New York theater community retired from the business.[45]

The last phase of Philipp's American career was bitter. He traveled to Hollywood, hoping for a film career he had been promised some three years earlier. Then he had been the toast of "tinseltown," as producers fell over themselves in their attempts to "secure [Philipp's] highly desirable list of comedies for motion picture production," the *Dramatic News* had reported in 1915. Some months later, the same trade publication noted that film mogul Lewis J. [father of David O.] Selznick had outbid all others. "None offered me the lavish expenditure of money, the powerful support which has been assured by Mr. Selznick," the newspaper quoted Philipp, then went on: "contracts have been signed with several noted stars to support Mr. Philipp and work will begin at once by an especially picked staff on Mr. Philipp's productions. [Selznick's] World Film Corporation has engaged a special studio for Mr. Philipp and scenery, properties and special electrical effects have been manufactured for each of his productions."[46] Yet when Philipp arrived in 1918 to claim his right, he was to be disappointed. Selznick did in fact produce a film version of *Der Corner Grocer,* but the role of Hein Snut went not to Philipp but to his erstwhile rival as America's most beloved stage-German, Lew Fields (of Weber and Fields fame). Adding insult to injury, Fields did not even enact the role in trademark "Dutch" vein. *Variety* noted of "this simple and direct story of fun and pathos . . . Lew Fields . . . is enabled to prove on the screen what he was never permitted to show in the speaking theater—that he can portray the more serious emotions with quite as much facility as the broad fun with which he has been so long associated."[47]

Through in New York and snubbed by Hollywood, Philipp next tried his hand at a radio career but failed anew. For some years he fell into utter obscurity, then resurfaced in New York in 1933 with a play called *Kultur.* Written in opposition to the Hitler regime, the play did not do well on the New York stage. Three years later Philipp died, virtually forgotten. In its front-page obituary, the *Staats-Zeitung* reviewed his career and emphasized the integral part he had once played in New York's world of German-language theater. In a display of hypocrisy, the publication that had once called upon its readers to boycott Philipp's plays and that had all but driven him out of town now lamented the fact that the younger generation did not even recognize his name. Few people came to his funeral, and the wake of the man who had once brought riotous laughter to the German-American community was reportedly a quiet and depressing affair.[48]

For one with as many triumphs as Adolf Philipp an end so ignoble seems cruel indeed. If with this chapter I have helped spark interest in a man who was for more than twenty years the *enfant terrible* of New York theater and whose plays celebrated phenomenal runs on both sides of the Atlantic, then I shall consider my efforts to have been partially successful; even more so if this chapter inspires others to continue researching the history and impact of immigrant (self-) parodists such as Philipp, and thereby deepen our understanding of the role of linguistic amalgamation and ethnic self-parody within the process of different immigrant groups' integration into the mainstream of American society. It has long been conventional wisdom that the American ethnic parodies staged in vaudeville (such as those of Weber and Fields) were a crucial transitional link for immigrants who, in their quest for assimilation through popular culture, shifted their allegiance from the ethnic stage, via vaudeville, to mainstream American theater. Yet the work of ethnic *self*-parodists such as Philipp (and he is only one; similar personalities can be found in virtually all other immigrant groups) adds another, even more crucial transitional link to the larger trajectory. Comfortably laughing at themselves in the self-consciously American environment of vaudeville would, I believe, be an accomplishment considerably eased for those who had already laughed at similar portrayals of themselves in a more familiar, ethnic environment, such as—for German-American immigrants—Philipp's Germania Theater. Thus the trajectory is complicated, covering four rather than just three bases in the route from ethnic to American theater: from the immigrant stage (such as the Irving Place Theater) via ethnic self-parodies, to American ethnic parodies, and finally to the mainstream American stage.

Having achieved what on at least one level they set out to do—readying the immigrant audience for participation in American culture and the use of the American language—Philipp's plays ultimately became anachronistic, lost their audience (now patrons of the American stage), and like Philipp himself, slipped into obscurity. After Philipp's departure and the folding of the Irving Place Theater, German-language theater in New York was never again to attain the widespread prominence and popularity it had enjoyed around the turn of the century. Unquestionably, the war had a great deal to do with this decline. Just as unquestionably, however, it was a decline that had begun long before the United States entry into the war. Philipp's first success, it will be recalled, 1893's *Der Corner Grocer*, had celebrated a run of 750 consecutive nights a full two decades before the "shadow of the Hun" ever darkened America's image of the German immigrant population. Looking back, Philipp himself remarked to the *New York World* in 1913, "Germans in New York want something typically American . . . they prefer it to highbrow drama or even comedies by the leading German authors."[49] This, in the end, remains what to me seems most significant about Philipp and what little we know of his work: the intriguing glimpse it affords us of an immigrant community torn between two different versions of culture—and ultimately two different versions of itself—during a crucial moment of its history.

NOTES

The author gratefully acknowledges the generous assistance of Marty Jacobs, Acting Curator of the Museum of the City of New York's Theater Collection, as well as that of the staff of the Billy Rose Theatre Collection at the New York Public Library for the Performing Arts.

1. An important note: what I call "Dutch English" here and throughout (I use the term interchangeably with "German-English" and, sometimes, "German-English pidgin") is not to be confused with "Pennsylvania Dutch," the amalgamation of English and what Don Yoder has called "the dialect of the Palatinate," whence many eighteenth-century German immigrants to Pennsylvania came. While Pennsylvania Dutch, which has a grammar and syntax of its own, experienced a revival in the 1930s and is still spoken in some sections of Pennsylvania today, "Dutch English" was what Carl Wittke once called a "strange mixture of German and English vocabulary and grammar." We find it parodied in the German burlesques of such vaudeville artists as Joe Weber and Lew Fields, as well as in the ethnic parodies of Adolf Philipp, both of which are discussed below. Though more of a trope than an actual language, we may assume that Dutch English was in fact quite close to the vernacular of urban German immigrants of the nineteenth and early twentieth centuries. Its popular stage version fell into disuse toward the end of the second decade of the century, when most German immigrants were fully integrated into American society and became fluent in English, and when, we may assume, the pidgin also lost its currency within the community. Carl Wittke, *The German-Language Press in America* (Louisville: University of Kentucky Press, 1957), p. 200. On Pennsylvania Dutch, see Don Yoder, "The Pennsylvania Germans: Three Centuries of Identity Crisis," in Frank Trommler and Joseph McVeigh, eds., *America and the Germans: An Assessment of a Three-Hundred-Year History* (Philadelphia: University of Pennsylvania Press, 1985), pp. 40–65; in the same volume, see also Jürgen Eichhoff, "The German Language in America," pp. 224–240, and Marion L. Huffines, "Language Maintenance Efforts among German Immigrants and Their Descendants in the United States," pp. 241–250.

2. *New York World*, March 2, 1913. Unpaginated clipping, Robinson Locke Envelope # 1751: "Philipp, Adolf," Billy Rose Theater Collection, New York Public Library of the Performing Arts (hereafter: RL#1751/BRC).

3. What follows is a list of Philipp's plays provided by himself in an article written for the *Dramatic Mirror,* to which I have added, where available, the probable production date. Where no such date is available, I have noted "n.d." ("no date") after the title: " 'A New Yorker Brewer' (856 nights) [1894], 'The Pawnbroker of the East Side' (150 nights) [n.d.], 'New York in Wort und Bild" (450 nights) [1896], 'Die Landlady' (150 nights) [n.d.], 'New York at Night' (250 nights) [1896], 'The Butcher of First Avenue,' (300 nights) [1902?], 'Klein Deutschland' (300 nights) [n.d.], 'Dollars und Cents' (125 nights) [n.d.], 'A Day in Manilla' (100 nights) [n.d.], 'Secrets of New York' (250 nights) [n.d.], 'The Happiest Man in New York' (150 nights) [n.d.], and 'The Journey to America' (150 nights) [n.d.]." Adolf Philipp, "A Remarkable Triple Identity," *Dramatic Mirror*, November 20, 1915. Unpaginated clipping, RL#1751/BRC. I have also found mention of the following plays credited to Philipp: *Alma, Wo Wohnst Du?* (1909, Philipp's most successful play, performed in English across the nation as *Alma, Where Do You Live?*), *Auction Pinochle* (based on his German-language play of the same title, 1910, and also performed in English as *The Card Party*), *Das Mitternachtsmädl* (1912, performed in English as *The Midnight Girl*), *Two Lots in der Bronx* (1913), *Therese, Sei Mir Nicht Boes* (1915, performed in English as *Theresa, Don't Be Angry*), *Zabern* (1914), *Das Mädchen, das gerne lacht* (1915, performed in English as

The Girl Who Smiles), *My Shadow and I* (n.d.), *Sh! It's A Secret* (1915), *That Night* (1915), *The Masked Marvel* (1916), *Sadie vom Riverside Drive* (1916), *O! Emilie!* (1918), *Tell That to the Marines* (1918), and *Kultur* (1933).

4. In the context of New York's German-language stage, the story of Rudolf Christians and the Irving Place Theater (which he managed from 1913 to 1918) are of equal significance and interest as the career of Adolf Philipp, yet including it here would go beyond the scope of this paper. Like Philipp's, Christians's career is relatively obscure, and the interested reader is hereby referred to my own "The Translated Community: New York City's German-Language Press as an Agent of Cultural Resistance and Integration, 1910–1918" (Ph.D. diss., Yale University, 1996), chap. 8. For the best discussion of the pre-Christians period of the Irving Place Theater, see Norman Hapgood, *The Stage in America* (New York: Macmillan, 1901), chap. 7; see also Edwin Hermann Zeydel, "The German Theater in New York City" (M.A. thesis, Cornell University, 1915).

5. *New York Telegraph,* December 9, 1913. Unpaginated clipping, RL#1751/BRC.

6. *Brooklyn Eagle,* undated, unpaginated clipping, probably 1910, RL#1751/BRC.

7. On the Arion, see Wirt Howe, *New York at the Turn of the Century, 1899–1916* (Toronto: Ryerson Press, 1946), p. 15. See also LaVern J. Rippley, *The German-Americans* (Boston: Twayne, 1976), p. 113; and Stanley Nadel, *Little Germany: Ethnicity, Religion and Class in New York City, 1845–80* (Urbana: University of Illinois Press, 1990), p. 114.

8. See Adolf Philipp, "A Remarkable Triple Identity," *Dramatic Mirror,* November 20, 1915. Unpaginated clipping, RL#1751/BRC.

9. Unidentified, unpaginated clipping, probably 1907 (the year the play was performed in English), RL#1751/BRC.

10. As immigrant historian William Carlson Smith noted in 1933, the ability to speak and understand the English language constituted an important "instrument of [cultural] participation" for immigrants: "Undoubtedly the most baffling and embarrassing obstacle the immigrant encounters upon his arrival in America is his inability to use the current speech . . . acquisition of the common language by the members of an immigrant group may be considered a criterion or rough index of Americanization." William Carlson Smith, *Americans in the Making* (New York: D. Appleton Century, 1933), pp. 146–147.

11. *New York Telegram,* 9 September, 1907. Unpaginated clipping, RL#1751/BRC.

12. "Adolf Meets Fritz," *Philipp Eno,* September 1, 1910. Unpaginated clipping, RL#1751/BRC.

13. *New York Herald,* October 30, 1912. Unpaginated clipping, RL#1751/BRC.

14. Joe Weber, "My Beginnings," *Theatre Magazine,* March 1907, p. 81; obituary of Joe Weber, *New York Times,* May 11, 1942, p. 15. In fact, it is unlikely that Weber and Fields made the transition from Irish to German parody overnight. Here, Weber's own recollections are perhaps more to be trusted: "On the Bowery . . . we changed our act to suit the taste of the audiences. If they didn't care for us as Irish boys we tried black face. And when we thought they had had enough of that, we put together a Dutch turn." *Theater Magazine,* March 1907, p. 82.

15. On the purely violent aspect of their act, see, for example, Richard O'Connor, *The German-Americans: An Informal History* (Boston: Little, Brown, 1968), p. 302. Certainly, the physical appeal of their comedy is undeniable. Weber himself recalled, "Sometimes we hurt each other in the murdering act that the audience seemed to like so well. Once I dressed in such a hurry that I forgot to put on the piece of iron I wore under my skull pad and Lew hit me a blow that laid my scalp open. Another time when I aimed at Lew's chest I struck his mouth. The compensation was that the audience seemed to like us better when we bled."

Weber, "My Beginnings," p. vii. Yet for all its physicality, we must bear in mind also what the *New York Times* noted of Weber and Fields's brand of humor on the occasion of the latter's death, "No doubt, the action was enhanced by the language, the German dialect of 'variety.' " *New York Times,* July 22, 1941, p. 18. In any case, it is for their dialogue—and specifically their "Dutch" dialogue—that the two are best remembered today. Of their most memorable skits, one of Fields's biographers listed (next to the famous "Pool Hall" skit quoted below) " 'The German Senators,' 'At the Bowing Alley,' 'Senators at Work,' 'Senators at Play,' and their inimitable 'German Schuetzenfest.' " *National Cyclopedia of American Biography,* vol. 14 (New York: James T. White, 1910), p. 317.

16. Quoted in Robert Allen, *Horrible Prettiness: Burlesque and American Culture* (Chapel Hill: University of North Carolina Press, 1991), p. 222. According to myth, this is how Weber and Fields were inspired to create this, possibly their most famous skit: "They were lounging in the pool room of Miner's Bowery, ten days before their Baltimore opening, when they heard two German players quarreling over the table. The spat ended in a barrage of three, five, and eight balls, during which the comedians sanely ducked; but in the meantime they had sensed opportunity and grasped it. They began to work on the poolroom skit, which was one of their most famous." *New York Times* obituary of Lew Fields, July 22, 1941, p. 19.

17. O'Connor, *Informal History,* p. 300.

18. Francis G. Couvares, "The Plebeian Moment: Theater and Working-Class Life in Late Nineteenth-Century Pittsburgh," in Bruce A. McConachie and Daniel Friedman, eds., *Theatre for Working-Class Audiences in the United States, 1830–1980* (Westport, Conn.: Greenwood Press, 1985), p. 52. O'Connor, *Informal History*, p. 300; Miriam Hansen, *Babel and Babylon: Spectatorship in American Silent Film* (Cambridge: Harvard University Press, 1991), p. 59. For a particularly insightful analysis of ethnic parodies, see Werner Sollors, *Beyond Ethnicity: Consent and Descent in American Culture* (New York: Oxford University Press, 1986), pp. 132–133.

19. "Jenes lächerliche, unmögliche Zerrbild, das einen kleinen dickbäuchigen Gesellen mit hängendem Schnurbart und blöden Augen, mit Holzpantoffeln, Ballonmütze und langer Pfeife, mit Bierglas und Pretzel zeigt. Wo hat man jemals einen derartigen Deutschen gesehen. . . . Wir Deutsch-Amerikaner lachen nicht darüber." *New Yorker Staats-Zeitung,* September 19, 1913, p. 6. (translation mine, as are all that follow).

20. On the *Staats-Zeitung's* self-proclaimed mission of protecting the German language from corruption, see Wittke, *German-Language Press,* p. 200. Wittke also provides a useful summary of the newspaper's early history on pp. 44–46; 62–75. For a more detailed account, see my "Translated Community," chap. 2, especially pp. 90–113.

21. "Um diese Zeit entstand das neue Germania Theater Adolf Philipp's an der 8. Straße, eine kleine Episode, die neun Jahre dauerte. Philipp war als Operettensänger herübergekommen und glaubte das Bedürfnis für eine Volksbühne entdeckt zu haben, deren Leiter, Hausdichter und erster Darsteller er sein wollte . . . da schlug er dann im 'Corner Grocer' lustige Saiten an—allerlei Posseneffekte und englisches Melodrama, das er konnte, bestrich es mit humorvollem Lokalkolorit—und siehe da, die Sache machte sich. Das 'Volk' der Avenue A und Umgegend, das er gerufen, kam in Schaaren, auch noch zum 'Brauer,' der 'Landlady' und anderen Stücken, die eine merkwürdige Familienähnlichkit miteinander aufwiesen. Als aber die Stücke von Neuem allzu rührselig und die darin aufgetischten Späße immer plumper wurden—einmal wurde ein Limburger Käse auf der Bühne buchstäblich todtgeschossen— da mundeten die Philipp'schen 'Volksgerichte' selbst der 'Avenue A' nicht mehr und die 'Volksküche' hörte auf, gute Geschäfte zu machen. 1897 verschwand Philipp temporär . . .

ging nach Berlin, wo er 'Ueber'n Großen Teich,' einen Extrakt aus seinen besten New Yorker Lokalpossen . . . nebst braunem Gerstensaft verzapfte. Die alte Kost seiner 'Volksstücke' wurde im vorigen Jahr im 'Schwarzen Adler' wieder hergerrichtet und erwies sich dort noch als nahrhaft. . . . Jetzt wohnt bei ihm die 'Alma.' " *New Yorker Staats-Zeitung,* April 24, 1910, p. 34.

22. *New York Times,* July 31, 1936; *New York Sun,* July 31, 1936; Adolf Philipp, "A Remarkable Triple Identity," *Dramatic Mirror,* November 20, 1915. All unpaginated clippings, RL#1751/BRC.

23. *Moving Picture World,* January 15, 1916. The following is the full text of the passage: "It is interesting to note that Mr. Philipp, with unusual modesty for a prominent impresario, has up to the present time kept his own dramatic and literary ability behind the nom-de-plumes of Paul Hervé and Jean Briquet. These two 'successful authors' had risen to dizzying heights of fame based on such international musical plays as 'Alma,' 'Adele' and 'The Midnight Girl,' before Mr. Philipp was cornered and finally admitted that he himself was practically [*sic*] the author of these productions." Around the same time, we may assume, the *Los Angeles Examiner* similarly noted, "On the programs Mr. Philipp's name always appears as the author and the composer is printed as G. Briquet. G. Briquet was Mr. Philipp's mother; he used her name so as to avoid, as he says, 'having Adolf Philipp sprinkled all over the program as author, composer and adaptor; that would look immodest!' Sure! He is a theatrical producer! You can't believe it of a man who won't put his name at every opportunity? You cannot be blamed, but remember I told you he is a cultured educated man, and with these the final ultimate joy is not in publicity." *Los Angeles Examiner,* undated. Both articles are unpaginated clippings, RL#1751/BRC.

24. Unidentified, undated clipping (probably 1907), emphasis mine. RL#1751/BRC.

25. Adolf Philipp, "A Remarkable Triple Identity," *New York Dramatic Mirror,* November 20, 1915. Unpaginated clipping, RL#1751/BRC.

26. *New York Dramatic Mirror,* February 4, 1914. Unpaginated clipping, RL#1751/BRC.

27. *Los Angeles Examiner,* March 22, 1914. Unpaginated clipping, RL#1751/BRC.

28. *Zabern* was based on an episode that had taken place in a small Alsatian town of the same name the previous year, after the commanding officer of the German occupying troops had offered a reward to any German soldier who ran through a native Alsatian guilty only of having been impolite. Fierce riots that almost led to a war with France ensued, and the situation was worsened when the same commanding officer wounded a lame Alsatian shoemaker a few days later. In a decision that was debated in the German *Reichstag* and that elicited international comment, the officer was court-martialed but later freed when Prince Heinrich, the kaiser's son, spoke on his behalf. See the *New York Times,* November 30, 1913, sec. ii, p. 1; December 2, 1913, p. 4; December 8, 1913, p. 3; December 20, 1913, p. 4; December 21, 1913, sec. iii, p. 4; January 24, 1914, p. 3; January 25, 1914, sec. iii, p. 3; January 26, 1914, p. 6.

29. "Blöde Dialog . . . schlechtester Witzblatt-Ulk . . . ein geradezu bösartiges . . . antideutsches Stück . . . da[s] in dem dritten Akt die Trikolore glorifiziert und die schwarz-weiß-rothe Flagge figürlich mit Füßen tritt." *New Yorker Staats-Zeitung,* January 29, 1914, p. 10. "Allerlei sogenannte 'Würze' . . . allerlei abgegriffene Burleske, die schon in diversen Philipp'schen New Yorker 'Volksstücken' hergehalten hat." *New Yorker Staats-Zeitung,* February 1, 1914, p. 16.

30. For further anti-*Zabern* editorials urging readers to boycott Philipp, see, for example, *New Yorker Staats-Zeitung,* February 3, 1914, p. 7; February 4, 1914, p. 6.

31. *New York Review,* January 2, 1915. Unpaginated clipping, RL#1751/BRC.

32. On Philipp's success in California, see *Dramatic News,* March 1, 1914; *Los Angeles Examiner,* March 22, 1914; *Variety,* April 15, 1914. All unpaginated clippings, RL#1751/BRC.

33. "Man ärgert sich gelegentlich wohl ein wenig, daß man gar so leicht in die Falle gegangen ist, aber man lacht, lacht, lacht . . . einschmeichelndste Tonwellen, bei denen man nicht nach dem Ursprung fragen darf . . . unangenehme Frage. . . . Lachstürme von so ursprünglicher Gewalt und Unwiderstehlichkeit sind schon lange nicht durch ein hiesiges Theater gebraust." *New Yorker Staats-Zeitung,* December 26, 1916, p. 8.

34. "Man amüsiert sich königlich und auch die der deutschen Sprache nicht mächtigen Zuhörer können der Handlung leicht folgen, da unzählige englische Ausdrücke gebraucht werden, die den Zusammenhang herstellen." *Deutsches Journal,* January 7, 1917, sec. ii, p. 5. On this fascinating German-language newspaper, virtually unknown to most historians of the immigrant press, see my "Translated Community," chap. 3.

35. On this sad chapter in German-American history, see, for example, Erik Kirschbaum, *The Eradication of German Culture in the United States: 1917–1918* (Stuttgart: Academic Publishing House, 1986). See also my "Translated Community," chap. 9; John A. Hawgood, *The Tragedy of German America* (New York: Arno Press, 1970); Frederick C. Luebke, *Bonds of Loyalty: German-Americans and World War One* (DeKalb: Northern Illinois University Press, 1974); and Andrew P. Yox, "The Fall of the German-American Community: Buffalo, 1914–1919," in William Penack, Selma Berrol, and Randall M. Miller, eds., *Immigration to New York* (New York: New York Historical Society, 1991), pp. 126–143.

36. On the American Defense Society and the National Security League, see Luebke, *Bonds of Loyalty.* The independent National Security League was the most radical of the many wartime "loyalty leagues," "attack[ing] German-American churches, schools, societies, and newspapers indiscriminately as inhibitors of assimilation and as agents of a world-wide Teutonic conspiracy." The American Defense Society was an offshoot of the Security League—both were based in New York—and had singled out as its special enemy the German language, in which it heard the echo of "the murder of a million helpless old men, unarmed women, and children." The title of one of the society's many pamphlets, "Throw Out the German Language and All Disloyal Teachers," is indicative of the sort of patriotism it promoted. Luebke, *Bonds of Loyalty,* p. 216. On American "superpatriotism" in general, see ibid., pp. 199–259.

37. "Superpatriots' " suspicion that the Irving Place Theater was a pro-German (and by extension anti-American) institution were voiced as early as 1914; see, for example, *Brooklyn Eagle,* November 1914, and *New York Herald,* November 14, 1914. The final death knell for Christians came when, five years later, the *Musical Courier* announced in an open letter that it would join forces with "all the patriotic societies to fight you [Christians] tooth and nail," should he ever attempt to stage German-language drama in New York again. *Musical Courier,* January 23, 1919. All three articles are collected as unpaginated clippings in *Robinson Locke Theater Scrapbook,* vol. 64, Billy Rose Theatre Collection, New York Public Library for the Performing Arts. On Morris Schwartz and the Yiddish Repertory Theater, see Irene Bachalenik, *East Side Story* (Lanham, Md.: University Press of America, 1988).

38. *New York Telegraph,* August 21, 1918; *New York Star,* August 28, 1918. Both unpaginated clippings, RL#1751/BRC.

39. On Mrs. William Jay and her anti-*Kultur* crusade, see Alan Howard Levy, "The American Symphony at War," *Mid-America,* 71,1 (January 1989); see also my "Translated Community," chap. 7.

40. Quoted in the *New York Times,* June 5, 1918, p. 22.

41. "Da die Presse sowohl, wie der weitaus größere Teil der amerikanischen Bevölkerung, ein deutsches Theater unter den obwaltenden Umständen als nicht existzenzberechtigt betrachten, unterwerfen wir uns freimütig diesem Urteil, umsomehr, da die Eigenthümer des deutschen Theaters uns keine Theatervorstellungen in deutscher Sprache erlauben." *New Yorker Staats-Zeitung,* August 19, 1918, p. 1.

42. "Eine Rechtfertigung all jener, die . . . unentwegt zu dem Lande ihrer Wahl standen." *New Yorker Staats-Zeitung,* September 1, 1918, sec. ii, p. 3. "Tell That to the Marines" first announced August 25, 1918, sec. ii, p. 1. For further advance publicity, see, for example, September 8, 1918, sec. ii, p. 3.

43. "Eine eminente Tat . . . ganz New York sollte die große Idee, die gewaltvolle, spannende Handlung und den kräftigen Humor von 'Tell That to the Marines' bewundern. Es ist ein Stück, das alle treuen Bürger dieses Landes gleichweise interessieren muß, den Yankee sowohl als den Fremdgeborenen!" *New Yorker Staats-Zeitung,* September 25, 1918, p. 10. For the follow-up article claiming positive reception in the English-language press, see September 29, 1918, sec. ii, p. 3.

44. *Dramatic Mirror,* October 5, 1918. Unpaginated clipping, RL#1751/BRC.

45. *Variety,* September 27, 1918, and *Dramatic Mirror,* October 5, 1918. Both unpaginated clippings, RL#1751/BRC. On Philipp's departure, see *New Yorker Staats-Zeitung,* October 6, 1918, sec. iii, p. 5.

46. *Dramatic News,* May 29, 1915; January 15, 1916. Both unpaginated clippings, RL#1751/BRC.

47. *Variety,* September 28, 1917, p. 37.

48. See *New York Times* obituary, July 31, 1936, unpaginated clipping, RL#1751/BRC. See also *New Yorker Staats-Zeitung,* July 31, 1936, p. 1 (obituary), and, for an account of Philipp's funeral and wake, August 31, 1936, p. 5.

49. *New York World,* March 2, 1913. Unpaginated clipping, RL#1751/BRC.

Chapter Fifteen

The Formation of an Italian-American Identity through Popular Theater

Anna Maria Martellone

The Italian-American theater offers many clues for a study of the self-representation of Italian-American identity by Italians transplanted to the United States. The studies on the Italian-American theater by Emelise Aleandri evidence the active presence of several Italian-American theatrical companies in New York already at the beginning of the twentieth century, and similar situations could be found in most American cities, large or small, with flourishing Italian districts from Boston, Chicago, Detroit, San Francisco, and Pittsburgh to Utica and even to small centers in the environs of Pittsburgh with settlements of Italian miners.[1] Several of these companies specialized in the Neapolitan repertoire because so many Italian immigrants came from villages in Campania, but there were also farces presented in the several dialects spoken in southern Italy. These strongly regional forms of popular theater did not completely ignore northern Italy, but the prevailing southern Italian composition of Italian emigration to the United States was reflected in the southern accents of most Italian-American theater.[2] This strong regionalism of the Italian popular theater should not make us forget that on the other hand the foremost Italian professional companies active on American stages presented a rich and varied repertoire in standard Italian, which included not only dramas by important Italian authors such as Giacometti, Giacosa, Cavallotti, Pellico, and Verga but also such international theatrical musts as plays by Dumas, Hugo, Sardou, and, of course, Shakespeare. And some Italian-American actors did not hesitate to put their talents to the test of all-American theater by choosing to act in English.

Soon several new forms of popular theater developed on American soil and took their place among the offerings of the Italian-American circuits, alongside ubiquitous vernacular *macchiette* and farces. These new forms of theater were the fruit of the creativity of Italian actors transplanted to the United States and of Italian-American journalists and writers living amid the hustle and bustle of one or another Little Italy. The *cronaca nera* (crime news) of the Italian ethnic press, always redolent of crime and passion, offered a wealth of materials reminiscent of the stuff of serials and pulp fiction, especially fit for dramatization. A well-known example of this tendency to write what we might call "local dramas" is *La tragedia di Bartolomeo Capasso* by Edoardo Pecoraro, the dramatic transposition of a crime that had actually occurred in Mulberry Street, the heart of one of New York's Little Italys. At the opening night of this drama (performed at one of the most popular venues for Italian-American theatricals, the café Villa di Sorrento), the level of audience approval ran so high that the owner of the place, seeing that the enthusiastic patrons gave no sign of leaving their seats at the end of the performance, seized this golden opportunity to make a pile of money through the continuing sale of refreshments and forced the actors' manager Guglielmo Ricciardi and author Pecoraro to add on the spot another act featuring the trial of Capasso's murderer. This impromptu addition met with the same uproarious success, so much that it was deemed necessary to improvise a fifth act, showing in two scenes the funeral of the murdered man and the last few hours of the convicted murderer waiting for the electric chair.[3] Superlative extemporizing skills were indeed a must for all Italian-American actors facing popular audiences, whose level of participation in the performances was always very high and found expression in frequent repartees to the actors, in booings and stampings of feet, and even in demands to change the end of a play to suit their fancies and sometimes very concrete threats to beat the "villain."

The success of "local dramas" such as *La tragedia di Bartolomeo Capasso* (or the similar *I misteri di Mulberry Street* by the well-known Italian-American journalist Bernardino Ciambelli) leads us to observe that the Italian-American audience that crowded the *caffe concerto* and the halls where such *pièces* were performed seemed to identify with situations highly charged with strong feelings of passion, hatred, and revenge, thus perpetuating a negative stereotype of an impassioned, even violent and primitive, southern Italian immigrant population that fed American nativist and restrictionist propaganda. It was difficult for Americans to grasp that violence and revenge (*vendetta*) could also be part of a rather complicated web of ancestral values centered on the cult of familialism and honor, not just an end in themselves. Revenge might be a form of redressing the balance of justice when one's honor had been injured. At this juncture the truculence of the *instant drama* originating in the "crime news" yields to the social implications of the "problem play" (*dramma a tesi*) at the hands of journalists with socialist leanings and willing to deal with *la questione sociale*.

A case in point is the drama *L'onore perdulto* (Honor lost) by the well-known poet and journalist Riccardo Cordiferro. The lengthy play aims to denounce the exploitation of newly arrived Italian immigrants by their own compatriots, the ill-famed *banchieri* (bankers) who profited in hundreds of ways from the ignorance and good faith of those who entrusted them with their hard-earned savings. The male protagonist, Alberto, has just lost his cashier job in the outfit of one of those "bankers" because he is unjustly suspected of stealing one hundred dollars. Alberto is married to Sofia and they have a child. They had left Naples following the invitation of their *compaesano* and friend Giuseppe Esposito, who had emigrated earlier and made money in America in the manner of the *banchieri*, by exploiting Italian workers. Giuseppe is a false friend and the "villain" of the play. In fact, when they all still lived in Naples he had fallen in love with Sofia and courted her, but she had preferred Alberto. Still bent on obtaining Sofia's favors, Giuseppe had persuaded them to come to America, and there he had procured a job for Alberto.

While Alberto is in jail under false accusation, Giuseppe repeatedly tries to seduce Sofia by offering her money, but the woman, though she now lives in poverty, rejects him and even resorts to threatening him with a revolver to defend her honor. In the long run, need drives her to yield to Giuseppe, and this surrender deprives her of honor and self-respect but releases Alberto from jail. Upon Alberto's return home, relatives and friends convene to express their joy. Sofia, haunted by the thought of her dishonor, drinks a vial of poison and dies. Before dying, however, she reveals to Alberto the name of the man who dishonored her and asks for forgiveness. Alberto knifes Giuseppe and proclaims his satisfaction for avenging his own and Sofia's honor, although that means a return to imprisonment.

This rather turgid drama provides us with the opportunity to observe the Italian-American identity as it is perceived and represented by an author who was himself rather critical of some aspects of that identity. Cordiferro intended to write a denunciation of the exploitation of Italian immigrants at the hands of dishonest "bankers"; at the same time he needed a dramaturgical focus that could be understood easily by a popular audience and could evoke immediate emotional involvement and participation. Thus he resorted to two protagonists, Alberto and Sofia, who have brought from their native country a set of values centered on the sanctity of honor. Honor is frequently mentioned and discussed in this drama: Sofia kills herself because she thinks she has betrayed and lost it, Alberto kills Giuseppe to avenge his own and his wife's honor. It is a value to which the author obviously attached much importance as a "marker" of Italian-American identity that Italian-American audiences would willingly appropriate.

We have mentioned the important role played by regional influences in shaping Italian-American self-perceptions and their representations in the theater. The *macchietta* (sketch) is another form of Italian theater that met with great success among the Italian-American communities. Sketches portraying and making fun of regional types were a vital part of the Italian theatrical tradition, derived from the *commedia dell'arte,* and a favorite entertainment for Italian emigrants who had no sense of allegiance to a national fatherland, of which they had experienced little more than vexations, taxes, and compulsory military service, and were instead deeply rooted in their regional and *paesano* origins. The *macchietta* had enjoyed an especially rich development in Naples, and it elicited enthusiastic responses in the Italian-American music halls and cafés through the acting of Edoardo Migliaccio, alias Farfariello. The emergence of an Italian-American identity that, although based on regional stereotypes, reflected that mingling of Italian regional and American elements that characterized the Italian-American experience in the Little Italys of American cities is best captured in the *macchietta coloniale* ("colonial sketch," where "colonial" indicates the reality of the Italian "colonies" in the United States), created and perfected by Migliaccio. This original form of theater, perhaps the "only original form of art produced by the Italian prose theater in New York,"[4] portrayed and made fun of the habits, inadequacies, pretensions, and speech of the first Italian immigrant generation, which delighted in Farfariello's creations. The language of his many characters was a funny mixture of southern Italian dialects—a sort of southern Italian *koine*—and of mangled English, an "Italo-Americanese" or "Italglish."[5] Here is an example of it, from Farfariello's *La lingua "Taliana"*:

> Sono vent'anni e piu che so'arrivato
> Direttamente qua, dal mio paese
> Anzi vent'uno e nun m'aggiu imparato
> Ancora 'e di' mezza parola inglese.
> Biccosa, mi no llaico lengue storte
>> Ca nun so'taliane, e tezzo guai
>> lo rimarraggio qua nfino a la morte
>> Ma na parola nun m' 'a mparo mai . . .
>> quanno me fu promessa
>> La carta cittadina
>> Mi fecero aspettare
>> Due anni, e la mattina
>> Andai al seti holo, e non la prese
>> Biccosa il giogge mi parlava inglese.
> Mia moglie invece, la scannata ncanna
> Mi parla quasi sempre americano.
> Quando io la chiamo, dice: "Guario guanne?"
> Ma "Guario guanne" nn è italiano! . . .
> E essa mme risponne, oh "iu giachesse!"
> Giachesse? Ma "Giachesse" è pure inglese.
> E dice spesso spesso "Ai brecche iu fesse!"
> Comm' i' nce la rompette a lu paise.[6]

Here, *bicossa* stands for "because," *mi no laiko* for "I don't like," *set holo* for "city hall," *giogge* for "judge," *guario guanne* for "what do you want," *iu giachess* for "you jackass," and so on.

The portrayal of Little Italy in Farfariello's sketches is an embarrassment of riches. He was able to observe the changes in values and behavior among second-generation Italian Americans and to create ever new *macchiette*. He acquired many imitators, but none could rival his truly creative genius and keen perception of the Italian-American universe.

The fortunes of the Italian-American theater in all its forms—comedy, drama, farce, sketch—were of course bound up with the continuous inflow of Italian immigrants who could understand and enjoy performances in the Italian vernaculars. In the twenties, when Italian immigration was severely curtailed by the Quota Acts, the genre experienced a decline, but in the thirties the diffusion of radio broadcasting gave Italian popular theater a boost. There were several Italian radio stations in New York and other cities, which broadcasted Italian drama and farces. The gramophone also lent a hand; many records were issued that presented Italian *pieces* spoken in dialect or standard Italian with English phrases interspersed within.

One of the many agencies created by the New Deal, the Federal Theater Project (FTP), addressed itself to, among other things, promoting the activities of ethnic theatrical groups. While the most numerous and important results of this government sponsorship concern black and Yiddish theater, there were a large number of

Italian productions, even though, according to a recent study, there emerged discrepancies and contrasts between the theatrical preferences of the Italian communities, still devoted to intricate plots of love, jealousy, honor, and revenge, and the inclinations of the government agency toward the diffusion of an "Americanizing" theater centered on American patriotic events.[7]

In the aftermath of World War II the development of cinema and especially of television, with its Americanizing impact, together with the dying off of the first generation and the lessened interest in Italian culture of the second generation, provoked a new decline in the Italian ethnic theater, a decline that even the ethnic revival of the sixties and seventies could do little to assuage, since the use of the Italian language among American-born Italian Americans was not sufficiently developed to guarantee a large theatrical audience. There are still, however, performances in private clubs and during Italian festivities, and the enormous development of cable television has opened a venue for a wide variety of ethnic broadcasting.[8]

To conclude these notes on the representations of an Italian-American identity in the Italian-American theater, it is important to recall that the transplanting of the Italian theater to American soil followed two paths. The first is the mere reproduction on foreign soil of a theater in the Italian language offering works by internationally known European theater authors, while some Italian professional actors even dared to act in English in the American theatrical circuits. The second is the adoption and then the new elaboration of several popular Italian theatrical genres, such as farces, sketches, and truculent drama derived from pulp fiction and "crime news," which portray the conditions and use of the language of Little Italy and contribute to the construction of an Italian-American identity based on a largely southern *koine* and on its gradual acculturation to America. This form of theater is still pursued by a few Italian-American comedians, who act in English but with frequent interpolations of passages in dialectical Italian, use of double meanings, and references to Italian foods,[9] all to elicit the interest and applause of Italian-American audiences whose identity by now differs widely from that of the average Italian, who has a different and updated image of Italy.

NOTES

1. Emelise Aleandri and Maxime Schwartz Seller, "Italian American Theater," in *Ethnic Theater in the United States*, ed. M. Schwartz Seller (Westport, Conn.: Greenwood Press, 1983), and Emelise Aleandri, *A History of Italian American Theater: 1900 to 1905* (Ann Arbor: Univerity Microfilms International, 1984).

2. Aleandri, *History of Italian American Theater*, pp. 331–332.

3. Ibid., pp. 50–51.

4. Giuseppe Cautela, "The Italian Theater in New York," *American Mercury*, 12 (1927): 1–2, 110.

5. Mario Maffi, *Nel mosaico della città. Differenze etniche e nuove culture in un quartiere di New York* (Milano: Feltrinelli, 1992), p. 131.

6. Aleandri, *History of Italian American Theater*, pp. 456–457.

7. Chris Newton, "The Italian American Theater in Boston, 1935–1939," in *Italian*

Americans and Their Public and Private Life, ed. F. J. Cavajoli, A. Danzi, S. J. LaGumina, eds. (Staten Island: American Italian Historical Association, 1993), pp. 137–148.

8. Salvatore Primeggia and Joseph A. Varacalli, "Southern Italian Comedy: Old to New World," in *Italian Americans and Their Public and Private Life*, ed. F. J. Cavajoli, A. Danzi, and S. J. LaGumina (Staten Island: American Italian Historical Association, 1990), pp. 241–252.

9. Salvatore Primeggia, Salvatore Vivino, Joseph A. Varacalli, "Southern Italian-American Comedy: The Cases of Matteo Cannizaro, Lou Monte, Louis Prima and Dom DeLuise," in *Italian Americans and Their Public and Private Life*, ed. F. J. Cavajoli, A. Danzi, S. J. LaGumina (Staten Island: American Italian Historical Association, 1993), pp. 194–211.

Chapter Sixteen

Crossings and Double-Crossings
Polish-Language Immigrant Narratives of the Great Migration

Karen Majewski

In Alfons Chrostowski's *Niewolnik Polski* (The Polish slave), a young man fleeing the Prussian army service has just bribed his way past the border guards. Suddenly, he retraces his steps and crosses back onto Polish soil:

> He knelt and kissed the cold, hard ground. It was his farewell to the country of his fathers, to his poor mother—the land. She was truly poor. Concealed in her womb was the dust of his forefathers, once wealthy and free. But, unfortunately, she was not in a position to gladden the grandsons mumbling about in her borderless spaces— today's Polish slaves. They were compelled to look for their bread in the wide and foreign world.[1]

Niewolnik Polski, serialized in 1893–1894 in Cleveland's *Jutrzeńka*, is one among hundreds of Polish-language plays, poems, short stories, and novels produced in America before World War II. Appearing only in Polish and sidestepping Anglophone publishing and distribution networks, these works offer an insider's view not only into the workings of immigrant community life but also into the formation of ethnic and national consciousness among Poles in America.

One subset of that literature is the "immigration saga" that, by fictionalizing the act of migration, attempted to direct the immigrant audience's reading of its own experience. By looking at the ways in which these works address the social and cultural pressures that resulted in and from migration, we can not only position them within a common genre but also identify ways in which they delineated sets of specifically Polish concerns. Like the immigrant tales of other ethnic groups, these Polish-language works treat the Old World contexts that spurred migration, as well as community issues like language maintenance, religious practice, family relations, and working conditions. But their discussion of these concerns is heavily colored by Poland's unique situation under political partition and, later, as a newly restored nation. In particular, urbanized, politicized journalist-authors encouraged immigrants to read their flight in the context of political oppression and to form new alliances in America based on national ideologies.

By the nineteenth century, for an audience of mostly peasant, first-generation readers that drew its identity from the *okolica*—the parish or neighborhood—or from a narrow geographic region, the immigrant intelligentsia quite consciously set about defining and instilling a sense of *polskość*, or Polishness. The components of this national identity were by no means universally agreed upon and were the continuing source of often vicious contention. Before the partitions Poland had been a multiethnic state, and Polish identity had remained a matter of social class and even of choice, with members of the same family sometimes claiming different ethnic identities. Under partition by Prussia, Russia, and Austria-Hungary, former Polish citizens faced varied pressures to denationalize. But after the failed uprising of 1863–1864, the grassroots Organic Work movement sought to educate and "polonize" the peasantry, and it was these efforts that writer-journalists continued in America.

Although the visions, methods, and priorities of leaders remained at odds, their broad goals, particularly before Polish nationhood was reinstated with the conclusion of the First World War, were largely the same: to transform the immigrant into a "true Pole" and American Polonia into Poland's fourth partition.[2] Since most Polish immigrants considered themselves sojourners in America, intending to return to their villages, ethnic leaders wanted to ensure that those who returned did so with loyalties to a national ideal, and that those who remained in the United States used their economic and political power on Poland's behalf. Even after the nation's political resurrection, when disillusionment with the new state began to make apparent American Polonia's own cultural and political independence, writers continued to emphasize loyalty to Poland, demonstrating new ways in which that loyalty could be expressed without compromising one's allegiance to America.

Thus, Chrostowski's *Niewolnik Polski* is more than the literary enactment of an experience of Polish immigration. Like other Polish-language fiction of the Great Wave immigrants, its purpose is as much polemical as it is literary, encouraging a political reading of migration that has as its moral touchstone the reestablishment of Polish sovereignty and the affirmation of Polish identity. Even as these works shift their focus to events in America, conditions in Europe continue to supply the terms of negotiation and struggle and to shape the creative impulse, with the adaptation of familiar literary conventions to new conditions and opportunities.

The short tale or *gawęda* (literally, a chat) was one familiar formula well suited to immigrant storytelling: concise, exemplary, and entertaining. In America, new *gawędy* helped link Polonian with Polish popular cultural expression and refocused village codes of value within an urban-village framework, encouraging an emblematic reading of immigrant experience. Kazimierz Nauman's weekly *gawędy* for *Dziennik Chicagoski*, a major Polish-language daily published by the powerful Resurrectionist Order of Roman Catholic priests, used the form's lightly humorous tone to dramatize competing and conditional definitions of Polishness. In an 1899 episode, a Galician immigrant vents his indignation over businessmen in Chicago's "Polish downtown" who lure customers with "false" claims to Polishness. "Where can I really find Poles around here?" he demands. "What are you talking about?" answers Nauman's fictionalized newspaper editor. "There are fifty thousand of us here." "Then where can one speak Polish?" the newcomer persists. "What do you mean, where? Everywhere."

But their Polish, complains the Galician, is only semi-intelligible, and as for their ethnicity, "One was an Americanized German Czech, and the other, damn it, a pure-blooded Jew from the depths of Russia. Each of them argued that he's a born Pole." The jaded editor points out that even "a Polish name doesn't mean that someone is a Pole," and calls the immigrant a "grynhorn" for not understanding America's situationally malleable and commercially utilitarian ethnicity.[3]

A reading of this episode is complicated along some of the fundamental lines of demarcation over which definers of Polishness skirmished: Was one a Pole by virtue of birthplace, of genealogy, of language, of religion, social class, political affiliation, of ideology, of inclination, of opportunism? American Polonia's varied voices might argue for any of these. In addition, the matter is complicated by rivalries between immigrants from the three partitions who brought with them different cultural experiences and economic skills. However, the question of Polish identity generally coalesced around issues of language, religion, and politics, issues to which Nauman himself must have been particularly sensitive. The Resurrectionists for whom he wrote and the powerful Polish Roman Catholic Union (the PRCU) with which they were allied held a hard line: to be a Pole meant to be a Catholic. But the slippery irony of Nauman's narrative voice suggests his more uneasy position. Not only is his name German (the Polish equivalent would be "Nowak"), but several years earlier, when he left Milwaukee's *Kuryer Polski* for the rival paper *Słowo*, the *Kuryer* had editorialized, "Everyone here already knows that [Nauman] is of Jewish extraction; . . . it's also known that he . . . lived in Poznan, where he passed as a Pole."[4] Accusations of Jewishness were one of the most frequent weapons which Polonian religionists used to undermine their rivals' claims to Polishness. But the forces of exclusion were not the only ones attempting to delineate the boundaries of a national consciousness.

Other factions opposed the PRCU's insistence on Roman Catholicism as a criteria for Polishness. The American-born Polish National Catholic Church, for instance, had broken with Rome over issues of language, parish control of clerical appointments, and the ownership of church property. The PNCC, calling Roman Catholicism the "Church of the rich and the capitalists,"[5] produced its own sizeable literature. "I'm a Pole, my son is a Pole, and my husband's a Pole—so our place is there [in the PNCC], not in a foreign, hypocritical church,"[6] explains a convert before returning to Poland to spread the National Catholic movement there. And other major institutional voices, most notably the Polish Women's Alliance and Polonia's most powerful fraternal organization, the Polish National Alliance, drew attack by refusing to limit membership on the basis of religious or political affiliation.

If immigrants were being warned against those among them who might be posing as Poles, they were also cautioned against strategically disguising their own Polishness. Julian Czupka's study in ethnic tricksterism, *"Tyrolczyk"* (The Tyrolean), describes an immigrant's plan to dress up like an Austrian and yodel for spare change in German-American saloons. Wearing the Hungarian tunic and Polish priest's hat he buys at an "Arabian bazaar" from a Jewish shopkeeper posing as an Arab, the hero tries to pass off Polish drinking songs as Italian opera.[7] Although this story ends happily enough, Czupka shows his characters as displaced in America, painfully alienated from nation and family, wandering in search of bread and of self. According to Czupka, the surest way to regain one's bearings and reorder this anomic world was to return to Poland.

Czupka's purpose, to "restrain the desire to emigrate,"[8] places his stories in counterpoint to the letters from America that were passed around so eagerly in Polish villages and that spurred so much chain migration. Given the importance of these letters, it is not surprising that authors found the epistolary form particularly suited to the circumstances of immigrant literary creation, to the expression of immigrant experience, and to the understanding of the immigrant audience for which they wrote. The specific conventions of the peasant immigrant letter, which like the newspaper was essentially community property to be passed around and read aloud, had literal and symbolic meanings that all were likely to comprehend and that consequently provided an immediate window of understanding into the epistolary tale. It is entirely appropriate, for instance, that in a 1907 series of letters, the fictional Katarzyna follows peasant oral and written conventions by beginning each of her letters to her husband with the greeting, "Let Jesus Christ Be Praised!" His letters follow with the required response, "For ever and ever, Amen!"[9]

The epistolary form rearticulated the national family dialogue, reinforcing and reconfiguring relationships. Its episodic, situational, and dialogical possibilities were especially appropriate for juxtaposing the shifting and contradictory claims of emerging ethnicity. Alternating fictional letters between the immigrant and loved ones at home, authors contrasted conditions and experiences in both countries, demonstrated immigration's power to transform the individual and the culture, and attempted to direct that transformation. Nauman's anonymously printed "*Listy Wojtka do starego kraju*" (Wojtek's letters to the old country), for instance, comment ironically on community issues like local church wars, the Lattimer massacre and trial, and Jan Rybakowski's Coxey-inspired march of the immigrant unemployed.[10] When he enlists in the Spanish-American War, as many Polish immigrants did in order to gain battle experience for an anticipated independence campaign, Wojtek is acting on the lessons he has learned from Polish nationalists in America: "In Cuba Negroes live," he explains to his parents, "and other people, and they're under the Spanish, like the Old Country is under the Muscovites and the Germans."[11]

This need to interpret the Polish emigrant perspective for the folks back home is a recurring source of comedy and social criticism. Among the common targets are misunderstandings resulting from the Americanization of the Polish language. This attention to linguistic transformation is not merely disapproving but illustrative of new concerns, values, and meanings that defied Old World understanding. In answer to parental complaints about his corrupted Polish, Wojtek attempts to map out a new linguistic geography:

Orejt, I have a little time today so I'll explain to you. A *sztryta* is a road along which the *treki* lie, and the *kara* runs on them, either electric or *kebel*. . . . In the *hauzach* there are *sztory, buczernie, grosernie, zaluny*, Jewish *kloting sztory*, cigar *sztory* and others. Every *sztryta* has a different name, and every *hauz* a number so you can find a person.[12]

His neighborhood, he explains, is Stanisławowo, where everyone is a good Pole and a Catholic, not like the schismatics in nearby Jadwigowo.[13] Wojtek's letters demonstrate his attempts to locate himself within the contested and ambiguous boundaries of a new social and moral order. For the narrator of Nauman's *Moi trzej przyjaciele* (My three friends), it is America's multiplicity of directions and possibilities, its "forty different railway lines," that bewilder and disturb: "One and the same street presents itself as wonderful, as horrible. Twenty-story iron-faced buildings neighbor on little wooden houses glued together out of sticks. Here you have glistening-clean asphalt pavement, and on the next street dirt and mud. On another street there's no pavement at all."[14]

Implicated in the disorientation of Nauman's narrator is a lack of clearly defined social boundaries. While Polish society was strictly ordered along lines of class, the immigrant community accommodated all strata, from the peasant to the landowner, within a shared neighborhood, and sometimes on the same factory floor. Old hostilities and suspicions persisted but needed to be contained for both practical and ideological reasons. When writers turned from forms like the *gawęda* and epistolary to the realistic, full-length novel, they tended to shift their focus from former peasant to gentry or middle-class characters. This is partly, no doubt, a matter of audience: these more sustained works were probably perceived as appealing to more educated readers. But some of these works also attempt to diffuse old-country class antagonisms by constructing a shared experience of immigration necessitated by common oppression. The undifferentiated misery described in Wojciech Morawski's *Na dwóch półkulach* (On two hemispheres), published in 1897, asks readers to see in their exploitation as immigrants a continuation of Poland's national exploitation under the partitions: "He well remembered that ship, crammed with emigrants fleeing their homeland because of injury and misery, that ship-prison in which the German sailors treated the poor Polish peasant like a dog. . . . Jan also remembered his first disappointments with America. The people there were treated like cattle, as the Moscow gendarmes might treat them."[15]

The well-educated young heroes of Bronislaw Wrotnowski's *Szlakiem dolara* (On the trail of the dollar),[16] serialized in 1927–1929, come to America because they see no opportunities for personal fulfillment and career advancement in partitioned Poland. Similarly, failed exams, boring jobs, and work assignments in foreign posts are the factors that propel the emigrants in Nauman's aforementioned *Moi trzej przyjaciele*, who find their success in Poland blocked and themselves "wanderers among their countrymen, without a tomorrow, without a past."[17]

Despite these claims that the immigrant gentry and peasantry were equally oppressed, attempts to establish a unified Polish identity were complicated by the class antagonisms lurking never far below Polonia's surface. Helena Staś's 1910 novel

Na ludzkim targu (In the human market) lays out the opposing cultural positions in a conversation between a working-class immigrant woman and a community activist. When the "great-little literary woman" is appalled to learn that her hostess does not know who poet Adam Mickiewicz is, the poor housewife tries to explain:

> "We don't have those books in the house because we don't understand them. But even though we don't know how to express ourselves very well, we still feel our Polishness inside. *By God, it is true*! When we heard they were going to build monuments to Pułaski and Kościuszko, my family and I cried with joy and we sent the President a handful of Polish soil that our mother left us on her deathbed. We gave the Poles the most precious gift we had."
>
> The great-little literary woman snorted: "But what does that mean if you don't know who Mickiewicz, Słowacki, Krasiński and so many other Polish writers are?"
>
> "Even though we don't know, we still feel our Polishness."
>
> "You don't know anything! . . . You are a lost nation for Poland."[18]

But, Staś's narrator wonders, "[C]ould all the works of Mickiewicz, Słowacki, and Krasiński have produced a greater love for the fatherland in that good soul? . . . The language is broken American, but the heart and soul are Polish."[19] This episode illustrates what historian Mary Cygan has termed the "cud" and "lud" debate, in which Polishness was conceived to derive from either the common people—the "lud"—or from the gentry and intelligentsia.[20]

If Staś perceives these social and cultural distances as unbridgeable, other authors suggest that America offered opportunities for coalescence. For instance, Czesław Łukaszkiewicz's rich novel, *Anioł stróż i djabel stróż* (Guardian angel and guardian devil), published in 1931, treats immigration as a process of growing dissatisfaction not just with economic pressures but with village parochialism. As the peasant Jacek crosses ever wider geographic, social, and theological borders, he is brought closer and closer to a national consciousness. Informed by the author's anticlericalism, this story of Jacek's coming of age, of which his emigration is a crucial component, is framed by the competition between two spirits for his mind, body, and soul. His guardian angel, Durniel (roughly, Dumb Ass), argues against Jacek's natural curiosity, the physical needs of his body, and his innate sense of justice. Durniel calls emigration a sin, a disruption of divine order:

> Oxen like these go to America, earn three dollars a day, and right away they get used to all the comforts, to extras, to clothes, but they only offend God with it. . . . They hardly earn money before they spend it on a six-room house, they put up a porch, they fix up a bathroom [pfe] and at night instead of going to sleep and not offending the Lord God with sinful thoughts, these beasts trudge out to the theater. . . . But that's nothing. Many of them even feel like going to school.[21]

Each phase of the immigrant journey, propelled by his guardian devil, takes Jacek and his fellow travelers farther and farther away from their provincial conceptions of themselves and the world. At every step, there are new sights and experiences to assimilate, from drinking coffee at an inn, to crossing their first river, to negotiating the streets of Kraków, where Jacek is amazed by the statue of the poet

Mickiewicz; he assumes all statues (including the Statue of Liberty) to be images of saints. He is taking his first steps into a secular world whose saints are icons of freedom, enlightenment, and national culture.

The ocean voyage, during which he begins teaching himself to read, leads Jacek toward manhood and independence. But the movement is neither unqualified nor unambiguous. As their ship passes another headed back to Europe, the emigrants do not know whether to envy those on board or not. Already the sense of their firm place in a static world has been compromised, and they are not sure where they belong, or what their direction should be. But while the personal freedom that America offers inevitably changes the immigrants, these changes can also bring them culturally and spiritually closer to a unified homeland. It is in America that Jacek is Polonized. His mountaineer dialect is replaced by standard Polish. He joins the quasi-military Falcons, is made manager of the organization's library, and works as an immigrant book agent. He gives up on the village sweetheart, who has been seduced by America's superficial promise of riches and amusement, in order to marry a cultured young widow who is proud to kiss the hand of Jacek's peasant mother. And by the end of the novel, his road to maturity will lead Jacek back to Poland, to fulfill his dying father's request to reconcile with the villainous village priest. America has transformed Jacek into "a real man," and a Pole.

Polonia's fictional immigrant narratives tend to conflate the boundaries of family, community, and nation, in order to highlight their literal and figurative crossing and recrossing. But the betrayal—the double-crossing—of the national family is a continual threat to its regeneration. Helena Staś's *Marzenie czy rzeczywistość* (Dream or reality) follows a misguided young woman of the impoverished gentry whose parents decide to emigrate in order to separate her from her Russian lover. "Are you so emancipated that religious and national feelings have died in you?" asks Wanda's scandalized father. "I don't acknowledge national or religious feelings," Wanda answers. "Not one nation and creed, but all humanity should be our motto—and we should endeavor for its union." "Renouncing national or religious feeling is the same as renouncing family feeling," old Kęszycki objects. "Oh, this world is so backwards," insists Wanda. "I want to belong to the universal, to move freely, to be a child of the whole world, and to love everyone equally."[22]

But Wanda's idealism leads not to union but to separation and rootlessness. When she abandons her parents aboard the ship and returns to the village, she discovers not only that the Russian has betrayed her but that without her family she has no place in the community. So she goes to America after all, tries in vain to find her parents, makes two unhappy marriages, contributes to the suicide of her teenage son, and is finally pursued by the police as an anarchist before she stumbles back into the family and the national fold. Staś's remarkable story ends with a description of this prodigal daughter's new worldview. Entitled "Dream or Reality?" an embroidered canvas over her bed depicts the Polish eagle held by three potentates who each stand with one leg in his own country and the other in Poland. But a Polish army is shown standing over the ocean in America, ready to fight for the violated motherland. The fourth partition is merely waiting for the opportunity to return.

For Staś and other immigrant writers, the personal was fundamentally political, and in the family drama of betrayal and reconciliation is implicit the national tragedy of partition. This widening of the family romance suggests webs of significance with which the movement across geographic and conceptual boundaries was weighted, and ways in which national and ethnic identities were molded through the revisioning of a collectivized experience of migration. In the continuing process of immigration, alliances and identities, constantly in flux, were being formed, reformed, complicated, and affirmed. Family ties, stretched and challenged by emigration, were sometimes broken but might also be reevaluated and revalued. Literature contributed to this process by rearticulating the interchange between emigrant and old country in ways that encouraged sanctioned responses to experience and memory, and a continuing and politicized relationship to the old country. That Polonian writers continued to produce immigration narratives well into the 1930s, even as other novels were exposing abuses of entrenched institutional authority and exploring the manners and morals of the second generation, testifies to the continued potency of the issues these novels raised.

The narrative frames through which authors created and readers perceived these stories reflect the relevance and utility of literary devices based on community and village models of communication, as Polish immigrant writers reshaped traditional forms to meet new cultural challenges.[23] The *gawęda*, epistolary, serialized novel, and other forms of early immigrant fiction should not be viewed as evidence of American Polonia's rudimentary literary development but, rather, as the consequence of artistic and political strategies emerging from the very particular circumstances of Polish and Polish-American history. In short, these forms, bridges between the oral and written word, offered authors a way to conduct a highly nuanced conversation in ways that could "speak" to an audience of generally poorly educated readers.

Finally, these works compromise conventional definitions of the act of immigration by treating it as a circular process, a continuing engagement with varied sets of boundaries and lines of demarcation: physical, emotional, historical, ideological, and theological, ending not in assimilation and comfortable success in America but in a renewed relationship to Poland. The authors of these narratives reconstructed the immigrant journey in order to provide readers with moral and ideological maps by which to trace the paths that had led them from Europe, to position themselves in American Polonia, and, ultimately, to find a way back to Poland.

NOTES

1. M. Alfons Chrostowski, *Niewolnik polski: na tle stosunków polsko-amerykańskich* (The polish slave: based on Polish-American conditions), *Jutrzeńka*, 10 January 1894. All translations are my own.

2. Although "Polonia" can refer to a specific Polish-American neighborhood, it is used here in its broadest sense to refer to the "Polish diaspora," that is, to Poles and their descendents living outside Poland's borders.

3. Kazimierz Nauman, (Dada, pseud.), *"Gawęda tygodniowa"* (Weekly chat), *Dziennik Chicagoski*, 16 September 1899.

4. *Kuryer Polski*, 18 September 1893.

5. Jozef, *"Dzielny Michałek, sierotka: opowiadanie z życia polskich robotników w Ameryce"* (Brave Mikey the little orphan: a story from the life of Polish workers in America") (Scranton: Nakl. Towarzystwa Przyjaciol Polskiej Narodowej Szkoly, n.d.), 45.

6. Ibid., 46.

7. Julian Czupka, "Tyrolczyk," in *Obrazki z Ameryki* (Pictures from America) (Wilkes-Barre: Górnik, 1897).

8. Czupka, *"Przedmowa"* (Introduction), ibid., 3.

9. A. K., *"Listy Bazyłego Szturkajly do żony w starym kraju i jej odpowiedzi"* (Bazyli Szturkajla's letters to his wife in the old country and her replies), *Ameryka-Echo*, 7 September 1907. For a discussion of the conventions of letter writing, including the importance of "bows," see "The Peasant Letter" in William I. Thomas and Florian Znaniecki, *The Polish Peasant in Europe and America*, ed. and abridged by Eli Zaretsky (Urbana: University of Illinois Press, 1984).

10. *"Listy Wojtka do starego kraju"* (Wojtek's letters to the old country), *Dziennik Chicagoski*, 2 February–7 April 1898.

11. *Dziennik Chicagoski*, 28 February 1898. For a discussion of Polish-American literary constructions of this war, see Matthew Frye Jacobson, "Martial Art: Literature and Romantic Militarism in Turn-of-the-Century Polonia," *Polish American Studies* 51, 1 (1994): 5–19.

12. *Dziennik Chicagoski*, 16 February 1898. Italicized words are Americanisms that appear (unitalicized) in the original text.

13. Stanisławowo refers to the area surrounding Chicago's first Polish church, St. Stanislaus Kostka. In 1895 the Reverend Antoni Kozłowski led parishioners from neighboring St. Hedwig's in a secession over issues of financial and administrative control of ethnic parishes.

14. *Dziennik Chicagoski*, 4 December 1902.

15. Wojciech Morawski, *Na dwóch półkulach: szkic powieściowy na tle prawdziwego zdarzenia* (On two hemispheres: a novelistic sketch based on true events) (Chicago: Nakł. Zjednoczonej Prasy Polskiej w Ameryce, 1907), 65–66.

16. Bronisław Wrotnowski [Marjan Bronisławski, pseud.], "Szlakiem dolara: przygody dwóch młodych Polaków w Ameryce" (On the trail of the dollar: the adventures of two young Poles in America), *Jaskółka*, November 1927–January 1929.

17. *Dziennik Chicagoski*, 2 December 1902.

18. Helena Staś, *Na ludzkim targu: szkic polsko-amerykański* (In the human market: A Polish-American sketch) (Chicago: Autorka, 1910; Warsaw: Księgarnia St. Sadowski, 1911), 177.

19. Ibid., 178.

20. Mary Cygan, "Inventing Polonia: Cultural Activists and the Polish American Community, 1870–1990," forthcoming.

21. Czesław Łukaszkiewicz, *Anioł stróż i djabel stróż: powieść satyryczna* (Guardian angel and guardian devil: a satiric novel) (Toledo: Paryski, 1931), 85.

22. Helena Staś, "Marzenie czy rzeczywistość: obrazek polsko-amerykański" (Dream or reality: A Polish-American picture), *Gazeta Polska w Chicago*, 29 August 1907.

23. Thomas S. Gladsky makes a similar argument for Polish-American literature written in English in *Princes, Peasants, and Other Polish Selves: Ethnicity in American Literature* (Amherst: University of Massachusetts Press, 1992).

Part V

"Melting Glots"

William C. Spengemann has asserted that, as opposed to English-speaking citizens, "Americans who speak different languages not only belong to different cultures by definition, they are culturally connected more closely with non-Americans who speak their respective languages than they are with each other by virtue of such non-linguistic, non-cultural links as political citizenship or geographical propinquity."[1] Yet though English-speaking Americans may perceive other American languages to be identical with those spoken in various motherlands, these American languages are actually different from their various origins and show their at least partly American location in many ways, for example, in English loanwords with the plurals and conjugation patterns from the original languages. H. L. Mencken directed his attention pioneeringly to the recording of what he referred to as "Finglish," "American-Greek," or "Negro-French," and of twenty-five other "non-English dialects in America."[2]

Literary texts are particularly nuanced in recording the new American languages that have emerged in the United States, and their existence has been a steady presence in *Multilingual America*. Øverland, for example, reported the case of Waldemar Ager, whose character Mrs. Omley "knows little English but peppers her Norwegian dialect with the few English words and phrases she has picked up." Dahlberg called attention to the problem of editorial corrections of what seem to be "errors" in Spanish, but may in fact be nuanced language differentiations of New Mexican and Comanche speakers. Taubenfeld examined the case of Abraham Cahan's American Yiddish: "The characters' speech is written in their native Yiddish, and the English words they insert into their language are given in English in the midst of the Yiddish text," rendered "in Hebrew characters." In his English-language journalism, Cahan highlights such examples of a new, mixed language as the following: "*Ich vel scrobbin dem floor, klinen die vindes, un polishen dem stov.*" Martellone reported Farfariello's La lingua "Taliana," which is not identical with Italian-Italian and includes such American elements as "*set holo* for 'city hall,' *giogge* for 'judge,' *guario guanne* for 'what do you want,' " or "*iu giachess* for 'you jackass.' " Majewski gave the example of a Polish-American "grynhorn," and instances of other "hybrid tongues" have appeared throughout this collection.

In the present section, these "mixed languages" move to the foreground of analysis. Marc Shell's "Hyphens: Between Deitsch and American" examines the features of the "Germerican" language and the debates surrounding hyphenation. World War I, popular comic poetry in the manner of "gemixte pickles," melancholy German-language verse, the parallel case of Yinglish, and the linguistic arguments against the hyphen made in Fowler's handbook *The King's English*, provide rich contexts for a new appreciation of "die schönste Lengevitch." Shell's approach, informed by his long-standing interest in language rights and the languages of America, offers a possibility for a new understanding of the aesthetic of "hyphen-ate" cultures, in literary texts as well as in images. In "Portinglês in the United States: The Luso-America of José Rodrigues Miguéis," Michela Corradini offers an in-depth study of the Portuguese immigrant author Miguéis, who translated F. Scott Fitzgerald into Portuguese, produced fascinating American stories in Portuguese, and included such Luso-American words as *dolas* (dollars) or *cracas* (crackers) in his works. Corradini appends to her essay a fully developed system of the "Luso-American" or "Portinglês" language. The American location of various American languages is not just marked by Anglicisms, of course, but the various non-English languages also exert pressures upon one another. Heike Paul also devotes her essay "Not 'On the Backs of Blacks': U.S.-American (Im)Migration and Jewish Diaspora in the German-Language Writings of Jeannette Lander" to the close examination of a twentieth-century American writer; and in her reading of Jeannette Lander's German-language writing, she pays particular attention to Lander's positive representation of black characters and to her transnational linguistic mix of German, English (and especially, Black English), Hebrew, and Yiddish.

Doris Sommer's "Choose and Lose" focuses on the case of Spanglish and resonates with the other essays in this section while taking a more theoretical approach to the issues. For Sommer, Du Bois's concept of "double consciousness" opens up a possibility of turning the "double bind" of Americanization (of which Øverland wrote earlier in this volume) into a subtly utopian stylization of difference that comes with the "neither . . . nor" location. She shows the political implications of the bilingual pun, be it in Gloria Estefan's ambiguous exhortation to "speak the same language" or in the title of Tato Laviera's collection *AmeRíca* that, as Sommer comments, "transforms what for English and Spanish is just a word into a *mot juste* in Spanglish."

In reviewing the many examples presented in this section of code switching, Anglicisms and other neologisms shaped by languages in contact, the reader may notice that some instances constitute "errors" in a given linguistic system and suggest flaws in spelling, grammar, and general language competence; and such "errors" may create among speakers who make them a sense of belonging to imagined communities that are identified by speech patterns that are neither those of other mother tongues nor those of pure English. Other examples are carefully chosen artistic vehicles employed by bilingual writers with a precise sense of the differing, often comic, effects of such mixed languages on readers in several languages. Perhaps it is the view, in many ways inadequate, of mixed languages as a sign of "overassimilation," weakness, and language loss that has sometimes impeded the understanding of such linguistic formations as viable languages in their own right, as media for carefully crafted artistic expression, and—though they appear to be deceptively simple and are easily laughed off for their comic effects—as ideal subjects for the serious study of cultural processes in what Shell sees as the cultures of the hyphen and Sommer suggests may be a world of double consciousness.

Thinking of hyphenated American tongues only in terms of their "impure" locations between "standard English" and one other nationally standardized language may render them invisible since their comic-seeming violation of linguistic purity seems so self-evident as to be overdetermined in such contexts; it is noteworthy that in many cases texts that seem located between two languages also draw on a "third language" that is outside such a confining dichotomy.[3] The comparative analysis of many "melting glots" may offer new ways of approaching linguistic interaction between English and other American languages, as well as among those other languages themselves.

NOTES

1. INTERROADS thread, July 1997, http://www.georgetown.edu/crossroads/interroads/spengemann.html.

2. *The American Language* (1919; 4th ed. 1936; repr. New York: Knopf, 1951), Appendix, 616–697. Mencken's approach has found many followers, and the discussion of features of hybrid languages is a recurring staple in journalism. See, for example, Lizette Alvarez, "It's the Talk of Nueva York: The Hybrid Called Spanglish," *New York Times*, March 25, 1997; or the Spanglish discussion thread on http://www.eunet.es/listserv/spanglish.

3. See Alide Cagidemetrio's introduction to "Peppino" in the *Longfellow Anthology of American Literature* (Baltimore: Johns Hopkins University Press, forthcoming).

Chapter Seventeen

Hyphens
Between Deitsch and American

Marc Shell

"Mixed languages" are often spoken by people who live in areas of interlinguistic contact where there is a dominant language other than their own.[1] For such languages in the United States nowadays the particular terms include "Greeklish," "Yinglish," "Spanglish," and "Franglais." The present chapter, "Hyphens," represents such languages by focusing on the German language in America. In the first part of this essay, we consider the role of German language in the United States, with special attention to the last decades of the nineteenth century and the first of the twentieth. In the second part, we focus on two by-products of German in America: German-accented American English, and Germerican. In the third, we consider the political debate in the United States about whether the languages of "hyphenated Americans" in general and German-Americans in particular ought to be tolerated. This anglophone debate about "hyphenated Americans" had a counterpart in a contemporaneous argument about whether the hyphen itself—that orthographic sign of tension between, say, Deitsch and American—was an alien diacritical mark that ought to be eliminated from the English language.

German in America

> We express our own free thoughts in our own language, adopted from the tongues of many nations, of our forefathers . . . , Consequently, language in the United States is polyglot—national with our people—not borrowed from one distinct tongue.   —James Herron, *American Grammar* (1859)

The history of the German language in the United States is an important part of understanding the development of a politics of linguistic unity in that country.[2] At the time of the American Revolutionary War, after all, not all that many people in the colonies were English-speakers. (Some scholars say that English-speakers numbered fewer than 40 percent; others point out that the German-speakers in one state numbered more than 50 percent.)[3] Many German-Americans believed that German would eventually become an official American language;[4] a few people argued that all Americans should learn to speak German;[5] several endorsed the view of Benjamin Rush (a "founding father") that there should be a German-language national college;[6] hundreds hoped to found a New Germany following the model of New France or New England.[7] In any event, by 1900, there were millions of German-speakers in the United States. German-Americans had published tens of thousands of German-language books and pamphlets. The German-American ethnic group was well educated, wealthy, and influential.

What happened to all these people? A complete answer is outside the purview of this essay, but its broad outline might be be summed up as follows: Thanks to fears of a German-American "third column" during the Great War, it became illegal in many parts of the United States even to teach German in American schools.[8] In 1917, President Theodore Roosevelt said that "we must have but . . . one language. That language must be the language of the Declaration of Independence."[9] The problem was one of "language loyalty."[10] Roosevelt's view was that the United States has to have only one language and that this language must be English. German-American appeals for linguistic tolerance—many eloquent ones were published during the Great War[11]—fell on deaf ears.

By the mid-1930s, most American German-language writers, especially in Chicago and Cleveland,[12] were worried about a precipitous decline in German immigration to the United States. This decline meant a general change in expectations about the linguistic future of the United States. At one time many people had believed that the American language would eventually become polyglot, a sort of linguistic melting pot.[13] In this tradition, Noah Webster had asserted that the United States would "produce, in course of time, a language in North America, as different from the future language of England, as the modern Dutch, Danish, and Swedish are from German, or from one another."[14] This belief in a non-English American language emerging from polyglot ethnic populations in America had remarkable counterparts in the modernist cosmopolitan literatures of the early twentieth century. Thus a specifically American "babel of languages" characterized basically anglophone "ethnic" literature of the period (Henry Roth's *Call It Sleep*, for example) as well as "modernist" writing. Ezra Pound uses Chinese and writes prose pamphlets in Italian. T. S. Eliot closes "The Waste Land" with a series of multilingual quotations. James Joyce's *Finnegans Wake* is a babel-like "language of the devil." (And elsewhere there is Paul Celan, say, or Samuel Beckett.)[15]

Many German-American writers and visual artists of the 1920s and 1930s were interested in developing a tradition at once multilingual and cosmopolitan. Their work included theory of translating German texts that contain English words into English, and vice versa; concern with "transfugee" writers; fostering of German-language anthologies of American writers and bilingual journals; and studying the influence of American English on American German.[16] In such a setting, German-Americans often debated whether their bilingualism (or diglossia) was a temporary "way-station" along the road to German-language "extinction" (as one study of German-Americans considers it;[17] others called it "Americanization"[18]) or a permanent "end in itself." In the Chicago area in the 1930s, the political and linguistic implications of such questions were considered from several angles: Aron's study "Colloquial American German" (1930) explores some of the relevant ambiguities.[19]

By the early 1940s a once-fruitful "dialectic of dual allegiance" between Germany and America was dying.[20] German-Americans were exhorting themselves to "talk American"—that is, to speak without even a trace of "a German accent." They encouraged themselves to speak "the American way" (as Beulah Handler put it) and to imitate all "American words and ways."[21] Soon enough there were few Americans who could speak German.[22]

What was lost, besides the language? Some German-Americans believed an entire culture was lost. They recalled that Herder had said, "Jede Nation spricht, nach dem sie denkt und denkt, nach dem sie spricht" [Every nation speaks according to how it thinks and thinks according to how it speaks]. The sentiment attracted Chicago scholars like Georgiana Simpson in her *Herder's Conception of "das Volk"* (1921).[23] Many German-Americans anticipated or mourned the loss of their own culture by projecting that loss onto other peoples and their languages. Native American peoples provided an especially important screen. A brilliant German and German-American scholarly tradition focuses on the loss of "Amerindian" languages and adds to it, sometimes wittingly and sometimes not, a concern with German-Americans' loss of their own language.[24] The German-American Karl Heinzen, critic of Karl Marx and editor of several important journals, was much vexed by this problem many decades earlier:

> Sich amerikanisieren
> Heisst ganz Sich verlieren
> Als Deutcher Sich treu geblieben
> Heisst Ehre und Bildung lieben:
> Doch lieber indianis[c]h
> Als deutsch-amerikanis[c]h.[25]

A similar German-American tradition of opposing or contrasting German language loss with Amerindian cultural loss extends from the ethnologist Franz Boas's *Handbook of American Indian Languages* (1911) and *Race, Language, and Culture* (1940) to Edward Sapir's *Language* (1921)—Sapir was professor of anthropology and linguistics at the University of Chicago from 1925 to 1931—to Benjamin Whorf's *Language, Thought, and Reality* (1956). Much German-American anthropology ventriloquistically transforms Americans' general silence about Amerindian genocide into something like a self-reflexive whisper.

The German-Americans for whom the disappearance of German from the American scene was most painful was probably the last (and largest) generation of German-speakers. This generation was born in the 1880s and 1890s in the United States or emigrated from Germany at about that time.[26] For them, the disappearance of German was often the intellectually motivating fact of their lives. The German/American poet Lisa Kahn wrote "Mitgift" mindful of the triumph of English over German in the New World.

> Eicherne Truhe handschmiedeeisern beschlagen
> aus unbekanntem Dorf in Westfalen
> nach Texas verschifft—wann?—
> einst selbstgesponnenes Linen bergend

grossmüttervererbt
auch Schmuck in einem schmalen Seitenfach
jetzt voller veralteter Sammlungen
Briefmarken
Ansichtskarten
Münzen
Kinderfotos herzzugeklappt [?]
hat ein faustgrosses Schloss
das schaut aus
wie ein Frauengesicht:
alt
algenutzt
zugeschlossen
Der Schlüssel
ging schon lange verloren.[27]

The key was lost long ago for understanding fully "Mitgift" 's old collections of stamps, picture postcards, coins, and photographs of children. Best, when dealing with this language, to handle with care.

Germerican Graffiti

Da steit me uf der neue Wel
u seit scho englisch: Very well!
—Popular emigrant song in American
English and Allemanic dialect[28]

In the United States at the turn of the century many German-Americans spoke German-accented English and some spoke Germerican, a lexically and syntactically polyglot mixture of the English and German languages. German-accented English, to which we first turn our attention, played an important role in the literature of the period.

Accent

The *New York Commercial Advertiser* claimed in 1896 that "if one were asked what was the most familiar poem in the households of America today, it would not surprise some New Englanders if he were to say, [Charles Follens Adams's] 'Leedle Yawcob Strauss.' "[29] Another well-known example of German-accented English-language poetry is Charles G. Leland's poem "To a Friend Studying German":

Will'st dou learn de Deutsche Sprache?
Brepare dein soul to shtand
Soosh sendences ash ne'er vas heardt
In any oder land.
Till dou canst make parentheses
Intwisted—ohne zahl—

Dann wirst du erst Deutschvertig seyn,
For a languashe id eaal.[30]

Other poets included Gus Williams.

In this same humorous tradition, there were German-accented monologues and plays.[31] Examples from the period 1926–1931 include *Dot's Right*,[32] *Dis Is Mine Autogeografy*,[33] and *Dot New Baby*.[34] Writers of American "Dutch Dialect" stories and essays include Charles H. ("Carl Pretzel") Harris, Joseph C. ("Rube Hoffenstein") Aby, and George V. ("D. Dinkelspiel") Hobart.

Germerican

Germerican was a lexical and syntactical mixture of GERMan[35] and AmERICAN spoken by hundreds of thousands of German-speakers in the United States.[36] The term *Germerican* does not appear in the dictionaries, but it was common parlance by 1926 when Kurt M. Stein published in Chicago his *Die Lorelei vom Michigan Michigan-See: 33 Gedichte in Germerican: "Die schonste Lengevitch"* (1926).[37]

In *The American Language* (1937) Mencken gives a humorous example from a German-language daily newspaper published in the United States in 1935:

"Was machst du denn in Amerika?" fragt der alte Onkel.
Well, der Kuno was sehr onest. "Ich bin e Stiefellegger," sagt er.
"Bist du verrückt geworden?" rohrt der Onkel. "Was is denn das?"
"Das," sagt der Kuno, "is a Antivereinigtestaatenconstitutionsverbesserungsspirituosenwarenhändler."[38]

Such Germerican-language stories about *Händler* also appeared in English-language newspapers like the *Chicago Tribune* and the *Evening Post*.

Germerican poets published one-line bilingual epigrams of the sort that have long constituted a genre in itself in places of "syncretic" cultural interaction.[39] Among them was Stein, who wrote *Gemixte Pickles* (1927).[40] *Pickles* includes a Germerican version of Hegelian *Aufhebung*: in Stein's Germerican-language version of Shakespeare's *Hamlet*, for example, Horatio (known as "Raish") says, "Well, business wird schon starteh aufzupickeh."[41]

The mixed language tradition has counterparts in the visual realms. Consider three examples from the often similar Yinglish, or Yiddish-English, tradition.[42] In one Yinglish cartoon, *Nudnick* (Figure 2) means "a silly person" in Yiddish and "little Nick" in English; being "nude" makes little Nick a nudnick. In another cartoon, *Menschen* (Figure 3) means "real human beings" in Yiddish and "mansion" in English: owning a mansion makes one a mensch. In a third cartoon, *Goyeh*, or *Goih* (Figure 4), means "gentile" in Yiddish and in English it is the name of the painter Goya: "Goya is a Goih." The fun here—if fun there is—arises from more or less coincidentally similar sounds of two languages.[43] Such coincidence makes "Yinglish" out of Yiddish and English even as "Germerican" arises from German and English.

1. Cover illustration. Charles H. Harris, *Carl Pretzel's Komikal Speaker,* (New York: Beadle and Adams, 1873). Houghton Library.

Hyphenations

Sitting atop the hyphen provides a marvelous view, but no direction.
Does one face forward or backward? Look ahead or behind?
the hyphen is incomplete; there is no where to go.
the force of the dash,
the inconclusiveness of the parenthesis
the finality of the period.
The Hyphen only supports. It does not connect.
Japanese-American, Mexican-American, Italian-American—
lacking the two slight marks that gives the arrow its certainty
the hyphen is incomplete; there is nowhere to go.
Exiting between two cultures, it is an eternal bridge
with barriers and guards at both ends.

—Wendell Aycock, "Hyphen-nation" (1980)

2. Nudnick. In *Yankee English: 26 Cocktail Napkins.* 1953. Permission Stephen Lariar. Photo: Judaica Collection, Harvard College Library.

3. Menschen. In *Yankee English: 26 Cocktail Napkins.* 1953. Permission Stephen Lariar. Photo: Judaica Collection, Harvard College Library.

Questions of English-language orthography are nowhere more vexed than in the area of hyphenation.[44] The once-influential, would-be regulator of the English language, H. W. Fowler, took an especial interest in the controversy about whether to use hyphens. In such works as *Hyphens* (1921) and the exceptionally influential *The King's English* (1930) Fowler maintains that "there are three degrees of intimacy between words."[45] The first and loosest degree of intimacy between two words is expressed by their mere juxtaposition as separate words. "Over due" and "German American" would be examples. The next degree of intimacy between two words is expressed, according to Fowler, by their being hyphenated. "Over-due" and "German-American" would be examples. Bret Harte writes in *Lost Galleon* (1872): "Due she was, and over-due—/ Galleon, merchandise, and crew."[46] Finally, the closest degree of intimacy is suggested by the two words being written continuously as one "solid" word. ("Overdue" and "GermanAmerican" would be examples.)[47] The term "Germerican" would be off the charts.

Now, there are often distinct needs for some sort of hyphenation in English-language terminology. Sometimes it is ambiguous whether particular words are nouns or adjectives, for example. In such cases it is often helpful to include a space between words: "over all" (meaning "from one extreme point to another") thus comes to mean something different from "overall" ("including everything"). Likewise, it is helpful to insert a hyphen between words: the bipartite noun *German-American* suggests that the person so called is an American citizen or "permanent resident" whereas combinations of adjectives and nouns like *German American* and *American German* suggest ambiguity about the matter.

Fowler reluctantly admits to the need for hyphenation in the English language. But like many of his social class in America as well as in England, Fowler believes that hyphens are a regrettable foreign-language "intrusion" into the English language. According to him the hyphen is basically a "German-language" solution to a particular English-language problem of imprecision.[48] If only there had been no German immigration! Then, Fowler suggests, there would be no hyphens.

In the United States as well as England, issues of national- or blood-purity thus came to interact with those of linguistic-purity.[49] (Fowler was a supporting member of the Society for Pure English, which published his *Hyphens*.) Dislike of hyphens and dislike of hyphenated Americans went hand in hand. When the hyphen became a common visual sign of the supposed problem that the loyalties of German-Americans were divided dangerously between Germany and the United States, American citizens of German descent themselves adopted the term "hyphenated citizens" partly because they wanted to demonstrate resistance to its uglier connotations. Herman Ridder's *Hyphenations* (1915), Edward Steiner's *The Confession of a Hyphenated American* (1916), and George Seibel's *Hyphen in American History* (1916) are principal examples.[50]

In the 1930s the rhetoric of divided loyalty hearkened back to the Great War, when German-American culture had been under fire in America from both English-speakers and German-speakers. For example, the German-Texan writer Selma

4. Goyeh. In *Yankee English: 26 Cocktail Napkins.* 1953. Permission Stephen Lariar. Photo: Judaica Collection, Harvard College Library.

Metzenthin-Raunick published a cosmopolitan poetic memoir of the Great War. Her *Deutsche Grossmutter*, with its throngs both English and French, raises a still motivating political question about "barbarianism."

> Rah, rah—bum, bum—tei, tei!
> Amerikas Jugend marschiert vorbei
> Darunter viel tausend Deutsche,
> Darunter auch du, mein Enkelsohn,—
> Ach Gott, ach Gott, welch' Spott und Hohn—
> Zu Schlagen die "deutschen Barbaren,"
> Mit den Englisch-französischen Scharen.[51]

Across a generational divide the German grandmother sings about German-Americans marching off to war in order to fight against "German barbarians." *Barbarian* means a person who does not talk the same way as the dominant group or who knows no one language well: a commonplace charge against German-Americans and Germericans was that they themselves were linguistic barbarians, or stammerers.[52] So *alma mater*'s lament wonders about the hyphenated relationships in America between words (*German* and *American*), between languages (the German language and the American language), and between national groups (Germans and Americans).

NOTES

1. For relevant studies in this area: *Sprachkontakt und Sprachkonflikt = Languages in contact and conflict = Langues en contact et en conflict, Zeitschrift fur Dialektolotie und Linguistik*, no.32 (Wiesbaden, 1980); *Languages in Contact and Contrast: Essays in Contact Linguistics*, Trends in linguistics, Studies and Monographs, vol. 54 (Berlin and New York, 1991); and Uriel Weinreich, *Languages in Contact: Findings and Problems*, Publications of the Linguistic Circle of New York, no.1 (New York, 1953).

2. See Marc Shell, "Babel in America: The Politics of Linguistic Diversity in the United States," 20.1 *Critical Inquiry* (Fall 1993): 103–28.

3. For the population of Pennsylvania, see "Linguistic and National Stocks in the Population of the United States," American Historical Association Annual Report (Washington, D.C., 1931), vol. 1, pp. 291–294. See also Frank R. Diffenderffer, *The German Immigration into Pennsylvania Through the Port of Pennsylvania, 1770–1775* (Lancaster, Pa., 1990), pp. 102–106.

4. Franz Löher, *Geschichte und Zustände der Deutschen in Amerika* (Cincinnati, 1847), p. 198; Robert A. Feer, "Official Use of the German Language in Pennsylvania," *Pennsylvania Magazine of History of Biography*, 76:4 (October 1952), p. 395. See also Shirley Brice Heath and Frederick Mandabach, "Language Status Decisions and the Law in the United States," pp. 87–106 in Juan Cobarrubias and Joshua A. Fishman, eds., *Progress in Language Planning*, Contributions to the Sociology of Language, 31 (Amsterdam, 1983). For an example of the myth in its present-day format: "Despite folklore promulgated by subsequent writers there were no serious attempts to adopt some language other than English for the new nation" (Richard W. Bailey, *Images of English: A Cultural History of the Language* [Ann Arbor, 1991], p. 104).

See too *Annals of America,* vol. 14, *Third Congress* [1916–1928] (Chicago, 1968), 1009; *American State Papers, Miscellaneous,* 1:114: The committee recommendation followed an incident in the Third Congress of the United States: "a petition of a number of Germans, residing in the State of Virginia" was presented to the House, "praying that a certain proportion of the laws of the United States may be printed in the German language" (*Journal of the House of Representatives* [1793], 65; cited by Feer, "Official Use," pp. 398–399).

5. J. Ehrenfried argues in *Colloquial Phrases & Dialogues in German & English* (Philadelphia, 1834) that "the prevalence of the German language in many parts of the United States should form a powerful inducement of men in every situation of life to become, at least partially acquainted with it" (quoted by Shirley Brice Heath, "English in Our Language Heritage," in Charles A. Ferguson, Shirley Brice Heath, and David Hwang, eds., *Language in the USA* [Cambridge, 1981], p. 11).

6. Benjamin Rush, *Letters of Benjamin Rush*, ed. L. H. Butterfield (Princeton, 1951), 1: 356–366. See also Rush's *Information for Europeans Who are Disposed to Migrate to the United States* (Philadelphia, 1790).

7. Wilhelm Roscher, the German economist, tried to convince German-Americans to establish a New Germany—Teutonia in the New World (Roscher, *Political Economy*, trans. J. J. Lalor [Chicago, 1878]; quoted by John Hawgood, *The Tragedy of German-America: The German in the United States of America during the Nineteenth Century and After* [New York, 1940], p. 215).

8. Edward Sagarin and Robert J. Kelly, "Polylingualism in the United States of America: A Multitude of Tongues," 20–44, in William Beer and James E. Jacob, eds., *Language Policy and National Unity* (Totowa, N.J., 1985). See also Carl Frederick Wittke, *German-Americans and the World War (With Special Emphasis on Ohio's German-Language Press)* (Columbus, Ohio, 1936).

9. President Theodore Roosevelt, in "Children of the Crucible" (1917), continued: "The greatness of this nation depends on the swift assimilation of the aliens she welcomes to her shores" (quoted in *Annals of America*, vol. 14 [1916–1928], Chicago; cited in James Crawford, *Language Loyalties: A Source Book on the Official Language Controversy* [Chicago, 1992], p. 85).

10. See Joshua A. Fishman, *Language Loyalty in the United States: The Maintenance and Perpetuation of Non-English Mother Tongues by American Ethnic and Religious Groups* (The Hague, 1966); Serge Ricard, "World War One and the Rooseveltian Gospel of Undiluted Americanism," in *Hyphenated Diplomacy: European Immigration and U.S. Foreign Policy, 1914–1984* (Aix-en-Provence and Marseille, 1985); and Mark Ellis and Panikos Panayi, "German Minorities in World War I: A Comparative Study of Britain and the USA," *Ethnic and Racial Studies* 17:2 (April 1994), pp. 238–260.

11. See Gustavus Ohlinger, *Their True Faith and Allegiance* (Wister, N.Y., 1917).

12. The situation of German-Americans in Cleveland is a theme of David Ross's bilingual work, *Deutsch-amerikanische Heimatkunde Tagung* (Cleveland, 1937). On the German-American press in the 1930s, see Stephen Economides, *Der Nationalsozialismus und die deutschsprachige Presse in New York, 1933–1941* (Frankfurt am Main, 1982). The specific bilingual tradition of German-Americans in the Illinois area in the 1880s is treated in Beate Hinrichs, *Deutschamerikanische Presse zwischen Tradition und Anpassung: die Illinois Staatszeitung und Chicagoer Arbeiterzeitung, 1879–1890* (Frankfurt am Main and New York, 1989). There was a more-than-proportitate drop in the number of German daily newspapers (H. L. Mencken, *The American Language: An Inquiry into the Development of English in the United States*, 4th ed. [New York, 1937], p. 620 n).

13. See epigraph to this section, and Dennis E. Baron, *Grammar and Good Taste: Reforming the American Language* (New Haven, 1982), p. 14.

14. Noah Webster, *Dissertations on the English Language* (1789), intro Harry R. Warfel (Gainesville, Fla.: Scholars' Facsimiles & Reprints, 1951, pp. 22–23. Webster also said that in the Federal Procession there was "a scroll, containing the principles of a [new] Federal language" (see Bailey, *Images of English*, pp. 104–5). In the ensuing years, Webster and his followers came to realize that the English language would predominate—or they now argued outright that it should. Only later did Webster say that "our language is the English and it is desirable that the language of the United States and Great Britain should continue to be the same" (quoted in Richard N. Rollins, *The Long Journey of Noah Webster* [Philadelphia, 1980], p. 127; in Crawford, *Language Loyalties*, p. 35 n).

15. For Eliot: his "American Literature and American Language" (address delivered at Washington University, June 9, 1953, St. Louis). For Joyce: *The Languages of Joyce: Selected Papers from the 11th International James Joyce Symposium, 12–18 June 1988*, ed. R. M. Bolletierri Rosinelli, C. Marengo Vaglio, and Chr. van Boheemen (Philadelphia, 1992); Hugh MacDiarmid, *In Memoriam James Joyce: From a Vision of World Language* (Glasgow, 1955); and Constantin-George Sandulescu, *The Language of the Devil: Texture and Archetype in Finnegans Wake* (Gerrards Cross, Buckinghamshire, 1987). For Celan and Beckett: Shira Wolosky, *Language Mysticisms: The Negative Way of Language in Eliot, Celan, and Beckett* (Stanford, 1995).

16. For a related viewpoint: Stephen Clausing, *English Infuence on American German and American Icelandic*, American University Studies, Series 13, Linguistics, vol.13 (New York, 1986).

17. See Stephen Joseph Shaw, *The Catholic Parish as Way-Station of Ethnicity and Americanization: Chicago's Germans and Italians, 1903–1939* (Brooklyn, 1991). Compare the argument in Clausing, *English Influence on American German*.

18. See Board of Education of the City of Chicago cooperating with the Chicago Association of Commerce, *A Year of Americanization Work, July 1918–July 1919: Has it Paid? Read the Answer!* (Chicago, 1919).

19. Aron's work came out of the University of Illinois. As Mencken (*American Language*, p. 621 n) points out, although there had been many studies of the Pennsylvania-Dutch dialectic-version of American-German by 1937, there were very few of other forms of American-German. Otis Kaye's painting *Handel With Care* (1935) considers others.

20. See Helene Christol, "The Dialectics of Dual Allegiance," in *Hyphenated Diplomacy*.

21. For "German accent": Lewis Helmar Herman, *Talk American: A Practical Guide for Eliminating a German Accent* (Chicago, 1944). For "American way": Beulah Handler, *English the American Way for German Speaking Adults* (New York, 1940), and John Whyte, *American Words and Ways, Especially for German Americans* (New York, 1943).

22. For a description of the disappearance of the German-speaking community in Ohio, see Guido Andre Dobbert, *The Disintegration of an Immigrant Community: The Cincinnati Germans, 1870–1920* (New York, 1980).

23. Johann Gottfried Herder, *Ueber die neure Deutsche Litteratur. Fragmente erste Sammlung*, in *Sämtliche Werke* 2:18, ed. Bernhard Suphan (Berlin, 1878–1913). See also Herder, *Ideen zur Philosophie der Geschichte der Menschheit*, esp. *Sämtliche Werke* 13 (Erster Theil, 1784), 354–366. Simpson's "Herder's Conception of 'das Volk' " was her Ph.D. dissertation at the University of Chicago (1921).

24. One can sense a very little of the same thing, in relation to African-Americans, in obviously scurrilous German-American works like Henry J. Wehman's *Black Jokes, for "blue*

devils" (New York, 1897), which is "chock full of darkey fun!" together with "colored philosophy and nigger witticisms." There is also Wehman's *Brudder Bones' "4-11-44" Joker, Containing a Jolly Lot of Sable Conundrums, Ethiopian Jokes, Burnt Cork Comicalities and Darkey Dialogues* (New York, 1897).

25. "To americanize yourself / Means to lose yourself entirely / To have stayed true to yourself as a German / Means to love honor and heritage: / But better to be Indian / Than to be German-American." From the *Pioneer* (a journal published 1852–1879), cited in Paul Otto Schinnerer, *Karl Heinzen = Deutsch-Amerikanische Geschichtsblatter*, 15 (published by the Deutsch-Amerikanische Gesellschaft of Illinois, Chicago, 1915), pp. 84–145, and in Hawgood, *Tragedy*; translation adapted. For Karl Heinzen on Marx, see, for example, his *Die Helden des teutschen Kommunismus dem Herrn Karl Marx gewidmet* (Bern, 1848).

26. Walter D. Kamphoefner, "German American Bilingualism: *cui malo?* Mother Tongue and Socioeconomic Status among the Second Generation in 1940," *International Migration Review* 28:4 (Winter 1994), 846–865, writes: "Clearly, second generation Germans were an aging if not a dying group by 1940. . . . Mass immigration had ended with the Panic of 1893, and the two largest cohorts of their children were those born in the 1880s and 1890s."

27. "Trousseau": Oaken chest fitted with hand-wrought iron from an unknown village in Westphalia shipped to Texas—when?—at one time holding handspun linen from one's grandmothers and jewelry in a narrow compartment at the side, now full of dated collections: stamps, picture postcards, coins, photos of children in closed, heart-shaped albums. (See Hubert P. Heinen, "Consciousness of Being German: Regional Literature in German Texas," in Theodore Gish and Richard Spuler, ed., *Eagle in the New World* [College Station, Tex., 1986], p. 156.) At the time she wrote this work, Lisa Kahn had a home in and close ties to Texas. Some of her works are listed on the inside back cover of Lisa Kahn, *David am Komputer und andere Gedichte* (Providence, 1982).

28. Cited in Lutz Röhrich, "German American Emigrant Songs," in Gish and Spuler, *Eagle in the New World*.

29. *New York Commercial Advertiser*, 23 January 1896. The essayist continues: "The quaint humor, the tender pathos, the subtle something that speaks of humanity and loving kindness, combined with an attractive metrical form and an amusing dialect, unite to make it a delight to young and old."

30. Charles G. Leland, "To a Friend Studying German," in *Hans Breitman's Ballads* (1870; New York, 1965), p. 28.

31. Humor is paramount in such works about "Dutch"-American vaudevillian jokes and witticisms as *The German Joker* (1904), Wehman's *Budget of Jokes, Replete with English, Irish, and German Wit and Humor* (New York, 1893), and Edmund Phillipp Kremer's *German-American Handbook* (Chicago and Philadelphia, 1939). The latter was a Chicago-based collection of Germerican "idioms, colloquialisms, familiar quotations, localisms, dialectal and slang expressions, and words not generally found in German-English dictionaries" (front page).

32. In *Eight Snappy Vaudeville Monologues*, ed. Arthur LeRoy Kazer (Boston, 1926), pp. 43–47.

33. In *Webstein's Stendick Dictionera*, ed. Al Webstein (New York, 1931), pp. 9–11.

34. In *Direct Monologues, Readings, and Plays*, ed. Arthur LeRoy Kazer (Dayton, Ohio, 1928), pp. 197–198.

35. The term "Germerican" denotes a combination of the German- and English-American languages, but it is no such combination: "Germerican" itself is an anglophone amalgam of

two English words. "Deutsch-American" or "German-Amerikanisch" would be bilingual combinations. Such terms appear frequently on German and German-American paper Notgeld of the period; see *Deutsche-Amerika — Woche* (1923), discussed and illustrated in Marc Shell, *OVERDUE* (Chicago, forthcoming, 1998), chap. 5.

36. The term "Handel" in the ambiguously bilingual label "Handel With Care" in Otis Kaye's painting of 1935 is an example of Germerican. See Marc Shell, "OK; or, Handel With Care," *Common Knowledge*, Winter 1997, pp. 71–113.

37. It is worth remarking that the generally anglophone term "handle" is sometimes also spelled "handel."

38. Heinrich Reinhold Hirsch, "Der Charlie," *Staats-Zeitung* (New York City), March 28, 1935. For much earlier examples of the Germerican language of the Pennsylvania Dutch variety, see Edward H. Rauch, *Pennsylvania Dutch Handbook: A Book for Instruction* (Mauch Chunk, Pa., 1879).

39. See Marc Shell, "The Forked Tongue," *Semiotica* 4:4 (1978), pp. 259–269, which concerns the epigrammatology of bilingual and FrAnglais commercial advertising in Quebec in the 1960s and 1970s. On bilingual poetry in general, see Tino Villanueva, "A Brief History of Bilingualism in Poetry," *Imagine* 1:1 (1984), pp. xviii–xxxvii.

40. The German-language term "Mixed Pickles" has long been the only proper German translation for the English-language term "mixed pickles." A. O. Weber had already used the German (as opposed to Germerican) book title *Mixed Pickles* in Germany in 1924 (Muhlhausen i Thur., 1924). For other examples of "mixed pickles" as a book title, see Henrik Bernhard Jaeger's book published in Norwegian in the 1880s and 1890s (*Mixed Pickles: feuilletoner og skitser* [Oslo, 1889]) and Louise Frances Field's book published in American English (*Mixed Pickles: A Story for Girls and Boys* [New York, 1885]). The Dutch book-series "Mixed Pickles" was published by Nederlandsche Uitg. Mij. in Leiden beginning in the 1940s.

41. "Well, business will soon start to pick up" (Stein, *Hamlet*, Part I, l. 5, p. 79; in Kurt M. Stein, *Die Schönste Lengevitch*, introd. Richard Atwater [Chicago, 1925]).

42. For the relationship between Yiddish and English in the United States, see Rudolf Glanz, *Jews in Relation to the Cultural Milieu of the Germans in America up to the Eighteen Eighties* (New York, 1947).

43. Consider the recent Jewish-American craze for books like Jackie Mason's *How to Talk Jewish*, with Ira Berkow (New York, 1991); Mollie Katz's *Jewish as a Second Language* (New York, 1991); Marcus Martin's *Yiddish for Yankees: or, Funny, You Don't Look Gentile* (Philadelphia, 1968); Dana C'Cele Berkman's *Goyim My Way: A Gentile's Guide to Yiddish* (South Brunswick, N.J., 1966); and Gene Bluestein's *Anglish-Yiddish: Yiddish in American Life and Literature* (Athens, Ga., 1989).

44. University of Chicago Press, *A Manual of Style*, 12th ed., completely revised (Chicago, 1969), p. 130, advises: "Of ten spelling questions that arise in writing or editing, nine are probably concerned with compound words. Should it be selfseeking or self-seeking? is the word spelled taxpayer, tax-payer, or tax payer?—solid, hyphenated, or open. "Most such questions are readily answered by the dictionary. If the compound is used as noun, the chances are good that it will appear in the columns of the abridged Webster, in one of the three possible spellings. If it is used as an adjective, the chances of finding it are still fair. But there will yet be some noun forms and a great many adjective forms for which no "authoritative" spelling can be found. It is then that general principles must be applied."

45. See Henry Watson Fowler, *King's English* (Oxford, 1906), pp. 284–289.

46. Bret Harte, *The Lost Galleon and Other Tales* (San Francisco, Towne & Bacon, 1867).

47. Fowler adds a fourth sort of intimacy between words: uppercasing of letters in the middle of words. One writes "Anglo-SouthAmerican" instead of "Anglo-South-American," for example, or "OverDue" instead of "OVERDUE" (Fowler, *King's English*, pp. 286–287).

48. Fowler, *King's English*, p. 288. Fowler dislikes foreign words and also "foreign methods" within English. Scott wrote "A low door, leading through a moss and ivy-covered wall"; Lowell wrote of "A language . . . not yet fet-locked by dictionary and grammar mongers"; and Thackery wrote of "Those who take-human or-womankind for their study." Concerning these uses of the hyphen, Fowler notes unhappily that the only "quite satisfactory plan" is the Germans', who would write moss- and ivy covered. In the end, all he can say is that "it is a much commoner fault to over-hyphen [*sic*] than to under-hyphen [*sic*].

49. On the general rhetoric of this interraction between race and language, see Marc Shell, *Children of the Earth: Literature, Politics, and Nationhood* (New York, 1993), esp. "Both Sides Against the Middle," pp. 41–44. For Fowler, "Americanisms" corrupt British-English even as, for Americans, "Anglicisms" corrupt American-English. Writes Fowler: "Though we take these [Americanisms] separately from foreign words . . . the distinction is purely pro forma; Americanisms are foreign words, and should be so treated" (Fowler, *King's English*, p. 33).

50. See also various essays collected in *Hyphenated Diplomacy*. Herman Ridder, *Hyphen-ations: A Collection of Articles on the World War of 1914 which have appeared from time to time in the New-Yorker Staats-Zeitung under "The War Situation from Day to Day"* (New York, 1915), begins with a dedication that already suggests his subject: "To those Americans in whose veins German blood still flows, whose undivided sympathy and loyalty to the ideal of these United States of America is coupled with the immutable remembrances of all that is noblest and highest in the Fatherland, these pages are respectfully dedicated." In the painting *Handel With Care* the pictorial counterpart to the hyphen is the ambiguously planar border between Dutch and American sectors.

51. "Die deutsche Grossmutter" (The German grandmother): Ta-ra-ra boom! America's youth is filing in parade, among them thousands of Germans, among them you, too, my grandson. Oh God, what mockery and scorn to beat the "German barbarians" along with the English and French throngs. Selma Metzenthin-Raunick, "Die deutsche Grossmutter," in *Deutsche Schriften in Texas* (San Antonio: Freiepresse für Texas, 1935–1936). See Hubert P. Heinen, "The Consciousness of Being German," p. 151, whence the translation, and also Joseph Wilson, "Texas German and Other American Immigrant Languages" (both in *Eagle in the New World*).

52. "The Greek word [*barbaros*] had probably a primary reference to speech, and is compared with L[atin] *balbus* stammering" (OED, s.v. "Barbarian"). In 1827 Julius C. Hare and Augustus W. Hare wrote: "A barbarian is a person who does not talk as we talk" (*Guesses at Truth* [c. 1827; London, 1859] p. 325). In 1857, John Ruskin wrote in *A Political Economy of Art* (London, 1857), p. 9: "A wholly barbarous use of the word, barbarous in a double sense, for it is not English, and it is bad Greek." Both Hare and Ruskin wrote during the heyday of the British Empire.

Chapter Eighteen

Portinglês in the United States
The Luso-America of José Rodrigues Miguéis

Michela Corradini

In 1980, José Rodrigues Miguéis died in Manhattan after having spent the last forty-four years of his life in the heart of New York City. Born in Lisbon in 1901, he led, while there, an active political life as a writer-intellectual helping to consolidate the republic established after the overthrow of the monarchy. With the failure of the young regime, however, and the country's falling into the hands of a dictatorship that would last until 1974 (almost to the end of his life) he elected to go into exile in the United States, where he would dedicate his energies to writing fiction, much of which recreates the fevered Lisbon years of his youth. Publishing only in his native language (though his work has been translated into several others), he lived a dichotomized life with his physical being in New York and his mind in his native Portugal.[1]

Miguéis's college and university years (1919–33) were characterized by political activism.[2] Very early (1921) he started contributing articles, short stories, and essays to newspapers and magazines. He traveled to the United States, first as a visitor in 1935, and then as an immigrant the following year. During his first ten years in the United States he was exceptionally active politically. He joined the campaign to support the Spanish Republicans (1937–39) and participated in political groups in New England Portuguese immigrant communities. Soon, he became once again disenchanted with politics, but this time even more deeply, so he decided to devote himself to writing. He spent the remaining thirty years of his life chiefly as a translator: he translated into Portuguese Stendhal (*L'Abbesse de Castro*), Carson McCullers (*The Heart Is a Lonely Hunter*), F. Scott Fitzgerald (*The Great Gatsby*), and Erskine Caldwell (*A Lamp for Nightfall*). He became very much a prisoner of New York, the city onto which he projected the Portugal that he dreamed of.

O Grande Gatsby

Miguéis's preface to *O grande Gatsby*, his translation of *The Great Gatsby*, shows a particularly Portuguese focus on love. The Portuguese spin on this common subject in literature is nostalgic and painful. Love and *saudade*—a Portuguese word that means "a very deep nostalgia"—are pervasive in this literature.

In Fitzgerald's novel Miguéis could see the Portuguese way of loving: not sexuality but the romantic and passionate feeling one can find in Fado music. Miguéis writes that this kind of love has nothing to do with that of Hemingway's novels or of the novelists after the Second World War; he claims that the sentiment Fitzgerald discusses is always spiritual, even when very passionate.

In the preface to *O grande Gatsby* Miguéis writes, "In America everything is different. . . . (In Portugal) there are no upper classes. . . . There are no Bohemians like Fitzgerald in Portugal."[3] The big parties to which Fitzgerald was accustomed or the great quantities of alcohol and money, the wonderful houses and clothes and cars, in a word, the rich lives they led, were not so common for the Portuguese writer. There were no Bohemians even in Lisbon in that period.[4] Writers like Fernando Pessoa were addicted to brandy (and not "mint julep" or "highball"), and they used to drink in the taverns, but they could not conceive of the American kind of life; they even were against it, against that kind of social class, to which they addressed deprecatory remarks.[5]

Miguéis leaves many English words in his translation. Most of them are typical American terms of uppercrust and upstart society ("halls," "cocktails," "nurse," "butler," "pool-room"), and their presence helps to demonstrate that this kind of vocabulary did not exist in the Portugal of that period.

"Gente da Terceira Classe" ("Steerage")

Miguéis's use of Anglicisms in *O grande Gatsby* prefigures his employment of English words and expressions in his own most representative short story, "Gente da terceira classe" ("Steerage" in the published English translation), a shipboard journal written during a voyage on the transatlantic *Arlanza*, as it makes its way along the Portuguese coast. On the ship Portuguese, Polish, English, and other passengers are thrown together: rich and poor, disillusioned immigrants who are coming back from America without dreams, "chilled by disappointment,"[6] and others who are going to America full of dreams and hopes, and "still warm from the sun of illusion."[7]

In the Portuguese edition there are English words like "deck," "steward," "sensation," "leader," "smoking jacket," "evening jacket," and "college," and there are also entire sentences in English or French. This reflects a general trend in the Portuguese language. For the Portuguese immigrant, code-switching, the mixture between English and Portuguese has created a new kind of language called Portinglês, or Luso-American.[8] There are words in Luso-American that neither a native from Portugal nor an American can readily comprehend, such as *frisa* (freezer, *congelador* in Portuguese).[9] "Refrigerator" is first found in English in an American quotation of 1841.[10] In the period after the Second World War it was used by the Portuguese immigrants in California, but it was unknown in Portugal because there were no refrigerators. As Francisco Cota Fagundes writes, the word *frijoeira* is a phonetic and semantic assimilation of the English word "refrigerator". We can find the same assimilation in the word "frisa" from the English "freezer". For this reason, the immigrant assimilated the phonetic meaning and value of the English word, as he understood it, and he adapted it to the Portuguese phonology.[11]

Fagundes gives a list of Luso-American expressions and words used by Portuguese immigrants, parts of which are appended to this essay. There are many reasons that the immigrants use this new kind of language in the United States, according to Fagundes they have to express new concepts; they lose their mother tongue when they learn the new language, which they prefer, and which their children adopt.[12]

We can find other Luso-American words in "Gente da terceira classe" used by Portuguese immigrants after World War II—like *cracas* (crackers), *dolas* (dollars), *improvimentos* (improvements), *bossa* (boss), *contrata* (contract), and *racatias* (racketeers). This sampling gives an idea of Portuguese as spoken in America.

Miguéis's interest in language is developed in a series of encounters among the people in the third class aboard the *Arlanza*. The narrator comments on a Madeiran woman with three children who goes to join her husband in "Améreca" that "she has lost her mother tongue but has not yet discovered her mother-in-law."[13] She wonders why a "lord" like him is also going to the United States, "as if the land of opportunity were the Mecca of the hungry alone."[14] In Portuguese the expression sounds much stronger; *esfomeado* means "one who has starved to death" and not "one who is simply hungry." She is one of the first characters the narrator meets in the ship. Another encounter is with a pretend-French-but-really-Polish couple, who, like some Portuguese immigrants, try to hide their original nationality by assimilating another culture badly. There are also some Galicians who return from Argentina and the narrator tells us they are different from the ones in his Lisbon; they are not "like the Galicians of my old Lisbon, who I was used to consider docile, smiling, and of good disposition. The New World has soured them; it has aged them."[15] Paradoxically America, the New World, ages the European immigrants. Later, when the narrator meets a Turkish (or maybe Lebanese) woman, she is screaming in an unknown language and throwing overboard all the "fruits of long years of slaving."[16] She has been abandoned by her husband, who slipped back to the shore at the last moment, leaving her alone on the ship.

Sometimes the narrator gives free rein to his thoughts and judgments. He is sorry that the immigrants do not understand anything about America:

> They gained nothing of the spiritual values that America had to offer them; how much longer will the simple and deprived people continue to confuse civilization with the purely material values of acquisition? When will they learn that, without principles, everything else is chaos? In their idolatry of Things . . . they continue to be regressive and niggardly in Spirit.[17]

Miguéis disapproves of materialism and of the Portuguese who denies his own country, which his description of a peasant from Montalegre, who is going to meet her daughter in America because she does not have other relatives, illustrates. She brings with her a basket of provisions from her land, and the narrator imagines the moment in which she will meet her daughter and say, " 'Take it; these are from our place.' Maybe that's why no one on board will take what she offers them."[18] He is reproaching the habits of the immigrants who disown their own country.

Other Works

The story "Como se ama na América" (1947)[19] deals with love, marriage, the family, and prostitution, and continues Miguéis's interest in themes from *The Great Gatsby*.

"O anel de contrabando"[20] is a story within a story. The narrator is a writer in search of a theme when a man tries to sell him a diamond ring for practically nothing. Convinced it is worthless, he decides to buy it on a whim for four dollars. When he decides he has been taken in, he pawns it off on a girl for twenty dollars with a tale of woe. Just as he begins to feel bad about deceiving an innocent girl, the police arrest him: it seems the girl had called the police when she found out that the ring was worth at least two hundred dollars. The narrator, who has displayed a somewhat superior air, is the victim when the tables are turned, a technique that is common in these stories and which greatly adds to their charm. The story's ending is in keeping with its tongue-in-cheek tone: "What the devil could I say but declare that I had finally found an end for my story?"[21]

"O 'crime perfeito' "[22] takes place in Manhattan and reveals Miguéis's interest in psychology. A married man has fallen madly in love with a young girl nearly half his age. His unbridled jealousy causes him to follow her and plot the perfect crime in his imagination. Yet he realizes that his plans are in no way perfect: his numerous love letters and people who knew both of them would lead the police directly to his door. He suddenly sees her as he has not seen her before: as a cold, cruel, ambitious person. He returns to thinking of his wife and children and getting on with the business of living. Again the tables have been turned on the narrator/character, who considered himself to be just a little superior.

"Há sempre um bei em Tunes" (There is always a bey in Tunis)[23] is a humorous short story written in 1964 that focuses on national stereotypes that are often embodied by shorthand words—as when Americans are perceived as such types as the "traveling salesman," the "gangster" of St. Louis or Chicago, and the "racketeer" of New York.[24] Some of the words that seem to travel most easily from one linguistic system to another may also be the ones that represent deep cultural differences, in literature as well as in life. Miguéis's wife, Camila Campanella, an American of Portuguese origin, commented,

> We had lovely fights because between the Portuguese and the American culture there's such a big gap [she used the English word here] that a simple word gave out sparks. I remember I used the word "aggressive" for a person and "aggressive," in English, doesn't mean "agressivo" [fighting] in Portuguese: I was always stumbling over these kinds of expressions. When I was with some Portuguese people my behavior was shocking. He used to kick me under the table because I was asking intrusive questions. But they weren't intrusive in the United States. All these things made our life very interesting, but a little bit difficult.[25]

Miguéis went to the United States in 1935, and in 1942 he became a naturalized citizen. He spent half his life in his adopted country; and in many ways was an American. He could express himself fluently in both Portuguese and English, and wrote essays and fiction in which American acquaintances and friends appeared. But he also wrote about his native country and its people; and he traced the Portuguese-American interaction in his Luso-American tales. In New York he adapted himself to the American way of life, but still his eyes were directed at Lisbon. John Austin Kerr Jr. tells us that whenever someone took pictures of Miguéis he was always turned toward the East, where his Portugal was.[26]

Appendix: Luso-American Words and Expressions Compared to Portuguese and English

Portinglês	English	Portugese
Agriculture		
rio	rig	utensílios de ordenhar
ban(d)o	barn	edifício onde se ordenaham vacas
dixa	ditch	canal de esgoto
pampo	pump	bomba de pressão
troque	truck	camião
trela	trailer	atrelado
manjas	mangers	manjedouras
mechim/mechinho	(milking) machine	máquinha de ordenhar
fira/fida	feed	forragem
guete	gate	cancela, portão
famo	farm	fazenda
precha	pressure	pressão
clova	clover	trevo
estia	steer	bezerro
estaca	(hay) stack	meda de Fardos
belo	bail	fardo
Places		
dampo	dump	entulheira
poche	porch	varanda
draivuei	driveway	entrada para carros
tao	town	cidade, vila
goraz	garage	garagem
friuei	freeway	auto-estrada
chape	shop	oficina
raiuei*	highway	auto-estrada
canaria	cannery	fábrica de conservas
estoa	store	loja, mercado
marqueta	market	supermercado
beiqueri	bakery	padaria
cela	cellar	cave
iardo	yard	quintal
Farm Works, Verbs		
pampar	to pump	bombear
clampar	to clamp	aplicar o *clamp*
fencar/afencar	to fence	vedar
firar/fidar	to feed	alimentar gado
famar	to farm	cultivar
pinchar	to pitch (hay)	atirar (erva) com forcado
Cities		
Gastimas	Gustine	
o Antero	Ontario	
Pixelim	Pixley	

Portinglês	English	Portugese
o Raneforto	Hanford	
Corca	Corcoran	
Becasfile	Bakersfield	
Tepetim	Tipton	
Limoa	Lemoore	
Poravile	Porterville	

Groceries

crocarias	groceries	artigos de mercearia
beica	bacon	toucinho
esteique	beef (steak)	bife
romborga/ramboia	hamburger	sanduiche feita de bife de carne picada
jelo	jello	gelatina
cachopa	ketchup	tomatada
panequeques	pancakes	panqueca
reme	ham	presunto
açucrim/açucrinho	ice cream	gelado
bia	beer	cerveja
(e)stu	stew	carne guisada
clames	clams	ameijoas
abalonia	abalone	marisco do pacifico
vanela	vanilla	baunilha
candinhos	candy	bombons
coca	cookie	bolacha
juice	juice	sumo
paio	pie	torta, pastel de
carretes	carrots	cenoura
aice	ice	gelo

Furniture, Etc.

fenicha	furniture	mobilia/moveis
frijoeira	refrigerator	frigorifico
frisa	freezer	congelador
televeija	television	televisão, televisor
tosta	toaster	torradeira eléctrica
sinque	sink	bacia, lavadouro
rira	heater	aquecedor
cula	cooler	refrigerador, ventilador
arcandeixa	air conditioner	ar condicionado
banco	piggy bank	mealheiro
copo	cup	chavena
saparreira	separator	separador
vaquinclina	vacuum cleaner	aspirador
draia	dryer	secador
estero	stereo	giradiscos
clauseta	closet	guarda-roupa
recapleia	record player	tocadiscos
lipesteque	lipstick	baton
mechas	matches	fosforos

Cars, Etc.

mechim/mechinho	"machine," motorcar	carro
estara	starter	motor de arranque
papelotes	spark plugs	velas
pontas	points	plátinos
radieira	radiator	radiador
taias	tires	pneus
breique	brake	travão
trasmexa	transmission	transmissão
draivar/raivar	to drive	guiar, conduzir
fazer o estar(e)	to start (car)	por o motor em marcha
parcar	to park	estacionar

Portinglês	English	Portugese
baquear	to back up	fazer marcha atrás
gricar	to grease	lubrificar
grisse	grease	graxa
gaceteixa	gas station	posto de gasolina

Clothing, Etc.

sute	suit	fato
zepa	zipper	fecho éclair
slepas	slippers	chinelas
saize	size	tamanho, nümero

Relationships

rasbelo	husband	marido
cesta	sister	irmã
boifrende	boyfriend	namorado

Nationalities, Professions, Etc.

airixo	Irish (man)	irlandês
chinos	Chinese	chineses
xarefa	sheriff	policia
meia	mayor	presidente de câmara municipal
senara	senator	senador
anateca	undertaker	agente funerario
nilca	milker	ordenhador
plama	plumber	canalizador
bossa	boss	patrão
faleira	forelady	mulher capataz
folemano	foreman	capataz
maneija	manager	gerente
caraprata/cara de prata	chiropractor	quiroprático

Common Verbs

aplicar	to apply	requerer
jampar	to jump	saltar
registar	to register	matricular
considerar	to consider	crer/pensar

Miscellany

lanimoa, moa	(lawn)mower	cortador de relva
basqueta	basket	cesto
boquexe	box/mailbox	caixote/caixa postal
pasqueta	pocket	algibeira
trasquin	trash can	lata do lixo
saiuoque	sidewalk	passeio/ladril
olber	wheel barrow	carrinho de mão
garas	gutter	algeroz/goteira
scrudraiva	screwdriver	chave de fendas
acaunte	account	conta
incameteques	income tax	impostos
fogue	fog	nevoeiro
sno	snow	neve
testo	test (exam)	exame
junque/janque	junk	lixo, coisas sem valor
treche	trash	lixo

Different Expressions

perigude	pretty good	muito bem
aranon	I don't know	não sei
patetame	part-time	emprego parcial
tanquiu	thank you	obrigado
annauei	anyway	de todos modos
samepleisse	some place	em qualquer parte
perisune	pretty soon	dentro de pouco
tarreque	hell, to hell	com os diabos
tofe	tough	duro, rijo
rofe	rough	áspero, grosseiro

Portinglês	English	Portugese
samebari	somebody	alguém, pessoa importante
taia	tired	cansado
o boi	oh boy	ora essa
tru	through	através
o sim	oh, yes	sim
aiesse	I guess	penso que sim
oceleira	I see you later	até logo
ser suposto	to be supposed to	ter que

*Luso-American words like *raiuei* (highway), *romborga/ramboia* (hamburger), *retie* (ham), *rira* (heater), and *rasbelo* (husband) take the consonant "R" instead of "H" because the latter's pronunciation does not exist in Portuguese.
SOURCE: Francisco Cota Fagundes, in *First Symposium on the Portuguese Presence in California,* ed. Donald O. Warrin (Los Angeles: U.P.E.C. Cultural Center, 1974).

NOTES

1. Onésimo T. Almeida, ed., *José Rodrigues Miguéis: Lisbon in Manhattan* (Providence: Gavéa-Brown, 1984), 17.

2. He graduated from the University of Lisbon Law School in 1924 and went on a scholarship to the University of Brussels to study education in 1933.

3. Na América tudo seria diferente. Não havia de facto classes superiores fechadas. . . . Falta a boémia de Scott. F. Scott Fitzgerald, *O grande Gatsby*, trans. J. R. Miguéis (Lisbon, Editorial Presença, 1960), 16, my translation.

4. Ibid., 16.

5. Ibid.

6. J. R. Miguéis, *Steerage* (Providence: Gávea-Brown, 1983), 156.

7. Ibid.

8. Eduardo Mayone Dias, *Coisas da LUSAlândia* (Los Angeles, Instituto Português de ensino à distância, 1981).

9. Ibid., 117.

10. Albert C. Baugh, *A History of English Language* (London: Routledge & Kegan, 1959), 363.

11. É uma assimilação fonética e semántica do inglês *refrigerator*; o mesmo se aplica a 'frisa' do inglês *freezer*. Portanto, o que o imigrante fez foi assimilar o significado e o valor fonético da palavra inglesa, tal ele o percebeu, adaptando-la à fonologia portuguesa. Francisco Cota Fagundes, in Donald O. Warrin, ed., *First Symposium on the Portuguese Presence in California* (San Leandro, Calif.: U.P.E.C. Cultural Center, 1974), 8, my translation.

12. Ibid., 16.

13. Dir-se-ia que perdeu a língua materna, e ainda não descubriu a madrasta. J. R. Miguéis, *Gente da Terceira Classe* (Lisbon: Editorial Estúdios Cor, 1971), 14, my translation.

14. Como se a terra da Fortuna fosse apenas a Meca dos esfomeados. Ibid.

15. Como os galegos da minha Lisboa velha, que me habituei julgar dóceis, risonhos e bem dispostos. O Novo Mundo azedou-os e envelheceu-os. Ibid., 18.

16. Miguéis, *Steerage,* 166.

17. E nada ganharam dos valores espirituais que a América tem para oferecer-lhes. Por quanto mais tempo é que os simples e os privados continuarão a confundir cultura com os valores puramente materiais, de aquisição? Quando aprenderão eles que, sem o espírito, sem os princípios, tudo o mais é caos? Na sua idolatria das Coisas . . . permanecem retrógrados e de espírito tacanho. Miguéis, *Gente da terceira classe,* 28.

18. "Pega lá, que estas são da nossa terra." Talvez por isso ninguém aceite o que ela oferece. Ibid., 30.

19. J. R. Miguéis, "Como se ama na América" (How you love in America), in *É proibido apontar* (It is forbidden to point) (Lisbon: Editorial Estúdios Cor, 1964), vol. 1, 175–197.

20. J. R. Miguéis, "O anel de contrabando" (The contraband ring), in *Gente da terceira classe*, 121–135.

21. Ibid., 135, my translation.

22. J. R. Miguéis, "O 'crime perfeito' " (The "perfect crime"), in *Gente da terceira classe*, 139–60.

23. J. R. Miguéis, "Há sempre um bei em Tunes," in *É Proibido Apontar*, vol. 1, 155–174.

24. Ibid., 155.

25. E naturalmente tínhamos guerras deliciosas porque, entre a cultura portuguesa e a cultura norte-americana há um *gap* tão grande que uma simples palavra deitava chispas. Eu lembro-me de ter usado acerca duma pessoa a palavra aggressivo e *aggressive*, em inglês, não é 'agressivo' em português: Eu topava continuamente con essas expressões. . . . Quando eu estava com pessoas portuguesas, a minha conduta era chocante. Eu apanhei pontapés debaixo da mesa . . . não é verdade? por fazer perguntas indiscretas. Mas não eram indiscretas nos Estados Unidos. E tudo isso naturalmente tornou a vida muito interessante, mas um tanto trabalhosa. Mário Henriques, "José Rodrigues Miguéis, primeiro prémio 'Camilo,' " *Diário popular, quinta feira à tarde* (literary supplement), July 2, 1959, 194. "

26. John A. Kerr, *Miguéis — to the Seventh Decade* (University, Miss.: Romance Monographs, 1977).

Chapter Nineteen

Not "On the Backs of Blacks"

U.S.-American (Im)Migration and Jewish Diaspora in the German-Language Writings of Jeannette Lander

Heike Paul

U.S.-American immigrant writing looks back on a distinct, long-standing literary and popular tradition, and boasts an ever-growing and expanding literary canon, as well as a history of critical engagement and revision. A revision of a particular kind has been suggested by critic Dorothy Burton Skårdal, who has opted for an extension of the American literary canon of immigrant writing to include the literature of and about American immigration written in languages other than English.[1] Questioning the "most fundamental assumption" that American literature is—by definition—written in English, she offers the example of Scandinavian-American writing in Norwegian, Swedish, and Danish to show that "American literature is in fact . . . multi-lingual."[2]

Following Skårdal's call for an investigation of non-English immigrant narratives of diverse linguistic backgrounds, I take a closer look at the German-language writings of Jeannette Lander. In doing so, my agenda is threefold. First, I agree with Skårdal that the inclusion of non-Anglophone texts in the American canon of immigrant writing is desirable, as well as enlightening. Based on this premise, my aim is to show, second, how Lander's writings contrast with certain assumptions about American immigrant writing, its rhetoric and topicality, and how they contest particular paradigms of race and representation. Border crossing in Lander's case ceases to be linked merely to the physical movement of (im)migration; it is linguistic, stylistic, and thematic. Thus, third, a closer look at Lander's texts evidences how, in turn, Lander unfolds her own "immigritude":[3] a unique immigrant scenario in terms of setting, language, structure, and style.

The Presence of "Race Talk" and/or the Absence of African-Americans as an Immigrant Paradigm

" '[I]mmigration' focuses on the process of traversing space and leads to rather awkwardly forced discussions of people who came as slaves or who were on the American continent before 'America.' "[4] This observation by Werner Sollors positions immigration as one way of phrasing and capturing American ethnicity in a potentially conflicting relation to other U.S.-American narratives of national genesis, such as the Middle Passage or the history of colonial dispossession. These "awkwardly forced discussions" reflecting the arising discomfort of the various "national" experiences pitted against one another are mirrored in many literary and cultural U.S.-American productions and, as such, are taken up by writer and critic Toni Morrison. Focusing on the—to her—particularly problematic relationship between immigrants and African Americans, she observes a detrimental dynamic whose rhetoric works in favor of immigrants and at the expense of African Americans.[5] In her essay "On the Backs of Blacks," she takes up this conflict as a paradigmatically "American" one and offers a compelling analysis of how the immigrant is portrayed and how he or she functions in the national imagination and rhetoric of American (popular) culture. Morrison sees the immigrant and his or her success vis-à-vis an "Africanist presence"; while the immigrant emerges "on the backs of blacks," African Americans suffer their literal and metaphorical erasure in the American immigrant imagination.[6] She states that "it is the act of racial contempt that transforms [the immigrant] into an entitled white."[7] The "race talk" at work in the American plotting of the immigrant experience is

> the explicit insertion into everyday life of racial signs and symbols that have no meaning other than pressing African Americans to the lowest level of the racial hierarchy. Popular culture, shaped by film, theater, advertising, the press, televison, and literature, is heavily engaged in race talk. . . . Whatever the lived experience of immigrants with African Americans—pleasant, beneficial, or bruising—the rhetorical experience renders blacks as noncitizens, already discredited outlaws.[8]

Consequently, "race talk" figures as "the organizing principle of becoming an American. Star-spangled. Race-strangled."[9] Among Morrison's examples to demonstrate the workings of "race talk" is Elia Kazan's film *America, America*, in the ending of which she sees the characteristic figure of the "scorned black" epitomized: "Fresh from Ellis Island, Stavros gets a job shining shoes at Grand Central Terminal. . . . Quickly, but as casually as an afterthought, a young black man, also a shoe shiner, enters and tries to solicit a customer. He is run off the screen—'Get out of here! We're doing business here!'—and silently disappears."[10]

In addition to Morrison's diagnosis of the racialized rhetoric of immigration, there seems to be a second, alternative paradigm, which can be captured as one of "literary segregation": whereas in some instances, immigrant rhetoric displays the racial antagonism of "race talk," in other instances, the immigrant imagination is confined to dealing with and writing about ethnic groups of immigrants, while the ethnic group of the native-born black population is virtually absent from the various scenarios of immigrant fiction. Although this segregation in immigrant literature may be claimed to be in accordance with actual urban living conditions, it is no less striking, both as a supposedly "lived experience" and as literary topos.[11]

It is exactly these paradigms of "race talk," a dubious "Africanist presence," or a no less dubious "Africanist absence," a literary immigrant experience written on the backs of or in the absence of blacks, that I would like to contest with regard to

Lander's plotting of the American immigrant experience in German. Writing in German, Lander does not partake in certain conventions and traditions of American immigrant writing, while at the same time contributing quite successfully to the process of revising this realm of American literature. In contrast to Morrison's observation, Lander's writing offers a way for productively engaging the immigrant's experiences and realities with those of African-Americans in the United States.

Introducing Jeannette Lander

In introducing the writer Jeannette Lander, it seems legitimate to say that in many ways her writings are as unique as the neglect that has befallen them. Born in 1931 in New York City, the daughter of Polish-Jewish immigrants, Lander spends most of her childhood and adolescence not in New York but in the black quarter of Atlanta, where her father runs a grocery store. At age twenty-eight Lander leaves the United States to attend the Free University of Berlin in Germany, where she receives her doctorate in 1966. Berlin is also her current place of residency.[12]

Apart from various publications in the field of literary criticism, television scripts, and poetry, Lander has written a number of novels, three of which I would like to mention here: *Ein Sommer in der Woche der Itke K.*,[13] which I discuss below in greater detail, is—in my view—a fascinating and, at the same time, rather untypical (i.e., un-American) tale of immigration. Its treatment of race matters transcends and transforms some of the boundaries of the field of American immigrant writing that I have outlined above. Being both immigrant *and* emigrant, Lander brings a rather exceptional perspective to the American immigrant experience. *Auf dem Boden der Fremde*[14] and *Die Töchter*,[15] which I refer to briefly, can be viewed as sequels to *Ein Sommer*; in these two texts the national framework of immigration is superseded by a rather international context of diaspora: issues of racism and historical trauma are addressed beyond a particular national rhetoric and beyond a particular ethnic group.

All three books are written in German and have not been translated into any other language. All of them have been out of print for years. *Die Töchter* has only recently been republished in a German paperback version.[16]

Jeannette Lander's Immigrant Writing: "Race Talk" and the "Africanist Presence" Revisited

Ein Sommer in der Woche der Itke K.—somewhat reminiscent of Lander's own biography—narrates half a year (the summer of 1942) in the life of the adolescent Itke, who lives with her immigrant parents among the black community in Atlanta.[17] The novel opens with a characterization of the protagonist, Itke Kovsky:

Itke.

Nappy-haired, dark-eyed Itke lives in a ring in a ring in a ring. The innermost is Yiddish. The middle, black American. The outermost is whiteprotestantamerican in the Deep South.

Itke-I. In her fourteenth summer. Deep Southern summers start in May.

Lives in her apartment, the Yiddish apartment, above the grocery and the general store, the "Krom" store for a black clientele in the black quarter in the ever larger, faster, better growing city of Atlanta where an exception is made for the white grocer so that he can live in the apartment adjoining his store in the black quarter.

Doesn't live among her own. Itke, with long dark locks combed and arranged morning after morning by European motherhands (Oi ayoi, a yiddische Mammenui), goes to school with natives, 150% blond from the inside out for generations in the Deep South. Itke with Rebecca-eyes, Rebecca and Ruth, morning after morning, by black hands the cornbread muffins baked, in mama Kovsky's kosher kitchen chewed, in the sheetwhite school digested, in the outermost ring. Not among her own.[18]

In the course of the narrative, we witness Itke's coming of age in this particular summer, which involves rebelling against her parents, Max and Hannah Kovsky, and their Jewishness—Itke longs for participation in the (black) street culture, which is more appealing to her than the meetings of the Jewish "*Arbeiterring*." We witness her first sexual encounter with her cousin Sonny and a loss of innocence with regard to racism and the violence it triggers within Itke's urban geography.

Although Itke certainly figures as the main character of the book, the focus of the narrative is not only on one immigrant protagonist but also on the community Itke is part of. This concern is manifested in the narrative voice, which at times is identical with Itke's, and at other times is an observing third-person-singular narrator. Rather unique, the setting conditions a certain cast of characters. Apart from Itke and her family (parents and two sisters; the latter are hardly ever mentioned) and Sonny, the cousin visiting from New York City, the narrative presents only black characters; this constellation is extremely untypical of an immigrant narrative, where black characters often appear in the way described by Toni Morrison or do not appear at all.[19]

The individual black characters are introduced in detail and appear as highly individuated; thus, they do not figure as negative stereotypes or functionalized "Africanist presences" in Morrison's sense but rather as full-fledged characters. There is Biggs-Mamma, who is known as a conjure woman practicing obeah, and who—among other things—heals the clubfeet of babies, cures the whooping cough of children and mumps, and spirits away infected mosquito bites but is mainly in demand for her love potions.[20] We meet Beatrice, who is "twenty-five years old and had nine children with nine different last names and lived in a decaying hut with the one whose turn it was as long as it was his turn, didn't let any other in, and if he went to another, she locked the door for him."[21] Then there is Ty Jones, a womanizer and petty criminal, who seems continuously on the verge of being arrested; he voices strong opinions on questions of race and politics, which he discusses with Max Kovsky. The same can be said for Brother Wilson, who joins the military to fight in World War II, and sees segregation and racism at work in the institution that supposedly fights "against the German racism a holy war in the name of human rights."[22] Tessie, another neighbor of the Kovsky family, sells moonshine liquor and is married to George, an alcoholic who frequently falls prey to police racism and is arrested for "loitering." Then there is Jimmie Lee, admired by Itke for her looks and her daring, who loses her factory job to a white person, and Luther, who barbecues pork chops of an unmistakable flavor on the streets on Saturday evenings.

They all come to Kovsky's store to buy their groceries, to hang out and chat, to catch up with the news of the community. The lively, vibrant, playfully antagonistic but overall harmonious atmosphere in the store is characteristic of this "community-in-difference."[23] Running the store is Itke's father, an enthusiastic immigrant, helpful and respectful of his customers and generally accepted and appreciated. However, this apparent racial harmony is overshadowed, among other things, by the known fact that Kovsky's predecessor, Mr. Jägel, was killed by a "black thief"(16). Kovsky does not heed the warnings that caution him to carry a weapon in his store and makes a point out of not having one. He sees class, not race or religion, as the reason for violence in his neighborhood: "Kovsky am I and not a Jägel. A Jägel has had houses. Tessie's house and Mrs. Stevens' house und Biggs-Mamma's and Mr. Biggs' house, too. . . . But I am Max Kovsky and don't have no property. I pay my rent like the Blacks, my customers. They won't shoot at a Kovsky."[24]

Yet, while Kovsky is right about not being killed, the black quarter is indeed a site of conflict and of violence—in more than one way. The description of Tessie's rape by her husband George early in the narrative only anticipates more violence to come.

While narrating incidents of racism and violence that happen in the ghetto, the stories told by the individual characters also reach back to recapture the racism and the racially motivated violence of the past; both, the black and the Jewish history, seem fraught with those instances: lynchings by the Ku Klux Klan, police brutality, the flight from Poland. The narrative abounds with stories of violent encounters. Lander depicts the two ethnic groups as related and as having common ground in their mutual oppression, while also paying respect to their distinctions. The narrative marks the privilege the Jewish family enjoys through their ownership of the grocery store. The racism the African-American community is subjected to is depicted against the backdrop of the Holocaust happening in Europe. Cynically, the radio show that broadcasts the news of Joe Louis's being once again the boxing champion—the black community is cheering—is followed by a news broadcast to which only the Kovskys seem to listen in silence: "Reliable sources report that Hitler and his followers are solving the 'Jewish question' through persecution! through annihilation! Only the most rapid intervention by American bombers."[25]

It is a major characteristic of Lander's text that the characters reflect on the nature of racism and prejudice in dialogues (or "polylogues," as Adelson calls them),[26] lively debates, and private musings. It is not the reader who has to invest the narrative with these racial connotations; the individual characters self-consciously comment on and talk about the political implications of their situation. The result is a very different kind of "race talk" than the one analyzed by Morrison. In one of their numerous conversations, Ty Jones and Max Kovsky reflect on the presence of African-Americans and Jewish immigrants in the United States or, more precisely, on the urban ghetto of Atlanta—and how they got there: Kovsky: " 'Black people don't immigrate to America.' "—Ty Jones: " 'That's a goddam fact. And they know why!' ";[27] while, interestingly, Kovsky renders his own immigration almost in form of a Middle Passage: "On the huge ocean I've been for seven weeks, where I lay in the bottom of the ship deep down in the belly of the ship in the belly of the ocean with sixty-three men."[28]

The ethnic identities along the lines of "black" and "white" are confused still further in another instance. Talking about a fellow ghetto resident, Ty Jones reveals information that he believes to be common knowledge, stating: " 'Every Negro who is black knows that.' " Kovsky replies: " 'See, Ty, therefore I don't know it because I am a Negro who is white.' "[29] A number of interesting aspects are disclosed in this exchange. First, instead of presenting a racial signifier, "Negro" is used here to connote a specific cultural, marginal positionality within Atlanta's urban geography in particular and within American society in general—of both the African-American and the Jew. Second, Ty Jones's way of talking in this paragraph as well as throughout the novel can be characterized as a form of "signifyin(g),"[30] in which Kovsky's response seems to join in; curiously, the "common language" between the two men appears to be the black vernacular rendered in German. Third, Kovsky's own precarious situation is exposed. While he—as a white man—is in a position to act as a mediator between the black and white community in favor of his African-American customers (which he does to get George released from jail or to secure medical treatment for Blue, Beatrice's little daughter), he is nonetheless vulnerable both to white society and to the African-Americans whose rage he cannot escape. The novel culminates in a confrontation between the white police (who previously have killed Blue) and the community. In an atmosphere of violence and chaos, some members of the community turn against Itke's father and break into his store, tearing down the place. He is left with his shelves full of more or less damaged articles, with an injunction that his store is to remain closed for two weeks, and with knowing the black community cannot buy food anywhere else but from him. The novel's ending sees Kovsky pedaling through the streets, giving away the remaining goods that he is not allowed to sell.[31]

Lander's Languages of America

One of the most interesting features of the novel is certainly its language. Faced with the problem of dealing with as many as five languages or language varieties simultaneously and rendering these languages in intelligible German without losing the sense of difference, Lander expressively and skillfully achieves a linguistic blend and a genuine linguistic hybridity. Sentences are composed in Standard English, African-American Vernacular, German, Yiddish, and Hebrew. The narrative is heavily textured and includes proverbs, songs, poems, and prayers in all the different languages.[32] The result is "fantastic neologisms," a language "tailored to this very unique world."[33] The texture also includes several optical arrangements, such as frequent capitalization of words to emphasize their linguistic 'otherness.' Lander's strategy of writing separate words as one, for example, "Itkewhitejewish," "Littleblackgirleyes," "Sixdaystheweekshop,"[34] seems to re-create and incorporate the flow and rhythm of the English language into a usually more abrupt-sounding German text, effecting a particular intonation and a defamiliarization that reminds the reading audience, time and time again, of the linguistic differences.

The reader is challenged to keep track of the variety of languages spoken as the characters engage in code-switching and multilingualism. Not only the author is constantly "translating," so are the characters and so is the audience. It becomes apparent that at least linguistically there can be no segregation: not only is the language of the Jewish family infused with English words and structures, standard and black; the black community also has a command of the Yiddish and Hebrew phrases used by Kovsky. This is evident, for example, in a scene where Kovsky titles Tessie's husband as "Beheeme": "Oh, but Tessie has heard it. . . . She knows all the Hebrew words, with which Tatte daily feeds the store, the backyard, the street and the telephone."[35]

And Sonny, the visitor from New York City, is revealed as linguistic outsider in this blend and mixture of cultures and languages, of which he lacks understanding: "Stands in the fridaystore and pretends he helps. Doesn't understand one thing about how the blacks pronounce the words. Even when they point at the onions, while saying "onjens," he gives them oranges."[36]

Thus, the linguistic competence of this community is socially and culturally conditioned, and one of performance and interaction. On every level, Lander's effort seems to lie in the entangling of the characters, cultures, and languages. Rather than segregation, Lander's novel advocates interaction; rather than some sort of linguistic purity, she stages a constant "bastardization" or "mongrelization" of languages.

Part of this communal linguistic practice is also a metalinguistic commenting on the languages that are used. In a "rap on language," Ty Jones and Max Kovsky discuss Kovsky's inability to properly pronounce the English "th" (instead of thumbtacks he talks about "tumtacks") and the inability of the African-American customers to properly pronounce Kovsky's name (" 'How long do you come here into my store saying "Kovky", huh? My name is "Kovsky"! "Sk". One time I will teach you Polish!' ").[37] Itke critically describes her father's language as a "Yiddischenglisch," which fuses both languages to varying degrees: " 'Kimm arein, es is busy, Itke.' "(14); " 'Kim aher un schreib mir a Letter.' "(91). As an ironic consequence, the glossary of Yiddish words that can be found in the novel's appendix is of only limited usefulness for a German-speaking readership because it does not contain all the English or anglizized Yiddish words Kovsky uses.

*

As I have mentioned, Lander has—due to her choice of German as literary language and her publication in Germany—been received as a German writer. Leslie Adelson places Lander's writings in the context of postwar German women's writing and against the historical backdrop of the Holocaust. In her analysis, Lander's representation of Jewish and African-American relations displaces and disrupts the binary opposition of Jews and Germans in postwar Jewish-German literature.[38] Yet, referring to Lander as a German writer equates language with (adopted) nationality, an assumption, as in the case of American literature, I am hesitant to make. On the contrary, in a more dynamic framework of "nation and narration,"[39] the question of language, that is, in which language to write, seems to constitute not only a question posed to every immigrant, emigrant or exile, but also a question that— with regard to an international and multilingual diaspora—is a specifically Jewish one. Well-versed in several languages, yet also often detached from the national scenarios that accompany them, the Jewish writer is forced to choose a tongue in which to be creative. A nonliterary example attests to this: the memoirs of Ingrid Warburg Spinelli, a member of the Jewish Warburg family who during World War II finds exile in the United States, are prefaced by a text that describes the question of finding a language in which to write and to remember her life as "central" and as "crucially tied to the unsteady life of the author itself."[40] Not being able to write a multilingual autobiography, it seems, Warburg chooses German.

Lander also chooses German, yet, as a writer of fiction, she experiments with this language in a way that subverts her "choice." As I have pointed out, it is the multilingual and hybrid quality of the narratives that give Lander's German its distinct flavor.[41] In her expressive, experimental adaptation, Lander, one could argue, refrains from using the "German of the Germans"; instead she uses a language that is, literally or figuratively, the German of (American and Jewish) immigrants and exiles—positively and productively impure, disjointed, and adulterated.

Lander's Staging of Ethnicity

As has become obvious, much of Lander's narrative is organized in dialogue; its storytelling mode and multivoicedness are at times reminiscent of African-American women's writing.[42] Its portrayal of racial tension in an urban setting resembles Spike Lee's dramatizing and choreographing of racial conflict in *Do the Right Thing* (1989).[43] As a literary version of a somewhat similar constellation set and written in earlier decades, Lander's writing achieves this filmic or even theatrical quality by presenting the narrative not in a realist fashion but, at least partly, in the form of a play. The dramatic aspect of the text lies in a theatrical staging of the plot, as well as in a metaphoricity of musical performance, which also relates to the overall textual structure. At the same time, Lander's concern—to portray the community as one intermingled entity rather than as internally segregated—is reflected in this formal structure, which Lander in her preface daringly describes as a truly syncretistic blend, a hybrid form deriving from two different but in the author's view analogous sources of folklore. First, Lander draws on the "black folklore" later copied by whites in the form of black-face minstrelsy;[44] second, she models her book on a Yiddish play, *The Dybbuk*.[45] Dramatizing her narrative along those lines includes stage directions prior to every chapter that present a summary of every scene. Chapter 1, for example, is headed

> Minstrel Show, in which Itke describes the rings of her environment in order to find out about their boundaries.
>   1. SCENE: *Itke sings the song of a Rebecca-eyed woman among the clarinette voices of the Blacks.*
>   2. SCENE: *Father and mother play the melody of otherness with keys and windowshades.*[46]

After four chapters described as minstrel shows and four chapters presented as remodeled scenes from *The Dybbuk*, chapter 9 announces the coalescence of both: "At the same time a scene from the Dybbuk and a Minstrel Show, in which Itke and the Blacks both break out at the same time."[47]

Through this enactment of black and Jewish folklore, Lander manages not only to fuse culturally distinct art forms but also—in a nonhierarchical way—to alternately address an individual as well as a collective level of cultural and racial conflict. The narrative of Itke's coming-of-age, her increased alienation from her Jewish familial background, is paralleled by a development within the African-American community, which depicts the characters, socially marginalized and alienated through the racism they encounter, as increasingly prone to violent reactions. Both strive for means and strategies of self-assertion and for articulating resistance: Itke rebels against her parents, their Jewish orthodoxy and morality, and the African-American community turns against the white police who patrol the ghetto and abuse its inhabitants.

Further, Lander evokes minstrelsy for the same reason she calls upon the Dybbuk: to establish transnational references that reach beyond the American South and point to some sort of non-American, "nonwhite" cultural and spiritual resources rooted in folklore. Thus, minstrelsy, in Lander's understanding, points to Africa, whereas the Dybbuk refers to (Eastern) Europe. This transnational, or perhaps diasporic, quality that is alluded to here will be of increasing importance in her succeeding novels, which I mention briefly in the next section.

The invocation of minstrelsy, at the same time, signals Lander's concern with her own authorship. Writing about the African-American community in Atlanta, she, too, becomes a minstrel, a linguistic minstrel, who speaks for an "other," an ethnic group not her own.[48] Her staging of ethnicity as minstrel shows and scenes from *The Dybbuk*, thus, again results in a syncretistic and denaturalized view on ethnicity: Lander's textual ethnicity is a matter of performance and performing—theatrically, dialogically, musically.

In summary, linking Lander's text once more to Toni Morrison's argument, I believe that the author is indeed interested in the "pleasant, beneficial, or bruising . . . lived experience of immigrants with African-Americans"[49] rather than in a literal or metaphorical erasure of African-Americans as the ethnic other. The ethnic other of both groups is the white southern patriarchy, which figures mainly as a removed but powerful variable that is manifested in the few consequential appearances of the police, rendering both, the Jewish immigrants and the African-American community, helpless and powerless.

From Migration to Diaspora

In the novels *Auf dem Boden der Fremde* and *Die Töchter,* which also appear to be somewhat autobiographic, and together with *Ein Sommer in der Woche der Itke K.* form a loose trilogy, Lander expands her literary geography. Her treatment of intercultural coexistence in the aftermath of World War II and the Holocaust points to the ubiquity of racism and prejudice—between Germans and Jews, Jews and Palestinians, Jews and African Americans.

Auf dem Boden der Fremde narrates the coming to terms of the protagonist Yvonne with her life as an American Jew married to a German (formerly a soldier of the Third Reich) living in postwar Germany. During a fight, her husband vents his anger by using a racial, anti-Semitic slur against her. Yvonne leaves him and their rapidly deteriorating relationship and returns to her family in the United States. Among her Jewish family members she is confronted with the classic question "How can a Jew live in Germany?" Yet in turn, Yvonne observes that her family, while having moved socially and economically upward, has "lost [its] integrity by denying [its] history."[50] She is disillusioned by the racism she perceives directed toward another minority group, African Americans. The ending of the novel sees her returning to Berlin, however, seemingly detached from both family *and* husband.

Die Töchter is a truly diasporic novel and describes the reunion of three Jewish sisters, who, having settled down in postwar Germany, the United States, and Israel respectively, meet in Warsaw, Poland, to look for their father's grave. All three of them, Julie, Minouche, and Hélène, still live in environments characterized by racism, hatred, and exclusion. Julie lives in the anti-Semitic Berlin; Hélène, in the atmosphere of anti-Arab racial paranoia in Israel; and Minouche, again, is confronted with the racial, segregation and stigmatization of black and white. The narrative negotiates between the different national, racial and familial settings; the conversations and conflicts among the sisters in Warsaw range around the question of how to live and cope with the past. In reaction to Hélène, who defends family and nation as the pillars of life and, more specifically, of her own life in Israel, Julie responds "But you can't form a cocoon there! . . . There is world."[51]

Diaspora in Lander's writings does not figure as a conservative idea that is enacted to prevent change and to preserve a traditional, exclusive, and essential ethnic identity. Quite the contrary, it is seen as a way of communicating and empathizing across ethnic and national boundaries. In that sense, Lander's migrating women protagonists can be aptly captured as—in Caren Kaplan's words—"transnational feminist subjects."[52] This transnationality manifests itself in Lander's choice of literary topic and in the linguistic syncretisms she creates while writing in German. Thus, Lander's writing is beyond the classic tradition of American immigrant writing in a twofold sense. First, in a very banal way, simply because of the language she uses—because she writes in German, she has had no critical reception as an American writer at all. Second, as I have shown, because she interferes with assumptions about what is commonly referred to as American immigrant literature.

To close the circle, I would like to come back to Toni Morrison, this time as writer and not as critic. Paul Gilroy places Morrison's novel *Beloved* (1987) among the body of works that he sees as constituitive of the "black Atlantic," texts "belong[ing] . . . to the web of [black] diaspora identities and concerns" and "operat[ing] at other levels than those marked by national boundaries."[53] Writing about black historical experiences—experiences that *Beloved*, for instance, vividly commemorates—and about Jewish history, Gilroy cautiously suggests a potential link: not denying the uniqueness of either ethnic history, he contemplates the possibility—"without lapsing into a relativising mode"[54]—of "discuss[ing] these histories together."[55] Following Gilroy's remarks, I would like to think of Lander's writings, in particular of the novel I have discussed here in greater detail, as one example of a literary configuration of difference without racial segregation or, worst, antagonism.

NOTES

For comments on an earlier version of this essay, I am grateful to Werner Sollors, Hana Wirth-Nesher, Matthew Jacobson, Sabine Bröck, Alexandra Tischel, Johannes Fischer, and Raimund Schieß.

1. Dorothy Burton Skårdal, "Revising the American Literary Canon: The Case of Immigrant Literature," in *American Studies in Transition*, ed. David E. Nye (Odense: Odense University Press, 1985), 97–119.

2. Ibid., 97–98.

3. I have borrowed this term from Rosemary M. George, "Traveling Light: Of Immigration, Invisible Suitcases, and Gunny Sacks," *Differences* 4.2 (1992): 72–99.

4. Werner Sollors, *Beyond Ethnicity: Consent and Descent in American Culture* (New York: Oxford University Press, 1986), 39.

5. Following Morrison's argument and focusing on urban-based (not rural-based) immigrant literature, I will not be concerned with Native American presences in American immigrant literature, although this topic certainly warrants further research.

6. Toni Morrison, "On the Backs of Blacks," appeared originally in a special issue of *Time* in the fall of 1993 and is reprinted in *Arguing Immigration*, ed. Nicolaus Mills (New York: Simon & Schuster, 1994), 97–100. Morrison coins the phrase "Africanist presence" in *Playing in the Dark: Whiteness and the Literary Imagination* (Cambridge: Harvard University Press, 1992; rpt. London: Picador, 1993). The present argument with regard to the problematic relationship between African Americans and immigrants is voiced by Morrison for the first time in the interview "The Pain of Being Black," in which she supports her observations with her own personal experience when growing up in a community of blacks and immigrants in small-town Ohio. The interview, also originally published in *Time*, is reprinted in *Conversations with Toni Morrison*, ed. Danille Taylor-Guthrie (Jackson: University Press of Mississippi, 1994), 255–261.

7. Morrison, "On the Backs of Blacks," 97.

8. Ibid., 97–98.

9. Ibid., 100.

10. Ibid., 97. With regard to American film, immigration has functioned "on the backs of blacks" also in quite a different way. As Michael Rogin points out, early in the century accompanying and solidifying the "birth of Hollywood," millions and millions of immigrant newcomers were in fact assimilated into the racism of the American mainstream "on the backs of blacks" as viewers and mass audiences for *The Birth of a Nation* (1915): "Griffith used blacks not to restore plantation patriarchy but to give birth to a new nation. The immigrants absent from his screen were present in his audience, as *Birth* used black/white conflict to Americanize them." Michael Rogin, "Blackface, White Noise: The Jewish Jazz Singer Finds His Voice," *Critical Inquiry* 18 (Spring 1992): 420.

11. The issue with regard to "race talk" and "literary segregation" is not to drum up an unspecified charge of racism against immigrant writing in general. Morrison herself has stated that she is not interested in an "investigation of what might be called racist or non-racist literature" (*Playing in the Dark*, 90). Rather, Morrison's structural argument and my additional remarks serve, first, as an angle from which Lander's work can be fruitfully approached in its distinctiveness and, second, as a backdrop for mapping Lander's immigrant aesthetic and her treatment of race matters.

12. I owe the biographic as well as some bibliographic information on Lander to Tobe Levin, who has met Lander in person and includes some of this biographical data in her article "No Place for Identity: Jeannette Lander's Migrating Women's Aesthetic," *International Women's Writing: New Landscapes of Identity*, ed. Anne E. Brown and Marjanne E. Goozé (Westport, Conn.: Greenwood Press, 1995), 253–263.

13. *Ein Sommer in der Woche der Itke K.* (Frankfurt/M.: Insel, 1971). All quotations from Lander's books are given in an English translation in the text and accompanied by a footnote that provides the original German version.

14. *Auf dem Boden der Fremde* (On the soil of a foreign country) (Frankfurt/M.: Insel, 1972).

15. *Die Töchter* (The daughters) (Frankfurt/M:: Insel, 1976).

16. Jeannette Lander, *Die Töchter* (Berlin: Aufbauverlag, 1996). Apart from the usual number of reviews, Lander's novels have received very little critical attention. Recently, two literary critics have taken up Lander's writing from two different angles. In her essay "There's No Place Like Home: Jeannette Lander's and Ronnith Neumann's Utopian Quest for Jewish Identity in the Contemporary West German Context" and in her book *Making Bodies, Making History: Feminism and German Identity* (1993) Leslie A. Adelson rediscovers Lander as a neglected German writer. Tobe Levin, in her essay "No Place for Identity: Jeannette Lander's Migrating Women's Aesthetic" and "The Challenge to Identity in Jeannette Lander and Fran Ross," sees her in the context of international women writing. Yet, for instance, *Women of the Word: Jewish Women and Jewish Writing* (1994) does not once mention Lander's work, although the essay collection is not limited to English-language texts and discusses Jewish (and Jewish women's) writing of many different tongues.

17. This is not to suggest that the novel is an autobiographical account of childhood memories; rather, as will become obvious, it is a carefully crafted composition that collapses the laws of mimesis. The title of the novel is already a small indication for this: *Ein Sommer* presents one long summer, from May to September, narratively condensed to a week in Itke's life.

18. Although Lander's novels have not been translated into English, both critics, Leslie Adelson and Tobe Levin, have translated individual passages from Lander's book in their

essays. In some instances, I rely on their translations; in others, I have translated the quotations myself. The English translation of the present paragraph is Tobe Levin's ("No Place for Identity," 256).

Itke.

Itke mit krausem Haar, mit dunklen Augen, lebt in einem Kreis in einem Kreis in einem Kreis. Der innerste ist jiddisch. Der mittlere ist schwarzamerikanisch. Der äußere ist weißprotestantischamerikanisch tief im Süden.

Itke-Ich. Im vierzehnten Sommer. Tiefsüdensommer beginnen im Mai.

Lebt in ihrer Wohnung, der jiddischen Wohnung, über dem Lebensmittel- und Kolonialwarenladen, dem "Kromladen" für Negerkundschaft im Negerviertel in der immer größer, schneller, besser werdenden Stadt Atlanta, wo ein weißer Lebensmittelhändler ausnahmsweise in der Wohnung wohnen darf, die an seinen Laden anschließt, auch im Negerviertel.

Lebt nicht unter ihresgleichen. Erste Generation Itke, mit langen dunklen Locken Morgen für Morgen von europäischen Mammahänden gekämmt und gelegt (Oi ayoi, a jiddische Mammeniu), geht in die Schule unter Einheimischen, hundertfünfzigprozent blond von innen her seit Generationen im tiefen Süden. Itke mit Rebekkaaugen, Rebekka und Ruth, Morgen für Morgen Maismehlbrötchen, die Negerhände backen, in Mamma Kovskys koscherer Küche kauend, in der blaßweißen Schule verdauend, im Außenkreis. Nicht unter ihresgleichen (13).

19. The setting of the novel and the narrative focus on the grocery store are reminiscent of Bernard Malamud's *The Assistant* (1957). In support of my argument on literary segregation in American immigrant writing, it can be observed that Malamud's novel introduces its readership to Jewish, Italian, German, and Norwegian immigrants but does not mention any African-American characters.

20. "Gegen Silberblick und Klumpfuß bei Säuglingen konnte Biggs-Mamma an, gegen Rachitis und Hühnerbrust und Keuchhusten der Kinder; sie konnte den Ziegenpeter abwenden, wenn er schon überall in dem Häuserblock wütete; entzündete Mückenstiche fortzaubern und gegen Rattenbisse den Bann aussprechen; den Hexenschuß herausziehen, die Zähne festigen, die Geburt beschleunigen, den Tod abhalten. Alles das war aber Nebenverdienst. Hauptsächlich war sie für die Liebe da"(24).

21. ". . . fünfundzwanzig Jahre alt und hatte neun Kinder mit neun verschiedenen Familiennamen und lebte in der verfaulten Kate mit dem, der dran war, solange er dran war, ließ keinen anderen herein, und ging er zu einer anderen, verschloß sie ihm die Tür"(32). The English translation is my own.

22. ". . . gegen den deutschen Rassismus einen heiligen Krieg im Namen der Menschenrechte . . ."(200). The English translation is my own.

23. Levin, "No Place for Identity," 257. This genuine community formed by the black population (already a community in itself) and the Kovsky family is a precarious textual construction that contains some utopian elements in its envisioning of coexisting differences.

24. "Kovsky bin ich und nicht ein Jägel. Ein Jägel hat Häuser gehabt. Tessies Haus und Mrs. Stevens Haus und auch das Haus von Biggs-Mamma und Mr. Biggs. . . . Aber ich bin Max Kovsky und hab Besitztum nicht. Ich bezahle meine Miete wie die Neger, meine Kunden. Sie werden schon nicht schießen auf ein'n Kovsky . . ." (16). The English translation is my own.

25. ". . . nunmehr zuverlässige Berichte. Hitler und seine feilen Anhänger lösen das "Judenproblem" durch Verfolgung! durch Vernichtung! Nur das schnellste Eingreifen amerikan-

ischer Bomber . . ."(65). The English translation is Tobe Levin's ("No Place for Identity," 259).

26. Adelson, "There's No Place Like Home," 117.

27. "Asoi schwarze wandern nicht ein in Amerika arein."—"Das ist ein gottverdammter Fakt. . . . Und die wissen auch warum!"(74). The English translation is my own.

28. "Auf dem großen Meer bin ich gewesen sieben Wochen lang, wo ich lag im Schiffs-boden tief unten im Schiffsbauch im Meerbauch mit dreiundsechzig Mann"(16). The English translation is my own.

29. "Das weiß hier jeder Neger, der schwarz ist." . . . "Siehste, Ty, farderfar weeß ich es ober nicht, weil ich bin a Neger, weleche ich bin weiß"(72). The English translation is my own.

30. Quoting from Geneva Smitherman's *Talkin and Testifyin: The Language of Black Americans* (Boston: Houghton Mifflin, 1977), Henry Louis Gates Jr. describes "Signifyin(g)" as a "black mode of discourse" characterized by "indirection," a "rhythmic fluency and sound" and as a "play on words," "humorous [and] ironic." See Henry Louis Gates Jr., *The Signifying Monkey: A Theory of African American Literary Criticism* (New York: Oxford University Press, 1988) 94.

31. For a more nuanced positioning of Lander's text in a U.S.-American context, it should not go unmentioned that the constellation the novel offers does not only confront African Americans and immigrants in general but also, more specifically, African Americans and Jews, i.e., Jewish immigrants. Thus, the novel also summons up a historically extremely charged relationship. The Leo Frank case of 1915 comes to mind as one key incident of heavily racialized strife involving Jews and African Americans. See Elly Bulkin, "Hard Ground: Jewish Identity, Racism and Anti-Semitism," *Yours in Struggle* (Ithaca: Firebrand, 1984), 116–117 and Adelson, *Making Bodies, Making History*, 161 n. 32. In 1955 (roughly ten years after Lander's novel is set and almost twenty years before she writes it), James Baldwin captured the state of affairs between both groups in a rather pessimistic outlook. Wrapping up his argument of mutual scapegoating, he provocatively concludes: "Georgia has the Negro and Harlem has the Jew." See James Baldwin, *Notes of a Native Son* (Boston: Beacon Press, 1955), 69–72. In Lander's novel, the geographical setting overwrites this binarism of racial hostilities: set in Georgia as well as in the black ghetto, Lander's characters have to negotiate multiple racial tensions.

32. One linguistic climax of the novel is the rendering of a black church service Itke attends with Ruth, who works in the Kovsky household (179–190).

33. Salcia Landmann. "Juden vom Negergetto" (review of *Ein Sommer in der Woche der Itke K.), St. Galler Tageblatt*, January 1, 1973. Quoted in Levin, "No Place for Identity," 255.

34. "Itkeweißjüdisch"(14), "Kleinnegermädchenaugen"(14), "Sechstagediewocheladen" (41). The English translation is my own.

35. "Oh, Tessie hat es aber gehört. . . . Sie kennt alle hebräischen Wörter, mit denen Tatte täglich den Laden, den Hintergarten, die umliegenden Bürgersteige und das Telefon speist"(30). The English translation is my own.

36. "Steht im Freitagladen und tut so, als ob er mithilft. Versteht kaum einen Ton davon, wie die Neger die Wörter aussprechen. Auch wenn sie auf die Zwiebeln deuten, während sie "onjens" sagen, gibt er ihnen Orangen"(195). The English translation is my own. Sonny is revealed as outsider to this community in a variety of ways. In a heated discussion with Brother Wilson, it is he who articulates the common racist stereotypes of white Americans about black Americans (195–204).

37. "Wie lang kimmste aher zi mir in mein Krom arein un sagst 'Kovky', hah? As ich heeß 'Kovsky'! 'Sk'. Amol werd ich dir lernen Polnisch!"(74). The English translation is my own.

38. Adelson, *Making Bodies, Making History*, 90.

39. This phrase is Homi K. Bhabha's, editor of *Nation and Narration* (London: Routledge, 1990).

40. Ingrid Warburg Spinelli, *Erinnerungen: Die Dringlichkeit des Mitleids und die Einsamkeit, nein zu sagen* (Hamburg: Dölling und Galitz, 1990), 6. Having lived in Sweden, Germany, England, the United States, and Italy, the author has command of many languages.

41. Adelson sees the linguistic alienation of a German audience as the prime reason for Lander's neglect and lack of reception when she speaks of the linguistic "shock" a German audience must have experienced (Adelson, *Making Bodies, Making History*, 122). She further connects Lander's style and language to what Gilles Deleuze and Félix Guattari have described as the "deterritorialization" of language in Franz Kafka's writing ("There's No Place Like Home," 131). While I agree that Lander's language shares some of the alienating effects that are commonly referred to as kafkaesque, I believe the intertextual link between Lander and Kafka runs deeper than that. Not only does the name of Lander's protagonist, as it appears in the title of the book (*Itke K.*), echo the abbreviations of Kafka's main characters in *Das Schloß* und *Der Prozeß*; additionally, Kafka's fragment *Amerika* presents a noteworthy displacement of racial signifiers and an "Africanist presence" certainly known to Lander. On the last pages of the text, the immigrant protagonist Karl Roßmann, upon being asked his name, takes the fictional characters and the reading audience by surprise as he replies "negro." While this "name" reverberates strongly with regard to race relations in general and with regard to those depicted in Lander's text in particular, Kafka's source of "inspiration" seems to have been the photograph of a lynching that shows the African-American victim surrounded by the four white perpetrators in Arthur Holitscher's *Amerika heute und morgen* (Berlin, 4th ed., 1912), 353. See Klaus Hermsdorf's introduction to Franz Kafka, *Das erzählerische Werk*, 2 vols. (Berlin: Rütten & Loening, 1983), 30–31.

42. I agree with Tobe Levin, who finds in Lander's depiction "scenes reminiscent of Maya Angelou or Zora Neale Hurston" (Levin, "No Place for Identity," 256).

43. Despite the obvious differences in style, theme, language, and geographical and historical locale, this comparison is not as far-fetched as it may seem. Lander and Lee both conjure a hot urban summer (1942 and 1989, respectively) as the site of "heated" race relations; both depict their characters and their actions with a deadly serious as well as a playfully humoristic edge.

44. Viewing minstrelsy, as Lander does, solely as a form of "black folklore" is certainly problematic. Scholars of minstrelsy (in particular black-face minstrelsy), e.g., Berndt Ostendorf in *Black Literature in White America* (Sussex: Harvester, 1982), and, more recently, Eric Lott in *Love and Theft* (New York: Oxford University Press, 1993), have pointed to the implications, contradictions, and ambiguities of this art form.

45. David G. Roskies describes S. Ansky's *The Dybbuk* as an "all-time favorite of the Jewish theater repertoire." He adds that the original title of the play was "Between Two Worlds." Although the reference is to two worlds different from those presented in Lander's novel, the title captures the quintessential conflict. See David G. Roskies, "Yiddish Literature," *The Schocken Guide to Jewish Books*, ed. Barry W. Holtz (New York: Schocken, 1992), 259–273.

46. "Minstrel-Schau, in der Itke die Kreise ihrer Umwelt beschreibt, um festzustellen, welche Grenzen sie haben."

1. Auftritt: Itke singt das Lied einer Rebekka-äugigen unter den Klarinettenstimmen der Neger.

2. Auftritt: Tatte und Mamma spielen die Melodie vom Anderssein auf Schlüsseln und Rollo . . ." (11). The English translation is Tobe Levin's ("No Place for Identity," 258).

47. "Gleichzeitig ein Akt des *Dibbuk* sowie eine *Minstrelschau*, in denen Itke und die Neger gleichzeitig ausbrechen"(237). The English translation is my own.

48. As Lander's preface has it, *The Dybbuk* contains a similar momentum of literally and metaphorically slipping into somebody else's skin: the Dybbuk, the ghost of a young man who has died from disappointed love, enters his beloved on the day of her wedding and has her dance the dance of madness. Ansky's play is included in the anthology *The Dybbuk and Other Writings* (New York: Schocken, 1992).

49. Morrison, "On the Backs of Blacks," 98.

50. Levin, "No Place for Identity," 262.

51. "Aber du kannst dich nicht einspinnen da!" sagt Julie. . . . "Es gibt Welt"(226). The English translation is my own.

52. Caren Kaplan, "Resisting Autobiography: Out-Law Genres and Transnational Feminist Subjects," *De/Colonizing the Subject: The Politics of Gender in Women's Autobiographies* (Minneapolis: University of Minnesota Press, 1992), 116–138. The gender aspect in Lander's work, an aspect that I have largely neglected, merits closer examination in all three of the novels mentioned in the present paper.

53. Paul Gilroy, *The Black Atlantic: Modernity and Double Consciousness* (Cambridge: Harvard University Press, 1993), 218.

54. Ibid., 213.

55. Ibid., 213.

Chapter Twenty

Choose and Lose

Doris Sommer

One response to English-only campaigns in the United States was a 1992 gubernatorial campaign in Puerto Rico that would have made "Spanish-only" the official language of the island. The Popular Democratic Party had put linguistic autonomy at the center of its program to defend Puerto Rico's "freely associated" relationship to the United States. An electoral victory should have demonstrated Puerto Ricans' pride in the home culture they love and value. But the incumbent "populares" lost that election. Pride in one language evidently didn't amount to dismissal of another. Four centuries of inquisitorial Spanish-only requirements (to "speak Christian" or never to speak), centuries of slaves who knew too much when they could conspire in other languages, may have been a caution against restrictive preferences.[1] The linguistic slash-and-burn tactics of the mainland (where bilingual jurors could be dismissed for understanding too much, and hospital orderlies fired for translating complaints and advice)[2] were sadly familiar in the history of intolerant empires. So Puerto Ricans voted wisely, as they often do when faced with either/ or decisions; they declined to choose sides by electing the opposition in a narrow vote. The prostatehood party misconstrued its victory as a de facto endorsement to finally join the Union. It felt to its members like a vote to cure a national case of double-consciousness by becoming a normal American state. But the 1993 referendum that should have confirmed a coherent identity lost by a narrow margin, again.

Puerto Rico stays afloat, culturally and otherwise, because it has been too judicious to take drastic positions. If the dependent island were to become a state, it would probably lose cultural autonomy; and if it showed enthusiasm for dependence, maybe the prospects for full incorporation would vanish. Independence would disappear either way. Less a practical option than a powerful rhetoric of self-determination, talk of independence fuels the debates about political status. Meanwhile, Puerto Rico regularly decides not to be decisive about legal definition or about language. In the case of status, resolving the debate may someday mean choosing one option and eliminating others. But languages are not chosen by the process of elimination. They can and do exist together. Would choosing Spanish or English be more effective or more interesting than managing to live with both? Or would that choice impoverish the island, culturally as well as economically?

Syncopate the State

These questions certainly sound different inside the United States. The country is not a dependent territory that asks for a hearing but an empire that hears appeals. And far beyond the Caribbean connections, its power seems boundless today, after winning the Cold War against communism and maintaining American enterprise at the core of global expansion. If there is now an international lingua franca for business and politics, it is English with an American accent. So the question of linguistic coexistence (a matter of survival in Puerto Rico) might seem unnecessary and confusing in the United States. Or worse, it might seem to be a distraction from national purpose, a dilution of power. These very concerns about fragility and cultural instability make multilingualism good for democracy in the United States, where immigration turns out to be uncontainable and also good for the economy, in this and in other increasingly postnational societies.

Democracy values nonnormative procedure over political substance. The seam between particular cultures that fit badly together is where democracy can work procedurally to define universal rights and obligations. Good fits leave little room for serious play. But differences that are admitted show the gap where debate and procedure can work. Precisely because citizens cannot presume to feel, or to think, or to perform alike, their ear for otherness makes justice possible.[3] That is why political philosophy and ethics, from Benjamin and Arendt to Bakhtin and Levinas, caution against empathy, which plays treacherously in a subject-centered key that overwhelms unfamiliar voices to repeat solitary sounds of the self.[4]

I am certainly not in favor of a Tower of Babel that will quake and crumble with the frustrations of incomprehension. Instead, I want to defend code-switching as one of democracy's most effective speech-acts, along with translation and speaking English through heavy accents, because they all slow down communication and labor through the difficulties of understanding and reaching agreement. "Every person who reads this article has an accent," writes Mari Matsuda in her case for more procedure and less prejudice in America's courts of law. "Your accent carries the story of who you are. . . . [T]races of your life and identity are woven into your pronunciation, your phrasing, your choice of words. . . . Someone who tells you they don't like the way you speak is quite likely telling you that they don't like you."[5]

"Hablemos el mismo idioma," by Gloria Estefan, could sound like a manifesto for one language and one style if you miss the ironies of her performance. "Let's Speak the Same Language" (which means, in Spanish and English, let's not argue anymore), was a hit song of her 1993 CD called *Mi tierra*, the title of another hit.[6] The tellingly generic homeland of the title counts on our collective nostalgia, despite the fact that mi tierra may not be yours too, and "Hablemos el mismo idioma" wants to move the feeling of homesick unity toward a better future here. Played to a salsa mix, and published in a bilingual booklet to make good on the lyric's call for racial rainbows and musical fusions, the song nevertheless draws a line of difference in its mixed audience. "Universalism isn't what it used to be," Werner

Sollors said in response. He is right, of course, because the appeal to get beyond differences is pitched to decidedly Latin locutors. After the first few lines, the song disinterpellates some listeners when the "us" turns out to be "*nosotros hispanos*." Others are literally put off, even though Estefan had accounted for differences from the very first lines of her call to unity. She admitted that differences constitute her as a subject (*A pesar de las diferencias que me hacen quien soy*), as she enjoined us think about how much we have in common (*respiramos el mismo aire, despertamos al mismo sol, nos alumbra la misma luna, necesitamos sentir amor*).

But then her rhythm of moving from outside to inside falters. It skips a beat, breaks the movement to freeze it in a *syncope*, a term that Catherine Clément takes from musical notation (and from its medical meaning of "apparent death") to name a political or philosophical interruption of predictability. "The queen of rhythm, *syncope is also* the mother of *dissonance*; it is the source, in short, of a harmonious and productive discord. . . . Attack and haven, collision; a fragment of the beat disappears, and of this disappearance, rhythm is born."[7] The pause between strong beats, between unity and selective solidarity, is a break for reflection. Readers who may feel the sting of exclusion don't necessarily stop to think about it, not if they are too quick on the uptake.

Estefan's pitch for pan-Hispanic solidarity rehearses what Puerto Rican Willie Colón, Panamanian Rubén Blades, and Cuban Celia Cruz had been intoning for years, a "trans-Latino" identity that now characterizes urban centers like "the New Nueva York."[8] Improvising on the themes of sameness and difference, the way that musical mixes make salsa from different national styles, Latinos are also saying that universalism is not what it used to be. They are saying it with relief, because they had fit so badly into milky homogenizations. "Racism as Universalism" is one result of the colorless abstraction.[9] But universality has renewed hope, say defenders of the public sphere and pragmatists, if democracies can tune in to discord in order to develop an "interactive" politics. Discord among culturally and economically situated subjects locates gaps as the space of democratic negotiation.[10] Without gaps, negotiation would be unnecessary. And because of them, listening is not easy; it requires patience at the *syncope* of communication in a country where citizens do not always speak the same language. Even when they do speak English, as Matsuda argued, the range of culturally inflected accents fissures the language community. Happily, she adds, because our accents safeguard American diversity from the meanness of one standard sound. Cultural difference is something for democracy to celebrate, not just to tolerate. Theodor Adorno had already appreciated the "negativity" inside communities as boundary markers that resist the subject's "greedy thirst for incorporation" of difference into sameness.[11] If there were no difference, there could be no recognition of one subject by another but only the identification that reduces real external others into functions of a totalizing self. Yet the very gap that allows for enough autonomy to make mutuality possible also risks misrecognition and violence. The risk is worth taking because without it we allow the violence of forcing sameness on others. Either they are forced to fit or they are forced out.[12] The necessary risk of breakdown that democracies defend as the negative (autonomous) moment of mutuality, surely gives some universalists pause about the possibility of a coherent culture and a cohesive polity.[13] But a pause is not a bad thing, if it gives time for one to listen to another.[14]

Universalism is promising today because it depends on difference, Ernesto Laclau argues a bit provocatively, along with some critical legal scholars.[15] It has survived classical philosophy's dismissal of particularity as deviation, and it has outlived a European Enlightenment that conflated the universal (subject, class, culture) with particular (French) incarnations. Today's universalism is a paradox for the past because it is grounded in particularist demands. They unmoor any fixed cultural content and keep universalism open to an "always receding horizon."[16] Dissonance, then, isn't noise. It is a function of the *syncope*, of the "performative contradiction" that can sing "Hablemos el mismo idioma" (a universal theme in a particularist key) and risk liberal improvisation between the "apparent deaths" of the polity. Democracy works in unscored counterpoint.

Pauses and residues from translation, even the limits of comprehension (which still means grasping, owning), are more promising for democracy than we have assumed. Consider, for example, Homi Bhabha's concept of lag-time: it names the temporal gaps between an already existing center and peripheries that cannot (or will not) catch up. Bhabha does some urgent work of underlining the asymmetries and complicating the notion of empty or homogeneous modern time.[17] But time-lag can describe a particular asymmetry: not the inequalities that he decries against the drone of easy multiculturalism[18] but the rhythmic variations in speech, even when we speak the same language. Time-lag can name a musical notation, a deferred stress, or a delayed apprehension of meaning, the skipped beat in conversation that also marks the rhythm of a joke; time-lag can be the signature of one language through the medium of another. Skewed rhythms and dissonant notes are not noise but signs of liberal improvisation. We share a polity, after all; differences coexist in time as well as through time. Blockage comes from rushing to fill in the gaps, not from appreciating syncopated sounds.

Signs of difference and of contingent translations are everywhere, unless we continue to ignore them. The gesture that first made me pause was Rigoberta Menchú's peculiar stops and starts at the secrets of her 1983 testimony about Guatemala's war of Indian removal. Why proclaim her own silence instead of being silent, I wondered, as if declaring secrets mattered more than the ethnographic data she was giving? With all those secrets, no amount of information could let intimacy flow. Maybe that was her purpose, I began to think: to engage us *and* to interrupt our universalizing habit of identifying with the writer, sometimes to the point of replacing her. A formidable lesson. Still illiterate, the young woman who spoke a newly learned, halting, Spanish managed to turn an ethnographic interrogation into a platform for her own irreplaceable leadership. The stunning move made me think of other books that interrupt universalizing mastery. Among them were slave narratives commissioned by abolitionists, the Inca Garcilaso's chronicles, Toni Morrison's *Beloved*, Elena Poniatowska's novelized testimonio, stories about blacks told by self-consciously incompetent whites, even the accommodationist memoir of Richard Rodriguez, in his refusals of intimacy with readers. The examples that drew me back and brought me up short are almost arbitrary. Anyone can think of others. The point is that some ethnically marked writing refuses to keep universalizing time. It halts, syncopates, and demands cautious engagements.

Following particular guides is an important precaution, if we hope to avoid the muddle of mistaking one difference for another, or collapsing difference into homogeneous categories like "Hispanics." The very rhythm of efforts at solidarity is a cue to the divisions among constituencies usually identified by national origin.[19] Puerto Rico can continue to be my strong case of a nation that maneuvers along the fault line of grammatical shifters, in the space between here and there, now and then, Our America and theirs. An entire population stays on the move, or potentially so, so much so that Luis Rafael Sánchez makes a hysterical joke about Puerto Rican national identity being grounded in the *guagua aérea* (air bus) shuttling across the Atlantic puddle.[20]

Literally a nation of Luftmenschen, half is provisionally on the Caribbean island, and half on and around that other mad-hatter island, which has become a homeland that Tato Laviera calls *AmeRíca*.[21] His genius is to skip a beat, to unravel a seamless label by reading the English sign for America with an eye for Spanish. In Spanish this country looks like "América," because without a written accent on the "e" to give the word an irregular stress, a default, unwritten, stress falls on the "i." Laviera's hypercorrection displaces the logic of diacritical marks from one language to another and performs a time-lag of translation. The alleged omission of an accent mark is an opportunity to read the country in syncopation as AmeRíca, a time-lagged sound whose sign reforms the country's look too. With a foreign stroke if you read it in English (just as superfluous for Spanish), and with an intrusive capital "R" that fissures and then fuses a conventional name into a convincing compound, the orthographic encroachments push both standard languages slightly out of bounds. The result is a practically providential metaphor: AmeRíca transforms what for English or Spanish is just a word into a *mot juste* in Spanglish. Doubly marked mainland Ricans become the most representative citizens we've got.

Double Consciousness

Double identity has been the bane of minority citizens, at least since W. E. B. Du Bois named the problem in *Souls of Black Folk* (1903).[22] It is an unhappy consciousness, by definition, in its structural duplicity. It mocks the word "identity," which literally means something coherent, by splitting it into contending signs (African-American; Jewish-American; Hispanic-American; Irish-American . . .) held apart by hyphens. Or were they braced together by that hyphen in an unstable, transitional cluster, in the citizen's development toward a more perfect alignment with a universal spirit? Braces are an apt figure for growing pains in America, a necessary nuisance that is scheduled to disappear once citizens achieve an unencumbered and attractive maturity. The young country was absorbing citizens from many different backgrounds. And their lingering sense of belonging elsewhere interrupted a sense of belonging here. The unhappy, but understandable and transitory, result was a fissured "double consciousness" that could be straightened out through training and through time. But time wasn't bringing progress for blacks, Du Bois complained.

"How does it feel to be a problem?" is what white people were always asking, even when they were being compassionate or feeling vicariously outraged at things "that make your blood boil." Du Bois reduces his own boiling point to a simmer, as he puts it, in order to ventriloquize for whites who don't dare ask about the "problem" outright. Delicacy doesn't cover up the question; it obstructs any possible answer. So Du Bois asks on the first page of *Souls*, and responds: Feeling yourself to be a problem, he says, "is a peculiar sensation, this double-consciousness, this sense of always looking at one's self through the eyes of others, of measuring one's soul by the tape of a world that looks on in amused contempt and pity. One ever feels this twoness,—an American, a Negro; two souls, two thoughts, two unreconciled strivings."[23]

Double consciousness is a double bind for Du Bois, and for advocates of monocultural policies including English-only legislation. This wasn't the case for Ralph Waldo Emerson, who had used the term to describe a productive dynamic. Nor will it necessarily bind up postmodern citizens in self-destructive contradictions. On the contrary, as I have been suggesting, double consciousness and bilingualism may be our best safeguards against the meanness of one thought, one striving, one measure of value. Du Bois himself opens leads in this direction. But mostly, *Souls of Black Folk* complains that seeing double means losing focus. Emerson's solution to *double consciousness* amounted to social bankruptcy for Blacks, who were pulled in opposite directions and getting nowhere.

For Emerson, the term had meant the dynamics of American progress, the principle of coordination between opposing forces. It was the productive relationship between nature and freedom, between racial inheritance and universal purpose: "one solution to the old knots of fate, freedom, and foreknowledge, exists, the propounding, namely, of the double consciousness. A man must ride alternately on the horses of his private and his public nature, as the equestrians in the circus throw themselves nimbly from horse to horse."[24] He formulated this mixture of optimism and resignation in "Fate," written during the troubled decade before the Civil War. The first draft was a lecture in 1851 (just after the war that annexed half of Mexico), and the published essay appeared in 1860. Instead of cures, Emerson commissioned monuments to the grand solution: "Let us build altars to the Blessed Unity which holds nature and souls in perfect solution, and compels every atom to serve an universal end. . . . Let us build altars to the Beautiful Necessity, which secures that all is made of one piece; that plaintiff and defendant, friend and enemy, animal and planet, food and eater, are of one kind. . . . Why should we fear to be crushed by savage elements, we who are made up of the same elements?"[25]

This is not a rhetorical question for everyone. Those who are crushed ask it differently from those who benefit by the crushing. Emerson's abstract, universalist language (loosely Buddhist, even more loosely Hegelian, or a Schopenhauerian turned perversely optimist) builds toward this final coordination of universal "Fate" with particularism. But the movement has been so effortless, the fit between his particular and triumphalist racial consciousness with consciousness of Divine Law has been so seamless that the concluding exhortation to praise the design seems callow if not downright cruel. "We like the nervous and victorious habit of our own branch of the family," he had proudly said early in the essay:

> Cold and sea will train an imperial Saxon race, which nature cannot bear to lose, and, after cooping it up for a thousand years in yonder England, gives a hundred Englands, a hundred Mexicos. All the bloods it shall absorb and domineer: and more than Mexicos,—the secrets of water and steam, the spasms of electricity, the ductility of metals, the chariot of the air, the ruddered balloon are awaiting you.[26]

Meanwhile, other races deteriorate when you dislodge them, and become fertilizer for our heartier selves: "The German and Irish millions, like the Negro, have a great deal of guano in their destiny. They are ferried over the Atlantic, and carted over America, to ditch and to drudge, to make corn cheap, and then to lie down prematurely to make a spot of green grass on the prairie."[27] All this makes the closing injunction suspiciously self-serving. Blameless, in the big picture, the Anglo-Saxon race smiles triumphant, effortlessly aligned with the Universe, while other races can share the design by embracing humility, resigning themselves to an appointed role, wisely grateful for the service they perform.

Emerson's steadfastness daunts anyone who isn't moving along. Americans who embrace his goal of coordination but who cannot make their double consciousness budge are frustrated by the desire. And others may be offended by the very program to brace the doubleness in a movement towards coherence. They may intuit that double consciousness is no problem at all but, rather, Americans' most promising feature. Without the experience of cultural contradictions, one might mistake the empty space of politics for a place occupied by one particular culture, the way Emerson did. Anti-Emersonians will refuse to count themselves either among conquistatorial Anglo-Saxons or among the vanquished who fuel progress with their own expendable existence.

Du Bois has seemed more frustrated to readers than offended, though we will see him complicated enough to occupy both positions. It is true that *Souls of Black Folk* begins at the end of Emersonian optimism, without lifting the now hopeless burden of coordination. "The history of the American Negro is the history of this strife,—this longing to attain self-conscious manhood, to merge his double self into a better and truer self" (215). The first pages eulogize the slaves' limitless faith in freedom, then follows a long and bitter review of the anticlimax to that faith, when Reconstruction broke one promise after another. Du Bois lingers on the rash of local sabotage that undid the federal government's ambitious program of reparations for blacks and their initiation into a market economy; the lynchings; and the experiences of former slaves themselves, unable to adapt to these unpromising circumstances.

A Republic of Hyphens

Doubleness has not always been a predicament, though. A long history of some premodern societies is instructive. Nor does doubleness necessarily mean trouble for a postmodern society, where the overload of cultural differences demands, as I said, an empty, public space for coordination. Consider medieval England, where Normans were wise enough to know that they ruled a nation of foreigners. Jews, Germans, Danes, and others could not "speak the same language" in any literal way, but they were enjoined to deal fairly with one another. Prudent listening for the "differend" was a medieval practice long before it became Lyotard's postmodern hope. A medieval mixed jury, which combined local subjects and foreigners as members of the same tribunal, would hear cases between culturally different litigants who could not be subject to one existing rule.[28] The mixed jury predates the contradiction between a monocultural nation and a procedural republic that Lyotard locates at the inconsistent core of modern polities (Declaration of 1789, 6).[29] Perhaps American law would do well to retrieve and adapt medieval respect for cultural specificity as a vehicle and safeguard for justice.[30] Now that our postmodern nations are adjusting to culturally mixed populations, unstoppable waves of immigration, the continuing sounds of different languages in public places, we might take a lead from the Normans, and from the Moors in Spain, to cite one more example. They used to tax thriving infidels rather than eliminate them as so much guano for conquest. More rational than Christian tradition has portrayed them, Moslem empires have traditionally been hosts to the cultural differences that Christendom does not abide. Spanish modernity came with cultural and political coherence: the consolidation of reluctant and even embattled kingdoms, the expulsion of miscreants, and the continued surveillance of private devotions by public authority. Modernity drove England to overcome internal differences too: a uniform Common Law replaced the ad hoc mixed jury, and Jews were expelled (as elsewhere) because they preferred double consciousness over the coherence of one intolerant culture.

Today, universal rights is an idea that parts company with what Europeans had assumed to be a universal culture. This is no time for Emerson's agile Anglo-Saxons who drive others aground, no time to revive his easy and airless fit between Americans and America. Nor is this the time to follow Du Bois in vicious circles as race and nation dig each other into a ground that requires acculturation but does not permit it. Today we might notice that double consciousness (and its often bilingual expressions) is a normal and ever more universal condition of contemporary subjects. It is also, I have been saying, a structure of democratic feeling. Du Bois called it a curse, we know, but he hinted that double consciousness could also be a double blessing, for blacks in particular and for America in general. Anything less impoverishes both:

> In the merging he wants neither of the older selves to be lost. He would not Africanize America, for America has too much to teach the world and Africa. He would not bleach his Negro soul in a flood of white Americans, for he knows that Negro blood has a message for the world. He simply wishes to make it possible for a man to be both a Negro and an American, without being cursed and spit upon by his fellows, without having the doors of Opportunity closed roughly in his face.
> This, then, is the end of his striving; to be a co-worker in the kingdom of culture, to escape both death and isolation, to husband and use his best powers and his latent genius. (215)

I want to risk an unlikely but still possible reading of this passage, to underline a reluctance have blacks disappear, rather than a desire for dialectical resolution. I hesitate at the point before differences would merge, and linger on the tension between ill-fitting partners. This slightly willful reading follows from Fernando Ortiz's improvement on effortlessly friendly words like *syncretism* and *hybridity* with the concept of "transculturation."[31] Transculturation is creativity derived from antagonism. But my reading also departs from Ortiz, along the very fault line that he described between cultural partners trapped in a forced marriage. Du Bois's scorn for the requirement to bleach one's soul and to ignore racial antagonism is an expression of pride in difference, a pride that keeps cultural particularity in productive tension with others. And thanks to this tension, to incommensurability itself when one thinks of history, taste, preferences, the empty space opens up for a truly universal, nonnormative, public sphere of rights and obligations. This is postmodernity's response to the dialectics of modernization. Does the modernizing Du Bois convince postmodern readers? Do we believe in an incrementally truer and more coherent consciousness, along with the eugenic arguments for merging and mestizaje?

If you allow me to pose the question in perhaps impertinently personal terms, I might ask if you would cure your double consciousness if you could. Or would you prefer to continue under its burden. Suppose that you could wake up tomorrow, no longer a Jewish-American, lesbian-American, Latino-, African-, Asian-, gay-, Moslem-American, or any other particular variation but simply American, would you do it? If you could suppress the hyphen of your oxymoronic, more than single, "identity," would you want to? Well, . . . would you? Almost everyone else I have asked has answered no, even when they show surprise at their own response. What would predict the resistance when so much of our civic and cultural training in the United States demonizes the doubleness. Even Du Bois showed reluctance to cure the problem at the cost of racial pride. Perhaps we sense, sometimes without saying it, that the cure is far worse than the complaint.

Some contemporary theorists do say it, urgently and boldly. I mentioned Ernesto Laclau, an Argentine in Europe (in the contradictions between universal rights and a presumptively universal culture) who defends an empty nonnormative universality opened up by the bad fit of cultural particularities. I mentioned Mari Matsuda too, a Japanese-Hawaiian legal scholar who also defends the play of cultural differences as America's best safeguard for democracy. Without it, fairness will continue to be mired in a practice of monocultural intolerance for difference. To these and other theorists, one could add a variety of authors who live happily on the hyphen between languages and countries, cultivating the space for personal self-fashioning and for political flexibility. Gustavo Pérez Firmat (delighted with the paradox) easily becomes American *because* he already is Cuban. Cuba, after all, coined the word *transculturation*, the self-conscious process of admitting difference into the self.[32] But his postmodern *biculturation*, "The Cuban-American Way," holds off the merging that Ortiz had described and that Du Bois had probably desired. Pérez Firmat doesn't fuse the contending cultures but braces them together, on either side of a spacing device that leaves room for creativity. Coco Fusco continues the game in *English Is Broken Here* (1995), a manifesto for keeping the country fractured, linguistically, and open to the play of difference. Even Richard Rodriguez, infamous among Chicano-rights advocates for arguing against bilingual education and for seamless assimilation, in *Hunger of Memory* (1981) keeps his distance. In afterthoughts to Anglos about his tenacious home culture, Rodriguez writes, "I might surprise, even offend, you by how inconveniently Mexican I can be." And like Pérez Firmat, Rodriguez credits his home culture, not the United States, for promoting assimilation. "As someone whose blood springs from Mexico, I am created by an assimilationist culture. Mexico, not the United States, is the true assimilationist example. Most Mexicans do not belong to a single race";[33] they aspire to become *la raza cósmica*.[34] In this country, though, Rodriguez remains inconveniently different, bicultural, and incoherent. Is this an unhappy consciousness that double identities define, as they did for Du Bois? Or is it more defiant to monoculturalism than disappointed at not fitting in?

Double consciousness may indeed be a challenge today for the United States, and for other countries reluctant to let go the dialectical dream of coherence. But it is no longer a rush of contrary forces that human progress should gradually coordinate, as it was for Emerson. Instead, double consciousness is the challenge to develop stamina for the incoherence. Matsuda and others will not be satisfied by mere tolerance for different accents in the courtroom, different flavors of food on street-corner stands, and complicated personal webs of belonging and sympathies. America needs to value these differences, to celebrate them as the fissures that keep the country from congealing into the meanness of one standard style. Now that Mexican and Central American immigration is virtually uncontainable, that African Americans are taking stock of what is to be gained through assimilation, now that class struggle throughout the hemisphere takes on ethnic inflections, it is time to admit that the dream of cultural coherence is a greater danger to democracy than any obstacle it could hope to overcome.

Is double consciousness in fact bad for democracy? Du Bois evidently worried that it blocks responsible conversation in a vertigo of particular self-hatred and universal contempt for misfits. But there is reason to believe that double consciousness instead enables conversation between parties who respect the differences that separate them, because they acknowledge stubborn differences that fissure their own identities. Perhaps double consciousness ensures democracy by embracing the particularities of citizens who must be tolerated in their difference from others. Otherwise, what would tolerance mean? Anyone who imagines that it means reducing difference to more of the same "universal" human character is surely more afflicted by an unhappy consciousness than those of us who learn to live happily with double identities and to deal fairly with other fissured subjects.

NOTES

1. Arcadio Díaz Qiñones argues this poignantly in his piecing together of *La memoria rota* (Rio Piedras, Puerto Rico: Huracan, 1993).

2. 111 Supreme Court 1859. I am grateful to Professor Bonnie Honig for leading me to

the following information: See also the reference in 60 U.S. Law Week 4339, 1992; and in American Law Reports 2nd, 540 vol. 89, a publication by lawyers about constitutionally important cases.

3. This is a commonplace of political philosophy, one that Mari Matsuda has developed. See John Rawls, "Justice as Fairness: Political Not Metaphysical," *Philosophy and Public Affairs* 14 (1985): 223–251. "[L]iberalism as a poltiical doctrine supposes that there are many conflicting and incommensurable conceptions of the good, each compatible with the full rationality of human persons." (248). Also Robert Dahl, *Dilemmas of Pluralist Democracy: Autonomy Versus Control* (New Haven: Yale University Press, 1982); Milton Fisk, "Introduction: The Problem of Justice" in Fisk *Key Concepts in Critical Theory: Justice* (Atlantic Highlands, NJ: Humanities Press, 1993) 1–8. "There has to be at least a conflict based on an actual lack of homogeneity for what is distinctive about justice to become relevant" (1). See also Seyla Benhabib, *The Situated Self: Gender, Community and Postmodernism in Contemporary Ethics* (New York: Routledge, 1992), 2.

4. Walter Benjamin, *Illuminations*, ed. and intro. Hannah Arendt, trans. Harry Zohn (New York: Schocken, 1969) In thesis VII of "Theses on the Philosophy of History" 253–264, at 256, Benjamin disdains historicism for cultivating empathy, that lazy attachment to the past that has survived in documents, necessarily to the oppressive winners. Hannah Arendt, *On Revolution* (New York: Viking Press, 1963), see the long section in Chapter 2, "The Social Question" 69–90. Because compassion abolishes the distance where politics can happen, it is irrelevant for worldly affairs (81) and worse, speaking for (weak) others may be a pretext for lust for power (84). M. M. Bakhtin, *Art and Answerability: Early Philosophical Essays*, ed. Michael Holquist and Vadim Liapunov. (Austin: University of Texas Press, 1990), 64, 81, 88; and Emmanuel Levinas, *Totality and Infinity: An Essay on Exteriority* trans. Alphonso Lingis (Pittsburgh: Duquesne University Press, 1969). For a proceduralist critique of grounding politics in positive feeling, see, for example, Dahl, *Dilemmas of Pluralist Democracy*, especially chapter 7, "Changing Civic Orientations," 138–164, at 147: "To love a member of one's family or a friend is not at all like 'loving' abstract 'others' whom one does not know, never expects to know, and may not even want to know."

5. Mari J. Matsuda, "Voices of America: Accent, Antidiscrimination Law, and a Jurisprudence for the Last Reconstruction," *Yale Law Journal* 100, no. 5 (March 1991): 1329–1407. She celebrates cultural difference beyond the tolerance that liberals like Rorty defend. I am grateful to Professor Susan Keller for this reference.

6. "Hablemos el mismo idioma" is song 10 on Estefan's very successful CD *Mi tierra*; music and lyrics are by Gloria Estefan and Emilio Estefan Jr., the 1993 copyright is held by Foreign Imported Productions and Publications, Inc.

7. Catherine Clément, *Syncope: The Philosophy of Rapture*, foreword by Verena Andermatt Conley, trans. by Sally O'Driscoll and Deirdre M. Mahoney (Minneapolis: University of Minnesota Press, 1994), 4, x.

8. For an excellent review of the sociological literature, see Juan Flores, "Pan-Latino/Trans-Latino: Puerto Ricans in the 'New Nueva York,' " *Centro* (Center for Puerto Rican Studies), 8, nos. 1, 2 (1996): 171–186.

9. Etienne Balibar, "Racism as Universalism" in *Masses, Classes, and Ideas*, trans. James Swenson (New York: Routledge, 1994), 191–204. See also Marc Shell's excellent *Children of the Earth: Literature, Politics, and Nationhood* (New York: Oxford University Press, 1993). "All men are brothers," is the slogan that Shell considers throughout the book. The danger is that if some are not brothers, or do not want to be, then they are not "men" and can be eliminated.

10. See Benhabib, *Situating the Self*, 3, 5. See also Richard Rorty, *Objectivity, Relativism, and Truth* (New York: Cambridge University Press, 1991), e.g., his defense of Dewey as clearing the ground for liberal democracy (13).

11. T. W. Adorno, *Negative Dialektic* (Frankfurt: Suhrkamp, 1966), 172. The greedy subject is Freud's formulation. See Diana Fuss, *Identity Papers* (New York: Routledge, 1996).

12. Jessica Benjamin, "The Shadow of the Other (Subject): Intersubjectivity and Feminist Theory," *Constellations* 1, no. 2 (1994): 231–254, at 245. Her entire discussion is most useful; I am grateful to Kerry Riddich for the reference.

13. See, for example, Naomi Schor, *Bad Objects: Essays Popular and Unpopular* (Durham: Duke University Press, 1995), xiv.

14. Levinas, *Totality and Infinity*, 57–58: "The real must not only be determined in its historical objectivity, but also from interior intentions, from the secrecy that interrupts the continuity of historical time. Only starting from this secrecy is the pluralism of society possible." Jean-François Lyotard, "The Other's Rights," in *On Human Rights: The Oxford Amnesty Lectures 1993*, ed. Stephen Shute and Susan Hurley (New York: Harper Collins, 1993), 136–147, at 142. "How to share dialogue with *you*, requires a moment of silence: 'Aristotle said: The master speaks and the pupil listens. For that moment, the status of *I* is forbidden to me, . . . ' The suspension of interlocution imposes a silence and that silence is good. It does not undermine the right to speak. It teaches the value of that right."

15. See Neil Gotanda, "A Critique of 'Our Constitution Is Color-Blind,' " *Stanford Law Review* 44 no. 1 (November 1991): 1–68. Citing Robert Paul Wolff in "Beyond Tolerance," in *A Critique of Pure Tolerance*, ed. Robert Paul Wolff, Barrington Moore, Jr., and Herbert Marcuse (Boston: Beacon Press, 1965), 4–17.

16. Ernesto Laclau, "Universalism, Particularism and the Question of Identity," in *The Identity in Question*, ed. John Rajchman (New York: Routledge, 1995), 93–108, at 107.

17. Bhabha attributes this notion of time to Walter Benjamin (although we should say that Benjamin named the bourgeois temporal tidiness in order to blast it apart with the interruptions of *Jetztzeit*). See Homi Bhabha, *Location of Culture* (London: Routledge, 1994), 95. But he will give Benjamin credit for the critique in "Translator Translated: W. J. T. Mitchell talks with Homi Bhabha," *Artform* #7, March 1995, 80–119, at 110.

18. Homi Bhabha, "Race Time and the Revision of Modernity," *Oxford Literary Review* 13, nos. 1–2 (1991): 193–219, at 204–205.

19. In "Do 'Latinos' Exist?' *Contemporary Sociology* 23 (May 1994): 354–356, Jorge I. Domínguez reports this observation derived from two books under review (Rodolfo O. de la Garza et al., *Latino Voices: Mexican, Puerto Rican, and Cuban Perspectives on American Politics* [Boulder: Westview Press, 1992], and Rodney E. Hero, *Latinos and the U.S. Political System: Two-Tiered Pluralism* [Philadelphia: Temple University Press, 1992]): "Very large majorities of Mexicans, Puerto Ricans, and Cubans identify themselves by their national origins, not as 'Latinos' or Hispanics" (354).

20. Luis Rafael Sánchez, "La Guagua Aérea: The Air Bus," trans. Diana Vélez, *Village Voice*, January 24, 1984.

21. Tato Laviera, *AmeRícan* (Houston: Arte Público Press, 1985).

22. For helpful recent explorations of the philosophical origins of the term *double consciousness* and of its meanings in contemporary America, see Shamoon Zamir, *Dark Voices: W. E. B. Du Bois and American Thought, 1888–1903* (Chicago: University of Chicago Press, 1995); Gerald Early, ed., *Lure and Loathing: Essays on Race, Identity, and the Ambivalence of Assimilation* (New York: Allen Lane, Penguin Press, 1993); and Robert Gooding-

Williams, ed., *W. E. B. Du Bois: Of Cultural and Racial Identity*, special issue, *Massachusetts Review* 35, no. 2 (Summer 1994).

23. William E. B. DuBois, *The Souls of Black Folk* (1903) in *Three Negro Classics* (New York: Avon Books, 1965), 213–390, at 215.

24. I thank Sacvan Bercovitch for leading me back to Emerson on the question of double consciousness, and for locating "Fate," wherein double consciousness is named. See Ralph Waldo Emerson, "Fate," in *The Conduct of Life* (Boston: Ticknor and Fields, 1860), 1–42. A version existed in 1851, delivered as a lecture; in *The Norton Anthology of American Literature*, ed. Ronald Gottesman et al. (New York: Norton, 1979), 794–816, at 815.

25. *Norton Anthology*, 816.

26. Ibid., 808.

27. Ibid., 801.

28. Marianne Constable, *The Law of the Other: The Mixed Jury and Changing Conceptions of Citizenship, Law, and Knowledge* (Chicago: University of Chicago Press, 1994).

29. Lyotard, "The Other's Rights," 139.

30. See Constable, *The Law of the Other*.

31. Fernando Ortiz, *Cuban Counterpoint of Tobacco and Sugar* (Havana: J. Montero, 1940). Originally published as *Contrapunteo cubano del tabaco y el azviar*.

32. Gustavo Pérez Firmat, *Life on the Hyphen: The Cuban-American Way* (Austin: University of Texas Press, 1994).

33. Richard Rodriguez, "An American Writer" (1987), in *The Invention of Ethnicity*, ed. Werner Sollors (New York: Oxford University Press, 1989), 9–10.

34. José Vasconcelos, *The Cosmic Race (The Mission of the Ibero American Race)*, trans. Didier T. Jaén (Los Angeles: California State University Press, 1979), 15.

Part VI

Multilingualism and English-Language Writing

Multilingualism has also left its traces in American English, and the investigation of "multilingual America" is not limited to noting the pressures of English on "foreign-language" texts or to identifying aspects that can be discussed under the term "Americanization." In attempting to correct the blind spots of the "English-only" past, it makes little sense to demand only the study of "non-English" literature of the United States; it makes more sense to stimulate new collaborative work toward a fuller history of American literature in English *plus* other languages. This does not mean a diminished importance of the study of English-language literature of the United States but perhaps the development of some new contexts for English-language texts in light of Benjamin Franklin's, Thomas Jefferson's, or Henry Wadsworth Longfellow's—not to mention Isaac Bashevis Singer's, Joseph Brodsky's, Czeslaw Milosz's, or Vladimir Nabokov's—multilingualism, and in light of the multilingual printing presses and newspapers in such historical centers as Philadelphia, New Orleans, and New York.

Contributors to this volume from Øverland to Sommer, and from Corradini to Taubenfeld, have therefore included English-language texts and such authors as William Dean Howells, F. Scott Fitzgerald, and Richard Rodriguez in their reflections. Steven Kellman has proposed the study of "the traces of Cantonese in Maxine Hong Kingston's English prose, of Yiddish in Bernard Malamud's, of Spanish in Oscar Hijuelos's." Hana Wirth-Nesher has recently undertaken something of the sort in her subtle analysis of "linguistic inscription" in Saul Bellow; and in this section Wirth-Nesher's "The Language of Memory: Cynthia Ozick's 'The Shawl' " shows how important multilingual contexts can be for English-language writing in the United States as she examines the ways in which language and linguistic inscription work against the traumatic background of Holocaust memory in Cynthia Ozick's *The Shawl*, in which English and Yiddish are represented while Polish makes itself felt by translation, and Greek and Latin are summoned by allusion.

Lawrence Rosenwald's "American Anglophone Literature and Multilingual America" focuses on such examples as James Fenimore Cooper's employment of Indian languages, Mark Twain's language games in Huck and Jim's dialogue about languages in *Huckleberry Finn*, Anzia Yezierska's rendering of Yiddish, and Kate Chopin's representation of Louisiana Creole, in order to ask some larger and important questions about the English-language tradition—mainstream and ethnic—in light of American multilingualism and the pervasiveness of linguistic assimilation. Jules Chametzky, in his "Reflections on Multilingualism," looks back at the history of American studies and his participation in it, recording his eye-opening recognition that a striking trope in a *Partisan Review* essay by Isaac Rosenfeld was actually a direct translation of a common Yiddish expression, and his hope that the contemporary prevalence of multilingualism among the best American writers may lead to a growing recognition of America's richer multilingual ancestry.

The section as a whole suggests how the further exploration of American multilingualism may affect the future study of authors who have written in English, too. This constitutes a step toward overcoming past approaches to American literature that isolated English-language writing as the sole subject of study.

Chapter Twenty-one

The Languages of Memory
Cynthia Ozick's The Shawl

Hana Wirth-Nesher

There is One God, and the Muses are not Jewish but
Greek.   —Cynthia Ozick

Since the coming forth from Egypt five millenia ago,
mine is the first generation to think and speak and write
wholly in English.   —Cynthia Ozick

The first of Cynthia Ozick's epigraphic assertions concerns the relationship between
Judaism and artistic representation; the second concerns the means of representation
and of communication within Jewish civilization. The first concerns what Jews may
say; the second, how they say it. It is clear in the first statement that there is an
ethical imperative, that certain forms of representation are antithetical to Judaism.
Ozick has repeatedly argued that invented fictional worlds are forms of idolatry,
reenactments of paganism. Ozick's only recourse out of the paradox of inventing
fictions that defy her own dictum is to seek forms that will require continuity, that
will make literature liturgical in that it evokes the texts of Jewish civilization. What
this means is that "liturgy" becomes a dynamic concept, one that requires reexamination within Jewish culture, and that English as a monolingual rupture with the
past must be recontextualized within the many languages that have made up that
Jewish culture for millenia.

To test her ideas within her own represented and invented worlds, Ozick sets up
the most extreme case imaginable: she writes a novella about the Holocaust, one in
which a mother is witness to the murder of her own child. The main character's
loss and her subsequent idolizing and fetishizing of the child's shawl is at the center
of a text that is itself a weaving together of texts in many languages that constitute
one version of the fabric of Jewish civilization. *The Shawl* as a work of literature
tests its readers both in terms of the idolatry of placing Holocaust representation at
the center of Jewish civilization and in terms of recognizing the strands of textuality,
beyond English, that comprise Jewish history and culture and that defy translation.
It is as if the injunction not to create idols is ameliorated by the presence of many

languages and many texts. One of the lessons of Babel so appealing to modern readers is its denial of the rational transparency of monolingualism.[1] If the idolized shawl at the center of the text is the temptation of idolatry, then the text of *The Shawl* itself, crosshatched with the languages of Jewish civilization, requires historicity and collective memory, thereby making Ozick's work a continuous part of that civilization. "When a Jew in Diaspora leaves liturgy . . . literary history drops him and he does not last." [2] Intertextuality restores Jewish fiction to its Aggadic role.[3]

In this chapter, I will be concerning myself with fiction as a means of collective memory, and more specifically with an American Jewish writer's invented account of a Holocaust survivor's act of remembrance. In choosing Cynthia Ozick's work "The Shawl," I am interested in two aspects of this act of remembering: (1) the role played by different languages in both the invented world of the characters and the historical context of the writer, and (2) the role of language itself in the representation of mother-child bonding. Although *The Shawl* evokes and partially reproduces a multilingual world, it is written almost entirely in English. And like other works of minority discourse, it appears to be alienated from the language of which it is constituted, estranged from its own linguistic matrix. In *The Shawl* this is compounded by its subject matter, for it is the story of the murder of a child at the very moment that she is making her entry into the world of language and the prolonged grieving of the surviving mother, who denies the loss by addressing and enveloping her phantom daughter in lost languages.

I am reading Ozick's work, then, from two main points of departure: as an example of Holocaust literature in America, and as an example of Jewish-American ethnic literature to the extent that such a literature "remembers" a pre-American and non-English Jewish past. These categories dovetail in *The Shawl* in that the main character is depicted first in a concentration camp and then as an immigrant to the United States. Here, the Old World is not simply lost through the act of emigrating; it is completely annihilated physically but is present as a phantom for the survivor.

Since the early part of the century, Jewish-American writing has often located itself between languages, primarily because it was an immigrant literature.[4] The writers who actually had some knowledge of an alternative Jewish literary tradition, in Hebrew or in Yiddish, located their own works between two traditions, the English and the Yiddish, the Christian and the Jewish. This has expressed itself not only in linguistic borrowings by incorporation of phrases from the other language but also by allusions to the other traditions, or to the borrowing of models and types from the other canon.[5] Just as Yiddish poets in America placed themselves in the line of Whitman and Emerson, so writers like Henry Roth, Abraham Cahan, Saul Bellow, and Delmore Schwartz, composing in the English language, often drew on quotations from Jewish sources, interspersed Yiddish words, and turned their characters into types between two different frames of reference.[6] The extent to which Cynthia Ozick engages with such material is evident in her story "Envy—or Yiddish in America," in which the imminent extinction of Yiddish language and culture is the very subject of the story because the Yiddish writer is left wholly dependent on translation to ensure some precarious survival.

As for the category of Holocaust literature, Jewish-American writers have felt the need to incorporate the subject of the Holocaust into their fiction, often with results that reflect their discomfort in presuming to give voice to survivors.[7] Philip Roth, for example, has abstained from even taking that step as he focuses, instead, on the Jewish-American *response* to the Holocaust, and not the historical trauma itself. His character Zuckerman is haunted by his mother's deathbed legacy to him, a scrap of paper with the word *Holocaust* on it, a legacy that paralyzes him as an artist. Earlier, Roth gave us the fantasy of Anne Frank as Holocaust survivor in *The Ghost Writer* and the Holocaust survivor as the last remaining embodiment of authentic Jewishness for the Jewish-American community in "Eli the Fanatic." It is precisely this collapse of Jewish identity into Holocaust remembrance, with its dangers of mystification and sanctification, that has produced Bellow's antisentimental character Sammler, who shares many traits with Ozick's Rosa. Products of the Polish-Jewish upper class, of an assimilated and urbane world, Sammler and Rosa find themselves in an American urban nightmare that has embittered them further.

Let me turn to the work itself. The acknowledgment page of *The Shawl* refers to the "two stories that comprise this work" as having been previously published in the *New Yorker*.[8] It is a deceptively simple statement, for it suggests that these two separate stories are now two parts of one artistic whole, and the relation between them is left for the reader to determine. The only connecting devices offered by the author are the title, which gives preference to the first story in the sequence, "The Shawl," and the German epigraph from Paul Celan's "Todesfuge": "Dein goldenes Haar Margarete / dein aschenes Haar Sulamith," to which I shall return. What connects these two narratives remains the central question before the reader not merely as a problem in aesthetics but as a moral problem in the representation of the Holocaust by an American author for an American audience. I believe that in this work Ozick has to date provided the most self-conscious and challenging fictional work in the Jewish-American repertoire on the subject of Holocaust representation in language.

Tying the two stories together is the assumption that there is continuity in biography, and that the narrative of two episodes in the life of one individual is sufficient to insure coherence and unity. In this particular case, the individual is a Holocaust survivor by the name of Rosa Lublin. The first story is an account of the death of her baby daughter at the hands of the Nazis in a concentration camp; the second story is a series of incidents in her life more than forty years later in Florida. The former records the child's first utterance; the latter is a fall into a babel of languages, as Rosa belatedly and compulsively communicates with her dead child. To what extent the second story can be understood only in the context of the first is Ozick's main concern and eventually ours. And if we hastily conclude that it is "necessary" to read "The Shawl" first, what does that mean? and what exactly does it explain?

In a failed attempt to protect her infant daughter from detection by Nazi guards in "The Shawl," Rosa Lublin also denies her child's entrance into speech, into the symbolic order. The sound uttered by the one-year-old Magda that betrays her to the Nazis, "Maaaa," is a cry provoked by the loss of her shawl, but within Ozick's text as filtered through the mind of the mother, it is the first syllable of "maamaa," later hummed wildly by the electric wires against which the girl is hurled. Having retrieved the shawl too late to quiet her daughter's wail, Rosa stuffs it into her own mouth to prevent her outcry and detection by the Nazis after they have already murdered her child. Swallowing the "wolf's screech" and tasting the "cinnamon and almond depth of Magda's saliva," she internalizes both the child's cry and the child's muteness. In "Rosa," the sequel "The Shawl," and the second part of the divided text—*The Shawl*—Rosa Lublin writes letters in Polish to her imaginary adult daughter in an attempt to connect the two parts of her life, before and after the Holocaust, and to give her daughter a life in her own fantasies. The first part of the combined work, then, as an American author's account of a Holocaust experience, is the context for reading the multilingual narrative that follows.

What distinguishes Ozick's treatment of this issue from those of her fellow Jewish-American authors is the degree of her self-consciousness about the inadequacy of language to render these experiences and her choice of a female character so that the narrative circles around maternity and the woman's relation to language and loss.[9] Let me return to that moment in "The Shawl" when the one-year-old child whom Rosa has been successfully hiding from the Nazis wanders into the open square of the concentration camp and screams as soon as she discovers that she has lost the shawl that has hidden, enveloped, and nurtured her from birth. Up to that point,

> Magda had been devoid of any syllable; Magda was mute. Even the laugh that came when the ash-stippled wind made a clown out of Magda's shawl was only the air-blown showing of her teeth. . . . But now Magda's mouth was spilling a long viscous rope of clamor.
>
> "Maaaa——-"
>
> It was the first noise Magda had ever sent out from her throat since the drying of Rosa's nipples.
>
> "Maaaa . . . aaa!"
>
> . . . She saw that Magda was grieving for the loss of her shawl, she saw that Magda was going to die. A tide of commands hammered in Rosa's nipples: Fetch, get, bring! But she did not know which to go after first, Magda or the shawl. If she jumped out into the arena to snatch Magda up, the howling would not stop, because Magda would still not have the shawl; but if she ran back into the barracks to find the shawl, and if she found it, and if she came after Magda holding it and shaking it, then she would get Magda back, Magda would put the shawl in her mouth and turn dumb again. (8)

Rosa at first chooses to hear the one syllable cry "Maaa" as an expression of pain for the baby's separation from the shawl. But when she fails to save the child from death, Rosa hears the electric voices of the fence chatter wildly, "Maamaa, maaamaaa," a reproach to her—for if the outcry was the girl's first act of communication rather than merely a wail, if she called out to her mother, then her mother failed her.

The verbal development of the infant, according to Lacan, begins as "a demand addressed to the mother, out of which the entire verbal universe is spun."[10] This moment in "The Shawl" is left suspended between sound and language, between undirected pain and an appeal to the mother, the beginning of a dialogue the price of which is death. Rosa's response to that cry for the rest of her life is to answer it obsessively in the most articulate language known to her, to write eloquent letters to her dead daughter in Polish.

Her letter writing is both a repeated recognition of her child's tragic entry into language and a denial of the war that murdered her, for Rosa's letters to a daughter whom she imagines as a professor of classics, specifically a professor of Greek—a dead language (and an indecipherable one for Rosa)—are primarily elegies for the lost world before the war, a world of elegant turns of phrase, of literature and art. Magda becomes for her the self that has been stolen from her, the self that she might have become. Rosa grieves as much for herself as lost daughter as she does for herself as lost mother.

Before I take a closer look at the languages that serve as various substitutes for the shawl, I want to turn to the shawl itself. What sort of language is it? For Rosa it signifies the preverbal bond between mother and daughter, as it becomes an extension of the mother's body for the infant Magda, a miracle of maternity that appears to nurture the sucking child after the mother's breasts are dry, "it could nourish an infant three days and three nights." Yet it also seems to serve as a denial of maternity, the means whereby Magda's presence is denied to the rest of the world.[11] Denial of Magda's birth is Rosa's way of protecting her and herself. After Magda's death, Rosa stuffs the shawl into her own mouth, an act that muffles her cries and that, metonymically, devours her daughter and returns her to the womb. Thus, the shawl is both mother to the child and child to the mother, their prenatal inseparability. The choice before Rosa when she spies her unprotected daughter whose cries are bound to reveal her presence to the Nazi guards is to retrieve the child or retrieve the shawl for the child. Rosa does not do the first because she believes that Magda cannot be comforted by her actual mother, that her only comfort is the shawl, metonym for womb and breast. Yet when the girl is murdered, Rosa believes that the child had actually cried out to *her*, that the pause between the utterances was not the interval of a repeated and meaningless wail but, rather, Magda's first word, "Maamaa."

Attempting to swallow that sign of maternity while also becoming that lost child in the act of sucking it—this image marks the end of the account of Magda's death and the end of the first text, "The Shawl." The second text, "Rosa," is made up of a series of discourses and languages that are responses to the traumatic events of "The Shawl": the responses of Rosa to her past and the responses of the American community of which Ozick is a part.

First, there is English, the language of the novella *The Shawl*, the language that Rosa shuns, "Why should I learn English? I didn't ask for it, I got nothing to do with it." Much of the English expression that surrounds Rosa seems to mock her and her past, primarily the lingo of advertising, journalism, and psychology. Kollins Kosher Cameo in Miami appeals to nostalgia to lure clients into the restaurant.

"Remembrances of New York and the Paradise of your Maternal Kitchen." Aimed at an American-born clientele, the sign is read by Rosa knowing that she left New York because it drove her mad and that her own daughter never experienced the "paradise of a maternal kitchen." The accumulated grief and despair that drove her to destroy her own livelihood in New York is recorded in the newspaper as "Woman Axes Own Biz," an account of her action that never refers to her traumatic past. This is "Rosa" without "The Shawl." The most humiliating English discourse for Rosa, however, is that of clinical psychology's language of disease for Holocaust victims. The letters that she receives from Dr. Tree, who is applying a model of "Repressed Animation" to his study of "Survivor Syndrome," offer a catalogue of terms—"survivor," "refugee," "derangement," "neurological residue"—but never, Rosa is quick to observe, the term "human being." In short, English in this novella is represented as a language of parody, a fall from some authentic primary language. It is the place of Rosa's exile, a maimed language that distorts and perverts her experiences.

Rosa seeks her protection in languages that are never represented mimetically in the text but are there either in translation, as is the case for Polish, or by allusion, as in Latin and Greek. They represent oases of cultivation. Her father, she recalls, "knew nearly the whole first half or the *Aeneid* by heart"; her imaginary adult daughter Magda is a professor of Greek philosophy.[12] She writes to her daughter "in the most excellent literary Polish." If Magda is killed in the moment of her entry into speech, then she will be forever associated with eloquence, language cut off from the flow of life around Rosa. "A pleasure, the deepest pleasure, home bliss, to speak in our own language. Only to you." Just as the shawl signifies the prespeech bond between mother and child, these languages cut off from community—Polish, Latin, and Greek—become the medium of intimacy between Rosa and her Magda, as if they envelope Rosa in a world of her wishing. But they are not the languages of dialogue; they are the languages of the dead.

Rosa's letters to her imaginary daughter are conveyed in apostrophe, which always "calls up and animates the absent, the lost, and the dead."[13] Addressing her child as "Butterly," she continues, "I am not ashamed of your presence; only come to me, come to me again, if no longer now, then later, always come" or elsewhere, "in me the strength of your being consumes my joy." Magda's imaginary future in America, as projected by Rosa, is an extension of Rosa's past—a non-Jewish world of intellect and aesthetics. The apostrophe to a Polish-speaking daughter who is a professor of classics is a denial of the Jewish identity that marked both mother and daughter as enemies of that European civilization by Polish and German anti-Semites responsible for her murder.

The only other language actually represented in the novella apart from English is Yiddish, much despised by Rosa and her assimilated family. "Her father, like her mother, mocked at Yiddish: there was not a particle of ghetto left in him, not a grain of rot" (21). In *The Shawl*, Yiddish is associated in the past with Rosa's grandmother, and in the present with Simon Persky, the Eastern European immigrant to America, former manufacturer, and retired widower in Miami who takes a romantic interest in her and gently admonishes her, "You can't live in the past."

Rosa looks condescendingly at his Yiddish newspaper in the laundromat where he makes his first move.

> "Excuse me, I notice you speak with an accent."
> Rosa flushed. "I was born somewhere else, not here."
> "I was also born somewhere else. You're a refugee? Berlin?"
> "Warsaw."
> "I'm also from Warsaw! 1920 I left. 1906 I was born."
> "Happy birthday," Rosa said." (18).

> "Imagine this," he said. "Two people from Warsaw meet in Miami, Florida."
> "My Warsaw isn't your Warsaw," Rosa said. (18)

Rosa is intent on distinguishing her Warsaw from Persky's on two grounds, one prewar and one postwar:

The prewar difference is based on rank, for Rosa's denial of any knowledge of Yiddish is her badge of honor in terms of social class. Rosa stems from an affluent assimilated Warsaw home, where the family spoke eloquent Polish and was steeped in Polish culture. Her parents, she recalls, enunciated Polish "in soft calm voices with the most precise articulation, so that every syllable struck its target" (68). Considering the fate of these parents, the trope of Polish syllables striking their target works against Rosa's intense nostalgia. In America, she is deeply offended by the homogenizing of the Old World that places her in the same category with Persky. "The Americans couldn't tell her apart from this fellow with his false teeth and his dewlaps and his rakehell reddish toupee bought God knows when and where—Delancey Street, the Lower East Side. A dandy." Rosa's continuing denial of her Jewishness and her romanticizing of her Polishness results in this peculiar misplaced rage. The American tendency to ignore differences among Jews seems to her a benign repetition of European racism. "Warsaw!" Rosa argues in her mind. "What did he know? In school she had read Tuwim: such delicacy, such loftiness, such *Polishness*" (20).

The irony of Rosa's evocation of pure Polishness in the poetry of Julian Tuwim is that he was a Polish-Jewish poet who wrote in New York in 1944, "So it is with mourning pride that we shall wear this rank, exceeding all others—the rank of the Polish Jew—we, the survivors by miracle or chance. With pride? shall we say, rather, with pangs of conscience and biting shame." The man who served Rosa as the embodiment of quintessential Polishness eventually reached the conclusion that "I shall deem it the highest prize if a few of my Polish poems survive me, and their memory shall be tied to my name—the name of a Polish Jew."[14]

The postwar difference dividing them is that Persky, who left well before the Second World War, has no firsthand experience of the ghetto, the transports, the death camps. As she says to the hotel manager whom she accosts for the presence of barbed wire on the Florida beaches, "Where were you when we was there?"

When asked her name by Persky, Ozick's character replies, "Lublin, Rosa." "A pleasure," he said. "Only why backwards? I'm an application form? Very good. You apply, I accept." Despite Persky's amusement at her self-naming, we recognize that this is not backwards at all, that Rosa first associates herself with Lublin, with her Polishness, and only secondly with Rosa, her Jewishness.[15] In her last letter to Magda she reminds her daughter of their aristocratic background, injured by the social leveling of the Warsaw Ghetto: "[I]magine confining *us* with teeming Mockowiczes and Rabinowiczes and Perskys and Finkelsteins, with all their bad-smelling grandfathers and their hordes of feeble children!" But it is only Persky with his Yiddish paper and his garbled English who has the power to separate her from her Polish phantom child and bring her back to the land of the living.

Despite Rosa's rebuff, Persky persists in his attempt to engage her in conversation:

> "You read Yiddish?" the old man said.
> "No."
> "You can speak a few words, maybe?"
> "No." My Warsaw isn't your Warsaw.

At the very moment that she denies any knowledge of Yiddish, in her mind she recalls her grandmother's "cradle-croonings," and Ozick adds the Yiddish words in transliteration, a rupture in the text because it is the only instance of a language other than English actually represented in the work. "*Unter Reyzls vigele shteyt a klorvays tsigele*," the first words of the popular Yiddish lullabye "*Rozhinkes mit Mandlen*" (Raisins and almonds). In this lullabye a little goat sets out on a journey from which it will bring raisins and almonds to the sleeping child who is destined to be a merchant of raisins and almonds himself but is now urged to sleep in his cradle. The cradle rhymes with the little goat; it rocks the child to sleep while the goat under his cradle is an ambassador of far-off lands of sweets, the Eastern European Jewish equivalent of sugar-plum fairies. In the story "Rosa," the almonds hark back to the previous text, "The Shawl," and to the "cinnamon and almond depth of Magda's saliva" that Rosa drank from the shawl after her child's death.[16] The clear little white goat under Rosa's cradle is merged in her own mind with the little innocent child, uncradled, to whom she writes in Polish to keep her pure of the Yiddish world that marked her as a Jew, but whom she also links with her grandmother, cradle-crooner in that tongue.

The choice of "*Rozhinkes mit Mandlen*" as the only Yiddish intertext in *The Shawl* adds further to both the gender and historical dimensions of the work. The first stanza of the lullabye, taken from the 1880 operetta by Abraham Goldfaden entitled *Shulamis* (Shulamith), frames the account of the baby and the goat by depicting the following scene:

> In a corner of a room in the Holy Temple [in Jerusalem],
> a widow named Daughter of Zion sits all alone
> —and as she rocks her only son to sleep,
> she sings him a little song.[17]

Within the masculine setting of the Holy Temple itself, a small corner has been domesticated, appropriated by mother and child. And in this woman's space the kid that is traditionally offered for sacrifice, or that takes the community's sins upon itself, has been transformed into the sustaining and nurturing creature who provides raisins and almonds. During the Second World War, the lullabye was adapted to conditions under the Nazis—one ghetto version being "In the Slobodka yeshiva an old sexton is reading his will. . . . When you will be free, tell your children of our suffering and murder, show them the graves and inscriptions of our extermination."[18]

While Rosa reminisces about a home comprising only Polish, Latin, and Greek, she shies away from any image of home that contains Yiddish. But in Miami decades later it is Persky, the Yiddish speaker, who tells her in fractured English, "Wherever is your home is my direction that I'm going anyhow."

Perhaps American-Jewish authors writing in English have invented cultivated and assimilated Holocaust survivors like Rosa and Mr. Artur Sammler as their main protagonists for in their prewar lives these characters inhabited a linguistic world as far removed from the Jewish languages of Hebrew and Yiddish as the authors themselves. Beauty, cultivation—civilization itself appears to be synonymous with the languages of their assimilation. For many American-Jewish authors and readers, such as Philip Roth, Yiddish is a language frozen socially and historically, embedded forever in a milieu of poverty, parochialism, and salty vernacular. Regardless of the historical facts that testify to a variegated Yiddish cultural and literary world before the Second World War, for the American-Jewish writer, product of immigrant parents or grandparents, Yiddish has tended to signify a maternal embrace, a home long since outgrown. For her or him, the lure of Yiddish seems to lie in its inarticulateness, in the rusty and homespun English of its translation.[19] In *The Shawl* the route to Rosa's grandmother's lullabye and to her own cradle is through social decline, through dialogue with the likes of a Persky. It is as if the well-crafted English of the Jewish-American fictional text is kept in its place by the admonition of the lost mother culture evident only in the scrappy sentences of non-English speakers.

No surprise then that the epigraph is in German, taken from a poem entitled "Death Fugue" by Paul Celan, a Rumanian-Jewish Holocaust survivor who chose to write in the language of his people's murderers. For most well-educated or assimilated Jews in Europe, Yiddish was scorned as a corrupt form of German, frequently dubbed a bastard or stepchild born of writers unfaithful to the legitimate language, Hebrew.[20] Because Yiddish did evolve from Middle German, while retaining the Hebrew alphabet, it is indeed a joining of these two languages. The Yiddish words of a lullabye in a book recounting the murder of a Jewish child constitute the opposite pole to the words of the epigraph, which also connect German and Hebrew. That Magda herself may be the product of rape by a Nazi adds a further grotesque dimension to the linguistic and historic analogues in *The Shawl*.

> Death is a master from Germany his eyes are blue
> he strikes you with leaden bullets his aim is true
> a man lives in the house your golden hair Margarete
> he sets his pack on to us he grants us a grave in the air,
> he plays with the serpents and daydreams death is a
>   master from Germany

·

your golden hair Margarete
your ashen hair Shulamith [21]

Margarete's golden hair is close enough to be that of Magda's, child of a roman-
ticized (for Rosa) non-Jewish world that aimed to be Judenrein; as the object of
desire of Goethe's *Faust*, Margarete is the incarnation of German romantic love.
Shulamith, a "female emblem of beauty and desire celebrated in The Song of Songs,
is an incarnation of Jewish biblical and literary yearnings. But there is a bitter
difference and shocking irony in the echoing resemblance."[22] One is the fair-haired
maiden of the Aryan ideal, the other the darker, ashen features of the Semitic
woman. Moreover, the figurative ashen hair is brutally undercut by its literal allusion to Shulamith's burnt hair reduced to ashes. In fact, this may be the source for
the ash-stippled wind that encircles Magda in the concentration camp. Shulamith is
associated with the "Rose of Sharon" in the biblical text, in Hebrew "Shoshana,"
and hence with Rosa.[23] Just as Rosa's series of letters to her dead daughter are
apostrophic, so too these lines in the poem are apostrophic, animating what is lost
and dead, both the language of Goethe, contaminated by Nazi Germany, and Jewish
civilization in Europe. But it also implicates Goethe's language, implying that the
idealization of Margarete's golden hair leads inevitably to the ashes of Shulamith's
hair. To add a tragic ironic twist to this entanglement of languages and texts,
Goethe translated the Song of Songs from Hebrew into German, and in the Wal-
purgis Night scene in *Faust*, the young witch's lewd remarks to Faust echo some of
the most sensuous lines of the biblical text. Earlier, Mephistopheles mocks Faust's
love of Margarete by his sexual jests about her body that allude to the Songs of
Songs as well, particularly to the often-quoted lines likening Shulamith's breasts to
two fawns feeding among the lilies (4:5), which Goethe translated more accurately
as among the roses ("*shoshanim*"). Margarete's being identified with Shulamith as
mediated through Geothe's romanticism makes her signification as the antithesis of
all that is Judaic particularly striking. Celan's poem severs Shulamith from Margarete, recovering the former for Semitic civilization and implicating the latter in anti-
Semitic atrocity. He sunders the German-Jewish symbiosis that yielded rich cultural
products, among them the first German-language periodical for Jews, significantly
called *Sulamith*.[24] Celan explained his own loyalty to the German language by
insisting that "only in one's mother tongue can one express one's own truth. In a
foreign language, the poet lies."[25] Bonded then to the language of the murderers of
his own parents, Celan seeks "to annihilate his own annihilation in it."[26]

As the work of a Holocaust survivor poet, Celan's epigraph lends the authority
of testimony to Ozick's novella, as well as the legitimacy of rendering this subject
matter in art. The link to Celan, and through Celan to Goethe, is striking in two
other respects. (1) In 1943 while a prisoner in a labor camp, Celan wrote a poem
originally entitled "Mutter" and then retitled "Black Flakes" ("Schwarze Flocken")
in which his mother addresses him: "Oh for a cloth, child / to wrap myself when
it's flashing with helmets / . . . hooves crushing the Song of Cedar / . . . [sic] A shawl,
just a thin shawl." In his reply to her envisioned plea a few lines later, he offers her
his poem as shawl: "I sought out my heart so it might weep, I found—oh the

summer's breath, / it was like you. / Then came my tears. I wove the shawl."
Ozick's *Shawl* is a response and continuation of the one woven by Celan. An
apostrophe to his dead mother, who instilled in him the love of Goethe, his poem
mirrors the apostrophic letters of Ozick's Rosa to her daughter and her fixation on
her shawl. (2) In *Faust*, the imprisoned near-insane Margarete raves about her dead
child as if it were alive and pleads to be allowed to nurse it. Margarete is thus not
only the incarnation of German romantic love, she is also a female victim of male
brutality and a child murderer haunted by her deed. Associated with the Song of
Songs, victimized by forces of evil, and finally reduced to infanticide and madness,
Margarete could appear to be a parallel of Rosa as well as her antithesis, were it
not for the decisive and colossal difference dividing myth from history, metaphor
from victim.

The medium for the coexistence of Margaret and Shulamith, Magda and Rosa,
is Paul Celan's German, the medium for the story of *The Shawl* is English, and the
medium for Rosa's reentry into the world of the living is Yiddish, through Perksy's
gentle insistence and her grandmother's voice. And the medium for prespeech bonding is the shawl itself, not the masculine prayer shawl that it evokes by association
but the feminine wimple of the cradle, the swaddling clothes that, like the tallit,
also serve as a shroud. As a Jewish-American woman writer, Ozick creates a
common ground in her book for her audience and her subjects, for the American
readers and the Holocaust survivor protagonists, through a barely remembered
mother tongue, Yiddish, and woman's translation of the tallit into the maternal
wimple. Stemming from the same Persian root, the word "shawl" is used in
German, English, and Yiddish for the same garment. Moreover, the word "shawl-
goat," occasionally used interchangeably for "shawl" in earlier periods, refers to a
goat that furnishes the wool for shawls. The "tsigele," then, the pure-white little
goat in the Yiddish lullabye, can be the source of "the shawl," mother for both
Rosa and Magda, and finally, not a child merchant, after all, but a provider of
shawls as well as of milk.

And this brings me to my final observation about Ozick's work, namely, the
dimension that she brings to this material as a woman writer. Although by now the
literature of the Holocaust is voluminous, Elie Wiesel's testimony in *Night* of the
murder of a child in Auschwitz remains central in any discussion of this subject, in
part because it is witnessed by a child and in part because the adult who remembers
interprets this atrocity as the equivalent of the death of God. No image conveys the
unspeakable horror more than the murder of children. Wiesel speaks with the
authority of the eyewitness; Ozick, moved to write literature about the Holocaust,
must do what every fiction writer does—act the ventriloquist for characters of her
own making. Faced with an ethical dilemma, the fiction writer must choose either
to abstain from all fictional portrayals of the Holocaust (as Philip Roth does
repeatedly by invoking the subject and then backing off), or to find a means of
conveying Holocaust experience that at the same time conveys awareness of the
debate on the subject. D. M. Thomas's deliberate retreat from fictionality in the
Babi Yar scene of his novel *The White Hotel*, in which he substitutes the testimony
of a survivor of the massacre recorded in Kuznetsov's documentary report, is,

according to Thomas, his reluctance to place his own words in the mouth of a character.[27] Ozick's *The Shawl* is clearly a work informed by this debate, and by the indictment of poetic language in Adorno's by now declaration-turned-axiom "After Auschwitz, it is no longer possible to write poems."[28]

Ozick begins by placing before the reader that searing moment of the death of a child: the death of a daughter witnessed by the mother. The reader is positioned with the mother, sharing the mother's excruciating decision as to which strategy will offer more protection, and then witnessing the failure to protect. The mother, and reader, are left with the first wail of a mute child, that demand addressed to the mother from which the entire verbal universe is spun, the demand for a presence that stems from the first sensibility of absence. The silence preceding the wail, the silence of mother-child preverbal inseparability is transformed, by that one utterance of pain, into the self-inflicted silence of Adorno's dictum, as Rosa muffles her own voice and attempts to swallow her daughter back into her own body by taking the child's muteness into herself. The babel of languages in the second part, the weaving together of a text that offers a variety of languages, each with its own claim to solace or heal, does not displace the wail in Part I. Rosa's spinning out of the letters to Magda stems from her guilt-ridden decision to hear Magda's cry as the moment of her entry into language, thereby intensifying the pain of her failure to save her, and also treating that moment as the first verbal communication of her child addressed to her, which requires a lifetime of reply and denial. The Yiddish lullabye, the maternal legacy denied to Magda, is the melody (and it is as much song as it is lyrics) of the mother tongue that cannot soothe away Magda's wail. By placing us within ear's range of the child's cry and with the shattered mother, Ozick insists on demetaphorizing the language of Holocaust literature. If her subsequent evocation of a Yiddish lullabye, in what is by now nearly a dead language, in a work of Holocaust literature written by an American seems sentimental, it is also a means for that community of readers, two or three generations removed from Eastern Europe, to identify with the Old World culture that was destroyed. And if her evocation of European Jewry's entanglement in the languages and cultures of their annihilators appears to blur the lines dividing Jewish from non-Jewish culture (as in Celan's poetry), it also provides American Jewish readers with another face of that community that is no more. "Then came my tears. I wove the shawl."

NOTES

1. For the paradoxes inherent in the Babel story and the double-edged effects of multi-lingualism, see Jacques Derrida, "Des Tours de Babel," in *Difference in Translation*, ed. Joseph F. Graham (Ithaca: Cornell University Press, 1985).

2. Cynthia Ozick, "America: Toward Yavne," *Judaism* (Summer, 1970), reprinted in *What Is Jewish Literature?*, ed. Hana Wirth-Nesher (Philadelphia: Jewish PubIcation Society, 1994), p. 28.

3. For a discussion of Ozick's struggle for historicity and her relation to Jewish memory, see Norman Finkelstein, *The Ritual of New Creation: Jewish Tradition and Contemporary Literature* (Albany: State University of New York Press, 1992).

4. Both Baal-Makhshoves (Isidore Elyashev) and Shmuel Niger have argued that bi- and multilingualism have been intrinsic features of Jewish literature in all periods. See Baal-Makhshoves, "One Literature in Two Languages," trans. Hana Wirth-Nesher and reprinted in *What Is Jewish Literature?* and Niger, *Bilingualism in the History of Jewish Literature*, trans. Joshua Fogel (New York: University Press of America, 1990).

5. For an analysis of poetic strategies of translation within narrative, see Meir Sternberg, "Polylingualism as Reality and Translation as Mimesis," *Poetics Today* 2 (1981), pp. 225–232.

6. Benjamin Harshav has argued that the work of many Yiddish poets in America should be considered a branch of American literature in the introduction to *American Yiddish Poetry: A Bilingual Anthology,* ed. Benjamin and Barbara Harshav (Berkeley: University of California Press, 1986). For discussions of the multilingual aspects of the writings of Henry Roth and of Saul Bellow, see Hana Wirth-Nesher, "Between Mother Tongue and Native Language: Multilingualism in *Call It Sleep,*" *Prooftexts: A Journal of Jewish Literary History* 10 (1990), pp. 297–312, and Hana Wirth-Nesher, " 'Who's he when he's at home?': Saul Bellow's Translations," in *New Essays on Seize the Day*, ed. Michael Kramer (Cambridge: Cambridge University Press, 1998).

7. Among the many works on this subject, the following have had a significant influence on my own writing: Sidra DeKoven Ezrahi, *By Words Alone: The Holocaust in Literature* (Chicago: University of Chicago Press, 1980); Lawrence Langer, *The Holocaust and the Literary Imagination* (New Haven: Yale University Press, 1975); Alan Mintz, *Hurban: Responses to Catastrophe in Hebrew Literature* (New York: Columbia University Press, 1984); Alvin Rosenfeld, *A Double Dying: Reflections on Holocaust Literature* (Bloomington: Indiana University Press, 1980); David Roskies, *Against the Apocalypse: Responses to Catastrophe in Modern Jewish Culture* (Cambridge: Harvard University Press, 1984).

8. Cynthia Ozick, *The Shawl* (New York: Random House, 1990), copyright page. All further page numbers will be cited in the text.

9. Ozick's sensitivity about representing the sufferings of Holocaust victims is evident in her letter to a survivor reprinted in Sarah Blacher Cohen, *Cynthia Ozick's Comic Art* (Bloomington: Indiana University Press, 1994), p. 148.

> Every Jew should feel as if he himself came out of Egypt . . . The Exodus took place 4000 years ago, and yet the Haggadah enjoins me to incorporate it into my own mind and flesh, to so act as if it happened directly and intensely to me, not as mere witness but as participant. Well, if I am enjoined to belong to an event that occurred 4000 years ago, how much more strongly am I obliged to belong to an event that occurred only 40 years ago.

10. Barbara Johnson, "Apostrophe, Animation, and Abortion," in *A World of Difference* (Baltimore: Johns Hopkins University Press, 1987), p. 198.

11. Sarah Blacher Cohen traces the source of this to the account of a devastating narrative of the denial of the maternal instinct in Tadeusz Borowski, *This Way for the Gas, Ladies and Gentlemen*, trans. Barbara Vedder (New York: Penguin, 1976), p. 43.

12. For a detailed analysis of the *Aeneid* as a central intertext in *The Shawl*, see Elaine Kauver, "The Magic Shawl," in *Cynthia Ozick's Fiction* (Bloomington: Indiana University Press, 1993), pp. 197–199.

13. Johnson, p. 187.

14. Julian Tuwim, "We, the Polish Jews . . ." (Fragments) in *Poems of the Ghetto: A Testament of Lost Men*, ed. and with introduction by Adam Gillon (New York: Twayne, 1969), p. 83.

15. Kauver notes that the choice of the name Lublin stresses the fate of Rosa's assimilation. "Originally planned as a reservation for the concentration of Jews by the Nazis, Lublin became one of the centers for mass extermination and was the site of a prisoner of war camp for Jews who had served in the Polish army. The Nazis made no distinction between Jews who abandoned their Jewishness and Jews who celebrated it" (187).

16. Berger suggests that the cinnamon-and-almond flavor evokes the scent of the spices in the decorative box used for the Havdalah service marking the end of the Sabbath; it thereby signifies liturgy as spiritually invigorating. Kauver associates cinnamon and almond with the sacred anointing oil in Scripture and a biblical symbol of divine approval, so that Magda becomes a holy babe for Rosa. I believe that two intertexts are evoked in these two scents: the almonds are obviously an allusion to the Yiddish lullabye "Raisins and Almonds"; the cinnamon is a reference to "The Cinnamon Shops" by the Polish-Jewish writer Bruno Shultz, murdered by the Nazis and the inspiration for Ozick's novel *Messiah of Stockholm*.

17. Abraham Goldfaden, *Shulamis: oder Bat Yerushalayim* (New York: Hebrew Publishing Company), p. 10 (my translation).

18. Introductory notes for "Rozhinkes mit Mandlen," in *Mir Trogn A Gezang: The New Book of Yiddish Songs*, 4th ed. (New York: Workmen's Circle Education Department, 1982).

19. While Ozick is aware of this tendency in American-Jewish culture generally, her excellent translations of the works of Jacob Glatstein, Chaim Grade, and Dovid Einhorn are proof of her knowledge of and commitment to Yiddish literature. See also her essays on Yiddish literature and on the problems of translation, "Sholem Aleichem's Revolution" and "A Translator's Monologue," in *Metaphor and Memory* (New York: Knopf, 1989), pp. 173–198; 199–208.

20. For an excellent discussion of Celan's multilingual upbringing and its cultural resonances see, "Loss and the Mother Tongue," in John Felstiner, *Paul Celan: Poet, Survivor, Jew* (New Haven: Yale University Press, 1995), pp. 3–22. The cultural significance of linguistic choice in Eastern European Jewish civilization is explored at length in Dan Miron, *A Traveler Disguised: A Study in the Rise of Modern Yiddish Fiction* (New York: Schocken, 1973).

21. Paul Celan, "Death Fugue," Michael Hamburger's translation, in Paul Celan, *Poems*, selected, translated and introduced by Michael Hamburger (New York: Persea Books, 1980), p. 53.

22. Shoshana Felman, *Testimony: Crises of Witnessing in Literature, Psychoanalysis, and History* (New York: Routledge, 1992), p. 32.

23. Cynthia Ozick's Hebrew name is Shoshana. The Hebrew original of "I am the rose of Sharon, the lily of the valleys" is "Ani havazellet hasharon, shoshonat ha'amakim."

24. Felstiner, p. 298.

25. Israel Chalfen, *Einer Biographie seiner Jugend*, 1979, quoted in Katherine Washburn's introduction to *Paul Celan: Last Poems* (San Francisco: North Point Press, 1986), p. vii.

26. Felman, p. 27.

27. For a discussion of this issue, see Hana Wirth-Nesher, "The Ethics of Narration in D. M. Thomas's *White Hotel*," *Journal of Narrative Technique* (Winter 1985).

28. Theodor Adorno, "After Auschwitz," in *Negative Dialectics*, trans. E. B. Ashton (New York: Continuum, 1973), p. 362. As Langer has noted, "Adorno never intended it to be taken literally as his own elaborations of the principle demonstrate" (see pp. 1–3).

This research was supported in part by a grant from the Israel Science Foundation.

Chapter Twenty-two

American Anglophone Literature and Multilingual America

Lawrence Rosenwald

American literature is wonderfully rich in scenes of language and dialect contact, but to make sense of these scenes we need to look at them as belonging both to the specific history of American linguistic life and to the general history of literary representation. The first approach has a political urgency to it, an urgency beautifully stated in a recent article by Marc Shell:

> Thus the story of America's social language-engineering is there to be understood and perhaps wisely redirected. It is a remarkable, and some would say heroic, story of immigrations: forced, illegal, and voluntary; of treaties, purchases, and constitutions by which Spanish- French-, German-, and Amerindian-speakers' languages, among many others, were subsumed; of a once new and powerfully nationalist literary movement that still informs devotedly monoglottal American university departments. Most Americans, however, cannot yet tell the story, or they do not want to tell the real story, not so much because the languages are forgotten (which they are), but mainly because forgetting language difference—and hence, more critically, partly suppressing the category of "language" itself—is still the urgent component of unofficially anglophone America's understanding of itself.[1]

The second approach has a theoretical fascination to it. It entails questions like these: what strategies have writers found for representing the diversity of languages, dialects, and idiolects? Where and how do these strategies work, and where and how do they fail? What attitudes toward language and literature do these strategies imply? What sorts of representation of dialect and idiolect do the various alphabets of the world make possible? What does it mean to speak of representing the speech of an invented character? And, most generally and poignantly, Why does the literature of so multilingual a world give so imperfect a portrait of that world's linguistic complexity?

Both approaches are necessary. The first without the second is too abstract, too schematic; the second without the first is weightless.

On Some Encounters between the Languages of Europe
and the Languages of America

A central fact about the linguistic history of America is that the first European travelers to this continent found themselves in the presence of languages radically unlike their own. Columbus himself knew Italian, Latin, Spanish, and Portuguese; his interpreter, Luis de Torres, knew Hebrew and Arabic, and by some accounts Chaldaean. None of these languages helped at all.

Columbus dealt with the problem of a radically alien language by declaring it not to be a language at all. He writes at the end of his account of the first landing, "I have caused six of [the inhabitants] to be taken on board and sent to your Majesties, that they may learn to speak." Editors and translators have often wrongly amended this to "that they may learn to speak Spanish." But the Spanish text is clear: *"para que deprendan fablar."*[2] Columbus proposes to treat the Caribbeans like so many *enfants sauvages.* He proposes this even though he has just recorded the Caribbean name of the island he has landed on.

Cortés dealt with the problem through two interpreters working in tandem. One was Jeronimo de Aguilar, a Spaniard who had been shipwrecked in Yucatan in 1511 and by the time that Cortés ransomed him eight years later had learned to speak Mayan. The other was La Malinche, also called Doña Marina, a native of the Gulf Coast who spoke both Mayan and Nahuatl, the language of the Aztecs, and is said to have joined Cortés's expedition not only as his translator but also as his mistress. Octavio Paz writes of how La Malinche haunts the language of Mexico:

> The symbol of [the violation brought about by the Conquest] is Doña Malinche, the mistress of Cortés. It is true that she gave herself voluntarily to the conquistador, but he forgot her as soon as her usefulness was over. Doña Marina becomes a figure representing the Indian women who were fascinated, violated or seduced by the Spaniards. . . . There is . . . nothing surprising about the curse that weighs against La Malinche. This explains the success of the contemptuous adjective *malinchista* recently put into circulation by the newspapers to denounce all those who have been corrupted by foreign influences.[3]

In Columbus's story, native Americans are said to have no language, so the only linguistic relation imaginable is the imposition of Spanish upon the languageless. In Cortés's story, Native Americans are acknowledged to have languages, but the task of negotiating between them and the languages of Europe is understood in later tradition as the abandoning of indigenous culture. In the one story, translation is impossible. In the other, translation is treasonous.

The history of relations between European and American languages involves a linguistic history that begins in the seventeenth century with Roger Williams and John Eliot, continues through the nineteenth with John Heckewelder and Peter Duponceau, and extends into the twentieth with Edward Sapir and Benjamin Whorf; a translational history that begins in the seventeenth century with John Eliot, continues through the nineteenth with Longfellow and Henry Rowe Schoolcraft, and extends into the twentieth with Dennis Tedlock and Jerome Rothenberg; and a representational history that begins in the seventeenth century with the Indian captivity narratives, continues in the nineteenth with the novels of James Fenimore Cooper, and extends into the twentieth with the films of Kevin Costner and Michael Mann. Each of these histories is rich and varied. But to a saddeningly large extent, they all take place in the territory between Columbus' vision and Cortés', between a language denied and a language betrayed.

On Some Passages in James Fenimore Cooper's The Last of the Mohicans

In most of the extraordinarily influential novel *The Last of the Mohicans*, Cooper represents Native American languages as being something less than language. Consider, for example, a celebrated conversation between Magua, the Huron villain, and Duncan Heyward, the white leading man. Magua is asking Heyward what has become of the Mohican Uncas, son of Chingachgook, also called *Le Cerf Agile*.

> " 'Le Cerf Agile' is not here?"
>
> "I know not whom you call the 'nimble deer,' " said Duncan, gladly profiting by any excuse to create delay.
>
> "Uncas," returned Magua, pronouncing the Delaware name with even greater difficulty than he spoke his English words. " 'Bounding elk' " is what the white man says when he calls to the young Mohican."
>
> "Here is some confusion in names between us, le Renard," said Duncan, hoping to provoke a discussion. "Daim is the French for deer, and cerf for stag; élan is the true term, when one would speak of an elk."
>
> "Yes," muttered the Indian, in his native tongue; "the pale faces are prattling women! they have two words for each thing, while a red skin will make the sound of his *voice* speak for him." Then changing his language, he continued, adhering to the imperfect nomenclature of his provincial instructers [*sic*], "The deer is swift, but weak; the elk is swift, but strong; and the son of 'le serpent' is 'le cerf agile.' Has he leaped the river to the woods?" (91)[4]

Magua accurately states Uncas's epithets in French and English. Duncan argues that the English and French epithets for Uncas do not mean the same thing, and attributes the disparity to a "confusion." Magua objects not to Duncan's pedantry but to the nature of white languages; white languages, he says, "have two words for each thing."

We might at this point expect Magua to celebrate Native languages for having only one word for each thing. If he did so, we might read his argument as an attack on what Tocqueville was to call the "unsettled condition" of words in a democracy.[5] But in fact Magua does something different; he makes Native American languages nonlinguistic. He draws a contrast, that is, not between two names and one, but between names and sounds: "a red skin will make the *sound of his voice* speak for him" (my emphasis). By this he implies that a Native speaker can do all the ordinary work of language by sound alone, without the distinctions of words.

The usually conventional idiom "red skin" for "red person" intensifies the sheer physicality of this idea of Native communication: the skin stands in place of the being as the sound in place of the words.

Elsewhere, Cooper brilliantly dramatizes Magua's theories. In chapter 10, for example, the white hero Hawk-eye and his two Native companions, Chingachgook and Uncas, are holding a debate in Delaware.[6] The subject is whether to continue their journey by land or by water. Hawk-eye prefers water; the others land. At the beginning of the debate, Hawk-eye is losing—because, Cooper tells us, "he rather affected the cold and inartificial manner, which characterizes all classes of Anglo-Americans, when unexcited" (199). To win the debate, he has to change his manner. He becomes more animated, adopts "all the arts of native eloquence" (199), and persuades his companions to follow his advice.

Now European-American admiration for "native eloquence" is nothing new; Thomas Jefferson, for example, had challenged "the whole orations of Demosthenes and Cicero . . . to produce a single passage, superior to the speech of Logan, a Mingo chief."[7] But what Jefferson admired was Logan's power over words. In Cooper, on the other hand, "the arts of native eloquence" turn out to be the arts of gesture. The debate is conducted in Delaware, which Heyward does not know, but "the language of the Mohicans," Cooper writes, "was accompanied by gestures so direct and natural, that Heyward had but little difficulty in following the thread of their argument" (198–199). Hawk-eye, on the other hand, is "obscure" (199); that is, he does not make many gestures, so Heyward cannot fully understand him. When he adopts the arts of native eloquence, though, his meaning becomes miraculously clear:

> Elevating an arm, he pointed out the track of the sun, repeating the gesture for every day that was necessary to accomplish their object. Then he delineated a long and painful path, amid rocks and water courses. The age and weakness of the slumbering and unconscious Munro, were indicated by signs too palpable to be mistaken. Duncan perceived that even his own powers were spoken lightly of, as the scout extended his palm, and mentioned him by the appellation of the "open hand;" a name his liberality had purchased of all the friendly tribes. Then came the representation of the light and graceful movements of a canoe, set in forcible contrast to the tottering steps of one enfeebled and tired. He concluded by pointing to the scalp of the Oneida, and apparently urging the necessity of their departing speedily, and in a manner that should leave no trail.
>
> The Mohicans listened gravely, and with countenances that reflected the sentiments of the speaker. (199)

This is, frankly, preposterous. It is, first, preposterous to suggest that Native American speakers accompany speech with gesture—Cooper writes in another place of "those significant gestures with which an Indian always illustrates his eloquence" (106)—and that European American speakers do not. We know perfectly well that all speech is accompanied with gesture. And, more important, Cooper's contemporaries knew it too. The Moravian missionary John Heckewelder, Cooper's chief source, makes the point clearly:

It has been asserted by many persons that the languages of the Indians are deficient in words, and that, in order to make themselves understood, they are obliged to resort to motions and signs with their hands. This is entirely a mistake. I do not know a nation of whom foreigners do not say the same things. (128)[8]

Lewis Cass criticized both Heckewelder and Cooper for their too-flattering portraits of Indians, but even he knows that Cooper's distinction here is false:

"They number," says one of the speakers in [Cooper's 1827 novel] *The Prairie*, "as many as the fingers of my hand." No Indian from Patagonia to Hudson's Bay ever used this periphrastic expression for the simple word *ten*. It is rather difficult to believe the author can be serious. An Indian will hold up his fingers if apprehensive he cannot be understood, and appeal by significant gestures to the eye; but to those who understand him he will use the proper numeral.[9]

Cooper's radical distinction between a speech always accompanied by gesture and a speech devoid of it is his own reductive invention

Nor in Cooper is Native American speech merely *accompanied* by gesture. In the passage quoted, and in several other scenes of the novel, the meaning of a Native American utterance is entirely *translated* by gesture; the language itself becomes unnecessary. And this too is preposterous. What gestures could Hawk-eye possibly be making to "delineate a long and painful path, amid rocks and water courses"? What is he doing to represent "the light and graceful movements of a canoe"? He is not, after all, Marcel Marceau; and presumably he is making only the sort of gesture used to accompany speech, rather than the sort of gesture that mimes use to replace it. Here again Heckewelder is sensibly skeptical, claiming that Native Americans

seat themselves promiscuously around a council fire, some leaning one way, some another, so that a stranger on viewing them, might be led to conclude they were inattentive to what was said, or had become tired of attending. . . . They are all ears, though they do not stare at the speaker.[10]

Heckewelder knows, that is, that gestures, like language, are culturally specific

We might find a source for Cooper's ideas here in French theorists of language like Condillac; Cooper probably had not read them, but their influence was widely diffused, and they do talk about a universal language of gestures. The gestures they have in mind, however, though they "constitute a rudimentary mode of expression and communication . . . do not constitute the language peculiar to man."[11] They can express pain or pleasure, but not, say, "the light and graceful movements of a canoe, set in forcible contrast to the tottering steps of one enfeebled and tired." What is distinctive about Cooper's universal language of gesture is that it can express everything that can be expressed by "the language peculiar to man."

Moreover, similar ideas have different meanings in different contexts. Condillac and Rousseau found much to admire in the universal language of gesture Cooper presents. Clearly, Cooper does too. But when writers like Condillac and Rousseau assess the universal language of gesture, they do not have to deal with anyone they actually believe to be speaking it. Cooper does; he is writing during one of the many shameful periods in the relations between the American government and Native Americans, a period in which the majority of Native Americans in the eastern parts of the continent are being forcibly or fraudulently driven west of the Mississippi. And it is hard not to feel that Cooper's representation of Native American languages makes such relocation morally plausible. He represents these languages as something admirable, but also as something less than European languages; he represents the speakers of these languages as noble savages, but as savages rather than members of a society or nation.

Cooper is interesting as a dramatizer of language partly because he sometimes so sharply contradicts himself, thus bearing out Fitzgerald's remark that an artist is someone who can entertain two contradictory ideas without going crazy. Toward the end of the novel, in scenes centered on the doomed Uncas, Cooper represents Native American languages as verbally complex, culturally specific, and resistant to translation. The most striking of these scenes is the account of Uncas's "war-song," that is, the chant he makes and performs to prepare himself for what will be his final battle:

> If it were possible to translate the comprehensive and melodious language in which he spoke, the ode might read something like the following:
>
> > Manitto! Manitto! Manitto!
> > Thou art great—thou art good—thou art wise –
> > Manitto! Manitto!
> > Thou art just!
> >
> > In the heavens, in the clouds, Oh! I see!
> > Many spots—many dark—many red –
> > In the heavens, Oh! I see!
> > Many clouds.
> >
> > In the heavens, in the clouds, Oh! I see!
> > The whoop, the long yell, and the cry –
> > In the woods, Oh! I hear!
> > The loud whoop!
> >
> > Manitto! Manitto! Manitto!
> > I am weak—thou art strong—I am slow –
> > Manitto! Manitto!
> > Give me aid. (319)

This is at odds with everything we have so far seen. To begin with, Cooper calls red language not only "melodious" but also "comprehensive"; it has not only sound and music but also sense. Probably the principal sense of "comprehensive" is "containing much in small compass, compendious"; but present also is "characterized by mental comprehension . . . that grasps or understands (a thing) fully" (OED). And, appropriately enough, a comprehensive language cannot communicate without being comprehended. Elsewhere in the novel, Cooper would have written that "though the words were unknown to the listeners, nothing could have been clearer than the martial spirit and valiant nobility of the speaker"; but here that *topos* is not in force, and translation is both necessary and difficult.

Cooper's actual "translation"—he was of course making up Uncas's song, not translating a Delaware original—makes that necessity and difficulty clear. Consider, by way of comparison, a celebrated translation made by Cooper's contemporary Henry Rowe Schoolcraft, a considerable European American authority on Native American life. In his 1845 *Oneota*, he presents as an example of Native American poetry the Ojibwa "Chant to the Fire-Fly." He describes it as follows: "metre there was none, at least, of a regular character: [the lines were] the wild improvisations of children in a merry mood" (61). He then presents a transcription of the poem, what he calls a "literal" translation of it, and, in a footnote, a verse translation:

> Wau wau tay see!
> Wau wau tay see!
> E mow e shin
> Tshe bwau ne baun-e wee!
> Be eghaun—be eghaun—ewee!
> Wa wau tay see!
> Wa wau tay see!
> Was sa koon ain je gun
> Was sa koon ain je gun.
>
> Flitting-white-fire-insect!
> Waving-white-fire-bug!
> give me light before I got to bed!
> give me light before I go to sleep.
> Come little dancing-white-fire-bug!
> Come little flitting-white-fire-beast!
> Light me with your bright white-flame-instrument—your little candle.
>
> Fire-fly, fire-fly! bright little thing,
> Light me to bed, and my song I will sing.
> Give me your light, as you fly o'er my head,
> That I may merrily go to my bed.[12]

The transcription and "literal" translation, together with some explanatory notes, give us the poem as a complex artifact.[13] The transcription reveals unfamiliar but evidently ordered sound patterns; the translation, unfamiliar but intelligible ways of naming. But Schoolcraft hides these truths. For one thing, even before we get to the poem he has told us that it has no regular meter, and that it is "wild," that is, not cultured or disciplined; we are then less ready to see the intricate formal patterning that the transcription reveals. For another, even his "literal" translation blurs the formal order evident in the transcription; for example, lines 1–2 and 6–7 are identical in the transcription but different in the translation. Schoolcraft's explanatory notes defend this, but the effect of the blurring is still to say that the evident formal order of the poem does not matter.

The inept verse-translation obscures the original poem still further. It substitutes regular meter for irregular, and familiar sound patterns and ways of naming for unfamiliar ones; its implicit argument is that if the Ojibwa chant is a poem, it is a

poem of a familiar English sort. Moreover, the verse translation has material that
the transcription and literal translation do not; the only "complete" version, that is,
is the verse translation. The account as a whole seems to imply that the chant is
either an English poem or no poem at all.

Cooper's "translation" suggests a different vision. Without being great poetry, it
is at least unfamiliar poetry; the lines of unrhymed anapests, the unashamed repetition of the divinity's name, the recurring numerical structures (the first two lines of
each quatrain are composed of three sense-units, the third of two, the fourth of
one), the complex syntax of the second quatrain all suggest what Cooper elsewhere
seems to deny: that Native American language has complex, artificial, and unfamiliar structures and requires complex, artful, and unfamiliar translations. The makers
of such poems are not identical to white makers of poems; they are not undeveloped
versions of such makers; they are adult, artful, social, and different.

Cooper thus anticipates the best anthropological translators of this century. Dell
Hymes, for examples, has reshaped the translation of Native American poetry and
storytelling through his passionate attention to "the structure of the original
poem."[14] By structure he means *particularly the form of repetition and variation,
of constants and contrasts, in verbal organization*;[15] and his retranslation of the
firefly song, animated by his concern with such matters, is more Cooper's sort of
text than it is Schoolcraft's:

> Flitting insect of white fire!
> Flitting insect of white fire!
> Come, give me light before I sleep!
> Come, give me light before I sleep!
> Flitting insect of white fire!
> Flitting insect of white fire!
> Light me with your bright white instrument of flame.
> Light me with your bright white instrument of flame.[16]

Hymes's concern with structure has been complemented by Dennis Tedlock's
concern with performance, with the circumstances in which poems are enacted and
the theatrical and rhythmical details of the enactment. Here, for example, is Tedlock
on "voice quality in Zuni narratives":

> When a character is trying to pull some tough blades loose from a yucca plant, the
> narrator may render "He pulled" with the strain of someone who is trying to speak
> while holding his breath during great exertion. When a passage involves intense emo-
> tion, the narrator may combine . . . softness . . . with a break in his voice, as if he felt
> like weeping.[17]

And Cooper has anticipated Tedlock's work too; he follows the text of Uncas's
song with this strikingly Tedlockian commentary on its performance:

> At the end of what might be called each verse, he made a pause, by raising a note
> louder and longer than common, that was peculiarly suited to the sentiment just ex-
> pressed. The first close was solemn, and intended to convey the idea of veneration;
> the second descriptive, bordering on the alarming; and the third was the well-known

and terrific war-whoop, which burst from the lips of the young warrior, like a combination of all the frightful sounds of battle. The last was like the first, humble and
imploring. Three times did he repeat this song, and as often did he encircle the post,
in his dance. (319–320)

Cooper's account of performance takes its meaning from being joined to an account
of the text performed. By itself, an account of performance can, as we have seen,
reduce language to gesture. Joined to an account of text, however, it becomes the
thick description of a speech-act. Uncas's tones and gestures make sense here,
because they do not have to do all the work; they are illustrating, rather than
replacing, the texts they accompany.

Cooper has so many strategies of portrayal partly because more than any other
American author he was haunted by the multilingual character of America. But
there is another reason too. He changes course at the end of his book because the
battle is over, and all red resistance to white domination has been overcome, and
whereas the language of the active adversary has to be treated with ideological
vigilance, the language of the defeated adversary can be treated with anthropological respect. Geronimo, the last great Indian antagonist of the United States government till the American Indian Movement, died in 1909. Franz Boas's *Handbook of
American Indian Languages* came out in 1911; Benjamin Whorf's celebrations of
Hopi came out in the 1920s, and both of these remarkable linguistic accounts are
as much elegy as advocacy. Cooper too, at the end of his book, can celebrate the
complexity of a Native American language whose speakers pose no political threat
to American expansion.

On Recording the Dialects of American English

The American debate over the representation of dialect in literature has been surprisingly even. Eminent writers have argued that writers of literature ought, when
presenting characters likely to speak something other than standard English, to
present their speech in the dialect they are likely to speak, in all possible acoustical,
lexical, and grammatical specificity. Equally eminent writers have argued the opposite.

The argument on behalf of recording dialect is simply the argument for realism:
that's the way they speak. It is thoughtfully elaborated by William Stanley Braith-
waite:

[Dialect]may be employed as the langue d'oc of Frederic Mistral's Provencal poems,
as a preserved tongue, the only adequate medium of rendering the psychology of character, and of describing the background of the people whose lives and experience are
kept within the environment where the dialect survives as the universal speech; or it
may be employed as a special mark of emphasis upon the peculiar characteristic and
temperamental traits of a people whose action and experiences are given in contact
and relationship with a dominant language, and are set in a literary fabric of which
they are but one strand of man in the weaving.[18]

The argument against recording dialect is more varied. It may be specific to a particular dialect at a particular moment, as when James Weldon Johnson argues against the representation of black dialect because of "the limitations on Negro dialect imposed by the fixing effects of long convention."[19] (Johnson is thinking of the "long convention" of the minstrel show, with its "unrealistic—indeed, insidious—archetypal portraiture of the black man as a head-scratching, foot-shuffling, happy-go-lucky fool" [ibid.].) It may also be general, as in Henry James's vexing and brilliant critique of "the riot of the vulgar tongue"

> One might state it more freely still and the truth would be as evident: the plural number, the vulgar tongues, each with its intensest note, but pointed the moral more luridly. Grand generalised continental riot or particular pedantic, particular discrimi-nated and "sectional" and self-conscious riot—to feel the thick breath, to catch the ugly snarl, of all or of either, was to be reminded of the only conditions that guard the grace, the only origins that save the honour, or even the life, of dialect: those precedent to the invasion, to the sophistication, of schools and unconscious of the smartness of echoes and the taint of slang. The thousands of celebrated productions raised their monument but to the bastard vernacular of communities disinherited of the felt difference between the speech of the soil and the speech of the newspaper, and capable thereby, accordingly, of taking slang for simplicity, the composite for the quaint and the vulgar for the natural. . . . The monument was there, if one would, but was one to regret one's own failure to have contributed a stone? Perish, and all ignobly, the thought![20]

There is an obvious problem with the argument against dialect: if we believe with Buffon that *le style, c'est l'homme*, we probably believe that part of a person's style is his or her idiolect, and have to concede that not representing idiolect hinders representing style and human identity. (By "idiolect" I mean, to quote David Crystal's *The Cambridge Encyclopedia of Language*, "the linguistic system of an individual—a personal dialect; also, more narrowly, the speech habits of a person as displayed in a particular variety at a given time."[21] There is a vast, fascinating, and, so far as I know, unexplored difference between understanding a person as summed up by an idiolect and understanding a person as summed up by an expressive style.)

But there is also a problem with the argument on behalf of dialect. In that argument, the representation of dialect is justified in relation to the representation of characters. But that justification implies strict limitations. If dialect is justified as a means of representing character, it is not justified, in fact it is already compro-mised, as an independent literary language. We celebrate the Greek of Homer, the Italian of Dante, the French of Montaigne, the English of Shakespeare or Melville not as accurately representing the author or his people but as marvelously describing the world.

The relations between orthography and pronunciation are complex. A fair amount of literary dialect is "eye dialect"; that is, a nonstandard spelling that doesn't indicate a nonstandard pronunciation. In such cases the nonstandard spelling says only, "Let me tell you again that this speaker is a dialect speaker." Nor does standard orthography adequately represent standard pronunciation, that is, the actual pronunciation of standard-speakers. Examples of this last might be the pronunciation in most contexts of "just" as "jist" or "jest"; the general tendency in pronunciation to reduce unstressed vowels to shwas; the variety even of nondialectal pronunciations of words like "children" or "interesting"; the general tendency to condense consonant clusters; even what is in general the failure of standard orthography to represent contraction.

Robin Lakoff in a lecture told of a journalist who quoted George Wallace as saying, "I could of told you etc." Lakoff pointed out that "I could of" is in fact an accurate transcription not only of Wallace's pronunciation of "I could have" but also of that of most standard-speakers, and suggests that the journalist's mode of transcription reflects in fact not a differentiation of Wallace's speech and a standard-speaker's but a means of degrading Wallace. She also suggested, accordingly, that the left-wing journalist would probably have transcribed Adlai Stevenson's enunciation of those words as "I could have" and Lyndon Johnson's as "I could've," expressing by these variations not differences in the speaker's sound but differences in the transcriber's attitude.[22]

If we think it important to represent dialect and idiolect on the ground that people are what they say, we would in theory have to represent every speaker's pronunciation, all the time. In fact no important author does this. Why not? The dialectologist Sumner Ives dismisses such possibilities: "[A]t some point," he writes, "the author must restrain his desire to be comprehensive and give some thought to the patience and understanding of his readers."[23] But this is clearly not a sufficient reason; reading a book in which no character spoke standard, even reading a book written in the International Phonetic Alphabet, could hardly be more difficult than reading *Finnegans Wake.*

Isn't it simply wrong to speak of "representing" the language of a character? After all, the author is not a transcriber but an inventor. But "language" means two things here, one of which the author invents and one of which he or she does not invent but reproduces. Twain invents the particular utterances Huck makes, and invents Huck's style. But he does not and cannot invent Huck's dialect. He cannot, that is, make Huck say what Dickens's Joe Gargery says; Huck cannot in speaking of some joyous expedition say to Jim, "[W]hat larks," because "lark" in that sense is not part of his dialect. The author of realistic fiction who identifies characters by class, by region, by race, by education must honor the pledges implicit in those identifications; someone identified as a poor white boy in Missouri before the Civil War, with a scanty education, must speak in accord with those constraints, whatever he actually says.

Of course, many authors do invent the dialects and idiolects of their characters. But we feel often feel that there is something inauthentic in this. And when we pursue the matter, an abyss opens up, because in fact most characters in most fictions do not speak in accord with the constraints laid on their speech by the asserted facts of their identity. What would an analysis of the novel lead to that took this grand falsification perpetrated by the novel as its subject?

On a Dialogue in Huck Finn

At the end of chapter 14 of *Huck Finn*, there is a wonderful dialogue, as good as almost anything in Plato:

"Why Huck, doan' de French people talk de same way we does?"

"*No*, Jim; you couldn't understand a word they said—not a single word."

"Well now, I be ding-busted! How do dat come?"

"*I* don't know; but it's so. I got some of their jabber out of a book. Spose a man was to come to you and say *Polly-voo-franzy*—what would you think?"

"I wouldn' think nuff'n; I'd take en bust him over de head. Dat is, if he warn't white. I wouldn't 'low no nigger to call me dat."

"Shucks, it ain't calling you anything. It's only saying do you know how to talk French."

"Well, den, why couldn't he *say* it?"

"Why, he *is* a-saying it. That's a Frenchman's *way* of saying it."

"Well, it's a blame' ridicklous way, en I doan' want to hear no mo' bout it. Dey ain' no sense in it."

"Looky here, Jim; does a cat talk like we do?"

"No, a cat don't."

"Well, does a cow?"

"No, a cow don't, nuther."

"Does a cat talk like a cow, or a cow talk like a cat?"

"No dey don't."

"It's natural and right for 'em to talk different from each other, ain't it?"

" 'Course."

"And ain't it natural and right for a cat and a cow to talk different from *us*?"

"Why, mos' sholy it is."

"Well, then, why ain't it natural and right for a *Frenchman* to talk different from us? You answer me that."

"Is a cat a man, Huck?"

"No."

"Well, den, dey ain't no sense in a cat talkin' like a man. Is a cow a man?—er is a cow a cat?"

"No, she ain't either of them."

"Well, den, she ain' got no business to talk like either one er the yuther of 'em. Is a Frenchman a man?"

"Yes."

"*Well*, den! Dad blame it, why doan' he *talk* like a man? You answer me *dat*!"

I see it warn't no use wasting words—you can't learn a nigger to argue. So I quit.[24]

This is a dialogue *about* languages, and a dialogue *in* languages.

In the dialogue about languages, Huck's position is that foreign languages exist. He bases this partly on what he's gotten out of a book. In defending what he's gotten out of a book, he makes an analogy between language difference and species difference; as there are different species, so there are different languages. In pursuing this analogy, he uses "natural and right" as a term that authorizes his view of things.

Jim's position is that foreign languages do not exist. He has not gotten this out of a book; he does not know how to read. His position is empirical. (Later he will ask the King, who has fraudulently passed himself off as the Dauphin, to speak some French; the king will claim that he has forgotten all his French, and thereby lend empirical support to Jim's position.) He rejects Huck's analogy between language difference and species difference in favor of an analogy between language unity and species unity: all those who belong to the same species will speak the same language. In pursuing this analogy he uses "sense" and "business" as terms that authorize his view of things.

Huck's position is correct, but Jim wins the argument. The paradox leads to three questions. What sort of argument does Huck need to make Jim see what is in fact the truth? Why can't Huck make that argument? Why can't Jim see that truth?

For Huck to win the argument, he needs to be able to draw an analogy between language difference and cultural difference. So why can't Huck do that? The maybe surprising answer is that he doesn't really understand cultural difference. He has a spectacularly good sense of how to deal with the various figures he meets from within his own culture, pretty much regardless of their social standing within that culture. But the one time he tries to do an impersonation outside his own culture, that is, of an English servant, he fails. (Appropriately enough, the one place in the book where he says he cannot reproduce someone's speech is when he is dealing with someone speaking British English: "I can't give the old gent's words, nor I can't imitate him" [155].) And of course he fails when he tries to cross that other cultural barrier constituted by gender, when he tries to fool Judith Loftus into thinking he's a girl.

What Huck does have, and what Jim also has, is a sense of social difference—of the difference between free whites and enslaved blacks. And we might imagine that a sense of this difference would help them here, would provide a useful analogy. In fact, though, a sense of social difference will not help here, for the obvious reason that for Huck and Jim the difference between free white and enslaved black is empirically *not* connected to language difference. As far as Huck and Jim know or say, they are speaking the same language. Huck and Jim do not know, but we do, that in this particular case the difference between free white and enslaved black has *annihilated* differences of culture and thus differences of language. The barriers between English and the languages of Africa, between American culture and the cultures of Africa, were broken down by the imposition of differences of power. All that remains in this dialogue of those vast differences of culture and language are the important but barely intelligible traces of the African sources of Black English.[25]

If either interlocutor has a sense of cultural difference, it is Jim. His distinguishing between a white and a black enunciation of "polly-voo franzy" is a first step toward that sense. So is his use of social terms like "sense" and "business" in place of Huck's "natural and right." But we can see in Jim's reaching toward a sense of cultural difference how unlikely he is to get there. If a black said "polly-voo franzy" to him, Jim would treat the statement as forbidden nonsense. He has no reason to think of it as foreign; black speakers are part of his world. If a white were the speaker, Jim would treat the statement as permitted nonsense. Here, perhaps, he would have some reason to think of it as foreign; white speakers move outside his world, and Jim is curious. But there is no room for him to turn his curiosity on white nonsense, because his differences from whites are so purely differences of power that treating them, and investigating them, as differences of culture would be an impossible luxury.

This is also a dialogue *in* languages. Specifically it is a dialogue between what Twain in the preface to *Huck Finn* calls "the Missouri negro dialect" and "the ordinary 'Pike-County' dialect" (2). And as a representation of the former, it is, so far as we can tell at this historical distance, stunning; William Labov singled it out for praise in a regrettably unpublished lecture, and Labov's pioneering investigations of Black English Vernacular give his judgment a lot of weight.

But if we want to understand what is going on in this dialogue, we have to look not only at Twain's rendering of Jim's dialect but also at his rendering of Huck's, and above all at the relation between the two, and at the way that relation works for the reader. Standard spelling is only partly a means of representing pronunciation; it is also a means of representing morphology, and ends up also representing history.[26] But dialectal spelling, that is, the alterations of standard spelling brought about by the attempt to present dialect, is essentially a means of representing pronunciation; and for that end it surrenders its other functions and becomes a single-value system, which when juxtaposed to the multiple-value system of standard spelling is likely to seem impoverished. Consider, for example, Jim's occasional "doan' " and Huck's consistent "don't." Twain's presentation of Huck's utterance reveals the morphological information that "don't" is a contraction derived from "do" and "not." Twain's presentation of Jim's utterance blurs that information. Huck's association with standard spelling makes him the bearer of information. Huck the hater of book learning becomes in Twain's transcription the conveyer of morphology and etymology; Huck the truant becomes Huck the schoolmaster. What sharpens the point here is that Twain's distinction of spelling is probably unwarranted by a distinction of pronunciation corresponding to it. That is, I don't think there's likely to have been any significant difference between Huck's pronunciation of that word and Jim's. The reason I don't think that is that if I were speaking these sentences, my own enunciation of "don't" on the previous two occurrences of the word wouldn't sound that word's final *t* any more than Jim's does. So Huck and Jim probably make the same sound. Twain chooses, then, to get that sound right with Jim and wrong with Huck; and as a result of that choice, Jim is stigmatized.

Other distinctions between Huck's speech and Jim's have similar effects, though these often record what seem likely to be real differences in pronunciation. Jim's "gwyne" for "going" obscures the participial character of the word and thus its affinity with other participial forms. Jim's "pint" for "point" obscures the history of the word and in particular its derivation by way of French from Latin *punctum*. Huck's pronunciation of those magisterial words "natural" and "different" is unlikely to be represented accurately by the standard spelling with which Twain represents it. (If Twain were not using the alphabet to portray Jim's pronunciation, we might not take it here as portraying Huck's. But he is, and we do.) And perhaps it is significant that Huck's utterance, but not Jim's, is articulated by Twain through that refined mark of punctuation the semicolon. Not in his presentation of Jim's dialect, then, but in the contrasts he sets up between Jim's dialect and Huck's, Twain is disturbingly like Lakoff's journalist.

To summarize: as a dialogue about languages, this exchange between Huck and Jim brilliantly evokes the constraints on thought about language imposed by living in a society founded on thoughts about race. As a dialogue in languages, however, it reinforces those constraints. Twain as the greatest American advocate and portrayer of dialect may ironically be confirming Henry James's suspicions.

On English and Other Non-Native Languages

H. L. Mencken in the 1937 edition of *The American Language* lists the following "non-English dialects in America": German, Dutch, Swedish, Dano-Norwegian, Icelandic, Yiddish, French, Italian, Spanish, Portuguese, Rumanian, Czech, Slovak, Russian, Ukrainian, Serbo-Croat, Lithuanian, Polish, Finnish, Hungarian, Gaelic, Arabic, Greek, Chinese, Japanese, Armenian, Hawaiian, and Gypsy.[27] Obviously, the list has grown since then, and the name of each language stands for a dramatic encounter between its speakers and anglophone America.

Each encounter is unique, but surely there are some useful categories for grouping some encounters with others. In one large group of cases, the encounter is usually described as follows: to unofficially but predominantly anglophone America comes a nonanglophone immigrant group. The nonanglophone-speakers retain their language for a while; probably their nonanglophone literature records the pressures exerted by English on their language, probably the English vocabulary is expanded by loanwords taken from their language, and probably, as members of this group begin to write of themselves in English, these English texts dramatize the linguistic encounter. Probably, after a while, the intensity of the encounter diminishes, the number of speakers of the immigrant language diminishes, the texts dramatize the linguistic encounter less often.

It is this sort of encounter that many narratives of American ethnicity make central. There is good reason to regard it as central. But there is no good reason to regard it as natural or universal. The American anglophone power to make nonanglophone languages disappear is without parallel; Kenji Hakuta points out that "at the rate of change observed in other nations, it would take 350 years for the average nation to experience the same amount of [language] loss as that witnessed in just one generation in the United States."[28]

An example of this sort of encounter would be the American history of Yiddish. In Poland and Russia, speakers of Yiddish kept the language alive and flourishing for hundreds of years, not giving it up in favor of the reigning local language but instead developing it there into a great literary language. So the fact that speakers of Yiddish in America *have* given it up here says something about the sheer magnetic power of American linguistic assimilation.

In another group of cases, involving fewer languages but large populations, the encounter is between two languages neither of which can be regarded as the immigrant to the other, because both have immigrated early and been established independently. Spanish, for example, has been spoken in this hemisphere, and in some territories of what is now the United States, for longer than English has. Much the same is true for French, and something of the same is true for German. American linguistic assimilation has had its effect on these languages too, but their story has to be told in different terms.

These differences of historical situation shape different modes of storytelling and language-representing. But so do the different relations authors may stand in to those situations. Authors may, that is, be outsiders or insiders to the nonanglophone cultures they depict in English, and their fictions may, to the extent that biographical situation determines literary form, tend on the one hand toward anthropological investigation, on the other toward autobiographical witness.

On Texts by Anzia Yezierska and Kate Chopin

Anzia Yezierska grew up in Russia as a native speaker of Yiddish, then came to America and learned English. As a writer in English about the Jewish community of the Lower East Side of New York, she is an insider to the depicted culture, an outsider to the depicting language. In *Bread Givers*, her best-known novel, she tells the story of, among other things, how to become an insider to English. The most dramatic moment in that linguistic story is near the end of the novel, where the narrator Sara Smolinsky, having gone away from Hester Street to college, and having come back to Hester Street to teach school, is giving a lesson on pronunciation:

> On the board I wrote, S-I-N-G.
> "Aby! Pronounce this word."
> "Sing-gha," said Aby.
> "Sing," I corrected.
> "Sing-gha," came from Aby again.
> "Rosy Stein! You can do better. Show our lawyer [Aby wants to be a lawyer when he grows up] how to speak. Make a sentence with the word 'sing.'"
> "The boids sing-gha."
> "Rosy, say bird."
> "Boid," repeated small Rosy with great distinctness. "Boid."
> "Wrong still," I laughed. "Children, how do you pronounce this?" And I wrote hastily on the board, OIL.
> "Earl," cried the class, triumphantly.
> "You know how to make the right sounds for these words, but you put them in the opposite places." And I began to drill them in pronunciation. In the middle of the chorus, I heard a little chuckle. I turned to see Mr. Seelig himself, who had quietly entered the room and stood enjoying the performance. I returned his smile and went right on.
> "You try it again, Rosy. The birds sing-gg."
> "Sing," corrected Mr. Seelig, softly.

There it was. I was slipping back into the vernacular myself. In my embarrassment, I tried again and failed. He watched me as I blundered on. The next moment he was close beside me, the tips of his cool fingers on my throat. "Keep those muscles still until you have stopped. Now say it again," he commanded. And I turned pupil myself and pronounced the word correctly.[29]

Many readers of this novel, myself included, find an intense literary energy in the novel's Yiddish-influenced English, as in this sentence from early in the novel: "But from always it was heavy on my heart the worries for the house as if I was mother" (1). The linguistic norm, though, is set in the dedication: "To Clifford Smyth, to whose understanding criticism and inspiration I owe more than I can express." And the passage quoted above makes clear that the mellifluous, formulaic English of the novel's beginning is also its goal. Yiddish has no magic for Yezierska.

In that passage, Sara is teaching her class "that better speech that the teachers in college had tried to knock into [her]" (271). The speech that she is trying to get rid of has more sources than just the influence of Yiddish. But it is the influence of Yiddish that Sarah cannot shake. She does not carelessly say "ain't it," or "boids" for "birds," or "earl" for "oil." None of these usages is due to the influence of Yiddish. But the vocalized *shwa* after the "ng" of "sing" is due to that influence; and that *shwa* is what she cannot quite get rid of. Yezierska is subtle here; Sara produces not the fully vocalized *shwa* represented by "gha" but the partly suppressed gurgle represented by "gg." Yet even this gurgle induces her to say that she is "slipping back into the vernacular," and the vernacular is so much a part of her, and so much an encumbrance to her, that to be rid of it she gladly suffers the principal Hugo Seelig's cool fingers on her throat. To be sure, Hugo is there to help his colleague out; twenty pages later the two become friends, and twenty pages after that they are engaged. But this does not in the least diminish the bitter taste of Sara's submission to Hugo's correction. I know of no scene in which an immigrant language is so vividly presented as the taint that must be washed away, or in which American *glottophagie*, to borrow Louis-Jean Calvet's term, is manifested so powerfully.[30]

Kate Chopin grew up in St. Louis; there is evidence that her first language was the Louisiana Creole, that is, the language resulting from contact between white francophone slave-owners and their black slaves, but she also spoke Parisian French with her influential great-grandmother Madame Charleville, and of course she also spoke English and wrote only in English.[31] She married the Louisiana planter Oscar Chopin and moved to Louisiana with him, and after his death wrote stories about the world of francophone Louisiana she had come to know with him. She is, then, both an outsider and an insider to the world she is depicting, and perhaps both an insider and an outsider to the language she is writing in; and in her one great story about language, it seems that her ambiguous status gave her a way of seeing.

That story is "La Belle Zoraïde," which is structured as a narrative within a narrative. In the outer narrative, there are two characters: a black slave named Man-Loulou, and her white mistress, Madame Delisle. The outer narrative tells how Man-Loulou chooses a tale to tell her mistress to help her sleep; after that tale

has been told, the outer narrative begins again, and recounts these characters'
remarks about the tale. The inner narrative tells the life of La Belle Zoraïde, a
young mulatto slave of great beauty. Her mistress wants to marry her to a mulatto
slave belonging to one of her friends, but La Belle Zoraïde does not love him;
instead, she falls in love with a black slave named le beau Mézor, finds ways to
meet with him, and bears him a child. Her mistress flies into a rage, arranges with
her friend to send le beau Mézor away, and steals the baby, telling Zoraïde that he
is dead. Zoraïde goes mad, takes a doll and treats as if it were her baby, her "piti,"
and passes the rest of her life in this state of harmless delusion.

The inner narrative, then, is a melodramatic anecdote. The outer narrative,
especially the end of the outer narrative, is something different, because it obliges
us to remember that the inner narrative is a Creole tale, that Chopin is imagining a
translation of that tale, and that her "translation" may well be a distortion and her
story a misrepresentation.

Here is the ending:

> "Are you asleep, Ma'zélle Titite?"
>
> "No, I am not asleep; I was thinking. Ah, the poor little one, Man Loulou, the
> poor little one! better had she died!"
>
> But this is the way Madame Delisle and Manna-Loulou really talked to each
> other:-
>
> "Vou pré droumi, Ma'zélle Titite?"
>
> "No, pa pré droumi; mo yapré zongler. Ah, la pauv' piti, Man Loulou. La pauv'
> piti! Mieux li mouri!" (200)[32]

There is something haunting here. Most obviously, there is the fact that this
passage is in fact the ending, that the Creole gets the last word; the story breaks the
standard linguistic frame of realistic anglophone fiction, in which an anglophone or
standard-speaking narrator records the nonanglophone or nonstandard utterances
of characters in dialogue. In Chopin's story, the nonstandard language gets the last
word.

And in getting the last word, the patois finally becomes a language. At the
beginning of the story, the patois is represented in a song; it has exotic charm but
does not need to have precise meaning. These associations are maintained even
when the patois is being spoken rather than sung; it is, says Chopin, that "soft
Creole patois, whose music and charm no English words can convey" (196). But at
the end, the patois is represented in a dialogue; it is used to express not only moods
but also information and judgment. It is no longer music but language.

More subtly, to indicate that the Creole is "the way they really talked to each
other" implies that what has gone before has been only appearance, has been
something else than "the way they really talked to each other." And by that
implication Chopin gets at the weakness of her own story, and the weakness of
local color stories generally: that they are a familiarization, a conventionalization,
of something more alien than the writer is willing to record. This is a characteristic
passage from Manna-Loulou's story:

> La belle Zoraïde's sorrows had now begun in earnest. Not only sorrows but sufferings,
> and with the anguish of maternity came the shadow of death. But there is no agony

that a mother will not forget when she holds her first-born to her heart, and presses her lips upon the baby flesh that is her own, yet far more precious than her own. (198)

In light of the ending, we realize that this cannot have been very like "what she really said," not just because what she really said was said in the Creole but because Chopin's mellifluous, sentimental "translation" of it is so aggressive an annexation and distortion of it. In particular her "translation" of the ending moves it in the direction of standard syntax, taking it as far as the elegant subjunctive of the last exclamation. A translation more interested in the unassimilable traits of the language might read like this:

> "You after sleeping, Ma'zélle Titite?"
> "No, not after sleeping: I after thinking. Ah, the poor little one, Man Loulou. The poor little one! Better she died!"

Or compare this Negro French folktale's account of a father's grief for his son's death:

> Popa Florimond lévé mais li té vé pas consolé et li crié tout la journin pou so piti garçon. . . . Ein jou li tapé marché dans la cou, li gardé temps en temps la tombe so piti garçon et délarme coulé dans so zié. Nita tapé chanté on ein nabe a coté li et so chanson té si triste qué pove nommé la senti plis triste que jamin. Ça té sembe li c'était Florimond que tapé chanté, et li vancé coté la tombe la et gardé li longtemps.

> [Poppa [of] Florimond got up but he did not want [to be] consoled and he cried all the day for his little boy. . . . One day he walked in the yard, he looked now and then at the grave [of] his little boy and tears ran in his eyes. The Nita sang on a tree beside him and his song was so sad that [the] poor man felt sadder than ever. It seemed to him it was Florimond who was singing, and he came beside the grave there and looked at it a long time.][33]

Chopin invites us to imagine a better, stranger story than the one she has told, and a more richly multilingual literature than we have as yet seen.

As a polyglot critic, obsessed with the relations among languages and among dialects, I can find a social utopia in any cosmopolitan city: Luxembourg, Jerusalem, Montreal, New York, or the Rustchuk Elias Canetti vividly describes in the early pages of *Die gerettete Zunge*. I find a domestic utopia in any good polyglot conversation, in which every participant is perpetually and expertly switching codes, and every other participant understands the switches. It is surprisingly hard, though, to name a literary utopia. There are great multidialectal novels like *Moby-Dick* or *Huck Finn*, or *Berlin: Alexanderplatz*, or practically anything by Dickens or Scott. But it is harder to name a great multilingual text. The authors who come to mind, like Rabelais or Mann or Nabokov or Canetti himself, are really writing not multilingual novels but cosmopolitan ones, unilingual puddings with lots of multilingual plums. No novel that I know is in this sense as linguistically complex as the ordinary conversation at any Cuban-Chinese restaurant in New York.

Accordingly, studying the literary depiction of multilingual America reveals not a collective triumphant accomplishment, not a pantheon of masterpieces, but particular, remarkable successes and failures in a difficult task. It is not, probably, very surprising that the task should be so difficult. Literature is what it is and not another thing, and in particular it is not essentially an instrument for the depiction of something outside itself: not right action, not history, not consciousness, and not languages. But it also is not indifferent to the depiction of any of these things, and even its failures are revelatory. The literature of America gets at subtle truths about the linguistic map and history of America, in its tenacious, imprecise approximations and stubborn inconstancies.

NOTES

1. Marc Shell, "Babel in America: Or, The Politics of Language Diversity in the United States," *Critical Inquiry* 20:1 (Autumn 1993), p. 127.

2. *The Diario of Christopher Columbus's First Voyage to America, 1492–1493, Abstracted by Fray Bartolomé de las Casas* (Norman: University of Oklahoma Press, 1989), ed. and tr. Oliver Dun and James E. Kelley, Jr., p. 68.

3. Octavio Paz, *The Labyrinth of Solitude* (New York: Grove, 1962), tr. Lysander Kemp, p. 86. On La Malinche, see also Frances Karttunen, *Between Worlds* (New Brunswick: Rutgers University Press), pp. 1–23.

4. James Fenimore Cooper, *The Last of the Mohicans* (New York: Penguin, 1986), ed. Richard Slotkin, p. 91. For subsequent quotations from this work, the page number will be given in the text.

5. Alexis de Tocqueville, *Democracy in America* (New York: Vintage, 1990; Knopf 1945), tr. Henry Reeve, rev. Francis Bowen, ed. Phillips Bradley; 2 vols., p. 2:67.

6. Cooper consistently calls Uncas and Chingachgook "Mohicans" but calls their language "Delaware."

7. Quoted in Helen Carr, *Inventing the American Primitive: Politics, Gender and the Representation of Native American Literary Traditions, 1789–1936* (New York: New York University Press, 1996), p. 58.

8. John Heckewelder, *History, Manners, and Customs of the Indian Nations Who Once Inhabited Pennsylvania and the Neighbouring States* (Philadelphia: Historical Society of Pennsylvania, 1876; repr. 1990), p. 128.

9. Lewis Cass, "Structure of Indian Languages," in *North American Review* 26 (April 1828), pp. 374–375.

10. Heckewelder, *History*, p. 110.

11. Hans Aarsleff, *From Locke to Saussure* (Minneapolis: University of Minnesota Press, 1982), pp. 108–109.

12. Henry Rowe Schoolcraft, *Oneota, or Characteristics of the Red Race of America* (New York: Wiley & Putnam, 1845), p. 61.

13. This is a famous case and has been the subject of a number of studies. See A. Grove Day, ed., *The Sky Clears: Poetry of the American Indians* (Lincoln: University of Nebraska Press, 1951); John Greenway, *Literature among the Primitives* (Hatboro, Pa., 1964); Dell Hymes, "Some North Pacific Coast Poems: A Problem in Anthropological Philology," in *"In vain I tried to tell you": Essays in Native American Ethnopoetics* (Philadelphia: University of Pennsylvania Press, 1981); and Arnold Krupat, "On the Translation of Native American Song and Story: A Theorized History," in Brian Swann, ed., *On the Translation of Native American Literatures* (Washington, D.C.: Smithsonian Institution Press, 1992). Most of these do less than justice to the complexity of Schoolcraft's text.

14. Hymes, "Some North Pacific Coast Poems," p. 42.

15. Ibid.; emphasis Hymes's.

16. Ibid., p. 41.

17. Dennis Tedlock, *The Spoken Word and the Work of Interpretation* (Philadelphia: University of Pennsylvania Press, 1983), p. 47.

18. Quoted in Henry Louis Gates, "Dis and Dat: Dialect and the Descent," in *Figures in Black: Words, Signs, and the "Racial" Self* (New York: Oxford University Press, 1987), p. 181.

19. Quoted ibid., p. 179.

20. Henry James, "Preface to *Daisy Miller*," in *The Art of the Novel: Critical Prefaces* (New York: Scribner's, 1934), ed. R. P. Blackmur, pp. 279–280.

21. David Crystal, *The Cambridge Encyclopedia of Language* (New York: Cambridge University Press, 1987), s.v.

22. The linguist Geoffrey Nunberg suggested to me in a private communcation that the journalist might argue that Wallace would have *written* "could of."

23. Sumner Ives, *A Theory of Literary Dialect*, Tulane Studies in English, vol. 11 (1950), p. 148.

24. Mark Twain, *The Adventures of Huckleberry Finn* (New York: Norton, 1977), ed. Sculley Bradley et al., pp. 66–67. For subsequent quotations, page numbers will be given in the text.

25. On this, see J. L. Dillard, *Black English* (New York: Vintage, 1973), pp. 73–138.

26. See on this, Geoffrey Sampson, *Writing Systems* (Stanford: Stanford University Press, 1985), pp. 194–213.

27. H. L. Mencken, *The American Language* (New York: Knopf, 1937), p. xi.

28. Kenji Hakuta, *Mirror of Language: The Debate on Bilingualism* (New York: Basic Books, 1986), pp. 166–167.

29. Anzia Yezierska, *Bread Givers* (New York: Persea, 1975), pp. 271–272; for subsequent quotations, page numbers will be given in the text.

30. On this see Louis-Jean Calvet, *Linguistique et colonialisme*: *Petit traité de glottophagie* (Paris: Payot, 1974). The term means "the eating of language."

31. See Per Seyersted, *Kate Chopin: A Critical Biography* (Baton Rouge: Louisiana State University Press, 1969), pp. 13–15. Interestingly but confusingly, "Creole" also refers to the French-speaking white Louisiana aristocracy.

32. Kate Chopin, *The Awakening and Selected Stories* (New York: Penguin, 1984), p. 200. For subsequent quotations, page numbers will be indicated in the text.

33. Alcée Fortier ed., *Louisiana Folk-Tales in French Dialect and English Translation*, vol. 2, *Memoirs of the American Folk-Lore Society* (Boston: Houghton Mifflin for the American Folk-Lore Society, 1895), pp. 78–80; the translation is my own.

Chapter Twenty-three

Reflections on Multilingualism

Jules Chametzky

A personal and perhaps intellectual breakthrough of sorts occurred for me when I encountered a strange phrase in an article by Isaac Rosenfeld in the *Partisan Review* in the late '40s or early '50s. Writing about East European literature and the futility of a certain action, he wrote that "it would help like cupping the dead." Only when I was a few pages further on did it occur to me that this was a direct translation of a Yiddish expression about futile gestures: " *'s vet helfen vi a toyten bankes.*" It was an expression that lay buried in my own consciousness, and the effect upon me was a revelation. It opened up a whole buried world, of language, experience, culture, an Atlantis of the spirit.

Using a language—an "ethnic" language—that was not French, Latin, or Greek, those sure signs of an elite and civilized education, was not so common in those days. At least I had never noted anything like it in the high criticism of the time— this casual sprinkling of a Yiddish word or Yiddishism in one's serious discourse. What excited me was the sudden awareness that it might be O.K., kosher in a manner of speaking, to mine and honor the material of one's own life and culture— even such a kitchen tongue (as it seemed to some of us then) as Yiddish—the beginnings of my own lifelong interest in ethnic and multicultural literature.

When I met and became friendly with Rosenfeld shortly afterward at the University of Minnesota and told him about my reaction to his slight multilingual (in translation) trope, he said something very interesting. He said, in words to this effect, that Yiddish was his first language, compared to which his English (however bright his reputation) always seemed to him flat and that all his various linguistic excursions, into popular culture (he was an early user), jazz idiom, Reichianism were efforts to enliven the language. This insight into a writer I much admire opens up to comparable situations in others. Now that some scholars have embarked upon their ambitious project of legitimizing the many languages in which Americans have lived, felt, thought, and written, the prospect before us is exciting with promise.

But the subject is also American studies and monolingualism. When and how exactly did scholars of all persuasions, left and right, paleface and redskin (to use Philip Rahv's playfully offensive binary opposition) get so monolingual in American literary studies? That is a subject requiring serious research and analysis—what I can offer here are only some personal reflections as a prolegomena to such an inquiry.

In the beginning ("barayshit") there was the sense of America as a "civilization." In the '20s, '30s, '40s, a discovery of an indigenous (meaning non-European) language (*pace* H. L. Mencken), customs, myths, and symbolic structures created a base of legitimate objects of study. This was part of a continuing struggle to get out from under "Europe" and especially England. It was also a result of, fascination with, even love for, the bits and pieces of American behaviors and creations—folklore, dialects, artifacts—all given a boost during the depression years and a turn inward toward "the people" and their creations when "the system" seemed otherwise falling to pieces. Out of that time and study, Tremaine MacDowell at Minnesota (my first academic job was as his assistant), a pioneer in the movement, thought change would occur in his students, a reordering of their consciousness. He offered no systematic method—*Does* American studies *have* a method? asked Henry Nash Smith, MacDowell's successor. Or only a desire to see the culture whole?—but he legitimized a focusing upon these materials. Perhaps this was a nationalistic impulse, as some later observers have claimed, that fed into the great nationalist fervor of World War II and beyond, but it was surely a populist and democratic one.

The question of language acquisition and knowledge were not primary, although both MacDowell and Smith were highly cultivated men and not monolingual (Smith was my very knowledgeable examiner in French when he was director of the graduate program). But the acquisition of other languages, especially the dead ones or those associated with snobbish elites, did not sit well with their followers. For them (for us) coming to terms with the new world opening up meant more intimacy with the vernacular, the real language being spoken and sung on the highways, streets, and back alleys of the United States. The foundational texts, taught by Smith so memorably, were *Roughing It* and *Life on the Mississippi*. In *Roughing It*, the dandy from the East (a displacement for Europe and England) must discard his high hat and white gloves if he is to parley with the Pawnees and, most significantly, toss out into the desert the heavy unabridged dictionary that keeps buffeting and bruising him in the stagecoach. In *Life on the Mississippi*, the cub must learn the new language of the river if he is to survive its treacherous rocks and turns—an image of the need to observe and learn the true nature of America and its vernacular realities, not the idealized version of the official and "high" culture. These are seductive and ambiguous lessons: a justification for discarding the baggage of other "civilizations" but, also, in its farthest reaches, a potential source of respect for truly indigenous languages and cultures (in what language would the dude converse with the Pawnees?). Perhaps now we can move along this latter path.

Meanwhile, back East, other roots of American studies and its monolingual emphases might be seen in the efforts of a post-'30s generation to break loose from, create some liberating space, in traditional English departments. Many of these departments were still philological in approach, antimodernist, anticontemporary literature, later in the '40s and '50s formalist and New Critical if they were adventurous, but in reaction against certain kinds of historical and social scholarship and criticism (the straw man of the day was "vulgar Marxism" of the '30s variety). Scholars like Daniel Aaron, Leo Marx, Alan Trachtenberg, and J. W. Ward were not "monolinguists," per se, but their battle was with these other, older confining elements. Indian languages were exotic and marginal concerns, "foreign" languages useful as tools for reading foreign scholarship, which, however, with certain notable exceptions, did not much concern itself with American culture, let alone "civilization."

Conditions of the depression, the rise of fascism, the war, and immediate postwar were overriding concerns in the formative years of American studies. Unfortunately, this could lead to a kind of unreflective nationalism. In the general triumphalism that followed World War II, in which the United States enjoyed an unparalleled position of power and influence based on a tremendous industrial engine never damaged or destroyed as almost all others were and its capitalism dominant worldwide, American studies suddenly became a very popular and exportable commodity (the early success and influence of the Salzburg seminars on young European scholars was paradigmatic). There was, too, of course, the Cold War and an enemy worth arming against and confronting—ideologically as well as militarily and economically. In such a climate, why bother with complexities and contradictions in our so manifestly superior a system? The unity of America—*e pluribus unum*—was the basic theme, despite unexamined peoples and pasts, buried languages and cultures. Problems could be swept under the rug, or if acknowledged as "American dilemmas," the assumption was that they would be resolved in time. For the most part, there was a general consensus of this sort into the early '60s. As one of my senior professors and mentors put it succinctly and wryly, "American Studies is a gravy train circling the globe." That blacks were still sitting in the rear of the train was only noticed and struggled with by a few hardy souls. Why rock the train?

And then the civil rights movement, the Vietnam War, 1968 in Paris, Prague, Chicago—things were never the same again. American studies began to lose its sense of a coherent center—though it still flourished and went abroad as "a hothouse product of the Cold War," as it once was described to me in Berlin. And the monolingual beat went on.

But now the Cold War is over, our best writers are multiethnic, multicultural, and increasingly multi (or bi) lingual. I think of Leslie Silko, Maxine Hong Kingston, Toni Morrison, Gloria Anzaldúa, Martín Espada, Irena Klepfisz, and a host of others. Our sense of ourselves as a society is more complex (and more interesting?) than ever—our newer writers as pilots navigating the ever-changing river of America are showing us new depths, and through the new and expanding work of scholarship, a richer multilingual ancestry. To which this would-be multilingualist says *Shantih, Selah, Salud, Sholem Aleichem*!

Part VII

Languages and Language Rights

If the language of the United States is viewed as English only, other languages become similarly identified with fixed places of origin, and American languages other than English become cast as marginal, diasporic, or impure parts of these origins. But this is a faulty view, for, to start with the most obvious example, American Indian languages have no other place of origin. Some languages have also migrated to America: the United States, after the Holocaust, has become the world's center of Yiddish speakers. Other languages, like Gullah, have emerged in America— as have many that were discussed in the section "Melting Glots." And some languages were formalized or received significant impulses of modernization in the United States. Thus H. L. Mencken listed (in an appendix to *The American Language*) modern Anglo-Arabic terms that were coined by Arabic-speaking communities in the United States; some of these "melting glot"–type words were later adapted by modern standard Arabic (as John Edward Philips pointed out).[1] And Daiva Markelis has investigated the formalization of modern standard print–Lithuanian (a forbidden language in Czarist Russia from 1864 to 1904) as the result of a public contest in a Lithuanian newspaper in Chicago.[2]

While the previous sections focused on literary expressions and articulations in multilingual America, attention now turns to languages themselves, and especially the political issues of language loss, universal languages, and language rights. Of course, the political issues surrounding American languages informed earlier sections, most notably Sommer's contribution; and the theme of language suppression has emerged in several essays—from Fabre's brief mention that French was no longer allowed for speeches in the Louisiana legislature after 1880 and Conolly-Smith's account of the hostility to German-language theater and journalism during World War I to Shell's poignant comments on the same period. In the present section these issues appear again and again, reminding readers of the need for a new and comprehensive study of language suppression.

In "Tigua Pueblo: Materializing Language, Transmitting Memory," Shelley Armitage chooses as her subject one of America's "almost lost" languages, that of the Tigua Indians who live in Ysleta del Sur Pueblo (in El Paso, Texas) and who have had to confront Spanish, Mexican, and Anglo-American encroachments. Armitage reconstructs the tragic history of the Tiguas (of whom only few members have survived to the present) and their struggle to defy language loss and suppression. The similarities between the history of "ethnic" tongues and that of other languages in the United States become apparent in the next two contributions. Douglas Baynton's "Out of Sight: The Suppression of American Sign Language" traces the sad history of the suppression of American Sign Language for deaf people, beginning in the second half of the nineteenth century, at a time when Alexander Graham Bell (who counted on communication by sound waves) could describe sign language as "essentially a foreign language." Conevery Bolton's essay "ISOTYPE: An Introduction" calls attention to an immensely popular form of sign language, created for the pictorial representation of statistical information, called ISOTYPE by its inventor Otto Neurath, and promoted by such American reform journals as *Survey Graphic*. Its creators saw ISOTYPE as a universal language like Esperanto, but as its success became more widespread, its reformist edge was weakened. The provocative "Statement on Language Rights" (1996) by the Linguistic Society of America is included at the end of this section in the hope that it will suggest broader historical, comparative, and political contexts for the work presented here and inspire students and teachers to enter the field of American multilingualism.

NOTES

1. H. L. Mencken, *The American Language* (1919; fourth ed. 1936; repr. New York: Knopf, 1951), 683–685; and Philips on the INTERROADS thread, July 1997.

2. Markelis's presentation in Longfellow Seminar, March 18, 1997; Mencken, 669–673, however, reports a young Lithuanian coming to America and complaining about the "Pidgin Lithuanian" surrounding him here.

Chapter Twenty-four

Tigua Pueblo
Materializing Language, Transmitting Memory

Shelley S. Armitage

Ysleta del Sur Pueblo, inhabited by Tigua (tiwa) Indians descended from the refugees of the 1680s, is located within the southern boundary of El Paso, Texas. Formerly, the inhabitants of this Texas pueblo spoke a language of the Southern Tiwa subgroup of the Kiowa-Tanoan language family. Since the early 1900s, Spanish has replaced the indigenous language, yet Tiwa persisted in the form of numerous words, phrases, and songs. Though the Tigua accepted English as a second language, they find themselves oddly at a crossroads linguistically. The Tiwa language is taught in elementary school at the reservation as part of a cultural awareness and education program that began in the early 1970s, after the tribe was officially recognized by the federal government. A few of the elders still converse in Tiwa, so that the young, learning the language as a cultural and historical experience, and the very old speak a little of the original tribal tongue. Yet the majority of Tiguas participate in the language through their ceremonies, chants, dances, and feast days. Therefore, though the language has essentially disappeared, it remains a formalized part of ritual within the cultural life of the tribe.

In 1540, when Spanish explorer Francisco Coronado reached the banks of the Rio Grande, there were numerous settled villages of native Indian farmers along the river from the Mexican state of Chihuahua to northern New Mexico. Today there are nineteen pueblos in New Mexico, from Taos in the north, to Isleta, just south of Albuquerque. The twentieth—Ysleta del Sur—is in El Paso, Texas, largely unknown and outside Native American, state, and federal auspices. The Tiguas, residents of this southern-most division of Pueblo Indians (the Southern Tigua or Tiwa, the language group of which they are a part), tell in one of their tribal stories of the pursuit and attempted murder of Coronado.[1] However, when the story is told, the language of its telling is Spanish or English, for the native language of the Tiguas appears to be all but dead to the observer. However, Tiguas today, young and old, still know enough words and phrases to continue to use them in certain ceremonies, religious events, and in chants, dances, and songs. Like the ceremonial materials they managed to bring south with them when removed by the Spanish in a retreat following the Pueblo Rebellion in 1680, the Tiwa language—suppressed, almost lost—has remained a part of the material and expressive culture of the

Tigua, surviving Spanish, Mexican, and Anglo-American encroachment. The language ironically has been transferred because of the cultural continuity of other aspects of their native life and memory, rather than being the means itself for perpetuating culture. The fact that some of the Tiwa expressions have absorbed Spanish, perhaps even English sounds or meanings, is further evidence that the Tiguas were able to assimilate without losing tribal ways. Isolated (250 miles from their nearest Tiwa-speaking neighbor, the mother pueblo Isleta) and finding themselves an ethnic island within Hispanic, Mexican, and American culture for three hundred years, nevertheless they continue to innovatively remember and articulate themselves.[2]

The town of Ysleta, first settled by the Tigua Indians in 1682, is one of the oldest continuously settled communities in the nation and the oldest Texas town. Located in the fertile valley of the Rio Grande, Ysleta is bounded by the river and the international border on the west and barren sand hills to the east. Once a small agrarian community surrounded by vineyards, corn fields, orchards, it has been engulfed since World War II by a sprawling El Paso's oil refineries, factories, and expressways, which typify the urban center in which Ysleta now finds itself. Traditional rituals and ceremonies have been hampered through time by such urban and environmental effects. A traditional rabbit hunt is now impossible due to the contamination of hunting grounds by industrial and other wastes that have changed desert habitats.[3] Deer hunts, customarily held at Hueco Tanks, a sacred ancestral site, ceased when the Texas Parks Service assumed the management of these grounds, allowing rock climbing and other activities that could deface prehistoric and sacred petroglyph and meeting places. Yet, although now completely encircled by dominant Mexican, Hispanic, and Anglo populations, Ysleta still has the feel of its pueblo past. Clinging to the sixty-six acres left from the original thirty-six square miles deeded in a land grant by the king of Spain in 1751, the Tiguas are involved in numerous land suits. Since 1993, however, when they were allowed by the state to open Speaking Rock, a casino for bingo and gaming, fortunes of the pueblo have changed because of this new income-generating activity that has provided for health, social, and cultural needs.

Only in April 1968 did the federal government officially recognize the Ysleta Indians as a surviving tribe.[4] There are many reasons recognition came so late for the Tiguas. One is that they have typically been peaceful and independent. Such resourcefulness has allowed them to survive three centuries despite colonization and removal by the Spaniards, raids by the Comanche and Apache, land disputes with the United States and Texas, and an increasing minority status among Hispanic and Anglo majorities. Never previously having reservation or government assistance, the history of these people still may be pieced together only through military, church, civil records, travelers' reports, and the oral traditions of the tribe. The persistence of this small group of people—numbering more than three hundred after the Pueblo Rebellion (1680) and only fifteen hundred today—is a tribute to tribal organization and identity.

Most recent studies of the Tiguas have been by anthropologist Nicholas Houser and photographer/documentarian Bill Wright. However, several pioneering ethnologists of the American Southwest visited the Tiguas through time, if unfortunately only for a short duration. They include John G. Bourke in November 1881; Dr. H. F. C. Ten Kate, Jr., in December 1892; Adolph F. Bandelier in April 1888; James Mooney in December 1897; Walter J. Fewkes in October 1901; and John P. Harrington in August 1909. Not surprisingly, Indian agent John Calhoun pleaded that governmental agents visit Tigua and learn more about the people and that a regional office be established closer to them, which, of course, was not done.[5] Corroborated through these early observations and the later photographic evidence were two crucial elements that allowed the Tiguas to argue for their tribal status in the 1960s: continued ceremonial and religious events that revealed in dress, demeanor, behavior, and beliefs certain features from the mother pueblo of Isleta, and recognition by Isleta pueblo representatives themselves. Other than the above observers and their studies, however, no major work exists on the Tiguas.

Written History

The factors that led to almost total language loss began with the Pueblo Rebellion against the Spanish in 1680. The Tiwa (later Tigua), then living at Isleta Pueblo—one of the villages that shared the language, along with the Piro Pueblos to the south—did not become actively involved in the revolt. However, during the uprising, more than two thousand Spanish colonists congregated at these two pueblos, the Rio Abajo southern district receiving temporary asylum at Isleta. When the Indian people there revolted against the Spanish, the intruders retreated southward, taking a number of Isletans with them, finally uniting with Antonio de Otermin's contingent, who had also fled Santa Fe. Three hundred seventeen Indians, including Tiwas and Piros, their ranks already augmented by an undetermined number of Indian refugees from pueblos abandoned before 1680, including eastern Tiwa, Tompiro, Jumano, and Saline Province peoples, established three camps at Guadalupe del Paso in an area of the Manso Indian Mission by the same name.[6]

Though oral tradition differs in the Isleta and Tigua versions of this escape, the Indians likely shared no Spanish loyalties and retreated because of fear of more reprisals in the North. After an attempt in 1681 by Governor Otermin to reconquer New Mexico, Isleta Pueblo again was attacked and yielded 385 captives, who were forced to march back to El Paso. Presumably, these captives were resettled that year at the new Pueblo of Sacramento de la Ysleta, later called Corpus Christi de la Ysleta.

By this time the peoples originating from the upper Rio Grande pueblo were organized into settlements among Spanish refugee colonists and in the vicinity of two other Indian groups already Christianized—the Manso and Suma Indians—in the El Paso area. Though Fray Francisco de Ayeta, the procurado general and custodian of New Mexico missions, maintained a policy of ethnic separation to protect the Spanish from arguments over livestock and land and from the possibility of disease, from this period on—1681–1881—the Ysleta del Sur village people mixed with the Spanish, the Mexicans, and the Americans. (Still, census records show that a majority of village dwellers were natives.) Governor Diego de Vargas had planned to return refugee Tiguas and Piros to their homeland, but these valley pueblos prospered and were never abandoned. Particularly during the eighteenth century, numerous civil and ecclesiastical reports mention the prosperity of the missions and the industry of the Indians.[7] To survive so well, the Indians quickly learned the Spanish language, so that gradually—given the mixing of various Indian groups, the distance from Isleta, and the necessity of accommodating Spanish, Mexican, and later Americans—the Tiwa language was no longer functional as the language of commerce. Tigua scouts, demonstrating their bilingual skills, defended the El Paso settlements against Comanche and Apache raids, took part in the New Mexico reconquest, and even helped quell uprisings by local Manso and Suma groups. Later, Tigua scouts soldiered with the Texas Rangers and the United States Cavalry during the Apache campaigns in Texas.[8]

While the Tiguas were adjusting themselves to live among outsiders, another factor threatened their language and culture: the gradual loss of their lands. The Ysleta Grant was made by the king of Spain, deeded by royal decree to the Pueblo of San Antonio de Ysleta on March 13, 1751. Indian title to the land was recognized by the Mexican state of Chihuahua, and Indian possession was even mentioned in the land disputes between Ysleta and Senecu pueblos following the American annexation. Though some land loss had occurred during the Mexican period, by 1871 a series of land transactions and schemes sought to defraud the Tigua of the grant of thirty-six square miles. Anglo opportunists indulged in fraudulent deeds of sale and arranged with the state of Texas for the incorporation of Ysleta into the city of El Paso, so that the lands could be taxed and disposed of. In 1892, the people of Ysleta petitioned the governor of Texas for protection from the injuries suffered from Americans who ignored the law. Though the state acted to stop the land investments, lost land was not restored to its rightful owners.[9] The Tiguas, who still own a piece of the oldest continuously farmed land in the United States, lost most of their agricultural lands and began to experience a poverty untypical of their self-sufficiency before the maneuvers of the Anglo interlopers. As late as 1881, when John G. Bourke visited Ysleta, the old Indian governor complained that "the American and Mexican [are] crowding into our beautiful valley taking up, without recompense, land belonging to the people of the pueblo."[10]

Earlier, another factor affected the Tiguas' landholdings and their economic loss. Because the state of Texas had been part of the Confederacy, the Tiguas had been doubly punished after the war. Texas had joined the Union in 1845 with uncertain western boundaries. The 1848 Treaty of Guadalupe Hidalgo had fixed the U.S.-Mexico boundary in the middle of the Rio Grande channel, and the Organic Act of 1850 had set the present limits of Texas and New Mexico, making Ysleta, along with the entire Trans-Pecos region, part of Texas. But a decade later Ysleta lay in the Confederacy, with unfortunate consequences for the Tiguas, since it was during the Civil War that Congress addressed the status of the Rio Grande pueblos. President Abraham Lincoln invited the tribal governors from New Mexico Territory to Washington and presented them with canes (symbols of authority) and official documents, and ultimately granted them land patents. Because they lived in a

Confederate state, the Tiguas were not included, and thus failed to gain a reservation or official recognition.

Nevertheless, before the early twentieth century, the Tiguas managed to live with little change in their daily habits—farming and hunting—even as they seemed to blend into the local Hispanic population. Perhaps expecting to see the manifestations of a more outwardly distinct pueblo life, comparable to the pueblos to the north, Bourke described a Tigua household in 1881: "I saw a shield, bows, arrows, guns, and a bundle of eagle feathers and a pair of wooden spurs, hanging from the rafters. But beyond these, nothing whatever led me to suspect I wasn't in the house of an humble and industrious family of Mexicans."[11]

Despite the exterior signs of adaptation to certain aspects of the dominant culture, there is no doubt that throughout this time the Tiguas continued their Pueblo rituals privately, engaging in hunts, feast days, dances, and the very private events of the *tusla* or kiva. When the Dutch anthropologist Dr. H. F. C. Ten Kate visited Ysleta in 1882, he recorded evidence of tribal dances and governing, and he took back to the Netherlands several ceremonial items—gourd rattles, a drum, sacred arrows—which were only later rediscovered by the Tiguas in 1990. He documented what he saw by writing an account of his experiences.[12] Other documentation verifies that the Tiguas persisted in their Isleta Pueblo past. In 1907, the anthropologist J. W. Fewkes made note of the condition of the tribe, reporting, for example, about housing. He detailed the arrangement of houses around a central plaza, which were constructed of vertically placed wooden branches chinked with mud, as in the early day *jacales*. In fact, the Ysletans had built the first Catholic church in this fashion. Fewkes also claimed to have seen a constitution that the tribe adopted in 1895, listing the officers of the tribe and their responsibilities, as he reflected on typical Pueblo government influenced by Spanish colonial civil titles and duties. Photographic evidence corroborates both the traditional elements of the Tiguas' expressive and material culture along with the hybridizing that was typical of the colonized and Christianized Pueblo people.[13]

By the 1930s, the Tiguas were again visible to the public, appearing at various exhibitions and folklife festivals. From the 1930s through the 1950s, their lives were chronicled from the point of view of an amateur El Paso historian and Catholic charity partisan, Cleofas Colleros, who was made an honorary tribal member for his championing of Tigua indigenous but Catholicized beliefs and rituals.

In 1965, the fortunes of the tribe improved as the 59th Texas State Legislature established the Commission for Indian Affairs. Following this action, on 23 November 1966, with help from attorney Tom Diamond and anthropologist Nicholas Houser, the Texas State Historical Survey passed a resolution recognizing the Tiguas as a tribe, and the Texas legislature passed two bills in 1967 placing the Tigua Indian Tribe under state care. Finally, on 12 April 1968, President Lyndon Johnson signed Public Law 90-287 recognizing the Tiguas as a federal tribe. After the termination of the Texas Commission on Indian Affairs, the federal government agreed to extend trust status to the tribe, and currently tribal matters are administered by the Bureau of Indian Affairs in Washington, D.C.[14]

By 1996, there were few full-blooded Tiguas left. With the government's terms of trusteeship requiring that persons of at least one-eighth blood quantum be carried on official tribal rolls, the pressure is either to marry one's cousin or to marry outside the tribe. Yet the Tiguas alone among the Piro, Sumas, and Mansos of the area are still identifiable.

Because of publicity arising from a land claim case, the 1960s proved to be a time for the tribe to recognize and strengthen its own identity. This resulted in a revitalistic spirit at the village, which included the revival of dances and songs as well as motivation to learn more of the Tiwa language. Though many individuals had, over the years, disassociated themselves from the tribe, due to outside pressures, discrimination, and negative circumstances locally and in the state, as pride in Native American heritage grew, so did the tribal rolls. A tribal census compiled by Nicholas Houser for a study funded by the Office of Economic Opportunity recorded 166 tribal members in 1966; in 1971, a census compiled by the superintendent for the Tiguas Indian Community, an employee of the now-defunct Texas Commission of Indian Affairs, recognized 348 tribal members. But both in 1966 and in 1971, federal and state officials reported that the economic status of most Tigua families was within the poverty level as then defined by the federal government. The industrialization of agriculture affected the tribe, as did the lack of available opportunities for retraining or working as unskilled wage laborers. For this reason, as the Tiguas sought to redefine themselves culturally, the state of Texas had as an objective an economic stability that might come from instruction in "Indian culture." Some Tiguas were encouraged to take up arts and crafts not native to their pueblo heritage, such as the making of bolos and Plains-style beadwork. The objective of the commission, as in the case of one of the other three Native American tribes recognized in Texas, the Alabama-Coushatta in East Texas, was to promote the Native American community as a tourist attraction. Nevertheless, the result was positive in that the Tigua Tribal Museum and Gift Shop were established along with tourist-oriented projects for the Hueco Tanks region.

Tribal Traditions/Oral History

George Trager documented in an article in 1967 that a Tiwa speaker from Isleta pueblo certified that the language spoken at Ysleta in the 1930s was indeed Tiwa. Nevertheless, in reports both in the 1930s and the 1950s, only five or six native speakers or tribal members who understood Tiwa were deemed to exist. Yet the oral and material history of the tribe demonstrates that as long as the feast days, social and ritual dances, songs, stories, and chants existed, the language was spoken and passed down in these enactments. Both the pattern of continuously held rituals and the reintroduction of them at different points during the tribe's history have allowed for the transference of words and phrases that, despite their limitations, are symbolic for the Tiguas of their resilience and cultural identity.

The calendar of traditionally observed dances for Ysleta del Sur, connecting their indigenous dances and chants to religious activities at the Catholic church, includes

Salida de los Santos (June 4), San Antonio (June 13), San Juan (June 24), San Pedro and San Pablo (June 25), Santa Ana (July 26), San Andres (November 30), and two dances at Christmastime, Inocentes (January 1) and Santo Reyes (January 6). Though these are tied, obviously, to Catholic/Christian periods or saint's days, Ysleta, like the other pueblos, has always maintained a double-affinity, for its own native religion and its adopted Catholicism, in elements of celebration, bilingualism, and biculturalism.

An example of this fact is a dance typically performed on January 6, Santos Reyes day. The *awelos* (Spanish *abuelos*, "grandfathers") perform this dance. One is a grandfather and the other, a grandmother. The male *awelo* may carry a whip to symbolically scare the children, and the female dancer carries a rag doll. The masks of these katchina-like figures are of buffalo hide, sacred and therefore handled with great care. A photograph taken in 1912 shows two *awelo* masked dancers standing behind two young Tigua girls.[15] The continuity of this dance is verified through the stories of the sacred commitment to the dance. In one interpretation, a man made a promise to God to serve as an *awelo* dancer and, following the dance, to remove his dress and swim in the Rio Grande to purify himself.[16]

In addition to dances and feast days, ancestral stories, which tie the Tiwa-speakers of Isleta to those of Ysleta, also exist. Some Tiguas believe their forefathers migrated from a homeland, either California or Gran Quivira of the Salina pueblos. These displaced Indians arrived at Isleta, where they were accepted into that village. In one of the stories, a rift developed within the village based on the attempt of a Spaniard to steal the village drum. The new arrivals therefore killed him and traveled south to what is now called Hueco Tanks.

Located in the desert plain, some thirty miles east of El Paso, the "tanks" comprise numerous caves and natural cisterns due to the large igneous knobs in the formation. They have provided shelter and a water source for Indians from Basket Maker times until the historic Comanche and Apache period. One legend holds that the Tiguas had to continually defend their ancestral grounds from Kiowa and Apache. During the Anglo period, the Butterfield Stageline maintained a station in the area from 1857 to 1861. Even into the twentieth century, Tiguas traveled from their village back to Hueco by burro, horse, and wagon to camp in the summer months, to hunt and to gather herbs and food plants. That practice is continued sporadically today as the Tiguas persist in returning to Hueco, where numerous sacred petroglyphs tell of their origin and cultural events, and the hunting and gathering grounds remain important to local potters and others.

One reason Hueco Tanks is so important is that, for some Tigua traditionalists, this is the home of the *awelo* or grandfather to the people. He resides at Cerro Alto, the highest peak in the Hueco Mountains. A kachina-like figure, he watches over the behavior of children and keeps the elder leaders in line. Parents warn unruly children that the *awelo* may punish them. Some Tiguas remember that the *awelo* would sometimes enter the *tusla* and join people in dancing. He also periodically joined the old people when they made a trip back to Isleta, reinforcing the connection between the original Tiwa-speaking people.

Another important ceremony also connects the Tiguas with another village, perhaps a daughter pueblo to them. The nearby Tigua community of Tortugas in Las Cruces, New Mexico, probably was founded before the turn of the century by a composite of Tigua, Piros, and Manso Indians from the El Paso-Juárez region. This village still is able to conduct the rabbit hunt that is so important to the Tiguas, and often the Ysletans join Tortugas in this ceremony.

Thus, though the first language of the Tiguas is Spanish even today, there persists, through stories, ceremony, and even Christianized feast days, the connection with ancient Tiwa grounds, people, and rituals. Some elders continue to remind present-day Tiguas that if ever the tribe approaches extinction, the drum, bows, arrows, and rattles, and other religious paraphernalia must be taken to Isleta, New Mexico, because these things remain sacred to the Tigua Indians. The canes of office, originally given by the king of Spain to signify the authority of the Tigua in their lands, must be given to the waters of the Rio Grande along with the *bastones* (willow staffs) that the officers carry during the feast day of San Antonio and that are thrown each year into the river. Today, the sacred ritual paraphernalia—masks, bows and arrows, ground rattles, and the sacred drum—are kept in the *tusla*. The drum, brought originally from the removal period in the 1600s from Isleta, is particularly sacred. Called *juan-chee-ros*, it may be bowed to during dances and is fed regularly by the war captain, who blows smoke into a small hole on one side. Typical of other Rio Grande pueblos that were colonized but not conquered or assimilated by the Spanish, the Tiguas have retained the Spanish names for the tribal leaders—*cacique* or governor; *alguacil*, or sergeant at arms; the war chief and four captains. Three sets of *mayordomos* (a man and woman each) are selected to serve for the fiesta of San Antonio.

Though two hundred years of acculturative influences from Spanish, Mexican, and Anglo contact have resulted in many changes in traditional Tigua culture, as evidenced by the survival of the form of civil government received from the Spaniards centuries ago, the Tiguas still retain a matrilineal system of family names and land ownership. Marriages are still conducted in traditional ways, as are funerals. Ceremonial dress for women and men is the same as in the earliest photographs. Typical of the genius of the pueblo people and perhaps most responsible for their survival through time is their ability to adapt yet not lose the essential core of their culture.

This cultural core, says Albert Alvidrez, the youngest tribal council member at age twenty-four, has always been in the Tiguas' lives. Alvidrez points to the fact that survivals and revivals of activities as linked to language and memory are part of this cultural continuity. In 1970, Nicholaus Houser, an anthropologist who has worked closely with the Tiguas for years, wrote: "Pottery was made as late as 1930, mainly in the form of bowls of different sizes and tortilla irons or flatteners. This pottery was quite simple, though not unlike the pottery manufactured in the pueblos to the north. Women as well as men were potters."[17] The 1860 federal census recorded several female potters for the town of Isleta. But in 1971, John Hedrick noted that the last Tigua potters had died in the 1930s.[18]

Alvidrez—himself a student of anthropology at University of Texas at El Paso—

is also a potter who recently has "retaught" the making of pottery to his own mother in the pueblo. Such activities demonstrate the genius of the Tiguas through time and how, if saved in the memory of the people, cultural elements seemingly lost may be reactivated later. In his explanation of the historical patterns of surviv-als and revivals, Alvidrez points to the fact that the oldest members of the village, who were Tiwa speakers, had children who were enormously impacted by the pressures of the outside world. Because the pueblo was not recognized as an Indian reservation and because of economic factors, little land, and other influences, Alvi-drez says that his father's generation had to work hard just to survive. The pueblo faced many non-Indian influences, and the Tigua cultural fabric began to weaken. Foreign customs were introduced into the community. The general appearance and cultivation of the land base was altered. The Tigua people were forced to incorpo-rate modern changes or face the consequences of extinction. However, with his own generation, Alvidrez says, has come a revitalization of the old ways coupled with new means of ensuring that ceremonial events, feast days, language, and other aspects of the Tiguas will be celebrated and understood. Born in 1972, Alvidrez is a product of the initial revitalization of the tribe ensuing from recognition by the federal and state governments. He has a particular interest in arts and crafts that communicate the cultural realities of the Tiguas through time. As a boy, he learned both pottery and the Tiwa language by participating in educational programs. Today, he is helping perpetuate and augment the meaning of such activities in very innovative ways for all the age groups within the tribe.

The Tiguas Today

When the Tiguas were recognized as a tribe in 1968, a new sense of identity began to be expressed by the tribe in terms of a new emphasis on tribal arts and crafts. Under the aegis of the state of Texas, the Tiguas experienced unprecedented oppor-tunities to reexplore their cultural past. Though language was not particularly emphasized, the Texas Indian Commission encouraged the reintroduction of arts and crafts. In an effort to promote tourism, and therefore self-sufficiency, pueblo craftspersons were invited to instruct the Tiguas in pottery making, textiles, and even beadwork. Though the Pueblos had historically borrowed from outside cul-tures, adapting elements that enabled them to survive and prosper, during this decade the outside influences were often based on a stereotype of "the Indian"— often Plains Indians—and hence included the effort to introduce beadwork, a Plains hallmark. As a result of this opportunity, however, the Tiguas did build a cultural center, which began a thirty-year effort to concentrate on cultural identity

However, it must be understood that despite all manner of historic challenges to its culture, the tribe had managed to maintain that culture. For instance, Alvidrez emphasizes that, with their removal by the Spanish in 1680 and 1682, the Tiguas, like the other pueblo people, learned quickly how to keep their ways secret while outwardly accommodating the Spanish enough to survive. Therefore memory of their past, reenacted in ceremonies and sacred events that they never lost, was the unseen repository of the culture. And that was passed on, whether wholly in the Tiwa language or not.

Early federal funding and state recognition allowed the Tiguas to improve their economy as a tribe, particularly in the 1970s and 1980s. Their local visibility increased, and as early as 1978, the Tiwa language was taught in the local elementary school, giving a whole generation of young people the chance to learn the language. Several elders had never completely forgotten the language, and by 1992—when gaming was allowed at the Texas pueblo, and when Speaking Rock, a casino, was opened—economic improvement again provided the chance for the tribe to better their social conditions, including education, housing, and health. Today, the remaining elders meet at their own elder center, where the bingo games are keyed in Tiwa and native drumming guides an exercise class. While very few of the Tiguas can actually converse in their original language, up to two hundred words are known, and such creative educational approaches encourage the daily use of their language. An after-school class in Tigua culture, including the language, is taught at the local elementary school. Helping the young and old retain the language are Tiguas now in their twenties who were the ones first impacted by the initial cultural and language programs in the 1970s.

Unlike some of the other Native American groups, the Tiguas decided not to divide their gaming proceeds on a per capita basis. Rather, they prioritized the collective use of the money to meet the needs to acquire land and to place an emphasis on education, college scholarships, health matters, and housing, and to address cultural concerns. In addition to the feast and religious days, a new cultural center, built in 1995, provides for dancing by the young people, a museum, the baking of traditional bread, and various events that have included Pueblo Tribal Council meetings for the nineteen northern pueblos. Dancers have visited from other tribes, including the Kiowa, with whom the Tiguas exchanged dances and native chants years ago. The story is etched in the stone walls at Hueco Tanks, recounting battles and exchanges in the tribes' shared history. Such events in the 1990s remind the Tigua participants of the cultural sharing that occurred in prehistoric and historic times. In this case, the Kiowa "gave" a "friendship dance" which is depicted at Hueco Tanks,[19] the ancestral home of the Tiguas when the Kiowas and Tiguas were at war. Thus, the earlier marking of peace between the tribes is symbolically reenacted in the dances shared by the two tribes.

The Tiguas also are planning to teach their language and other cultural aspects by computer in the schools. They are on the Internet with the other tribes. Currently, they offer summer educational programs that feature native arts such as pottery making and involve language use and symbology. The tribe provides an educational booklet to help in the learning and practice of the language through newsletters and word puzzles. It plans to make a video, with tribal elders speaking in Tiwa, and to compile an archive based on audiotapes.

Since their first encounter with the Spanish, the Tiguas have surmounted many obstacles in order to survive as a tribe. Other pueblo groups—the Mansos and Piros—were absorbed into the local population and disappeared as distinct cultures, but the Tiguas have remained. They have held fast to their cultural identity even though they have lost most of their language and intermarried with other Native Americans and Hispanics. However, intermarriage signals another formidable problem. Under the federal government's terms of trusteeship, persons must have a "blood quantum" of at least one-eighth Tigua ancestry to be carried on the tribal rolls. Because the tribe is so small, it is virtually impossible to marry inside the tribe without marrying a cousin. Therefore, today, consideration of *cultural identity and practice* figures even more in the official identification of who is a Tigua Indian. Over time, various theorists have interpreted the content and meaning of cultural practice and its relationship to language. In "Folk History and Cultural Reorganization," Thomas A. Green uses the Tiguas as an example of a tribe constructing positive nativist stories to counter not only assimilation but also the view of some members of other tribes that the Tiguas were a "Judas tribe," fleeing by choice with the Spanish south from Isleta Pueblo to El Paso. Though neither Isleta nor others of the southern groups—the Piro, Senecu, or Saline pueblos—participated in the revolt in 1680, because the Tiguas moved with the Spanish retreat, a negative story has emerged that could call into question their social and cultural integrity.

Green demonstrates through selected interviews how tribal members recount other reasons for the evacuation and the consequent resettlement in the El Paso area. One story posits that the Tiguas' fearless warriors followed Coronado, attempting to kill him because they perceived him as a danger to the pueblo people. Embedded in this story is an even more profound thought: the Tigua were already in the El Paso del Norte area in ancient times, as borne out by some physical evidence at Hueco Tanks, where the Tiguas identify petroglyphs detailing part of the tribal prehistory. Because the Tigua, despite language loss, continued to assert their cultural distinctiveness from both their Anglo-American and Mexican-American neighbors in the eighteenth and nineteenth centuries, Green argues that Ralph Linton's definition of a nativist movement fits the experience of the Tigua, a "conscious, organized attempt on the part of a society's members to revive or perpetuate selected aspects of its culture."[20]

The existence of Tigua cultural identity today may also signify the ability to adapt to outside necessities for survival while simultaneously challenging stereotypes. Alvidrez, who often speaks in public schools, tries to get non-Native American children to recognize and dispel their own false notions. Wearing typical Western dress in the school room, he says, "This is a Native American too." His major goal is to deconstruct the pervasive Hollywood imagery, largely of a pseudo-Plains-type, which is still perpetuated in the public mind as representing all Native American peoples. But his actions further indicate that cultural identity may also be bound up in the attitudes of outsiders.

Scholar Roger Abraham effectively argues that there is an intimate relationship between the problems commonly faced by a group and the communicative interaction they develop. He also argues that in certain cases physical and geographical separation increases the sense of community, particularly if a group is a minority that feels a threat from outsiders or must cope with an exoteric stereotype imposed upon it by the dominant culture. Where the group is threatened, traditional practices and expressions are often the most salient means of proclaiming and reinforcing group identity. In this regard, the Tiguas today are performing a very crucial role. Having survived the near-extinction of their language, they are now in the unique position of advising not only non-Natives, but also some of the other pueblo peoples. Though themselves seemingly an isolated, forgotten tribe, they have found ways through time of meeting the challenges of urban change, encroachment, economic swings, and disbelievers.[21]

As the northern pueblos today finally face the drain on traditional pueblo life of their young's being drawn to nearby urban centers, they are experiencing many of the disruptive forces the Tiguas have confronted throughout their history at Ysleta. Perhaps they will find, as the Tiguas have in transferring language through significant activities, that the *nature* of their cultural transference will reflect the kinds of tensions and anxieties experienced in common by members of their group.

Lacking a land base that for other pueblos has been honored since the Spanish land-grant period and reservation status and recognition during the mid-nineteenth century, the people of Tigua pueblo have contended with extraordinary tensions and challenges to their cultural integrity. It is nothing short of amazing that they survived, either according to the "blood-quantum" requirement for certification by the U.S. government or in their own cultural identity, which, despite its various characteristics through time, has constituted a continuity.

Many scholars have concluded that pueblo peoples in general were ready and eager to include in their cultural behavior the techniques they learned about, and that this kind of acculturation took place rapidly and easily, regardless of the original culture of the acculturating group or the language spoken. As Trager points out:

> All have traditions of movement in many directions. And for all, the specific Puebloan developments—their becoming city states—took place recently and quickly, and with retention of basic differences. The whole Pueblo development may very well have been induced by constant influx of new peoples, and the movements of the old. Rather than being arch "conservatives," these people perhaps were all eager innovators, constantly seeking new places to go, and new ways to do the things they always have been doing.[22]

Certainly the reconsideration of how Tigua pueblo peoples have survived language loss and suppression, by inventing a new dialect of the Southern Tiwa and transferring this cultural core throughout their materialized world, is a study in Puebloan innovation.[23] Instead of letting their culture disappear under the weight of colonization, the people of Ysleta del Sur Pueblo have continued their culturally and historically creative lives.

NOTES

The author wishes to thank Albert Alvidrez, Tribal Council member and director of the Tigua Cultural Center, and his assistant, Deborah Alvidrez, for their generosity, warmth, and sharing of information, all of which made this chapter possible. Special thanks are given to Rosa Holquin-Hernandez, daughter of Francisco Holquin, a Tigua Indian. The Holquin family name dates from the 1840s, when they first farmed land in Ysleta. Mrs. Holquin-Hernandez suggested invaluable contacts and background, and introduced me to Mr. Alvidrez. Special Collections librarian at the University of Texas of El Paso, Claudia Rivers, also was instrumental in providing information for this chapter.

1. See Thomas A. Green, "Folk History and Cultural Reorganization: A Tigua Example," *Journal of American Folklore* 89 (Summer 1976), 310–318.

2. For studies of the Tiwa language as related to the Tiguas and Isleta del Sur, see John R. Bartlett, "Senecu Piro Vocabulary," Manuscript 1627, National Antrhopological Archives, Smithsonian Institution, Washington, D.C. (1897); John R. Bartlett and James Mooney, "Kiowa and Tiwa (Isleta del Sur) Linguistic Notes and Vocabularies," Manuscript 454, National Anthropological Archives, Smithsonian Institution, Washington, D.C. (1897); J. P. Harrington, "Notes on the Piro Language," *American Anthropologist*, 2 (1909): 563–594; Carol Rosen, "Rethinking Southern Tiwa: The Geometry of a Triple-Agreement Language," *Language* 1 (December 1966); George L. Trager. "The Tanoan Settlement of the Rio Grande Area: A Possible Chronology," *Studies in Southwest Ethnolinguistics* 45 (1967), 338–365.

3. Interview with Albert Alvidrez, Tigua Tribal Council member, September 28, 1996, Ysleta Pueblo Cultural Center. See also Patrick H. Barrett, "A Tiwa Rabbit Hunt as Held by the Tortugas Indians," in *Awanyu* 2, no. 5 (1974), 40–46.

4. For accounts of the events leading to official tribal status, see Nicholas P. Houser, "Tigua Pueblo," in *Handbook of North American Indians*, vol. 9 (Washington, D.C.: Smithsonian Institution Press, 1979), 336–342, and Bill Wright, *The Tiguas: Pueblo Indians of Texas* (El Paso: Texas Western Press, 1993).

5. *The Official Correspondence of James S. Calhoun*, ed. Annie H. Abel (Washington, D.C.: Government Printing Office, 1915).

6. See Joe S. Sando, "The Pueblo Revolt," in *Handbook of North American Indians*, vol. 9 (Washington, D.C.: Smithsonian Institution Press, 1979).

7. See Wright, *The Tiguas*, for a very good bibliography and interpretation of this early period. Wright applies the logical historical categories of "Beginnings to 1540," "The Spanish 1590–1680," "Rebellion 1680–1836," and "The Americans: 1836–1993."

8. J. B. Gillet, *Six Years with the Texas Rangers, 1875–1881* (New Haven: Yale University Press, 1963).

9. The best chronological account of this period is in Alan Minter, "The Tigua Indians of Pueblo del Sur, El Paso County, Texas," in *West Texas Historical Association Year Book* (1969), 30–44.

10. Quoted in L. B. Bloom, "Bourke in the Southwest," *New Mexico Historical Review* 13 (1938), 200.

11. See Bloom, 204.

12. H. F. C. Ten Kate, Jr., *Reizen en Onderzoekingen in Noord Amerika* (Leiden, Denmark: 1885).

13. W. J. Fewkes, "The Pueblo Settlements Near El Paso, Texas," *American Anthropologist*, 4 (1902), 57–75.

14. Certain popular articles of this period give insight into the attitudes surrounding the final acknowledgment of Tiguas as an Indian group. The local newspapers in El Paso carried several articles during this time, including pieces highlighting the resilience of Tigua pueblo culture. See "Tigua Indians Celebrate; Dances Planned at Ysleta," *El Paso Herald-Post* (10 June 1960); "New Tigua Indian Plans Study of Tribal Culture," *El Paso Times* (20 June

1960); Bob Miles, "Tiguas Have Retained Tribal Customs, Songs," *El Paso Times* (27 February 1966). Local curiosity and supportive articles also appeared during the ˙1950s, prior to tribal recognition, when local writers such as Cleofas Calleros published *Tigua Indians Oldest Permanent Settlers in Texas* (El Paso: American Printing, 1953). Calleros went to great lengths to remind readers of the vitality of the Tigua culture by reproducing photographs of Tigua elders investing President and Mrs. Franklin D. Roosevelt with the titles of cacique and squaw at the Cotton Bowl in Dallas, June 12, 1936, during the Texas Centennial Exposition. Before and after federal and state recognition as a tribe, the Tiguas were and have been invited to attend various expositions, national folk festivals, and the Festival of American Folklife in Washington, D.C., where they danced and demonstrated bread making.

15. An invaluable bibliography of existing photographic records and documentation's exists in Wright's *Tiguas.*

16. Nicholas P. Houser, "The Tigua Settlement of Ysleta del Sur," *Kiva* (1970), 23–32.

17. See Hauser, *Kiva,* 29.

18. See John A. Hedrick, "Investigations of Tigua Potters and Pottery at Ysleta del Sur, Texas," *Artifact,* 9 (1971), 1–17.

19. See Gordon Dickson, "Pottery Craft Spans Generations in Tribe," *El Paso Times* (28 September 1996).

20. Green, "Folk History," 312.

21. Roger D. Abraham, "The Negro Stereotype," *American Folklore,* 83 (1970).

22. Trager, "Tanoan Settlement," 365.

23. Of a generation affected by the first wave of revival of Tigua culture in the late 1960s and 1970s, Albert Alvidrez and others of his age group are instrumental in the current renewed interest and activities among the Tiguas. Having learned the craft of pottery making when he was eighteen years old from visiting tribal elders who molded, painted, and sold their wares to tourists, he has maintained contact with many of the elders and fifty or so Tiguas making pottery today at the reservation. But he was also influenced at an earlier age by the arts and crafts revival at the pueblo during the early days of tribal recognition. Tribal elder, Santiago Bustamante, seventy-five, remembers how family members would grind corn for tortillas in their handmade pottery. Though Alvidrez's mother married into the tribe, she was willing to learn from him in order to help prevent the decline in the craft. "We must keep the tradition," she says (see *El Paso Times,* 28 September 1996). "This is the most important thing," Alvidrez adds. "Pueblo people are tied to the earth and pottery is the earth itself. Without what we have here, we would be no one." Alvidrez and the Tribal Council are currently supporting an effort to preserve the house of one of the last full-time potters at Tigua. Her pottery sherds, bearing suggestions of method, materials, and design, may be found around the house and in the adobe walls. Such projects, along with cultural programs on the reservation taught by other young women of the tribe, Laura Soto and Connie Ortega, are ways in which the generations are working with and influencing one another in the preservation and perpetuation of expressive and material culture.

Chapter Twenty-five

Out of Sight
The Suppression of American Sign Language

Douglas C. Baynton

The story of the suppression of American Sign Language (ASL) is a familiar one in the rich folkloric history of the American deaf community. Few scholars, however, are aware of the campaign to eradicate ASL that began in the late nineteenth century and was led by such luminaries as Alexander Graham Bell, Franklin Sanborn, and Gardiner Green Hubbard. While ultimately a failure, the campaign was successful to the extent that the knowledge accumulated about ASL over the course of the nineteenth century—indeed the very knowledge that ASL constitutes a true language—was forgotten for nearly a hundred years. As a result, the suppression went unrecognized for what it was, and was remembered only euphemistically as educational reform. The reasons for the suppression were various and complex. They included perceived similarities between the deaf community and ethnic communities at a time of intense nativism, an imagined hierarchy of languages constructed from the new theories of evolution, and the rise of the concept of normality.[1]

One consequence of the long suppression of ASL is the number of current misconceptions about this language. For example, many people assume that there is one universal sign language. This notion often coexists, curiously, with the incompatible and equally erroneous belief that ASL was invented for the purposes of educating deaf children and that its signs correspond to English words. ASL is a natural language that has evolved, just as spoken languages do, within a linguistic community. Like any other language, it has a unique syntactic structure and is governed by a unique set of grammatical rules. The sign languages of different countries differ from one another just as their spoken languages do, both in lexicon and grammar. Having developed independently from the spoken languages of their respective countries, sign languages neither correspond to nor represent them. ASL is often confused with the manual communication systems invented recently for the purpose of teaching English to deaf children, which attempt to represent English on the hands. Several varieties of these "Manually Coded English" systems exist today. These are artificial codes, not true languages.[2]

The main source for ASL was French Sign Language, and while ASL and FSL have diverged considerably over the years, they are still mutually intelligible to a limited extent—somewhat like modern Spanish and Italian. British Sign Language and ASL, on the other hand, are mutually unintelligible.[3] The historical relation of FSL and ASL came about in 1817, when the Reverend Thomas H. Gallaudet returned to Hartford, Connecticut, from Paris intent upon establishing the first school for the deaf in the United States. He was accompanied by Laurent Clerc, a deaf man educated at the National Institute for Deaf-Mutes in Paris and subsequently a teacher there, who was to become the head teacher of the new school, the American Asylum for the Deaf and Dumb.[4]

Clerc brought with him the sign language of Paris, a city with a large deaf community and sophisticated sign language. This language had apparently been in existence for some time. A deaf Parisian, Pierre Desloges, wrote in 1779 that while the communication ability of a deaf person living isolated in the provinces was "limited to physical things and bodily needs," in Paris, through "intercourse with his [deaf] fellows he promptly acquires the supposedly difficult art of depicting and expressing all his thoughts" using sign language. Desloges maintained that deaf Parisians expressed themselves "on all subjects with as much order, precision, and rapidity as if we enjoyed the faculty of speech and hearing."[5] Clerc brought this sign language to the United States and taught it to Gallaudet and the other teachers at the new school. FSL became the official language of the school.

The United States was a rural country with no great cities such as Paris, but it nevertheless had at least one well-developed sign language. On Martha's Vineyard, from the seventeenth to the nineteenth century, an unusually high rate of inherited deafness resulted in a community in which both hearing and deaf islanders knew and used a signed language. The hearing members of the community switched back and forth from speech to sign depending upon who was present. Most of the deaf students who came to the new school at Hartford were from rural areas and learned for the first time how to communicate in a language rather than with pantomime and gesture. But some came from Martha's Vineyard and brought with them the sign language of the island. Modern American Sign Language was formed from the encounter of this and possibly other indigenous signed languages with FSL.[6]

The school at Hartford was the first of many residential schools that soon opened around the country. Within forty years there were twenty, and by the turn of the century, more than fifty schools for the deaf. Thousands of young deaf people were brought together and, aside from school vacations, spent years living and studying together. More than a new sign language came into existence with these schools. A new culture was born. Deaf people created a rich folklore, passed on from generation to generation, that included stories, poetry, oratory, games, and jokes in ASL, as well as distinct rules of etiquette and naming practices. By the latter half of the century, the deaf community had its own periodical press, with dozens of newspapers such as the *Silent World*, the *Deaf-Mute Journal*, and the *Silent Worker*. Most of these were locally oriented; a few were national in scope and distribution. Deaf people across the country established local clubs, statewide organizations, and in 1880 the National Association of the Deaf. They attended churches where sign language was the medium of sermon and song alike. And the great majority found not just their friends but their spouses within the deaf community.[7]

For a complex variety of reasons that had little to do with the realities of deaf education or the actual lives of deaf people, in the years following the Civil War many hearing people became increasingly uneasy with the existence of this community and its language. A coalition of hearing parents and hearing educators of deaf children began a campaign to suppress ASL. Given the difficulties and obstacles involved in regulating the activities of independent adults, the campaign to eradicate sign language concentrated, as most such campaigns do, on children and the schools. In the case of deaf children, this seemed a choice likely to be effective since it was known that the great majority—about 90 percent—of deaf children had hearing parents. For these children, sign language was learned at school, not at home. If the schools forbade its use, most deaf children presumably would never acquire it. Central to this project, then, was a campaign to abolish "manualism"— the use of sign language in the schools for the deaf—and to replace it with "oralism," the exclusive use of lipreading and speech.

The deaf community fought back against the attack on sign language. At the 1890 convention of American Instructors of the Deaf, a deaf member declared that "Chinese women bind their babies' feet to make them small; the Flathead Indians bind their babies' heads to make them flat." Those who would prohibit sign language in the schools, he charged, "are denying the deaf their free mental growth . . . and are in the same class of criminals." In 1896, Robert P. McGregor, first president of the National Association of the Deaf, indignantly asked, "By whom then are signs proscribed?" His answer was, "By a few educators of the deaf whose boast is that they do not understand signs and do not want to; by a few philanthropists who are otherwise ignorant of the language; by parents who do not understand the requisites to the happiness of their deaf children and are inspired with false fears by the educators and philanthropists."[8]

The deaf community did not control the schools, however. By the turn of the century, nearly 40 percent of American deaf students were taught entirely without the use of sign language. By the end of World War I, that number was approaching 80 percent, and deaf teachers, who had numbered nearly half of all teachers of deaf children in the 1860s, had been almost entirely purged from the profession.[9] Oralism remained orthodox until the 1970s.

Why did hearing Americans turn against sign language at this particular time? Manualist educators earlier in the century, such as Gallaudet, had been chiefly concerned with the spiritual life of deaf people. Most of them were evangelical Protestants, many of them ministers, and they explicitly described themselves as missionaries to a people cut off from the Christian gospel. They learned the sign language of deaf people just as other missionaries learned the languages of American Indians, Africans, and the Chinese, and went to preach among the heathen.

Those of the oralist generation were concerned more with national unity than with salvation. During the ardent nationalism that followed the Civil War—the sense that divisions or particularisms within the nation were dangerous and ought to be suppressed—educators and others began to express concerns about the "clannishness" of deaf people. In 1873, for example, Edward M. Gallaudet (son of Thomas H.) criticized the conventions, associations, and newspapers of deaf people for discouraging intercourse "with their race and the world," and deplored the existence of a deaf " 'community,' with its leaders and rulers, its associations and organs, and its channels of communication." He nevertheless did not advocate abolishing sign language.[10] That came soon enough, however, when "clannish" gave way to "foreign," a more ominous charge.

By the 1890s, the rhetoric of deaf education conjured images of foreign enclaves within American society. Articles about deaf people mirrored proliferating articles on the dangers of immigration, warning that deaf people "must be made people of our language," attacking "the foreign language of signs," and insisting that "the English language must be made the vernacular of the deaf if they are not to become a class unto themselves—foreigners among their own countrymen." Indeed, "no gesturer can become an American" because his or her primary and native language would never be English; "the gesturer is, and always will remain, a foreigner."[11]

Alexander Graham Bell described sign language as "essentially a foreign language" and asserted that "in an English speaking country like the United States, the English language, *and the English language alone*, should be used as the means of communication and instruction—at least in schools supported at public expense." In a letter drafted to send to a journal of deaf education, Bell objected that the use of sign language "in our public schools is contrary to the spirit and practice of American Institutions (as foreign immigrants have found out)." He added it was "un-American," but apparently thought better of it and crossed the word out.[12]

Bell was especially disturbed that, according to his research, the rate of intermarriage among deaf people was more than 80 percent. This issue brought together for Bell the three great interests of his life: elocution, eugenics, and deaf education. He and his father before him had spent their lives studying the physiology of speech. He thought it ought to be possible to teach the deaf to speak and not only maintained this in a steady stream of letters and articles but opened his own school and began to instruct teachers in his methods. He also wrote about his concerns that the influx of immigrants into the country and intermarriage among the deaf were damaging the genetic stock of the nation. In an 1884 paper published by the National Academy of Sciences, Bell warned that the intermarriage of the deaf was producing a "great calamity," the "formation of a deaf variety of the human race." The chief cause of deaf marriages, he argued, was "segregation for the purposes of education, and the use, as a means of communication, of a language which is different from that of the people." Bell's fear of a proliferating deafness was based upon a faulty understanding of the genetics of deafness. Marriages between deaf people on average do not produce greater numbers of deaf offspring than mixed hearing/deaf marriages. However, the image of a foreign, inbred, and expanding deaf community was widely repeated in both professional and popular periodicals for years to come.[13]

Foreignness was a powerful metaphor for Americans of the late nineteenth century. References to deaf people as foreigners reflected apprehensions about the massive influx of new immigrants at the time, most of whom concentrated in urban ethnic neighborhoods. Many were from the East and the South of Europe and brought with them cultural practices that native-born Americans regarded with hostility and suspicion. The nativism that is never far from the surface of American life resurged with calls for immigration restriction and the proscription of languages other than English in the schools. To say that sign language turned deaf people into "foreigners" was for many a compelling argument against it.

Oralists were concerned, however, not only with the use of a *language* other than English. Any form of manual communication, whether a distinct language such as ASL, a manual code for English, or finger spelling, was objectionable to them. To understand their total opposition to talking with hands rather than with tongues, it is necessary to turn from the question "What makes an American," to a knottier question: "What makes a human being?"

The central cultural divide that separated the generations of teachers who used sign language from later teachers who opposed it was the rise of evolutionary theory. Most manualist teachers were of a generation that came of age before the publication of Charles Darwin's *Origin of Species* in 1859. The manualists' world-view was constructed on the theory of immediate creation; the oralists' was built on an evolutionary understanding of the world. The mechanism that Darwin advanced in 1859 to explain how evolution worked—natural selection—was not widely accepted in the United States until after the turn of the century, but evolution itself quickly found a remarkably widespread acceptance.[14] Evolutionary analogies, explanations, and ways of thinking were ubiquitous by the 1870s, one result of which was a radical change in attitudes toward language—specifically toward the relative standing of spoken and gesture languages.

During the eighteenth and nineteenth centuries the origin of language had become an important topic of philosophical discussion in both Europe and America; many people speculated that humans had used gestural language before turning to spoken language.[15] Manualist teachers, as experts on sign language, were naturally interested in the idea that gestures preceded speech and discussed it in their professional journals and conferences. As evangelical Protestants, they interpreted the theory in terms of a biblical history according to which humanity was created in its present form. The theory that sign language preceded speech did not therefore imply inferiority; on the contrary, the antiquity of sign language was taken as an indication of its superiority over modern, degenerate languages. The fact that "many philologists think that it was the original language of mankind" meant that sign language might have been "in the designs of Providence, the necessary forerunner of speech," which was for them a mark of honor.[16]

Later in the century, however, oralists interpreted the theory quite differently. If to the manualist generation, "original language" had meant "closer to the Creation," to post-Darwin oralists, it meant "closer to the apes." Humanity had risen rather than fallen and represented the culmination of history rather than its beginning. Antiquity was no mark of honor but, rather, one of inferiority. Sign language was transformed into a language low on the evolutionary scale, antedating even the most "savage" spoken language.

Language scholars began to promulgate a kind of "linguistic Darwinism," arguing that inferior languages were continually being eliminated and replaced by superior ones in the "struggle for existence." Gestural communication had suffered an early defeat in that struggle. The American philologist William Dwight Whitney, for example, believed that human communication once consisted of "an inferior system of . . . tone, gesture, and grimace," and it was through the "process of natural selection and survival of the fittest that the voice has gained the upper hand." The British anthropologist Edward B. Tylor noted that "savage and half-civilized races accompany their talk with expressive pantomime much more than nations of higher culture," indicating to him that "in the early stages of the development of language, . . . gesture had an importance as an element of expression, which in conditions of highly-organized language it has lost." Garrick Mallery, an expert on American Indian sign languages, believed that the "most notable criterion" for distinguishing between "civilized" and "savage" peoples was to be found in the "copiousness and precision of oral language, and in the unequal survival of the communication by gesture signs which, it is believed, once universally prevailed."[17]

The language used by deaf people became increasingly linked with the languages of "savages." Tylor wrote of "the gesture-signs of savages and deaf-mutes." Darwin referred to the gestural communication "used by the deaf and dumb and by savages." Mallery suggested that "troglodyte" humans communicated "precisely as Indians or deaf-mutes" do today. A contributor to *Science* noted that sign language was common among "the less cultured tribes, while the spoken language is seen in its highest phase among the more civilized," adding that sign language was used "in the training of the deaf and dumb."[18] In an article on the gestures of Italian immigrants, a reporter for the New York *Evening Post* wrote that "among most savages the language of gesture is extensive," that this was commonly taken as a "sign of feeble intellectual power," and that deaf people communicated in the same way.[19]

Educators began to echo the notion that sign language was "characteristic of tribes low in the scale of development," and that the sign language of deaf people "resembles the languages of the North American Indian and the Hottentot of South Africa." They began to argue that because "as man emerged from savagery he discarded gestures for the expression of his ideas," it was time that deaf people discarded them as well. They declared that spoken language was the "crown of history"; to permit deaf children the use of sign language was to "push them back in the world's history to the infancy of our race."[20]

Manualists had not been unaware that American Indians also used a form of sign language. Delegations of Indians occasionally visited the schools for the deaf where they conversed with the residents via pantomimic gestures, at which both were adept.[21] While manualists often noted the parallels between the sign languages of deaf people and American Indians, they also noted parallels with the art of pantomime cultivated by the ancient Romans, and syntactical resemblances to ancient Latin, Greek, and Hebrew. None of these comparisons demeaned sign language for them, for the past did not connote inferiority. First, their understanding of progress did not include improvement in physical or intellectual capacity. And second, many of their generation believed that history was cyclical, that both languages and peoples had "their birth, growth, and culmination, like the language of the Hebrews for instance, or the splendid tongues of Greece and Rome." The examples of Sanskrit, Hebrew, Greek, and Latin were evidence that all languages finally "passed into that doom of death and silence which awaits alike the speaker and the speech." Since the "tendency of every language is toward change, decay, and ultimate extinction as a living organism," there was no reason for them to assume that present forms of communication were superior to those of the past.[22] Americans coming of age in the late nineteenth century, however, lived with a different past than this. For them, sign language had been superseded by speech, was therefore necessarily inferior, and deserved extinction.

Sign language came to characterize not only the lower human but the nonhuman as well. A writer in *Science* repeated the common speculation that the "creature from which man developed in one direction, and the apes in another" probably used rudimentary forms of both gesture and speech. While in humans gesture was largely supplanted by speech, "in the apes the gesture-language alone was developed."[23] Manualists found themselves defending sign language against charges that it was nothing more than "a set of monkey-like grimaces and antics." They complained about the persistent insult "You look like monkeys when you make signs," and protested attempts to "impress [deaf people] with the thought that it is apish to talk on the fingers." Oralists scoffed that "these signs can no more be called a language than the different movements of a dog's tail and ears which indicate his feelings."[24]

Like all ideas, this interpretation of evolutionary progress did not travel alone. One of its most influential traveling companions was the emerging concept of normality. The word *normal* first began to acquire its modern meaning of *typical* or *average* in the middle decades of the nineteenth century. *Normality* has never adhered to its dictionary definition, however. It is much more than a norm or an average. As Ian Hacking has noted, it functions simultaneously as both description and prescription, signifying both the *is* and the *ought*.[25]

What has gone unnoticed about the emergence of normality as a concept is that it became a culturally powerful idea only with the advent of evolutionary theory. The ideal of the *natural*, which normality to some extent displaced, had been a static concept for an essentially unchanging world, at a time when "the book of nature" was represented as the guidebook of God. Normality, on the other hand, was a dynamic concept for a changing and progressing world, premised upon the notion that one could discern from the observation of human behavior the direction of human progress, or evolution, and use *that* as a guide. Its ascendance signaled a shift in the locus of faith, from a God-centered to a human-centered world, from a culture that looked within to a core and backward to lost Edenic origins, to one that looked outward to behavior and forward to a perfected future.

In response to the manualist belief that sign language was the natural language of the deaf, oralists countered that speech was the evolutionary norm. All people, hearing or deaf, have "an undoubted constitutional tendency toward speech," resulting from "the cumulative inheritance of a thousand generations of ancestors who have employed this means of communicating their thoughts." The normal was defined according to the perceived direction of evolution; whatever diverged from that direction was both abnormal and undesirable. Consistent with the ability of the concept of normality to function as both description and prescription, oralists asserted not only that people *should* do what has been done by past generations but that they *will* do so out of an inborn tendency—unless they are somehow corrupted and turned away from their evolutionary heritage, which is what they believed had happened to deaf people.[26]

Furthermore, while normality ostensibly denoted the average or the usual, in actual usage it stigmatized those defined as *below* average or in some way undesirable. "Is the child normal?" was never a question that expressed fear about whether a child had *above* average intelligence, motor skills, or beauty. *Normality* was an ideal more than an average, and *abnormality* signified the *sub*normal. In the context of a pervasive belief that the tendency of the human race was to constantly improve itself, that barring something out of the ordinary, humanity moved ever upward, away from its animal origins and toward greater perfection, normality was implicitly defined as that which advanced progress (or at least did not impede it). Abnormality, conversely, was that which pulled humanity back toward its past, toward its animal origins.

Physical or mental abnormalities have been commonly depicted as instances of atavism, reversions to earlier stages of evolution. Down's syndrome, for example, was originally called Mongolism by the doctor who first identified it in 1866 because he believed the syndrome to be the result of a biological reversion by Caucasians to the Mongol racial type.[27] When teachers of the deaf spoke of making deaf children more like "normal" people and less like savages and animals by forbidding them the use of sign language, when they worked to prevent deaf marriages with a rhetoric of evolutionary progress and decline, they were expressing a sense that normality was tied to progress and that the abnormality of deaf people threatened that progress.

Educators' nomenclature began to change, as "hearing people" became "normal people." Teachers compared the development of deaf children—their speech, English skills, social behavior—to "normal children," and discussed how their work, as teachers "of the abnormal child," compared with "ordinary work with the normal child."[28] Deaf people never accepted this use of the term "normal" and continued to refer to "hearing" people, but the concept of normality came to dominate the way that professionals and the public thought and spoke about deaf people. "Our first and foremost aim," wrote a teacher in 1907, "has been the development of the deaf child into as nearly a normal individual as possible."[29]

While most oralists reluctantly conceded that deafness precluded *complete* attainment of the ideal of normality, they held it to be a goal worthy of unending pursuit. Even if deaf people inevitably fell short of normal, they might nevertheless be made less *obviously* abnormal. An optimistic writer for *Scientific American* proclaimed in 1907 that, with oral instruction, "congenital mutes are . . . able to speak so perfectly, that it is difficult to distinguish their voices from those of normal persons."[30] The new measure of success was to *pass* for a normal person.

Of course, most deaf people either could not or did not desire to pass for hearing. The deaf community responded to oralism with both overt and covert resistance, in the fashion common to beleaguered minorities. The organized deaf community perennially lobbied legislatures and school boards in support of sign language.[31] Deaf organizations issued passionate statements that in spite of attempts to "banish signs from the schoolroom, from the churches, and from the earth . . . as long as we have Deaf people on earth, we will have signs."[32] Deaf parents passed sign language on to their children, and those children who were deaf taught others in the dormitories, behind school buildings, away from the censorious eyes of their hearing guardians. Deaf adults acquired the habit of signing surreptitiously while out in public, knowing hearing people's disapproval, relaxing and communicating freely only at the deaf club or at home. More than 90 percent of deaf people continued to marry within the community, deaf community organizations continued to thrive, and ASL continued to be the language of that community.[33]

Nevertheless, because deaf adults were excluded from the formation of school policy, sign language continued to be excluded from the classroom, and generations of deaf children grew to maturity poorly educated, on average reading at a third-grade level upon graduation, with a knowledge of the world gleaned largely from secret conversations with other children. Oliver Sacks has described the "dramatic deterioration in the educational achievement of deaf children and in the literacy of the deaf generally" that resulted from oralism. Fortunately, that damage was mitigated by the existence of the deaf community, which saved a great many deaf children from severe linguistic impoverishment.[34]

The suppression of ASL is a continuing story to this day. The "mainstreaming" or "inclusion" of deaf students into local public schools has increased dramatically in the last decade. Approximately 80 percent of deaf students now attend local public schools, with "interpreters" who are rarely competent in ASL and who generally employ a cumbersome manually coded English system of communication. Alexander Graham Bell maintained that the ideal school "would contain only one deaf child."[35] Nearly one hundred years later, his dream is in many places being realized. While "mainstreaming" and "inclusion" cover a wide variety of actual circumstances—in some cities, "magnet schools" might have several dozen deaf children in attendance—for the majority of deaf children, mainstreaming means being the only deaf student in the class. For many, it means being the only deaf student in the entire school.

Even during the long years of oralism's ascendancy most deaf students continued to attend residential schools, so that in private and away from supervision they could steal moments of genuine, relaxed, and easy communication. Today this is no longer the case. Thousands grow up with no contact with other deaf people, children or adults, with no access to American Sign Language or to the knowledge of the deaf community, accumulated over generations, of how to live successfully in a mostly hearing world.[36]

Deaf adults, the products of the educational system, have a wealth of experience to draw on, yet the education of each generation of deaf children has operated almost entirely in ignorance of, or in conscious opposition to, what they advise. Deaf people argued strenuously against oralism for the better part of a century. When, in the 1970s, the educational establishment finally abandoned its attempt to eliminate sign language, acknowledging that oralism had been a devastating failure, the deaf community enjoyed a brief period of optimism, thinking that finally its words would be heeded. That optimism was short-lived.

Whatever hearing educators choose to do, it is clear that the deaf community will go on using ASL. It will also continue to repair as best as possible the damage done by an educational establishment intent on suppressing what Thomas H. Gallaudet more than a century and a half ago called the natural language of the deaf. For more than one hundred years there was a concerted effort to eradicate any use of sign language in this country and for all of that time American Sign Language was passed down, from generation to generation, without break, without faltering. Today, deaf children leave school after years of instruction with awkward manual English systems and turn to ASL as their primary means of communication. Exposure to ASL can be delayed and linguistic competence can be thereby injured, but the great majority of deaf people will continue to use it as best and as soon as they can.

NOTES

1. Readers who wish a fuller exposition of the ideas sketched here may turn to my book, *Forbidden Signs: American Culture and the Campaign Against Sign Language* (Chicago: University of Chicago Press, 1996).

2. James Woodward, "Historical Bases of American Sign Language," in Patricia Siple, ed., *Understanding Language Through Sign Language Research* (New York: Academic Press, 1978), 333–348; Joseph D. Stedt and Donald F. Moores, "Manual Codes on English and American Sign Language: Historical Perspectives and Current Realities," in Harry Borstein, ed., *Manual Communication: Implications for Education* (Washington, D.C.: Gallaudet University Press, 1990), 1–20. For reasons I explain in my book, neither nineteenth-century deaf people nor their teachers distinguished between the sign languages of various countries, referring to all generically as "sign language." While it is usual today to attach a qualifier, as in French Sign Language and American Sign Language, to avoid anachronism I use the term "sign language" as it was used by my subjects. I also use the term "sign" as they did, to denote a gesture sign, the basic morphemic unit of sign language and the equivalent of "word" in spoken language.

3. Susan D. Rutherford, "The Culture of American Deaf People," *Sign Language Studies* 59 (Summer 1988): 133; Woodward, "Historical Bases," 333–348.

4. Originally called Connecticut Asylum, it was soon renamed American Asylum, and in the 1890s took on its present name, American School for the Deaf.

5. Desloges's book, *Observations d'un sourd et muet sur 'Un Cours elementaire d'education des sourds et muets'* (Amsterdam and Paris, 1779), is translated in Harlan Lane, ed., *The Deaf Experience: Classics in Language and Education*, trans. Franklin Philip (Cambridge: Harvard University Press, 1984), 36.

6. Nora Ellen Groce, *Everyone Here Spoke Sign Language: Hereditary Deafness on Martha's Vineyard*, (Cambridge: Harvard University Press, 1985); Woodward, "Historical Bases."

7. "Tabular Statement of Schools for the Deaf, 1897–98," *American Annals of the Deaf* (hereafter cited as *Annals*) 43 (Jan. 1898): 46–47; Jack Gannon, *Deaf Heritage: A Narrative*

History of Deaf America (Washington, D.C.: National Association of the Deaf, 1981), 237–254. An excellent account of the contemporary American deaf community can be found in Carol Padden and Tom Humphries, *Deaf in America: Voices from a Culture* (Cambridge: Harvard University Press, 1988). For a concise history of the community in the nineteenth century, see John Vickrey Van Cleve and Barry Crouch, *A Place of Their Own: Creating the Deaf Community in America* (Washington, D.C.: Gallaudet University Press, 1989); see also Harlan Lane, *When the Mind Hears: A History of the Deaf* (New York: Random House, 1984); John Vickrey Van Cleve, ed., *Deaf History Unveiled: Interpretations from the New Scholarship* (Washington, D.C.: Gallaudet University Press, 1993); Renate Fischer and Harlan Lane, eds., *Looking Back: A Reader on the History of Deaf Communities and Their Sign Languages* (Hamburg: Signum, 1993).

8. Quoted in Lane, *When the Mind Hears*, xvi, 371. It was often noted that deaf adults almost universally opposed oralism, a claim oralists did not dispute. See Amos G. Draper, "The Attitude of the Adult Deaf Towards Pure Oralism," *Annals* 40 (Jan. 1895): 44–54; Sarah Porter, "The Suppression of Signs by Force," *Annals* 39 (June 1894): 171; Anonymous ["A Semi-Deaf Lady"], "The Sign Language and the Human Right to Expression," *Annals* 53 (March 1908): 148–149.

9. Alexander Graham Bell, "Address of the President," *Association Review* 1 (Oct. 1899): 78–79 (in 1910 renamed the *Volta Review*); Edward Allen Fay in "Progress of Speech-Teaching in the United States," *Annals* 60 (Jan. 1915): 115; "Statistics of Speech Teaching in American Schools for the Deaf," *Volta Review* 22 (June 1920): 372. On the oralist movement, see Van Cleve and Crouch, *A Place of Their Own*, 106–141; Lane, *When the Mind Hears*, 339–414; Richard Winefield, *Never the Twain Shall Meet: Bell, Gallaudet, and the Communications Debate* (Washington, D.C.: Gallaudet University Press, 1987).

10. Edward M. Gallaudet, " 'Deaf-Mute' Conventions, Associations, and Newspapers," *Annals* 18 (July 1873): 200–206.

11. Katherine T. Bingham, "All Along the Line," *Association Review* 2 (Feb. 1900): 27, 29; Edward C. Rider, "The Annual Report of the Northern New York Institution for the Year Ending September 30, 1898," reprinted in the *Association Review* 1 (Dec. 1899): 214–215; S. G. Davidson, "The Relation of Language to Mental Development and of Speech to Language Teaching," *Association Review* 1 (Dec. 1899): 132; Z. F. Westervelt, "The American Vernacular Method," *Annals* 34 (July 1889): 205, 207; Gardiner G. Hubbard, "Introduction of the Articulating System for the Deaf in America," *Science* 16 (Dec. 19, 1890): 337.

12. Letter from Bell to Miss Mary E. Bennett of Los Angeles, Calif., dated August 30, 1913, in the Alexander Graham Bell Family Papers, Library of Congress, Manuscript Division, Container 173, Folder-Gen. Correspondence A–C. Letter draft to the editor of the *Educator* (Philadelphia), titled "The Question of Sign Language: Some Remarks upon Mr. Jenkins Letter," dated Feb. 1894, Alexander Graham Bell Family Papers, Manuscript Division, Library of Congress, Container 198.

13. Alexander Graham Bell, *Memoir Upon the Formation of a Deaf Variety of the Human Race* (Washington, D.C.: Government Printing Office, 1884).

14. Peter J. Bowler, *Evolution: The History of an Idea* (Berkeley: University of California Press, 1989), 188.

15. Gordon W. Hewes, "Primate Communication and the Gestural Origin of Language," *Current Anthropology* 14 (Feb.–Apr. 1973): 5; Alf Sommerfelt, "The Origin of Language: Theories and Hypotheses," *Journal of World History* 1 (April 1954): 886–892; James H. Stam, *Inquiries into the Origin of Language: The Fate of a Question* (New York: Harper

and Row, 1976); Renate Fischer, "Language of Action," in Fischer and Lane, *Looking Back*, 429–455.

16. B. D. Pettingill, "The Sign-Language," *Annals* 18 (Jan. 1873): 9; Remi Valade, "The Sign Language in Primitive Times," *Annals* 18 (Jan. 1873): 31; Harvey P. Peet, "Notions of the Deaf and Dumb Before Instruction," *Annals* 8 (Oct. 1855): 10; J. C. Covell, "The Nobility, Dignity, and Antiquity of the Sign Language," *Proceedings of the Seventh Convention of American Instructors of the Deaf, 1870* (Indianapolis, 1870), 133–136.

17. William Dwight Whitney, *The Life and Growth of Language: An Outline of Linguistic Science* (New York: D. Appleton, 1876), 291; Edward B. Tylor, *Researches into the Early History of Mankind* (New York: Holt, 1878 [London, 1865]), 15, 44, 77–78; Garrick Mallery, "The Gesture Speech of Man," *Annals* 27 (Apr. 1882): 69; Garrick Mallery, *Introduction to the Study of Sign Language among the North American Indians as Illustrating the Gesture Speech of Mankind* (Washington, D.C., 1880), reprinted in D. Jean Umiker-Sebeok and Thomas A. Sebeok, eds., *Aboriginal Sign-Languages of the Americas and Australia*, vol. 1 (New York: Plenum Press, 1978), 13.

18. Edward B. Tylor, "On the Origin of Language," *Fortnightly Review* 4 (Apr. 15, 1886): 547; Charles Darwin, *The Expression of the Emotions in Man and Animals* (Chicago: University of Chicago Press, 1965), 61; Mallery, *Introduction*, 12–14; Jastrow, "Evolution of Language," *Science* 7 (June 18, 1886): 556.

19. Quoted in Thomas Francis Fox, "Speech and Gestures," *Annals* 42 (Nov. 1897): 398, 400. The reporter was noting a common attitude but disagreed with the modern disdain for gesture.

20. J. C. Gordon, "Dr. Gordon's Report," *Association Review* 1 (December 1899): 206; Gardiner G. Hubbard, "Proceedings of the American [Social] Science Association," *National Deaf Mute Gazette* 2 (Jan. 1868): 5; J. D. Kirkhuff, "Superiority of the Oral Method," *Silent Educator* 3 (Jan. 1892): 139; Susanna E. Hull, "Do Persons Born Deaf Differ Mentally from Others Who Have the Power of Hearing?" *Annals* 22 (Oct. 1877): 236.

21. Garrick Mallery, "The Sign Language of the North American Indians," *Annals* 25 (Jan. 1880): 7; for other accounts of such visits, see "Institution Items: Pennsylvania Institution," *Annals* 19 (Jan. 1874): 48–49; Warring Wilkinson, "The Development of Speech and of the Sign-Language," *Annals* 26 (Jan. 1881): 171; Mallery, "The Gesture Speech," 75.

22. Harvey P. Peet, "Preliminary Remarks—Signs versus Articulation," *National Deaf Mute Gazette* 2 (Feb. 1868): 4, 6–7; Thomas H. Gallaudet, "On the Natural Language of Signs—I," *Annals* 1 (Oct. 1847): 59; Isaac Lewis Peet, "The Relation of the Sign Language to the Education of the Deaf," *Silent Educator* 1 (Jan. 1890): 214; Warring Wilkinson, "The Development of Speech and of the Sign-Language," *Annals* 26 (Jan. 1881): 167.

23. Joseph Jastrow, "The Evolution of Language," 555–556.

24. Pettingill, "The Sign-Language," 4; Sarah Harvey Porter, "The Suppression of Signs by Force," *Annals* 39 (June 1894): 171; R. W. Dodds, "The Practical Benefits of Methods Compared," *Annals* 44 (Feb. 1899): 124; John Dutton Wright, "Speech and Speech-Reading for the Deaf," *Century Magazine* (Jan. 1897): 332–334.

25. Georges Canguilhem, *The Normal and the Pathological* (New York: Zone Books, 1989), 39–64, 125; Ian Hacking, *The Taming of Chance* (Cambridge: Cambridge University Press, 1990), 160–166.

26. Bingham, "All Along the Line," 22; Mary S. Garrett, "Helps and Hindrances of Deaf Children in Acquiring Speech and Language at the Natural Age," *Association Review* 10 (June 1908): 274–275.

27. Daniel J. Kevles, *In the Name of Eugenics: Genetics and the Uses of Human Heredity* (Berkeley: University of California Press, 1985), 160.

28. Mary S. and Emma Garrett, "The Possibilities of the Oral Method for the Deaf and the Next Steps Leading Towards its Perfection," *Silent Educator* 3 (Jan. 1892): 65; Richard A. Johnson, "Annual Business Meeting of the Association," *Association Review* 9 (Feb.–Apr. 1907): 281–282; Jennie L. Cobb, "Schoolroom Efficiency," *Annals* 58 (May 1913): 208; Caroline A. Yale, *Formation and Development of Elementary English Sounds* (Northampton, Mass.: Gazette, 1914), 3–4.

29. Grace C. Green, "The Importance of Physical Training for the Deaf," *Association Review* 9 (Feb.–Apr. 1907): 180–181.

30. Anon., *Scientific American* 96 (June 8, 1907): 474.

31. W. Earl Hall, "To Speak or Not to Speak: That Is the Question Behind the Bitter Deaf-Teaching Battle," *Iowan* 4 (Feb.–Mar., 1956); John Van Cleve, "Nebraska's Oral Law of 1911 and the Deaf Community," *Nebraska History* 65 (Summer 1984): 195–220; Van Cleve and Crouch, *A Place of Their Own*, 128–141.

32. Quoted in Padden and Humphries, *Deaf in America*, 36.

33. Ibid., 5–6; Beryl Lieff Benderly, *Dancing Without Music: Deafness in America* (Garden City, N.Y.: Doubleday, 1980), 218–239; Jerome D. Schein, *At Home Among Strangers: Exploring the Deaf Community in the United States* (Washington, D.C.: Gallaudet University Press, 1989), 72–105, 106, 120.

34. Oliver Sacks, *Seeing Voices: A Journey into the World of the Deaf* (Berkeley: University of California Press, 1989), 28, 110–111.

35. Bell, *Memoir*, 222.

36. For a variety of viewpoints on inclusion, see *Annals* 139 (April 1994): 148–171.

Chapter Twenty-six

ISOTYPE and the Project of Universal Graphic Language

Conevery A. Bolton

Underlying contemporary American graphic sensibility is a far-reaching program for social uplift through "picture language." The information symbols, traffic signs, and illustrated bar charts that inform and direct the late-twentieth-century United States have their roots in an innovative educational and design venture of 1920s "Red Vienna."

As Austria struggled to rebuild itself from World War I, a young mathematician, philosopher, and social critic named Otto Neurath sought to create ways to empower and educate the working class. Neurath was fascinated by the power of statistical information. He felt that if quantified facts about economic and social conditions were presented in an engaging way to a broad public, citizens would better shape government to their needs. Neurath's political goals stretched beyond the socialism of his day to encompass a vision of socially emancipated life made possible by public education.[1]

Leading a group of artists, statisticians, and researchers in the 1920s and '30s, Neurath created a system for the pictorial representation of statistical information.[2] Neurath and his team named the system "ISOTYPE," standing both for the system's full name, International System for Typographic Picture Education, and for the isotypes, or standardized forms, that were its hallmark.[3]

This graph, from the 1939 Neurath volume *Modern Man in the Making*, illustrates many of the principles of ISOTYPE.[4] Icons stand for numbers, making rates of change and rough comparisons—here, of population—easily visible. The shifting numbers and composition of the silent male figures spur the reader's own conclusions about intercontinental disease transfer and cultural conflict. "Guide-pictures" place Latin America in tropical and subtropical parts of the world—note the palm trees—while also offering subtle commentary on technological and social change through the juxtaposition of tall ship and ocean liner, temple and oil rig. "Race" is unproblematic, and gender invisible: the graph invites some kinds of societal critique while eliding others. A product of faith in quantified number and in scientific fact, ISOTYPE is a product of its time, ever alert to chronicle and forward the onward march of "Modern Man in the Making."

The basic principle behind the system was the use of repeated icons, each of

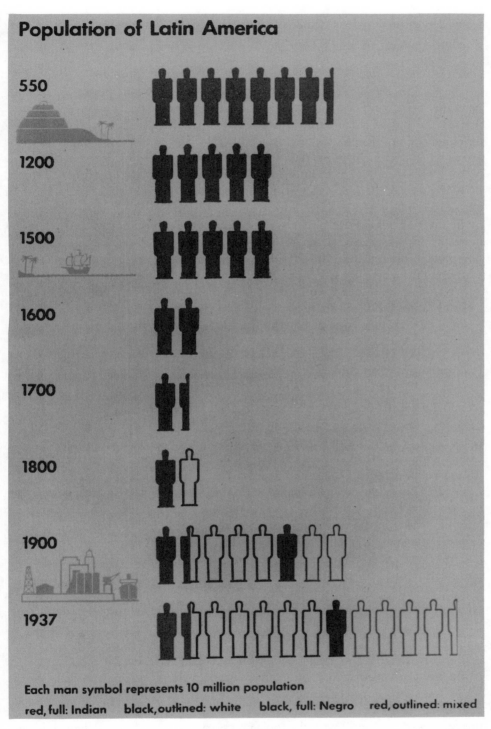

Population of Latin America

Each man symbol represents 10 million population

red, full: Indian   black, outlined: white   black, full: Negro   red, outlined: mixed

1. "Population of Latin America," from Otto Neurath, *Modern Man in the Making* (New York: Alfred A. Knopf, 1939), 33.

which represented a given quantity. These stylized, easily recognizable shapes were arranged in bar charts or combined with other graphic elements.[5] Sacrificing precision for immediacy, the images and diagrams of the ISOTYPE team made statistical comparisons intuitively easy to grasp (see Figure 1 for one example).[6]

The system was designed for an innovative city museum project headed by Neurath. Eschewing conventional exhibits, the "Social and Economic Museum" offered the public a constantly updated set of materials about the history and development of Vienna's culture and economy. The project was intended to be accessible and thought-provoking. It allowed people of varying degrees of literacy to have access to statistical information about their city and the broader world. ISOTYPE exhibits addressed pressing social issues: one quantified the number of coal miners needed to produce a load of coal when assisted by varying degrees of mechanization, while another charted the connection between social class and infant mortality in Vienna. Amid the grim rebuilding of the postwar period, displays in the museum offered whimsical insight into the processes of city planning. Exhibits scattered throughout the city in small "vest-pocket museums" featured minidisplays and extended the museum's mission by bringing education to working adults who had only a lunch hour to spare.[7]

ISOTYPE exhibits focused on what people knew best: their lives and their city. Yet the goals of ISOTYPE's creators for their work were ambitiously broad. ISOTYPE was to be an "international picture language," a universal graphic vocabulary accessible to people of all languages and levels of literacy. Designed to need minimal textual explication, ISOTYPE diagrams were intended to be easily translated, transcending linguistic boundaries.[8] Like a language, the system was based on repeated, constant elements. Images represented the same things in different graphs, so that every ISOTYPE chart would be "readable" by someone familiar with others. Education would be accessible to peoples of widely disparate cultures through this demonstrative tool.[9]

ISOTYPE was the concrete manifestation of Neurath's far-reaching goal of unification across boundaries. His colleagues in the Vienna Circle, a discussion group later influential in the philosophy of science, had little use for his enthusiasm for colorful statistics. Yet Neurath himself drew many links between the goals of ISOTYPE and the Vienna Circle's Unity of Science movement, which proposed the universalization of all scientific observation and language.[10]

In conjunction with their promotion of ISOTYPE as a universal picture language, Neurath and his colleagues worked closely with C. K. Ogden to publicize BASIC— British American Scientific International Commercial—English.[11] An English with simplified grammar and vocabulary, BASIC was intended to provide a practical, easily learned second language for businesspeople, scientists, and politicians the world over.[12] Armed with a "fundamental vocabulary" of one thousand words, BASIC's creators hoped to democratize communication across national boundaries. Promoting their two systems together, Ogden and Neurath attempted to provide the peoples of the world with the tools necessary for radical social change through education.

Despite their efforts, however, the linkage between the two systems attenuated.

BASIC never achieved even the success of created languages like Esperanto, while ISOTYPE caught the imagination of many educators of the interwar period. The Vienna museum provided a model for civic museums around the world.[13] ISOTYPE staffers trained designers in a number of countries, including the Soviet Union, to produce their own educational materials in the ISOTYPE style.[14] ISOTYPE was ultimately to become a widespread, if not universal, system—but one divorced from many of the linguistic and pedagogic aims that fired its creators.

The rise of the Third Reich fractured work on ISOTYPE. A core team fled to the Hague in 1934. In 1940, Neurath and designer Marie Reidemeister were forced to make a dramatic escape to England, where they continued to popularize and promote the system.[15]

Meanwhile, the system's bold graphics and its potential for popularizing statistical information caught the imagination of Neurath's contemporaries in the United States. Social reformers and educators promoted and emulated ISOTYPE.[16] *New York Times* science writer Waldemar Kaempffert praised the system.[17] The influential social-reform journal *Survey Graphic* promoted ISOTYPE as an educational and analytic tool.[18]

In 1934, Rudolf Modley, an Austrian refugee who had worked with the Vienna museum project in the late '20s, started his own version of ISOTYPE, a for-profit company called Pictograph, Inc.[19] He produced charts and diagrams very similar to ISOTYPE's. Soon Pictographs appeared on behalf of reform efforts in the United States and in the syndicated newspaper feature "Telefact."[20] In 1936, United States Surgeon General Thomas Parran used Pictograph images to lead the charge in his "War on Syphilis" (see Figure 2).[21]

This illustration, "A Community Program for Tuberculosis and Syphilis Control," is from a 1938 article written by Parran as part of his dramatic campaign against these diseases.[22] The Pictograph images used by Parran, legacies of the ISOTYPE system first developed in 1920s Vienna, were seen by other public health educators as important tools in promoting Parran's message. Only a few brief captions are necessary to sketch the process of examination, case tracing, and treatment necessary to combat these insidious ills—and the happy, wholesome, "healthy community" that would result from increased vigilance against disease.

The anthropomorphized figures convey a host of messages about the power of science and medicine and the role of expertise in confronting social problems. At the same time, the diagrams speak of a powerful optimism about public response to education. They reveal the faith of interwar educators that images had the power not simply to quantify but to convince.

These images are the forerunners of a broadly used set of graphic principles. Their stylized human shapes gave rise to the standardized images that label public facilities and direct traffic. Similar images reappear throughout charts and graphics in contemporary popular media. This style of image is a powerful example of the ways in which many kinds of language—graphic as well as word-based—shape and structure the world.

By 1945, the ISOTYPE style had become a part of the visual vocabulary of American designers and educators.[23] Not simply educational diagrams but filler

2. "A Community Program for Tuberculosis and Syphilis Control," from Thomas Parran, "No Defense for Any of Us," *Survey Graphic* 27, number 4 (April 1938): 200.

graphics were soon influenced by the Neurath project. In 1942, breaking with the emphasis upon coherent style that had characterized the ISOTYPE project, Pictograph published a book of "clip art" intended to be used independent of other design elements.[24] A subtle but important shift had taken place: no longer thought-provoking technique, the style was promoted instead as a labor-saving graphic tool.

Seventy years after the Neurath team embarked upon its mission to reform Austrian pedagogy, images in the ISOTYPE style have become an international symbolic vocabulary. International information signs use the principles of ISO-TYPE. Desktop publishing and computer-based design take the iconic style of Neurath's system for granted. Neurath's "little men" parade in the almost unseen background of contemporary visual perception. *USA Today* and the *New York Times* chart troop strength and quantify American consumables with a visual vocabulary once intended to effect social uplift. In their progress, however, the images have lost much of their social critique and educational daring. Little of the social idealism of interwar Vienna seems to resonate in contemporary ISOTYPic images. No longer idealistic social project, the ISOTYPE system is nonetheless a near-universal graphic language, powerful in ubiquity if not in content.

NOTES

1. For biographical material on Otto Neurath, see Nancy Cartwright, Jordi Cat, Lola Fleck, and Thomas E. Uebel, *Otto Neurath: Philosophy between Science and Politics*, Ideas in Context, ed. Quentin Skinner (Cambridge: Cambridge University Press, 1996); Robert S. Cohen, "Otto Neurath," in Paul Edwards, editor in chief, *The Encyclopedia of Philosophy*, vol. 5 (New York: Macmillan and Free Press; London: Collier-Macmillan, 1967); William M. Johnston, "The Eclipse of a Universal Man: Otto Neurath," in *The Austrian Mind: An Intellectual and Social History, 1848–1939* (Berkeley: University of California Press, 1972); Elisabeth Nemeth and Friedrich Stadler, eds., *Encyclopedia and Utopia: The Life and Work of Otto Neurath (1882–1945)*, Vienna Circle Institute Yearbook No. 4, ed. Friedrich Stadler (Dordrecht: Kluwer, 1996); Otto Neurath, *Empiricism and Sociology*, ed. Marie Neurath and Robert S. Cohen (Dordrecht: D. Reidel, 1973); Paul Neurath and Elisabeth Nemeth, eds., *Otto Neurath, oder, Die Einheit von Wissenschaft und Gesellschaft*, Monographien zur österreischen Kultur- und Geistesgeschichte No. 6, ed. Peter Kampits (Vienna: Böhlau, 1994); Friedrich Stadler, ed., *Arbeiterbildung in der Zwischenkriegzeit. Otto Neurath und sein Gesellschafts- und Wirtschaftsmuseum in Wien, 1925–1934. Politische Grafik von Gerd Arntz und den Konstruktivisten* (Vienna: Löcker Verlag, 1982); and Thomas E. Uebel, ed., *Rediscovering the Forgotten Vienna Circle: Austrian Studies on Otto Neurath and the Vienna Circle*, Boston Studies in the Philosophy of Science No. 133, Robert S. Cohen, ed. (Dordrecht: Kluwer Academic Publishers, 1991). A near-complete listing of Neurath's many publications is contained in Stadler, *Arbeiterbildung in der Zwischenkriegzeit*.

2. Marie Reidemeister and Gerd Arntz were particularly crucial figures in the development of ISOTYPE. Reidemeister, who later married Otto Neurath, worked with him until his death in 1945 and then continued to create ISOTYPE texts at their Institute for Visual Education in Reading, England, until her retirement in 1972. Gerd Arntz, too, continued his work on his own in the Netherlands after the war. See Robin Kinross, "Marie Neurath

1898–1986," *Information Design Journal* 5, number 1 (1986): 69–71; and "On the influence of Isotype," *Information Design Journal* 2, number 2 (1981): 122–130.

3. In 1935, Marie Reidemeister devised the name, and graphic designer Gerd Arntz the iconic logo for the system they had worked with Neurath to create. Otto Neurath, *International Picture Language. A Facsimile Reprint of the English edition*, Psyche Miniatures General Series No. 83 (London: Kegan Paul, Trench, Trubner, 1936), with a German translation by Marie Neurath (Reading: Department of Typography & Graphic Communication, University of Reading, 1980), 6.

4. Otto Neurath, *Modern Man in the Making* (New York: Knopf, 1939), 33.

5. Otto Neurath, *International Picture Language*, 47; and Marie Neurath, "ISOTYPE," *Instructural Science* 3 (1974): 127–150.

6. On ISOTYPE's graphical innovations, see James R. Beniger and Dorothy L. Robyn, "Quantitative Graphics in Statistics: A Brief History," *American Statistician* 32, number 1 (February 1978): 6; H. G. Funkhouser, "Historical Development of the Graphical Representation of Statistical Data," *OSIRIS* 3 (1937): 350; Robin Kinross, "Otto Neurath und die Humanisierung des Wissens mit Hilfe der Bildpädagogik," *Kultur & Technik: Zeitschrift des Deutschen Museums München* 2. Jahrgang, Heft 3 (September 1978): 32–35; Ellen Lupton, "Reading Isotype," in Victor Margolin, ed., *Design Discourse: History/Theory/Criticism* (Chicago: University of Chicago Press, 1989); Calvin F. Schmid and Stanton E. Schmid, *Handbook of Graphic Presentation*, 2d ed. (New York: John Wiley and Sons, 1979), 224–229; and Peter Wildbur, *Information Graphics: A Survey of Typographic, Diagrammatic and Cartographic Communication* (New York: Van Nostrand Reinhold, 1989): 51–52.

7. Kinross, "Otto Neurath und die Humanisierung des Wissens mit Hilfe der Bildpädagogik"; Otto Neurath, *Empiricism and Sociology*, 221; Otto Neurath, "Das Gesellschafts- und Wirtschaftsmuseum in Wien," *Minerva-Zeitschrift* 7. Jahrgang, Heft 9/10 (September/October 1931): 153–156; Otto Neurath, *International Picture Language*, 42–46; and Otto Neurath, "Museums of the Future," *Survey Graphic* 22, number 9 (September 1933): 458–463, 479, 484, 486.

8. Neurath, *International Picture Language*, 16–21.

9. As Otto Neurath succinctly and frequently admonished, "Words divide, pictures unite" (in the original: "Worte trennen, Bilder verbinden." Neurath, "Das Gesellschafts- und Wirtschaftsmuseum in Wien," 156). Or, in BASIC English, "Words make division, pictures make connection." (Neurath, *International Picture Language*, 19). This translation of the phrase gives some indication of the euphony of BASIC.

10. On the links between Otto Neurath's political and philosophical work, see Jordi Cat, Nancy Cartwright, and Hasok Chang, "Otto Neurath: Politics and the Unity of Science," in Peter Galison and David J. Stump, eds., *The Disunity of Science: Boundaries, Contexts, and Power* (Stanford: Stanford University Press, 1996), 347–369.

11. See, for example, Otto Neurath, *BASIC BY ISOTYPE*, Psyche Miniatures General Series No. 86 (London: Kegan Paul, Trench, Trubner, 1937).

12. For an introduction to BASIC, see the textbooks and reference works published in the Psyche Miniatures General Series: C. K. Ogden, *The ABC of Basic English (in Basic). with An Account of the Sounds of Basic English by A. Lloyd James*, Psyche Miniatures General Series No. 43, 6th printing (London: Kegan Paul, Trench, Trubner, 1938); C. K. Ogden, *The Basic Dictionary: Being the 7,500 most useful words with their equivalents in Basic English for the use of Translators, Teachers, and Students*, Psyche Miniatures General Series No. 42, 5th ed. (London: Kegan Paul, Trench, Trubner, 1939). Also see The Orthological Committee, *Notes on Basic English, number 1. A Short Account of the System of*

Basic English (Cambridge, Mass.: privately published, October 1940). All four gospels and many novels and works of literature were translated into BASIC in an attempt to prove its feasibility and boost its popularity. See, for instance, Leonhard Frank, *Carl and Anna,* translated into Basic English by L. W. Lockhart, Psyche Miniatures General Series No. 32 (London: Kegan Paul, Trench, Trubner, 1930).

13. By 1933, museums on the Vienna model had been established in Berlin, Amsterdam, and London, and ISOTYPE was in use in Montessori schools. Otto Neurath, "Pictorial Statistics—An International Problem," *Listener* 10, number 246 (Wednesday, 27 September 1933): 471–472.

14. Otto Neurath established the "Institut Isostat" in Moscow in 1932, staffing it with newly trained Austrians who then trained Soviet workers. For examples of charts designed by workers in the Institut Isostat, see Walter Duranty, "U.S.A. and U.S.S.R." a "visual essay" in *Survey Graphic* 21, number 8 (November 1932): 538–539. The following year, standard statistical symbols based on ISOTYPE were established by government decree in the Soviet Union for use in schools and public information materials (Beniger and Robyn, "Quantitative Graphics in Statistics," 9). On the international spread of ISOTYPE, see Marie Neurath, "ISOTYPE," 127–128 and 146–147.

15. Supporters in the United States helped raise enough money to reestablish the International Foundation for the Promotion of Visual Education in Holland ("The Neurath Museum," *Survey* [later *Survey Graphic*] 70, number 6 [June 1934]: 205). See Cartwright, Cat, Fleck, and Uebel, *Otto Neurath,* 82–88.

16. See, for example, Marguerite E. Schwarzman, "Statistics for All: The Fact Picture from Vienna Is a Significant Visual Aid," *Educational Screen* (Chicago) 12, number 7 (September 1933): 189–190; and [unsigned], "Isotype: What Is It?" *Bulletin of the National Tuberculosis Association* 22, number 12 (February 1936): 26.

17. Waldemar Kaempffert, "Staccato Speech for Silent Statistics: The Pictograph, From Vienna, Gives New Meaning to the Facts of Everyday Life," *New York Times Magazine,* 22 January 1933, 9, 16; and "THE WEEK IN SCIENCE: . . . A Language of Symbols," *New York Times* Sunday "Science" section, 17 January 1937.

18. Waldemar Kaempffert, "Social Showman," *Survey Graphic* 25, number 11 (November 1937): 618–619; "The Thrust of Invention. ISOTYPES by Otto Neurath," *Survey Graphic* 22, number 12 (December 1937): 643–647, 714, 715, 717, 718; and "Facts March On—With Neurath," *Survey Graphic* 28, number 9 (September 1939): 538–540, Harlow S. Person and Beulah Amidon, "Economics Makes the Front Page," *Survey Graphic* 22, number 3 (March 1933): 156–159; and Merle D. Vincent, "Coal at the Cross-Roads," *Survey Graphic* 23, number 4 (April 1934): 181–187. Brief notices in *Survey Graphic* tracked the activities and political turmoil associated with the project: see "The Neurath Museum," *Survey* 70, number 6 (June 1934): 205; a capsule review of *Modern Man in the Making,* *Survey Graphic* 28, number 12 (December 1939): 758; and "Among Ourselves," *Survey Graphic* 33, number 12 (December 1944), 483.

19. Rudolf Modley founded Pictorial Statistics, Inc., in 1934 (it became Pictograph Corporation in 1940). Rudolf Modley and Dyno Lowenstein, Director of Pictograph Corporation, in Collaboration with Jane Fiske, Frederick Jahnel, and Norman Levit, *Pictographs and Graphs: How to Make and Use Them* (New York: Harper & Brothers, 1952), 6–7. See also Louis M. Hacker, with pictorial statistics by Rudolf Modley and statistical research by George R. Taylor, *The United States: A Graphic History,* Modern World Series No. 1, Louis M. Hacker, ed. (New York, Modern Age Books, 1937). On the influence of Pictograph, see Rudolf Modley, "The Challenge of 'Symbology,' " in Elwood Whitney, ed., *"Symbology":*

The Use of Symbols in Visual Communications, report on the fourth communications conference of the Art Directors Club of New York (New York: Communication Arts Books, Hastings House, 1960); and Schmid and Schmid, *Handbook of Graphic Presentation,* 226.

20. See many of the covers of *Survey Graphic,* 1936–1940; "The Nation's Biggest Business," a pictographic essay on state of U.S. education, *Survey Graphic* 28, number 10 (October 1939): 583–586; Hacker, *The United States: A Graphic History;* Luther Gulick and Rudolf Modley, *The New York Primer: A Picture Book for the More Easy Attaining an Understanding of New York's School Problems* (The Regents' Inquiry into the Character and Cost of Public Education in the State of New York, 1939); and Maxine Sweezy, *Medical Care for Everybody?* (Washington, D.C.: American Association of University Women, 1945). The back cover of *1000 Pictorial Symbols Designed and Copyrighted by Pictograph Corporation* (New York: privately published, 1942) contains an advertisement for Telefact. On the efforts and popular reception of Pictograph, see also Rudolf Modley, "Language in Pictures," reprint from *P.M.* (September 1937): 26–30; File Folder 281, Thomas J. Parran Papers, Record No. 90/F–14, University Archives, Hillman Library, University of Pittsburgh.

21. Thomas Parran, "The Next Great Plague to Go," *Survey Graphic* 25 (July 1936): 405–411, 442–443; "Why Don't We Stamp Out Syphilis?" (condensed from *Survey Graphic*), *Readers Digest* 29, number 171 (July 1936): 65–73; *Shadow on the Land: Syphilis* (New York: Reynal & Hitchcock, 1937); and "No Defense for Any of Us," *Survey Graphic* 27, number 4 (April 1938): 197–202, 248–253.

22. Parrah, "No Defense for Any of Us," 200.

23. ISOTYPic images were used by a variety of public agencies: see, for example the front cover of the 1934 report on the Henry Street Visiting Nurse Fund in New York, reproduced in *Healing at Home: The Visiting Nurse Service of New York, 1893–1993,* catalog of an Ellis Island Exhibit, 15 (courtesy of Elizabeth Watkins, Senior Historian at the Senator John Heinz Pittsburgh Regional History Center) and a chart by the Civil Aeronautics Administration in "Wings for the Future," text by Charles I. Stanton, *Survey Graphic* 32, number 5 (May 1943): 197. Pictograph books for children were produced by a major publishing house: see Picture Fact Associates, Alice V. Keliher, ed., with Franz Hess, Marion LeBron, and Rudolf Modley, *News Workers* and *Movie Workers* (New York: London: Harper & Brothers Publishers, 1939).

24. *1000 Pictorial Symbols Designed and Copyrighted by Pictograph Corporation.*

Chapter Twenty-seven

Statement on Language Rights

Linguistic Society of America

The Linguistic Society of America was founded in 1924 to advance the scientific study of language. The Society's present membership of approximately 7000 persons and institutions includes a great proportion of the leading experts on language in the United States, as well as many from abroad. Many of the Society's members have experience with, or expertise in, bilingualism and multilingualism. Despite increasing interest in these topics, public debate is all too often based on misconceptions about language. In this Statement, the Society addresses some of these misconceptions and urges the protection of basic linguistic rights.[1]

1. The vast majority of the world's nations are at least bilingual, and most are multilingual, even if one ignores the impact of modern migrations. Countries in which all residents natively speak the same language are a small exception, certainly not the rule. Even nations like France, Germany, and the United Kingdom have important linguistic minorities within their borders. Furthermore, where diverse linguistic communities exist in one country, they have generally managed to coexist peacefully. Finland, Singapore, and Switzerland are only three examples. Where linguistic discord does arise, as it has with various degrees of intensity in Belgium, Canada, and Sri Lanka, it is generally the result of majority attempts to disadvantage or suppress a minority linguistic community, or it reflects underlying racial or religious conflicts. Multilingualism by itself is rarely an important cause of civil discord.

2. The territory that now constitutes the United States was home to hundreds of languages before the advent of European settlers. These indigenous languages belonged to several language families. Each native language is or was a fully developed system of communication with rich structures and expressive power. Many past and present members of the Society have devoted their professional lives to documenting and analyzing the native languages of the United States.

3. Unfortunately, most of the indigenous languages of the United States are severely threatened. All too often their eradication was deliberate government policy. In other cases, these languages have suffered from biased or uninformed views that they are mere "dialects" with simple grammatical structures and limited vocabularies. The decline of America's indigenous languages has been closely linked to the loss of much of the culture of their speakers.

4. Because of this history, the Society believes that the government and people of the United States have a special obligation to enable indigenous peoples to retain their languages and cultures. The Society strongly supports the federal recognition of this obligation, as expressed in the Native American Languages Act. The Society urges federal, state, and local governments to continue to affirmatively implement the policies of the Act by enacting legislation, appropriating more adequate funding, and monitoring the progress made under the Act.

5. The United States is also home to numerous immigrant languages other than English. The arrival of some of these languages, such as Dutch, French, German, and Spanish, predates the founding of our nation. Many others have arrived more recently. The substantial number of residents of the United States who speak languages other than English presents us with both challenges and opportunities.

6. The challenges of multilingualism are well known: incorporating linguistic minorities into our economic life, teaching them English so they can participate more fully in our society, and properly educating their children. Unfortunately, in the process of incorporating immigrants and their offspring into American life, bilingualism is often wrongly regarded as a "handicap" or "language barrier." Of course, inability to speak English often functions as a barrier to economic advancement in the United States. But to be bilingual—to speak both English and another language—should be encouraged, not stigmatized. There is no convincing evidence that bilingualism by itself impedes cognitive or educational development. On the contrary, there is evidence that it may actually enhance certain types of intelligence.

7. Multilingualism also presents our nation with many benefits and opportunities. For example, bilingual individuals can use their language skills to promote our business interests abroad. Their linguistic competence strengthens our foreign diplomatic missions and national defense. And they can better teach the rest of us to speak other languages.

8. Moreover, people who speak a language in addition to English provide a role model for other Americans. Our national record on learning other languages is notoriously poor. A knowledge of foreign languages is necessary not just for immediate practical purposes, but also because it gives people the sense of international community that America requires if it is to compete successfully in a global economy.

9. Furthermore, different languages allow different ways of expressing experiences, thoughts, and aesthetics. America's art and culture are greatly enriched by the presence of diverse languages among its citizens.

10. To remedy our policies toward the languages of Native Americans and to encourage acquisition or retention of languages other than English by all Americans, the Linguistic Society of America urges our nation to protect and promote the linguistic rights of its people. At a minimum, all residents of the United States should be guaranteed the following linguistic rights:

A. To be allowed to express themselves, publicly or privately, in the language of their choice.

B. To maintain their native language and, should they so desire, to pass it on to their children.

C. When their facility in English is inadequate, to be provided a qualified interpreter in any proceeding in which the government endeavors to deprive them of life, liberty, or property. Moreover, where there is a substantial linguistic minority in a community, interpretation ought to be provided by courts and other state agencies in any matter that significantly affects the public.

D. To have their children educated in a manner that affirmatively acknowledges their native language abilities as well as ensures their acquisition of English. Children can learn only when they understand their teachers. As a consequence, some use of children's native language in the classroom is often desirable if they are to be educated successfully.

E. To conduct business in the language of their choice.

F. To use their preferred language for private conversation in the workplace.

G. To have the opportunity to learn to speak, read, and write English.

11. Notwithstanding the multilingual history of the United States, the role of English as our common language has never seriously been questioned. Research has shown that the newcomers to America continue to learn English at rates comparable to previous generations of immigrants. All levels of government should adequately fund programs to teach English to any resident who desires to learn it. Nonetheless, promoting our common language need not, and should not, come at the cost of violating the rights of linguistic minorities.

NOTES

1. The statement was prepared by the Committee on Social and Political Concerns, approved by the Executive Committee, and ratified in June 1996 by the membership of the Linguistic Society of America, Archibald A. Hill Suite, 1325 18th Street, N.W. #211, Washington DC 20036–6501.

Part VIII

Researching Multilingual America

The existence of electronic library catalogues and easily available databases means—among many other things—that there are now completely new possibilities of researching multilingual literature or of quickly compiling extensive bibliographies of single-language works. Steve Love's "Researching Non-English Literature of the United States with the Modern Language Association (MLA) Database" presents strings of keyword searches in the case of the electronic bibliography of the Modern Language Association (on SilverPlatter CD-ROM) that serve as a model to enable readers to access up-to-date bibliograpic information on multilingual literature of the United States. If applied to German-language writing of the United States alone, for example, the command he suggests—"american literature in de and (german-language* or german-american*)"—would generate a 150-page bibliography with subject divisions and keywords that provide much help in searching other databases and electronic library catalogues. The relevant library keywords might be, for example, "find kw Germanamerican" at the American Antiquarian Society (or on the EUREKA electronic search vehicle); "German-American" at the Library of Congress; or "Germans—United States" in the Harvard University On-Line Library system. From there one can also proceed to somewhat more specialized subject searches such as "German American newspapers," "German imprints—United States—Bibliography" or "German American literature."

Other catalogue descriptors vary: Russian-language American literature descriptors include disparate phrases such as "Russian language and United States" or "Slavic languages—foreign countries." In the case of American Indians, such keyword strings as "Native Americans—languages" may be successful; for Native American poetry, the search command "American poetry—Translations from Indian languages" might yield more results. In other cases, the general opening "find kw literature, United States, foreign language" may take the researcher to a long string of further leads, though it is often hard to exclude such items as Hawthorne translations from these searches.

The various search engines on the world wide web will produce further findings. For example, projects such as the Yamada Language Center at the University of Oregon (http://babel.uoregon.edu/yamada/fonts.html, with fonts for many languages that users can download); web pages such as "The Voice of the Shuttle: Literatures Other Than English" (http://humanitas.ucsb.edu/, woven by Alan Liu); "The Human-Languages Page" (http://www.june29.com/HLP/); or "Multilingualism and the Internet" (http://wwli.com/library/localize.html), and aids such as the "Internet Explorer Multilingual Browsing Tools" will be helpful to the researcher in this field. It is probably true that the electronic availability of library catalogues and other archives has given a tremendous boost to studies in American multilingualism. To bring more students to this field, however, much will depend on the presentation of easily available, platform-neutral sites that offer access to a great variety of sources and research tools. A "webliography" for American multilingualism would be most desirable, and I hope that the Longfellow Institute web page (http://www.fas.harvard.edu/~lowinus/) will soon be able to make research simpler by providing the easiest-now-possible access to multilingual America.

Chapter Twenty-eight

Researching Non-English Literature of the United States with the Modern Language Association (MLA) Database

Steve Love

NOTE: The discussion that follows refers to the electronic version of MLA available on the SilverPlatter CD-ROM, which covers the years 1963 to the present.

Here are some suggested strategies for searching the MLA database in order to retrieve citations to articles, books, and dissertations related to the topic of non-Anglophone American literature. Although you will be retrieving secondary critical materials, this can be an effective way to unearth primary source materials, as well as the names of still untranslated authors and works. Since MLA provides no overarching terminology for research in the area of non-Anglophone American literature, you will need to perform a number of different searches for specific language categories.

1. Limit the term "american literature" to the descriptor (subject heading) field, as in the following example:

american literature in de

This descriptor will accompany all citations that pertain to American literature, and will help to exclude a number of irrelevant references.

2. Next, link this term with a specific language:

american literature in de and norwegian

The search results will be mixed, and not everything will be relevant to your topic. However, some of these citations may be useful in that they will pull up the names of untranslated authors and works, as well as the titles of specific monographs and journals—for example, *Norwegian-American Studies* — that would bear close scrutiny; in a few instances, the retrieved citations may provide you with the names of special collections.

3. If you were to use the same search strategy with German, French, or Spanish, you would retrieve an even greater number of irrelevant citations, and, in these instances, you will want to make your connecting terms more specific:

american literature in de and (german-language* or german-american*)

Note that "german-language" and "german-american" are not restricted to the descriptor field, which means that you will retrieve them not only as descriptor terms but as phrases that might appear in the titles of articles, books, etc., as well as in the names of journals and scholarly societies.

Hyphens are used to search bound phrases; without the hyphens, you would retrieve not only the bound phrase but any occurrence of these words as separate unrelated terms.

Asterisks are used to retrieve variant endings of words—German-American* also retrieves german americans, german-americana, etc. When you use hyphenated bound-phrase searching, asterisks are also used to retrieve any extensions of phrases—for example, German-language* will also retrieve german-language-literature. Without the asterisk, you would retrieve *only* german-language.

"Or's" and "And's." Parentheses must be used if you are linking an "or" statement with another term or set of terms on the same search line. However, you also have the option of combining terms on different search lines by combining the set numbers: #1 and #3. In these instances, parentheses are not required.

4. MLA on SilverPlatter provides an online thesaurus of descriptors. Consulting this may help you in formulating your search strategies.

5. MLA on SilverPlatter is divided into two segments: 1963–1980; 1981–present. You can search both together, or you can search them separately; however, it is important to remember that the pre-1981 citations provide fewer descriptors than the 1981 forward segment.

Contributors

Shelley S. Armitage is Professor of American Studies at University of Hawaii at Manoa. She has held appointments in American literature, cultural studies, and served as director of women's studies. Author of seven books, including critical studies of American visual artists, popular culture, women's "work," and ethnic and regional texts, her most recent focus is the relationship between material culture and folk traditions to multicultural issues, place, and creativity.

Douglas C. Baynton is Assistant Professor of History and American Sign Language at the University of Iowa. He is the author of *Forbidden Signs: American Culture and the Campaign Against Sign Language* (University of Chicago Press, 1996). His current project is an exploration of the concept of disability and its use in the cultural construction of ethnicity, gender, and race in American history.

Aviva Ben-Ur is a Ph.D. candidate in Near Eastern and Judaic Studies at Brandeis University and specializes in Ladino and Sephardic Studies. A founding member of the New York theater group The Ladino Players, she is the author of *The Ladino (Judeo-Spanish) Collection of the Lubavitcher Rebbes: A Descriptive Bibliography* (forthcoming) and a contributor to *Jewish Women in America* (Carlson), to the *Sephardic House Newsletter* (New York), and to *Los Muestros* (Brussels).

Menahem Blondheim teaches American Studies and Communications at the Hebrew University of Jerusalem. His research interests include the history of communications, contemporary telecommunications, and American Rabbinics. Among other publications he is author of *News over the Wires* (Cambridge: Harvard University Press, 1994) and is preparing, with Michael P. Kramer, a critical edition of American Orthodox sermons.

Conevery A. Bolton is a Ph.D. candidate in the Department of the History of Science at Harvard University. Bolton's dissertation, " 'The Health of the Country': Environment and Sense of Place in the Making of Arkansas and Missouri, 1800–1850," explores American and European emigrants' understandings of human health as related to the natural environment in the early-nineteenth-century trans-Mississippi American West.

Alide Cagidemetrio is Professor of American Literature at the University of Udine (Italy). Among her recent works are *Fictions of the Past: Hawthorne and Melville* (University of Massachusetts Press, 1992) and a bilingual edition of *John Davis,*

Captain Smith and Princess Pocahontas (1995). She is a contributor to the forthcoming *Longfellow Anthology of American Literature*.

Jules Chametzky, Professor of English emeritus at the University of Massachusetts/ Amherst, is the author of *From the Ghetto: The Fiction of Abraham Cahan,* as well as coeditor, with the late Sidney Kaplan, of *Black and White in American Culture: Ten Years of the Massachusetts Review.*

Peter Conolly-Smith is Assistant Professor of the Humanities at the DeVry Institute in New Brunswick, N.J. He received his Ph.D. in American Studies from Yale University in 1996, has taught at Columbia and Yale, and was a fellow at the Longfellow Institute in 1997. His dissertation, "The Translated Community: New York's German-Language Press as Agent of Cultural Resistance and Integration, 1910–1918," is forthcoming in the Smithsonian Institution Press Series on American Studies.

Michela Corradini graduated from the University of Venice with a thesis on José Rodrigues Miguéis.

Sandra L. Dahlberg is Assistant Professor of English at the University of Houston- Downtown, where she teaches Mexican-American literature. Her research focuses on colonial-era literature of the Southwest and the dialogues these works create with contemporary life. Dahlberg published a previous article on "Los Comanches," titled, "Having the Last Word: The Cost of Conquest in 'Los Comanches,' " in *Recovering the U.S. Hispanic Literary Heritage.*

Michel Fabre is Professor Emeritus at the Sorbonne Nouvelle (Université Paris III), where he has long been the Director of the Center for African American Studies. His books include *From Harlem to Paris: Black American Writers in France, 1840–1980* (University of Illinois Press, 1991) and *The Several Lives of Chester Himes,* written in collaboration with Edward Margolies (University of Mississippi Press, 1997).

Melinda G. Gray is a Ph.D. candidate in Comparative Literature at Harvard University. She is working on language and national belonging in late-nineteenth- and early-twentieth-century England, Wales, and the United States. The Longfellow Institute awarded her a John E. Sawyer Fellowship for 1997–1998 to complete her dissertation. Her research interests also include feminism and psychoanalysis; literary canons and revisions; and translation.

Matthew Frye Jacobson is Associate Professor of American Studies and History at Yale, and author of *Special Sorrows: The Diasporic Imagination of Irish, Polish, and Jewish Immigrants in the United States* (1995) and *Whiteness of a Different Color: European Immigrants and the Alchemy of Race* (Harvard University Press, forthcoming, September 1998). He is currently at work on a volume on United States confrontations with "the other" through immigration and imperialism, 1876–1919.

Steve Love is Reference Librarian at Hilles Library, Harvard University.

Mario Maffi teaches American Literature at the University of Milan (Italy). He is the author of several books on the history and culture(s) of the United States, among them *Gateway to the Promised Land: Ethnic Cultures in New York's Lower East Side* (New York University Press, 1995). He has recently edited two anthologies of Asian-American and Latino authors. After publishing *New York: L'isola delle colline* (1995), he is currently writing another book on New York.

Karen Majewski is a graduate student in the American Culture Program at the University of Michigan. Her dissertation, "Traitors and True Poles: Narrating a Polish-American Identity, 1880–1939," examines Polish-language fiction written and published in the United States. She has written and lectured on Polish teaching sisterhoods, on Polish immigrant women writers and activists, and on Polonia's immigrant texts and publishing industry. Majewski teaches at St. Mary's College in Orchard Lake, Michigan.

Anna Maria Martellone is Professor of American History at the University of Florence. She has written books and essays on Italian-Americans, immigration, ethnicity, both in Italian and in English. Her most recent work includes the contribution of "Italian Mass Emigration to the United States, 1876–1930: A Historical Survey" to *Migration in European History* (1996) and the edited volume *Towards a New American Nation? Redefinitions and Reconstruction* (Keele University Press, 1995).

Orm Øverland is Professor of American literature at the University of Bergen in Norway and has a Ph.D. in American Studies from Yale University. His books include a study of J. F. Cooper's *The Prairie* (1971), Johan Schrøder's *Travels in Canada, 1863* (1989), three volumes of immigrant letters (1992/1993), and *The Western Home: A Literary History of Norwegian-America* (1996). He is now writing a book on "homemaking myths," the stories told in immigrant groups to prove their special right to a home in America.

Heike Paul has been a member of the interdisciplinary doctoral studies program ("Graduiertenkolleg") on "Gender & Literature" at Munich University. She wrote her dissertation in the field of American literature on "Mapping Migration: Women's Writing and the American Immigrant Experience" and currently teaches in the American Studies Department at Leipzig University.

Gönül Pultar is a member of the Department of English at Bilkent University (Ankara, Turkey), founding editor of the *Journal of American Studies of Turkey*, and vice-president of the American Studies Association of Turkey. She is the author of *Technique and Tradition in Beckett's Trilogy of Novels* (1996), of two novels, and of numerous articles on fiction, with an emphasis on ethnic and postcolonial authors. Her current interest centers around multilingual American literature in French and Turkish. She is a fellow at the Longfellow Institute in 1998.

Lawrence Rosenwald is the Anne Pierce Rogers Professor of English at Wellesley College. He has written extensively on American diaries, on the relations between words and music, and on translation. His current project, from which his contribution is drawn, is a book-length study of scenes of language and dialect contact in American literature.

Te-hsing Shan received his Ph.D. degree in comparative literature from National Taiwan University in 1986 and is currently Research Fellow and Head of the Division of the Humanities, Institute of European and American Studies, Academia Sinica, Taiwan, Republic of China. His research interests include American literary history, Chinese-American cultural studies, and cultural expressions of the Chinese diaspora.

Marc Shell, a John D. and Catherine T. MacArthur Fellow, is Chairman of the Department of Comparative Literature at Harvard University. His books include *The Economy of Literature* (1978), *Money, Language, and Thought* (1982), *The End of Kinship* (1988), *Elizabeth's Glass* (1993), *Children of the Earth* (1993), and *Art and Money* (1995). A forthcoming book, *OVERDUE* (Chicago), concerns German-American literature and art. With Werner Sollors, Marc Shell is codirector of the Longfellow Institutute for the Study of the Languages and Literatures of the United States.

Werner Sollors is Henry B. and Anne M. Cabot Professor of English and Afro-American Studies and Chair of the History of American Civilization Program at Harvard University. Recently, he published *Neither Black Nor White Yet Both: Thematic Explorations of Interracial Literature* (1997), edited Mary Antin's *The Promised Land* (1997), compiled and introduced *Theories of Ethnicity: A Classical Reader* (1996), and coedited, with Marc Shell, *The Longfellow Anthology of American Literature* (1999).

Doris Sommer is Professor of Latin American Literature at Harvard University. Among her publications is *Foundational Fictions: The National Romances of Latin America* (University of California Press, 1991), about the mutual construction of Eros and Polis as fundamental to the consolidation of modernity. Her forthcoming *Proceed with Caution: A Rhetoric of Particularism* considers the politics and esthetics of pausing before the universal embrace of modernity, to point to asymmetries of language, race, gender, and historical experience.

Aviva Taubenfeld is a doctoral candidate at Columbia University. She is the recipient of a Mellon Fellowship in Humanistic Studies and the Columbia University President's Fellowship, the Barnau Fellowship, and the H. C. Bunner Award for best essay in American Literature.

Hana Wirth-Nesher is Associate Professor of English and American Literature at Tel Aviv University. She is the author of *City Codes: Reading the Modern Urban Novel* and the editor of *What Is Jewish Literature?* and *New Essays on Call It*

Sleep. She has published articles on English, American, and Jewish literature and is currently writing a book on multilingualism in Jewish-American literature.

Xiao-huang Yin is Associate Professor of Asian American Studies at Occidental College in Los Angeles. His writings on Asian Americans and United States-Asia relations have appeared in such books, journals, magazines, and newspapers as *Asian American Encyclopaedia*, *American Quarterly*, *Journal of American-Asian Relations*, *Atlantic Monthly*, and *Los Angeles Times*. His book *Gold Mountain Dreams: Socio-Historical Aspects of Chinese American Literature* is forthcoming from the University of Illinois Press.

Index